Dictionary of Symbolism

D0815725

The Wordsworth
Dictionary of Symbolism

–

Hans Biedermann
Translated by James Hulbert

Wordsworth Reference

First published 1992 by Facts on File, Inc. New York.

This edition published 1996 by Wordsworth Editions Ltd.
Cumberland House, Crib Street, Ware, Hertfordshire SG12 9ET.

Copyright © 1989 by Hans Biedermann.
Translation © 1992 by Facts on File, Inc.

All rights reserved. This publication may not be
reproduced, stored in a retrieval system,
or transmitted, in any form or by any means, electronic,
mechanical, photocopying, recording or otherwise,
without the prior permission of the publishers.

Wordsworth® is the registered trademark
of Wordsworth Editions Ltd.

ISBN 1-85326-391-5

Printed and bound in Great Britain by Mackays of Chatham PLC.

Contents

Preface

When we talk about symbols and symbolism, we usually reveal one of two very different attitudes toward them. To some the subject is utterly antiquated, the sort of thing to which no sensible person should give a second thought in this day and age. Others go to the opposite extreme: they believe that symbolism is the key to understanding the intellectual world. Symbols, they claim, enable people to bring the incomprehensible into the realm of the tangible, where they can deal with it.

Symbols and metaphors extend into the realm of everyday language and figures of speech. They also permeate images from the world of advertising, as well as political slogans and emblems, the parables of our religions, the icons and writing of foreign and prehistoric cultures, legal customs and artworks, poetry and historical figures—wherever a "signifier" communicates anything beyond its own superficial exterior. The wedding ring, the cross, the national flag, the colors of a traffic light, the red rose, the black of mourning, the candles on a dinner table—countless objects, gestures, images, and figures of speech are linked to complex ideas and traditions. The increasing abstractness and mechanization of our intellectual world seems to be drying up what was once an almost limitless flow of symbols. Of course, the language of computers cannot dispense with symbols. And yet older intellectual systems and intuitive structures were rich in images in a way that their newer counterparts are not. The new "order" is a constructed one that is not spontaneously appealing; it is something that we have to learn. The purpose of this book is to acquaint the reader with the symbols that have been most significant throughout the history of civilization.

It hardly needs to be said that a single volume cannot provide an exhaustive account of the topic. Although I have spent years writing and lecturing about this and related matters, I find it very difficult to delimit the subject matter. Almost anything can be called a symbol and demand an entry in these pages. I confined myself to the most significant symbols and used an admittedly subjective selection process most noticeable when it comes to symbolic figures (historical or legendary persons). Sherlock Holmes, Tarzan, and E.T. are also symbolic figures—but I focused my attention on those who had left deeper impressions in our cultural life. It is clear that we all have our own mythologies and raise certain (real and mythical) persons to the level of symbols. It is likely to be in these areas that individual readers will find gaps in this dictionary.

In other respects, however, this volume seeks to be as inclusive as possible, primarily through the material that goes beyond "Eurocentric" concerns. Other cultures have extraordinary symbolic traditions, and they are included here to suggest the universality of many of these images and their meanings. There are many discussions of the psychological basis for various symbolic associations, as well as material from disciplines that are not always included in discussions of symbolic traditions. The articles and illustrations in this volume are intended to stimulate the reader to explore areas of special interest.

For years now, readers with serious interest in the study of symbols and symbolism have been able to choose from a great number of basic and specialized works on the topic. All of these works, however, have adopted a particular perspective, emphasizing one aspect or another of these great traditions. Until now there has been no single work offering an overview of symbolism in Europe, Asia, Africa, and the New World, from earliest times until the present; no introduction, in words and pictures, to this fascinating topic. I have tried to portray the history of symbols not simply as an accumulation of abstruse thought processes and associations but as a way to ask questions about how artists and thinkers of earlier times worked in the ways they did. A person viewing the various forms of older symbolic thought from a purely rational, scientific standpoint will wonder how such apparently strange notions ever came into being. Our cool reason and our scientific way of thinking have long functioned differently from the authors of the early Christian text *Physiologus*, the medieval bestiaries, or the emblem books of the baroque period. They do not seek rational definition and documentation but a deeper, more "human" meaning for the world that God formed for his creatures.

A highly developed civilization will offer written documentation of an entire world of images, often wondrous and strange. In dealing with images of less developed cultures, we must resort to a process of interpretation and analogy, but there, too, our conclusions have a certain degree of authority.

Jungian psychology, which posits a universal store of archetypes, serves as a tool for "reading" symbolic thought and can itself profit from the rich and varied material of cultural history. Archaeology, anthropology, heraldry, mythology, folklore, and the history of religion together provide a wealth of symbolic tradition that expands our knowledge of what is constant and what is variable in the ways that people think.

Those who are familiar with work in the area of symbols and symbolism know all too well that entire volumes could be (and in some cases have been) written about the interpretations offered in any one of these articles. Within the limits of this project, however, it is possible to offer only the "essential"— enriched, in many cases, by little-known primary data. This dictionary is addressed to the general reader who seeks to know more about how images have been experienced and how their meanings have been extended. Certain concepts treated here might be thought of as strictly religious or theological in nature. And yet "heaven," for example, is also an image that goes back to the archetypal duality of "above and below"; it is not an exclusively theological concept, and it is entirely appropriate to discuss it here in its symbolic as well as religious dimension.

Many traditional symbols are ambiguous: they cannot be explained as having a single, constant meaning. Not every dragon in every culture is an evil enemy; the heart does not always stand for love. Indeed, real symbols, at different stages, are sources of very different, but always relevant, "information." Sometimes we can also discover why a certain symbol has come to have a certain meaning, why it is related in this particular way to *Homo sapiens*— whose interpretations have always been egocentric and anthropomorphic, or, more precisely, "theomorphic": people have long seen in the events and images that surround them a chance to understand their place in a divine plan. A present-day observer who does not appreciate the joy that symbols gave our ancestors would completely miss the purpose served by symbolic thinking.

Such intellectual enslavement has provided us with inhumane products of every sort, including "the atom bomb, and we are starting to grow distrustful. Once again we leaf through the dream book of humanity, look for codes whose significance we have lost—for guides to help us flee the playing fields of the society of production. Our problem is that the ways of life in which religion flourished have become anachronistic for us, along with the rituals of nomads, knights, farmers, and artisans, as they continue to exist in the Third World and, strangely enough, in our own Christian churches" (Adolf Hall, 1982).

This dictionary is itself a "dream book" of codes and images that people of earlier times experienced at times intuitively, at times rationally. Quoting Manfred Lurker, "The meaning of the symbol does not lie in the symbol itself but points to something else outside it. According to Goethe, true symbolism is found wherever 'the particular represents the general, not as a dream or shadow, but as a living, momentary revelation of the inexplicable.' For the religious person the symbol is a concrete phenomenon in which the idea of the divine and the absolute becomes immanent, in such a way as to be more clearly expressed than in words. . . . In the story of salvation, the symbol expresses the unbroken link between Creator and creature. . . . When the individual images are revealed from out of the fullness of the divine original, then they are literally *sym-bolon*, a 'throwing together' of time and eternity. . . . The symbol is at once concealment and revelation" (1987). Admittedly, Goethe was referring to religious symbolism. The present volume also treats images and signs that are formed in the imagination, and abstractions that claim no connection with spirituality. Moreover, when studying other cultures it is difficult to distinguish between experience, myth, and the speculations of priests and scholars. Sources often make it impossible to penetrate deeply enough into ancient and exotic intellectual traditions.

A final word about the previously mentioned polemic against all symbolism. Certain symbols have deadly consequences. The Aztec civilization is not the only one to have had ritual symbols like "sacrificial blood, heart, sun" that led to the destruction of human beings. In modern times other symbols, like "flag, *Führer*, blood and soil," have exacted their terrible price. Yet, symbols are among the most valuable possessions of the human race. They have made possible some of the greatest products of civilization: cathedrals, pyramids, temples, symphonies, sculptures, paintings, religious practices, festivals, dances. The symbols that are rooted in personality have the power to take on lives of their own and, in a curious reversal, influence their creators. It is the responsibility of those of us who are aware of this to discuss symbols that are truly valuable.

"The 'hidden persuaders' of modern advertising," writes Gerhart Wehr (1972), "know how to use the power of images. They know how to subject the Average Joe to an even greater loss of freedom—by manipulating symbols that lead the unsuspecting fellow to spin fantasies." Usually discussing symbols is a benign activity, one that points the way to the intellectual treasures of the past and revitalizes them. But unscrupulous use of this coded world can trap people and turn them into robots.

A few remarks of a more practical nature: It was not possible to document each detail in these articles. The documentation in each case would have been longer than the article itself. At the end of this volume the reader will find a list of important source materials, especially those in English and those that are cited in abbreviated form in the individual articles. In this bibliography I have also stressed books that offer general discussions of issues; only in rare cases did I include highly specialized studies.

A project like this one would have been impossible if standard works rich in primary materials had not been reissued in the last few decades. Let me mention here only the contributions of the Akademische Druck- und Verlagsanstalt (Graz, Austria), whose reprints of the works of Cartari, Hohberg, and Boschius, along with facsimile editions of early codices, were indispensable for this volume.

Finally, not merely as a matter of duty but in all sincerity, let me express my gratitude to those who assisted me in the preparation of this volume, especially in obtaining often elusive primary materials: first of all, my wife, Sibylle, who also was responsible for the illustrations; the late Annette Zieger, Braunschweig; Liselotte Kerkermeier, Freiburg-im-Breisgau; Dr. Friedrich Waidacher, Graz; Edith Temmel, Graz; Erich Ackermann, Bruchenbrücken; Rector Josef Fink, Graz; Ralph Tegtmeier, M.A., Bonn; Gerhard Riemann, Pentenried; Dr. Leonhard Eschenbach, Vienna; Ingeborg Schwarz-Winklhofer, Graz; Kurt Edelsbrunner, Graz; Octavio Alvarez, Enfield, New Hampshire; Dr. Karl A. Wipf, Frauenfeld, Switzerland . . . and many friends and acquaintances. If this book stimulates the reader to reflection, they share the credit.

HANS BIEDERMANN

DICTIONARY
OF
SYMBOLISM

above/below A pair of polar opposites, perhaps the most important and most widespread of all symbolically significant DUALITIES. It may have already taken root in the human psyche when our distant ancestors began to walk upright. *Homo erectus:* FEET "planted in the dust, head raised to the STARS," and the dirt below, from which there seems to be no escaping, is "an earthly remnant, painfully borne." The upper regions—the HEAVENS, the STARS, the source of LIGHT and fertilizing RAIN—are readily associated with the "higher powers": God or the gods, ANGELS. The EARTH remains the realm of mortals, and under it, through an extrapolation from the vertical duality already in place, there comes to be a lower region: Sheol, Hades, HELL. In many cultures this vertical organization of the human cosmos calls for a central AXIS MUNDI or a world TREE to link these different levels; the skilled shaman will then be able to communicate (and interact) with the extrahuman powers and creatures in all of these realms. Since all good things come from above (compare such expressions as "to gain the upper hand," "to be on top of the heap"), male-dominated societies think of the heavens as masculine and the earth and underworld as feminine. (The reverse was the case, for example, in ancient Egypt: the heavens are personified by the goddess Nut; the earth, by the male god Geb.) The upper realm is usually that of the spirit, and the lower that of matter; humans see themselves as "creatures of two worlds," between which they must find their way. Our way of thinking about heaven or the heavens is linked to our religious and ethical views, and even agnostic ideology does not dispense with vertical polarities: they recur, for example, in astrological versions, or quests for contact with extraterrestrials who might, on the basis of their "higher" intelligence or degree of development, come to the aid of beleaguered humanity. (See also MOON, SUN.)

Abraham Biblical patriarch who according to Old Testament accounts, lived around 1800 or 1400 B.C., depending on the starting point for calculation. Presumably a shep-

herd and clan chieftain in the region of Hebron, he is a central figure in many legends. The name 'Abram or 'Ab-raham means "The Father is sublime" or "He is sublime by reference to the Father." Abraham is considered the ancestral father of the people of Israel, called by God, and in the terms of their covenant, to be the bearer of revelation and salvation, "the rock whence [the people of Israel] are hewn" [Isaiah 51:1]. "The numbers in accounts of Abraham's life—at 75 immigration, at 100 the birth of his promised son, at 175 death—are ideal and not meant literally. . . . Were it not for Abraham's faith, the history of religion on earth would have taken a different course. . . . Abraham's key position concretizes the fact . . . that God does not reveal himself to every individual but to one initiator who

Abraham: Sacrifice of Isaac. Mosaic, Synagogue Beth-Alpha, 6th century A.D.

Abraham: Sacrifice of Isaac. Bible illustration, 16th century

passes that revelation on to the community and thus takes responsibility for all" [Schilling, quoted in J. B. Bauer, 1959]. In the New Testament it is noted that what is critical is not corporeal but spiritual and moral descendancy, as John the Baptist preaches: "And think not to say within yourselves, We have Abraham to our father: for I say unto you, that God is able of these stones to raise up children unto Abraham" [Matthew 3:9]—which has been interpreted to mean that God is not limited to the people of Israel but can make followers even out of dead stones (Gentiles). In the Islamic tradition Abraham was to be killed by NIM-ROD, who had been warned in a prophecy about the birth of a child by this name who would be mightier than gods or KINGS. Abraham, the son of the angel Gibreel (Gabriel), was hidden by his mother in a CAVE for fifteen years. There he was nourished by the fingers of Allah, from which he received WATER, MILK, date juice, and curds, until he was old enough to leave the cave and come to know the Creator. There is a similar legend in the Jewish tradition [bin Gorion, 1980].

Abraham, bosom of A symbol for the safe refuge that believers find in the care of a patriarchal figure. Much Romanesque and early Gothic sculpture (Moissac, Reims, Notre-Dame, etc.) depicts the Biblical progenitor (see FATHER), with a cloth across his lap, in which the souls of the just and faithful sit like little children. Although the

"bosom" is usually associated with woman and MOTHER, there has been in the Occident considerable interest in the later Jewish conception of the "patriarchal bosom" of a male progenitor, treated with particular respect in HEAVEN and even on earth richly blessed with wealth and progeny. There is a further context in which Abraham himself is of interest to medieval Christian typology, which sees events in the Old Testament as symbolic anticipations of those in the New: his readiness to sacrifice his son Isaac, in accordance with the will of God, is considered an "imitation before the fact" of the sacrifice of Christ, the Son of God. (See LAZARUS.)

acacia Primarily because of its hard, durable wood, the acacia (in symbology often confused with the locust tree or the mimosa) is a symbol for the victory over death. In this sense it is of particular importance in the symbology of FREEMASONRY: in the "craft-legend" of the murdered master-builder Hiram Abif (Churam Abî), a martyr for the "word of the master," who was murdered by three jealous journeymen and buried under a mound of earth marked by an acacia branch. Because the murdered man lives on symbolically in each new master, the acacia branch suggests the flourishing of the idea even beyond death. Masonic death-notices bear this symbol, and acacia branches are placed in the grave at burial. Botanical distinctions are of little importance here: "The acacia branch on the coffin is an image of the acacia or thistle branch that our brethren laid atop the mound by the head of our worthy father; . . . these are the laurels, the palm fronds, that he received . . ." [Baurnjöpel, 1793].

Actaeon In Greek mythology, a symbolic figure warning humans against approaching the sphere of the gods in a spirit of curiosity or irreverence. The hunter Actaeon, who had been brought up by the CENTAUR Chiron, came by chance upon Artemis (Latin DIANA) bathing with her nymphs in a stream near the city of Orchomenos. Instead of withdrawing in awe, he observed the spec-

Actaeon transformed into a stag. Copperplate, *Musaeum Hermeticum*, 1678

tacle intended for no human eye. The furious goddess of the hunt transformed him into a stag, and his own dogs tore him limb from limb: a frequent subject of mythological paintings. The essence of the myth may be the sacrifice of a human to honor a goddess of the hunt or the forest. Plutarch recounts that as late as the first century A.D. a man dressed in buckskin was hunted and slain on Mount Lycaeus in Arcadia.

Adam and Eve In the Biblical tradition the progenitors of the human race; the European symbol of the original couple (appearing in the myths of many nations and cultures) with whom the human race begins. In many versions the creation of the first man and woman comes only after a variety of attempts to create beings pleasing to the gods. The motif of the loss of immortality through error or violation on the part of the first humans is similarly frequent. In the Biblical account, this takes the form of Adam and Eve's arrogant disregard for the "taboo": at the Serpent's urging (see SNAKE) they eat the fruit (see APPLE) of the TREE of Knowledge. The creation of the first humans out of EARTH and mud recalls the ancient Egyptian myth in which the RAM-headed god Khnum formed all the earth's creatures on a potter's wheel. The more familiar version

of the Biblical story of creation, according to which God molded only Adam out of earth, gave him life, and later made Eve from Adam's side (or rib), does not agree entirely with Genesis 1:27: "So God created man in his own image, in the image of God created he him; male and female created he them." It is of critical importance for symbology, in this context, that Adam and Eve prefigure all of the humans that descend from them both in their free will and in their need for salvation after their sinful deviation from God's plan. For Origen (185–254) Adam symbolizes the mind and Eve (Hawwa, Mother of the Living) the soul.

In depictions of the Crucifixion Adam's skull often appears at the foot of the CROSS, which was similarly said to be made of the wood of the Tree of Knowledge. According to the apocryphal *Gospel of Nicodemus* and the *Golden Legend*, the buried Savior, in his "descent into the kingdom of death" (formerly referred to as his "descent into HELL"), broke open the bars that imprisoned those who had died before his time and in his own Resurrection led Adam and Eve with him to the light. The motif of the creation of Eve from Adam's rib is explained in medieval Jewish legend through the following considerations on the part of the Creator: "I shall not make her from his head, lest she hold her head up too high; nor from his eye, lest she spy about her in every direction; nor from his ear, lest she harken unto one and all; nor from his mouth, lest she speak in excess; nor from his heart, lest she be-

Adam and Eve: Creation of Eve. Saxon chronicle, 13th century

come haughty; nor from his hand, lest she reach out to seize all that surrounds her; nor from his foot, lest she roam in every direction; but from a virtuous part of the body, covered even when one stands naked. And with every part that the Lord formed, he said: Be a godly woman and chaste." Latter-day speculation as to a symbolic connection between rib and lunar crescent (see MOON) is less persuasive than the hypothesis that the apparently varying number of "floating ribs" (Latin *costae volantes*) led to the explanation that one rib, perceived as missing, had been used to create Eve.

Adonis In ancient myth, Adonis is the archetypal symbol of young male beauty, Phoenician in origin (*adon* meaning "lord"), one of the "gods who die and are resurrected," a demon of perennial growth. As the lover of Aphrodite (Latin VENUS) he was killed by an angry BOAR; in some traditions, by the god Aries (Latin MARS), who had taken on animal form. From Adonis' BLOOD grew anemones or pheasant's eye (a variety of Ranunculus), and his soul descended into Hades (see AFTERLIFE). The goddess of love implored Zeus to let Adonis spend only a part of the year in the underworld and return to her in the spring. Her request was granted, and the annual resurrection of youthful nature was celebrated with festivals, songs, and the planting of little "gardens of Adonis." Adonis is the Greek form of the Sumerian god of vegetation, Dumuzi (in Aramaic, Tammuz), the lover of the goddess Inanna. Many religions and cultures symbolize the annual cycle of vegetation with divinities who descend into the underworld and are periodically resurrected.

afterlife There are symbolic designations for the "next" life, life after death, that do not yet characterize its specific nature (as do, for example, the notions of PURGATORY, HELL, HEAVEN, the ISLANDS OF THE BLESSED). We speak of "the Great Beyond" or the "other shore," meaning the opposite bank of a RIVER that marks the boundary between the realm of the living and that of the dead. In Norse mythology that river is Gjöll; in Greek, Acheron, Cocytus, or Styx; other cultures had analogous rivers. The river could be crossed only by boat, usually after the survivors had observed specific ceremonies for the dead and included a coin for the ferryman (Greek Charon) in the coffin. DOGS were frequently killed and buried with the dead to guide them through the unfamiliar terrain ahead. The custom of underground burial and perhaps also the knowledge of great CAVES led to the development (in cultures throughout the world) of the symbol of a subterranean realm of the dead (Hebrew Sheol; Greek Hades; Latin Orcus; Aztec Mictlán), conceived as dark and joyless, and, in some circumstances, taking on the characteristics of hell. In exceptional cases, for example in Native American cultures of North America, the afterlife was placed in a heavenly setting (but with no implication of moral evaluation) or in a distant terrain where life went on much as it had in this world. In civilizations believing in multiple souls (EGYPT, ancient China) it was said that one of the souls remained at or in the grave and required sacrifices, while another had to seek out the other world. Where theories of reincarnation were developed, however, this "other world" was only a sort of holding station where the soul awaited rebirth. In revealed religions with ethical bases (Judaism, Christianity, Islam), but also in a number of other religious contexts (e.g., Egypt), the dead are judged in the afterlife on the basis of their actions while alive and their souls condemned or exculpated. (See SCALES and PARADISE.)

Adonis: Etruscan urn cover, Tuscany, ca. 190 B.C.

In ancient Greece there were frequent expressions of the wish that the deeds of the living might be requited in the afterlife. This explains the following proverbial punishments in Hades for famed evildoers: the "tantalizing" cup of Tantalus (King Tantalus of Lydia provoked the gods by slaughtering his son and serving them his flesh; in Hades he stands in WATER up to his chin but suffers from an unquenchable thirst, because it disappears the minute he tries to drink it; splendid fruits dangle before his mouth, but the wind blows them out of reach when he attempts to seize them; his punishment is never to be able to reach what seems so near), the "ROCK of Sisyphus" (Sisyphus, who built the city of Corinth, tried to trick Hades, the god of the underworld, and was punished by having to roll a boulder uphill, only to have it slip from his grasp and roll back down: the torment of eternal frustration), a Danaidean task (the DANAIDES were the daughters of King Danaus of Argos, who murdered their husbands on their WEDDING night; their punishment in Hades was to pour water into a bottomless container: an endless, senseless task).

In Catholic areas of Central Europe the image of purgatory has become proverbial: a place where lesser sins are expiated by the "poor souls" suffering for a limited period of time, which can be reduced by the prayers of the living, whom the souls of the dead also have the power to help. In popular art purgatory is portrayed as resembling hell, with ANGELS leading the souls (depicted in human form) off to heaven after they have completed their expiation. An impressive image of the afterlife is also that of Jesus Christ, between his death and resurrection, "harrowing hell," or the limbo (Sheol) in which the pious souls of the Old Testament await salvation, as the apocryphal Gospel according to Nicodemus portrays it: "The bronze portals were smashed, the iron crossbeams broken, and the bonds of the dead all loosed. . . . The King of Glory came in like a man, and all the dark corners of Hades were filled with light. . . . The Savior now blessed Adam, making the sign of the cross on his forehead, and he did likewise with

Afterlife: Charon, ferryman of the dead. Cartari, 1647

the elders, prophets, and martyrs. Then he arose with them from out of the underworld." This "anastasis," or resurrection, is frequently portrayed in the art of the Eastern Church.

agate Already in antiquity a prized gem, symbolically associated with the MOON or the planet MERCURY, depending on its coloration. Its bands were seen as representing mythological figures, and it was believed to possess magical powers—warding off storms, keeping RIVERS from overflowing their banks, bringing luck against an opponent, exerting aphrodisiac powers over women. The early Christian text *Physiologus* reports that pearl-fishers (see PEARL) tie a piece of agate to a string and drop it into the sea. "The agate goes to the pearl and does not budge." Divers can follow the line and recover the pearl. The pearl is a symbol of Christ, but "the agate refers to St. John, for he showed us the holy pearl with words: 'Behold, this is the Lamb of God, who carries away the sins of the world.' " The medieval scientist Lonicerus was thinking of the colorful band-structure of agates when he wrote that they would produce richly varied dreams if placed by the heads of sleeping persons. Jean de Mandeville attributed to agate the power to make its possessor clever and eloquent. Pseudo-Albertus Magnus writes of the black-banded agate in 1581 that it helps to repair damage "and fortifies the heart and makes for a powerful person, pleasing and admired of all, glad-hearted as well, and helps [against] disagreeable things."

Ahasuerus: The "Wandering Jew," woodcut, Caën, 1820

Alchemy: Androgyne, pelican, lion, snakes. *Rosarium Philosophorum*, Frankfurt, 1550

Ahasuerus In the Book of Esther, the King of Persia, Xerxes I (reigned 486–465 B.C.), who "reigned from India even unto Ethiopia, over an hundred and seven and twenty provinces." However, in the legend of the Wandering Jew, Ahasuerus was the symbolic figure condemned to roam eternally over the face of the earth. One version of this medieval tale identifies him as the cobbler of Jerusalem who refused to let Christ rest on his way to Calvary and who therefore must wander the earth until Christ's second coming. Tyrolean woodsmen were said to strike crosses with their axes in the flat surfaces of tree stumps to provide a resting station for Ahasuerus; in another version, this was to provide refuge for wood-nymphs fleeing the "Wild Huntsman." (Compare CAIN.)

alchemy and its symbols Alchemy is by no means merely "the fraudulent art of turning base metals to gold," but rather a non-ecclesiastical philosophy seeking the refinement of the soul, obliged by its unorthodox doctrines to take its symbology from the realm of the laboratory (notwithstanding the fact that some alchemists did hope to synthesize precious metals). Until Carl Gustav Jung (1875–1961), alchemy was generally seen only in the context of the history of science, as an "erroneous pre-chemistry," its ideological aspect hardly ever received ap-

propriate attention. Alchemy was primarily striving to extend the spiritual realm of LIGHT by systematically pushing back the world of matter, felt to be heavy and dark; in this respect, alchemy resembles some of the diverse sects of early Christian Gnosticism. The bewildering proliferation of symbolic and allegorical images in late-medieval manuscripts and in Renaissance and baroque books of engravings, seeks not to inform outsiders but to provide initiates in alchemy with guidance in their meditations. From primal matter (*materia prima*), via several purifying steps, the philosopher's STONE (*lapis philosophorum*) is to be formed, which will enable its possessor, among other things, to turn base metals into GOLD and SILVER—the

Alchemy: Circle, triangles, hexagram, mercury-gold. *Musaeum Hermeticum*, 1678

Alchemy: Elements, planets, hexagram, circle. *Trithemii güldenes Kleinod*, 1782

metals of the SUN and the MOON—and to produce a universal medicine for all disease. Many symbols link this ideology with the images of the Rosicrucians (see ROSE) and of FREEMASONRY. The most important motifs from the world of alchemy include the ANDROGYNE, the CADUCEUS, CORAL, the DOVE, the DRAGON, the EAGLE, GOLD, the HEXAGRAM, LEAD, the LION, the MOON, the PEACOCK, the PELICAN, the PENTACLE, the PHOENIX, the QUINTESSENCE, SATURN, SILVER, SULFUR and MERCURY, SUN, TOADS, and the UNICORN.

Alexander the Great Even more in the Orient than in Europe, the Macedonian King Alexandros III (356–323 B.C.) is the

Alchemy: Putrefaction enabling elevation. Basilius Valentinus, Azoth, Paris, 1659

symbolic figure of the brave commander and ruler whose conquests extend to the limits of civilization. The imagination of mythographers East and West was captured by the conqueror of Persia and of Darius III (the Alexander mosaic of Pompeii); the founder of the city of Alexandria, who visited the shrine of Zeus Ammon (Jupiter Ammon) near Memphis and received divine honors; the man who cut the Gordian KNOT; who penetrated with his troops all the way to the Indus delta. The "Alexander romance," legendary narratives that originated in Greece in the second century B.C. and whose popularity extended into medieval times, attributed to Alexander and his men fantastic

Alexander the Great with ram's horns. Coin, Lysimachus

feats of heroism in their struggles against the SAVAGES at the edges of the civilized world; in medieval Byzantium it was given poetic form in the *Song of Alexander*. Syrian versions of the romance were paraphrased in the Persian *Iskander-nameh*. Legendary poems sing of the "bicorn" (see RAM), from the HORN attribute of Zeus Ammon, called in Islamic Arabia and in the Inner Asian Uighur region "Sulkharnai": "In ancient times in the East/ In the city known as Misir/ Lived a man named Sulkharnai/ Who grew to be a thousand years old . . . ." It is said that he crossed over the long bridge of life, climbed a high mountain, and (like the hero Gilgamesh in Sumerian myth) in search of the secret of longevity explored the depths of the sea, turned the TREE of life green again, and went through the land of darkness. He is also said to have ascended into

Aloe. Hohberg, 1675

the HEAVENS by means of a basket borne by EAGLES. Jewish legends reproach him for hubris (arrogance), and report that he ultimately came to know mortal limits (he died suddenly of an attack of fever in BABYLON). In Islamic legend his travels to the limits of the inhabited world become symbolic for the hero who accomplishes great deeds in remote lands. Muhammad developed a stylized version of Alexander as "the archetype of the just and godly king. The consequence of his exploits is the conversion or punishment of the infidel. . . . His greatness is not earned but comes through the grace of Allah" [Beltz]. In the *Gesta Romanorum* (around 1300), however, the emphasis is on the transitory nature of Alexander's glory: "Yesterday he oppressed the earth, and today he lies under it; yesterday the entire earth was not enough for Alexander, and today three or four yards of cloth suffice."

aloe A plant in the lily family, in ancient and modern symbol-books frequently called "agave." Both plants are erroneously said to cure constipation, and the bitterness of each is referred to as a symbol of penitence and suffering. It was also used in embalming, since it was believed to protect against decomposition. The plant continues to grow for many years but blooms fully only once, and thus it was also taken as a symbol for the Virgin Birth in its uniqueness. The bitterness of the aloe inspired Hohberg (1675) to imperfect verse: " 'Tis bitter on the tongue and bitter going down,/ And yet the aloe keeps us healthy and most sound./ Thus Christian's cup is bitter, and he might wish it pass,/ And yet, as Scripture teaches, it saves us at the last."

Alpha and Omega The first and last letters of the Greek alphabet, said to be created by the three Fates; in Hellenistic times a symbol for God as the beginning and the end of the universe, as in such Biblical verses as "I am the first, and I am the last; and beside me there is no God" [Isaiah 44:6]. It is characteristic of late antiquity that it viewed letters, sounds, and words as the elements of creation, with letters (Greek and Hebrew) receiving numerical value as well (see NUMBERS). This opened the door to every sort of cosmogonic speculation, which especially in the Cabala forms the core of "speculative gnosis." In the Book of Revelation the Creator, the "Lord, which is, and which was, and which is to come" calls himself Alpha and Omega [1:8]. The two letters frequently adorned Christian graves as an indication that those buried there had seen in God their beginning and their final goal. In medieval depictions of the Last Judgment, Alpha and Omega, left and right, often adorn the aureole of Christ the Judge.

Alpha and Omega; God Almighty in mandorla. Farmer's almanac, Austria, 1913

Alpha and Omega, ankh-like cross. Tombstone, Fayum, Egypt, 6th century A.D.

Amazons The name of a legendary nation of women warriors; in modern times, the collective symbol for aggressive womanhood. The ancient legend tells of a nation of women by the river Thermodon. They supposedly had occasional relations with men of neighboring nations only for purposes of reproduction, mutilated male offspring, and made slaves of them. They undertook great military campaigns on swift HORSES, armed with bows and ARROWS and double-headed AXES. The historian Diodorus Siculus writes that Amazons from northwestern Africa made conquests through Egypt to Asia Minor. In Greek legend they are repeatedly defeated by male heroes (Hercules, Theseus, Bellerophon, Achilles) and put to death as punishment for their extravagances. There seems to be little historical basis for the myth, although among certain ancient peoples it was not uncommon for women to participate in battle. Such nations often were matriarchies in which name and property were inherited through the mother's side of the family. Mythic exaggeration apparently transformed this social order, which to the Greeks seemed barbaric and unnatural, to the symbolic image of man-hating, bellicose womanhood. The Attic orator Lysias (ca. 450–380 B.C.) portrays the Amazons and their fate as follows: "Masters of many nations and subjugators of their neighbors, they heard of the great prestige of Greece. In hopes of great glory they joined forces with warlike peoples and rode against Athens. But since they came up against valiant men, able warriors, the Amazons' mettle proved no greater than did befit their sex.

Here they died, bore the punishment for their rashness, gave us Athenians the chance to win forever the name of brave victors. . . . Thus did they in their unjust pursuit of an alien goal [i.e., military glory] rightfully lose that which would have been theirs." The myth apparently seeks to warn against excessive political influence by women, such as Athenians felt prevailed in Sparta; starting with meager facts, they constructed a fantasy vision of bloodthirsty women warriors. (Compare VALKYRIES.)

amber (Greek *elektron*) Fossilized resin from coniferous trees that flourished millions of years ago, especially around what is today the Baltic Sea; in Neolithic times already prized for use in jewelry. Amber trade routes once extended overland to distant regions. The Greek nature-philosopher Thales of Miletus (ca. 600 B.C.) was already familiar with the ability of *elektron*, after rubbing, to attract lightweight objects; hence, our word "electricity." This property, along with its combustibility and yellowish color, made amber—in Mediterranean regions an exotic substance—a prized material from which amulet jewelry (against ghosts and all demons) was manufactured. Even today it is thought by some to ward off headaches and bad dreams; yellowish, polished pieces of amber are, after all, said to be "solidified SUNBEAMS" (in antiquity, tears of Phaeton,

Amazon queen Penthesilea with Achilles. Hellenistic vase painting (detail)

the son of Helios). Astrologers associate amber with the PLANET MERCURY. In ancient China as well imported amber was known, and it was apparent from material trapped in the amber that it had once been PINE resin. The Chinese word *(hu-po)* means "TIGER'S soul," in connection with the belief that the soul of the beast sank underground at death and was transformed into amber.

amethyst A cherished jewel, a pale blue or violet variety of quartz (see PRECIOUS STONES), the amethyst was considered a symbol of modesty, peace of mind, and piety, but was also associated with powers of mental healing. In ancient times it was thought to protect against drunkenness (from the Greek a-methysios, not intoxicated); similarly, Eduard Mörike wrote in 1853 in "The Story of Beautiful Lau" that the amethyst "quickly drives the heavy fog of wine from the head, indeed checks tipsiness even in a serious drinker; for this reason it is often used to adorn the fingers of laymen and clergy." Its VIOLET COLOR, associated with atonement, made it the ideal material for expensive rosaries. Conrad of Megenburg ascribed to it the power of warding off evil thoughts and bringing "good reason" (14th century). Traditional books of stone-lore, or "lithica," associate the amethyst with the planet SATURN and mention the stone's supposed ability to protect its possessor against poison and black magic. In more recent esoteric doctrines it is the stone whose cool, mystic emanations best suit the "age of Aquarius," which is soon to replace the "age of Pisces" (see FISH, STARS).

anchor For Mediterranean seafarers, a device symbolizing sea gods, even in ancient times. An anchor promised stability and security and thus became an image of trust and confidence. In pre-Christian burial imagery an indicator of occupation, marking the graves of sailors, it became in the early Christian era, by virtue of its resemblance to a CROSS, a covert symbol of salvation (Latin *crux dissimulata*). The horizontal bar under the ring to which the anchor-cable

Anchor and fish. Early Christian catacomb mosaic, Sousse, North Africa

was tied, was suggestive of the cross, which only the lower parts of the anchor dissimulated. In Christian burial carvings the anchor is often flanked by equally symbolic FISH or DOLPHINS. The anchor is used as an attribute of saints (Clement of Rome; Nicholas, patron saint of seafarers; Placidus; John of Nepomuk), and in heraldry, in which it often designates seaports, or in the arms of the German city of Solingen, whose patron saint, the martyr St. Clement, was drowned at sea with an anchor around his neck. The baroque poet W. F. von Hohberg (1675) proposed this analogy: "As, when a sailor spies a storm at sea,/ He drops his anchor and it holds him fast,/ So when a soul finds strength and trust in Thee,/ No cross, no fear, no woe it can't outlast."

Anchor. Cruciform with olive branches, fish, doves. Early Christian cameo

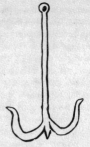

Anchor. Early Christian engraving. Priscilla catacomb, Rome

androgyne (Greek) Both man and woman, a creature of both sexes, the androgyne is often called a hermaphrodite, which more properly designates a creature with intermediate sexual characteristics. In early symbologies the two expressions are generally used interchangeably. Whereas the modern conception here is of a "neither-nor," for ancient civilizations it was primarily a "both-and," a figure simultaneously masculine and feminine, like the pantheistic Zeus in the Orphic hymn: "Zeus is male, Zeus is an immortal woman . . . ." Ancient myths of the creation of the world frequently tell of an original being who only later is divided into two complementary halves. Even ADAM, in Jewish legend, was at first androgynous, until Eve was separated from him and made autonomous. For symbologists this becomes a matter for speculation in the area of duality and totality, with bipolar tension understood as referring not exclusively to sex but also to other pairs of opposites. In the imagery of alchemy for example the androgyne personifies the primal elements SULFUR AND MERCURY (by extension, that which burns and that which is volatile), which are present in the philosopher's STONE, and represent ideal totality at its most elevated. Androgynous figures as symbols of the bringing together of opposites (*coincidentia oppositorum*) in divine, autonomous unity, appear in the divinities of Asia (Shiva-Shakti) and the South Seas, some composed of male and female halves on either side of an imaginary

vertical axis, some male figures with female breasts. In Western depictions we occasionally find gods in female clothing or BEARDS on goddesses and on women saints. The image of the androgyne always signifies the original totality of the maternal and paternal realms (see MOTHER and FATHER) in divine perfection: all tension is resolved, and primal unity is restored. Ovid's *Metamorphoses* tells of Hermaphrodite, whose body becomes inseparably merged with that of the water-nymph Salmakis; as a result, everyone who bathes in Salmakis's SPRING must likewise become a "hermaphrodite."

angel Since "angelology" is more in the domain of theology than of symbology, we must restrict ourselves here to a few general observations. The *maleachim* (messengers of God) mentioned in the Old Testament received the Greek designation *angeloi* (Latin *angeli*); they were viewed at first as personifications of the will of God, then as members of a HEAVENLY host (i.e., army) or of the court of God the King. They were divided into nine orders: seraphim, cherubim, thrones, dominations, virtues, powers, principalities, archangels, and angels. This heavenly hierarchy goes back to Dionysius Aeropagita (ca. A.D. 500), who thus established the basis for the concentric-sphere structure of medieval cosmology: cherubim

Androgyne of alchemy. M. Maier, *Symbola*, 1617

Angel: John the Baptist, portrayed in the iconography of the Eastern Church

as winged creatures, which was long avoided in early Christian art (presumably to avoid confusion with personifications such as Nike/Victory, Glory, and Agatha Tyche, the good-luck goddess of the emperor). Around the fourth century, pictures of angels begin to appear, with halos and wings, as youths clad in white, holding messenger's staffs, LILIES, PALM-branches, fiery SWORDS (for fighting the DEVIL), censers, FLAGS, and TRUMPETS (to announce the Last Judgment). In the Middle Ages and early Renaissance, angels became increasingly ANDROGYNOUS or girl-like. Also, as early as the 12th century, angels were portrayed symbolically as winged

and seraphim are responsible for the *primum mobile* (first movement) and the sphere of the fixed stars, thrones for that of SATURN, dominations for JUPITER, principalities for MARS, powers for the SUN, virtues for VENUS, archangels for MERCURY, and angels for the MOON, the heavenly body closest to the EARTH. Somewhat different orderings appear in some medieval sources. Ancient Eastern depictions of WINGED human forms as embodiments of spirits and supernatural beings influenced the Christian portrayal of angels

Angel: Six-winged seraph on one of the wheels. Didron, *Christian Iconography*, 1866

heads (an expression of "incorporeality") and as children (innocence), which culminates in the *putti* (see CUPID) of the baroque period. There are many portrayals of cherubim with fiery swords as guardians at the locked gates of PARADISE, seraphim as servants at God's THRONE, the archangel Gabriel at the Annunciation, Michael fighting the DRAGON Lucifer, Uriel at Christ's empty grave, angels with Jacob's ladder, and in the baroque, angels leading the souls cleansed in purgatory as they float to heaven. In the 19th century there was a dramatic increase in depictions of guardian angels, especially for children. (See also BOOK (Rasiel) and DEATH, SYMBOLS OF.)

Angel: Michael does battle with the Satanic dragon. W. Auer, 1890

Ankh held by the goddess Hathor. Memphis, Egypt, ca. 1500 B.C.

ankh (Latin *crux ansata*) An important Egyptian symbol for life. It can be interpreted as a CROSS in the form of a T (tau cross or St. Anthony's cross), with a loop attached by which it can be held. The gods—or, in the solar religion of Akhenaton, the life-giving rays of the SUN—may hold the ankh by the loop when they extend it to humans, or the ankh may appear in isolation in depictions of surviving corporeal death. In early Christian (Coptic) times in Egypt, the ankh was used as a symbol of eternal life, granted to humanity by the sacrificial death of the Savior. Because its form suggests a key, it is also called the "key of life" or the "key of the Nile." In recent years it also has become an emblem of various organizations.

Anthony of Egypt, Saint (251–356 A.D.) A symbolic figure on the basis of the many paintings showing his temptation by the forces of Satan; the first documentable figure in the history of monasticism in the desert of Egypt. He is said to have withdrawn to a CAVE to lead a solitary life of prayer and meditation. For the DEVIL, this way of life, so pleasing to God, constituted a challenge, and he sought to lead Anthony astray, first in the guise of irresistibly beautiful women, then with the help of demons—but in vain. At the age of 90, guided by a WOLF, he went into the desert to seek a 110-year-old

hermit named Paul. Subsequently Paul died the death of a holy man and Anthony buried him, then later died himself, a model of the pious man who defies every temptation. His day is the 17th of January. *The Golden Legend* of Jacobus of Voragine (ca. 1270) contains numerous legends of St. Anthony with symbolic details. For example: "A monk had withdrawn from worldly life, but not completely, for he secretly retained a portion of his possessions. To him St. Anthony said: 'Go and buy meat.' And he went and bought meat; but as he was carrying it, DOGS fell on

St. Anthony in the desert. W. Auer, 1890

him and bit him. Then St. Anthony said to him: 'If a man renounce the world but would have its goods, he will be attacked by devils and torn asunder.'" Anthony of Egypt is not to be confused with Anthony of Padua (1195–1231), of whom it is said that he preached to the FISHES and that a DONKEY knelt when Anthony stood before him holding the consecrated wafer. Anthony of Padua is thus the patron saint of animals; he is popularly believed to provide reliable assistance with the recovery of lost property, if he is invoked with a believing heart.

Antichrist In present-day usage, an allegorical designation for an enemy of the

Antichrist. Woodcut from *Des Entkrist Leben*. Strasbourg, ca. 1480

Church or of humanity, or for a corresponding power. The personification of evil (called by Luther "End-Christ") as Christ's opponent in the final struggle at the Last Judgment, goes back to ancient dualistic notions (compare GOG AND MAGOG). In the Essenian sect of Kumran on the Dead Sea, books were written about the battle between the "Sons of LIGHT" against Belial ("spite" in Hebrew) as leader of the forces of darkness. Later, heretics and persecutors of Christians (such as the emperor Nero) were referred to as embodiments of the Antichrist. Irenaus of Lyon (second century A.D.) writes that the Antichrist will come with the might of the DEVIL, cast aside the idols, and be worshipped as a god, ten KINGS giving him the power with which to persecute the Church; he is to establish himself in the temple at JERUSALEM and rule three years and six months, until the Lord appears in the HEAVENS and casts him and his followers into the fiery slough. His name is the subject of much speculation, taking off from the "666" prophecy in the Book of Revelation 13:18 ("Let him that hath understanding count the number of the beast: for it is the number of a man; and his number is six hundard threescore and six"); Euanthes, Lateinos, and Teitan are among the hypotheses. According to a Jewish legend, an Antichrist named Armillus resulted from the coupling of heathen scoundrels with a marble pillar depicting a beautiful maiden. Beginning in the 13th century, reformers and founders of new sects often designate the papacy as an institution of the Antichrist. Of interest to cultural historians are the incunabulum *Life*

of the Antichrist (ca. 1480, printed in German with no date or place of publication) and Sebastian Franck's *Chronica* (1536). The Antichrist also appears frequently as the leader of Satan's legion in popular legends of the great final battle (see END OF THE WORLD)

ant Despite their size, ants are by no means insignificant in symbology. The early Christian text *Physiologus* quotes Solomon— "Go to the ant, thou sluggard" [Proverbs 6:6]—and makes the ant, along with the BEE, the symbol of diligence. It also mentions that ants not carrying bits of food do not beg from their fellows who are, but rather go and get their own, which supposedly shows their wisdom, as does their biting seeds stored in the anthill to keep them from sprouting, and the fact that they store food just before winter storms (a symbol of foresight). Finally, it is said of the ant that it recognizes barley and rye by smell but collects only the true grain (wheat) and not the fodder. "So must you shun food for animals and take the grain that is set aside to be kept. For the barley is as heretical doctrine, the grain however as steadfast faith in Christ." In India, however, the ant, so esteemed in the West, is a symbol of the aimless terrestrial scurrying of unenlightened humanity. For a variety of other peoples, the diligent insect is a helper of the divinity who created the world. In ancient Greek myth the first inhabitants of Aegina are called "Myrmidons," ants, because they farmed the soil with antlike patience, endurance, and diligence. A Thessalian legend traces plow-farming back to the invention of the important farm implement by a nymph named Myrmex, ant; in this civilization ants were honored as holy creatures.

ape Various species of apes (Greek *pithekos*, Latin *simia*) were known in the ancient world and were occasionally trained and exhibited in theatrical performances. "Ape" was a pejorative epithet, and the animal was a symbol of malice and physical ugliness. Nevertheless apes were often kept as exotic pets. It was popularly believed that an ape's

EYE rendered its possessor invisible, and that an ape's urine, spread on the door of an enemy, would make the person generally hated. In ancient Egypt, apes (long-tailed monkeys, and especially caped baboons) were viewed with great respect; Nubian tribes had to provide them as tribute, and it was said of the apes that they understood human speech and could learn better than many schoolchildren. The screeching of baboons at dawn was interpreted as the pious animals' prayer to the sun-god coming over the horizon. Thoth (Djhuty), the god of wisdom, though usually portrayed with the head of an IBIS, also appears as an old, white caped baboon, sitting behind a scribe and overseeing his transcription of important texts. The ape was a holy animal in ancient India as well, as is seen from the worship of the ape-god Hanuman, who appears in the epic *Ramayana* as Rama's powerful assistant and emissary. He is the symbol of strength, loyalty, and self-sacrifice. Although Indian farmers suffer from plagues of apes, they eagerly celebrate the festival of Hanuman-Jayanti, Hanuman's birthday. The ape was revered in China as well. In South China and Tibet families proudly trace their ancestry back to simian forefathers who abducted women and had children by them. The ape Sun Wu-k'ung is famous for the acts of bravery and the many pranks he is said to have carried out while accompanying the Buddhist pilgrim Hsüan-tsang on his journey to India. Apes were often portrayed with the "PEAR of longevity" in their hands.

Ape: The devilish ape "drinking tobacco." London, 1618

Because of similarities of pronunciation, pictures of apes on Scots pines or on horseback signify the wish for high social rank. In the Chinese zodiac the ape is the ninth sign. The ape is a calendar symbol in ancient Mexican cultures also, lending its name (in Aztec *Ozomatli*, in Mayan *Ba'tz*) to the 11th day of the month. The ape was a god of dance, and those born under this sign were expected to become jugglers, pranksters, dancers, or singers. In ancient Mexico the ape has a not entirely explicable symbolic connection to the wind. In the ancient Mexican myth of periodic "ends of the world," the second era or "sun," the wind-sun, was ended by devastating tornadoes, and the humans of this era were transformed into apes.

In Christian symbology the ape is seen negatively, as a caricature of the human and as an emblem for the vices of vanity (with a mirror in its hand), greed, and lechery. Apes in chains symbolize the DEVIL vanquished. They also stand for uninhibited, filthy humans, a metaphor probably derived from the early Christian text *Physiologus*, where the ape is portrayed as wicked but also as prone to imitation. The hunter pretends to rub glue into his own eyes, then hides; the monkey descends from the tree and, "aping" the hunter, glues its own eyes shut, and thus can be easily snared. "Thus, too, does the great hunter—the devil—hunt us. With the glue of sin he dazzles the eyes,

Ape: Caped baboon. Fresco, grave of Tutankhamen, 18th dynasty

makes our spirit blind and sets a great snare, ruining us body and soul." In the psychology of the unconscious, the ape is taken to be a symbol of insecurity and doubt about one's own role, as well as of immodesty. In the language of dreams, any species of ape is "that which is like the human without being human" but which seeks to attain humanity; "a person who dreams of an ape approaches this possibility from a starting-point held in contempt" [Aeppli]. Asian sculptures now sold widely portray three monkeys with their hands over their mouths, eyes, and ears. Although in some countries this is widely taken to mean that it is better to see, hear, and say *nothing,* this of course is incorrect: it is precisely *evil* that one is to avoid seeing, hearing, and speaking. These monkeys supposedly originate with simian spies that the gods sent among humans to get information about their actions; charms to ward off this spying supposedly portrayed the monkeys as blind, deaf, and mute. In Japan the three monkeys are also explained by the homonymy of the word *saru,* which means both "monkey" and "not do," thus symbolizing conscious abstinence from evil.

apple   A fruit with a core and multiple symbolic meanings. Wild crab-apples were gathered in ancient times, and full-sized varieties were already found in Central Europe in the Neolithic era. In ancient myth the god of intoxication Dionysus was the creator of the apple, which he presented to Aphrodite, goddess of love. Erotic associations liken apples to women's breasts, and the core of an apple cut in halves to the vulva. In this way the apple acquired a somewhat ambiguous symbolism. The goddess Eris called for "the judgment of Paris" when she threw down a golden apple marked "for the most beautiful" (the "apple of discord" that in other languages corresponds to the English "bone of contention"); Helen of Troy was Paris' reward for choosing Aphrodite, but his abduction of Helen led to the Trojan War. Hercules had to brave great danger to retrieve the apples of the Hesperides from the far reaches of the west (compare ISLANDS OF THE BLESSED). On the

other hand, the earth-goddess Ge (or Gaea) gave Hera an apple as a symbol of fertility upon her engagement to Zeus. In Athens newlyweds divided and ate an apple when they entered the bridal chamber. Sending or tossing apples was a part of courtship. The Old Norse goddess Iduna guarded apples that brought eternal youth to whoever ate them. In the Celtic religion the apple was the symbol of knowledge handed down from ancestors.

Chinese symbology starts with the homonymy of the words for "apple" and "peace" (*p'ing*), but the word for disease (*ping*) is also similar, and thus it is considered inappropriate to bring apples to the sick. Apple blossoms, on the other hand, are a symbol of feminine beauty. In Europe the apple of the Garden of Eden, from the TREE of Good and Evil, is the symbol of temptation and original sin. In European representations of the Fall (see ADAM AND EVE) the serpent holds an apple in its mouth, although Genesis refers only to "fruit"; our apple was unknown east of the Mediterranean. Various traditions replace the apple with a FIG, quince, or POMEGRANATE. Paintings of Christ's birth show him reaching out for an apple, symbolically taking the sins of the world upon himself; apples on a European Christmas tree suggest that Christ's birth

Apple held by Eve. Jewish book illustration, ca. 1350

makes possible a return to the state of innocence that preceded the Fall. The enticing sweetness of the apple, however, was first associated with the enticements of sin, also in the surface similarity of the Latin words for "apple" (*malus, malum*) and for "bad, evil, sin" (*malum*). Thus in baroque art the skeleton of death often is holding an apple: the price of original sin is death.

In the secular realm the apple, with its almost perfectly spherical form, functions as a symbol for the cosmos; thus many emperors and KINGS hold an "imperial apple" along with their scepter. In ancient times some coins showed three spheres representing the three continents known to the emperor Augustus—Asia, Africa, and Europe; the imperial apple was crowned by an image of the goddess of victory (Nike, in Latin Victoria). In the Christian era a CROSS assumed this role, so that the astronomical symbol for earth is a circle with a cross on it. In the legends of Celtic Britain, Avalon (Appleland) is a symbol for divine joy. Thus Robert Graves takes the apple as a symbol for springtime and lovers' bliss: "It grants admittance to the Elysian Fields, those apple orchards where only the souls of heroes may go. . . . An apple is the gift of the three Hesperides to Hercules, and the gift of Eve, 'mother of all the living,' to Adam. Finally, Nemesis, the goddess of the holy grove, who in later myths became a symbol of divine vengeance wrought upon arrogant kings, carries an apple-bough, her gift to heroes. Every Neolithic or Bronze Age paradise was an island of orchards. . . ." It should be noted that even the unpalatable crab-apple found its place in heraldry: "A crab-apple is harsh and tart, is also particularly useful for keeping WINE from turning. Thus rigor that seems harsh chastises evil and conserves virtue" [Böckler].

Ark (from Latin *arca*, box or chest) The vessel that, according to the Bible, saved NOAH and his family, as well as two of every sort of animal, from the FLOOD. Christian symbolic exegesis interprets the Ark as the way of saving believers from the engulfing sea of godlessness: i.e., baptism, a sort of

Ark: "It sinketh not but is borne upwards." J. Boschius, 1702

ship that does not go under, however tempest-tossed the seas of the world. "The Ark is the Church, Noah is Christ, the dove the Holy Ghost, the olive-branch God's goodness" [St. John Chrysostom, ca. 360 A.D.]. In the symbolism of FREEMASONRY, one branch of the order was called the "Royal Ark Mariners," and in a manual for an order of nuns the Ark is explained as follows: the Ark signifies "the human heart, which is as tossed about by the passions as this box was by the Flood" [Baurnjöpel, 1793]. "Arcane" teachings are secret knowledge, locked up as if in a chest, a tradition to which outsiders have no access. The chest containing the Ten Commandments, carried by the Hebrews during their wanderings, is also called the "Ark of the Covenant." In psychoanalysis the Ark, like a house, is an image of refuge in the womb. (See also CHEST.)

Arma Christi The "weapons of Christ"; designation of the baroque period for the implements of Christ's torment and crucifixion. They were considered powerful weapons against sin, leading sinners to contemplate Christ's suffering and thus capable of rooting out every germ of evil from the human soul. These "weapons" included, in

Arma Christi, and Christ himself, in the Tree of Salvation. Ulm, 1485

addition to the CROSS itself, HAMMER, NAILS, tongs, scourges, spears, a staff with a sponge attached, the CROWN of Thorns, and a HAND, with which Jesus was slapped. Such Arma Christi not only appeared as attachments to rosaries, especially in the 18th century, but also appear on crucifixes of the period, which thus became composite symbols of Christ's sacrifice for the redemption of the world.

Armageddon A symbolic battleground, the site of the final conflict between the forces of Satan (see GOG AND MAGOG) and the faithful. In reality, this apocalyptic setting is in the ruins of the ancient city of Megiddo (in Arabic Tell el-Mutesellim), east of Haifa. From the early Bronze Age on, Megiddo was an often heavily fortified settlement on the border between the Egyptian and the Syrian and Babylonian spheres of influence. It was thus the site of numerous major battles. Here, for example, the army of Thutmosis III annihilated a Syrian-Palestinian coalition in 1478 B.C., and Josiah, king of Judah, tried to hold back the troops of Pharaoh Necho that were marching toward BABYLON: it was an utter rout, and Josiah himself was killed. The enemies of EGYPT were made to pay a forfeit of "a hundred hundredweight of silver and one hundredweight of gold," which apparently so impressed the authors

of the Bible that Megiddo (Armageddon) was made the site of the final conflict [Revelation 16:16].

arrow A weapon fired from a distance to penetrate its prey, the arrow, for psychoanalysts, is a symbol of phallic sadism; in other contexts it may be associated with impulse, speed, menace, and determination. Surprisingly, not all ancient civilizations used the bow and arrow; in pre-Columbian Central America, for example, they were replaced by a spear hurled with a throwing stick (Aztec *atlatl*). Arrows are often associated with the rays of the SUN, and of course with hunting. They were the weapons of the Greek divinities Apollo and Artemis (DIANA); the Hindu weather god Rudra, in his dark phase, sent arrows of disease, and in his benevolent form (Shankara) warming rays of sunlight. In ancient Egypt the LION-headed goddess Sekhmet, associated with the hot WINDS of the desert, loosed arrows with which she shot through hearts, and the goddess Neith had crossed arrows as her attribute. The experience of being wounded by love is brought about by arrows of the god of love in his various forms (Greek Eros, Latin Amor or CUPID, Hindi Kama), but the arrows of ecstatic love of God likewise penetrate the human HEART [St. Theresa of Avila, St. Augustine]. Held by SKELETONS, the bow and arrow become symbolic of DEATH, as in depictions of the rider on the pale horse of Revelation 6:8. In his great

Arrow and target: "Some will hit, some will miss." J. Boschius, 1702

Arrow: Death as archer. Woodcut (detail) from *Ackermann aus Böhmen*, 1463

trials, JOB says, "The arrows of the Almighty are within me, the poison whereof drinketh up my spirit" [Job 6:4]. Great plagues were often personified by avenging ANGELS shooting arrows. In architectural sculpture of the Middle Ages, archers are often portrayed alongside animals associated with lechery (the GOAT or the ROOSTER), apparently suggesting Cupid's arrow.

The tradition that a single arrow can be easily broken while a bundle of them holds strong, symbolizes strength through unity, in China as well as in the Occident. When treaties were agreed upon, in China as among the Native American peoples, arrows were broken to express the renunciation of war. Bundles of arrows were the heraldic symbol of Queen Isabella I of Spain (ruled 1474–1504); later, they appear in combination with the YOKE in the arms of Spain and the Spanish Falange. A CROSS with the head of an arrow at each extremity was the POLITICAL SYMBOL of the Hungarian Nyilaskereszt ("arrow cross") Party before the Second World War; three arrows were the emblem of the Austrian Social Democrats. In modern convention the arrow simply indicates direction, and no one associates it with weaponry. A heart pierced by an arrow appears frequently on trees or walls as the symbol of a love match.

The FEATHERS on arrows (for hunting or war) seek to stabilize their course and may also go back to an attempt to impart to them birdlike qualities (speed, lightness).

The arrow lives on in our day in expressions like "straight as an arrow" and in the names of swift, sleek vehicles (e.g., Silver Arrow). The modern counterpart of the arrow as an aggressive weapon (with far greater potential for intimidation) is the long-range missile with its tapered nose and feather-like stabilizers.

Among the saints associated with arrows, St. Sebastian, his body pierced by the arrows of a nonbeliever, is the best known.

Asclepius, staff of A staff with a serpent around it; in Europe, the present-day symbol of pharmacy, in memory of the Ancient Greek god of healing Asclepius (Latin Aesculapius); the symbol, also, of the medical profession. The relevance of the serpent lies in the SNAKE's annual shedding of its skin, traditionally thought of as a process of rejuvenation. Snakes ("Asclepius-adders") were sacred creatures in the hospitals of antiquity set up especially at medicinal springs. One astral myth holds that Zeus put Asclepius and the serpent into the heavens as the constellation Ophiuchus ("holder of snakes"). It is said that when an epidemic was devastating ancient Rome her people brought the god of healing there from Epidaurus (Greece) in the form of a gigantic snake and that the contagion was immediately snuffed out. The staff of Asclepius should

Asclepius with his staff. Cartari, 1647

Staff of Asclepius: The Old Testament "serpent of brass." Hohberg, 1675

not be confused with the CADUCEUS, the staff of the messenger Hermes or Mercury, with its two intertwined serpents. In modern times the pharmacist's staff of Asclepius was modified by the addition of a bowl at its higher end, from which the serpent is drinking; this was to distinguish the pharmaceutical emblem from that of the medical profession. An earlier prototype of the staff of Asclepius is the staff, also with two serpents entwined, of the Sumerian-Akkadian god of healing and the underworld, Ningizzida, portrayed in other contexts with a horned serpent; Ningizzida was the tutelary god of King Gudea of Lagash (ca. 2100 B.C.). Eshmun (Jasumunu), a Phoenician god of healing honored in Carthage as well, is considered a manifestation of Asclepius and was portrayed with the staff and serpent. (Compare THYRSUS.) The orientalist A. Jirku associated the staff of Asclepius both with the magic rod of Exodus 7, which transforms itself into a serpent and with which Moses brings down the plagues upon Pharaoh's land, and with the "brasen serpent" on a pole in the desert, the sight of which cures those who have been bitten by poisonous snakes [Numbers 21:9; II Kings 18:4].

ashes   It was believed in many older civilizations that what remains when FIRE has consumed everything else contains the concentrated powers of that which was burned; ashes, however, also symbolize the transitory nature of all earthly form. The pure, cold

remains of a fire, ashes also provide an image of death, matter returned to dust, or something close to it. In rituals of death and rebirth, for example puberty rites of preliterate peoples, the candidates are frequently dusted with ashes, to give them a "ghostly" appearance. Ashes are here the mark of a rite of passage. In Mediterranean civilizations ashes are a familiar symbol of death, purification, and reflections upon the transitory nature of life on earth. As a sign of mourning the Egyptians and the Greeks covered their heads with ashes, or sat or rolled in ashes (and Arabs and Jews similarly). On the other hand, the power of purification was ascribed to the ashes of sacrificed animals (perhaps because of the cleansing power of lye, made from ashes). The ashes of the statesman Solon were strewn over the island Salamis to bind it eternally to Athens. The ashes of supposed WITCHES, however, were often scattered in streams to wash away every trace of their existence and to prevent the return of their ghosts. Ashes symbolize not only humility (sackcloth and ashes), mourning, and penitence (the CROSS of ashes on the forehead of the devout Catholic on Ash Wednesday) but also hope for new life: the PHOENIX is purified by the flame and rises rejuvenated out of the ashes. The Rosicrucians teach that the form of a flower burnt and reduced to dust can be reconstructed from the ashes that remain.

asphodel   A plant of the LILY family, with dark green leaves and pale blossoms; in Greek mythology, it grew in the meadow of the underworld as well, bringing joy to the souls of the dead. The asphodel was associated with the goddesses Demeter and Persephone; its tubers, according to the mythology of the AFTERLIFE, were the food of the dead in Hades, but they were also eaten by the living in times of want and were thought to have medicinal powers to treat poisoning. Clusters of the pale flowers, given the Latin name *hastula regia*, were used to adorn images of the gods. In Mediterranean countries, the "affodil," which still has its traditional symbolic association with mourning, was believed by the ancients to dispel evil spirits, and was associated with the planet SATURN.

astrological symbols Astrology is in general a study or doctrine of analogies relating cosmic events to events in our lives: it seeks to define how we are influenced by or dependent upon astral displacements and the astral calendar. It would appear, moreover, to be the only ideology with a paralogical basis to have attracted interest from the times of the earliest civilizations onward; even today, despite rejection by representatives of the empirical sciences, it has more adherents than in any previous age. Fixed STARS were long ago observed to move about the celestial pole and were thus distinguished from the PLANETS, in whose number the SUN and the MOON were included (the source of the sacred number SEVEN: sun, moon, MERCURY, VENUS, MARS, JUPITER, and SATURN). The zodiac was divided into 12 signs not only in the Occident but also in China, to establish a doctrine of compatibility in relations between persons born under the respective signs. Ancient Mexican civilizations also used signs (mostly of animals) to characterize individuals by their birthdays; their system, however, consisted of 20 day-signs that recurred cyclically: CROCODILE, WIND, house, LIZARD, SNAKE, death, DEER, HARE, WATER, DOG, APE, grass, reed, jaguar, EAGLE, VULTURE, earthquake, stone knife, RAIN, and FLOWER. Four of them (house, hare, reed, and stone knife) also appeared as year-signs.

The quest for cosmic laws that would define a harmony between "HEAVEN and EARTH" led many civilizations to come up with heavenly images of which humans then tried to develop analogues in their own world. The figures that resulted are generally highly impressive and appealing; even in the age of technology their effect seldom fails. It should be of interest to semanticists that in all "Western" civilizations the astrological symbols for the planets and signs of the zodiac have gone virtually unchanged for many centuries.

Traditional Chinese astrology differs from Occidental astrology in many respects. In

Astrological symbols: sun, moon, Mars, Mercury, Jupiter, Venus, Saturn

the Chinese system there are 28 moon-stations and 12 star-stations, to which 12 earth-branches correspond. Neither set of 12 coincides with the 12 signs of our zodiac, which however has also been known in China since the Middle Ages, presumably through the influence of Westerners (see STARS). The observation of FIVE ELEMENTS in connection with the 12 star-stations led to a cycle of 60, which repeats indefinitely. Horoscopes were done in China as well as in the West, primarily to attain the greatest compatibility between the partners in carefully arranged MARRIAGES. Violations of the ensuing prescriptions were interpreted as a breach in the harmony of heaven and earth. India and Indonesia also had complex astrological systems; some have used similarities between them and the calendar and astrological symbologies of ancient Mexico to support the hypothesis of a pre-Columbian Asian influence in the New World.

Atlantis According to two dialogues of the philosopher Plato (427–347 B.C.), an island kingdom submerged in the ocean west of Gibraltar; its capital, Basileia, was con-

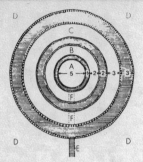

Atlantis: Map of the capital, following Plato's description

structed upon concentric CIRCLES of land and WATER. Atlantis was said to have been originally a sort of PARADISE, blessed by nature and ruled by wise KINGS, until the inhabitants became presumptuous and wicked and the gods decided to submerge it. Aristotle (384–322 B.C.) considered the account to be pure fiction, but since then countless scholars have tried to determine a factual basis for the myth and to discover the location of the island kingdom. Since Plato claims that the story of Atlantis came to his ancestor Solon from Lower Egypt, it is conceivable that the ancient Egyptian mythic geography of a land of bliss (see ISLANDS OF THE BLESSED) located in the distant West, was the basis upon which Plato set about erecting his detailed mythic structure. A

once-accessible island paradise, vanished through human weakness, along with the concentric circles of its capital, suggest both the symbolic nature of this Platonic myth (the subject of countless books) and something of its force, its appeal. The myth seems to go back to the widespread image of a primeval GOLDEN AGE, a topos of great importance in the myths of ancient civilizations. The Atlantis CROSS is a combination of concentric circles and a cross-like structure, corresponding roughly to Plato's description of the layout of the capital, Basileia, in *Timaeus* and *Criteas*. It is an emblem of esoteric groups tracing their heritage back to the mythical civilization of Atlantis.

Atlas Today, the word for a bound collection of maps, after the title and frontispiece of Mercator's volume (1595). There are many artistic representations of the Titan who bears the world, or the heavens, on his shoulders. In various versions of the Greek myth, Atlas is a brother of PROMETHEUS, a king of the island nation of ATLANTIS, or a personification of the AXIS MUNDI or of a stone PILLAR separating HEAVEN and EARTH. He is also described as knowing intimately the sea and its depths. In Hesiod's mythology he is an ally of Cronus (Latin SATURN) against the latter's son Zeus (see STONE); when the army of the Titans was defeated, Atlas was condemned to carry the sky on his shoulders (which is reminiscent of myths

Atlantis: The so-called Atlantis cross, an esoteric emblem

Atlas. Detail from a drinking bowl. Greece, ca. 540 B.C.

from Asia Minor about the giant Upelluri; see ROCK). In the legend of Perseus, however, Atlas was a KING of Mauritania (today Morocco) who refused hospitality to the hero. As punishment Perseus revealed to him the head of Medusa (see GORGONS), whereupon the king was transformed into a gigantic rocky mountain, which has borne his name ever since. The legendary high mountain far off to the west may have been inspired by the volcano Pico de Teide on Tenerife (see ISLANDS OF THE BLESSED).

Attila The "Scourge of God" became a symbol for the barbarian who threatens the Occident. We do not know the real name of this king of the Turkish tribe of the Huns (from the Chinese *Hsiung-nu*); "Attila" is the diminutive of the Gothic word *attar*, "father," thus "daddy" (corresponding to the figure Atli in Nordic myth; in the *Nibelungenlied* [see SIEGFRIED] Etzel). The king of the Huns ruled from 434 onward with his brother Bleda; from Bleda's death (445) onward Attila was the sole ruler of his peoples and ancillary groups. His domain extended from the Caucasus to Hungary, and from there he pushed westward. When he arrived in Gaul an army of Franks, Burgundians, and Visigoths led by the Roman general Aetius opposed and defeated him on the Catalaunian Plains near Troyes (451). An incursion into Italy took him up to the gates of Rome, but he retreated to his Pannonian headquarters, where he died in 453 on his wedding-night hours after marrying his Teutonic bride Ilkido. His empire was soon broken up, but his memory lives on in legend and epics. The jacket or cape that was part of the hussar's dress uniform bore Attila's name until World War I.

ax Since the Neolithic Age an important and thus richly symbolic instrument for battle and work. As a weapon wielded by gods of the sky or of THUNDER against their enemies, the ax in early depictions, such as rock drawings, is often difficult to distinguish from a club or mace (see HAMMER). The observation that blows of the ax often produce sparks led to the association of storm-

Ax used as a religious insignia. Dahomey, West Africa, 19th century

gods with LIGHTNING and the destruction of demonic creatures (e.g., GIANTS). In Africa a decorative, and thus nonfunctional, ax is often symbol of the rank of chief and of executive power in general. Since large sacrificial animals in many metal-age civilizations were killed with an ax, it often came to symbolize BLOOD sacrifice, and often judicial authority, as in the fasces of ancient Rome. In Christian times the ax became the symbol or attribute of Joseph (the carpenter) and of St. Boniface, who used it to cut down the oak-tree near Geismar dedicated to Donar, the god of thunder. The ax applied to the roots of a tree is also a symbol of the Last Judgment. The old German custom of striking a blow with an ax to establish building sites or borders links the ax in the Austrian tradition especially with legends of St. Wolfgang. Martyrs executed with an ax, like Barnabus, Matthew, Matthias, and

Ax as an attribute of Sts. Matthew and Wolfgang. W. Auer, 1890

Ax, Double-headed: Head of a Shango dancer's club. Yoruba, West Africa

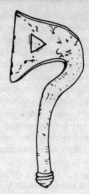

Ax: Bronze votive ax, 3 inches long. Martigny (Switzerland), Gallo-Roman

Thomas Beckett, were often portrayed with one. One special form is the *labrys* (see AX, DOUBLE-HEADED). The proverbial hatchet of the Native American was originally a club; the ax blade was added to it only after contact with European colonists.

ax, double-headed (Greek *labrys*, from a pre-Hellenic word) The symmetrical *labrys* was used as a carpenter's tool, and Homer refers to its use on the battlefield by enemies of the Greeks. It was of particular importance as a religious symbol, probably at first as a whetted stone-AX, and, according to Robert Graves, was originally associated with the female Titan Rhea, then usurped by the Olympic gods and attributed to Zeus as his THUNDER-bolt. Earlier it was important in the religious cult of Minoan Crete; the two whetted blades with their half-MOON shape suggest that the *labrys* may have been a lunar

symbol, but some have taken it as an indication that every sort of power "cuts both ways." The symbol of the *labrys* was carved into the stone blocks from which Minoan palaces were built, perhaps to indicate that they were under divine protection. The weapon itself probably originated in Asia Minor and is often depicted in the hands of the legendary AMAZONS. Modern feminist literature associates the *labrys* with the phases of the moon and with matriarchy (see MOTHER). It was later used as a tool for animal sacrifice, and in the Roman era the

Ax: Hephaestus splits Zeus's head and Athena is born. M. Maier, *Atalanta*, 1618

Ax, Double-headed: On the head of a bull (Bycranion). Mycenaean Greece

war-god JUPITER Dolichenus carried it as his attribute. The Etruscan god of the dead, Charon, has a similar insignia, which is, however, closer to a HAMMER. When performing dances to honor the thunder-god Shango, the Yoruba of West Africa carry ceremonial clubs that also suggest the *labrys* of the ancient cults of the eastern Mediterranean region. The same is true for the wooden *oxé* of the Afro-Brazilian Candomblé ritual honoring Xangô, the god of thunder and LIGHTNING; this New World ritual constitutes a modification of the Yoruban original [Kasper].

axis mundi The "axis of the world," a wide-spread image from the cosmology of ancient civilizations. Their own realm was thought of as a sort of middle kingdom, the center of the (flat) EARTH; the zenith was Polaris, the pole star, about which all the other stars seem to rotate. An imaginary support was referred to as holding up the heavenly firmament—in some versions a crystalline pillar rotating like a spindle; in others a world-MOUNTAIN or -TREE. In cultures including shamanistic trance religions, the axis mundi was also thought of as a pathway along which the shaman could journey from one layer of existence to another in order to communicate with subterranean and celestial deities or demons on behalf of the community. Visual representations of the axis mundi make it a symbol of the orderliness of creation, of humanity securely positioned in a well-organized universe. The sacred POLE, the MENHIR, and the OBELISK were all originally expressions of similar cosmologies. (See also OMPHALOS, SQUARE, PILLAR, and TEMPLE.)

tals to "re-establish the broken axis linking HEAVEN and EARTH, against God's will if need be" [Lurker, 1987; see AXIS MUNDI]. A Jewish legend from the Talmud makes the misanthropy of the builders responsible for God's punishment: a worker is said to have fallen to his death from the heights of the structure, but "the master builders are totally caught up with their own concerns and the wish to make quick work of this structure, for which they plan to become famous. Thus they pay little attention, just have the body carted away without any interruption of work. A few days later a stone comes loose and a

Babel, Tower of Designation given to Etemenanki, the ziggurat-TEMPLE of the city of BABYLON, or perhaps a similar structure, over 150 feet tall, in Borsippa (today Birs Nimrud) south of Babylon, temple of the god Nabu or Nebo, babylonian god of wisdom and writing. A canal linked the two cities. The Biblical "Tower of Babel" symbolizes the hubris or presumption of humanity's seeking to "reach for the stars" by terrestrial means—from the standpoint of the Bible a vain, extravagant effort of mor-

Tower of Babel: "Unfinished because of discord." J. Boschius, 1702

Tower of Babel as a spiral. G. Doré (1832–1883)

piece of wall collapses: a moment of great consternation for the builders, concerned with schedule and costs. That stone matters more to them than a laborer who falls to his death. This is one reason for God's decision to punish them" [Aron]. The Biblical name Babel is associated with the root *bll* (confusion), with the legendary origin of mutually incomprehensible human languages to impede forever such arrogant projects to reach the heavens. The miracle of Pentecost, the descent of the Holy Ghost (see TONGUE), symbolizes the ability of divinely inspired persons to master foreign languages spontaneously and overcome the limits imposed in the Old Testament. FREEMASONRY also associates the Tower of Babel with the

Tower of Babel: Ziggurat (Babylon), reconstructed as in 6th century B.C.

subsequent spread of architecture to all the countries of the earth. An instructional guide for Masonic "sisters" interprets the reference to the tower morally, as an image of the arrogance of the "children of the earth," a failing against which we can be secure only if we "oppose it with a reasonable and upright heart" [Baurnjöpel, 1793]. Esperanto, the (artificial) international language, is a Masonic attempt to overcome the confusion of languages; "Esperanto-Fremasona" was established in 1905 to do away rationally with the linguistic boundaries that separate us.

Babylon One of the most important cultural centers of the ancient East, on the lower course of the Euphrates RIVER. The old name of the city was Bab-ilu or Bab-ili, "HEAVEN'S GATE" or "gate of the gods." The Bible speaks of the great "whore of Babylon," because Babylon was the enemy power that under King Nebuchadnezzar in 598 B.C.

Babylon, City of Satan, battles City of God. From St. Augustine, *City of God*, Basel, 1489

plundered JERUSALEM and took the majority of its people into the "Babylonian captivity," where they mourned for their lost homeland until they could return to it. The king rebuilt the temple district Esagila with the terraced (ziggurat) TEMPLE (see STEPS) Etemenanki and thus in the eyes of the Jews conspicuously served "idolatry." The prophet Isaiah places these words in the mouth of the proud king: "I will ascend into heaven, I will exalt my throne above the stars of God: I will sit also upon the mount of the congregation [i.e., of the world], in the sides of the north: I will ascend above the heights of the clouds: I will be like the most High" [Isaiah 14:13–14]. This hubris or presumption and the humiliating captivity of the Jews continued until the defeat of the Babylonian king Bel-shar-usur (Belshazzar) by the Persians in 550 B.C., which ended the exile of the Jews. Babylon still remained a symbol of idolatry: "The wine of her whoredom made the whole world drunk." In the Book of Revelation Babylon is the antitype of the holy city of Jerusalem, portrayed as a woman "arrayed in purple and scarlet colour [. . .] having a golden cup in her hand full of abominations and filthiness of her fornication [. . .] drunken with the blood of the saints, and with the blood of the martyrs of Jesus" (Revelation 17:4, 6). Here Babylon admittedly functions only as a cover-name for the capital of the ancient world in the prophet's time: Rome.

Bacchus Transformed from the ancient god of wine-induced ecstasy to a symbol for taverns, along with the beer-god Gambrinus, who has no antecedents in the ancient world. Bacchus or Dionysus was, according to myth, a son of Zeus, who introduced the grapevine, dispelled care, and roamed with his followers—satyrs, Sileni, and maenads (women in mad ecstasy)—from country to country. His attributes were vines, vine leaves, and his staff, the THYRSUS; powerful animals like BULLS and GOATS often appear at his side. Myths of his death (as Zagreus) and rebirth place him in the ranks of divine figures who are resurrected after death. The name Dionysus, in the form "di-wo-no-so-

Bacchus as a drunken god, with followers. Cartari, 1647

chins covered THRONES and altars, and were translated by church architects into stone canopies for altar tables and tabernacles. Pulpits, too, perhaps for better acoustics, had similar shells arching over them, often decorated with STARS, as did saints' graves and images. Representations of scenes from the Gospels place canopies over especially important figures, e.g. the Virgin Mary. In Judaism, the bridal canopy is known as a *chupah*, which is symbolic of the bride entering the groom's house and becoming his wife.

jo," is documented in preclassical times on tablets in Cretan-Mycenaean Linear B script. The Latin "Bacchus" and related forms may go back to Lydia (Asia Minor). (See also LIGHTNING.)

badger The animal's symbological interest lies in the fact that it lives in a dark underground home (is afraid of the light) on its own body fat. This made it a symbol of vice: like the mole, the badger often represented avarice. German popular speech is somewhat kinder to the animal ("to sleep like a badger" corresponds to the English "to sleep like a log"; in German not only foxes but also badgers are proverbially sly; "cheeky" young men are often likened to badgers) than English (where "badgering" refers to particularly unwelcome nagging). The English word "badger" may refer to the white mark or "badge" on the animal's forehead. The fat of the badger was used for medicinal purposes as far back as classical antiquity.

baldachin The canopy carried on four poles in church processions is descended from the awnings that protected Eastern dignitaries from sun and rain; it is associated metaphorically with the HEAVENS (the firmament as a "canopy"). In ancient China heaven was likened to a (round) umbrella covering a CHARIOT. The occidental baldachin is more nearly square, suggesting the "four corners of the earth," and believed to provide, for persons of high rank, a shelter not unlike a little microcosm of the sky. Similar balda-

Baldachin offers protection against "both sun and rain." J. Boschius, 1702

ball Games played with a ball made of rubber (ancient Mexico), leather, wool, or cloth, have special symbolic significance in

Ball: Drawing of a Mexican "rumpball" player. C. Weiditz, colonial era

the cults of many older civilizations: the ball is associated with the SUN, that ball which moves through the HEAVENS. A "game with the ball thrown upward" played by two dancers at the Phaeacian royal court is mentioned in Homer's *Odyssey* [VIII, 370–80, translated Lattimore].

In Church customs the ball played with in cloisters symbolized Christ, the "resurrected Easter sun." This "Easter pilota" was celebrated in Auxerre (France) until 1538: to the accompaniment of song and organ music clerics danced around the monastery, throwing the ball back and forth.

bamboo plays an important role in Far Eastern art and symbolism. Its "empty HEART" stands for modesty; its leanness and evergreen [see GREEN] for constancy and advanced age. Pieces of bamboo placed in a FIRE burst with a loud noise and drive off evil spirits. A bamboo branch is the attribute of the gentle Kuan-yin, goddess of mercy. Chinese watercolors thus frequently portray the bamboo tree (along with chrysanthemums, pines, and plum-blossoms). Its joints are widely understood to be steps along the way to higher knowledge. In Japan the proliferous plant symbolizes eternal youth and indomitable strength.

basilisk (Greek, "little KING") A mythical creature, rich in symbolic resonance, from the world of serpents (see SNAKES). Saint Hildegard of Bingen (1098–1179) wrote of the basilisk as follows: "A TOAD, feeling

Basilisk. Hohberg, 1697

herself pregnant, saw a serpent's EGG, sat upon it to hatch it, until her [own] young were born. They died; but she continued to sit upon the serpent's egg, until life began to stir within it, which was immediately influenced by the power of the serpent of Eden. . . . The young broke the shell, slipped out, then suddenly let out a blast of breath like FIRE. . . . [It] kills everything that comes near." Other traditions have the egg laid by an old rooster and hatched by a "venomous" toad. As the basilisk is the king of serpents, so the DEVIL is king of demons, writes St. Augustine. In medieval bestiaries the basilisk is a CROWNED serpent to whom its subjects pay homage. It symbolizes lust (*luxuria*), one of the seven deadly sins, and Christ is portrayed as doing battle against it, along with the LION and the DRAGON. At the end of the 15th century, the rapidly spreading syphilis was referred to as the venom of the basilisk. Baroque books of emblematology indicate that the only weapon against the basilisk is a MIRROR to turn the creature's "venomous gaze" back upon it: "To eye of Basilisk that e'er with venom slew/ Returns the looking-glass the beast's death-bringing gaze;/ So to themselves returns the evil sinners do,/ And what more meet than that its poison end their days?" [Hohberg].

Bamboo. Detail from a Chinese watercolor, 17th century

bat An animal of multiple symbolic significance, whose dual nature (as a winged mammal) has attracted attention in many cultures. In the Occident the bat is an eerie creature, believed to become entangled in

Bat god of the Mayas. Acanceh, northern Yucatán

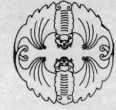

Bats in ancient Chinese symbol for "double good fortune"

people's HAIR. Reports from South America of BLOOD-sucking vampire bats have made Europeans view their own bats (who are harmless except to gnats and the like) as terrifying creatures. The DEVIL as a fallen ANGEL is portrayed in art with bat's wings (he, too, flees the LIGHT), and the same is true for demonic creatures of every sort (e.g., Invidia, the personification of envy, who dare not show herself by day). Bats are seldom omitted from paintings of WITCHES' Sabbaths. And in modern English the creatures appear in derogatory idioms referring to the mentally ill ("to have bats in one's belfry," "to be batty") and older women ("an old bat"). Bats fare better in other cultures. Among the Maya of Central America the bat (z'otz) is revered as a tutelary god, especially by the Zotzil tribes. In the mythology of the Quiché Maya a "beheading bat" from the underworld appears frequently. In ancient China the bat was a symbol of good fortune, primarily because of the homonymy of the words for "bat" and "luck" (fu). FIVE bats mean five forms of earthly happiness: a long life, wealth, health,

love of virtue, and a natural death; there are many depictions of a kindly magician producing five bats from an urn. RED bats were considered to be particularly lucky: their color could frighten away demons. In African myths the bat was often considered especially intelligent, since it never collided with anything in flight.

In classical antiquity the bat symbolized vigilance, and its eye was believed to offer protection against drowsiness. At the same time bats were already being nailed to doors as protection against night demons and black magic; this practice continues even today in some rural areas. Drops of bat's blood under a woman's pillow were thought to assure that she would bear many children, and bats furnished miraculous remedies for snakebite and plagues of ANTS, LOCUSTS, and caterpillars. In Greek fable and legend the bat is portrayed as shrewd but timid. "Bat" (Latin *vespertilio*, Greek *nykertis*) was also a humorous term for a night reveller. In the *Odyssey*, the souls of the dead are described as fluttering through the underworld and emitting cries like those of bats. In medieval

Bat-like "Z'otz" painted on Mayan vessel. Chamá, Alta Vera Paz

Bats combined with symbol for longevity to denote good fortune. China

bestiaries the bat is still presented in a positive light: "When bats decide to stay in one place for an extended period of time, they hold on to one another and form clusters—an exchange of favors of a sort quite rare in human society" [Unterkircher]. Yet this admiration for the bat, unlike other views expressed in the bestiaries, did not carry over into popular attitudes. St. Hildegard of Bingen (1098–1179) also wrote that the bat, which she classified as a bird, "flies especially at the time when ghosts choose to travel: while people sleep," and she offers a treatment for jaundice that will not appeal to animal lovers: the sufferer "should carefully impale the bat so that it remains alive, then attach it with its back to his or her own. Immediately thereafter, the bat should be attached to the sufferer's stomach until the animal dies." The bat was apparently supposed to draw the disease out of the sufferer's body and become infected itself.

baths and bathing Even in very early times baths served to do more than just clean the body; "cleanliness" became associated with purity, symbolizing freedom from the "dirt of sin," which WATER washed away. For example, the "great bath" of the Indian cultural city Mohenjo-daro (in the Indus Valley, ca. 2500 B.C.), measuring 40 feet by 23 feet, was famous, and not unlike later

Baths: Philosopher's stone conceived in water, born in air. M. Maier, *Atalanta*, 1618

Indian temple pools for ritual cleansing. Nocturnal baths for similar purposes were the custom in ancient Mexico, as well. Even more common in almost all civilizations was the ritual washing of parts of the body, as is still the case in Islam. In ancient China bride and groom bathed before the wedding ceremony; on one day in the 12th month the Buddhas in the temples were bathed, and baths marked each new phase of a person's life. In the course of celebrating the Mysteries of Eleusis participants were to bathe in the sea. In Judaism, a woman is obligated to take a ritual bath known as a *mikveh* seven days after the conclusion of her monthly menstruation. For a minimum of 12 days, a woman is not permitted to have sexual relations with her husband. Baptism as performed by John the Baptist involved not merely a sprinkling of the head but total immersion in the river, and Jesus himself was so baptized. Secularly, bathing in the fountain of youth (see SPRING), in European art, especially of the Renaissance, symbolizes rebirth; in the ecclesiastical sphere, confession and absolution function as cleansing baths for the soul, which is also washed clean by tears of repentance. Martyrdom is considered a "baptism in BLOOD." In the imagery of ALCHEMY the dissolving together of SULFUR AND MERCURY are referred to as the conjugal "bathing" of KING and QUEEN. In early Christian times the public baths of Rome assumed, for the converted, negative symbolic associations as places of enervation and lechery. The bath-culture of the Middle Ages, which is indicated even in the illustrations of the oldest German illuminated manuscript of the Bible (the "Wenzelsbibel" in the Austrian National Library), ended abruptly with the spread of venereal disease at the beginning of the modern period. In analytical psychology the image of the bath is associated with the return to the womb (see MOTHER).

Baubo A quite puzzling figure of ancient Greek myth and symbology. According to the mythology of the Eleusinian mystery-cult, she was a maidservant who, completely baring her abdomen in an obscene belly

Baubo. Terracotta statuette. Priena, Asia Minor, 5th century B.C.

dance, made the goddess Demeter laugh, cheering her even in her mourning after her daughter Persephone had been carried off by the god of the underworld. Baubo is portrayed either as a figure consisting only of a face and an enlargement of the body from the waist down, or as a *dea impudica* (shameless goddess), riding on a pig with her legs spread. Baubo is also called "the vulva personified," a blunt expression of female sexuality, corresponding to phallic god Priapus, symbol of male sexuality. Diachronically speaking, she appears to have originated in Asia Minor as a frightening divinity, a nocturnal demon, perhaps associated in particular observances with the exposing of the genitals and with ritual laughter, all of which in the classical period was transformed into a coarsely comic scene within the context of the Eleusinian mysteries. In the Walpurgis Night scene in Part I of Goethe's *Faust*, Dame Baubo appears as the leader of the witches. (Compare BES.) Interestingly enough, there is in ancient Japanese mythology a figure corresponding to Baubo: the goddess Ame-no-uzume lured the sun-goddess Amaterasu out of a CAVE (in which she had hidden, out of resentment over the storm-god's ragings) with an obscene dance that aroused the sun's curiosity, so that she soon restored her light to the earth. (See RICE.)

bean Cultivated doubtless as early as grain, with its many varieties an important food in Mediterranean countries and in the Neolithic Age north of the Alps as well. Because of their flatulent and supposedly aphrodisiac properties, beans were considered unclean in Egypt, especially by priests; but they do have a place in the Dionysian and Apollonian mysteries of the Greeks. PYTHAGORAS forbade eating them, because they were thought to harbor the souls of the dead. Roman priests were not allowed to look at or even to mention them, because "letters of [i.e., spelling] mourning" were in their flowers. On the Feast of Parentalia (February 13) the spirits of the dead were permitted to visit the world of the living, and WITCHES took advantage of this ghostly time to restrain "malicious tongues" using black beans. Because the plants yield so many seeds (beans), these legumes have in other contexts come to symbolize fertility and wealth, in Japanese superstition for example. In European idioms, beans, which are used in lieu of chips as a sort of play-money, are taken as having little value; someone who "doesn't know beans" about a topic knows nothing at all. A bean baked into a cake foretold good fortune for whoever found it (the "bean-KING"), or else revealed who would be the first to become engaged.

bear One of the less significant animals to symbologists, although humans have always been familiar with bears, as is demonstrated by Neanderthal sacrifices of the skulls of cave bears. In cave art of the Ice Age, the bear appears far less frequently than wild cattle (see BULL) and HORSES. In the myths of northern Asia and northern North America, bears play a major role as creatures who resemble humans physically and who can also mate with women and beget human offspring (many legends about SAVAGES may have their origin in these bear myths), but in more advanced civilizations they are less important; they are also no longer to be found in the vicinity of urban centers. Still, Athena, the Greek goddess of the hunt, is occasionally shown with bears, and the priestesses of Artemis Brauroneia were called "she-bears." Greek astral legend (see STARS) tells of the Arcadian princess Callisto ("the most beautiful," originally probably a local wood-nymph), who while a servant of Artemis (Latin DIANA) was made pregnant by Zeus, whereupon Artemis turned her into a bear. She gave birth to a perfectly formed human son, Arcas, who later felt threatened by his ursine mother. Lest one should kill the other, Zeus transported mother and son into the heavens: Zeus' jealous wife Hera, determined to prevent Callisto from ever being able to refresh herself by bathing in the sea, placed her (as Ursa Major) among the circumpolar stars, which never set; Arcas lives on in the constellation Boötes.

In Norse myth Odin appears at times as a bear (Björn). The word "berserk" comes from "berserkers," warriors who wore bearskins and fought (presumably under the influence of drugs) with frenzied violence; they were sometimes thought to be only part human, like werewolves (see WOLF). Among the Celts, the Helvetii referred to a divinity named Artio as goddess of wild game; her attribute was the bear. In Christian symbology we frequently encounter the fable of the she-bear who gives birth to shapeless offspring; she must lick them to give them form. Similarly, we are ignorant creatures who find our way only through spiritual knowledge. The bear's hibernation is seen as symbolizing the old age of humans, which

Bear: Companion of the goddess Artio. Gallo-Roman, Muri (Switzerland), ca. A.D. 200

will be followed by their resurrection. Otherwise bears appear anecdotally, as in the legend of St. Gall, at whose side a bear stood ready to aid him, ever since the saint removed a thorn from his paw. A bear is also the attribute of saints like Columban, Ursinus and Sergius; a bear with pack-saddle, of Corbinian, Hubertus, and Maximin of Trier. In heraldry the bear is of greatest importance in Switzerland (Bern) and southern Germany. As a dangerous animal, the bear is at times the embodiment of the devil's power. The young David's fight with a bear, mentioned in the Bible, is taken by Christain exegesis to be a prototype of the triumph of Christ over the forces of darkness. Bears also appear as the avengers of the bald prophet Elisha: they maul boys who have mocked him (II Kings 2:23–24).

In psychology, for example in dream symbolism, the bear is interpreted as an embodiment of the dangerous aspects of the unconscious; for Jung, the bear often represents the negative aspect of the superposed persona. Aeppli adds that the bear, although dangerous, contains a greater, positive potential: although the word for "bear" is masculine in gender in most languages, the bear can also stand for feminine, EARTH-like qualities (warm fur, BROWN like the earth itself, stockiness, care in rearing offspring). (See also TOTEM.) In ancient China, however, the bear (hsiung) is a masculine symbol embodying strength, whose feminine antitype is the SNAKE. Dreaming of a bear foretold the birth of a son. In Chinese fairy tales the bear plays the role of the Occiden-

Bear: Attribute of Sts. Columban and Gall. W. Auer, 1890

tal "big bad wolf." The bear symbolizing Russia is in modern China a polar bear.

beards and mustaches Symbols of manhood. Heroes, KINGS, and gods, unless their youthfulness was to be expressed, were always portrayed with beards. The Egyptian queen Hatshepsut was often shown with an artificial beard on her chin, as an indication of her royal function. Occasionally women wear beard-like tattoos, for example among the Ainus, aboriginal inhabitants of northern Japan. In northern China a red beard was a sign of strength and valor. Although the Chinese are not naturally disposed to have full beards, famous men are always portrayed as bearded on stage and in paintings. In pre-Columbian Central America, beards were also rare, but specific gods, like Quetzalcóatl (Kukulcan to the Mayans, literally, "feathered serpent"), were portrayed with beards. In Andes civilizations, too, there are clay images of gods with long beards on their chins, which has been taken by some to indicate forgotten contacts with Europeans. In the art of ancient Europe, hostile Celts were almost always portrayed with mustaches. In Minoan Crete man were portrayed without beards, but in Homeric times it was primarily only the upper lip that was still shaved. In Rome shaving was customary up into the time of the emperor Hadrian, then returned with Constantine the Great. In the Byzantine realm, the emperor was clean-shaven, whereas Eastern Orthodox priests wore beards. Roman Catholic priests, not wishing to display distinctly masculine attributes, were almost always clean-shaven, unlike monks, both cenobites and HERMITS, who saw shaving as a sign of vanity. In early Christian art Christ was portrayed (like an ANGEL) as a beardless youth. The mode of portrayal common today, with long hair and beard, prevailed only later. A "bearded VIRGIN" in Christian legend is St. Cummernus, also known as Wilgefortis or Liborada. A portrayal of the Crucifixion in Italy (Volto Santo in Lucca) shows Christ in long Byzantine robes. Because of language difficulties foreign pilgrims to Italy mistook it for the representation of a maiden who refused to obey her father and marry a heathen; in response to her prayers, the legend went, God disfigured her with a beard, whereupon her angry father had her crucified. ("Cummernus" could be a version of the Byzantine name Comnenus.) In the world of Islam the oath "by the beard of the Prophet" is proverbial; a hair from Muhammad's beard is a treasured relic in the city of Srinagar. That a man's beard and his dignity are equivalent (the part for the whole) in the European world as well, is indicated by colloquialisms like the medieval oath "by my beard" (i.e., on my honor).

bee Few creatures are as important in symbology as this insect and the life of its colonies. Virtually as soon as there were humans they began gathering wild HONEY. Soon, too, they discovered the possibility of beekeeping, a great step forward toward ensuring the continuation of life. Honey was used not only as a sweetener and in fermentation but also in making medicines; the wax, to make candles, and later in casting metal (the lost-wax, or *cire perdue*, process), and in Egypt in mummification. Beekeeping has been documented in Egypt as far back as ca. 2600 B.C.; the bee was the hieroglyphic symbol for the kingdom of Lower Egypt. In India wild honey is plentiful, and thus beekeeping did not develop there as it did in China, where it is an ancient art. Since the Chinese word for bee (*feng*) sounds like the word for the rank of count, the bee has a certain association with professional advancement. Otherwise the bee was less

Beards and Mustaches: Advertisement for mustache wax, 1911

the symbol of diligence than of a suitor with an eager fondness for the FLOWERS of young womanhood. In Chinese (as in European) fairy tales, bees help young men find the right bride. In the Occident the bee is often called "the bird of Our Lady" or "of Our Lord"; it symbolizes the soul. Dreaming of a bee means that one's death is near: one's soul is buzzing off. But if a bee flies into the mouth of a dead person, that person will come back to life. The "path of bees" was a Germanic way of referring to the air as filled with the souls of the dead. In Mediterranean civilizations there were often curious notions about the life of bees: they were thought to be unsexed, to be spontaneously generated from the rotting bodies of animals, to have no blood, and not to breathe. They were seen anthropomorphically as brave, chaste, industrious, clean, living harmoniously in the political entity constituted by the hive, and aesthetically gifted (the "birds of the Muses"). The priests and priestesses of the Eleusinian mysteries were called "bees." Because the hibernation of the bees equated with death, they also became an image of resurrection.

Christian iconography could hardly pass up these analogies. Working unflaggingly for its community, the bee was exemplary. St. Ambrose likened the Church to the beehive and devout parishioners to the bees, who collected only the best from all the flowers and eschewed the smoke of arrogant pride. The belief that bees lived from the fragrance of flowers alone, made them symbols of purity and abstinence, and, for Bernard of Clairvaux, of the Holy Ghost. In the secular world the bee was a royal symbol, especially

Bees. Hohberg, 1675

since the QUEEN bee was long regarded as a KING. It has been speculated that the French *fleur-de-lis* (see LILY) goes back to a stylized image of the bee. The sweetness of honey came to symbolize the "honey-sweet" eloquence of St. Ambrose and St. John Chrysostom (literally, "Goldmouth"). This sweetness also served as a symbol for Christ and his mercy, but in the context of the painful sting to be felt at the Last Judgment. An additional belief taken over from antiquity, that bees do not procreate their young but instead gather them up from the flowers they visit, made the bee a symbol of the Virgin Mary as well.

Medieval bestiaries also describe the "technical skill and beauty of the honeycomb structure, the regular hexagons of the cells which [the bees] separate with hard wax and fill with honey, which flows from the dew that they bring from the blossoms. [. . .] The honey is for the benefit, in pleasing equality, of kings and commoners. It is not only for pleasure but also for health, sweet to the palate and a healer of wounds. Thus though a bee is weak in body, yet is it strong through the power of wisdom and the love of virtue" [Unterkircher]. "The bees work busily to flowers' nectar find,/ Thus full of honey sweet their waxen kingdom grows,/ So where in unity the hearts of many bind,/Blooms sweet utility, and useful sweetness flows" [Hohberg]. In heraldry bees usually appear in groups, as in the arms of the Corsican Buonaparte family, symbolizing diligence and a sense of order. In ancient

Bee on a coin of ancient Ephesus, symbol of the mother goddess

Egypt the king of Lower Egypt was "he who belongs to the bee"; the rushes growing in the south symbolized Upper Egypt.

beggar　Symbolic figure for the lowest level of the traditional social pyramid of EMPEROR, KING, noble (see KNIGHT), townsman, farmer, beggar. In the absence of any "social safety-net," those who have nothing, whether through misfortune or their own doing, can be seen either as ideal figures of scorn for things of this world (like St. Alexios, a Syrian ascetic) or as pariahs whose only use is to provide the more fortunate with an opportunity to practice charity. Several saints are portrayed in the company of beggars, such as Elizabeth of Thuringia, St. James of Alcalá, and especially St. Martin of Tours,

Beggar at the Door. Etching, Ludwig Richter (1803–1884)

Beggar as heraldic figure (ca. 1340) and seal (ca. 1352)

who gave away half of his cape. The beggar's staff, a familiar attribute along with the beggar's sack, was originally a white stick designating alternatively persons forced to abandon their lands, prisoners of war, or surrender (compare the later white FLAG): at the time of the Peasants' Wars the German expression "to go forth with a white stick" meant to surrender unconditionally. In the modern era, beggars came to understand themselves as a sort of guild, using simple but discreet marks to share information about the prospects of handouts. Both Christian and Buddhist monks, scornful of worldly possessions and ways, have made the deliberate rejection of property and comfort their ideal. Members of mendicant orders are to live entirely from voluntary contributions.

bells　In many Old World cultures, not only musical instruments but also religious implements for summoning both worshippers and supernatural beings; thus they became symbols in the cults that used them. In East Asia they were struck on the outside with a rod. There were many ancient Chinese legends about bells: they can fly through the air to a specific place (compare the references of Central European Catholics to the silenced bells of Good Friday as having "flown

Beggars: Christ and the poor. Lucas Cranach, 1521

Bell ("ghanta"). Lamaist religious implement, Tibet

to Rome"), and they indicate happiness or unhappiness by their pitch. Chariots were strung with little bells, as were ornamental birds in GARDENS so that their jingle might lift people's spirits. The word for bell (*chung*) is a homonym of the word meaning "to pass a test"; thus images of bells are often punning references to advancement in the civil service hierarchy. In Japan bronze bells (*dotaku*) date back to ca. A.D. 300. They hang at the entrances to Shinto shrines and are rung by pulling a string; worshippers then donate a small coin, clap their hands twice, and make a wish, which is supposed to be granted. In the early Christian era bells (often SILVER) were used in the Roman catacombs to summon worshippers to Mass. Larger bells were first used in monasteries and are mentioned from the sixth century onward, although the difficult casting of enormous bells is documented only toward the end of the Middle Ages. In many leg-

ends bells drive away supernatural beings, such as DWARFS, or keep the DEVIL from seizing a human soul that he desires; they were also believed to ward off storms (i.e., the WITCHES who produced them). Bells also played a role in exorcisms and in rites of excommunication (hence Shakespeare's reference to "bell, book, and candle" in *King John*, III,iii,12). Goethe's ballad "The Roving Bell" and Schiller's "Song of the Bell" suggest something of the importance of bells in symbolism and superstition. A bell hanging on a tau (or T-shaped) cross is an attribute of the Egyptian anchorite St. Anthony; the bell served to dispel the demons

Bell. Illustration in Goethe's *Wandering Bell*, Ludwig Richter (1803–1884)

who were seeking to tempt him. In America it is common to speak of bells of freedom, such as the Liberty Bell.

Bell used in casting spells. French ms. of a book of magic, 18th century

belt, sash, and girdle English designations for what in older languages was a single concept: the Latin *cingulum* (or *cingula*), for example, was whatever literally "girded the loins" or resembled the accessories so worn. In English "belt" has replaced the older "girdle" in this sense, the latter reserved in present-day usage for the world of the foundation garment; otherwise, belts usually have clasps and pass through loops, whereas sashes are tied or pinned in place. The symbolic associations of the *cingulum*, of course, date

Belts: Part of a Frankish belt clasp showing crosses. 7th century

one's loins" is an image of preparation for from many centuries before the nearly universal wearing of trousers; its first use was as a sword- or tool-belt. In the Bible "girding travel or battle, and also of proper and moral attire, since the girdle, whatever its variations, encircled the body like a RING and separated the lower parts from the upper (see ABOVE/BELOW). Buckles and clasps were often adorned with heraldic symbols or symbols of military victories. The Milky Way (see MILK) is often called "the Girdle of the Firmament"; the "Girdle of Aphrodite," in Homer, seems to symbolize love "conquering all." In Jewish tradition a sash made of wool and byssus lent special solemnity to the girding of a priest. The various forms of "girdle" can be associated with an attempt to enclose or confine the sexual element; they soon came to symbolize sexual abstinence and chastity (e.g., in the monk's habit or the cingulum worn by the priest celebrating Mass). The ceremony of induction into the Order of St. Benedict includes the following: "May righteousness be the girdle of your loins. Be mindful that Another will gird you. . ." (submission to a higher law than that of one's own will). The "bridal sash," along with the veil, symbolized the bride's virginity; prostitutes (*meretrices*) were forbidden to wear either, under penalty of law. In ancient China civil servants had their own sash or belt (*tai*) with a metal clasp. The removal of the bridal sash on the wedding night symbolized the consummation of the marriage. Fans and calligrapher's brushes were bound to the sash and held in place by an ornate toggle; these toggles are now prized by art historians and collectors. A Mongolian custom of symbological interest is that of the "girdle child": a man who has a relationship with a woman leaves his belt behind upon departure; if she has a child, the two lovers are considered to be married, and she and the child take the name of the absent father.

Bes Grotesque demonic figure of ancient Egypt, a symbol of protection against the evil eye, black magic, and dangerous animals. Bes was portrayed with a squat, dwarflike body, contorted face and pointed, animal ears, often as a phallic figure (with an erect penis) or dressed in animal skins. It is not surprising that with time this figure was seen not only as warding off evil but also as bringing pleasure to merrymakers and as symbolizing sexual potency. From ca. 2000 B.C. on, there was also a parallel female figure named Beset, who corresponded roughly to the Greek BAUBO. Bes' grotesque appearance was amusing, but his image also appeared on the outbuildings of major temples. He was thought to protect childbearing women, especially, against harmful influences of every sort.

In Coptic (Christian) Egypt, before Islamization, Bes' presence was felt as a reality, but by this time he was thought of as

Bes, Egyptian tutelary spirit, ca. 500 B.C.

an eerie figure who frightened or harmed people.

bird St. Hildegard of Bingen (1098–1179) wrote in her natural history *(Liber de Subtilitatum)* the following sentences about birds in general: "Birds are colder than animals that live on the earth, because they are not conceived in such intense and heated desire. Their flesh is purer than that of land animals because they do not emerge naked from their mothers' bodies but rather covered by a shell. Many live from fiery air and for this reason are constantly stretching upward, like a fire. High-flying birds contain more fiery air than those that fly close to the earth." (See also BIRD OF PARADISE.) "Birds symbolize the power that helps people to speak reflectively and leads them to think out many things in advance before they take action. Just as birds are lifted up into the air by their FEATHERS and can remain wherever they wish, the soul in the body is elevated by thought and spreads its wings everywhere."

In mythology and throughout symbological tradition birds have mostly positive associations. Exceptions, however, include the Stymphalian Birds, swamp dwellers representing fever demons and which HERCULES expelled with bronze castanets, and the birdlike Harpies, who catch criminals and turn them over to the FATES for punishment. (Although the Harpies serve the greater moral order, they are figures of dread.)

Bird with human head: "Ba," symbol of the soul. Book of the Dead, ancient Egypt

Bird-headed monster "Makemake" with egg. Stone relief, Easter Island

Otherwise, these creatures that use their WINGS to approach the HEAVENS often embody the human desire to break free of gravity and to attain higher spheres like the ANGELS. The legend of ICARUS, who flew too close to the SUN and plunged into the sea, offers a symbolic warning against the hubris that leads us to ignore our own limitations. The disembodied human soul is often depicted as a bird, or as a bird with a human head (the partial soul Ba of ancient Egyptian philosophy) or, in many prehistoric rock drawings, as a human with the head of a bird (explicable in part as a representation of hallucinations of flying when in altered states of consciousness). Birds played an important role in ancient Roman augury, in which priests interpreted their flight patterns as an expression of divine will. A bird doing battle with a SNAKE (e.g., Garuda in India) represents the overcoming of base instincts through spirituality. In the Upanishads of ancient India it is written that two birds sit in the branches of the great world-TREE: one eats the fruit (symbolizing the active life) while the other watches (the meditative seeking after knowledge).

In FAIRY TALES those who understand the language of birds are often privy to special knowledge; people are also transformed into birds, and birds bring food to good or holy persons.

In the idioms of various languages, birds are given sexual connotations (e.g., the Chinese word *niao,* "bird," also means "penis") or associated with insanity (in Ger-

Bird: Legendary roc transporting elephant. Etching, J. Stradanus, 1522

man, *einen Vogel haben*, literally "to have a bird," is to be not quite sane)—despite the values generally attached to birds, which are most clearly expressed in the symbolic traditions of the PHOENIX and the EAGLE. See also BIRD OF PARADISE, CRANE, CROW, CUCKOO, DOVES AND PIGEONS, FALCON AND HAWK, HERON, HOOPOE, IBIS, MAGPIE, NIGHTINGALE, OSTRICH, OWL, PEACOCK, PELICAN, PHEASANT, RAVEN, ROOSTER, STORK, SWALLOW, SWAN, VULTURE; FEATHER.

bird of paradise Featured in baroque emblem-books as a symbol of lightness, closeness to god, and removal from worldly concerns, as well as of the Virgin Mary, the bird of paradise owes its reputation and its older name, *paradisea apoda* ("footless bird of paradise"), to the New Guinean and Indonesian practice of preserving intact the skin and feathers removed from their carcasses and smoking them so that they keep their form without bones or feet. They were sold in this form and found their way to

Birds, tree in stylized symmetrical design. Carpet pattern, Turkoman

Europe, where they came to be known as "sylphs" (spirits of the air). It was said of them that they lived only from the DEW of HEAVEN (see PHOENIX), spent their entire lives in the air, remained "pure and sinless from birth onward," and knew nothing of doings on earth: "'Tis named for paradise, this one ethereal bird,/ Which floats so close to heav'n and never touches earth" [Hohberg]. Even scientific books of the 18th century conserved the myth of the pure bird of the heavens; only in the 19th century did zoologists uncover the truth behind the symbol.

Bird of paradise "soaring weightlessly." J. Boschius, 1702

bivalves Although there were Latin words to distinguish individual bivalves (e.g., *ostrea, pecten,* and *teredo,* for oyster, scallop, and shipworm, respectively), the general word for them was *concha,* which also meant "vulva": symbologically, the bivalve has long been associated with female genitalia and reproductive organs (see also PEARL). After the end of the Ice Age, bivalves were a staple food of coast dwellers, as we can tell from heaps of shells several yards high (in Danish, *Kjökkenmöddinger;* in Spanish, *concheros*) that survive this epoch. In ancient Indian representations, the god Vishnu holds a conch to represent the ocean, the first breath of life, and the first sound. The birth of VENUS (Greek Aphrodite) from the sea foam was the subject of Pompeian frescoes,

Bivalve "marrying" sea and sky. J. Boschius, 1702

black A color symbolically associated (like its opposite, WHITE) with the absolute: in Jungian dream analysis, for example, black is the color of "total lack of consciousness, the descent into darkness and mourning. In Europe black is a color with negative associations. A black man, a house in shadows, a dark snake—all of these dark things offer little hope" (Aeppli). In ancient times, pitch-black animals were sacrificed to the divinities of the underworld; later, a black ROOSTER or GOAT was sacrificed to the DEVIL or his demons. "Wotan's horde" ride black HORSES, and the devil himself is often portrayed as being black (if not RED). Satanic rituals mocking God are referred to as "black masses." A chimney-sweep looks suspicious, or even diabolical, at first glance, but through a reversal of opposites has come to be seen as a symbol of good fortune. Black is also the negation of worldly vanity and ostentation; thus black became the color of priestly garments and, by extension, of conservative (Church-oriented) political parties. The black of mourning and penitence is also a promise of future resurrection, in which it will be turned to gray, then white. In ALCHEMY the blackening (Medieval Latin *nigredo*) of primal matter is a necessary first step in its metamorphosis into the philosopher's stone.

In other contexts black is often the color of awesome divinities (e.g., Mahakala, the "great black one" in the mythology of In-

then of Botticelli, who represented Venus is standing on a shell, as did Titian. Because of its association with WATER (see WATER SPIRIT), the bivalve combines sexual symbolism with notions of procreation and fertility, which makes it a natural attribute for the goddess of love. Christian symbolism shunned these associations and preferred to make the bivalve a symbol of the grave, which encloses a person from the time of death until resurrection. The idea of the fertilization of bivalves (viewed as having two sexes) by DEW from the heavens, also made them a symbol for the VIRGIN Mary. (See also PEARL.) The scallop (Latin *Pecten pilgrimea*) was a symbol for pilgrims (see PILGRIMAGE) and was an attribute of such saints as Sebastian, Roch, Coloman, and James (in Spanish: Santiago) the Greater, whose shrine in Santiago de Compostela (Spain) has drawn many pilgrims, as well as of the archangel Raphael accompanying Tobiah on his long journey to Media (Book of Tobit, chapters 5–12). In medieval bestiaries we read that "nature, following God's orders, secures the fleshy part of the bivalve within mighty walls, so that its shell constitutes its fortress"; nevertheless, CRABS—symbolizing the wicked who lead the innocent astray—overcome this protection by jamming gravel between the two halves of the shell and devouring the bivalve inside [Unterkircher].

Black Kali, frightening Hindu diety. India, 19th century

Black: Chimney-sweep. Children's book illustration, F. Pocci, 1846

dia). In ancient Chinese cosmology it is associated with the ELEMENT WATER and the north. The great EMPEROR Shi Huang-ti, who overthrew the Chou dynasty (whose color was red), chose black as his symbolic color, "just as water puts out fire." The frequent "black Madonnas" often associated with European shrines (e.g., Czestochowa, Chartres, Tarragona, Einsiedeln, Montserrat, Guadelupe) are puzzling within Western traditions; they may have their origin in the Middle East, in association with the dark visage of a pre-Christian maternal deity, perhaps one of the manifestations of Hecate, who was associated with "the dark of the MOON." These Madonnas are also reminiscent of the black goddess Kali of the Hindu pantheon; they, however, do not inspire fear, but seem rather to be associated with fertility. Another dark female figure is the black Sarah (Sarah-la-Kali), the patron saint of the Gypsies at the shrine Les Saintes Maries de la Mer in the south of France, sacred to a TRIAD of Marys: Mary Jacobaea, the sister of Christ's mother; Mary Salome; and Mary Magdalene—all of whom are said to have landed in Provence when they fled the Holy Land. One of the archaic "black Madonnas" may be the origin of the cult of "black Sarah," whose memorial is celebrated on May 24.

blindness   There are multiple symbolic associations: ignorance, "bedazzlement," im-

partiality, a complete vulnerability to fate, scorning the outer world in favor of the "inner LIGHT." Because of this last association, prophets (Tiresias) and gifted poets (Homer) were portrayed as blind in ancient Greece, often with an indication that they had been struck blind upon penetrating secrets reserved for the gods. In ancient Rome Amor (CUPID) was often represented blindfolded (see EYES), suggesting that earthly love disdains all reason. Early Christians understood references in the Gospels to Christ making the blind see, as allegorical expressions of spiritual enlightenment through the Savior's teachings. For St. Isidore of Seville (570–636 A.D.) the fall from grace of Adam and Eve brought a blinding darkness over the world, which only the coming of Christ could lift. Thus "Synagogue," the medieval personification of Judaism, is portrayed blindfolded, symbolizing a refusal to see the LIGHT of salvation. JUSTICE (because its decisions were to be weighed [see SCALES] "without regard for person or rank") and the goddess FORTUNA (Fortune) were also blindfolded. In Masonic (see FREEMASONRY) initiation rites the removal of the blindfold upon entry into the "light" is a crucial symbol of being freed from blindness to higher values. "The practice of blindfolding aspirants was begun in Hamburg in 1763. Goethe refused to be blindfolded, promising only to keep his eyes closed during the initiation, which was found acceptable" [Lennhoff-Posner].

Blindness: "Synagogue." Gothic sculpture, south portal of Strasbourg Cathedral

Blood sacrifice (ram). Assyrian, Nineveh, ca. 680 B.C.

blood may play a greater role in rituals than in symbolic traditions, but it is nevertheless of symbolic significance, referring globally to life itself. It is often represented by materials (like ocher) that reproduce its COLOR, to symbolize the continuation of life and its effects. RUNES were magically enlivened with red paint (see COLOR) to be more effective, as if they were filled with blood. Blood is widely considered the element of divine life that functions in the human body. As such there was a taboo in many cultures to shed it: "For the life of the flesh is in the flood: and I have given it to you upon the altar to make an atonement for your souls: for it is the flood that maketh an atonement for the soul. Therefore I said unto the children of Israel, No soul of you shall eat blood" [Leviticus 17:11–12]. Again and again blood is referred to as having magic powers and as the exclusive food of supernatural beings; it also associated with a variety of non-rational notions (see DRACULA). Examples include blood brotherhood, blood vengeance, blood baptism (of a martyr), and an array of popular idioms: "something in the blood," "bad blood between them," "hot-blooded," "cold-blooded," "bloodthirsty," "blood on his hands." In the classical theory of the humors, blood was the decisive factor for the "sanguine" (from *sanguis*, Latin for "blood") personality. In Hitler's vocabulary, blood meant "race," heritage, genetic information, when he wrote for example about the "recognition of blood, i.e., of the racial foundation in general." (In *Mein Kampf*: "The simple loss of blood-purity destroys

inner happiness forever, pulls a person down eternally.")

In many ancient peoples participants also drank the sacrificial blood to transport themselves into a state of ecstasy. In the cults of Mithras and Cybele, bulls were sacrificed and their blood poured over the faithful, who were believed to take on the animals' life-force. In the classical theory of procreation, menstrual blood is one of the two components (along with sperm) from which new life comes about. Yet it is considered "impure" by many peoples and charged with negative power, so that menstruating women are often separated from the community. "Pure blood," on the other hand, was the symbol of unfaltering vitality. In medieval legend it even had the power of healing lepers who bathed in it. Ancient Chinese legends tell of painted DRAGONS who actually took off in flight when their EYES were painted in with blood. In the tradition of European magic blood was considered a "special liquid," saturated with the individual aura of the donor; this is why pacts with the DEVIL had to be signed in, or sealed with, blood. When blood is spoken of in alchemy, however, this refers to a reddish solution of a formerly solid substance.

Blood: Andreas of Rinn, pseudohistorical victim of blood sacrifice. W. Auer, 1890

In Christian imagery the blood of Christ is of central importance through the sacrament of Communion (flesh and blood, BREAD and WINE); wine mixed with WATER symbolizes the Church, eternally united with the water of the faithful, producing unity in Christ: the members of the Church become imbued with the purifying and saving power of the blood of the Savior. In portrayals of the Crucifixion, ANGELS often collect this blood in chalices, which in turn were associated with the legendary GRAIL. The Aztecs of ancient Mexico believed that human blood was necessary to fortify the sun (which had become powerless making its nocturnal way through the underworld), and thus indispensable if cosmic order was to be maintained. This explains the excessive sacrifice of prisoners, whom the Aztecs forced to die "the flowery death" (see FLOWER). References to the "blue blood" of nobility are supposedly explained by the fact that members of higher social classes were not suntanned and their bluish veins were visible through their genteel pallor. The original Spanish expression, *sangre azul,* was widely translated into other European languages by the middle of the 19th century.

blue is the COLOR that most frequently is seen as a symbol for things of the spirit and the intellect. Unlike RED, blue seems "cool" and makes most people reflective. Analytical psychologists associate it with a detached way of giving form to one's life. It is the color of the sky, associated in ancient Egypt with the sky-god Amon. G. Heinz-Mohr calls blue the "deepest and least substantial color, the medium of truth, the transparence of the void to come: in air, WATER, CRYSTAL, DIAMONDS. This is why it is the color of the heavens. Zeus and Jahweh plant their feet on sky blue." Blue amulets are supposed to neutralize the evil eye. The Norse god Odin has a blue mantle, like the cloak of the VIRGIN Mary, who herself is addressed poetically as a "blue LILY." Vishnu in ancient Indian myth is colored blue as Krishna; Jesus teaches in a blue garment. "Blue, the symbol of the truth and the eternity of God (for what is true is eternal), will always remain the symbol of human immortality" [Portal]. Ancient China had an ambiguous attitude toward the color. Blue-faced creatures in traditional art were demons and ghosts or the god of literature, K'ui-hsing, who once out of frustrated ambition had committed suicide. Originally there was no specific Chinese word for blue: instead, *ch'ing* referred to all shades from dark gray through blue to green, as well as the life of scholars, who devote themselves to their studies by lamplight. The present-day word *lan* actually means indigo, the color of simple work-clothes. Blue FLOWERS, EYES, ribbons, and stripes were considered ugly and unlucky, whereas in Europe the famous "blue flower" of the Romantics suggests the greatest aspirations of the spirit. In China the ELEMENT wood was grouped with the East and the color blue. In illuminated manuscripts of ancient Mexico the gem TURQUOISE and WATER were represented by a light blue-green, but blue had no place in the symbology of the points of the compass.

In Central European popular symbology blue is the color of fidelity, but also of mystery (the fairy tale "The Blue Light"), deception, and uncertainty (numerous German idioms; compare the English "out of the blue"). The association between the color and intoxication (the German adjective *blau* is also a colloquialism for "drunk") is hard to explain but may have to do with the bluish coloration of the cheeks and noses of heavy drinkers. In political symbology blue is the color of liberals (or, in the Germany of Bismarck and after, National Liberals). The traditional "blue" system of FREEMASONRY is the basic, three-degree hierarchy (compare RED). In the art of prehistoric and nonliterate peoples blue is seldom used, for lack of raw materials with which to produce pigments. Cloth dyed blue is popular in the western reaches of the Sahara and in the Sahel region to the south, e.g., among the ReGleibat nomads of the (formerly Spanish) Western Sahara, among the Tuareg, and in Mauritania.

In colloquial English, the color is associated both with mild depression and with the risqué (as in "a blue movie").

boar Unlike the PIG, which in symbolic portrayals is usually the female domestic pig, the wild variety (*Sus scrofa*), in the form of the male boar, connotes an aggressive animal, raging through the underbrush, and is the image of a fearless band of warriors. In Norse mythology both the goddess Freyja and her brother Freyr were associated with the boar; Freyr was said to ride on a boar with golden bristles. Warriors often wore helmets in the form of boar's heads, as in Mycenaean Greece helmets were covered with boar's teeth. In ancient Greece, the boar was spoken of as the dangerous prey of Hercules and as the slayer of ADONIS and Attis, but also as the attribute of the goddess Demeter and the heroine Atalanta, and, in ancient Rome, of the war-god Mars. Its status as a symbol of unflinching courage and ferocity on the battlefield explains the presence of *Eber* ("boar") in so many Germanic personal and placenames. In heraldry the boar symbolizes "the dauntless and well-armed soldier, who in battle opposes the enemy with valiant courage and never thinks of taking flight" [Böckler]. In Christian iconography, astonishingly, the boar is also a symbol of Christ, through a false etymology that traced *Eber* to Ibri, the ancestor of the Hebrews or Ibrim. It is, however, primarily a symbol of unreined savagery and the rule of diabolical forces, as in the case of tyrants. The boar took on positive symbolic associations when it sought protection against hunters among devout FOREST settlers; it thus became the attribute of St. Columban and St. Aemilian. It was an important sacred animal for the Celts; for them,

Boar: "The teeth inspire fear." J. Boschius, 1702

too, it symbolized military courage and strength. Images of boars decorated helmets and shields; boar meat was buried with the dead to give them strength on their journey to the AFTERLIFE. Stone and bronze sculptures of boars (Euffigneix and Neuvy-en-Sullias, France, respectively) attest to the great symbolic importance of this animal in Western Europe.

bones In many ancient cultures, bones are the last earthly traces of the dead, and they are of critical symbolic and ritualistic importance. Since they seem almost to last forever—in any case, long after the flesh has turned to dust and, under ideal circumstances, can be preserved for thousands of years—they came to be seen in many cultures as "seeds of the body to be resurrected": after the Last Judgment, when the TRUMPET

Boar. Small bronze figure, La Tène period, Prague-Sarka

Bones: The "coat of arms of death." From the *Heiligtumbuch*, Vienna, 1502

is blown and the graves spring open, the bones that they contain will be joined together and covered with new flesh. The bones and skulls of ancestors were often preserved as insignias or for ritual use. The Stone Age custom of erecting massive STONE structures (megalithic dolmens) to house the remains of great ancestors, may go back to a desire to protect the skeletons from being crushed by the weight of the soil. A Middle Eastern Jewish curse was "May your bones turn into air." Among populations who live by hunting, all of the bones of the prey were often returned whole to the EARTH, so that new life might replace the old. According to the *Prose Edda,* the GOATS that pulled the CHARIOT of Thor, the Norse god of THUNDER, could also be restored to life (through the magic of Thor's HAMMER) from just their bones. Thus human bones can function not only as symbols of DEATH but also as tokens of a belief in the resurrection to come. In other civilizations, their use in ritual served to diminish the fear of death. We find a completely different notion in cremation, which seeks a maximal disintegration of the bodies of the dead in FIRE, the purifying ELEMENT.

book   A symbol of high culture and religion; as the container of revealed wisdom, designated as "the Holy Book." Even more than Christianity, Islam is a "book-religion": the devout Muslim is obligated to read and copy the Koran (Qur'an, literally "reading, recitation") over and over. But Muslims also recognize adherents of the book-religions (revealed religions) Judaism and Christianity, as long as they are ready, under Muslim domination, to pay for religious freedom, as were the Mozarabian Christians

Book as symbol of the Eight Precious Things of ancient China

Book: Shelves with four Gospels. Grave mosaic, Galla Placidia, Ravenna, 5th century

in Moorish Spain. Jews read through the Torah (the five Books of Moses) every year. In the Christian world there was an early distinction between codices (books consisting of pages glued together) and scrolls (Latin *volumina*), the latter often shown in the hands of the Apostles, who are receiving from Christ these symbols of his teachings. The four EVANGELISTS, however, usually appear (with their symbolic animals) writing books in the modern sense. The universal judge (Greek *pantocrator*) of the Last Judgment is usually portrayed with a book in his hand in which all of the deeds of humanity are recorded; it bears the ALPHA AND OMEGA on its cover. The Book of Revelation is considered a "book with SEVEN SEALS" which can be broken only with divine inspiration. Scenes of the Annunciation show the VIRGIN Mary reading or opening the Bible (to Isaiah 7:14: "Behold, a virgin shall conceive"). The prophet John swallowing the Book of Revelation is a primal symbol of the internalization of a divine message. Scholarly saints were often portrayed with books (e.g., Bernard of Clairvaux, Anthony of Padua, Dominic, Thomas Aquinas, Catherine of Alexandria, as well as the Evangelists); the Sibyls, similarly, with scrolls, allegorical representations of astronomy and faith.

Jewish mysticism is so oriented toward the book that even ADAM, the first man, is confronted with one. In the Book of Rasiel (Hebrew Sepher Razielis) of the 13th century, the angel Rasiel appears to Adam, who has been driven out of PARADISE, and tells him: "I have come to give insight into pure teachings and great wisdom, to make you familiar with the words of this holy book. . . . Adam, take courage, be not anxious or afraid. Take this book from my hand and use it wisely: for from it you will gain wisdom and knowledge and convey them to whoever is worthy of them and is destined to receive them. . . . Adam, keep it holy and pure." Transmission of higher knowledge was apparently possible only with the aid of a book originating in higher spheres. In ancient China the book (shu) was the attribute of scholars. If small children reached for a book rather than any other of the objects laid out before them (including SILVER, money, a banana), this presaged success in a scholarly career. The four books of Confucius and the "five classical books" (see I-CHING) were especially esteemed. There are reports of repeated book-burnings (e.g., in the Ch'in dynasty in 213 B.C., under the aegis of the chancellor) as a gesture of "wiping the slate clean" of traditions that had come to be seen as superfluous. The possession of only chronicles and books on practical life was permitted. Ancient Mexico also had sacred books, some of which survive today (including Codex Borgia, Codex Laud, Codex Vindobonensis mexicanus 1); the fourth Aztec king, Itzcóatl (reigned 1427–1440), ordered a book-burning to eradicate the traditions

Book: Portrayal of a scribe with quill and inkhorn. Ca. 1170

of other Aztec nations and city-states and thus leave only the glory of Tenochtitlán. There were further destructions of tradition in the missionary period: under Bishop Juan de Zumárraga in Tezcuco or under Diego de Landa in Yucatán, who in 1562 in the city Maní had numerous Mayan codices burned.

In FREEMASONRY the "Book of Holy Law," the Bible, lies on the altar table of the lodge next to the law-book of the Great Lodge (these are two of the "Great Lights"; the others are the carpenter's square and the drafting compass). In heraldry the open book appears in the arms of university cities and in Richental's chronicle of the German city of Constance. The LION in St. Mark's Square in Venice is holding a book in its paws (the Gospel according to St. Mark). The German city of Bochum has a book as its (rebus-like) emblem. The book is of importance in visionary experiences, including those of illiterates like Joan of Arc (1412–1431), who opposed her experience to theological book-learning: "My Lord has a book, in which no cleric has ever read, however clerically perfect he may be." Paracelsus also preferred reading "the book of nature" to theoretical studies. Today the fundamental symbolic meaning of the book (in dreams, for example) is positive: "Nature and intellect appear to the unconscious as the great powers of life. The book appears especially often as the container of intellect. At times it is massive, worn, its print impressive: this is the book of life" [Aeppli]. In the Christian world the Bible is called "the Book of Books," from biblia, the Greek plural of biblios, book.

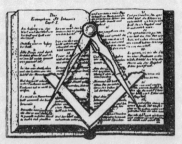

Book: Gospel according to John, compass, square. Masonic emblem, ca. 1830

This word, in turn, comes from the name of the Phoenician city Byblos, the most important ancient trading center for papyrus, the paper of the day.

box-tree (Greek *pyxos*, Latin *buxus*) An evergreen often planted (along with CYPRESSES and YEWS) to adorn the cemeteries of classical antiquity, and thus sacred to the divinities of the underworld and to the mother-goddess Cybele. The wood of the tree was used to make small boxes (*pyxis*, from *pyxos*) and statues of the gods (especially to honor the Olympian Apollo), and in the modern era the master-hammer of the FREEMASONS. The leathery leaves of the tree remain green and, as a symbol of that which is lasting, are often consecrated with palm fronds in the Palm Sunday bouquets of alpine regions, where they are kept throughout the year. *Buxus* is the ancestor of the English word "box": among the earliest boxes were pillboxes made from wood.

bread For all peoples with a knowledge of grain agriculture and baking, bread was the most important food. (The original Canary Islanders did not bake bread but worked grain into a sort of "Cream of Wheat" called "gofio.") In ancient Egypt there were some 40 varieties of bread and other baked goods, and the formulaic expressions for making sacrifices to the dead, refer to "bread and beer" as the staples of the AFTERLIFE. East of the Mediterranean, bread was not sliced but broken off; hence the expression "to break bread together." This meal soon came to be understood as a sacred observance, and the 12 loaves of showbread (see Exodus 25:30) in the tabernacle stand for spiritual nourishment. The New Testament recounts the miracle of the loaves and FISHES. Because "man does not live from bread alone," the "bread of life" of the Holy Eucharist, along with the WINE, nourishes his soul. For missionaries to peoples with different staple foods, it was often difficult to make the sacramental symbol comprehensible. (In China, the primary staple is rice; in Native American cultures, corn; those who first preached to the Inuit or Eskimos spoke of

Bread-kneading. Phoenician clay statuette, Achzib, ca. 1000 B.C.

"our daily seal blubber.") The entire process that culminates in bread—reaping, threshing, baking the processed grain from which the sacred bread is prepared—came to symbolize the Christian's laborious life on earth, which was to culminate in the blessed sanctity of HEAVEN. The manna falling miraculously from heaven as the Israelites made their way through the wilderness was later considered by Christians as a prefiguration of the Communion bread.

It was a popular custom to bless each new loaf of bread with the sign of the Cross. Countless idioms reflect the figurative importance of bread ("to take the bread out of someone's mouth," "that's my bread and butter"). Bread turned the wrong way on the table was considered unlucky: the DEVIL was said to ride on it, and the sight of it to produce quarrels and "make ANGELS weep" at this reversal of the proper order of things. As a dream symbol bread has only positive associations. Aeppli notes that it is "the most common of foods, and yet hallowed": "The path that extends from the grain of wheat being placed in its dark furrow, the gentle greening of the field, the sea of grain undulating, through the work of the reaper and thresher, the milling, sifting, kneading, then the passage through the fiery heat of the oven, and finally the sharing of bread at the family table—every station along the way is richly symbolic and, if applied to humanity, refers to the entire course of civilization." In the Neolithic Age, settlement, clearing of forests, and agriculture began to replace hunting and fishing: instead of appropriating food, humans began to produce it, creating in the process a new world and a new cultural landscape. With the possibility of accumulating food for future use came increased free time and opportunities for contemplation. The unbounded quality of nomadic life was replaced by delimitations, literally and figuratively, of cultivated and cultural space; it was now possible to be aware of the structure of a manageable microcosm. The bread produced therein was indeed the bread of life, and "all essential, 'nourishing' values can be handed us in our DREAMS in the form of bread. To receive bread is to take on value, value that must not be squandered" [Aeppli].

breasts The female breast is portrayed in Christian iconography without any erotic implication, as in images of *Maria lactans*, the MOTHER of God nursing the baby Jesus. St. Bernard of Clairvaux (1090–1153) also had a vision in which he was nourished by spiritual MILK from Mary's breast, a gift that could also be distributed to the multitudes of the faithful or be used to refresh the poor souls in purgatory. We occasionally see, as in 15th- through 17th-century representations of the Last Judgment, Mary baring before her son the breasts that had nursed him, in order to make him more lenient, while he himself shows the wounds of his

Breasts: Juno adopts Hercules. Etruscan mirror engraving, 4th century B.C.

Passion to God the FATHER. Amputated breasts on a platter are the attribute of brutally tortured women martyrs, e.g., St. Agatha, who died in Sicily in 251 for her faith. In classical antiquity a significantly portrayal of the mother's breast was the famous DIANA of Ephesus, "Artemis *polymastos*" (many-breasted), the universal mother nursing all of humanity; Macrobius speaks of her as a many-breasted Natura. The recent hypothesis that the grape-like breasts of this Artemis are the testicles of sacrificed BULLS, seems unlikely in view of the classical notion of the primeval mother nursing the world. Ancient Chinese symbolism paid little attention to female breasts, but a highly developed male chest resembling a woman's bosom is referred to as a lucky symbol. Wen-wang, who founded the Chou dynasty, is said to have been distinguished with FOUR breasts. (See also CHARITY.)

bridge A symbol of transition or passage, for example over the water that separates this world from the next (see AFTERLIFE). It replaces the ferryman who in other versions transports souls. In Norse myth this bridge trembles when one who has not yet died tries to cross it, and it is guarded by a sentry who sounds a horn of warning if enemy legions approach. The bridge between the secular world and the divine is so significant

Breasts: Libation vessel depicting mother goddess. Mochlos, Crete, ca. 2000 B.C.

that it requires a special bridge-builder (*pontifex* in Latin, also "priest") to bring the two realms into communication. Because of the deep symbolic significance of bridges, their construction required sacrifices: in ancient Rome the vestal virgins threw rush-dolls into the Tiber from the old bridge when work began on a new one. The RAINBOW and the Milky Way (see MILK) were seen as bridges between the terrestrial and the heavenly world. In Islam there is an image of a bridge to HEAVEN that is as narrow as the edge of a SWORD; only a person who is free from sin can walk along it without plunging into the depths below. There are similar motifs in Native American tales, in which a narrow wooden beam serves as the bridge. In the imagery of ancient China the bridge to the other world is again very narrow, and sinners plunge into a filthy stream of BLOOD and pus. The pilgrim Hsüan-tsang also had to cross over a bridge consisting of a single tree-trunk in order to obtain Buddhist scripture from India (see APE). A bridge-divinity protects those crossing bridges from disease-bringing demons. In the religion of Parsiism the dead must cross Cinvat Bridge, which is no wider than a HAIR. The unjust plunge from it into HELL. Bridges do more than just link one space or realm with another: they also symbolize transition to a new way of existence that can be achieved meaningfully only through firmly established rites of passage. A wealth of idiomatic expressions that vary from language to language (but usually include some version of "to burn one's bridges behind one") suggest something of the symbolic importance of the bridge. In HERALDRY bridges appear on the rebus-like arms of certain cities (e.g., Innsbruck, whose arms contain the bridge [*Brücke*] of a ship).

broom Implement for sweeping rooms; in oldest times already invested with magical powers and symbolic import. The fairy tale of the sorcerer's apprentice, who transforms a broom into a water-carrier, itself dates back to the classical world and derives from certain ancient Egyptian motifs. Following an old superstition, PYTHAGORAS said that it was forbidden to step over a broom. As part

Broom as witch's transportation. Book illustration (*Le Champuis des Dames*), 1451

of the Athenian festival Anthesteria, the souls of the dead visited the houses of the living and were received with hospitality but then driven out by a thorough sweeping of the houses with brooms. In ancient China it was taboo to leave a broom in a room where someone was dying, lest the person return as a long-haired ghost to haunt the living. Gamblers also avoided brooms, which could sweep away their luck. On the other hand, the goddess of clear weather, honored at New Year's, was esteemed for sweeping away the rain-CLOUDS. Europeans focused particularly on the life-force that was believed to emanate from the twigs of the besom; these were thought to ward off bad weather, which is why "WITCHES' brooms" were placed on rooftops. On the other hand, the broom was a symbol and attribute of witches themselves, who flew off on them to witches' sabbaths after rubbing themselves with (presumably consciousness-altering) ointments. The broom between the legs of the naked witch was widely understood as a phallic symbol; admittedly, pokers, benches, and other household objects were portrayed as alternative means of air travel. In ancient Mexico, a broom festival, Ochpaniztli, dedicated to the old earth-goddess Teteo-innan, supposedly swept away disease and harm. In Christian iconography the broom is the attribute of St. Martha and St. Petronilla, patron saints of household employees. Familiar expressions include "a clean sweep" and "a new broom sweeps clean."

brown is not a primary color and has relatively little significance within the symbology of COLORS. Nevertheless it is the color of clay soil (see EARTH), replaced only in ancient China by YELLOW (the color of loess) as a symbol of the center. To psychologists the simple brown seems "warm, calm, maternal, close to the simple facts" [Aeppli], but Portal (1847) described it as a mixture of red and black and thus a "symbol of subterranean love," "devilish garb," "dark FIRE" with evil import: he saw the RED of the ancient Egyptian enemy Seth (Setesh; Greek Typhon) as brown; in fact, the color abhorred by the Egyptians was reddish ocher. In the Christian world brown is the "color of the earth, autumn, sorrow, humility [from *humus*, "earth"], poverty (and hence the brown cowl of many mendicant orders)" [Heinz-Mohr]. It has negative associations, however: with smoke from fires (see SODOM AND GOMORRAH) and with the DEVIL. It was also a symbol of Nazi Germany: Hitler's Storm Troops were called Brownshirts.

Buddha, Fat, or *Mi-lo fo* Today countless Asian import stores sell porcelain figurines of a happily grinning, bare-chested, bald man. This is the Chinese *Mi-lo fo*, i.e., actually a later incarnation of Buddha (in Hindi *Maitreya*) who will relieve future ages from the sufferings of existence. This Buddha seems to have taken on different associations in China from what would have been possible in India. Around A.D. 1000 the *Mi-lo fo* became popular throughout East Asia as a symbol of carefree bliss, holding a bag of presents and often surrounded by children at play. The misfortune and sorrow of the real world were to be overcome by

Bull (Zeus) abducts Europa over the sea. Etruscan vase decoration, ca. 580 B.C.

this friendly antitype and make room for the prospect of an entirely secular state of bliss. In Japan he is called *Hotei* and is believed to bring peace and prosperity, also as one of the seven GODS OF HAPPINESS.

bull In many ancient cultures, a symbol of great importance. In Paleolithic religious CAVE drawings, wild cattle (specifically, the aurochs) are one of the most common motifs, second only to HORSES. The primeval bull must have been a powerfully impressive symbol of vitality and masculine strength, but the animal's symbolic significance is ambiguous. While untamed strength is impressive, the brutality of the attacking bull, as experienced by humans, is intimidating. The bull is of particular importance in the history of religion: bulls were worshipped in a variety of cultures, especially as symbols of potency and for their horns, which suggest the lunar crescent (a common association with COWS, as well). On the other hand, there are countless symbolic rites in which a bull is defeated or sacrificed. In ancient

Fat Buddha: Hotei. Japanese porcelain, 19th century

Bull. Cave painting, Lascaux, France, Ice Age

Bull. Copper, El Obeid near Ur, southern Babylonia, Sumerian

Cretan ritual (which presumably had its counterparts in other cultures) the bull was used in athletic/artistic leaping dances in which humans sought to demonstrate their superiority as they overcame the supposedly dull animalistic nature of the "beast." Such rituals are also related to the efforts of the human race to domesticate cattle. Even when OXEN were put to work, uncastrated bulls often remained sacred (e.g., the Egyptian Apis, which was also mummified) and were worshiped as symbols of natural forces. Fertility, death, and resurrection were commonly associated with the bull (e.g., in the Mithraic religion of late antiquity). The minotaur of ancient Crete (a mixture of man and bull) was first hidden in the LABYRINTH, then killed by the hero Theseus. The bull-

Bull: Minotaur. Coin, Crete

fight of southwestern Europe should not be understood primarily as a sporting event but rather as a stylized version of the bull rituals of the ancient Mediterranean world, which ended with the sacrifice of the equally respected and feared symbol of the forces of untamed nature. (See also RED.)

In ASTROLOGY the bull, Taurus, is the second sign of the zodiac (April 21– May 21; see STARS), an earth sign. Those born under this sign are believed to be clumsy, earthbound, tenacious, and powerful. The PLANET VENUS is said to rule Taurus—an echo of mythological connections between the love goddess and the bull. In the astral legends of the Greeks, the constellation Taurus was associated with the minotaur, but also with the wild bull that devastated the fields around Marathon and was slain by the hero The-

Butterfly (stylized). Arms of the Taira family, Japan, ca. 1150

seus. On the back of the astral bull are found the Pleiades, an indistinct cluster of stars traditionally identified with the SEVEN daughters of ATLAS, who were pursued by the hunter Orion (see SCORPION) until they were transformed first into DOVES, then stars. The bright eye of the bull is the fixed star. (See also HORNS.)

butterfly (Greek psyche, Latin papilio) A symbolic creature in many cultures, standing in some contexts for beauty and metamorphosis and in others for the transitory nature of happiness. "The miracle of its successive life stages, of metamorphosis from the larval existence of the plodding caterpillar to the delicate beauty of the butterfly, has moved us deeply, becoming a metaphor for the

Butterfly (stylized). Ceramic decoration, Teotihuacan civilization, ancient Mexico

Butterfly: Swallowtail. T. Moffet, *The Theater of Insects*, 1658

transformations undergone by our own souls: this is one source of our hope that we may one day leave behind our terrestrial prison and ascend into the eternal light of the heavens" [Aeppli]. This is why butterflies often adorn old tombstones. (See symbols of DEATH.) As its Greek name indicates, the butterfly, like the BIRD, is an analogue for the human soul (another meaning for the Greek word *psyche*). In its "flightiness" it resembles elves, genies, and cupids. Pixies, like dream or fantasy figures, are often depicted with butterfly wings, as is HYPNOS (Latin SOMNUS), the god of sleep. In depictions of the earthly PARADISE, the soul placed by the Creator in Adam is sometimes shown as having such wings.

In Japan the butterfly is a symbol of young womanhood; two butterflies dancing about

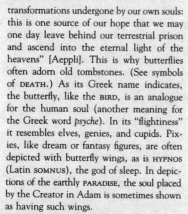

Butterfly. Stone relief, Acalpixan, Mexico

one another mean marital happiness. In China, on the other hand, the insect symbolizes a young man in love and is portrayed drinking from the (female) FLOWERS and blossoms; however, if the woman he loves dies, she may be represented coming out of her grave as a butterfly. In combination with the PLUM, the butterfly symbolizes longevity and beauty; when used punningly (*tieh* is the word for "seventy"; *hu-tieh*, for "butterfly") it expresses the wish that the recipient might reach the age of 70 (and is often paired with a cat, *mao*, which is also the word for "eighty"). In ancient Mexico the butterfly (in Aztec *papalotl*, suggestive of the Latin *papilio*) was one of the attributes of Xochipilli, the god of vegetation, but also symbolized flickering firelight and was associated with the SUN. The goddess Itzpapalotl, a butterfly surrounded by STONE knives (*itzli*), was a night spirit associated with fiery STARS and also a symbol of the souls of women who had died in childbirth.

There is a line of Japanese poetry expressing sorrow over the lost pleasures of the past, a response to the maxim, "The fallen blossom never returns to the branch": "I thought that the blossom had returned to the branch—alas, it was only a butterfly." (See also JOAN OF ARC.)

caduceus (Greek *karukeion*) Staff and symbol of the god MERCURY (Greek Hermes), the messenger of the gods. It consists of a magic wand or herald's staff, around which two serpents are twined, their heads turned toward each other (compare ASCLEPIUS, with whose staff the caduceus is often confused; and see SNAKE). On occasion the caduceus is topped by a pair of WINGS. The staff is said to have originally been adorned with fluttering ribbons in place of the serpents. Symbological speculation along psychoanalytic lines sees the caduceus as a phallus (see LINGA) along which two serpents are mating. In fact zoologists have noted a mating ritual in some varieties of snake (e.g., cobras) in the course of which both partners rise vertically part way. In modern times the

caduceus has become the symbol for the world of trade and transportation and, through its resemblance to the staff of Asclepius, a symbol of the medical profession. In the imagery of ALCHEMY the two serpents are interpreted as an image of the balance of the primary elements SULFUR AND MERCURY, i.e., as a DUALITY of that which burns and that which is volatile; the element mercury is also represented by the divine messenger of the same name. Not only Hermes but also Isis, the goddess of dawn, was portrayed with the caduceus, because she heralds the SUN. The ancient myth explaining the caduceus is reconstructed as follows by G. S. Böckler (1688): Mercury had received a staff from Apollo. When he came to Arcadia with it, "he found two serpents biting one another; he threw the rod between them and they became reconciled. Thus the rod or staff came to be seen as a symbol of peace, which means simply that the venom of war can be contained and drawn off by means of good, peaceful discourse. Others liken the staff to dialectics, which seek to determine right or wrong out of the confusion of an argument."

Caduceus and horns of plenty as symbols of commercial success. Cartari, 1647

Cain A symbolic figure in the Bible, kills his brother Abel when God is displeased with Cain's sacrifice but has "respect for Abel and his offering" [Genesis 4:4]; the text does not explain the reason for God's differing responses to the two sacrifices. The fratricide between the sons of ADAM AND EVE was a frequent subject in medieval art, with Cain often serving as a prototype for the Jewish people as the killers of Christ— a characterization of them that ignores, of course, the fact that Christ himself was Jewish. Abel, conversely, the innocent victim, served as a prototype for Christ, "the good SHEPHERD." Cain must become "a fugitive and a vagabond in the earth" [4:14]; (see also AHASUERUS) but must not be killed for revenge: the "mark of Cain," placed upon him by God, protects him, and "east of Eden" he becomes the progenitor of a line of highly productive, creative individuals, such as Tubalcain, "an instructor of every artificer in brass and iron" [4:22].

Cain questioned after Abel's death. Relief (detail), Hildesheim Cathedral (ca. 1015)

According to a symbolic myth in the Gnostic text *Apocryphon of John* (as discovered at Naj Hammadi), one that appears strange to Christian readers, Adam sired two figures: Yahweh, the BEAR face, and Elohim, the CAT face. "They are the ones who are known to all peoples as Cain and Abel." Their

Cain, slayer of his brother Abel. Gustave Doré (1832–1883)

names are the Old Testament names for God. They govern the four material ELEMENTS: Elohim FIRE and WIND; Yahweh WATER and EARTH. Of the children of Adam, only Seth represents redeemed humanity; for this reason, Gnostics of this orientation were also called "Sethians." Cain is seen as "the bear face Yahweh," governing those elements more contaminated with materiality. According to Leland, the popular 19th-century witches' cult of DIANA also included incantations to Cain: "I entreat you, O Cain, you who will never find peace until you are freed from the MOON, which is your prison, I implore you, let me know my fate." (Cain here seems to be thought of as "the man in the moon.")

calumet or "peace pipe" The "sacred pipe" of Native Americans around the Upper Mississippi; references to "smoking the peace pipe" (a designation for the end of hostilities between two parties) are common in most of the languages of the Western world, dating back to the first half of the 19th century and since then attributable mostly to the international influence of such widely read authors as James Fenimore Cooper and, in Central Europe, Karl May (1842–1912). In reality the sacred pipe was a ritual and symbolic object. In addition to its other meanings, the calumet was the Native American analogue of the CADUCEUS, the messenger's staff of European antiquity. WHITE FEATHERS on it meant peace; RED, war. Contrary to the implications of present-day linguistic usage, not every tobacco pipe of the Native Americans was, strictly speaking, a calumet. In the primary sense of the word, calumets come in pairs, portraying a duality, one HEAVEN (male), the other EARTH (female)— with the possible variant (found among the Omaha, for example) of the "heaven" pipe being thought of as female and the "earth" pipe male. The two pipestems (feather staffs) together represented the symbolic EAGLE. In ceremonies of blessing they were waved over the gathered members of the various Plains nations. In the ritual smoking of the calumet, the pipe was lit and passed to the speaker, who took a few puffs and then blew

Calumet bowl with bear figure. Iroquois, 17th century

smoke toward heaven, "mother" earth, and the four points of the compass, extending the mouthpiece of the sacred pipe in the same direction each time. Finally he passed the pipe on to the next person; it went around the circle like the sun moving from east to west. This ceremony protected the guest who had participated in it against any act of hostility—at least while in the camp. A sacred pipe was strictly a symbolic object, withdrawn from everyday use; the bowl was usually made of pipestone (or steatite) into which figures had been carved. The Plains nations seem to have taken over this custom from the settled corn farmers of eastern North America. The tobacco (*kinnikinnick*) was prepared according to specific rules from a blend of sumac and bearberry leaves and the ground bark of certain trees. In 19th-century portraits chiefs are often shown holding sacred pipes.

Calumet of the Mandan tribe. George Catlin, 1839

camel   The animal that—largely by its undemanding nature—made it possible for humans to traverse the steppes and deserts of Asia and North Africa, plays an ambiguous role in symbolic traditions. It is not surprising that the camel became a symbol of moderation and sobriety and that St. Augustine (A.D. 354–430) made it a symbol of the humble Christian shouldering life's burden without complaint. Because of its physiognomy, however, which to the human eye appears haughty, it also came to symbolize arrogance and selfishness. In the Middle Ages, because it would accept only those burdens that it could actually carry, the

Camelus.

Camel. Woodcut in Pseudo-Albertus Magnus, Frankfurt, 1531

camel came to stand for *discretio*, or discernment; but for those who had little familiarity with the animal, the same behavior made it a symbol of laziness. Its ability to kneel "obediently" was taken as a positive characteristic. In images of the Magi (the "wise men from the east" of Matthew 2:1–12) the camel appears as a beast of burden. A camel began to speak in support of the wish of St. Cosmas and St. Damian that they might be buried in the same grave; the DEVIL, however, assumed the form of a giant camel to plague Macarius the Egyptian. Although it has been suggested that a mistranslation may have produced Christ's statement that "it is easier for a camel [in Aramaic *gamlá*, which also means "rope"] to go through the eye of a needle, than for a rich man to enter into the kingdom of God" [Matthew 19:24], it seems more likely that "camel" is correct, a—to Western ears especially "Eastern"—paradoxical hyperbole expressing utter impossibility. In the Babylonian Talmud a similar image is used in reference to those who achieve the impossible: they make "an ELEPHANT pass through the eye of a needle." In Asian symbology the camel does not play a major role. One occasion upon which it does appear, however, is when it joins the water buffalo, the elephant, and the TIGER in mourning the death of Gautama Buddha.

candelabra and candlesticks In antiquity the crucial holders of the candles that made it possible to see despite the dark of night, whenever oil lamps (themselves often adorned with symbols) were not used. The candelabra took on symbolic significance, especially the Menorah, the seven-branched candelabrum of Jewish tradition: "And thou shalt make a candlestick of pure gold: of beaten work shall the candlestick be made: his shaft, and his branches, his bowls, his knops, and his flowers, shall be of the same. And six branches shall come out of the side of it; three branches of the candlestick out of the one side, and three branches of the candlestick out of the other side: Three bowls made like unto almonds, with a knop and a flower in one branch; and three bowls made like almonds in the other branch, with a knop and a flower: so in the six branches that come out of the candlestick. And in

Candelabra: Menorah. Stone relief, Priena (Asia Minor) synagogue, ca. A.D. 300

the candlestick shall be four bowls made like unto almonds, with their knops and their flowers. And there shall be a knop under two branches of the same, and a knop under two branches of the same, and a knop under two branches of the same, according to the six branches that proceed out of the candlestick. Their knops and their branches shall be of the same: all it shall be one beaten work of pure gold" (Exodus 25:31–36). Originally each branch bore an oil lamp, but wax candles were frequently used in later times. The Menorah, with its botanical features, is presumably intended to suggest a sort of world-TREE in the Babylonian manner, its SEVEN branches referring to the seven PLANETS. The Menorah stood in the TEMPLE of JERUSALEM and was stolen after the Roman conquest (as depicted in the Arch of Titus at the Roman Forum). In medieval art it is often a symbol of Judaism. "The candelabrum is a tree of light in full bloom. The light shines up to God, and all other lights shine toward it, in order to dissolve into it. . . . This is the Menorah, which, according to tradition, at the time of the heroic Maccabees burned for a total of eight days when the second temple was consecrated—although it was fueled only from a small container of oil, which was found intact" [De Vries]. The lights of Chanukah number only eight; the middle branch holds not a candle but a figure (e.g., Judith with

Candelabra: Extinguishing the Sabbath candles. Jewish woodcut, ca. 1680

the head of Holofernes). The ninth arm holds the candle "shammash" ("the servant of light," also the name of the Babylonian SUN god), which is used to light the other seven. In the Christian world the large holder for the Easter candle (for example, in the Hildesheim cathedral, dating from 1015) is particularly splendid in design.

Capricorn The MOUNTAIN GOAT with its great curving horns has at times been associated with the MOON or with lunar deities, e.g. under the name Ta'lab in the Sheban tradition of southern Arabia. As a sign of the zodiac, this creature was first known as the "goat FISH," a WATER animal with horns and the tail of a fish. Only later did the tenth sign of the zodiac receive the name Capricorn. Augustus Caesar had coins stamped with the image of Capricorn because it was his birth-sign. The sign is ruled by the PLANET SATURN; its metal is LEAD and its COLOR BLACK. The SUN is in Capricorn from December 21 until January 19; because of the winter solstice and the lengthening of the day, the sign is considered to be a positive one. Nevertheless, Capricorn is still a male goat, and thus linked in the Christian era with the DEVIL; astrologers associated error, deception, greed, and narrowness with the sign, but also wealth, restraint, concentration, and the power of steadfastness. An EARTH sign, Capricorn is associated with the qualities "dry" and "cold," because of the time of the year when the sun traverses it.

Capricorn: Winged ibex. Cover of Persian vessel, ca. 350 B.C.

Capricorn: Ibex. From a drawing in E. Topsell, *The History of Four-footed Beasts*, 1658

carnations Flowers found in some 300 varieties and variously cultivated. The pink carnation appears frequently in depictions of the Madonna and Child, and the carnation is a frequent love token in Renaissance engagement paintings. In the modern era the RED carnation became a symbol first of the French Royalists, then, in German-speaking countries, of the Social Democrats (especially on May Day), whereas a WHITE carnation was the symbol of the Christian Socialists; the association of the red carnation with socialism eventually spread to the rest of Europe. In designs of Turkish and Caucasian carpets, the carnation symbolizes good fortune.

Casanova In current usage the symbolic figure of the vain adventurer who lives to seduce more and more women but is incapable of having a lasting, fulfilling relationship. Giovanni Girolamo Casanova, Chevalier de Seingalt (1725–1798), was a liberally educated, gallant confidence man and charlatan who boasted of his alchemistic and cabalistic knowledge, was a talented diplomat, and had more imagination and intelligence than most of his contemporaries. In his memoirs, along with references to fleeting amours with some 200 women, he tells of his escape from the reputedly escape-proof Piombi prison of the Venetian Inquisition, in which he had been sentenced

Carnation. B. Besler, *Hortus Eystettensis*, 1613

for five years for writing impious texts. He spent the last years of his life as the librarian of the Bohemian castle Dux, where he also wrote his memoirs.

Cassandra A tragic female figure of Greek myth, a daughter of King Priam of Troy and his queen Hecuba. A seer and a priestess, she revered the oracular god Apollo, who gave her the gift of prophecy and hoped to become her lover. She accepted the gift but rejected his overtures, and the disappointed Apollo amended the gift as follows: Cassandra's prophecies would be accurate, but no one would believe them. She warned that the child Paris would one day bring disaster to Troy, that his voyage to Sparta (where he was to encounter Helen) would have dire consequences, and that the wooden HORSE left by the Greeks must not be brought through the gates and into the city, but all of her warnings fell on deaf ears: Troy fell, and Cassandra was taken to Mycenae as a slave and soon murdered. Near Amyclae, where she was buried, a temple was dedicated to Cassandra (under the name Alexandra). A "Cassandra" is a person whose prophecies, however accurate, go unheeded.

cat The animal that is thought of today as a beloved pet (and hardly as an exterminator of RATS and mice any more) has a predominantly negative reputation in symbolic tradition. It was domesticated in ancient Egypt around 2000 B.C. from the Nubian *Felis sylvestris lybica*. A short-tailed cat, the so-called "reed cat," which was known there even earlier, is mentioned in *The Book of the Dead* as slicing up the evil SNAKE Apepi. The domestic cat soon replaced leonine deities: the cat goddess Bast or Bastet was a lioness in earlier times, but cats themselves came to be frequently mummified, and feline deities appeared, represented with a cat's head and a woman's body. In late antiquity cats were brought from Egypt to Greece and Rome and were viewed as attributes of the goddess DIANA. BLACK cats in particular were believed to have magic powers; even their ASHES, strewn over a farmer's fields, were believed to ward off harmful insects and animals. For the Celts cats symbolized evil forces and were frequently sacrificed, whereas the Norse goddess Freya was represented in a chariot drawn by cats. The eye of the cat, which appears to change as the light strikes it from different angles, was considered deceptive, and the animal's ability to hunt even in virtual DARKNESS led to the belief that it was in league with the forces of darkness. It was associated with lasciviousness and cruelty and was considered above all the "familiar" (Latin *spiritus familiaris*) of WITCHES, who were often said to ride black (tom-)cats to their sabbaths. Even today the superstitious believe the black cat brings bad luck. Interestingly, humorous or satirical papyri from ancient Egypt often portray a "world turned upside down" in which mice in CHARIOTS wage war on cats in their en-

Cat of sun god beheading the snake Apepi. Hunefer papyrus, ca. 1300 B.C.

Cat. E. Topsell, *The History of Four-footed Beasts*, 1658

trenchments—not unlike the humor we find in "Tom and Jerry" cartoons of our day.

For some psychologists the cat is "the typically feminine animal," a creature of the NIGHT, "and woman is, we know, more deeply rooted in the dark, intuitive side of life than man, with his simpler psyche" [Aeppli]; we are tempted to speculate that the negative valuation of the cat, which we have noted in many cultures, is related to an aggressive attitude toward that which is female. (Note the frequent feline metaphors in misogynist expressions and clichés: a "cat fight" between two women, a "catty" remark, "like a cat in heat.") In heraldic tradition cats appear frequently, and with associations that recall little of the ailurophobia we find elsewhere: "Cats, being difficult to catch or to confine, signify liberty. The cat is tireless and cunning when going after its prey—the virtues of a good soldier. This is why the Swabians, Swiss, and Burgundians of old had cats in their coats of arms, standing for liberty" [Böckler].

caves As secret passageways to a subterranean world, often filled with bizarre stalagtite formations, caves figure in many highly symbolic myths, legends, and cults. The oldest shrines, adorned with paintings and rock drawings, many of them were perceived already in the Ice Age as "otherworldly" spaces: they were not dwellings but sanctuaries. They are in many cases to be understood as images of the womb, as in many Native American myths of the origin of the world and of the human race (e.g., the *chicomoztoc* birth-caves of Aztec myth). They were widely thought of as birthplaces of gods and heroes, abodes of anchorites and prophetic sibyls. In ancient Egyptian cosmology the Nile came from a rock cave. In the religions of Mycenaean Crete many caves were believed to be sacred. One of them was later the site of the oracle of Heros Trophonius, which required that supplicants go through a special initiation ritual.

It was natural for caves to be seen as critical sites for chthonic (i.e., relating to the EARTH and the underworld) religion and symbolism, places in which to make contact with the powers and forces lodged below which will later make their way to the LIGHT. Thus the temple of the late Roman god Mithras was built in the form of a rock cave. Grottos (and grotto temples) are often artificially dug out and created "caves" (in Egypt, Abu Simbel; in India, Ajanta and Ellora). In Christian iconography the stable in Bethlehem is portrayed as a rock cave. According to the tradition of the Eastern Church, it was in a cave on the island of Patmos that John the Evangelist received his powerful vision of the Apocalypse. In the philosophical language of Plato (427– 347 B.C.), the cave metaphor is of great importance: it is as if humans were trapped in a cave, unable to see more than the SHADOWS of ideas, mere images of a higher and truer reality, which they with their limited capacities will never be able to view directly [*The Republic*, Book VII].

The chalky caves of what was the Mayan region of Central America continue to interest the present-day descendants of the ancient inhabitants. Many of the caves were sought out by the Maya for ritualistic purposes; vessels for sacrifices to the RAIN god have been found in them. Some of them have on their walls paintings in typical Mayan style, most notably the grotto of Naj-Tunich, whose paintings indicate rituals of a sexual nature. Pictures of DWARF-like creatures seem to belong to a complex of interrelated notions: fertility, RAIN, dwarfs, caves. Caves were associated with female genitalia (both vagina and uterus), as ancient chronicles indicate, and sexuality, in turn, with fertility in general. The dwarf-like Aztec rain gods, who carried phallic staffs, were also thought of as living in caves; the Mayan moon goddess was associated at times with caves, life-giving WATER, and sexuality (relations with the god of the planet Venus). In the most advanced civilizations of Central America (as in many other traditions) the cave "underworld," nestled in the belly of the earth, had female associations and thus was made part of the general conceptual domain of fertility. Similar associations in the Old World—which are also linked to the theme of the "primeval"—seem quite likely. In the Christian context sexual symbolism, of course, was often muted. A nonecclesiastical text of the early Christian era, called The Book of the Cave of Treasures (or The Christian Adam-Book of the Orient; ca. fifth century after Christ), reads like a vestige from the beginnings of human history when its narrative begins in a cave in which ADAM was buried at the end of his life's struggles (which followed his expulsion from Eden); old Noah, the survivor of the FLOOD, orders his son Shem to take Adam's remains

out of the cave and rebury them—"at the midpoint of the earth" (compare CROSS).

In popular legend caves usually house gnomes, mountain spirits, and DRAGONS guarding treasures; outsiders can reach them only with great difficulty and peril. KINGS of earlier, distant times (Charlemagne, Frederick I) were believed to lie in caves of specific MOUNTAINS (the Kyffhäuser Mountains, the Untersberg near Salzburg) awaiting resurrection at the moment of the final apocalyptic battle between the forces of good and evil (see DUALITIES). Cave legends are prominent in Irish myth (see STONE). Out of the cave Cruachan (also called the "gate of HELL") comes an immense flock of WHITE BIRDS whose breath withers humans and animals. Another cave housed the terrible goddess Morrlgan (RAVEN), and the heroes Conan and Finn became entangled in the yarn of witches who lay in wait there and almost managed to carry them off to the underworld. The most famous entry to the subterranean, hell-like world is "St. Patrick's PURGATORY," on an island in Loch Derg: in earlier times pilgrims had themselves enclosed in the cave for four hours so that they might experience the torments of purgatory, and legend had it that anyone who fell asleep there would be carried off to hell by the DEVIL. The medieval KNIGHT Sir Owen described visions of the AFTERLIFE similar to Dante's in The Divine Comedy. Present-day pilgrims who spend a sleepless night in the chapel that now surrounds the "purgatory" describe it as an eerie place "where two worlds meet." The cave of a legendary Scotish king is commemorated in Felix Mendelssohn's Hebrides Overture (1830–32), better known as Fingal's Cave.

In symbolic architecture recesses or niches often represent a "world-cave" enclosed in a greater cosmos: a prayer niche (mihrab) in a mosque or an apse in a church heightens one's sense of being in an enclosed haven. Psychologists interpret a dreamer's dangerous passage through dark caves as symbolizing the search for the meaning of life in the deep, hereditary strata of the maternal unconscious, or, in different contexts, a longing to return to the dark refuge of the

Cave drawing of wild bison. Niaux (Ariège, France), ca. 10,000 B.C.

dreamer's life before birth. Thus the cave fascination of amateur spelunkers could be understood not only as a matter of intellectual curiosity but also as a striving—explainable only through symbology—for self-knowledge through a descent into the hidden depths of their own personalities. This is suggested by the following psychological interpretation of the cave topos: "The retreat to the cave is primal; the cave is refuge, shelter. Going into it is returning to the womb, negating birth, submerging into shadow and the nocturnal world of nondifferentiation. It is the renunciation of life on earth in favor of the higher life of the unborn. . . . [In the cave] there is no time, neither yesterday nor tomorrow, for day and night there are as one. In seclusion there is, according to Eliade (1980), a 'larva-like existence,' like that of the dead in the afterlife" [Kasper]. For this reason as well, the cave—in various contexts and stages of cultural development—is an obvious site for symbolic rituals of initiation and of rebirth on a higher level of existence.

cedar (genus *Cedrus*) An evergreen of the Mediterranean region, prized like the CYPRESS for its durability; exported from Lebanon to Egypt in the earliest period of Egyptian history. Its wood, used in Egypt to build ships, furniture, coffins for mummies, and tools, was also prized for its fragrant

Cedrus.

Cedar. Hohberg, 1675

aroma. King SOLOMON used cedar for the construction of the great TEMPLE IN JERUSALEM. "The righteous shall flourish like the palm tree: he shall grow like a cedar in Lebanon" [Psalm 92:12]. One of the Church fathers, Origen (A.D. 185–254), based the following moral application on the durability of cedar wood: "The cedar does not decay. To use cedar for the beams of our house is to protect our soul from corruption." The patriarch Cyril of Alexandria (412–444) likened cedar to the flesh of Christ, which remained unspoiled. Only the wrath of God is mightier than cedar: "The voice of the Lord breaketh the cedars; yea, the Lord breaketh the cedars of Lebanon" [Psalm 29:5]. Hohberg, however, stressed the durability of the wood: "Of cedar Solomon did his temple build,/ Lest worm or blows its splendor should attack./ When God brings peace to bless all that He's willed,/ Fear no misfortune, nor the tempest's wrack."

The national tree of Lebanon is unfortunately close to extinction there.

centaurs Mythical monsters, each with a horse's body to which a (male) human upper body has been attached where the horse's neck would be; since Greek antiquity, these creatures have been thought of as embodiments of discord and (internal) tension. Their legend is believed to have originated as a recollection of the first sightings of nomads on horseback from the steppes of Asia—a terrifying sight for the settled inhabitants of Mediterranean countries. (Similarly, when the native peoples of Central America first saw the Spanish conquistadors arriving on horseback, they thought they were part man, part animal.) Centaurs, also called "hippocentaurs," were often portrayed in Greece as the opponents of the Lapiths, a (human) tribe of the mountains of Thessaly: drunken centaurs had tried to abduct Lapith women. (See also SAVAGES.) They consequently came to symbolize animality, untamed nature, and subservience to basic drives: their animal side, it seemed, was only partly tamed by their human side. In the *Physiologus* text of late antiquity, centaurs stand for heretics, who know

Centaur and Lapith doing battle. Parthenon frieze, Athens, ca. 445 B.C.

Christian doctrine but do not apply it properly and thus remain at odds with themselves. In medieval imagery the centaur, because he has failed to overcome his animal nature, is contrasted with the noble KNIGHT, and is also often made to embody the vice of pride *(superbia).*

On the other hand, positive qualities were ascribed to individual centaurs, primarily because of their close association with nature. Heroes like Jason and Achilles were in their youth pupils of the wise centaur Chiron, who teaches them about medicinal herbs. The plant centaury is so named because its medicinal properties were said to have been discovered by Chiron. Hercules accidentally struck the benevolent teacher with a poisoned arrow; Chiron renounced his immortality for the sake of Prometheus and was

Centaur-like Minotaur battling Theseus. In Plutarch's *Lives,* Venice, 1496

transported into the HEAVENS, where he became the constellation Sagittarius. One Greek family of doctors traced its lineage back to Chiron. In astrology the ninth sign of the zodiac, Sagittarius, is a centaur shooting an arrow, a FIRE sign; those born under this sign are said to be resolute, aggressive, spirited, and seekers of light, energy, and power.

chain Originally a symbol of imprisonment and slavery, or defeat. Thus in Christian iconography the DEVIL, in defeat after the Last Judgment, is portrayed plunging into the abyss in chains; but the chains that once held St. Peter are likewise an important symbol, in this case of the liberation of the

Centaur. Floor mosaic. Palestine, 5th century A.D.

believer through divine intervention. In many contexts broken chains symbolize the overcoming of servitude. The "golden chain" (in Latin *catena aurea*) was thought of in antiquity as linking HEAVEN and EARTH and, in Neoplatonism, represented the first principle along with its emanations; both have positive associations. Macrobius (ca. A.D. 400) expresses this as follows: "Since spirit emanates from God in the highest, and in turn creates and fills with life everything that comes after . . . and since all things follow in unbroken sequence, descending to the lowermost level of this series, the alert observer will discover a concatenation of these parts, from God in the highest to the lowest dregs, all of which are linked continuously. This is Homer's golden chain, which God, according to the poet, ordered sus-

Chain, toad, eagle: alchemist's image for duality "fixed"/ "volatile." M. Maier, *Symbola*, 1617

Chains both "oppress and adorn." J. Boschius, 1702

pended from heaven to earth." Dionysius Areopagita (ca. A.D. 500) speaks of the Christian's prayer itself as a golden chain whose luminescence bridges the abyss between creature and creator.

In the symbolism of FREEMASONRY, the "fraternal chain" is the bond between brother Masons, expressed at the conclusion of the WORK of the lodge by the joining of hands in a CIRCLE: the bond is understood as extending across international borders and encircling the globe. In 1817 it was noted that far earlier documents had mentioned the forming of the chain; the new initiate, when he "sees the LIGHT," sees the brothers "standing in the chain." In this connection, the symbolic "chain" often appears in the names of lodges. As for HERALDRY, Böckler sees the chain as a multiplying of RINGS: "The linked rings of the chain signify a

Chain: A seller of amulet chains. *Hortus Sanitatis*, 1493

powerful and lasting unity, or that in war a chain across a river or before a stronghold has been broken through . . ."

chaos   Since the Judeo-Christian notion of creation *ex nihilo* by means of God's word alone is difficult to visualize, it is usually replaced in the symbolic tradition by the concept of an ordering of a primal hodgepodge of elements, the Biblical *tohu wa bohu* [Genesis 1:2; King James Version: "without form and void"], out of which is produced the rationally ordered cosmos (as in "order out of chaos," the motto of the Scottish Rite of FREEMASONRY). The chaotic state of primal matter before the Creator takes it in hand is usually represented pictorially as swirls of fog, floodwaters, and flaming torrents (see FIRE), as in the works of the Rosicrucian Robert Fludd (1574–1637). Other systems of myths employ here an unbounded frothing ocean or, as in Norse myth, the "yawning abyss" Ginnungagap. In the imagery of ALCHEMY chaos is the designation for primal matter that has not yet been transmuted. The alchemist J. B. van Helmont (1579–1644) is said to have drawn his word "gas" from the word "chaos." As an abstract symbol, chaos means all that is not ordered, everything that is opposed to civilization, including a regression to the conditions that preceded the systematic organizing carried out by the Creator.

Chaos: Elements at the beginning of Creation. Fludd, *Utriusque Cosmi Historia*, 1617

Chariot of the sun god, in baroque style. J. Boschius, 1702

chariot Ever since the invention of the WHEEL in the earliest developed civilizations, chariots have been a common attribute of regal divinities, especially gods of the SUN and sky (Helios/Apollo and Zeus, but also the goddesses Cybele and Freya) and THUNDER (Thor/Donar; the rumble of a chariot rolling over uneven ground resembles that of thunder). The path of the sun across the heavenly firmament has often been associated with wheels and chariots, as in the Germanic myth of the "solar chariot of Trundholm." A "chariot of fire" carries the prophet Elijah off to HEAVEN [II Kings 2:11]; rotating wheels are central to Ezekiel's vision. Mystical chariots symbolize the mythic journeys and triumphant processions of the gods, with a tall female figure, holding a bowl, at its center. Gods and goddesses of fertility and vegetation (like Nerthus, a Nordic earth mother mentioned by Tacitus and whose chariot was pulled by COWS) were said to visit the fields on their chariots. A SHIP-like wagon *(carrus navalis)* played a role in the Isis cult of late antiquity. The animals pulling a divine chariot helped to define its character: Zeus' was pulled by EAGLES, APHRODITE's by DOVES or SWANS, Donar's by wild GOATS. Similarly, in one of Titian's paintings, Christ's triumphal chariot is pulled by creatures symbolizing the EVANGELISTS (EAGLE, BULL, LION, man).

The wheel as a solar symbol is often represented by a circle with a cross inscribed, the "wheel-cross."

Even in classical antiquity, the chariot driver symbolized a reasoned, self-possessed conduct of life. The Byzantine author Dionysius Areopagita interpreted the chariots in Ezekiel's Biblical vision as follows: "They signify that harmonic equality in which creatures of the same order are united."

Chariot of goddess Ceres, pulled by snakes. Cartari, 1647

charity (Latin *caritas*) Symbolic figure for caring love extended to one's fellow beings, one of the three personified Christian virtues (along with Faith, *fides*, and Hope, *spes*). Caritas is portrayed as a beautiful woman surrounded by children. The image of Pera, a Roman maiden, is also referred to as *"Caritas humana."* She is said to have nursed her aged father Cimon at her breast, in order to save him from dying of thirst in prison.

Chariot. Rock drawing. Frännarp, Sweden, Nordic Bronze Age

cherry (Latin *Malum persicum*, literally "Persian APPLE") In classical antiquity a highly valued fruit, imported from the East in the first century after Christ, confused on occasion with the apricot. When in the GARDEN of the EMPEROR Alexander Severus a LAUREL grew higher than a cherry TREE, this was seen as presaging a victory over the Persians.

In ancient China the cherry (*t'ao*) was considered a symbol of immortality or longevity; the cherry blossom, of maidenly freshness, but also of the wanton woman. "Cherry blossom madness" was a euphemism for the emotional upheavals of puberty. According to legend, the fairy goddess Hsi-wang-mu has a garden in which every thousand years the cherries of immortality become ripe, and for the spirits and "immortals" this is an occasion for great celebration. The wood of the cherry tree was believed to drive off evil spirits; thus cherry branches were placed on house doors on New Year's Day, and statuettes of spirits "standing guard" at doorways were carved from cherry wood. In legend, "cherry spring caves" are gateways to the AFTERLIFE; the "cherry spring" is the poetic expression for the female genitalia.

chest (Latin *cista*, Greek *kiste*) A box-like container, corresponding also to the Latin *arca* (see ARK). The mystic chest of Dionysus

(see BACCHUS)—probably a basket rather than a wooden chest—was filled with symbolic objects and carried by special priests known as *kistophoroi*; when the mysteries of Dionysus were celebrated, a SNAKE emerged from it. The image of Demeter (Latin Ceres) as worshipped in the Eleusinian mysteries shows the goddess seated on a chest. In the Roman period the *cista* became a general symbol for esoteric mystical religions. The anatomical meaning of the English word "chest" is an extension of this same etymology.

chi-rho A monogram derived from the first two Greek letters in the name of Christ, which resemble the Roman letters X and P; the chi-rho has been a symbol of Christianity since the time of Constantine I, frequently appearing on church banners (see FLAG), often within a CIRCLE or a victor's WREATH. On the LABARUM (the banner of the CROSS), the chi-rho was said to have accompanied Constantine's victory over Maxentius in A.D. 312, after the prophecy to Constantine "*In hoc signo vinces*" ("Under this sign will you be victorious"), but its earlier use has been documented. It symbolizes the universal victory of Christianity or the victory of the Savior over the domination of sin. The chi-rho is at times placed within a triple circle (a reference to the TRINITY), with the ALPHA AND OMEGA on either side. Within a circle the monogram also has the effect of a WHEEL-like symbol for the SUN, which heightens its triumphal character.

chimera or Chimaera In present-day usage only a symbol of imaginings or rumor; in

Chi-Rho: early Christian catacomb painting with doves and olive branches

Chi-Rho: the monogram of Christ

antiquity, a monster part LION, part GOAT, and part SERPENT (the Etruscan "Chimera of Arezzo" having one head from each of these animals). The Chimera is said to be the daughter of Echidna, who was part serpent and part woman, and Typhon, a monster from the underworld; her brother was the HELL-hound Cerberus. According to Robert Graves, her TRIADIC form symbolizes the divisions of the year: the lion corresponding to spring, the goat to summer, and the serpent to winter. In the myth, the Chimera was killed by the hero Bellerophon riding on his WINGED HORSE PEGASUS; Bellerophon was thus a pre-Christian prototype of such DRAGON-slayers as St. George and St. Michael. Chimeras appear occasionally in medieval mosaics (and in the capitals of pillars and columns) as embodiments of Satanic forces. In antiquity the terrifying monster appeared in the coats of arms of several cities, including Corinth and Cyzicus. The rationalistic interpretation of the tripartite creature saw her as the embodiment of the dangers of land and sea, but above all of the volcanic forces in the EARTH's interior.

Chimera. Etruscan bronze, 4th century B.C.

Christopher, Saint The personification of a saintly legend, behind which there stands no historically documented person. Nevertheless, the legendary saint was venerated as early as the fifth century and is counted among the "14 catholic saints." There are accounts that identify him as a GIANT named Offero or Reprobus of the savage race of the Cynocephali (dog-headed), who would offer his services only to the strongest; a KING and the DEVIL proved to be timid, and only the Christ child remained. The giant was to carry him across a RIVER (an image of transition; see AFTERLIFE), and the child became so heavy that he pulled the giant under the surface of the WATER, baptising him Christopher ("the bearer of Christ") in the process. He is said to have died a martyr's death

Chimera. Woodcut, Cartari, 1647

under the emperor Decius; his day was July 25. Christopher was portrayed as a giant with a leafy staff or stake in his hand (symbolizing justification through divine grace) and on his shoulder the Christ child, who is holding the imperial APPLE, symbol of the world. Frescoes depicting St. Christopher are common inside churches, which is explained by the popular belief that anyone seeing Christopher's image would not die on that day; this encouraged frequent visits to churches. Christopher thus came to be seen as offering protection against sudden death; hence his modern status as patron saint of travelers. Iconographic prototypes may include late Egyptian portrayals of the dog-headed Anubis with the child Horus, or

Saint Christopher. Woodcut, Buxheim, 1531

images of Hercules with the child Eros (CUPID) on his shoulder. The legendary saint is an image of the witnessing believer who bears Christ through the world and thus attains salvation. The *Golden Legend* of Jacobus de Voragine (ca. 1270) gives the following account of him: "He carried Christ in four ways: on his shoulders, when he transported him over the water; in his body, through the mortification to which he submitted himself; in his spirit, through his fervent prayers; in his mouth, through his witness and his sermons." In the Jewish and Islamic faiths the ancestral father ABRAHAM, who will serve only the greatest master and thus comes to know God, in this respect plays a role analogous to that of Christopher. (See also STARS.)

Chronus The personification of time, often not distinguished from the God Cronus (Latin SATURN); Saturn was thus often portrayed with symbols of transitoriness, which are properly the attributes of Chronus: the hourglass and the SCYTHE. Cronus, who devoured his children, became a symbol of time, which creates and then destroys. In ancient mysterious religions, Chronus was a primeval god of the cosmos, also known as Eon (originally Aîon or Aeon); this Chronus was believed to have emerged from the DARKNESS to create the world, making a primordial SILVER EGG out of the ether. The figure of the time-guardian Chronus appears on many baroque clocks. The fleeting nature of passing time is often suggested by his WINGS, its cruel inevitability by the scythe with

which Cronus (in Hesiod's theogony) had castrated the primeval god Uranus; drops of Uranus' BLOOD seeped into the ground, and from them the FURIES (Greek Erinyes) arose.

chrysanthemum In East Asia a prized flower: in Japan an imperial emblem, and in China a symbol of autumn, as the PLUM-blossom is of spring. Its Chinese name *(chü)* is a homonym for "wait, linger" and suggests reflective contemplation, an association that is found in poetry as well: "O yellow chrysanthemums, in the light from my little lamp you have grown quite pale," or "In late splendor do chrysanthemums bloom." State attire was often decorated with designs containing chrysanthemums. Rebus-like messages of good will or congratulations were built on homonymies linking "PINE" and "chrysanthemum" ("May you have long life"), or "nine," "quail," and "chrysanthemum" ("May nine generations live together in peace.") A European wildflower variety, the tansy *(Chrysanthemum vulgare)*, was used in folk-medicine against intestinal worms but is used today only for garden decoration.

cicada (Greek *tettix*) The "tree cricket" of the Mediterranean region. According to Greek myth, Tithonus, the brother of King Priam of Troy, was the lover of EOS, the goddess of dawn. She asked Zeus to make

Chronus as an angel. St. Hawes, *The Pastyme of Pleasure*, 1509

Cicada ornament, symbolizing immortality. China, ca. 1200 B.C.

Tithonus immortal but forgot to ask that he might remain forever young. He therefore lived forever, but became more and more feeble, mumbling to himself meaninglessly, until he shriveled up and was transformed into the constantly chirping cicada. The literature of antiquity sometimes describes the high-pitched drone of the insect as pleasant, sometimes as annoying. For Callimachus (ca. 300–240 B.C.), the sound symbolized "elevated" poetry; the cicada, in various contexts, stood for the tireless poet, was his helper, or appeared as an attribute of the MUSES.

In ancient China the cicada (*shan*) symbolized immortality or life after death; a JADE amulet representing a cicada was placed in the mouth of the dead. A queen of the vassal state of Ch'i in the east was said to have been transformed into a cicada when she died; for this reason, the insect was also known as "the maiden of Ch'i." A stylized cicada ornament also represented "loyalty to one's principles."

Circe A Greek demigoddess and the quintessential enchantress (see WITCH); the daughter of the SUN god Helios. She was said to have transformed men whom she loved into animals; she turned Picus, the son of SATURN, into a woodpecker. She did not manage to transform Glaucus when he requested a love-elixir from her, but she did change the nymph Scylla, whom he loved, into a hideous monster, the bane of seafarers (see WATER SPIRITS). Circe is best known for her adventure with Odysseus, whose men she turns into swine (see PIG). Only Odysseus himself—protected by the magic herb moly, which Hermes (see MERCURY) had given him—was impervious to her spell. He forced her to reverse the transformation of his men, spent a year with the enamored sorceress, and was finally freed by her and sent on with useful advice. Circe came to symbolize the seductive woman whose enchantment leads her admirers to forget their dignity.

circle Arguably the most important and most widespread geometric symbol; its form also corresponds to that of the SUN and MOON as they appear to us. In the specula-

Cicada singing from the summer heat. J. Boschius, 1702

Circle: Cosmos, zodiac. R. Lulli's *Practica compendiosa artis*, 1523

Circle: Mausoleum decorations. Ireland (Sess Kill-green), Brittany (Gavr' Inis)

dome (partly because of the circular trajectory of the STARS around the celestial pole), and thus the circle also stands for heaven and all things spiritual. When spokes are drawn in, it becomes a symbolic WHEEL, which however carries dynamic associations opposed to the permanence of the circle. The Egyptian symbol for eternity is a string tied to form a circle; the corresponding symbol in the world of the ancient Greeks was a SNAKE biting its own tail (UROBORUS). Concentric circles arise also when an object is thrown into the water. The frequent designs of this sort on megalithic gravestones can be interpreted as representations of sinking into the seas of death (see AFTERLIFE), or perhaps of miraculously re-emerging from them, suggesting a doctrine of death and rebirth, symbolized by concentric waves. A

tive philosophies of the Platonists and the Neoplatonists, the circle is the ultimate, the perfect form. The legendary Hyperborean temple of Apollo is described as circular (a reference to the prehistoric Stonehenge in southern England?), and the capital of Plato's "island of ATLANTIS" as a system of concentric rings of land and WATER. In mystic systems God is spoken of as a circle whose center is everywhere—an expression of perfection and of surpassing human understanding (limitlessness, eternity, the absolute). In the circle there is no beginning or end, no direction. The "canopy" of the HEAVENS (see BALDACHIN) is represented as a round

Circles inscribed with names of God, to repel demons. England, ca. 1860

circle with its center drawn in is the traditional astronomer's symbol for the sun, and the alchemist's for the solar metal, GOLD. In magic lore the circle (drawn around the conjuring magician and not to be crossed throughout the ceremony) is supposed to serve as protection against evil spirits.

The symbological opposite of the circle is the SQUARE, which is associated with the terrestrial world and things material. The circle stands for God and heaven, the square for humans and the earth. The proverbial task of "squaring the circle," constructing a

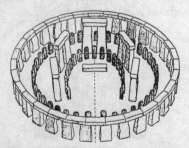

Circle: Reconstruction of shrine at Stonehenge. Southern England, ca. 1800 B.C.

circle (by purely geometric means) that has the same area as a given square, thus offers an image of human efforts to transform their own substance into that of God, and thus to render themselves divine. This insoluble problem in geometry was a frequent Renaissance allegory for human striving for divine perfection, one that was also of great importance in the symbolism of ALCHEMY. Without going into the problem of equal areas, the Cabala also treats the circle and the square: a circle inside a square is seen as symbolizing the divine "SPARK" within a material envelope. In Christian iconography the halo (NIMBUS) around the head of a saint is usually circular, and concentric circles also represent God's original creation. The first represents the earth, where humans will be placed only later, and God draws it with a drafting COMPASS (in the *Bible Moralisée* of the 13th century), or he reveals himself in the form of a HAND, which emerges from the center of multiple circles and breaks through them "transcendentally" on the periphery (Romanesque fresco, St. Climent de Tahull, Catalonia, ca. 1123).

Naturally, the importance of the circle as a symbol is not restricted to Occidental culture. For various Native American peoples, the orbit of the moon, and the apparent orbits of the sun and the stars, are round forms, and such forms appear in the way things grow in nature. Thus the camp, the teepee, and seating arrangements are all based on the circle. It is not uncommon to find traditional dances following (or generating) circles. In Zen Buddhism the circle stands for enlightenment, the perfection of humanity in unity with the primal principle. In the Chinese symbol of YIN AND YANG, duality is enclosed in a circle (*t'ai-chi,* the primal One). In Europe the notion of concentric cosmic spheres dominates medieval cosmology and is represented poetically in Dante's *Divine Comedy* in the form of the "circles" of HELL, PURGATORY, and heaven; the hierarchies of ANGELS serve as guardians of these spheres and thus of the entire structure. The TRINITY is often symbolized by three mutually intersecting circles. (See also MANDALA and SPIRAL.)

city One criterion for some cultural historians seeking to determine whether a nation or people can be referred to as having attained "civilization." A city is not simply an agglomeration of fixed houses; it is also defined by central civil and religious organization, and in some cases by the presence of city walls. For the symbologist, the city is a reflection in miniature of cosmic structures, not sprung up in a totally random way, but laid out systematically, having at its center a terrestrial counterpart of the midpoint of the heavens (see OMPHALOS, MUNDUS, AXIS MUNDI). At this center we often find the shrine of the tutelary god of the city (in China: *ch'eng huang-shen*) or of a god-like hero, a local deity who ranks with KINGS. We find this not only in the Greek city-state (*polis*) but also in ancient Mesopotamia and Egypt. When an empire is established, the tutelary god of the central *polis* often becomes the god of the entire realm, bringing the gods of other cities into the pantheon over which he presides; the EMPEROR is then the earthly representative of this ruling deity. To a very limited extent, in the Christian world the patron saint of a city takes on something of the role played by the tutelary gods of old.

The ideal city of the Western world is JERUSALEM, with BABYLON its ancient opposite, subsequently replaced by heathen

City: Assyrian portrayal of a Phoenician city. Nineveh, 8th century B.C.

Rome. The "city of God" is also a symbol of "Mary, Mother of God," and in the Middle Ages tabernacles and shrines for relics were often constructed like cities, with decorative walls and miniature towers.

In the symbology of the psyche, the city stands for the regularized center of a person's life, which can often be reached only after long travels, when a high degree of emotional maturity has been attained and the GATE to the spiritual center of one's life can be traversed.

clouds In the tradition of the Occident, symbols of concealment—covering, for example, the mountaintops where the gods dwell. God went before the Israelites "in a pillar of a cloud, to lead them the way" [Exodus 13:21], as they left Egypt. Similarly, a cloud conceals the risen Christ [Acts 1:9]. But on the Last Day humanity will "see the Son of man coming in a cloud with power and great glory" [Luke 21:27]. In paintings depicting HEAVEN, clouds form the THRONE of God, e.g. in the Last Judgment (see END OF THE WORLD). In Islam the cloud symbolizes the inscrutability of Allah.

In pantheistic religions clouds are generally seen as bringing rain and thus fertility, but needing to be struck by thunderbolts to release the water stored up in them. An ancient Mexican divinity bore the name "cloud SNAKE" (Mixcóatl).

In ancient China, clouds (yün) were objects of great interest, especially the "five-colored" ones known as "clouds of fortune," which were recognized as peace symbols. They were believed to come from the union of YIN AND YANG in the distant west. In the visual arts they were portrayed either as spirals or, realistically, as cumulus clouds. Fertility symbolism and a reference to the

Cloud mountains, rain comb, lightening snakes: a Hopi rain prayer. Walpi, Arizona

(masculine) MOUNTAIN around which clouds gather to come down as rainwater, led to the poetic metaphor "cloud and rain game" (yün-yü), used in erotic novels to refer to sexual intercourse. A woman's curly hair was referred to as a "fragrant cloud."

clover and shamrock The shamrock, a symbol of Irish and Celtic national consciousness, can in fact be any of a number of (generally three-leafed) plants, including wood sorrel and various clovers. By pre-Christian times Druids revered the shamrock as a sacred symbolic plant; it later came to symbolize the Christian TRINITY. It thus became an attribute of St. Patrick, who is often represented killing a SNAKE with a cruciform staff topped by a shamrock. The four-leafed clover is thought of today as lucky, which is explained superficially by reference to its rarity: one must be lucky to find one, therefore the clover itself is seen as bringing luck. The original symbolism probably goes back to the robust growth of the plant, which made it a symbol of vitality in general. In medieval love poetry, couples often met or made love "in clover"; today, perhaps because of the importance of clover for pasturage, to be "in clover" means to live well, to be free of care, and to be prosperous. Because clover, presumably as a reference to new life after resurrection, was at one time planted on graves, it also came to symbolize parting, often in combination with ROSES (the symbol of love) and VIOLETS (whose color is that of penance).

coats, capes, and robes Garments capable of enclosing the entire body lend optical unity to the human form and give it the appearance of power. Splendid garments of this sort thus are a part of the finery of rulers (e.g., coronation robes), often richly jewelled. The notion that something of the "aura" of the wearer is transmitted to the garment makes the robe of a prophet a precious inheritance. The mantle of the prophet Elijah divides the WATERS of the Jordan, and, after he is carried up to heaven in a CHARIOT of FIRE, his follower Elisha picks up the mantle in order to repeat the

Coats and capes help Sts. Raymond and Sebaldus to cross the water. W. Auer, 1890

Coats: St. Martin. Fresco, Church of Our Lady, Oberwesel, ca. 1520

miracle [II Kings 2:8–14; compare I Kings 19:19]. Various Christian saints (e.g., Francis of Paola) are said to have crossed over the water with the help of their capes, and St. Martin of Tours and St. Francis of Assisi divided theirs with beggars. Other saints (including Bridget, Goar, and Gotthard) had the power to hang their capes on sunbeams. Capes and cloaks have the further symbolic significance of protective enclosure, as in certain artistic representations of the cape of the Virgin Mary. Female founders of religious orders are also portrayed extending the protection of their capes to others. As a legal symbol, wrapping one's own coat around another person means that one will accord parental care and protection to the other. In DREAM psychology the coat is associated with warm enclosure and refuge. When the dreamer wears the coat of

Coats: In the Shelter of Mary's Cape. Study. Southern Germany, ca. 1830

his or her mother, "the second birth, in which one leaves the mother's warmth for the cooler regions of the outer world, has not yet taken place for the psyche" [Aeppli]. (See also BLUE.)

Cockaigne (French pays de cocagne, German Schlaraffenland) A fabled land of leisure and idle pleasures. The English and French names appear to be cognates of the word "cake," referring to the delicacies available in abundance to the inhabitants of Cockaigne. The German name suggests that those inhabitants are "lazy apes" who believe that they are entitled to all of life's luxuries. A tradition including Sebastian Brant (Ship of Fools), Hans Sachs, Grimmelshausen (Simplicissimus), and the Brothers Grimm portrays such a life as impossible anywhere except in far-off Schlaraffenland. There are more recent texts, however, in which Cockaigne or Schlaraffenland are depicted without satirical intention, simply as a world radically different from our own and having many features traditionally associated with the ideal AFTERLIFE. The most familiar French cocagne is the earthly paradise evoked as the travelers' destination in Baudelaire's "Invitation au voyage" (especially the prose version published in 1862).

The naive or playful aspect of such dreams of release from the harsh realities of everyday life is also reflected in the attitudes of the artists' group Schlaraffia (or "International

Union of Schlaraffians") founded in Prague in 1859.

Other cultural traditions also have their versions of Cockaigne. The Aztecs of ancient Mexico described the older Toltec empire, Tollan, as follows: ears of corn there were so heavy that they had to be rolled along the ground; cotton grew in colors; vegetable plants were the size of palm trees, and so forth—an apparent idealization of the "good old days" that preceded the disillusionment of the present. (See GOLDEN AGE.)

colors, symbolism of This is such a broad topic that only its contours can be suggested here. Clearly, colors have a significance all their own and an ability to influence the psyche directly, as is shown by recent research to develop color therapy to treat mental and psychosomatic disorders. It should be noted that colors do not have uniform emotional rankings and associations from one person to the next; differences in color preferences are used diagnostically, as in the Lüscher color test, in which the subject selects the most and least pleasing shades from 23 test colors. The Pfister-Heiss interpretation of the "color pyramid" associates for example with the color BLUE emotional moderation and an ability to master one's drives. RED, on the other hand, is an emotional color associated with the ability to receive and release external stimuli. The secondary color orange (for which there was no word before the fruit lent it its name) stands for striving to achieve, to "become somebody"; BROWN, for a positive relationship with "MOTHER EARTH."

Despite individual differences in the interpretation of colors, ancient civilizations worked out conventionally determined forms of color symbolism, usually as part of a search for basic principles with which to organize a world of multiplicities. Thus the primary colors were frequently associated with the points of the compass and the ELEMENTS, and arranged schematically in a CROSS or SQUARE. Popular speech has its own color symbolism—including "true" blue for loyalty, YELLOW for cowardice, GREEN for

inexperience, WHITE for innocence, and BLACK for death. Alchemy has its own system, in which green is a powerful solvent, and red and white represent the DUALITY of the primal substances SULFUR AND MERCURY. For the ancient Mayas of Central America, the directions east, north, west, and south were associated with red, white, black, and yellow, respectively; in ancient China east, south, west, north, and "center," with blue, red, white, black, and yellow. Whereas in European color symbolism red ROSES express passionate love, in ancient Egypt everything red (ochre) was considered menacing and harmful.

In HERALDRY all colors were originally indifferent, but in the Renaissance a complicated set of associations was introduced, linking colors to metals and "PLANETS": yellow—GOLD, SUN; white—SILVER, MOON; red—IRON, MARS; blue—TIN, JUPITER; black—LEAD, SATURN; green—COPPER, VENUS; purple—MERCURY (element and planet). According to Böckler (1688), the metal gold or the color yellow means virtue, intellect, esteem, and majesty; silver or white purity, innocence, joy; red "a burning desire for virtue" and a "devout heart, ready to shed its blood for the word of God"; blue constancy, loyalty, learning, and "sincere devotion to God"; black "sorrow, humility, misfortune, and danger"; green freedom, beauty, merriment, health, hope, and kindness; purple or VIOLET "royal garb"; orange fleeting personal glory; "flesh" tones "fickleness and inconsistency." He goes on to attribute highly imaginative symbolic meanings to combinations of colors: blue and gold—joyousness or amusement; blue and red—rudeness; black and gold—honor and long life; black and blue—a peaceable disposition; green and gold—obstinacy; green and blue—lasting joy; red and silver—longing for revenge; red and green—youthful courage; and so on and on. These speculations about color combinations, however, were unknown to medieval heraldry and arose only after coats of arms had nothing to do with knighthood in its original sense. It should also be noted that the choice of colors was also a matter of the availability

Columbine. Hohberg, 1675

of dyes and pigments. In prehistoric cave painting, for example, blue does not occur at all, because there was no way to produce the color.

columbine (*Aquilegia vulgaris*) In ancient times the sacred plant of the goddess Freya; in medieval panels, an attribute of the Virgin Mary. The columbine, once prized as a medicinal herb and a remedy for the "severe choler of jaundice," served also as an image for healing the sin of covetousness: "Thus where God's light the human heart illuminates,/ Is not for envy nor for worldly grasping space" [Hohberg].

compass, drafting An instrument for drawing a perfect CIRCLE; in the Western world, especially since the Middle Ages, a symbol for geometry, cosmic order, and planning—going back primarily to the secret traditions of those who built the great cathedrals. Medieval illustrated manuscripts depict the Creator as a geometrician constructing the globe with a drafting compass. The compass is an attribute of the personifications of such "liberal arts" as astronomy, architecture, and geography.

Even today the compass (along with the sacred BOOK and the carpenter's SQUARE) is one of the three "great LIGHTS" of the symbology of FREEMASONRY, referring to the ideal circle of "all-embracing love for others" and thus indicating the appropriate attitude toward fellow Masons and humanity

in general. In the rite of initiation, it is taught that one point of the drafting compass is fixed in the heart of the individual Mason and that the other establishes his bond to all of his brothers.

A frequent emblem combines the compass and the carpenter's square, which make it possible to draw the cosmic circle and the SQUARE, respectively. In a wide variety of speculative traditions, this combined emblem represents the union of HEAVEN and EARTH, e.g., in the architecture of the Temple of the Heavens in Peking (Beijing). In the symbolism of Freemasonry, the angle between the two arms of the compass is also significant (a right angle symbolizing the ideal balance between body and spirit), as is the question of which of the two symbolic instruments is placed in front of the other. If the square covers the compass, matter dominates spirit; if they are interlocking, matter and spirit are in perfect balance; if the compass covers the square, spirit dominates. J. Baurnjöpel notes that the symbolic tapestry of the lodge of initiation shows both arms of the compass pointing "toward the dawn" (eastward), because the "brother Mason" should open himself to the entire world as a "man of honesty and rectitude, bringing about peace and joy" (1793).

Compass, Drafting: "The center remains unchanged." J. Boschius, 1702

copper (Greek *chalcus*, Latin *aes cuprum*) In Latin, copper is "the metal from Cypress"—from the island on whose shore Aphrodite (VENUS) was born from the billows of the sea. In ancient metal symbolism copper is thus the terrestrial analogue of the PLANET Venus and is represented by the same ASTROLOGICAL symbol in alchemistic writings. In the Mithraic cult, however, the metal of Venus was not copper but tin—the element that was alloyed with copper to form bronze. According to the tradition of the Ancients (Hesiod, Ovid), the GOLDEN AGE was followed by one of SILVER, and before the present IRON Age came one of COPPER, as a transitional period between the epochs of the precious metals and the present one. Copper, occurring in nature in pure form, was often hammered cold (in prehistoric North America, for example), which produced a somewhat more solid metal than cast copper. In West Africa copper was revered as a chthonic symbol for warmth and LIGHT. In ancient China, as in Europe, there was hardly any distinction made between pure copper (*t'ung*) and its alloys, bronze and brass. Copper was used to produce coins ("cash") with a square hole in the center, through which a string was passed. Since the word *t'ung* also means "together," copper coins were placed in the bridal bed to assure the newlyweds a lasting union. In "hell" sinners were forced to drink molten copper or, in the case of lechers, to dance with partners who turned into red-hot copper pillars when embraced. Copper was also used to make drums and BELLS for religious use.

coral Despite its organic origin, coral is used like a PRECIOUS STONE and considered as such in popular symbology. In Ovid's *Metamorphoses* it is written that coral originated from the severed head of the GORGON Medusa when drops of her BLOOD struck the sand. This RED coral was used in amulets for protection against the "evil EYE." The ancient physician Pedanius Dioscorides wrote of its healing powers, calling it the "TREE of the sea." Coral symbolizes the intense vividness of the marine world, and, in ancient

Coral. Konrad of Megenberg's *Book of Nature*, 1350, reprint 1535

China, longevity. Because of the red color, polished coral came to be associated with MARS. It was also made into tiny hands making the sign of the FIG, to ward off the forces of evil, or the phallic form (see LINGA) of the "branches" was heightened by polishing, to the same end. Especially in Italy, amulets of red (and occasionally WHITE or dark) coral are still prized today. It was believed in ancient times that coral could make bitter water potable and provide immunity against poison. The alchemistic emblem book *Atalanta fugiens* (1618) shows a fisherman pulling red and white corals from the foaming sea—symbols of the *materia prima,* which is already potentially available but has not yet been hardened (fixed) by contact with the air.

cornucopia, or horn of plenty An attribute of FLORA and FORTUNA, and a symbol

Coral: "Tree of the sea," *Enalia drus.* From *Dioscorides' herbarium.* Byzantine, A.D. 512

Aurochs cow

of inexhaustible bounty freely bestowed upon mortals; a GOAT's horn, from which fruit and other refreshing gifts pour endlessly. In Greek myth it belonged to Amalthea (a nymph with the form of a goat), who nursed the infant Zeus in a cave on the island of Crete and provided him with everything he needed to survive. Hercules fought with the RIVER god Achelous, who had the form of a BULL, and broke off one of his horns; he generously returned the horn to his defeated opponent, who gave him Amalthea's horn of plenty in return. The use of horns as vessels for liquid offerings (libations) is documented even in prehistoric representations (e.g., the VENUS of Laussel).

courtesans, or concubines In Greek *hetaerae* ("companions") and in Latin *amicae* ("friends"). A superior class of prostitutes, rigidly distinguished in ancient times from "common" prostitutes or WHORES (*pornae*), to whom they bore little resemblance. The Greek *hetaerae* (unlike the married women of Athens, who were hardly more than child-bearing housekeepers) were often highly cultured, and there was no embarrassment associated with being seen in their company. They were accomplished students of philosophy, art, literature, music, and dance—the approximate counterparts of the *geishas* of Japan. Being truly "companions," they enjoyed a status that was denied to wives. Famed *hetaerae* (and the men with whom they were associated) included Aspasia (Pericles, whose second wife she eventually became), Phryne (Praxiteles), and Thais (ALEXANDER THE GREAT), and later, in Rome, Lesbia (Catullus) and Cynthia (Propertius). When they died they often were given fine gravestones and, in the case of Belistiche, the *hetaera* of Ptolemy II of Egypt, deification. But their class was in time to come under fire: Theodora, wife of the Byzantine emperor Justinian I and herself a former *hetaera*, despised her class and had *hetaerae* put into a "cloister of repentance." In Sparta there were no *hetaerae*, because married women as a group were far more respected and freer there. In modern times "courtesan" and *hetaera* (depending on the language involved) refer to women like the heroine of Dumas fils's *Camille* (later Violetta in Verdi's *La Traviata*), but such women have long been denied the social status of classical *hetaerae*. (See also FLORA.)

cow Whereas the symbolic meaning of the BULL is ambivalent, the cow (the female of the domesticated *Bos taurus*) is a uniformly positive force. She stands for the maternal (see MOTHER), nurturing powers of the earth, and, because of her horns and her sex, for the lunar attributes (see MOON) as well. (The Sumerians stressed the correspondence between cow's milk and moonlight.) In the Norse myth of creation, the cow Audumla licked the first man out of salty blocks of ice; she herself was the first creature to

Courtesan. Vase painting, Greece, ca. 520 B.C.

Cow nursing, symbol of maternity. Ivory. Phoenician, Arslan Tasch, ca. 900 B.C.

emerge from the "yawning abyss" Ginnungagap (see CHAOS). In ancient Egypt Hathor, a goddess of the HEAVENS, was worshipped as a woman with the HEAD of a cow, and the vault of the heavens itself was symbolized either in the form of Nut, a similar goddess, or as a cow that carried the STARS in her belly. Isis could also appear in the form of a cow. India's "sacred cow" is famous: this sacred nurturer of prehistoric times promises fertility and abundance (*prithivi* and *aditi*). As Aditi she is also the female counterpart of the bull Nandi and can grant wishes. The role of the cow in guaranteeing the survival of cattle-breeding humans is of paramount importance, hence her passivity, which implied that she could not play a major role in mythology or epics. In psychological symbolism she is, according to Aeppli, a "good creature of great endurance and modest dynamism . . . with her simple warmth, her patient gestation, she is a plain symbol for Mother Earth herself, an expression of the vegetative maternal principle.

Cow, pregnant. Wrought-iron votive figure. Styria, Austria, 19th century

. . . The cow's great rhythm is that of her humility. Her green food is manifestly natural. She has a primitive holiness all her own, which is addressed by the Indian cult of the 'sacred cow.' "

crab   (Latin *cancer*, Greek *carcinus*) This crustacean, because of its backward movement, was widely thought of as a bringer of misfortune, but it was also used in magical RAIN ceremonies. In Christian symbology the crab, because of its shedding of its shell, came to refer to the "casting off of the old

Cow: Guise of goddess Hathor, guarding Pharaoh Psammetich I (Egypt, 26th dynasty)

ADAM" and resurrection from the confines of the grave. A sea animal, the crab symbolizes great flooding. In the ancient world it was thought of as an enemy of SNAKES, which were thought to feel pain when the SUN was in Cancer; similarly, it was written that DEER ate crabs as an antidote to snakebite and that it was possible to protect seed from parasites by sprinkling it with water which had contained crabs for more than a week. The fourth sign of the zodiac is named for the constellation Cancer. The sun is in Cancer between June 23 and July 22; Cancer is a water sign, and "feminine." Cancer is the house of the MOON, and thus its metal is SILVER. Astrologers associate with Cancer

Crab-man. Decoration on a Chimu container, ancient Peru

pregnancy, imprisonment, baptism and rebirth, the awakening of consciousness, and a tendency to prefer seclusion. Hippocrates (ca. 460–370 B.C.), for reasons which he did not make explicit (but perhaps in reference to a demon of disease popularly believed to take on animal form), used the word for "crab" to designate tumors, and this is the source of our word "cancer." According to Greek myth, a crab sought to impede Hercules as he fought the Hydra of Lerna, a NINE-headed snake-monster; the crab pinched Hercules in the heel and was swiftly crushed by him, but the crab was transported into the heavens (becoming the

Crab. Zodiac symbol in *Liber Astrologiae*, ca. 1350

constellation Cancer) in recognition of its bravery in the face of death.

crane (Latin *grus*, Greek *geranus*) In the ancient world an object of marvel because of its ability to fly great distances without tiring; thus a crane's WING was believed to be an amulet against exhaustion or debility. The migration of cranes from Thrace to Egypt (in formation) attracted the interest of the Egyptians, who revered the bird. There are many portrayals of legendary battles waged by pygmies against cranes. For reasons that are unclear today, the crane was sacred to Demeter, the goddess of agriculture. Its migratory flight, which announced the coming of spring, made the crane a symbol of renewal and, in the Christian era, of Christ resurrected. Its mating dance provided the model for the "crane dance" *(geranicus)*, celebrated in the Greek

Crane as a symbol of vigilance. Hohberg, 1647

world as the sublime expression of *joie de vivre* and love. Like the IBIS, the crane became known as a killer of SNAKES. In ancient China the crane *(ho)* was one symbol of longevity (often standing on a STONE or a PINE TREE) and of the relationship between FATHER and son (because young cranes respond to the cry of their parents). It also stood for wisdom, presumably because of the "contemplative" posture of the bird at rest. A crane soaring toward the SUN expressed the wish for social elevation. The death of a Taoist priest was expressed indirectly with the syllables *yü-hua*: "he has been transformed into a feathered creature,"

Crane. Chinese woodcut, 17th century

i.e., a crane (see also BIRD). In Japan the crane *(tsuru)* was revered as symbolizing the eminence of the island nation, whereas in the legends of India the bird often appears as an embodiment of deceit and knavery. In Hohberg's emblem book of the baroque period (1675), the crane appears as a symbol of vigilance: "By night the crane a pebble gripped doth hold,/ Lest sleep surprise his watch and close his eyes./ So, lest this world should lull with pomp and gold,/ The Cross reminds us where our duty lies." In many older depictions it is not clear whether a crane or a HERON is portrayed; the heron is said to have a WHITE stone in its beak (a symbol of reticence). Cranes appear in Schiller's ballad "The Cranes of Ibycus" (1798) as instruments of divine will.

crocodile The large water reptile, whose form is suggestive of that of the DRAGON, is

Cranes battle pygmies. Olaus Magnus, *Historia,* 1545

thought to be identical with the monstrous "leviathan" mentioned in the Bible, one of the creatures of primordial CHAOS. In ancient Egypt it was represented by the god Sebek (Greek Suchos) and revered especially in the city of Shedit (Greek Crocodilopolis): "Praise be unto you, who arose from the primal ooze. . . ." Otherwise it was naturally thought of as a dangerous water predator and was counted among the followers of Seth, the god of misrule. Those who worshipped Sebek, however, revered the animal and mummified it after death. In Rome it was believed that a swimmer whose body had been rubbed with crocodile fat could swim among crocodiles unmolested, and that the skin of a crocodile over the yard gate would protect one's property

Crocodile god Sebek with scepter and feathered crown. Ancient Egypt

against damage by hail. In the Middle Ages the crocodile, with its tremendous mouth, came to symbolize the jaws of HELL. The early Christian *Physiologus* formed a DUALITY opposing the crocodile and the water SNAKE: the snake let itself be swallowed by the crocodile but then ripped apart the enemy's intestines from within and escaped with its own life. Thus the snake, otherwise associated with evil, here symbolizes the Savior, who between death and resurrection descended into limbo to free the souls waiting there. In other contexts the crocodile appears as a symbol of hypocrisy, since it was said to shed tears of compassion ("crocodile tears") once it had devoured its prey. In pre-Columbian Central America the first of the 20 day-signs of the calendar was named for a creature (Aztec, *cipactli;* Maya, *imix*) resembling the crocodile, a sign promising fertility and wealth, and, according to the oracular priests, great progeny, fortune, and power. In many ancient Mexican myths an animal like the crocodile also appears (along with the TOAD) as a symbol of the primordial earth, or simply as a mythical chthonic creature.

For Jungian psychologists, the crocodile is like the dragon, except that the former is "even lazier, more ancient life, snapping mercilessly at the individual, and thus a negative symbol of our inner energies, a dull, ill-tempered attitude toward life, lodged in the depths of the collective unconscious" [Aeppli]. Medieval bestiaries had a similarly negative view of the crocodile: it can move only its upper jaw, while the lower remains motionless in the mud; a cosmetic preparation is made from crocodile dung, but it washes away too easily; and then comes the moral lesson associated with this symbolic animal: "The crocodile is the figure of the hypocrite, the miser, the lecher. Even swollen up as they are with the drivel of pride, and scarred by the pox of lust, and obsessed with pathological greed, still they walk before their fellow beings, proud and as if beyond reproach in their fulfillment of the law. As the crocodile lives in the water by night, so do these people lead their unruly lives in secret. . . . With the upper part of their mouths, they hold up to others the examples and redeeming doctrines of the fathers of the Church, while the lower part remains immobile, for they by no means practice what they preach. As from the dung of the crocodile a salve is made, so do the evil enjoy the favor of this world, which would cosmetically paint their evil deeds as acts of heroism. Only when the severe judge lashes out in his wrath at their misdeeds will all the luster of the false salve vanish" [Unterkircher]. In fact it seems difficult for hu-

mans to approach the "saurian," ancient figure of the crocodile, and its apparently mechanical movements, so foreign to mammals, with anything other than feelings of estrangement and fear, or to evaluate the creature in human terms.

cross The most universal of the simple symbolic figures, its importance is in no way limited to the Christian world. First of all, it represents spatial orientation, the intersection of vertical (ABOVE/BELOW) and horizontal (RIGHT/LEFT) axes, the bringing together of multiple DUALITIES in a single whole that, moreover, suggests the human form with the arms extended. Its extremities are suggestive of a quaternity (see FOUR), or, when the point of intersection (one's own standpoint) is included, of a quincunx or pentad (see FIVE). Like the CIRCLE, the cross enters into the structure of many MANDALAS (see also YANTRA), as well as temples and churches. Crosses often figure prominently in the cosmological representations of a wide variety of cultures (see, for example, the ancient Mexican *Codex Fejérváry-Mayer*). The paradise of the Bible, with the four RIVERS flowing from it, was similarly represented. A cross inside a circle, in addition to its cosmological associations, also stands for the division of the year into four parts. With its vertical axis the cross links zenith and nadir, and is thus symbologically related to the AXIS MUNDI (see also TREE, MOUNTAIN, POLE). Laid horizontally, it divides a SQUARE into equal quadrants, as in the ideal plan for a Roman city, with the streets Decumanus and Cardo (common to all Roman encampments) intersecting at the center. Even in more recent times cities have traditional been laid out literally in "quarters"; the schematic world maps of the Middle Ages are often cruciform (when not in the form of a T), with JERUSALEM at the center. Crossroads are often thought of as symbolizing points of intersection between the path of the living and that of the dead, for example in various African traditions. Guides for conjurers and exorcists recommend that they pass through crossroads whenever possible, apparently because they

Cross statuette. Stone, 2½ inches, Lemba-Lakkous, Cyprus, ca. 2500 B.C.

detain pursuing spirits, who are uncertain which way to proceed.

Early Christians often misinterpreted crosses encountered in foreign cultures as an indication that forgotten Christian missionaries had sojourned there, as in the case of the "Temple of the Foliated Cross" in the Mayan city of Palenque (Yucatán), in which the "cross" is actually a world-tree, a tree representing the cosmos. Christian speculation on symbols associates cruciform positionings of geographical points with the image of Christ's cross, for example in the following account from the nonecclesiastical *Book of the Cave of Treasures* (see CAVES): Noah has his son Shem and grandson Melchizedek, under the guidance of an ANGEL, move the remains of ADAM from the cave where he is buried to the "midpoint of the earth. And there four ends come together. For when God created the earth, his strength ran ahead of it, and the earth came running out after his strength from four sides, like wind and light breezes. And there [at the center of the earth] his strength remained and came to rest. There will salvation come to be. . . . When they came to Golgotha, which is the midpoint of the earth, the angel showed Shem this place. . . . Four parts separated there, and the earth opened up in the form of a cross, and Shem and Melchizedek put Adam's body inside. . . . The four parts moved, and enclosed the body of our father Adam, and the door of the outer

earth closed. And this place was named 'the place of skulls,' because the head of all mankind was laid there. . . .'" In accordance with this narrative, medieval portrayals of the Crucifixion often show Adam's skull and the foot of Christ's cross on Golgotha [Müller]. The familiar Christian symbolism of the cross refers to the means of Christ's execution, an instrument of excessive cruelty that, however, through the Resurrection, came to symbolize eternal life. [See also NAIL.] In the early Christian era the cross was accepted as a symbol only hesitantly, because of the infamous nature of this particular form of execution (comparable perhaps, in the feelings it aroused, to the gallows of later times); only with time (in the Romanesque period) was the cross fully recognized as a symbol of the victory over death. The first dated cross in this sense is from the year 134 (Palmyra, Syria). Non-Christians found reverence for the cross grotesque, as a mock crucifix drawn on the Palatine (Rome), dating from ca. A.D. 240, demonstrates: it shows a crucified man with the head of a DONKEY and the inscription "Alexamenus worshiping his God." The figure of an ANCHOR (a cross standing on a U-shaped crescent) functioned also as a covert cross.

The cross on which Jesus was crucified was probably a tau cross (also called "St. Anthony's cross"), formed like the letter T,

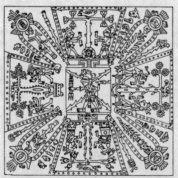

Cross: Cruciform cosmogram. Codex Fejérváry-Mayer, ancient Mexico

an ancient symbol of divine election, mentioned in the Old Testament, for example [Ezekiel 9:4; Vulgate: "signa thau"]. In form it resembles the HAMMER symbol (Thor's hammer, a popular Germanic amulet). Crowned with a circle or oval, it yields the Egyptian cross of life (ANKH, or *crux ansata*), which gods (e.g., the SUN god Aton in the monotheism of Akhenaton [Amenhotep IV]) or pharaohs were often shown holding. Egyptian Christians (Copts) took the ankh as a symbol of eternal life through the sacrificial death of Christ; it appears on gravestones of the sixth through ninth centuries. Today it is a frequent emblem of groups claiming a heritage of "ancient wisdom." Among the many variations on the cross, each with different symbolic associations, we should still mention the X-shaped St. Andrew's cross (*crux decussata*), on which it is said that the apostle Andrew was crucified (and whose form has been found scratched into prehistoric bones and on magical devices to ward off evil, such as the "witch-knife" that was thought to frighten away storm WITCHES), and the St. Peter's cross, whose horizontal pieces are attached near the bottom of the vertical piece, because the apostle Peter was said to have been crucified on an inverted cross. A cross formed from four tau crosses first appeared in the Merovingian period (ca. A.D. 500–751) and found its way into religious art as the "litur-

Cross: Christ's crucifixion. Byzantine psalter, British Museum, 1066

gical cross." The "Russian cross" goes back to a cross with a name-plate (Latin *titulus*) and diagonal supports at its foot. The Y-shaped "thief's" or "forked" cross often has branch-like ends and refers to ancient images of the "tree of life."

In heraldry we find crosses in many forms, often with specific symbolic significance. One that is particularly important is the Jerusalem cross, resembling a liturgical cross, with an additional small cross in each of the four corners: during the Crusades, this was the coat of arms of the Kingdom of Jerusalem. The FIVE crosses together refer to the five stigmata of Christ. The combination of the cross with a circle, with the extremities of the cross extending outside the circle, as in the Celtic cross, is called the "quest cross" or simply "quest," going back to the use of the word in the context of medieval chivalry. The "LILY cross" is a heraldic device in which each extremity of the cross is a stylized heraldic lily, or fleur de lys. There is also a variant of the lily cross in which the lower extremity has a pointed tip. The lily cross is the symbol of the chivalric Order of Alcántara, founded in 1156 in Castile. The "ARROW cross" has the head of an arrow at each tip of the cross; it is a political symbol, known in Hungary as the *Nyilaskereszt*, and was intended, as the symbol of the national fascist party of the 1930's, to

Cross: Mock crucifix with donkey; "Alexamenus worshipping his God." Graffito, Rome, 3rd century

Crosses (clover, arrow, and Jerusalem) used in heraldry

recall the arrows of the Magyar conquerors. Other crosses used in heraldry include the tree cross, the shamrock cross (see CLOVER) symbolizing St. Patrick, the quadruple cross, the Maltese cross (or cross of the Order of St. John) with its fanned extremities, and the APPLE cross.

Some indication of the universality of the cross symbol is offered in the account written by the Inca descendant Garcilaso de la Vega: "In Cuzco the Inca rulers possessed a cross made of reddish-white marble called 'crystalline jasper'; it is impossible to say how long they had had this cross. . . . It was square in its proportions, as broad as it was high; it was some three-quarters of an ell in each direction, or perhaps less, and each arm measured three fingers in breadth and thickness. It was masterfully hewn from a single block of marble, the corners neatly finished, the stone highly polished and gleaming. They kept it in one of the royal residences called *huaca*, which means 'sacred place.' Although they did not pray to it, they did revere it, presumably because of its formal beauty or for some other reason to which they could not put a name." A similar STONE cross was found in the ruins of Minoan Crete on the pedestal of a square architectural model. Such parallels indicate merely the presence of this basic symbol in different cultural worlds; the cross is apparently a framework for co-ordinates, giving the inhabitants of those individual worlds the possibility to orient themselves in space and time.

crow (Latin *corvus*, Greek *corone*), a bird virtually indistinguishable from the RAVEN in symbolic tradition. It is said of the crow, like the raven, that its FEATHERS were originally WHITE. According to Greek myth, the SUN god Apollo had his love, the princess Coronis, watched over by a snow-white crow. The bird, however, was unable to prevent Coronis, who was already pregnant by Apollo, from giving herself to an Arcadian prince. Apollo cursed the negligent guardian, turning its feathers BLACK, then killed the unfaithful princess with his arrows. Her body was placed on the funeral pyre to be burnt, but Apollo pulled from the flames his unborn son, ASCLEPIUS, the god of healing. In other contexts the crow was regarded as an oracular animal, and, on occasion, portrayed as an attribute of the god Cronus (Latin Saturn; compare CHRONUS) and the Celtic god Bran.

crown An adornment for the head, which seems to elevate its wearer above the level of others, legitimizing this person as a superhuman creature associated with the higher spheres. FEATHERED crowns, HORN masks, and the like are found in nonliterate civilizations, but ring-shaped crowns symbolize royalty. Their structure picks up the symbolic associations of the (infinite) CIRCLE, and glittering PRECIOUS STONES add those of sensory splendor, wealth, and election. The points of the crown are like sunbeams, as crowned rulers generally are to be understood as representatives of a (patriarchal)

Crown of Sassanid ruler. Bronze, Persia, 6th–7th century A.D.

16. Crown of nobility	17. Crown of a baron	18. Crown of an earl	19. Crown of a prince
20. Crown of an elector	21. Crown of a duke	22. Crown of a grand duke	23. King's crown (former)
24. King's crown (contemporary)	25. Crown of Holy Roman emperors	26. Papal tiara	27. Bishop's miter

Crowns

solar cosmology. The crowns of KINGS are thus usually made of GOLD, the solar metal. In Christian iconography the crown is associated not only with the majesty of the Lord but also with the highest attainable level of (human) existence, as in depictions of the coronation of Mary (whose crown often is made up of 12 STARS or 12 precious stones) or portraits of martyrs, whose HANDS often conceal crowns. In FREEMASONRY, the "Four Crowned Men" (Quattuor Coronati), the patrons of the research lodge which is named for them, were martyrs to their faith. In medieval sculpture the VIRTUES Faith and Hope, Wisdom (Sophia), and the Church (Ecclesia) were portrayed wearing crowns, whereas Synagogue, the personification of Judaism, is often made to wear a crown tilted sideways (and is also blindfolded). A triple crown (the tiara) marks the Pope, and a five-tiered crown, images of God the Father.

In East Asian symbolism a crown resembling a flower symbolizes the attainment of a high stage of development, the elevation of the spiritual element over the corporeal. Fantastically formed crowns were worn by the priest-princes of the Maya in the Yucatán; the ancient Egyptian double crown referred to the union of Upper and Lower Egypt. Jewish high priests and rulers of the Aztec kingdom wore crowns resembling diadems. Occidental bridal and burial WREATHS, which indicate the transition to a new state of existence, are related symbolically to the crown but are simpler adornments. See also VULTURE, HEADDRESS.

crystal Traditionally a symbol of the formal splendor of the mineral world. Crystals of every sort, especially PRECIOUS STONES when cut or semiprecious stones in their natural state, have an undeniable fascination that goes beyond their material value: they attract the eye of the beholder and can serve as aids to meditation and concentration, not unlike drawn or painted YANTRAS. Since crystals often refract and reflect light, they stimulate the imagination of receptive individuals and can induce visions that are of great importance in divinatory magic. The "crystal ball" of clairvoyants, however, is today rarely of mineral origin: it is usually clear glass, in a sphere as nearly perfect as possible. In Christian symbology, rock crystal, which is not itself a source of light but gleams with the light of the SUN, is a symbol of the Virgin Mary. Since crystals have tangible, material form but are transparent, they represent "the spiritual in corporeal form." (See also DIAMOND.)

cube For the symbologist, the three-dimensional counterpart of the SQUARE; an image of stability and permanence. Naturally occurring crystals of rock salt are cubical in form and offer persuasive evidence of the harmonious creativity of nature. This structure also surely explains the alchemist's considering the "ELEMENT" sal (literally "salt") to be "the principle of the tangible." Plato

Cube "always stands upright." J. Boschius, 1702

associated the cube with the "element" EARTH. In the symbology of FREEMASONRY the cube represents the "hewn stone" (the "journeyman" lodge brother), into which the "rough stone" (the apprentice or initiate) has been fashioned; it can now take its place in the foundation of the TEMPLE of humanity. The shaping of the stone symbolizes moral self-education; the harmonic form itself, the necessary observance of moral standards. This makes the stone cube a social symbol of Freemasonry.

A die is made by adding from one to six dots, or "EYES," to each of the six faces of a cube, in such a way that the dots on opposite faces always total seven. In the place of eyes, Etruscan dice had numerals on the six faces. The expression "The die is cast" goes back to Julius Caesar's use, when crossing the Rubicon in 49 B.C., of a quotation from Menander (342–291 B.C.), in Greek *"Anerrhiphto kybos"* ("let the die fall"), freely translated by Suetonius as *"Iacta alea est."* Through the flourishing of humanism in the Renaissance the saying became part of the symbolic vocabulary of the learned.

In many legends and FAIRY TALES dice are thrown to determine a person's fate; they are seen as a manifestation of the will of a higher power.

It often goes unnoticed that in the Book of Revelation the "heavenly JERUSALEM" is described as a cube ("The length and the breadth and the height of it are equal" [21: 16]) 12,000 furlongs (1500 miles) in each dimension, a perfect form based on the NUMBER 12.

The cubic shrine in Mecca is the Kaaba (literally "cube"), around which every faithful Muslim is supposed to walk.

cuckoo (Greek *coccyx*, Latin *cucullus*, German *Kuckuck*) The "bird that speaks its own name." For many peoples, it was the bird of the soul, a harbinger of the future in general or spring in particular. The SCEPTER of the goddess Hera bore a cuckoo because Zeus, before their MARRIAGE, had transformed himself into one. The bird's peculiar tendency to lay its eggs in the nests of other birds, was remarked upon even in ancient

times. Oliver Wendell Holmes wrote, "We Americans are all cuckoos—we make our homes in the nests of other birds"; in German, a "cuckoo's egg" is a gift of dubious value or a child sired by an "outside" father. It is popularly believed that the number of times the bird cries will predict the number of years a person has left to live, or until he or she marries. In present-day English, the most common extension of meaning of the word is to refer to extreme eccentricity or insanity; there are analogues for this in medieval German, presumably going back to the bird's monotonous cry. (It is a common alpine practice to jingle the coins in one's pocket when one hears this cry, because of the superstition that to do so assures that one will not run out of money in the year following; here, too, there seems to be a connection between the great number of repetitions of the bird's cry and the number of coins hoped for.) In modern German the word *Kuckuck* is a common euphemism for the devil, not unlike "deuce" in English.

In the Tibetan *Book of Birds,* which contains metaphysical poetry, the cuckoo is a veiled manifestation of the savior *(bodhisattva)* Avalokitesvara, who is otherwise embodied in the Dalai Lama.

cuckoopint (Latin *Arum maculatum*), also called "lords-and-ladies": A tuberous plant with a strikingly "phallic" (hence "-pint", penis) spadix; its tuber was formerly used as

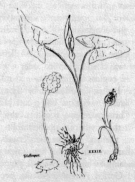

Cuckoopint. From L. Fuchs, *New Kreuterbuch,* 1543

a medicinal herb to relieve congestion and stomach disorders. Despite its form, it became a medieval symbol for the Virgin Mary, perhaps because of the phonetic similarity between *Arum* or *Aron-* (the cuckoopint is called *Aronstab* in German, a homonym of the expression for "Aaron's rod") and the name of the Biblical Aaron: Mary's kinswoman Elizabeth was descended from the house of Aaron. The blossom was also said to "point to heaven like a lily." It was believed that its tuber would also cure melancholy and "stimulate the passing" of harmful bodily secretions.

Cupids (amorettos) personifying the power of love. Cartari, 1647

Cupid. Gustave Doré (1832–1883)

Cupid or Amor (Greek Eros) The ancient embodiment of suddenly budding love in its merry, roguish form. He is usually portrayed as a naked, winged boy with bow and arrow, shooting not only mortals but also gods in the HEART and thus enticing them to love. The son of the god of war, MARS (Greek Aries), and Venus (Greek Aphrodite), he spreads such confusion that his mother often must confine or spank him. In Hellenistic times he was often multiplied to form whole groups of cupids or amorettos, as in the frescos of Pompeii or in ceramics. They are the forerunners of baroque and rococo *putti*—cupids Christianized to become baby ANGELS. In the myth of Cupid and Psyche, however, the god of love is a handsome young man, who brings his beloved at first many calamities but finally ideal happiness (in *The Golden Ass* of Apuleius, second century A.D.). In the medieval collection

Gesta Romanorum (ca. 1300) the god of love is described, as shown in a statue, with four WINGS; on the first was written: "First love is strong and mighty. For the sake of the beloved, it will bear every hardship, all distress." On the second: "True love seeks not to enrich the lover but to give all to the beloved." On the third: "True love eases woe and fear, and will not be deterred by them." On the fourth and last: "True love contains in itself that true law which grows not old but ever young again."

cypress In modern times, a TREE readily associated with death and burial ("Come away, come away, death,/ And in sad cypress let me be laid" *Twelfth Night*, II, 4), but in classical antiquity a symbol and attribute of Cronus (SATURN), ASCLEPIUS,

Cypress. Hohberg, 1675

and—perhaps because of its flame-like shape—Apollo, as well as many goddesses (Cybele, Persephone, Aphrodite, Artemis, Eurynome, Hera, Athena). The daughters of King Eteocles of Orchomenus are also said to have been transformed into cypresses, as is a youth named Cyparissus (in a different story) who had killed a sacred DEER. There are many indications that even before the period of Greek civilization the tree had been a religious symbol, and that it subsequently became associated with underworld cults. This is one reason for the custom of planting cypresses by graves. It was also believed to ward off black magic, and thus was frequently arranged in hedges. Cypress twigs were placed beneath seeds to protect them against vermin. This evergreen, with its particularly hardy wood, was also a symbol of longevity. Since it also appeared in depictions of PARADISE, the cypress could be planted by Christian graves as a symbol of hope for eternal life and portrayed on sarcophagi, although in earlier times IDOLS had often been carved from its wood. "The cypress wood endures time's ev'ry test,/ Defies, it seems, the law that all things die./ Prepare for life as for eternal rest:/ Naught but God's grace the two can sanctify" [Hohberg].

Danaïdes The daughters of Danaus (king of Argos). They murdered their bridegrooms, and in the underworld (see AFTERLIFE) their punishment was to fill a bottomless container with water, using sieve-like vessels. A Danaïdean task would be an endless or futile one, spoken of as an infernal punishment.

dance of death (French *danse macabre*) A symbolic expression of the idea that in death everyone is equal and that all social distinctions disappear. The series of images (executed by Holbein, for example) presumably is derived from customs of the Spanish Church. They typically show people of every age and social class made to dance feverishly (or led off in a sort of dance) by SKELETONS; those of elevated social rank usually resist the invitation to dance, while the poor are resigned to their fate. The dance motif, which flourished in the late Middle Ages, was later eclipsed by more peaceful depictions of the notion that *"media vita in morte sumus"* ("in the midst of life we are surrounded by death"). Depictions of the *danse macabre* were most common in times in which massive epidemics (cholera, bubonic plague) swept through Europe.

Images of dancing skeletons with musical instruments (flutes, noise-makers), however, were also produced in the Chimu dynasty of northern Peru; they appear to be depictions of the kingdom of the dead.

Daphne A powerfully symbolic figure of Greek mythology, the archetype of the VIRGIN who eternally disdains men. CUPID is said to have fired a GOLDEN ARROW into Apollo's heart, whereupon he fell madly in love with the nymph Daphne. She, however, was struck by an arrow with a LEADEN tip, so cold that she refused all male advances. Apollo pursued her fervently as she fled through the forests, pleading with the earth-goddess Gaea for assistance. When Apollo tried to embrace her, she turned into a LAUREL-tree (in Greek *daphne*). The disappointed god could only break off a branch and wear it as a WREATH on his head. From that time on, the laurel has been sacred to

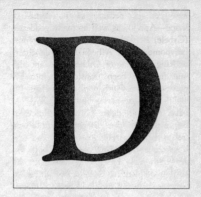

Apollo. In the allegorical system of ALCHEMY, the transformation of Daphne is an indication of all the transmutations that are possible in nature.

Daphnis Symbolizes the tragic aspect of love that ends in rejection. Daphnis is said to have played the reed-pipe as the pupil of his half-brother PAN; Daphnis, so handsome that he was loved by all the nymphs, swore eternal fidelity to one of them but soon broke this vow and was punished: the nymph pulled him into the WATER and drowned him. In another version, the love-goddess Aphrodite (Latin VENUS) filled him with such insatiable love that it killed him.

Daphne at the moment of transformation, courted by Apollo. Cartari, 1647

darkness The complementary opposite of LIGHT in a fundamental DUALITY, is first of all a symbol of primeval CHAOS before it was banished by the light emanating from the Creator. In this context darkness is primarily a symbol of removal from God and the light, of the dark underworld of the AFTERLIFE, and the enemies of illumination and enlightenment (embodied in ancient Persia, e.g., by Ahriman). Christians call the DEVIL "the Prince of Darkness," and eclipses of the SUN were interpreted, not only in the Judeo-Christian world (the "darkness over the land of Egypt" in Exodus 10:21, and the "darkness all over the land" upon the crucifixion of Christ, in Matthew 27:45) but also, e.g., in the Peru of the Incan period, as menacing omens. In the Book of Revelation darkness indicates that the END OF THE WORLD is imminent. In contrast to this readily understandable imagery, however, darkness can also express the ultimate, the ineffable, which is not to be perceived visually and which the mystic can no longer distinguish from the dazzle of the light. St. John of the Cross (1542–1591) spoke of the "dark CLOUD that illuminates the night" in a paradoxical image that attempts to put into words the coming-together of opposites in the fundamental essence of being: "It is a wondrous thing that this cloud, dark as it was, illuminated the night. This suggests that faith, which, for the soul, is at once a dark and ominous cloud, and night—since in the presence of faith the soul is blinded, robbed of its natural light—that faith, I say, illuminates with its darkness, and brings light to the darkness of the soul." This attempt to express ineffable mystical experiences by means of paradoxical (or apparently paradoxical) sentences, is found also in the context of the light symbolism of FREEMASONRY: "The primal opposition of light and darkness . . . fills all human existence. The secret fraternity believes that it has resolved this opposition and thus solved the most troubling of life's riddles: light and darkness are one and the same. Life is also death; darkness is also light! There is a constant effort throughout Masonic symbology to put this rationally incomprehensible

declaration into images and make it something that can be experienced; the symbols relate the struggle and wedding of light and darkness, of life and death" [Lennhoff and Posner]. Thus every aspirant must pass a lonely period of reflection in the "Dark Chamber," gazing upon symbols of transitoriness (skull, HOURGLASS, Bible) and considering his wish to become a Mason, before he is initiated and given the "Light." The "gruesome" symbolic objects of 18th-century Masonic rituals are no longer customary.

David A major figure not only in the Old Testament but also in artistic symbology. He lived in the tenth century B.C., was

David with his harp. Jewish book illustration, Italy, ca. 1460

KING Saul's armsbearer and harpist, and later himself became king of Judea and Israel, conquering Jerusalem and making it the center of his kingdom. His victory over the GIANT Goliath made him for some Christians a typological precursor of Christ, who overcame Satan; his harp playing, a prototype of the royal musician, often portrayed in ways reminiscent of ORPHEUS, the great musician of Greek mythology. His inspired poetry must also be mentioned, the Psalms of the Bible, which in the Middle Ages made up the most read book of the Bible, and the book most often copied in manuscripts.

death, symbols of The concentric CIRCLES found on the walls of megalithic graves (Neolithic period) suggest ripples in the surface of a lake when an object is dropped into the WATER, and thus seem to symbolize the descent of the soul into the waters of death. It was believed at one time that the AFTERLIFE would be spent in the regions over the sea or RIVER encircling the world of the living; this may explain the frequent cave drawings of death SHIPS, believed to transport the dead to the world beyond. In early Etruscan burial art DOLPHINS and seahorses are shown bearing the souls of the dead to the Elysian ISLANDS OF THE BLESSED; later, they are frequently replaced by demonic figures (Charon, with his HAMMER resembling a double-headed AX, or Tuchulcha, with SNAKES in his hands) that resemble DEVILS more than any creatures in nature. Alongside depictions of the dead themselves, the grave markers of classical antiquity often feature mourning women with their heads covered, or else a GENIUS with a lowered TORCH, or poppy capsules symbolizing sleep (see SOMNUS, THANATOS). More obvious symbols of death are SKELETONS and skulls (the latter also the sixth day-sign of the Aztec calendar, Miquiztli), although the "dry bones" of the dead can also be symbols of the resurrection to come: "O ye dry bones, hear the word of the Lord. . . . Behold, I will cause breath to enter into you, and ye shall live. . . . And the bones came together, bone to his bone. . . . And the breath came into them and they lived, and stood up upon their feet, an exceeding great army" [Ezekiel 37:4–10]. On the other hand, from the Middle Ages onward, "living" skeletons have figured in depictions of the DANCE

Death: Gravedigger, corpse. Graffito, Commodilla catacomb, Rome, early Christian

OF DEATH, which presents death as the great leveller, the equalizer of fortunes. The old symbol of the death ship becomes in Greek art a "church ship" with ANCHOR, CROSS (as a mast), and DOVE (like NOAH's, but leading the way to PARADISE). The olive branch, as a symbol of peace, is also included, as are the SNAIL (sleeping in its grave-like shell) and the BUTTERFLY, traditional symbols of resurrection; a WREATH symbolizes the reward in heaven for a life of devotion on earth. The scythe of the Grim Reaper (see SICKLE) represents the cutting off of life; at times he also carries a bow and ARROW (weapons of death) or an HOURGLASS (see also CHRONUS), a reference to the limited span of a person's life on earth. Especially in the Romantic period there were many depictions of the weeping WILLOW. In the Occident BLACK is the symbolic color of death; in the Far East, it is WHITE. (See LILY.)

In Islamic myth, a person's death is symbolized by Israfil, the ANGEL of death who stands next to Allah's THRONE and picks up

Death: Masonic emblem including carpenter's square and drafting compass

Death: Urn, weeping willow. A. Anderson (1775–1870)

the leaves fallen from the world-TREE bearing the names of those whom Allah has chosen to die. Thereupon Israfil, in a variety of forms, visits those who are to die: "He appeared to Adam as a goat, to Abraham as a sickly old man, and to MOSES as a man hale and hardy" [Beltz, 1980]. It was Israfil (who is not mentioned by name in the Koran) who provided the SEVEN-colored EARTH needed for the creation of humanity, whereupon Allah promised that Israfil could have the physical remains when each person died.

In the TAROT deck the XIIIth card of the Major Arcana shows death as a skeleton with a scythe or a bow and arrow, often in a monk's cowl or as a "horseman of the Apocalypse." The card is taken as a portent of "death, loss, change, the old giving way to the new."

deer (male), stag, hart, or buck   A symbolic animal prominent in Old World cultures. The stag seems to have been frequently paired with the BULL to form a mythic and cosmological DUALITY, not unlike the wild HORSE and the wild bull in Ice Age CAVE art in the hypothesis of French archaeologists. The stag's tree-like antlers with their periodic regeneration made him a symbol of rejuvenation, rebirth, and the passage of time. In Norse mythology four stags graze in the highest branches of the world-tree Yggdrasill, eating buds (hours), blossoms (days), and branches (seasons). The deer's antlers were seen as symbols of

Deer as attributes of Sts. Hubert and Eustace. W. Auer, 1890

the SUN's rays. In antiquity the stag was considered the enemy of poisonous SNAKES, its skin an amulet against snakebite, and powdered antler as protection for seed corn against black magic. In ancient China the deer (*lu*), through homonymy with the word for riches, came to symbolize wealth, and also filial piety (according to fable a young man disguised himself in a deerskin to obtain deer's milk as eye medicine for his blind parents); the animal accompanied the god of longevity, Shou-hsing.

Christian iconography is greatly influenced by the 42nd Psalm: "As the hart panteth after the water brooks, so panteth my soul after thee, O God" [verse 1]. According to the early Christian text *Physiologus*, the deer spits water into every crevice in which poisonous snakes are hiding; it

Deer, with wheel. Clay vessel fragment, early Iron Age, Asia Minor

thus floats them out and tramples them. "So too does our Lord strike the serpent, the DEVIL, with heavenly WATER. . . . In another sense, ascetics are like the deer: with tears of penitence they extinguish the flaming ARROWS of evil, and they trample the great serpent, the devil, and kill him." The deer is also said to be able to suck snakes out of their holes, protecting itself against the snakes' venom by drinking spring water within three hours; then, supposedly, the deer will live another 50 years. "If you have the serpent in your heart, namely sin, then rush to the springs, to the veins of Holy Scripture, and drink the living water . . . and die not of sin." Medieval bestiaries repeat all of this, adding: deer discovered the miraculous power of the herb dittany (*Dictamnus albus*, or gas plant) when they

Deer. Snuffbox engraving, southern Tyrol, 19th century

had hunters' arrows in them and found that eating dittany enables them to expel the arrows and their wounds to heal. When deer cross a stream each one "lays its head on the hindquarters of the deer in front of it, thus reducing its weight. If they come to a filthy place, they quickly leap away from it. Thus, too, should Christians . . . help carry one another; they should leap over a place of filthy sin, and when they have satanic venom in their bodies they should run to Christ, the true spring and source, to confess and be rejuvenated" [Unterkircher]. Deer horn, according to the same sources, is an effective medicine, the RIGHT antler being more potent than the left, and burnt deer horn drives away any snake. Deer meat heals fever, and a salve made from the deer marrow is also an effective remedy for it.

The stag appears frequently in heraldry, signifying "gentleness and mildness, because the deer is believed to have no yellow bile, the reputed reason for its long life, reaching a hundred years" [Böckler]. The antlers also appear alone (or a single antler, or a part thereof), referring, according to Böckler, to "strength." In this context he explains the symbolism of "putting horns on" a husband: "The Greek emperor Andronicus had horns placed on the houses of women with whom he had slept, authorizing them to hunt, and thus we speak even today of putting horns on a cuckold. Also in the time of Galeazzo Sforza, Count of Milan, women were not ashamed to sleep with princes, for their husbands came away not with paltry but

with golden horns and received great honors." In Celtic myth deer are "cattle of the fairies" and messengers between the world of the gods and that of mortals. The Celtic god Cernunnos was portrayed with antlers on his head like the shamans of ancient peoples. In Christian sculpture of the Middle Ages the deer is sometimes portrayed nibbling on grapes (see WINE), symbolizing humanity, which even on earth can already enjoy the fruits of God's grace. The animal's striving to reach springs symbolizes the desire for purification through baptism: "Just as the deer devours the snake,/ Then rushes off his thirst to slake,/ Lets spring the venom wash away,/ So all is well, can Christian say,/ For he is saved, sin's trace is lost,/ When in baptismal font he's washed." This is why the relief-work on such fonts often includes the representation of deer.

The imagery of ALCHEMY sees the deer as a symbol in the context of the classical myth of the hunter ACTAEON, who was transformed into a stag by the goddess DIANA (Artemis): for the alchemist the deer is a reminder of the possible transmutation of metals in connection with the lunar (see MOON), feminine world of SILVER. The animal is referred to figuratively in occasional idioms. Germans speak of "hunting the white deer" to indicate that a task is very difficult, or a goal unattainable; and in English "stag" refers to a man attending a social function unaccompanied by a woman: "to go stag," a "stag party." The legends of St. Eustace and St. Hubert tell of a CROSS appearing in the antlers of a hunted stag. Other saints (Meinulf, Meinhold, Oswald, Prokop of Bohemia) are portrayed with deer as their attributes. In pre-Columbian Central America antlered animals resembling the deer (in Aztec, *mazatl;* in Maya, *manik*) give their name to the seventh of the 20 day-signs of the calendar. Like these creatures of the wild, persons born under this sign are said to roam through nature, seeking distant regions and shunning fixed abodes. In the Shinto religion of Japan, the stag is the mount of the gods and is often portrayed with their symbols on scrolls at shrines. (See also DOE.)

devil (Greek *diabolus*) The great adversary (Satan) and "father of lies," is the counterpart in hell of God, who rules in heaven. The devil's attributes seem to come primarily from those of Charu, the Etruscan demon of the underworld: a NOSE like a VULTURE's beak, pointed EARS like those of an animal, WINGS, tusk-like teeth (like those of the demon Tuchulcha), carrying a HAMMER as a symbol of death. To these are added physical features of the GOAT: HORNS, legs, tail—making him resemble the Greek god of nature PAN. In some contexts he is portrayed with HORSE's hooves (or, to symbolize his divided nature, with one hoof and one human foot). His wings are often formed like those of the BAT to distinguish them from those of ANGELS. In paintings of witches' sabbaths (see MOUNTAIN) he is often shown with a second face on his buttocks, which his servants must kiss (the "kiss of shame," *osculum infame*). Legendary elaborations on Isaiah 14 trace the existence of the devil (Lucifer, Phosphorus, "bearer of light") back to his uprising against God and his fall into the underworld. (See GRAIL.) He is not always portrayed as a terrifying figure, however. In popular legend he appears as a hunter in GREEN or RED garments; in medieval sculpture, as the "Prince of this world," whose back, however, is being devoured by TOADS, SNAKES, and worms. Snakes and DRAGONS are associated with the devil in

LUCIFER, Empereur.

BELZÉBUT, Prince.

ASTAROT, Grand-duc.

LUCIFUGÉ, prem. Ministr.

SATANACHIA, grand général.

AGALIAREPT., aussi général.

FLEURETY, lieutenantgén.

SARGATANAS, brigadier.

NEBIROS, mar. de camp.

Devil: Names, symbols of the Princes of Hell. From *Le Véritable Dragon Rouge*, 1822

Devil: Demons (from "Against the Papacy . . . Established by the Devil"). Lucas Cranach, 1545

other contexts as well; saints are frequently portrayed in conflict with them. Because of Satan's power and his reign in the realm of godlessness, the otherwise usually positively valued LION is also associated with him, as in I Peter 5:8: "The devil, as a roaring lion, walketh about, seeking whom he may devour." The FOX (thought of as slyly destructive) is also a symbol for the devil.

As the opposite of the Holy TRINITY, the Prince of Hell is also occasionally portrayed with three faces, e.g. in woodcuts illustrating Dante's *Divine Comedy*. Creatures thought of as belonging to Satan may include a red BIRD, the reddish SQUIRREL, the BASILISK, and the CUCKOO.

The XVth card of the Major Arcana in the TAROT deck, The Devil, shows him with horns and bat wings, on a platform to which are chained two persons who have been turned into demons. It is interpreted as meaning punishment, guilt, bondage to physical urges.

dew The moisture traditionally believed to fall from the HEAVENS to rejuvenate and revitalize: "Thy dew is as the dew of herbs, and the earth shall cast out the dead" [Isaiah 26:19]. In classical antiquity dew was understood symbolically as traces left behind by the divine messenger Iris (see RAINBOW) or by EOS, the goddess of the dawn. In the Middle Ages, Isaiah 45:8 ("Drop down, ye heavens, from above, and let the skies pour down righteousness") was interpreted as a prophecy of Christ's coming. Dew and RAIN were almost always taken as synonymous and associated with blessings coming down from heaven. In the symbolic tradition of ALCHEMY, the dew from heaven (Latin *ros coelestis*) is also a symbol of the philosopher's STONE in embryo: "Thus our matter is our dew, fat, airy, and heavy, also found on the surface of the earth. . . . Another dewy general subject coming directly from a celestial source and indirectly from plants and animals. . . . It is celestial and terrestrial, fluid and stable [compare CORAL], white and reddish, light and heavy, sweet and bitter . . ." [*Hermetisches ABC vom Stein der Weisen*, 1779]. Dew is thus conceived of as a tangible watery aggregate of that *materia prima* from which all other matter comes. In the "silent book" [*Mutus Liber*, 1677] of the alchemists, the gathering of dewdrops in cloths is portrayed allegorically.

In the Christian symbolic tradition dew coming down from heaven symbolizes the gift of the Holy Spirit, which revitalizes parched souls.

Dew. Hohberg, 1675

diamond The "most precious of PRECIOUS STONES," also called "Regina gemmarum" (queen of gems), has the symbolic signature of perfection, purity, and imperviousness. In Buddhism there are references to a diamond THRONE as "the seat of enlightenment," and a diamond THUNDERBOLT destroys earthly passions. In Occidental antiquity Plato used the image of a diamond AXIS MUNDI. It was popularly believed that a diamond made a person invisible, drove ghosts away, and assured the winning of a woman's favor. According to the *Physiologus* (late antiquity, early Christian era), the "adamas" or "adamant" can be neither carved nor cut with IRON, but its otherwise unyielding hardness is softened by the hot BLOOD of a male GOAT; it is found only east of the Mediterranean, and only at night. This, the text continues, is why it is a symbol of Christ the Savior: he was born at night, in the Holy Land, and all the powers of the earth tried in vain to harm him, after the manner of Amos 7:8–9: "Behold, I will set a diamond in the midst of my people Israel: [. . .] and the sanctuaries of laughter shall be laid waste"; Christ, however, is softened only by (his own) warm blood. The Greek *adamas* means "unbreakable, untamable." In the traditional symbolism of precious stones, the diamond, like ROCK-CRYSTAL, corresponds to the SUN. Hildegard of Bingen (1098–1179) wrote: "The devil is the enemy of this stone, because it withstands his power; for this reason the devil detests it day and night." The Renaissance botanist Lonicerus believed it to be effective against war, strife, poison, and evil spirits. The alchemistic image of the "philosopher's stone" may have been influenced by such myths. Only positive qualities are attributed to the diamond: it symbolizes LIGHT and life, faithfulness in love and sorrow, unyielding sincerity and greatest purity. Naturally the diamond was always prized as a crown-jewel and talisman. (Diamond scepter: see THUNDER.)

Diana The Latin designation, popular in Europe since the Renaissance, for the goddess of the hunt, in Greek Artemis, who by this time had only allegorical or symbolic

Diana with the lunar crescent. Cartari, 1647

meaning. Statues of Diana with the crescent-MOON in her hair, bow and ARROWS in her hand, accompanied by hunting DOGS, adorned especially the gardens of the baroque period. On occasion, the legendary scene is represented in which ACTAON, having observed the chaste Diana bathing, is transformed into a stag (see DEER) and torn apart by his own hunting dogs. The crescent is explained by the fact that the early Italian goddess Diana was originally the goddess of the moon and only later were the myths relating to Artemis, the mistress of the animals *(potnia theron)*, carried over to her. Diana seems to have lived on not only in garden sculpture but also as a mythical figure in Italy. The American mythologist Charles G. Leland (1824–1903) reported in his book *Arcadia* (1899) about a cult of "WITCHES" *(streghe)* who revered Diana and appealed to her as a great goddess: "Diana! Diana! Diana! Queen of all magicians and of the dark night, the stars, the moon, all fate and fortune! You, mistress of ebb and flow, who shine at night upon the sea, throwing your light upon the water! You, commander of the sea, in your boat like a half-moon . . ." (from a hymn appearing in a legend in which Melampus has his mother ask that he be given the art of understanding the language of SNAKES).

djed-pole A mysterious symbolic object of ancient Egypt, also referred to as a fetish, whose meaning is "stability" or "that which endures." It is composed of a POLE or PILLAR with a broader base and four horizontal boards near the top that form layers. Egyptologists describe it as a tree from which most of the branches have been removed, or a notched tree-trunk, or a pole to which sheaves of grain have been attached so as to define multiple sections along its length. Others refer to sheafs of papyrus-sedge bound together in similar sections. The symbol seems to have originated in the Egyptian city of Memphis (Men-nefer-Pepi) and been associated with the cult of the god Osiris (Usire). The djed-pole was called "the backbone of Osiris," and the KING celebrated the cult festival known as "the raising of the djed," e.g., at the beginning of the celebrations of royal jubilees (Heb-sed). Djed carvings were worn as amulets and buried with the dead to ward off the dangers of the AFTERLIFE.

doe or hind A female DEER, stands in many myths for the female animal in general, which can have a demonic character, despite what we see as the gentleness of the doe. The second of the Labors of Hercules was to capture the Hind of Ceryneia. The chariot of Artemis (in Latin myth DIANA), the goddess of the hunt, was pulled by does. The animal is also important in Asiatic myth. In the Ural-Altaic regions she was the supernatural ancestor of several peoples

Djed-pole, personified as royalty with staff and scourge. Egyptian amulet

Doe as an attribute of St. Aegidius. W. Auer, 1890

(compare TOTEM). The Hungarian myth of origin tells of a fleeing doe who lured two primeval hunters into a swamp, where she transformed herself into two princesses who coupled with the hunters, becoming the progenitors of the Huns and the Magyars, respectively. Similarly, the family tree of Genghis Khan shows a doe and a WOLF as his progenitors. A doe was said to have rescued fleeing Frankish warriors by showing them a point at which they could ford the Main River. In many old European fairy tales young women and girls are transformed into does. In one ancient Chinese legend a doe gives birth to a human child, a girl who is later reared by a man; but when she dies her body disappears, revealing her supernatural origins. In prehistoric rites of passage does may have symbolized female initiates. In Mayan mythology of the Yucatán, Zip is a god of the hunt; under the name A Uuc Yol Zip he is portrayed in ancient hieroglyphic writings as a horned man having intercourse with a doe.

dog (Latin *canis*) The first domesticated animal; symbolically associated primarily with loyalty and vigilance, figuring often as a guardian at the portals of the AFTERLIFE

(Cerberus, a three-headed dog), or as a sacrifice to the dead, to guide them in the next world. Dogs are also believed to be able to "see ghosts" and thus to warn us of invisible dangers. Only rarely do dogs appear in a negative light: the HELL-hound Garm of Norse myth simultaneously kills the god Tyr and is killed by him at the END OF THE WORLD (Ragnarök); the dark goddess Hecate of Greek myth is accompanied by fighting dogs. BLACK dogs were also thought of as demonic companions of witches or necromancers (e.g., FAUST, Agrippa of Nettesheim [1486–1535]). In various non-European cultures the dog, because of its intelligence and ability to learn, receives credit for many of the attainments of human civilization, including technical skills. And although in classical antiquity we find references to "canine flattery and shamelessness," the loyalty of the dog as household guardian (*phylax*) and its sheep-herding abilities are the characteristics that are stressed. ASCLEPIUS and Hermes (Latin MERCURY) were accompanied by dogs, as were later St. Hubert, St. Eustace, and St. Roch. In the Muslim world the dog is considered "unclean," but the watchdog is tolerated. In ancient Egypt a large wild dog, similar to a jackal, was a manifestation of Anubis, a god of the dead, a further indication of the importance of the dog as a guide in the

Dog "protects and warns." J. Boschius, 1702

Canis.

Dog. Woodcut in Pseudo-Albertus Magnus, Frankfurt, 1531

Dog: Priest's mask representing Anubis, god of the dead. Woodcut, late Egyptian

afterlife for the souls of the dead. In the Middle Ages the dog usually appears as an image of feudal loyalty or marital fidelity, e.g., on tombstones. In sculpture it frequently stands for total belief in God but has an alternate negative association with uncontrolled wrath. Hell-hounds accompany Satan, the hunter of souls. Images of *Christophorus cynocephalus* are in a category all their own, showing the legendary medieval saint (see CHRISTOPHER) as having the head of a dog, presumably under the influence of depictions of the Egyptian god Anubis.

In the 20-day calendar of the ancient civilizations of Central America the dog (in Aztec *itzcuintli*, in Maya *oc*) is the 10th day-sign; in ancient Mexico dogs were buried along with the dead as sacrifices to them and as guides for the afterlife. Those born

Dog: Legendary cynocephalics. Hereford world map, Richard of Haldingham, 13th century

under the sign of the dog were believed to be destined to rule and to distribute valuable gifts. The god Xolotl ("twin") had the form of a dog; dogs were supposed to bring the dead across the "ninefold RIVER" to the underworld. Xolotl also accompanied the SUN into the west as it sank into the jaws of the EARTH, leading it through the underworld, back to the place where it rose the next morning; he died himself in the process but returned to life as he guided it up out of the realm of the dead. This dual role explains his name. (See also LIGHTNING.) In ancient China the dog was the 11th sign of the ancient Chinese zodiac (see STARS), but it had a variety of symbolic and mythical associations. Dogs were thought of primarily as repelling demons, but in certain areas they were seen as a source of meat and eaten. In other areas (South and West China) they were thought of as bringers of food (RICE or millet). The surviving Yao of South China consider their nation to be descended from a canine ancestor, which is reminiscent of totemic notions (see TOTEM). China, too, has its legends of humans with canine heads. Japanese shrines often have "Korean dogs" as guardian figures. Among the Slavic peoples the dog was especially esteemed; as late as 1560 a Samaite bishop reproached his people for "dog worship," but we know nothing of the symbolic or mythic significance of this dog. In Celtic myth the dog was also important, e.g. as the companion of Epona (the goddess of the hunt and of HORSES) and as an attribute of the god Nodon or Nuadu. The hero of the Ulster legends of Ireland is Cú-Chulainn, the hunting-dog of Ulster.

dolphin   This intelligent and human-friendly mammal of the sea has long attracted interest in the Mediterranean area. A dolphin is said to have saved the Greek bard Arion and brought him to the shore after a shipwreck. In mythology, Apollo is said to have assumed the form of a dolphin to carry Cretans to Delphi, where they built a temple to him. The name Apollo Delphinius ("Lord of the Dolphins") may mean that in Minoan Crete Apollo was honored with the symbol of a dolphin. It is not clear whether the name Delphi derives from this connection. Otherwise, the dolphin was an attribute of the sea-god Poseidon, and a dolphin is said to have matched him with his wife Amphitrite. Another attribute of Poseidon was the HORSE, images of dolphins were used at racetracks as counters to show how many circuits had been run. Dionysus, the god of drunken ecstasy, supposedly turned pirates into dolphins. Aphrodite (Latin VENUS), who was born from the sea-foam, is frequently portrayed with dolphins. In Etruscan burial art, dolphins often bear the souls of the dead to the ISLANDS OF THE BLESSED; only in later times did a darker conception of the AFTER-LIFE (on the order of Hades) come to prevail. In heraldry the dolphin appears covered with fish-scales, in the arms of Dauphiné (France), for example. The crown prince of France bore dolphins in his personal coat of arms (and was thus called "dauphin"). The note *"ad usum delphini"*

Dolphin: Boy on the Dolphin, Renaissance style. Cartari, 1647

(for the use of the crown prince) in books means that they are expurgated editions morally suitable for younger readers.

Don Quixote   de la Mancha (also spelled "Quijote")   The symbolic figure of the touchingly heroic, unworldly romantic, who confuses dreams and hard realities and therefore "tilts at windmills." The character was created by Miguel de Cervantes Saavedra (1547–1616) for his parody of pompous novels of chivalry but took on something of a life of its own in the process and grew beyond the limits of the project as originally conceived. In the first part (1605) of the novel that bears his name we already find all the characteristics of the "knight of the sorrowful countenance" in flight from reality; he is accompanied by Sancho Panza, his "grossly material," down-to-earth squire, the other half of this personified DUALITY. Their hopelessly divergent dialogues anticipate those of the comedy teams of our own day, but the tragic undertone remains in the "knight-errant's" lifelong quest for worthy adventures. In the second volume (1615) the author brings his hero back to grim reality and lets him die in favor with God and humanity. Cervantes clearly wanted to satirize the sentimental excesses of romance: he loved adventure and glory and deplored the hackneyed chivalric romances of his day. Thus the now proverbial Quixote is "a protest against the false poetry of literature in favor of the true poetry of life. . . . If we laugh with Cervantes and are moved by him, then we have already understood him, whether we read Don Quixote as entertainment, as assigned reading, or as a tower-

Dolphin. Ancient Greek coin, Lindos, 560–520 B.C.

Don Quixote and Sancho Panza. Gustave Doré (1832–1883)

ing—and profound—work of literature." [Karl Vossler].

donkey or ass An animal with highly divergent symbological associations. In ancient Egypt it was usually linked with Seth (Setesh), the slayer of Osiris, and a knife was added to the hieroglyph for "ass" (stabbing the animal in the shoulder) to make the pernicious sign harmless. In Greece, Dionysus (see BACCHUS) was portrayed as riding a donkey; the Romans understood an ass as a reference to Priapus, the god of procreation and fertility, and thus included the animal in the suite of the goddess Ceres.

Donkey: Demons with donkey heads. Fresco, Mycenaea, ca. 1500 B.C.

On the other hand, it appeared in stories and fables as a ridiculous creature, and there is a Palatine rock drawing that mocks Christians as "worshipping a crucified ass" (Christ portrayed with a man's body and an ass's head). In the Old Testament, Numbers 22 tells the story of Balaam's ass, who understands God's will before her master does; Jesus rides into Jerusalem on a (female) ass. The familiar image of the Nativity scene with the ox and donkey beside the cradle of the Christ-child comes from an apocryphal gospel purportedly written by Matthew; in a subsequent interpretation, the donkey symbolized the Gentiles, and the ox, the Jews. One tradition sees in the animal all that is humble and gentle; the opposing tradition, all that is stupid, lazy, stubborn, and lascivious. In Romanesque sculpture the donkey, like the male GOAT, symbolizes indolence and fornication. In the Middle Ages, "stupidity" also refers to insufficient faith, and for this reason the apostle Thomas, who doubted the reports of Christ's resurrection, and Synagogue, the personification of Judaism, were shown accompanied by donkeys. On the other hand, there are depictions of the scene in which a donkey kneels before the consecrated communion wafer carried by St. Anthony of Padua, thus recalling Balaam's ass from the Old Testament and her recognition of holiness. In the early Christian *Philologus* it is said that the wild ass bites off the genitals of male foals to make eunuchs of them, and that this is where the Persians learned castration; the text appends the moral that it is better to live a celibate life and beget "spiritual children," because the "new seed" is that of the ascetic life, "voluntary abstinence and self-mastery." A medieval legal custom obliged those convicted of adultery to ride through the streets on a donkey.

doves and pigeons Birds of major symbolic importance from ancient times to the present. The dove's reputed peaceful, gentle character (which bears little resemblance to its actual behavior) made it a symbol of love and tenderness—although it is also sometimes thought of as fearful or loquacious.

The dove, which in its most familiar incarnation—the pigeon—has become the polluting bane of many city-dwellers, is also a symbol of the peace movement; the opponents of "doves" are known as "hawks." In the ancient world, similarly, the dove was opposed to the EAGLE or the RAVEN (Horace, Martial, Juvenal). "Dove" or its diminutives were already established as erotic terms of affection for a woman with whom one was intimate—and nicknames for a woman of ill repute. This usage is explained primarily through the bird's association with the love goddess Astarte (Ashtoreth) in Semitic tradition, subsequently taken over by the Greeks in the fourth century B.C. Doves, as creatures sacred to Aphrodite, were kept at her shrines (Cythera, Paphos) and also associated with her lover ADONIS and with Cupid. Doves were also associated with augury: the priestesses in the sacred GROVE at Dodona, the Peleiades, were also called Peleiae ("doves"), going back to the time when a BLACK pigeon settled on an oak and ordered that a shrine be established there. Similarly, a dove figures prominently in the legend of how the shrine to JUPITER Amon was established in the Siwah oasis. Poor Jews generally used the dove as their sacrificial animal. The nesting instinct made pigeons ideal messengers for the ancient Chinese and Egyptians. Because of its use in augury, the dove often had ambiguous symbolic associations. The ancient Romans were fond of the flesh of the dove, even though the bird was sacred to VENUS and its EGGS were believed to have aphrodisiac powers. In ancient medicine it was believed that doves had no bile in their systems, making them especially docile, and that the medicinal herbs they ate (e.g., bindweed, vervain) rendered their flesh, blood, and organs therapeutic for the humans who ate them. Even

Doves as a symbol of romantic love. Children's book illustration, Franz Pocci, 1846

the droppings of pigeons and doves were used in making poultices.

In the Bible the dove symbolizes the end of the Great FLOOD when it brings an olive branch back to NOAH on the ARK. When Jesus is baptized in the RIVER Jordan a dove descends upon him [Matthew 3:16]. The Holy Spirit is almost always portrayed in the form of a dove, e.g., in depictions of the Annunciation, the Holy Trinity, or divine inspiration. The SEVEN gifts of the Holy Spirit (wisdom, understanding, counsel, fortitude, knowledge, piety, and fear of the Lord) are represented by seven doves; doves also stand for the newly baptized. On grave markers the soul of the person buried is represented by a dove soaring to HEAVEN, where it perches in the TREE of Life or drinks the WATER of eternal life; doves are also shown flying out of the mouths of dying martyrs or carrying the martyr's CROWN in their beaks. According to the early Christian text *Physiologus*, the turtle dove is loquacious by nature, but "when its mate dies, it dies immediately itself as well and never lives to take another mate." Christ is "our most eloquent spiritual dove, our mellifluously truthful bird: everything under the heavens resounds with His joyful message. . . . St. Basil says: Let women imitate the turtle dove, keeping their marriage vows sacred." The dove embodies the virtue of moderation and is an attribute of many saints: the Evangelists, Theresa of Avila, Gregory, Basil, Thomas Aquinas, Catherine of Alexandria, Columban (compare Latin *columba*, "dove"), Scholastica.

In the symbolic imagery of ALCHEMY the WHITE dove represents the whitening (*al-

Dove with olive branch. Early Christian catacomb painting, Sousse, Tunisia

Doves with Cinderella. Etching, Ludwig Richter (1803–1884)

bedo) of the *materia prima* as it is turned into the philosopher's stone: the BLACK RAVEN becomes the white dove.

The dove is a symbol for the soul in India, as well. In China it stood for marital fidelity and longevity: doves (*ko*) are usually found in pairs, and the male and the female divide parental responsibilities. They also appear in the headdress of the goddess of fertility, probably because doves multiply so rapidly.

In German, an alternate expression for "COCKAIGNE" is "the Land of Roast Doves": in this imaginary paradise, ready-to-eat doves fly into the mouths of the indolent sybarites who dwell there.

Dracula This archetype of the "undead" vampire, the BLOOD-sucking monster of Eastern European folklore, is only in part a literary fantasy of the Irish novelist Bram Stoker. (The much-filmed book was first published in 1897.) The model for the tale is a historical figure, the Transylvanian Vlad Tepes (called "Dracul"), who was notorious for his cruelty toward subordinates and, on the battlefield, toward the enemy Turks. His castle was destroyed in 1462 by Sultan Mehmed the Conqueror, but Vlad Tepes, "the Impaler," lives on in the folk tradition of Rumania. Memory became intermingled with legend, according to which the dead returned to the world of the living to suck

the blood (the elixir of life) from their veins and thus turned them into vampires as well. As early as 1745 J. H. Zedler's encyclopedia offered the following explanation for this notion: "An epidemic was raging among those people and bringing with it sudden death. But since this disease also produced confused fantasies, or nightmares, those inflicted came to imagine that the dead were attacking them and sucking their blood."

dragons provide an important ingredient in the symbologies of many peoples. They are always portrayed as reptilian in form, at times like winged CROCODILES or gigantic SNAKES. What are the origins of this symbol? The attempt to associate them with those "dragons" that once really existed—the dinosaurs of the Mesozoic era—does not constitute an immediately satisfactory explanation, since the dinosaurs were never the contemporaries of the human race, which first walked the earth some hundred million years after their extinction. Edgar Dacqué's theory (see GIANTS) thus posited a primal memory, reaching back far past the actual dawn of humanity, to preserve the image of the dinosaur. In myths of creation, dragons are usually violent primeval creatures who must be defeated by the gods. Later, heroes and ancestors of noble lines take on the role of dragon-slayers (the intellectually superior human overcoming the untamed natural world). In fairy-tales and legends, slaying the dragon is a frequent test of the hero's mettle; if he succeeds, he will obtain a treasure or free a captive princess. The dragon

Dragon of Satan. Hohberg, 1675

Dragon of the ancient Mexican calendar, Cipactli

Dragon. Children's book illustration, Franz Pocci, 1846

is here a symbol of the bestial element which must be defeated with strength and discipline. In Christian symbology the dragon embodies the diabolical element, or the satanic Lucifer, whom the archangel Michael defeated and plunged into the pit of HELL (see DEVIL, ANGEL). Dragons are therefore often associated with FIRE and portrayed as breathing fire, or else as creatures of that primeval CHAOS which was to be destroyed only through disciplined marshaling of mental and physical prowess.

In contrast to this Occidental conception, the dragon is usually understood in East Asia as a symbol of happiness, capable of producing the potion of immortality. It represents the primal essence *yang* (see YIN AND YANG) of Chinese philosophy—procreation, fertil-

Dragon of the Apocalypse with the Whore of Babylon. Hans Burgkmair, 1523

ity, activity—and thus is frequently used decoratively to ward off evil spirits. In many legends and fairy-tales dragons play a leading role, and in the fine arts and in artisanry they are a principal motif. The number of dragons on the brocade garments of the generals of ancient China was precisely regulated, and only the emperor's garment might have NINE. From the Han dynasty (206 B.C. – A.D. 220) onward, the turquoise dragon (*lung*) was the symbol of the emperor: it was the fifth sign of the Chinese zodiac, and the symbol of the East, the rising sun, and the spring RAIN; the WHITE dragon, on the other hand, governed the West and death. In winter, according to popular tradition, dragons live underground, but they come to the surface in the second month of the Chinese calendar and cause THUNDER and the first RAINS. There are frequently dragon festivals with fireworks on the second day of the second month. In decorative art two dragons are often shown playing with a PEARL (the thunder-BALL), with which they bring forth the fertilizing rain. In Japan, too, the dragon is the embodiment of the rain-divinity; fountains around temples often have bronze dragons as waterspouts.

In Africa and the Americas, however, we find no clear dragon symbology, although in ancient Mexico iguanas and mythical serpents did have great prominence.

drawing board   Used symbolically in FREE-MASONRY to represent the rank of master; one of the "immovable jewels" (see SQUARE, CARPENTER'S). Following symbolically the imagery of Gothic cathedral construction, it enables the Master to draw the plan of the "structure" to be erected. It is usually represented graphically by a sort of pound-sign above an X, usually identified only as "geometric figures" but in fact a grid used especially in the 18th century to encode and decode messages (see Biedermann, *Das verlorene Meisterwort*, 1986). In the Swedish system of Freemasonry the drawing board is part of the "curriculum" even for the "apprentice."

Baurnjöpel wrote that "every Master is to strengthen himself in his work by sketching out his structures on the drawing board: the lines he draws must remain indelible both for him and for all of those who labor under his direction" (1793).

Dream Symbols. Frontispiece, English dream book, 1821

dream symbols If studied scientifically, can help ethnological symbologists to understand the meanings of the cultural symbols they study. Jungian psychologists believe that the symbols in myths, fairy tales, legends, visions, religions, and various works of art, as well as dream symbols themselves, have their roots in the subconscious human psyche, thus the vast experience of analytic psychologists with the interpretation of dreams can help decipher the "other reality" of symbolic thought in general. Of course, ethnological symbologists take historical data into account, whereas analytic psychologists work ahistorically, focusing on a universally valid "other world" whose contents remain unchanged. The most important ancient documentation of the attempt to interpret the dreams of individuals is found in the five books of the *Oneirocriticon* by Artemidorus of Daldis (second century after Christ), which distinguishes between "thereomantic" (i.e., directly foretelling the future) and "allegoric" dreams (i.e., requiring interpretation or decoding; PEARLS, for example, stood for the shedding of tears, APPLES for sexual pleasure). Artemidorus takes into account the possibility that one dream symbol can have a variety of meanings, which makes his ancient text vastly superior to most modern popular guides to interpreting dreams.

Modern dream psychology includes studies of the duration of dreams, their occur-

rence in phases of rapid eye movement (REM), and their tension-reducing effect. Dream symbolism is explained differently by different researchers, according to their initial assumptions and approaches. Freudian psychoanalysis found in the world of dream symbols a "royal road," "a vital and flexible relationship to the various symbols of life" [I. Caruso, quoted by Lurker]. Since Freud's theory begins with the development of the libido and was elaborated in a period of sexual repression, he believed that the repression of sexual experiences and fantasies from early childhood, along with other sexual topics, were of critical importance for the interpretation of dreams. In more liberal times Freud's views have been and will continue to be modified. But according to a

Dream Symbols: Pharaoh's dream. Hans Holbein

Dream Symbols: Winged spirit of dreams. Cartari, 1647

popularized version of Freudian theory, long pointed objects (e.g., OBELISKS, lances, TOWERS, MENHIRS, ARROWS, SWORDS) are male or phallic symbols, whereas concave objects (baskets, goblets, CAVES) are female symbols. Such acts as climbing STEPS, horseback riding, swimming, or wrestling, are interpreted as veiled images of sexual intercourse. In Alfred Adler's psychology of the individual, the images in dreams refer to the dreamer's confrontations with issues of power and self-affirmation, whereas the psychology of Carl Gustav Jung (1875–1961) has been called (ironically) "psycho mythology" (see FAIRY TALES). For the symbologist, Jungian interpretations of dreams are of great importance, because they supplement traditional, received modes of interpretation with the clinical experience of analytical psychologists. In the present volume the Jungian approach is presented primarily in quotations from the psychologist Ernst Aeppli (1892–1954).

In ancient Egypt priests had already developed a technique of dream interpretation, based on the assumption that dreams contained milder versions of future events; thus, a dream of sitting in a GARDEN meant that the dreamer would experience great joy in the future. In ancient China, on the other hand, dreams (*meng*) were interpreted as predictions of events directly opposed to their contents; death in a dream, for example, predicted longevity in the waking

world. In the Bible certain dreams are taken very seriously, in accordance with the ancient Middle Eastern tradition that understands them as divine inspiration (e.g., the dreams of Pharaoh, interpreted by Joseph in Genesis 41), but a dream can also be a mere fantasy of "wish fulfillment": "As a dream when one awaketh; so, O Lord, when thou awakest, thou shalt despise their image" [Psalm 73:20]. According to Ernst Jünger, we glimpse in dreams "for a moment the wondrous tapestry of the world with its magic figures."

dualities Symbolic structures whose significance resides in the tension between two components, each one of these components being less expressive in isolation. The cave paintings of the Ice Age already made use of a dualistic program. Pairs of opposites of every sort can be the basis for similar bipolar orderings: day/NIGHT, man/woman, life/death, animal/human, in ancient China YIN/YANG (i.e., approximately, fertility/activity), HEAVEN/EARTH, God/DEVIL, ABOVE/BELOW, purity/sin, SUN/MOON, in alchemy SULFUR/MERCURY (i.e., that which burns/is volatile). The repeated ordering of the world into new dual structures is itself apparently "archetypal" and is universal. It is not clear where this tendency to organize material in terms of opposites originates. It is conceivable that the self's experience of the outer world, at the very beginning of the history

Duality male/female brought by alchemist to higher unity. M. Maier, *Atalanta*, 1618

Duality of fire and water intertwined in Aztec symbol for "war" (atl-tlachindli)

of the human race, was the basis for the division of the cosmos into pairs of opposites confronting one another. The more common hypothesis, however, which views the duality of the two sexes as the initial stimulus, is debatable. In many nonliterate civilizations the society is divided into two complementary halves which are defined by religion. The modern political arena usually features two powerful parties in opposition to each other. Absolutist religions divide the world into true believers and "heathens" (those who do not share this faith). This world-view of thesis (including the self) and antithesis is dynamic in nature and is so deeply rooted that it is unlikely that any ideal synthesis will resolve such dualism. In pictorial representation dualities are represented by such pairings as EAGLE/SNAKE or DRAGON/dragon-slayer. (See also OGDOAD, WEDDING.)

Duality sun/moon, alchemist's symbol for all polarity. M. Maier, *Symbola*, 1617

duck An aquatic bird and domesticated animal of less symbolic importance than the GOOSE. Ducks in the wild were first hunted, then domesticated (in Egypt as early as 1500 B.C.) and often depicted in art. The contexts in which ducks are portrayed there (and in Eastern art as well) suggest erotic allusions the precise nature of which can no longer be determined; we find something similar in Hellenistic art, which pairs Eros (see CUPID) or maidens with ducks. In Gaul the duck was the sacred animal of the Sequani people and their goddess Sequana (the deification of the Seine). In China the word for duck (*ya*) was taboo in many areas because it also meant "penis" or "homosexual," depending on the region. A "duck's

Duck. Hohberg, 1647

EGG sect" is said to have imposed a strict vegetarian regime (including duck's eggs) on its members, but it was outlawed because of supposed debauchery within the sect. The duck attracted the attention of Hohberg, the baroque author of emblematic verse: "As under water often ducks do dive/ But bob right up again all hale, alive,/ Might sinner, luckless, choose a wat'ry grave,/ Were not God present, life and soul to save." In East Asia the attractive mandarin duck (*yüan-yang*) has positive connotations: it always lives in pairs and symbolizes a good marriage (see WEDDING CUSTOMS). Figurines portraying these ducks are a popular gift to married couples, and similar designs adorn the blankets and curtains of nuptial beds.

dwarfs   Usually associated symbolically with secret powers, agility, and knowledge about hidden TREASURE, dwarfs play an ambiguous role in folk traditions. On the one hand, they are survivors of an earlier order of creation. Like GIANTS, they represent a pre-human world, and thus they flee when we approach and jealously hide their treasures underground (see CAVES). Heroes like Dietrich of Berne are their enemies and conquerors. Dwarfs, despite their short stature, often have great powers at their disposal: for example, the legendary dwarf-like Corrigans are said to have built the megalithic structures of Brittany. In Norse mythology dwarfs and elves, especially black elves, are extremely clever creatures, generally hostile to both gods and mortals. They also have magic powers and can be defeated only through trickery—e.g., by being trapped into having to solve a puzzle that keeps them rooted to the spot until a sunbeam strikes them, turning them into STONE. Living beneath the surface of the earth, they have ties to the world of the dead; these "little people" are often thought of as inhabitants of the underworld (see AFTERLIFE).

The dwarfs of popular tradition are usually inscrutable, stubborn, distrustful, little old men (sometimes with BIRDS' feet), but occasionally helpful to humans out of gratitude. In this sense the little stone figures in parks and gardens symbolize the secret but benevolent powers of nature that bless growing things. This view of the dwarf may go back to pre-Christian notions of secret guardians of the earthly kingdom, expressed in the modern area by the view of Paracelsus (1493–1541) that gnomes were guardians of the "ELEMENT" EARTH. Miners' legends portray dwarfs as guardians of precious metals who punish irreverent human intruders but free trapped miners. (Snow White's seven dwarfs are themselves miners, and clearly benevolent.) Nevertheless, symbolic tradition conserves the predominant image of dwarfs and similar creatures (e.g., goblins and leprechauns) as uncontrollably roguish, mischievous, even malicious.

In Central America, dwarfs (e.g., "Chanekes" in Veracruz, or the Tlaloques of the Aztecs) are traditional symbolic figures, usually associated with caves, forests, rain, and fertility or sexuality. (See also BES.) In Hindu myth the fifth avatar of the god Vishnu is the dwarf Vamana, who was nevertheless able to traverse the world in three strides and defeat the demon Bali.

All of these dwarfs are fantasy creatures with little connection to the medical phenomenon of dwarfism as it is understood today, although the existence of real-life dwarfs presumably was the basis for these traditions.

eagle The "KING of birds" is known as a symbol of titanic might and valor, thus primarily a HERALDIC symbol in many coats of arms and national emblems, for reasons of symmetry often bestowed with two heads (the double eagle). Ancient books of animal lore attributed to the eagle the power to gaze directly into the SUN without blinking and to traverse regions of the heavens to which humans had no access. One Old Babylonian text, of which unfortunately only a fragment survives, tells of the ascension of King Etana, borne into the HEAVENS by an eagle. Ancient sources report the custom of releasing an eagle at the funeral of a ruler: the flight of the eagle, as the body was cremated, symbolized the departure of the ruler's soul to dwell among the gods. In Palmyra in ancient Syria the eagle was associated with the sun-god. It was said to be capable of rejuvenation like the PHOENIX. One process of rejuvenation involved the bird's plunging three times into the water; hence the eagle as a symbol of baptism and depicted on baptismal fonts. Its high flying was seen as a parallel to Christ's ascension. The sun was also said to rejuvenate the eagle ("The eagle, when in time his feathers fly no more,/ Renews, restores himself, made young by solar flame" [Hohberg, 1675]), an indication of the salubrious effect of spiritual light. As a slayer of SNAKES and DRAGONS the eagle is a symbol of the triumph of light over the darker forces; eagles with snakes in

their beaks are portrayed in many cultures, e.g., in the national symbol of Mexico. Gothic windows portray the eagle carrying its unfledged young up into the sky to teach them to gaze into the sun. In Christian iconography the eagle appears frequently as a symbol of John the EVANGELIST, as an attribute of ascended prophet Elijah and the resurrected Christ; indeed, the eagle generally has only positive associations (energy, renewal, contemplation, acuity of vision, royal bearing), which made it for the Ancients the attribute of JUPITER. In the Christian era the masterly virtue of justice came to be associated with the bird, but also the sin of arrogance, presumably because it gazes into the distance and seems to ignore that which is at hand. In Freemasonry the double eagle is the symbol of the 33rd Degree of the Scottish Rite, with a crown atop the two heads and a sword held horizontally in its claws (motto: Deus meumque ius—God and my right).

"*Quauhtli*" (eagle) is the 15th of the 20 days of the Aztec calendar, a symbol presaging martial qualities in those born under this sign, but also a tendency to plunder and steal. Two elite "orders" of Aztec warriors were called "Eagles" and "Jaguars," embodying on earth the polar DUALITY of heavenly powers (sun and STARS), one taking as its symbol Mexico's largest bird, the other its largest beast of prey. The goddess Cihuacóatl (SNAKE-WOMAN) was also called Quauh-Cihuatl, or eagle-woman. She wore a crown of eagle's feathers and was believed to be the leader of all women who had died

Eagle as victor over the satanic dragon. Hohberg, 1675

Eagle plunging into water. Bestiary, Bibliothèque de l'Arsenal, Paris (11th century)

in childbirth (giving birth to a child was treated as an act of military heroism, the equivalent of capturing a prisoner). In ancient China, as well, the eagle was an image of strength and power ("ying," the word for eagle, is the homonym of the word for hero). An eagle on a rock was the symbol of a warrior poised for hand-to-hand combat; an eagle on a PINE-tree, that of longevity with undiminished powers. The eagle in combat with a snake goes back to the bird Garuda in Hindu mythology, which is also reminiscent of the insignia of the Aztec capital Tenochtitlán (now Mexico City).

The eagle is, with the lion, the animal appearing most frequently in European coats of arms, but always portrayed in a stylized, symmetrical manner most unlike the eagle in nature. The eagle's legendary heroic qualities led many rulers to take it for their insignia: kings of Germany and Poland, dukes of Bavaria, Silesia, and Austria, margraves of Brandenburg. A striving for symmetry in head-on two-dimensional depictions soon

favored the double eagle, already in evidence in Oriental antiquity and from 1433 on in the insignia of the Holy Roman emperor. After the empire was dissolved (1806) the double eagle was the symbol of imperial Austria (until 1919), czarist Russia (until 1917), the Serbian kings, and even today, part of the national insignia of Albania. It has been speculated that the two-headed eagle originally relates to the double function of Roman emperor and German king. The minnesinger Reinmar of Zweter used in his insignia a three-headed eagle with additional heads at the tips of its wings. The historian of heraldry A. G. Böckler in 1688 connected the German words *Adler* (eagle) and *Adel* (nobility) in verse: "And from that *Adler* German *Adel* came;/ Without the bird, were neither lord nor dame./ Imperial *Adler* keepeth *Adel* safe,/ 'Neath Eagle's wing doth Noble walk in state." Elsewhere Böckler writes: "The eagle is the king among feathered beasts. His stern gaze can regard the sun; he always gets his prey; he rejuvenates himself; he flies highest; and his passing overhead is a universal augur of victories to come. And because Romulus on the Aventine Hill was first to see an eagle, he took it as a good omen, and had an eagle rather than a flag borne before his army. There are six kinds of eagles, all of them birds of prey, but only the smallest and most inferior of them will attack a carcass. The eagle is not the personal symbol of the emperor but rather the symbol of the Holy Roman Empire. The eagle on a field of gold refers to God the Father, whose star shines bright, bringer of serenity, inspirer of awe."

In psychological symbology the eagle is seen as a "mightily winged creature in the heavens of the mind" [Aeppli]; dreams of

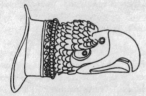

Eagle: Ancient Mexican lip plug, god, Aztec

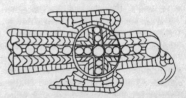

Eagle: Ostrogoth eagle brooch, ca. A.D. 500

Aquila.

Eagle: Woodcut in Psuedo-Albertus Magnus, Frank-furt, 1531

Ear: "Goddess" Heresy (=Reformation), donkey's ears. A. Eisenhoit, ca. 1580

eagles are thus viewed favorably, except when "thoughts of eagles" swoop down on ordinary objects, indicating the "consuming passion of the intellect" is producing doubts about the dreamer's everyday life. It is understandable also in this context that the eagle became the symbol for St. John, the evangelist most firmly established in the intellectual realm. There is little sense here of the compromises often expedient or unavoidable in everyday life. Medieval bestiaries compare the eagle to the first man, ADAM. The "king of all birds" floats high in the heavens but swoops down to earth the moment it spots food there. Adam, too, originally dwelt close to heaven but then caught sight of the forbidden fruit and was pulled down from the heights of glory. "After his incomparable flight through the heavens he once more drew close to the lusts of the flesh and lost all enlightenment" [Unterkircher].

ear A surprisingly important part of the body, from the viewpoint of the symbologist. "What the ear hears will shake a person's insides" [Hildegard of Bingen]. From antiquity onward the ear was thought of as the seat of memory, and in early medieval art the Annunciation was often portrayed naively as the penetration of the DOVE (representing the Holy Ghost) into Mary's ear. Because of the resemblance between the external ear and the spiral coil of a snail's shell (in human anatomy, the words "helix"

and "antihelix" are used), there came to be a symbolic association linking the ear, the snail, and birth (which resembled the emergence of the snail from its shell); it was said of some gods and demigods that they had been born from out of their mothers' ears. Ear lobes are pierced in many civilizations so that wooden, jade, or gold studs, RINGS, or other inserts can be worn. For this reason pendulous earlobes came to be seen as a symbol of nobility and merit: the highest-ranking Incas were called "*orejones*" ("big-eared") by the Conquistadors. In Europe, on the other hand, the DONKEY ears of KING Midas (and classroom dunces) were an object of ridicule. SAVAGES in remote parts of the world were once reported to have such inordinately long ears that they could wrap them around their bodies like a cape.

We speak of people "pricking up their ears" as DOGS and CATS literally do, or being "up to their ears" in debt; a person alert to shifting trends is said to have "an ear to the ground." The Pythagoreans of antiquity took a ringing in the ears as a sign of divine inspiration; in German and in Yiddish the phenomenon corresponds to the (English) "burning" of our ears when we are being discussed "behind our backs."

earth One the "four ELEMENTS" of classical tradition, and a concept charged with many symbolic associations ("down-to-earth," "earthiness," "earth mother," "I'll see you under the earth first" . . . .). In many ancient cosmologies the earth is represented by a maternal (see MOTHER) goddess (Greek Gaea, Latin Tellus, Germanic Nerthus, Polynesian Papa), and less often by a male divinity (Egyptian Geb). "Hail to thee, Earth, mother of humanity, may you grow in God's embrace, and be filled with fruit, for the use of your children" [Aeschylus, 525–456 B.C.]. The "holy MARRIAGE" (hieros gamos) of HEAVEN and earth appears in many ancient myths and rituals, especially in fertility rites and in the mysteries of the goddess Demeter. For the ancient Chinese the earth was a SQUARE, like the four-cornered chassis of a CHARIOT, and heaven was a circular canopy or BALDACHIN over it. Heaven and earth (t'ien-ti) were synonymous with the totality of the cosmos. There are often FOUR PILLARS or TREES at the four corners of the earth, protected by supernatural guardians, e.g., for the Maya of the Yucatán peninsula, four ceiba or kapok trees (yaxché, Latin Ceiba pentandra) and in the sacred center an AXIS MUNDI or a world-TREE; the four points of the compass (or five, when the center is added) are associated with particular COLORS. Earthquakes are always understood as expressions of powers, either divine or hostile to humanity, that threaten the cosmic order and must therefore be appeased. The desired stability of the earth is also symbolized by STONES and ROCKS. The structure of the TEMPLE is a common architectural translation of the ideal structure of the earth.

In the classical (Occidental) system of correspondences, the element earth is asso-

Earth: the god Khnum makes humans from clay. Egyptian relief

ciated with the melancholy temperament, "BLACK bile," autumn, and the spleen; in ancient China, on the other hand, with the center, the number two, yellow, the ox, and sweetness of taste. St. Hildegard of Bingen (1098–1179) expresses an original system of symbols in her De operatione Dei: "The living earth is the Church, which, with the teachings of the Apostles, bears the fruit of righteousness, as they originally preached to their disciples. They were to be like a plant, growing green with the vitality of the true faith, a plant the seed of which they received in God's word. And they were to be trees bearing fruit in accordance with God's law, so that neither fornication nor adultery should find their way into their seed, but that they might rightfully beget children and send them into the world." In classical antiquity the "holy goddess Tellus, who yields up nature's goodness," was also portrayed holding a CORNUCOPIA and—in the frequently copied text Medicina antiqua—implored to provide suffering humanity with medicinal herbs and their healing powers. In the Middle Ages the "heathen" text, which began "Dea sancta Tellus," was corrected to read "Deo sancto" ("Holy God") but not otherwise changed.

In Islamic tradition, earth is important as the material from which the first humans are made. Allah is said to have sent his ANGELS to gather earth in seven different colors. The earth refused at first to give up any of its substance, until finally the angel of death completed the mission, stealing soil of the seven colors. After the death of humanity, the earth's contribution was to be returned to it. Allah then created ADAM, and the various races came from him: WHITE, BLACK, BROWN, YELLOW, GREEN (the olive-skinned people of India), half-black (the Nubians), and RED (the "SAVAGE" peoples). In medieval Latin texts the material from which Adam was made is called limus, which was translated as "mud" ("loam") or "glue" ("[bird-]lime"). Hildegard of Bingen writes that the mud was "boiled" by the FIRE of the soul until it was flesh and BLOOD. Mud appears in many myths of creation as the material from which the gods made the first mortals, e.g., in ancient Egypt, the ram-headed god Khnum, or, in the Babylonian Gilgamesh epic, the goddess Aruru, who molded humans as if she were a Neolithic potter.

egg Its symbolic import is determined by a variety of characteristics: it is fragile, usually WHITE, a repository of new life, with a shape resembling that of the testicles. The legend that the world originated out of a primal egg is not only an Orphic myth of creation (black-winged NIGHT, after being courted by the Wind, brought forth an egg, out of which Eros or Phanes emerged; compare CHRONUS) but is found in Polynesian, Japanese, Peruvian, Indian, Phoenician, Chinese, Finnish, and Slavic traditions as well. Many heroes were also said to have not been born but rather come from eggs, e.g., the Dioscuri Castor and Pollux (the egg came from Leda, whom Zeus, in the form of a SWAN, had impregnated), or an ancient king of southern Korean legend. The new life that lies dormant in the egg came to be associated with life-energy, which led to the egg's importance in mystic healing and fertility rites, and to the burial of eggs along with the bodies of the dead, to nourish them on the journey into the next world (see AFTERLIFE). The SUN and the MOON were also frequently associated with heavenly GOLD and SILVER eggs, respectively. In general the egg symbolizes a primeval embryonic form from which the world later

Egg: Alchemist breaking down the "philosophical egg." M. Maier, *Atalanta*, 1618

emerged. As an image of a totality enclosed within a shell, it suggests that the creation was completely planned from the very beginning. In the Christian world the chick breaking out of its shell came to symbolize Christ rising from the dead; the white COLOR of the shell symbolizes purity and perfection. In the imagery of ALCHEMY, the "philosophical egg" is the primal matter which will later transform itself into the philosopher's STONE; this egg already contains in embryonic form everything that it will need to reach maturity, the yolk suggesting the anticipated GOLD. Many symbolic customs involve the egg, e.g., the use of the Easter egg as a sign of the fertile awakening of nature, but also through the already mentioned association with the Resurrection. In popular magic, an egg is sometimes buried as part of specific rituals which also refer to its fragility (hostile powers were believed to hold themselves in check lest they bring about its destruction). There is an Austrian custom of the *Antlassei*, an egg laid on Maundy Thursday and then blessed, which is buried to ward off misfortune. It can also be thrown over the roof of the house and then buried where it strikes the ground, to protect the house against LIGHTNING.

Egypt Presumably the oldest highly advanced civilization; often seen as a symbol for everything ancient and secret. The SPHINX or the pyramids are for many the proof that Egypt, with its mummies, its burial scrolls, its deities with the forms or heads of animals, embodied a spiritual mastery of the wisdom of vanished ages (see ATLANTIS) undreamt of today. The assumption that peoples of earlier ages were closer to divine wisdom than their descendants is reflected also in the image of a primordial "GOLDEN AGE." In fact, however, the struggle for existence then was generally harder than in modern times. In the Nile Valley permanent states and kingdoms, stone architecture, and written language were realities at a time when the civilization was still marked by ancient notions (including animal TOTEMS) that dominated spiritual life. Men and women of "modern" civilizations find these notions puzzling and suspect that they conceal sublime secrets. Since much in Egyptian culture was "mummified" for almost 3,000 years until the Mediterranean civilizations took notice of it in the Hellenic period, it was inevitable that Egypt should appear to the Greeks and Romans a repository of great secrets. Herodotus (485–425 B.C.) wrote in the second book of his *History*: "The Egyptians, they said, were the first to discover the solar year, and to portion out its course into 12 parts. They obtained this knowledge from the stars. (To my mind they contrive their year much more cleverly than the Greeks. . . .) The Egyptians, they went on to affirm, first brought into use the names of the 12 gods, which the Greeks adopted from them; and first erected altars, images, and temples to the gods; and also first engraved upon stone the figures of animals. (. . . .) They are religious to excess, far beyond any other race of men" (translated by Rawlinson). In modern times it became customary to call almost anything mysterious "Egyptian"—from DREAM books to the symbology of ALCHEMY. This was not taken seriously by historians, but on closer examination it has been determined that in fact many characteristics of early religions, religious mysteries, and symbols are ultimately of Egyptian origin.

Eight Immortals: fan, sword, gourd, castanets, flower basket, bamboo, flute, flower

Eight Immortals, The In the traditional Chinese system of symbols, eight residents of the ISLANDS OF THE BLESSED. Chang-kuo-lao is thought to have been a BAT that then transformed itself into a human. He carries a hollow bamboo pole (for making sounds), and frequently a PHOENIX feather and PEAR of longevity. Chung-li-chüan was an ALCHEMIST who turned mercury and lead into "yellow and white SILVER," possessed the "philosophers' STONE," and could float through the air. Han-tsiang-tse could accelerate the growth of FLOWERS; he is associated with the flute. Ho-hsien-ku is a woman with a magic LOTUS-blossom. Lan-ts'ai-ho is in some accounts ANDROGYNOUS, and carries a basket containing blossoms or fruit, and occasionally a flute. Li-t'ieh-kuai walks with a crutch like SATURN as depicted

in Western ASTROLOGY. His body is said to have been reduced to ashes once when his soul was traveling, so that he had to assume the body of a crippled BEGGAR; he is associated with a gourd from which a BAT emerges. Lü-tung-pin carries a SWORD capable of killing demons. It is said that in lieu of payment at an inn he painted on the wall two cranes that attracted many guests but flew away once they had made up for his debt. Ts'ao-kuo-chiu, the patron saint of actors, wears courtly dress and is usually seen holding a pair of castanets. These eight, the *"pa-hsien,"* are usually portrayed together on a terrace, greeting Shou-hsing, the god of longevity, as he flies in on a crane. They are a favorite subject of Taoist iconography. For the symbolism of the number eight, see NUMBERS.

El Dorado Refers, in general usage, to a symbolic place of great abundance, wealth, or opportunity; in some languages, it may refer to a "find" of a highly specialized sort ("a true El Dorado for stamp collectors"). Originally, however, the term referred to a person—in Spanish, it means literally "the gilded one"—a cacique, or chief, of the ancient Chibcha kingdom in what is today Colombia, whom the conquistadors sought to capture because of the tremendous quantities of GOLD that were said to be on his land. On a feast-day the ruler of a similar kingdom would cover his entire body with gold dust, ride a raft out into the Guatavita Lagoon, and then plunge into the WATER, washing off all of the precious metal as a sacrifice. After the Spanish conquests it was discovered that these territories were not as rich in gold as the Spaniards had believed. (Compare COCKAIGNE.)

elecampane   The composite *Inula helenium*, was prized not only as a medicinal herb: it is said that Helen of Troy was holding it when Paris carried her off (hence *helenium*). In Christian symbology the plant, because of its medicinal effects, came to stand for deliverance from the disease of sin: "As Helen's flower cheers us, turns the sickly fit,/ Is poison's antidote, restores us, makes us whole,/ So, too, doth hearten love of Church and Holy Writ,/ And bring through vale of tears unscathed the Christian's soul" [Hohberg].

elements   Not merely organizing principles of traditional cosmologies, elements have little to do with the modern concept of an element as defined in chemistry and physics: in the history of symbols, they are also

Plant. *Enula. Campana.*

Elecampane. Hohberg, 1675

points of reference, key terms within many interlocking systems of correspondences. Thus they are associated over and over again with COLORS and the points of the compass. What different past civilizations had in common in this regard was that they saw as interrelated concepts that today are the province of separate disciplines. Classical antiquity distinguished two primal qualities (*stoicheia*), the active and the passive (reminiscent of the East Asian DUALITY of YIN AND YANG), from which two active qualities, "dry" and "moist," and two passive qualities, "cold" and "warm," were derived. Combinations of these four yielded the actual elements: EARTH (dry + cold), FIRE (dry + warm), AIR (moist + warm), and WATER (moist + cold). This leads to numerous analogies. The element earth corresponds to autumn, BLACK bile, the spleen, and the color of LEAD, from which the melancholy "temperament" follows; air corresponds to spring, BLOOD, the HEART, bright colors, and the sanguine temperament; water corresponds to winter, phlegm, the brain, the color WHITE, and the phlegmatic temperament; fire, finally, corresponds to summer, yellow bile, the liver, the color of fire, and the choleric temperament. Ancient theories of healing, whose effects extended into modern times, sought to bring these components into harmony in each patient, not letting any one dominate and thus throw off the balance. Plato's *Timaeus* posits the symbolic equivalence of the "four elements" with geometric forms: "To earth, then, let us assign the cubical form; for earth is the most immovable of the four and the most plastic of all bodies. . . . And to water we assign that one of the remaining forms which is the least moveable [the icosahedron]; and the most moveable of them to fire [the tetrahedron]; and to air that which is intermediate [the octahedron]. Also we assign the smallest body to fire, and the greatest to water, and the intermediate in size to air; and, again, the acutest body to fire, and the next in acuteness to air, and the third to water" (55d–56a, translated by Jowett). The dodecahedron symbolizes the totality of the world. In the complex imagery of ALCHEMY,

Elements: The four-based system, associated with the seasons. Augsburg, 1472

a duality relating the two first principles SULFUR AND MERCURY, was of great importance: by adjusting the proportions and concentration of each (the balance of the "fixed" and the "volatile"), alchemists proposed to achieve the "solar quality" (see SUN) of GOLD. Paracelsus (1493–1541) added "sal" (literally, "SALT") as the third of these "philosophical elements," to express "palpability." Only with the progress of the natural sciences did it become clear that this symbolic view of nature was not in accord with chemical and physical fact and that its value was strictly theoretical and philosophical.

In East Asian cosmology, as developed in ancient China, the first principles are YIN AND YANG, and to the four occidental points of the compass is added the center. The elements in this system are water, wood, fire, earth, and metal; air is not included. An ancient verse notes: "Water breeds wood

but destroys fire; fire breeds earth but destroys metal; metal breeds water but destroys wood; wood breeds fire but destroys earth; earth breeds metal but destroys water." The *Book of Annals* (see FIVE) explains: "It is in the nature of water to moisten, and to flow downhill; in that of fire to blaze and shoot upward; in that of wood to be bent or straight; in that of metal to be submissive and to let itself be formed; in that of the earth to be planted and harvested." Wood is associated with the East and the color blue; fire, with the South and red; metal, with the West and white; earth, with the center and yellow. Thus in the Asian system, too, the elements (*wu-hsing*) form the plumbline for the symbolic organizing of the world, the five known PLANETS, qualities of taste (salty, bitter, sour, spicy, sweet), types of animals (hirsute, feathered, scaly, armored, unprotected), and principal human organs. In addition to this system of fives, a system of eights (see EIGHT IMMORTALS, I-CHING) was used for the philosophical organizing of the universe. For the Gnostic symbolic mythology of the four elements and their masters, see CAIN. In Sanskrit the elements are called collectively *tattwa* and individually *prithivi* (earth), *apas* (water), *tejas* (fire), *vayu* (air), and *akasha* (the ether). In our own time, following yogic and tantric teachings, meditational journeys into these "elemental cosmic states of vibration" have been combined with theosophical symbols (earth—a yellow square; water—a reclining silver crescent; fire—a red TRIANGLE with its apex pointing upward; air—a light-blue disk; the ether—a VIOLET oval) to form a system of "*tattwa* therapy" [Tetgmeier, 1986].

Elements: Man, where the four meet. Weiditz in Pliny's *Historia Naturalis*, 1587 ed.

elephant An animal with positive symbolic associations; in Asia it is tamed to carry kings, and esteemed for its intelligence. A WHITE elephant announced the birth of Gautama Buddha and is also the "Vahan" symbol of the bodhisattva, the one who brings salvation from worldly entanglements. In Hinduism, Ganesha, god of writing and wisdom in general, has an elephant's head (with a single tusk) and is the chief of the attendants of the god Shiva. In ancient

Elephant falls over with sawn tree. Hohberg, 1647

China the elephant was a symbol of strength and intelligence, much as in Occidental antiquity, for which this exotic animal, on the basis of its intelligence, was an attribute of the god MERCURY. Because of its longevity, moreover, it was considered a symbol of the victory over death. In the Christian imagery of the *Physiologus* of late antiquity and in medieval bestiaries, the elephant's chastity is celebrated; it will procreate only after eating MANDRAKE root. The same sources also relate that the female elephant gives birth in a swamp while the male protects it from deadly SNAKES. If the elephant leans against a tree that has been partly sawed through, and collapses, even 12 other elephants cannot set it back on its feet; but the newborn elephant lifts it with just its trunk. The symbolic interpretation: ADAM AND EVE knew nothing of sexuality in Eden and only after eating the APPLE (the fruit of the mandrake) did they come to know one another. Then Eve gave birth to Cain on the vile WATERS. Neither the Law of Moses

Elephant-headed Indian god of wisdom Ganesha. Bronze

nor all of the prophets can lift Adam up: only Christ, the holy and spiritual elephant. Hohberg's emblematology of the baroque period (1675) makes poetic use of the inflexibility of the elephant's legs (which in classical antiquity had also been a supposed attribute of the elk): "When foolish elephant doth lean against a tree/ Sawed halfway through, behold, it topples, beast and all./ Who feels the most secure, ill chance fells suddenly,/ And mocks and shames, who EARTHLY things his stay did call." The *Physiologus* also refers to an elephant attacked and weakened by a blood-sucking snake; the elephant collapses and, dying, crushes the oppressor as well. "Take care lest the serpent find you . . . , lest it suck the true faith out of you, and bring you down, even with

Elephant: Mammoth. Stone Age cave drawing, Les Comberelles, France

itself," and the sinner hears these words on the Judgment Day: "Away from me, ye who are damned, into the eternal FIRE which is prepared for Satan and his ANGELS!" Finally, the positive associations with the elephant are further augmented by reports that the burnt hair or bones of the animal effectively ward off demons.

The ancient Chinese lauded the "chastity" of the elephant, which supposedly procreated only in the water (in hiding). In Europe it was an exotic animal that appeared only occasionally in fable. The elephant was more common in depictions of PARADISE, and after the time of the Crusades even appeared on coats of arms (of the counts of Helfenstein; as a supporter, in the arms of

Elephant: Hindu stamp, ca. 2000 B.C.

Oxford). In 1464 an Order of the Elephant was established in Denmark. A white elephant appeared in the arms of the kingdom of Siam (today, Thailand) until 1910. In the symbolism of analytic psychology the elephant (because of its trunk) is viewed as a phallic creature, but also as embodying the wisdom of the ages and peacefully reposing strength. In dreams it symbolizes terrestrial reality for those whose relationship to reality is not clearly enough worked out, and a major statement about the power of life. In China the elephant (*hsiang*) has similar symbolic value: because of a similarity in Chinese pronunciation "to ride on an elephant" (as the heroes of legend often did) is synonymous with "happiness."

emerald "The emerald brings reason, wisdom, and dexterity," wrote the alchemist Leonhard Thurneysser (1583). It was associated with the sign of Virgo (see VIRGIN) and the planet JUPITER. Ancient volumes devoted to STONE lore attributed to the emerald the power to dispel STORMS and liberate slaves. Its GREEN color made it a powerful symbol for WATER and fertilizing RAIN. (Bluish emeralds were sacred to VENUS.) It was often said that the stone was especially powerful in the spring. According to medieval legend, emeralds actually come from the depths of HELL—in some versions, from Lucifer's CROWN—but this makes them even better suited to combat demonic forces. An emerald was often placed under the TONGUE of a magician pronouncing a ritual incantation. In later centuries, books on **precious**

stones recommend emeralds for children who suffer from bad dreams; in Christian symbology, the stone symbolizes "faith and hope."

In the writings of ancient Mexico we find many references to green gems, which may have been either emeralds (Aztec *chalchihuitl*) or varieties of JADE. As in Old World tradition, the green color was associated symbolically with the fertilizing rain.

emperor (German *Kaiser*) A figure less firmly established in European symbology than that of the KING, and appearing less often in fairy tales, legends, and figures of speech: the emperor, whose "divine right" is more significant in continental tradition than is that of kings, stands at an even greater remove from his subjects than does the king; moreover, the emperor himself, as we shall see, is already a symbol and thus ill-suited to take on new layers of figural associations. In the West we have two linguistic traditions for designating this personage. The English word "emperor" and the French *empereur* go back to the Latin *imperator*. The German *Kaiser* (and its Slavic cognate *czar*) are also of Latin origin, going back to the Latin name Caesar, the family cognomen of (Gaius) Julius Caesar (100–44 B.C.) before it became an imperial surname. Pliny the Elder is our source for the legendary etymology according to which Julius Caesar was so named because he was cut (*caesum*,

Emperor and electors. Incunabulum, Augsburg, 1472

Emperor fetched by Death. From a *Dance of Death* (*Danse Macabre*), Paris, 1486

Emperor: Shih Huang-ti, the first emperor of China, ca. 259–210 B.C.

past participle of *caedere*) from his MOTHER's womb, that is, delivered by what we have come to refer to as Caesarean section. Caesar had himself addressed as "JUPITER Julius," and Augustus Caesar (63 B.C. – A.D. 14), the first actual emperor of Rome, permitted himself to be revered even during his lifetime within the cult of Roma, the tutelary goddess of the city. Upon his cremation he was officially deified by the Senate and a separate priesthood created to worship him in perpetuity; an EAGLE soared up into the HEAVENS, symbolically carrying his soul with

Emperor Henry IV. Chronicle of Ekkehart of Aura, 1113–14

it. Commodus (A.D. 161–192) had himself revered as a god (namely Hercules) during his lifetime; Aurelian (A.D. ca. 212–275) called himself "lord and god" (*dominus et deus*). Divine legitimization was supposed to hold the empire together, but Christianity, which was then on the upsurge, could view these claims only as blasphemy. We see some reflection of the claim of imperial divinity in the subsequent notion that Charlemagne or the Holy Roman Emperor was a sacred figure—crowned by the Pope, and thus designated as the protector of the Church and the executor of divine power on earth.

In other cultures we encounter similar ideas, for example in ancient Egypt, where the pharaoh was a living god. (In 332 B.C. ALEXANDER THE GREAT was hailed there as "the son of Amon.") Sargon (or Sharrukin), the founder of the Babylonian empire (ca. 2300 B.C.), called himself "the king of the FOUR regions of the world," placing the symbol for divinity before his name. In ancient China the emperor was "the son of HEAVEN"; the *tenno* of Japan claimed to be descended from the gods. The emperor in each of these cases feels that he is an instrument of divine authority, with which he identifies himself to a great extent. It is in this sense that he is not merely the starting point for symbolic analogies (compare KING) but himself already a symbol.

end of the world Found in the myths of widely divergent cultures throughout the world, this symbol represents the transitory nature of all matter and all life—including the life of every person—none of whom endures forever. As the men and women of each epoch came to feel the approach of their own demise, their myths invariably situated the end of the world in the near future. Ancient civilizations favored the image of repeated cycles in which the world was first destroyed and then created anew; in the Occident, however, time is viewed linearly, as a straight path moving inexorably from the creation of the world to its ultimate destruction. (This is why the Occidental calendar numbers years in linear fashion, whereas the civilizations of ancient Mexico used cycles of years.) In Christianity the world as we know it ends with the Last Judgment, in which the Lord passes judgment on all men and women, sending the good to HEAVEN (the paradise lost in the GARDEN of Eden is thus restored) and the wicked to HELL.

The idea that the end of the world was an imminent catastrophe was often made more believable, especially in times of great change or upheaval, by reference to the calendar (millennia), astrology (conjunctions of the planets JUPITER and SATURN, as in 1524, and recurring after every five orbits of Jupiter and three of Saturn), prophecy, and visions.

In 13th-century Old Norse literature, the *Edda*'s famous prophecy of the "fate of the gods" (*Ragnarök*, usually mistranslated as "twilight of the gods") treats such ominous occurrences as the increase in numbers of hostile demons, the darkening of the SUN, more severe winters, CHAOS in the area of personal relationships, trembling of the world-TREE—ALL of them portents of the coming battle of the gods against giants and horrible creatures (the WOLF Fenris, the hell-hound Garm, the SNAKE Midgard). In this battle the cosmos is to be destroyed, the sun will drop from sight and the stars fall out of the sky—but a new age will succeed the old, and a new couple (Lif and Lifthrasir) will found a new cycle of human life. This vision

of the end of the world clearly shows traces of Christian influences: it is a Germanic reaction to the way that that tradition had envisioned the end of the world at the approach of the first millennium after Christ.

For the Christian world the most famous depiction of the destruction of the earth and the human race as we know them is found in the Book of Revelation (also called the Apocalypse, or the Revelation of St. John the Divine, although it is not clear that its author is the same as that of the fourth Gospel). This most puzzling text in the Holy Scriptures was often understood as a prophecy of the imminent Last Judgment, after which the new paradise, built around the "heavenly JERUSALEM," was to be established on earth. (See also GOG AND MAGOG.)

In Islam it is believed that all of those who are not adherents of the religion of the prophet Muhammad—all non-believers, heretics, and idolators, all those who live by violence, all rebellious spirits, demons, and DEVILS—will be condemned. Allah's seat of judgment will be the throne from the Kaaba (see CUBE), transported from Mecca to the temple mountain of Jerusalem. Israfil, the ANGEL of death, will blow his TRUMPET to summon all of the dead to the Valley of Jehoshaphat. A giant set of SCALES placed before the temple will weigh their deeds. A cord will be strung across the valley to serve as a BRIDGE; all of the just will be able to walk across, but the wicked will plunge into the fiery pit of hell.

In the TAROT deck, "Judgment" is the XXth card of the Major Arcana. An angel blows a trumpet over open graves from which naked people are emerging. The card is interpreted as representing renewal, rejuvenation, and the desire for immortality.

Eos The Greek personification of dawn (Latin Aurora), in Homer a "rosy-fingered" goddess; she was also called Hemera ("day") when in the morning, accompanied by the morning star (VENUS), she preceded the CHARIOT of her brother Helios (the SUN). She ran with the sun across the sky and, as Hespera ("evening"), left it at the far western edge of Oceanus, which circles the entire earth. Her husband was the Titan Astraeus, and their children were the STARS and the WINDS; but, as the result of a curse by the love-goddess Aphrodite, she had numerous lovers, including the hunter Orion (see SCORPION). With Tithonus, the brother of King Priam of Troy, she had a son named Memnon, who was killed by Achilles in the Trojan War; this caused her such sorrow that her tears still cover the earth with DEW. (See also CICADA.)

Eulenspiegel, Till (Low German: Dyl Ulenspegel) Said to have been a real-life German from Schöpenstedt in Brunswick, buried in Mölln in 1350. He became the title character of a beloved volume of folk tales recounting the pranks (see FOOL) that the cunning (if at times brutal) peasant plays on conceited guildsmen and townspeople; Till's humor often consists of carrying out literally instructions that were meant figuratively. Till (or Dyl, Tyll, Tile; compare TELL) was a common peasant name, whereas Ulenspegel (the source of the French word *espiègle*, "scoundrel") was apparently a vulgar nickname derived from *ulen* ("wipe, sweep") and *Spiegel* (literally "mirror," but in the language of hunters "buttocks"). The first Low German version of Till's adventures was published in 1478 in Lübeck; the

Eulenspiegel: Title page, first known edition. Strasbourg, 1515

first High German version, in 1515 in Strasbourg. "Eulenspiegel-ry" has become proverbial; Till figures prominently in many ballads, novels, comedies, and musical compositions (Richard Strauss, Reznicek). In Charles de Coster's *La légende d'Ulenspiegel* (1867) the hero is a rebel against the Spanish oppression of the Netherlands. In puppet shows and popular theater, the role corresponding to that of the earlier Till—the merry prankster—was subsequently assumed by the clown or "Kasperl" figure, who with wit and cunning prevails against powerful opponents and makes the audience laugh in the process. In the *commedia dell'arte* this is the role of Arlechino (Harlequin).

Evangelists, symbols of the In the Book of Ezekiel, the prophet recounts his vision as follows: "And I looked, and, behold, a whirlwind came out of the north, a great cloud, and a FIRE infolding itself, and a brightness was about it, and out of the midst thereof as the COLOUR of AMBER, out of the midst of the fire. Also out of the midst thereof came the likeness of FOUR living creatures. . . . And every one had four faces, and every one had four WINGS. . . . And they sparkled like the colour of burnished brass. . . . As for the likeness of their faces, they four had the face of a man [to the front], and the face of a LION, on the right side: and they four had the face of an OX on the left side; they four also had the face of an eagle [to the rear]" [1:4-7, 10]. This tetrad, or tetramorph, is doubtless influenced by the ancient Eastern notion of four guardians, or supporters of the HEAVENS, stationed at the four corners of the EARTH (or on the four sides of the firmament), which in turn go back to the STAR symbolism of the zodiac. Similarly, in the Book of Revelation, four "beasts" are positioned around God's THRONE: "And the first beast was like a lion, and the second beast like a calf, and the third beast had a face as a man, and the fourth beast was like a flying eagle" [4:7]. This appears to be a symbolic representation of the four signs of the zodiac in the "fixed cross," which today is made up of the signs Taurus, Leo, Scorpio, and

Evangelists: Luke as a painter, with the bull. Schedel's *Weltchronik*, 1493

Aquarius (the middle sign from each of the four seasons). The eagle replaces Scorpio; the man, Aquarius. Although the four Evangelists were originally associated with the four cherubim around God's throne, the identification of them with the tetramorph of Ezekiel and Revelation prevailed from the fifth century onward, apparently under the influence of astrological doctrine. St. Jerome (A.D. 348–420), Doctor of the Church, jus-

tifies this identification as follows: St. Matthew is symbolized by the (winged) man because his gospel begins with the human incarnation of Christ; St. Mark, by the lion, because his begins with "the voice of one crying in the wilderness" (John the Baptist); St. Luke, by the sacrificial animal, the calf, because his begins with the priest Zacharias; and St. John, finally, by the eagle, because his contains the most vivid account of the spiritual ascent to the heavenly heights. Even earlier Irenaeus of Lyon (ca. A.D. 180) had likened the four Evangelists, in terms of their ideal qualities, to the tetramorph, without assigning individual symbolic creatures to individual Evangelists; Irenaeus referred only to the quadruple effect of the Gospels: the lion was an expression of royal energy; the calf, of sacrifice; the man, of the human incarnation of Christ; the eagle, of the divine breath (*pneuma*) that blows through the Church. The four great prophets of the Old Testament (Isaiah, Jeremiah, Ezekiel, and Daniel) and the four fathers of the Church (Augustine, Ambrose, Jerome, and Gregory I) were soon likened to the four Evangelists. "Doubtless the very choice of creatures particularly embodying majesty, strength, insight, and mobility, goes back to ancient motifs and prehistoric traditions. There is also a connection to the long-

Evangelists: Symbols of John, Luke. Decoration, Calixtus baptistry, Cividale (ca. 770)

Evangelists: Symbols of Matthew, Mark. Decoration, Calixtus baptistry, Cividale (ca. 770)

established cardinal virtues of wisdom, courage, prudence, and justice" [Heinz-Mohr]. In the early Middle Ages the pictorial representation of the Evangelists as four philosophers in Roman togas, with BOOK and lectern, is often accompanied by the symbolic figures of the tetramorph. There are also texts comparing their gospels to the four rivers of PARADISE. Of the animal figures, the "lion of St. Mark" became especially famous, appearing in the coat of arms of the Republic (until 1797), then the city, of Venice. In its right forepaw it holds an open book with the inscription *"Pax tibi Marce evangelista meus"* ("Peace be with you, Mark, my Evangelist"). To this day St. Mark's lion adorns the flag of the Italian navy and merchant marine.

eye The most important organ of the senses, always associated symbolically with LIGHT and intellectual perspicacity; at the same time, the eye has long been considered not only a receptive organ but also the transmitter of "beams," the image of spiritual expressivity. Evil creatures or those with great magical powers were thought to have eyes whose gaze rendered others powerless or turned them to stone: for example, in Greek mythology, Medusa (see GORGONS), killed by Perseus with the aid of a MIRROR; in Celtic legend, King Balor of the Fomoriers, whose "evil gaze" did its work on the battlefield when four men raised his eyelid. The supposed emanations of the "evil eye" (in Italian, *malocchio*) led to the production

Eye: God sees everything. Hohberg, 1647

of countless amulets. Of greater symbological importance, however, are positive associations with the eye. In many civilizations the SUN is understood to be an all-seeing eye, or is symbolized by an eye, as is the case for Horus, the youthful EGYPTIAN sungod, who is portrayed elsewhere as a hawk or with the head of a hawk. The characteristic stylization of his eye, the Udjat-eye, was considered a powerful amulet. In Christian iconography the eye, surrounded by sunbeams or inside a TRIANGLE with its apex pointing upward, is a well-known symbol of divine omnipresence or of the TRINITY. Similarly, the highest orders of ANGELS (cherubim and seraphim) have eyes on their WINGS as signs of their pervasive wisdom. There were religious practices (specific blessings and votive candles) to alleviate eye ailments, and eyes were washed at holy shrines and SPRINGS. (See also BLINDNESS.) For St. Hildegard of Bingen (1098–1179) the eye

Eye: A demon with three eyes. Tibetan costume

Eye: Three idols. Alabaster, Tell Brak, Near East, ca. 3200 B.C.

Eye: The "Udjat" eye, a symbol from amulets of ancient Egypt

is an organ of multiple symbolic significance: "The eyes, which see so much, refer to the stars in heaven, which shine everywhere. The WHITES of the eyes symbolize the purity of the ether, their brightness its brilliance, the pupils the STARS above. Their moisture shows us the moisture that comes from the upper waters to sprinkle this same ether, lest it be damaged by the higher celestial fires [of the empyrean]." Every function of the eyes has its analogue in the macrocosm and in moral life. "Discernment, too, shines bright and clear, like the whites of the eyes. A person's insight sparkles within, like the eyes' power of radiation, and reason shines in each being like the pupil of the eye."

In the symbolism of FREEMASONRY, the "all-seeing eye" in the triangle and surrounded by sunbeams (a symbol of the Trinity, as mentioned above) appears in many lodges over the master's chair, a reminder that the wisdom of the Creator, the "Great Master Builder of All Worlds," penetrates all secrets; the eye is in some contexts also called the "eye of providence." In modern psychology the eye functions symbolically as the organ of light and consciousness, for it permits us to perceive the world and thus makes it real for us. "Eye-dreams have to do with this act by which we grasp existence. . . . We often dream of eye ailments. They naturally relate to the limits that our complexes place upon the visual acuity of the psyche; to our inability in this state to see

life properly. . . . When consciousness is in danger of dissolving (with the approach of death), then many eyes gaze upon the critically ill person" [Aeppli]. For psychoanalysts the eye (like the mouth) as a dream-image is often a veiled symbol for the female sexual orifice. There has been a great deal of discussion about the origin of the symbolic representation of a third eye in Indian and Lamaistic art, taken to signify supernatural vision and illumination. Fossils of reptiles of the Mesozoic era show an eye in the forehead, and in the tuatara of New Zealand it is still vestigially present. We are unable to say with authority, however, whether Asiatic iconography reflects the lost history of organisms and their vestigial body-parts, or whether the single round eye of the cyclops Polyphemus and the fairy tale of the Brothers Grimm ("One-Eye, Two-Eyes, and Three-Eyes") are somehow related to this motif.

eyeglasses In the emblem book *Atalanta Fugiens* (1618) by the Rosicrucian Michael Maier it is written that nature is to the alchemist in search of knowledge like "a guide, staff, spectacles, and lamps." His eyeglasses (Latin *perspicila*) symbolize the keen gaze of the educated seeker, who follows Nature's footprints as she carries along her FLOWERS and fruits. This keen gaze also characterizes sculptures and paintings of the personification of Temperance, who can distinguish between life's necessities and gluttony, as well as representations of Doctor of the Church St. Jerome (A.D. 348–420), patron saint of scholars—although such glasses were not yet in use in his lifetime. (Lens-grinding dates from ca. A.D. 1280) There have long been popular idioms in German that refer to charlatans as "eyeglass salesmen" (and which substitute "eyeglasses" for the English "bill of goods"). In any language, as far as idioms are concerned, spectacles often assure not a keen but a predetermined view of life: e.g., "looking at the world through rose-colored glasses."

fairy tales Treasure troves for the symbologist, and not only in the Western world. The documentation of the fairy tales of distant, nonliterate civilizations has brought to light a wealth of symbolically significant motifs. The cosmology that prevails in these stories is that of "a different reality; we find ourselves in the world of symbols, characteristic images each of which has special significance within it. . . . Research into fairy-tale motifs must begin with precise investigation of variants, going beyond the narrower confines of the genre. We must seek out the origins—e.g., Greek and Christian elements in German fairy tales. . . . We can arrive at an interpretation only with help from every possible discipline—specialized narratology, folklore, history of religion, legal history, and so on and on" [E. Hörandner, quoted by Lurker, 1979]. The approaches of the various (at times conflicting) disciplines have led in recent decades to different ways of understanding fairy tales. Analyses of individual texts have made psychological, especially Jungian, interpretations accessible to a broader audience. Their point of departure is the belief in the existence of archetypes, i.e., innate "molds" into which the contents of experience are "poured," always yielding similar symbolic formations and chains of motifs from culture to culture, even in the absence of historical influences or connections. These archetypes, according to Jung (1875–1961), are operative not only for fairy tales and myths but also for DREAMS, visions, and rituals, which are to be understood as "interpretations of symbols"; they have their origin not in individual experience but in the "collective unconscious," a repository that extends far beyond what any one person could ever experience. Historical ethnologists propose a completely different approach to the world of fairy tales and their symbols: they focus on the peculiarities of the storyteller, his or her personal and social environment, the manner of transmission of the tale, transformations imposed by the compiler, and so forth. Details of cultural history are also studied—details which, in the view of the psychologist, are insignificant. According to Lutz Röhrich, "establishing a parallel between the fairy tale and the dream is more useful for the psychiatrist than for the fairy tale," which is of course not necessarily an indictment of the psychological approach, since any way of coming to grips with a question has something to be said in its favor.

Fairy Tales: Little Red Riding Hood. Etchings, Ludwig Richter (1803–1884)

Recent decades have also seen the publication of anthroposophic-psychological attempts at interpretation: their ultimate goal is to document typologically the universal sequence of stages in the maturation of any individual personality, and they seek to do this by establishing parallels between those stages and the plot elements and symbolic motifs of fairy tales. In general, all of these approaches confirm our belief that the traditional fairy tale is not an arbitrary succession of images but rather a limited set of motifs tied together in a logical plot sequence that moves toward a preconceived goal in accordance with the laws of its internal structure. This belief holds true, of course, primarily for fairy tales that are preserved in their complete form: tales from distant civilizations have often undergone distortion and fragmentation before they reach those who seek to document them.

Many of the symbolic elements discussed in the present volume are prominent in fairy tales, and the reader is referred to the specific articles in question, such as ANGEL (helping spirits), ANT, APPLE, BALL (the golden ball of fairy tales), BATHS AND BATHING (as in the Fountain of Youth), BEAR, BEE (showing the way), BEGGAR (the supernatural being in disguise), BIRD, BLOOD, BOAR (symbol of savage nature), BREAD, BRIDGE, BULL, CAT, CHARIOT, DARKNESS, DEER, DEVIL, DOG, DONKEY, DOVE, DRAGON (the monster), DWARFS, EAGLE, EGG, EYE, FALCONS AND HAWKS, FEATHER, FIRE, FISH, FLOWER (sleep-inducing or miraculous), FOREST, FORTRESS, FOX, FROG, GARDEN, GATE, GIANT, GOLD, GOOSE, GRIFFIN, GROVE, HAMMER, HARE, HEART, ISLANDS OF THE BLESSED, KING, LADDER, LIGHTNING, LILY, LION, LIZARD, MAGPIE, MILL, MOON, MOUNTAIN (the glass mountain), NIGHTINGALE, OVEN, OWL, PEARL, PIG, PRECIOUS AND SEMIPRECIOUS STONES, QUEEN, RAVEN, RING, RIVERS (the border with the unknown world), ROBBER, ROCK, ROOSTER, ROSE, SALT, SHADOWS, SILVER, SPIDER, STARS, STORK, SUN, SWALLOW, SWORD, THUNDER, TORCH, TOWER, TREE, TRIADS, UNICORN, VIRGIN, WATER, WATER SPIRITS, WELLS (as gateways to the underworld), WINE, WINGS, WITCHES (negative female figures), WOLF.

falcon and hawk Words with similar and overlapping denotations but very different connotations in English; in most other languages and cultures, however, there is no separation of the noble keenness of the falcon from the rapacious predatory nature of the hawk. In mountainous regions, the symbolic import of the falcon is comparable to that of the EAGLE. Even today (especially in Arab countries) falcons or hawks are used for hunting, but only for reasons of sport, since modern rifles make it possible to hit small game even from a great distance. In ancient Egypt the falcon (especially the peregrine) was a royal symbol, because its gaze was said to paralyze birds as does the countenance of the Pharaoh his enemies. The falcon or hawk was most importantly a manifestation of Horus, the great god of the sky, presumably because the bird flew so high. Horus was portrayed as a hawk or with a hawk's head and a human body. Other divinities similarly portrayed were the sun-god Ruê (with a disk representing the SUN on his head); Mentu, with a double crown of feathers; Seker, the god of the dead (as a mummified hawk); and Hariêse with the crown of Upper and Lower Egypt. The noticeable markings in the feathers under the hawk's EYES create the impression that they are open even wider, and thus Horus' "all-seeing Udjat-eye" became a symbol for visual acuity and imperviousness to injury, as

Falcon-headed god Horus. Relief, Abydos, ca. 1290 B.C.

well as a treasured amulet. In Europe the hunting falcon is the attribute of several saints (e.g., St. Hubert, the patron saint of hunters), and less often, as the hunter of the "ever lustful" HARE, a symbol of the triumph over the sensual. In Norse mythology Odin could take on the form of a falcon to fly across the earth, but the tricky Loki could perform the same transformation. The hawk is presented as a negative symbol in medieval bestiaries. It drifts through the air around meat markets, they say, to snatch up scraps: an image of humans who think only of their stomachs. "Of larger birds the hawk is fearful, but he hovers around baby birds, spying his chance to seize them. So, too, do degenerates approach delicate young people and lead them into vice" [Unterkircher]. In our day a "hawk" is also one who favors a belligerent foreign policy, in opposition to the "DOVE" (the symbol of peace).

Fasces: "Fear augments honor." J. Boschius, 1702

Fama An allegorical-symbolic figure in the literature of ancient Rome, derived from the Greek goddess Pheme (in Hesiod). Fama is the personification of unverifiable rumor and an individual's (usually bad) reputation; Ovid describes her as a messenger of simultaneous and indistinguishable truth and falsehood. In Virgil, she is a hideous creature with multiple, constantly blabbering MOUTHS and TONGUES. In the fine arts she is portrayed with WINGS, so that rumors can spread quickly, and a TRUMPET, with which she "trumpets" truth and falsehood.

fasces ("bundles") An ancient Roman symbol of bureaucratic authority; in modern times a POLITICAL symbol. In public appearances high magistrates and some priests were preceded by attendants (lictors), each carrying a bundle of rods tied together with a leather strap. Six lictors preceded a praetor; 12, a consul. In the middle of each bundle was an executioner's AX symbolizing judicial authority—except within the city of Rome itself, since the citizens of Rome had the final word in questions of capital punishment. The fasces were of Etruscan origin, the Etruscans using a double-headed ax. Italian Fascism took its name from the fasces.

The bundle of sticks or rods symbolized the concentrated power of the different classes of Italian society; the blade of the ax, absolute authority.

Fates (Latin Parcae ["the allotters"] or Fatae, Greek Moirae ["the child-bearers"]; corresponding to the NORNS of Germanic myth). The three are referred to either as daughters of the NIGHT (the Greek goddess Nyx) or, along with their sisters, the Horae, as daughters of Zeus and Themis; here, too, the abstract symbolism is of greater importance than the religious aspect. In the fine arts the Fates are shown SPINNING the thread of life. The first of the three, Clotho, does the actual spinning; the second, Lachesis, catches up the thread; and the third, Atropos, "she who cannot be turned back," cuts it off, thus ending the life of the mortal in question. Occasionally, too, they are portrayed with spindle, scroll, and SCALES.

The Roman Parcae were originally two goddesses of birth named Decuma and Nona ("nine," for the NINE months of gestation), but under the influence of the Greeks the TRIADIC structure was introduced, along with the three corresponding roles in the allotting of human destinies.

father As a symbolic figure, the father— primarily, it seems, because our society is a

Father: Return of the Prodigal Son. Bible illustration, Ludwig Richter

patriarchy—stands for supreme authority and even divinity (God the Father, the "father of the gods," the *paterfamilias*, the "fatherland," etc.), and, in the symbology of analytic psychology, for the superego as the ultimate judge. KINGS and EMPERORS were long thought of as representatives or deputies of the "Heavenly Father" and as the father of their nations. The religion of the Bible has distinctly patriarchal features, which have been conserved in Christianity ("Our Father who art in heaven"). The theologian Friedrich Heiler (1892–1967) considered the relationship of a person in prayer to that of a child to its father; this relationship, for Heiler, was "an elemental religious phenomenon." Feminists, however, reject this view.

In the imagery of ALCHEMY, the SUN is considered to be paternal ("The sun is the father, and the moon the mother, of the philosopher's stone"—Tabula Smaragdina), whatever the gender of the word for "sun" (feminine in German, *die Sonne*, but masculine in French, *le soleil*).

Faust or Faustus, Dr. Johannes (English John; also Georg or, in Goethe's version, Heinrich). Symbol of the relentless pursuit of eschatological knowledge, undaunted even by HELL itself. The historical Faust, thought to be a wandering "magician" and astrologer (ca. 1480–1540), has not been precisely documented. Unlike the idealized Promethean hero of Goethe's drama (Part 1, 1808; Part 2, 1832), the Faust of earlier tradition (e.g., the anonymous German account of 1587, which was translated into English as

Historie of the Damnable Life, and Deserved Death of Dr. Iohn Faustus and provided one basis for Christopher Marlowe's *Doctor Faustus*, 1604) was more simply a man who made a pact with the DEVIL; Mephistopheles, a devil temporarily in service to humanity, supposedly brought about the downfall of the wandering scholar (in Staufen-im-Breisgau, Germany) and carried off his soul to hell. The legend is a manifestation of popular distrust of scholars and charlatans who carried around with them incomprehensible BOOKS in foreign languages and led comfortable lives without either being nobles or doing manual labor. The most obvious explanation to the "common man" was that this was possible only with the help of the devil—who would eventually reclaim the soul that had been pledged to him. Countless legends, books of charms, and literary works treat this timeless figure, probably originally, like his contemporary Paracelsus (1493–1541), a student of the occult, but a roving outsider.

feather The symbologically prominent characteristic of lightness, which was once believed to lift BIRDS into the air as if by magic (in many legends, garments made of feathers give their wearers the ability to fly); of particular importance as a symbol of Ma'at, the ancient Egyptian goddess of justice and

Faust in his study. Etching by A. Matham (detail), 1642

Feathers adorn Aztec warrior. Codex Mendoza

universal legal order. Ma'at wears on her head a single OSTRICH-feather, with whose weight that of the heart of the deceased is compared in the "judgment of the dead"; the deceased is found to be just only if guilt has not made the heart heavier than Ma'at's feather. The heart must be *ma'ati* (in accordance with Ma'at) if the deceased is to "become Osiris" (i.e., take on immortality). Four feathers adorned the headdress of the god Anhur (Onouris), a warrior-figure from the Upper Egyptian city of This. The dispeller of demons Beset (see BES) was also portrayed with a CROWN of feathers. Feathers were important in the civilizations of ancient Mexico, where they were used to make crowns, capes (see COAT), banners, and mosaics glued on shields. The polyvalent god and hero Quetzalcóatl was portrayed as a SNAKE (in Aztec, *cóatl*) covered with the iridescent-green feathers of the quetzal bird. These feathers also made up the insignias of Mexican kings. In the headdresses of the native inhabitants of the North American prairies, each feather originally recalled an act of bravery of the wearer. The expression "to deck oneself out with borrowed plumes" (i.e., to take credit for someone else's accomplishments) goes back to an ancient Roman fable, in which a CROW adorns himself with the feathers of a PEACOCK. In the Grimms' tale "Mother Holle," the feathers

shaken out of the bedding symbolize flakes of snow falling from the HEAVENS. (See also WING and ARROW.)

fig Mediterranean fruit-TREE frequent in depictions of the Garden of Eden (see PARADISE): fig-leaves constitute the minimal clothing with which the first humans, Adam and Eve, are to cover their nakedness. Figs and grapes (see WINE) are often named in classical antiquity as attributes of Dionysus, the god of intoxication, and of the phallic god Priapus, which suggests an erotic association. In medieval etymologies the Latin word *peccare* ("to sin") is associated with the Hebrew word *pag* ("fig"); see also FIG, SIGN OF. In Gnostic and Islamic traditon the two forbidden trees in the Garden of Eden were the OLIVE-tree and the fig-tree. In Christian symbology there are many portrayals of the "dried-up fig-tree," a symbol of heresy. The Bible mentions the fig-bearing tree, on the other hand, as one element (along with the olive-tree and the grapevine) of the carefree life to be lived in paradise. The baroque poet Hohberg expressed something of the religious symbolism of the fig in the following verses: "The fig tree's fruit is pleasing sweet and draws/ Both young and old its succor for to know./ Thus, too, we rush with even greater cause/ To taste the fruits that from God's grace do grow" (1675). In Buddhism the *bodhi* or fig-tree is a symbol of enlightenment, since it was under it that in 528 B.C. Siddhartha Gautama (Buddha) attained deep inner knowledge of nature and the suspension of earthly suffering.

Fig-leaf design on coin (stater) of ancient Greece. Camirus, ca. 550 B.C.

Ficus.

Fig. Hohberg, 1675

fig, sign of the A symbolic gesture, believed to ward off the evil EYE and offer general protection against hostile beings and powers; from the Italian *fica* ("vulva," "fig"). It consists in making a fist with the thumb protruding between the index and middle fingers, and is interpreted as an "obscene gesture" of contempt, symbolic of sexual intercourse (compare LINGA and YONI; and the use of the word "fig" in Shakespeare, e.g., in *The Second Part of Henry IV,* V, 3: "Fig me like the bragging Spaniard"). The belief in its power to ward off evil may go back to the reasoning that spirits are sexless and thus easily frightened by any allusion of a sexual nature (which may also explain the intermingling of genital images, PENTACLES, and Christian symbols on alpine rock drawings). In many regions a red coral amulet depicting the sign of the fig is popular even today on watch-chains and necklaces. Medieval depictions of the Passion show hostile bystanders along Christ's route mocking the Savior with the sign of the fig.

fire The apparently living ELEMENT, which consumes, warms, and illuminates, but can also bring pain and death, has conflicting symbolic associaitons. It is often a holy symbol of the hearth (as in the tradition of the vestal VIRGINS who tended the sacred flame in ancient Rome), of inspiration and the Holy Spirit (which in the form of "cloven TONGUES like as of fire" descended upon the Apostles at the first Christian Pentecost; see Acts 2); in ancient Mexico the lighting of the new fire to begin the new year was a sacred ritual. On the other hand, fire also has the negative aspect of the fires of HELL, the blaze and the lightning bolt (fire from the heavens) that destroy, and the volcanic fire that spews forth from the bowels of the earth. It should be noted that the very beginnings of civilization, of human life, millions of years ago, are marked by the successful "quest for fire"; prescientific theories of our origins used to speak of earlier "primal" humans, "living free in the wild," but these creatures cannot be called human. Fire is the only one of the "elements" that humans can produce themselves; it thus symbolizes the similarity of mortals and gods. Many Greek and Polynesian myths described it as having originally been the property of the gods, then stolen by or for mortals. Essentially divine, fire can thus be seen as "purifying": destroying evil or the physical

Sign of the fig: Rock-crystal amulet, set in gold. Southern Germany, ca. 1680

Fire-making ritual in ancient Mexico. Codex Nuttall

forms of witches and other possessed beings; erasing the blemish of sin in the PURGATORY of Roman Catholic doctrine; and similarly holy in Parsiism (the doctrine of Zoroaster, or Zarathustra) as well. The Assyrian incantations known as "Maqlu" and "Shurpu" series seek largely to counteract evil spells by enlisting the aid of fire: "Boil, boil, burn, burn! . . . I tie you up, I bind you, I give you over to Gila, who singes, burns, and binds, who lays hold of sorceresses. . . . As this goat's skin is torn asunder and cast into the fire, and as the blaze devours it . . . so too may the curse, the spell, the pain, the torment, the sickness, the sin, the misdeed, the crime, the suffering, that oppress my body, be torn asunder like this goat's skin! May the blaze consume them today. . . ." Both *maqlu* and *shurpu* are translated as "burning"; this is a particularly clear manifestation of the belief that fire can annihilate sorcery. Shakespeare used a similar incantation for his witches in *Macbeth.*

The custom of running barefoot (unharmed) over hot coals (Greek *pyrobasia*), which was practiced in many parts of the earth, is believed to have originated as a springtime purification ritual, which it still was even in the modern era in Tibet (15th day of the first month). Fire is generally considered a "male" element (in opposition to "female" water) and as an image for vital force, the HEART, potency, enlightenment, the SUN (see PHOENIX). The VIRGIN Ocrisia was supposed to have been made pregnant by a SPARK and to have given birth to King Servius Tullius. Incantations addressed fire

Fire: Elijah's burnt offering, before the priests of Baal (I Kings 18). Holbein, 1530

Fire: Two Dominicans are burned as Satanists. Woodcut, Geneva, 1549

as a supernatural being. At the highpoint of the ancient Roman shepherds' festival Parilia (April 21), those seeking purification leapt over burning straw; in Greek myth the goddess Demeter, wishing to cleanse the demigod Demophoon of the soot of the earth and make him immortal, placed him in a hearthfire. TORCHES were carried around the mentally ill or those in need of atonement. The ever-present threat of fire to ancient cities was combatted by the symbolic pouring out of water whenever anyone spoke the word *ignis* ("fire").

In general, because of the ambiguous nature of fire, the gods and other supernatural beings associated with the "element" (e.g., Loki in Norse mythology) are essentially "tricksters," never to be trusted. Still, the notion of fire as "the flame of life" dominates, especially with its progressive taming over the course of civilization: this is indicated by our preservation of ancient customs like torchlight processions and lighting midsummer's-night fires on mountaintops—or eating by candlelight in the era of electrification. In Church ritual as well, candles play an important symbolic role (e.g., at the altar, communion, baptism) as bearers of spiritual light. (See also THORNS AND BRIARS, and SALAMANDER.) In dream symbolism fire is closely associated with the hearth (the center of home and family), food preparation, and the melting down of metals, as well as romantic ardor. "When the dreamer approaches a great fire, or sees the sky lit up with the glow from a fire, this suggests the presence of divine powers"; but "the fire of passion, including the passion of the intellect, is also a flame that can consume us" [Aeppli]. (See also OVENS, STOVES, AND FURNACES.)

fish Since they inhabit the WATER, which in analytical psychology is understood to symbolize the unconscious, they thus embody "live" material from the depths of the personality, relating to fertility and the life-giving powers of the "maternal" (see MOTHER) realms within us. In many ancient religions fish were associated with love goddesses and the fertility of nature. But at the same time the fish is "cold-blooded," symbolically "not governed by the heat of passion," and for this reason is a sacrificial creature and particularly appropriate for sacred meals. In the modern era, the fish (Greek *ichthys*) as symbol is understood as an acronym for the Greek "Iesous Christos Theou Hyios Soter" ("Jesus Christ, Son of God, Savior"): the fish became a secret sign by which Christians recognized one another in the midst of hostile nonbelievers. It is a fact that the symbol appeared frequently in the early Christian world up till the end of the fourth century, but the acronym explanation is not the only one. The immersion in the baptismal font (Latin *piscina*, literally "fish pond") and the reference to the Apostles as "fishers of men" (see RING) may have been the primary sources; in Mediterranean cultures, moreover, the fish was a symbol of good luck, as it still is in some New Year's customs. A further interpretation involves the conditions of the "Age of Pisces": in A.D. 7 (which is thought to be the true year of Christ's birth) the "golden conjunction" of the PLANETS JUPITER and SATURN occurred three times under the sign of Pisces, and the beginning of spring also fell in Pisces; Christ was interpreted as the first embodiment of the Age of Pisces. Converts were referred to as *pisciculi* ("little fish"), in reference to the Christian *ichthys* (according to Tertullian, A.D. 150–230), and the fish itself, along with BREAD, came to symbolize Communion. Speculative Christian theologians argued that in the Flood of Noah's time the

fish were not afflicted by God's curse and that Christians became their equivalent by virtue of baptism. In medieval art a legendary fisherman named Trinacria, with three bodies with a common head, was interpreted as a symbol of the TRINITY. Fish are common attributes of saints, such as Brendan and Maclovius, the seafarers, as well as Peter, Andrew, Elizabeth of Thuringia, and Anthony of Padua, who is said to have preached to the fishes. In Christian Biblical typology, which sees anticipations of the New Testament in the Old, the great fish that swallows the prophet Jonah and then vomits him out, is related symbolically to the buried but resurrected Christ.

In ancient Egypt fish were eaten by the common people but forbidden to ordained priests and kings. Silent inhabitants of the deep, they were widely perceived as eerie creatures and associated with negative myths (e.g., as eating the phallus of the god Osiris, who was slain by Seth). Nevertheless, individual varieties of fish were considered divine and sacred, e.g., the eel (to the god of Heliopolis) and the perch (to the goddess Neith). This reveals our ambiguous attitude toward the deeper layers of the personality and their contents, which—like the SNAKE—can be interpreted positively or negatively. Legendary monstrous fish in old bestiaries illustrate clearly both fascination and fear of the inhabitants of the deep. In Hindu myth, the god Vishnu is said to have taken on the form of a fish in order to save Manu, the ancestral father of the human race. In an-

Fish as "Uroborus." Initial D, *Missale Gelonense.* Bibliothèque Nationale, Paris, late 8th century

Fish struck by arrows. Shell engraving, Spiro Mounds, Oklahoma

cient China, the fish (*yü*) symbolized happiness and plenty; the combination of fish and water were a metaphor for sexual pleasure. Fish (*sakama*) is a staple in the Japanese diet, either raw (*sashimi*), boiled, or fried in oil. Certain species are traditional symbols in Japan; the carp, for example, because it can make its way through eddies and waterfalls, stands for courage, strength, and endurance. On May 5 ("Boy's Day") a banner with a carp on it is mounted in front of each house, with an additional silk carp for each male child in the family. In the symbology of alchemy, two fish in a river represent the primal essences SULFUR AND MERCURY dissolved in water. In psychoanalytic theory the fish is a symbol for the penis, which in colloquial Turkish is also called "the one-eyed fish." Pisces, the sign of the fish, is the last sign of the zodiac (see STARS), and that of the present era ("the Age of Pisces"; compare WATER SPIRITS), which many astrologers believe is almost over. Those born under the sign are said to strive for fraternity, peace, and perfection; to be attentive; to pursue their goals patiently until they succeed; and to be "cheerfully productive."

The analytical psychologist E. Aeppli points out that the silent, cold-blooded fish is envied and admired for its agility in the water. Its edible tissue is not considered to be meat and thus can be eaten on certain fast days. The miracle in which Christ feeds the multitude includes "fishes" along with the "loaves" [Luke 9:12–17]. "Getting in touch with the fish in oneself means ulti-

mately confronting the cold-blooded primeval forms of human existence. . . . Thus the person who has a profound transformation to undergo, like the legendary prophet Jonah, is for a while swallowed up by his or her unconscious, by that huge fish with jaws like those of a whale, before being disgorged—a transformed being—upon the bright shore of a new consciousness" [Aeppli]. It is worth noting that the ancients, e.g., Aristotle, in their ignorance of the life and habits of fish, believed them to be unisexual, which doubtless influenced the symbolic connotations of these "cold-blooded" sea-dwellers. In early Christian murals in the Roman catacombs, the fish symbolizes Holy Communion, and in depictions of the Last Supper fish appears on the table along with bread and the WINE chalice. The Pope's signet ring, the fisherman's ring or *annulus piscatoris*, refers to Peter's miraculous "draught of fishes," and Christ's words, "From henceforth thou shalt catch men" [Luke 5:1–11].

five A NUMBER whose importance is suggested by the PENTACLE, which can be seen as containing the upright human form, with head, arms, and legs, when the STAR rests on two points with one going upward; in the inverted position, it is a symbol from the realm of "BLACK magic." The Pentateuch (the five BOOKS of Moses) of the Old Testament form the Torah. Jesus fed 4,000 with five loaves (see BREAD), and his five stigmata are commemorated by five CROSSES in altar STONES. Medieval symbolists saw a

Five-petaled blossom, symbol of good fortune (because of the five "gods of happiness")

reminder of the five senses in the five petals of many FLOWERS. In ancient China five *(wu)* was a sacred number: there were five each of "points of the compass" (including "center"), primary colors, tones, customs, spices, kinds of animals (hirsute, feathered, crustacean, scaly, and bare), human relationships, and "classics": *The Book of Annals, The Book of Songs, The Book of Changes* (I-CHING), *The Book of Rituals,* and *The Book of Ceremonies.* Five ELEMENTS (wood, FIRE, EARTH, metal, and WATER) corresponded to the five points of the compass and the five colors. Five forms of earthly happiness were wealth, longevity, peace, virtue, and health; five moral qualities, humanity, duty, wisdom, reliability, and observance of ceremony; five pure things, the MOON, water, the PINE, the BAMBOO tree, and the PLUM. There were also five degrees of nobility, kinds of grain, punishments, and mythical rulers of the distant past. This structure appears to have been worked out in the fourth century and to have been linked to classical Confucianism during the Han dynasty (206 B.C.– A.D. 220).

In the Japanese tradition there are five GODS OF HAPPINESS.

flags Like military banners, at first primarily strategic aids, used to make it easier to observe from a distance the movements of

Flags: Knight with lion banner at gate of city. *Lirer Chronik,* 1486

individual columns of troops. Only later did flags become symbols for the honor of the units displaying them. Whereas the original Roman standards *(signa)* were made of wood and metal, and often crowned by an EAGLE (the inscription "S. P. Q. R." stands for "Senatus Populusque Romanus," "the Senate and the People of Rome"), the present-day flag, consisting of a staff and cloth, originated in the East and was eventually taken over by the Greeks and Romans because it could be more easily carried by a cavalryman. Around the ninth century this form was familiar throughout Europe. In East Asia, too, there were flags with insignia. Genghis Khan's first flag was simply white, and then a black MOON was added. The flags of Chinese emperors were YELLOW; in later centuries a DRAGON and a RED SUN or PEARL were added. Feather-garlands frequently adorned Aztec flags. In Europe flags blowing in the WIND symbolize the charge to victory, and all the symbols of HERALDRY are put to use on them. Bertholet's dictionary of religions calls the flag a "fetish out of staff and cloth, used as a palladium of victory and majesty, especially in the military and in court ritual; also a symbol and attribute of the gods; later reduced to service as a purely politico-military symbol." In Christian iconography the resurrected Christ is often portrayed with a flag of victory (see

Flag bearer of "Lindau" (note linden tree). Jakob Köbel, 1545

Flags: Lamaist temple flag (*dhavaja*). Tibet

LABARUM), or as a (paschal) LAMB that has overcome the forces of darkness. Others with the labarum include the archangel (see ANGEL) Michael, who defeated the rebellious Lucifer, and warrior saints such as JOAN OF ARC; St. George, the DRAGON-slayer; Duke Leopold the Saintly of Austria; and John of Capistrano, who in Vienna raised an army with which to fight the Turks. The scientific study of flags, banners, standards, and the like is called "vexillology," from the Latin *vexillum*, "flag."

Flood, The Great A catastrophe exterminating most of the human race. This symbolically powerful theme, known to us from the Bible [Genesis 6–9], appears earlier in the Sumerian Gilgamesh epic, in which the hero meets the survivor Ziusudra, or Utnapishtim, on the island Dilmun (see ISLANDS OF THE BLESSED) and hears from him the story of his past. In many civilizations we find the theme of punishment for human shortcomings through a catastrophe bordering on the END OF THE WORLD, which is then reversed.

In India the first incarnation of the god Vishnu, in the form of a FISH, saves the earliest ancestor of humanity, Manu, from a great flood by bringing him high up in the Himalayas. In Greek mythology the survivors of the great flood are Deucalion and his wife Pyrrha; they create a new human race out of STONES. In many flood legends the imperiled mortals are saved in SHIPS, like the ARK (from Latin *arca*, literally "box") in which the Biblical NOAH and his family escape death; in the Middle Ages, Noah's ark was often the basis for an analogy with the Church, which was said to save humanity from drowning in sin and moral decay. In the Talmud the parting of the waters when the Israelites crossed the Red Sea (recounted in Exodus 14:15–31) is referred to as an "anti-Flood": in this case, "the waters recede from the earth and dry land appears. This reversal is a sign through which God shows humans that he has adopted a new attitude with respect to them. . . . [This constitutes] God's solemn declaration to the Israelites that he will come to their aid no matter what and will never destroy them again" [Aron].

Flood legends and other legends of catastrophes, mythic symbols of the general endangerment of humanity through natural catastrophes and its own admitted culpability, are found in almost all the cultures of the earth. They are also related to the ancient notion of a cyclical pattern of creation, in which the gods periodically destroy and rebuild what they have made. In ancient Mexico this was represented in the myth of

Great Flood. Illustration of Biblical account, Gustave Doré (1832–1883)

successive "suns": the age referred to as the "water sun" would end with a great flood, in the course of which humans would be turned into APES. (See also OMPHALOS.)

flora Our symbolic, collective designation for all vegetation (as in the expression "flora and fauna") was in ancient Rome the goddess of FLOWERS, portrayed with a CORNUCOPIA of blossoms that she scattered over the earth. Originally a goddess of the (Italic) Oscans and Sabines, she was in time honored by the Romans at the feast of Floralia, which lasted from April 28 until the beginning of May (thus corresponding temporally to Walpurgis Night and May Day festivities). It was a spring festival in which COURTESANS played a major role, and Flora herself was also referred to as a *meretrix* (prostitute). This period of moral laxity was apparently intended to conjure growth throughout the natural realm and can be understood as a specifically agrarian ritual that subsequently evolved into a general celebration. "Fauna," the collective designation for the animal world, goes back to a female counterpart of the nature god Faunus (Greek PAN). According to the poetry of Ovid (43 B.C.–A.D. 17), Flora was in the GOLDEN AGE a nymph named Chloris ("greening"), whom Zephyrus (the west WIND) abducted and made his bride. His wedding gift to her was eternal spring, and this is how she became the goddess and herald of spring. She is also supposed to have given the goddess Juno a miraculous flower with the help of which she became pregnant—without JUPITER's intervention—and gave birth to the god MARS.

flower The flower and the blossom are universal symbols of young life. (Their disappearance, in the song "Where Have All the Flowers Gone," stands for the loss of lives on the battlefield.) Because of the STAR-like arrangement of the petals, the flower is also associated with the SUN, the globe, or the center (e.g., the lotus-blossom in Southeast Asia). It is striking how many flowers are prized and revered not only for aesthetic reasons but also for their psychotropic properties. Sometimes flowers

Flowers as emblems. J. Boschius, 1702

are thought of as more than innocent harbingers of spring: they can designate carnal lust and the whole realm of the erotic, like the nicté-blossom *(Plumeria)* of the Mayas or the ROSE in the medieval French *Romance of the Rose.* Viewed neutrally, flowers are symbols of vitality, *joie de vivre,* the end of winter, the victory over death. In Christian symbology the calyx, open at the top, suggests the receiving of God's gifts, childlike joy in the GARDEN of Eden, but also the transitory nature of all earthly beauty, which can be lasting only in the gardens of HEAVEN. This helps to explain the long-standing customs of putting graves in gardens or planting flowers on them. Since early Christian churches were closely associated with revering the graves of martyrs, the churches themselves were also decorated with flowers. In the Bible flower-blossoms are a sign that God is pleased (as with Joseph and Aaron). A dry stem from which blossoms spring forth also appears in many stories as a sign of hope and divine pleasure. The custom of decorating POLES with flowers and then carrying them in processions may relate both to this tradition and to a general pleasure in springtime floral decoration. The COLORS of flowers are of great symbological importance (WHITE: innocence and purity, but also death; RED: vitality, blood; BLUE: secrecy, fervent devotion; YELLOW: sun, warmth, gold).

In Taoism a spiritual "golden blossom" growing out of the crown of the head symbolizes the highest mystical enlightenment. In the 20-day Aztec calendar, the 20th day-sign is "flower" (xóchitl), symbol of the artistic and the tasteful. Those born under this sign are believed to be gifted for all artistic and artisanal pursuits, but also for sorcery. "Flower Standing Upright" (Xochiquetzal) was the name of a goddess associated with sexuality and fertility. Among her attributes are a floral WREATH in her hair and a bouquet in her hand. "Flower wars" were the ritually limited struggles between neighboring Aztec kingdoms, undertaken only to capture prisoners for human sacrifice on the altars of each side. (See BLOOD.) In what survives of Aztec poetry, flowers symbolize both joie de vivre and transitoriness: "The flowers sprout, and bud, and grow, and glow. From your insides the stalks spring free. . . . Like a flower in the summertime, so does our heart take refreshment and bloom. Our body is like a flower that blossoms and quickly withers. . . . Perish relentlessly and blossom once more, ye flowers who tremble and fall and turn to dust. . . ." In the Bible, similarly: "As for a man, his days are as grass: as a flower of the field, so he flourisheth. For the wind passeth over it, and it is gone; and the place thereof shall know it no more" [Psalm 103:15–16]. Today the ecological threat to blooming plants may be such that the symbolism of many flowers will be accessible to coming generations only through historical literature, when, as the Psalmist wrote, the place thereof shall know them no more.

flowers, language of Especially in the early 19th century, it was not unusual to express difficult messages by means of flower arrangements. A playful flower-symbology had first emerged toward the end of the 18th century, and it was revived a century later. In 1899 G. W. Gessmann wrote that he hoped his guide to this Blumensprache would "remind especially our gracious ladies of this most sensible custom." Here are some samples of this overwrought code, which readers today may find more amusing than ingenious:

ACACIA (white): "Your good heart assures me that our friendship will last."

Agave: "I remain favorably disposed to you despite your knavery."

Amaryllis (red): "I respect you from the depths of my soul."

APPLE-BLOSSOM: "Will the glow of love finally redden your delicate cheeks?"

ASPHODEL: "I expect letters numerous and heartfelt."

Aster (white): "Your true friendship lessens the torment of my misfortune."

Bindweed: "No gaze in the world is so keen, so deep, as the hawk's eye of love."

Bur: "Be assured of my sympathetic attachment and sincerest wish to be of aid."

CARNATION (red): "You will be able to resist no longer, once you see the extent of my esteem and love."

CARNATION (white): "You are the symbol of the closest friendship, for your color remains unchanged until death strips away your petals."

Centaury: "It is bitter like the truth once told, but just as healing."

Cherry-blossom: "My blush at your arrival may reveal to you the quiet fondness that I have for you."

Chive-blossom: "I shall follow your sincere good advice."

Clover (FOUR-LEAF): "Fortune smiles upon me only when I can share it with you."

Corn-cockle: "I live for you alone."

Cotton-blossom: "The blossoms of our union are yet tender; thus do I tend them with careful love."

Cowslip, or "keys of heaven": "The KEY to my HEAVEN lies in your angelic HEART."

CUCKOOPINT: "Though life assail you, despair not! The knowledge that you are good and pure will exalt you."

Cyclamen (see VIOLET): "With purest inclination I respect you above all else."

Dahlia: "My heart is eternally with you; the heart is a thing of the homeland, not of the body."

Dead-nettle: "Your promises of love leave me cold; your promising and gallantry ring hollow."

Field clover: "Let me know when I can see you again."

Forest-rose: "One who is born for quiet happiness, finds contentment only in obscurity."

Forget-me-not: "Three words reveal the wish to meet again: Forget me not!"

Garlic-blossom: "What I feel for you is the utmost indifference."

GRAIN (an ear of): "What you ask, only time can bestow."

Guelder-rose: "However unfeeling you pretend to be, Cupid's arrow one day yet will reach you."

Hazelnut-blossom: "Fear not: innocent love is under God's protection."

Hyacinth (white): "My heart draws me to you, pale dreamer."

Iris: "You fill my heart with joyful hope, only then to plunge it into doubt."

Iris (blue): "Your feigned emotions scatter, and no trace of them remains."

LAUREL-leaf: "The victor's wreath befits you not, but the modest wreath of virtue."

Lavender: "The memory of you is my only quiet joy."

Lilac: "In your every look and word speaks the beauty of your soul."

LILY (white): "You are as innocent as this symbol of innocence."

Linden-blossom: "Sensual love vanishes like the night-dew; love from the soul abides like the golden star of day."

Lupine: "In you I found heavenly charms and splendrous blossoms of the spirit combined with those of the heart."

Marigold: "As eternal as the golden RING of this flower, is the purity of my love."

Meadow saffron: "My heart is kindled by love for you, and I gladly follow the divine emotion."

Mignonette: "Like this flower, quietly fragrant, without the pomp of color, you have pleasing talents without outward show."

Mimosa: "The great and beautiful soul that you contain is grounded in your noble, serious pride."

Mullein (yellow): "Take courage. Fortune yet will bloom for you."

Myrtle-shoot: "It is ever green, for the wreaths that true love weaves never wilt."

NARCISSUS (yellow): "Your being, flirtatious, enraptured, is like this beautiful flower, which arises proudly, only to sink its head in yearning."

Nasturtium: "How shall I suffer, when the prospect of seeing you no longer fills my spirit with joyful hope!"

OAK leaves: "The crown of morality and virtue."

Oleander: "In you jealousy and pomp reign, for nature gave you not a warm, feeling heart but only outer beauty."

Onion-flower: "You can win my love if you show me the tender respect that a gentleman must feel for a feminine creature."

Passionflower: "Your bitter pain will be transfigured in the afterlife by the crown of eternal bliss."

Peony: "Your pride is unbearable."

Peppermint: "Of false hearts, like yours, I can find a surfeit."

Poppy: "Your sleepy, phlegmatic temperament will let no more meaningful emotions emerge from your heart."

ROSE (red): "This is the pledge of love and fidelity."

Rose (white): "Its pale petals signify to you the joy of love eternal and pure, for it lacks all earthly glow."

Rose (yellow): "The color of this flower reminds me of the jealous gaze of your eye."

Rose-petal (red): "Yes!"

Rose-petal (white): "No!"

Rosebud (with thorns): "Love, hopeful, with the doubts of uncertainty. . . ."

Rushes: "Add this basket to the one you have already received."

Snapdragon: "Your wanton mischief will be avenged upon you bitterly."

Snowdrop: "Be glad of the present and future, and grant the memory of a melancholy past no place in your heart."

Sorrel-blossom: "I do not like knowing that you are always following me."

Spurge: "Your nature is so cold that one might think your heart made of stone."

Sunflower: "It turns ever toward the SUN. As sunlight is to it, so is your love to my life."

THISTLES: "The poetry of life sweeps over you, leaving no trace."

Thyme: "Unity of souls is the greatest good."

Tulip: "You silent thing of splendor! Where is your inner value?"

Turk's cap: "Will your stirring, roguish glances do much more mischief?"

Vetch-flowers: "To be envied are all to whom heaven gives the pearl 'loving friendship.' "

Vine-leaves (see WINE): "With your recurring merriment you can restore my high spirits."

Weeping WILLOW: "My heart trembles with the memory of your vanished presence."

Willow: "True friendship presents its arm to us, that we might take it as we walk and bear life's burden."

Yarrow: "Are you in fact as unaware as you would seem?"

Another collection includes the following equivalencies:

Apricot-branch: "Angel of your sex, I worship you!"

Carnation: "My bosom thrills in the rapture of longing."

Crown imperial: "Most adorable of your sex, goddess, I worship you!"

Elder-blossom: "You are becoming colder and colder."

Elm-leaf: "Our love must remain a secret."

Forget-me-not: "Give heed to what this little flower whispers."

Grapevine: "Move closer, and remain true to me."

Kale: "Explain yourself more clearly, if I am to understand you."

Lavender: "Your speech is puzzling."

Lilac: "Let us hurry to the altar, before our youth has passed!"

Moss: "Your obstinacy drives me to despair!"

Narcissus (white): "Frightful! Would you destroy me completely?"

Onion: "You are repugnant to me."

Peppermint: "Why make so much fuss over trifles?"

Poppy: "Why are you so tired?"

Rose: "As you are in bloom, let me rest on your bosom."

Snowdrop: "Purity of heart shines forth in your gaze."

Tobacco-flowers: "You awaken feelings that slumber sweetly within me."

Given the varying meanings that the same flower could carry, it was clearly necessary for both partners to be using the same code.

Only then could the secret messages of love be transmitted accurately.

fly (Greek *myia*, Latin *musca*) Flies of all species are creatures with negative symbolic associations; they can, however, be appeased through specific rituals. Beelzebub (literally "lord of the flies"), the "god of Ekron" referred to in II Kings 1:2, is a Syrian divinity associated with the control of swarming flies, like the Greek "Zeus Apomyios" (or "Myiodes" or "Myiagyros"). In certain cultural contexts the apparently invincible swarms were seen as embodiments of demonic powers. (Compare Sartre's use of them in place of the classical Eumenides—FATES—in his drama *Les Mouches, The Flies*.) The ancients believed that the image of a fly on jewelry offered protection against the "evil EYE." Its Greek name, used figuratively, was the equivalent of our "parasite"; the satirist Lucian (A.D. 120–180) spoke not of making mountains out of molehills but of making ELEPHANTS out of flies. In ancient Persian mythology the enemy of LIGHT, Ahriman, slips into the world in the form of a fly. Swarms of flies are harbingers of disaster in Isaiah 7:18: "The Lord shall hiss for the fly that is in the uttermost part of the rivers of Egypt." Flies are predominantly symbols of satanic beings and swarms of demons, which also plagued the anchorite monk, St. Macarius the Egyptian.

Flying Dutchman A symbolic embodiment of the eternally restless wanderer, a sea-going analogue of AHASUERUS; made fa-

Fly demon Beelzebub. Collin de Plancy, *Dictionnaire infernal*, 1863

mous through Richard Wagner's opera of 1843. The legend of a ghost SHIP whose sighting bodes ill for one and all, was associated with the protracted efforts of explorers to circumnavigate the Cape of Good Hope (1497). A Captain van der Decken is said to have sworn recklessly never to abandon this quest, for all the rest of time, and to have fired his pistol at the constellation Crux, or Southern CROSS (see STARS); from that time on (according to the legend, which became popular around the beginning of the 19th century), he was condemned to sail the sea eternally. Another legendary Flying Dutchman was Captain Barent Fokke, who took a BLACK DOG with him, had signed his soul over to the DEVIL, and was condemned to sail the South Atlantic forever, between Cape Horn and the Cape of Good Hope, without ever entering port.

Fool. Sebastian Brant's *Ship of Fools*, 1494

fog Generally symbolizes an uncertain "gray" zone between reality and unreality. In ancient Celtic myth, it covers the northwest region of the EARTH between the world of mortals and the ISLANDS OF THE BLESSED; in Norse myth, the polar regions of frigid, deathly DARKNESS. The name Niflheim ("foghome") designates those parts of the goddess Hel's domain (see HELL) into which the living cannot penetrate and in which dwell all of the dead except for those whom the VALKYRIES have chosen to fight alongside Odin in the final battle, Ragnarök (see END OF THE WORLD). In the poetry of the Far East, fog is usually a symbol either of autumn or of strange moods in which vulpine spirits (see FOX), for example, can manifest themselves. In Central European fairy tales fog is often explained as boiling, brewing, spinning, or other activities on the part of demonic creatures (DWARFS, WITCHES); the fog symbolizes human uncertainty about the future and the afterlife, and only LIGHT (spiritual illumination) can dispel it.

fool A figure appearing in many fairy tales and legends, and associated with the court jesters of old, who had a sort of "fool's license" to tell the truth without fear of punishment, provided that that truth was presented as humorous satire and jokes. The court jester carried a "fool's staff" (see SCEPTER) and wore grotesquely COLORED costumes (like the young Parsifal) and a "fool's cap" with bells—all of this frequently reproduced in modern-day Mardi Gras dress. The fool as prankster (the proverbial EULENSPIEGEL) has been a hero of popular fiction since the 16th century; the most famous fool in the English-language tradition is King Lear's jester in Shakespeare's play (1606). The fool is also the "O card" of the Major Arcana in the TAROT deck, portrayed as a traveler in rags and tatters, with a small DOG leaping up on him. The symbolism of the card is interpreted as follows: the fool, utterly spontaneous and natural, lacks experience, but also any trace of affectation; he has set out on a journey toward wisdom. This card is the predecessor of our "joker." In a Jewish legend recorded by E. bin Gorion, a wise man went out of his senses because he had concerned himself only with BOOKS and entirely neglected everyday life. He began to act like a fool, and was hired by a KING to serve as his jester. But when his foolishness left him, he reproached his master for narrow-mindedness; the king had him beaten and ejected from the palace. Now he understood the Bible verse "More weighty than wisdom or wealth is a little folly" [Ecclesiastes 10:1, New American Bible]. In the Middle Ages the mentally ill were labeled "fools" and were forced to wear the fool's cap and coat, and the principle of "fool's

Fool: Court jester before King and Queen. *Tristan and Isolde*, 1484

license" was also extended to them. The association of a jester's antics and the behavior of the mentally ill continued into modern times; traces of it are still found today, e.g., in characterizations of comedy as "wacky," or in "humor" that exploits and propagates stereotypes of mental illness. A "fool's paradise" is a state of blissful illusion, and a "fool's errand" is one that will be utterly unproductive.

foot and footprint   Even in prehistoric times footprints were an important symbol (found in pictures on rocks and in early sculptures) of the presence of humans, and especially of supernatural beings. Because of the contact between the foot and the EARTH, it was frequently believed that the foot transmitted personal emanations and powers to the ground upon which it walked. Explorers claimed territory simply by "setting foot" on it; the victor's foot was similarly placed upon the defeated foe, as a symbol of the latter's submission. The classical equivalent of our "getting up on the wrong side of the bed" was "getting up with the left foot" (compare our "getting off on the wrong foot"): a bad omen for the day to come. Subordinates and slaves had to kiss the feet of their masters as a sign of humility. Chinese women's feet were bound to keep them subservient to their husbands. On the other hand, loosening one's thongs and walking barefoot on holy ground [Exodus 3:5] was a sign of respect. The Maundy Thursday custom of "foot washing" in the Catholic Church is a symbolic expression of humility, following Christ's example, who washed the feet of his disci-

ples in accordance with the Eastern custom of hospitality. Barefoot orders of monks like the Carmelites are expressing voluntary poverty. Demonic beings were often given feet somehow different from those of ordinary people: they were turned the wrong way, or they were like those of a duck or goose (as were the feet of some WATER SPIRITS and DWARFS). The most famous in this connection is the DEVIL's, GOAT's or HORSE's foot: as a caricature of his former physical perfection, he is now forced to limp.

It was popularly believed in ancient China, as well as in the Buddhist, Islamic, and Christian worlds, that hollows in the surface of STONES (often of natural origin) were footprints of gods, heroes, prophets, and saints. The mother of the founder of the Chou dynasty was said to have become pregnant by stepping in the footprint of a god. In the year 1740 "God's footprint" was removed from the Swabian Rose Stone to prevent "superstitious worship" (especially by those with foot ailments). Similar footprints of saints, GIANTS, devils, and WITCHES are displayed in many places in Central Europe, mostly weather erosions in stone slabs and bearing some resemblance to footprints. "To walk in someone's footsteps" is to seek to follow that person in spirit, to take him or her as a model (see Romans 4:12). In our own day, a more playful version of this ancient veneration of the footsteps of great exemplary figures is the Hollywood custom of admiring movie stars' footprints in cement in front of Grauman's Chinese Theater. In psychoanalytic theory, the young child perceives a woman's foot as a substitute for the "missing penis" of her

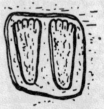

Footprints chiseled in stone. Megalithic grave, Petit Mont, Brittany, Bronze Age

sex; this is believed to explain the unusual form of male sexual deviation known as "foot and shoe fetishism." In Christian symbolism the cardinal sin of wrath (Latin *ira*) is sometimes represented by a noblewoman kicking a servant; in other contexts as well, a kick expresses extreme contempt for the person kicked. (See also HAND and SLIPPER.)

forest Symbologically distinct from the individual TREE, the FOREST stands in many traditions for an exterior world opposed to the microcosm of arable land. In legends and FAIRY TALES the woods are inhabited by mysterious, usually threatening creatures (WITCHES, DRAGONS, GIANTS, DWARFS, LIONS, BEARS, and the like)—symbols of all the dangers with which young people must deal if they are to survive their rites of passage and become mature, responsible adults. This image of the forest goes back to a time when great stretches of land were wooded and still had to be cleared for cultivation. In dreams the "dark woods" represent a disoriented phase, the realm of the unconscious, which the conscious person approaches with great hesitation. The LIGHT that in fairy tales often filters through the branches, symbolizes the yearning for a place of refuge. The forest itself, nature in the wild, devoid of human order, is felt to be unsettling and dangerous; in our imaginations, it is often peopled with SAVAGES and sprites, but also

Forest: Little Red Riding Hood. Fairy tale illustration, Ludwig Richter (1803–1884)

with fairies who can be benevolent. For a contemplative person, on the other hand, the forest can offer some seclusion from the hustle and bustle of the civilized world. Hermits do not fear the dangers of the woods: they are protected by higher powers.

Unlike the forest, the GROVE is not thought of as going on forever: it is "manageable" in its dimensions, and still a place in which mortals can come into contact with forces greater than themselves.

For analytic psychologists the forest often symbolizes the feminine as perceived by a young man: a disturbing terrain that he has yet to explore. In a more general sense, we find in the forest "the green half-light, the alternation of clearing and darkness that parallels the outwardly invisible life of the unconscious"; as a DREAM symbol, the forest contains "many creatures—harmless or dangerous—such as might yet enter the landscape of our personality by the light of day" [Aeppli]. ROBBERS, in this context, personify a "primal but dangerous part of our beings—which, after all, contain both good and evil."

Forest god (Silvanus) of Roman Illyria. Duvno, Bosnia, State Museum of Sarajevo

fortress Only in the Occident is a citadel viewed symbolically ("A mighty fortress is

Fortress assaulted and protected by the sea. J. Boschius, 1702

our God," Luther). The metaphor already appears in the Old Testament: the Lord is "my goodness, and my fortress; my high tower, and my deliverer" [Psalm 144:2]. If we consider the constant danger of wars and invasions in the Holy Land, we can understand the desire for a safe refuge and the recourse to faith in God. Christian faith as well should constitute a walled fortress against the DEVIL's crafty onslaughts. At times the "heavenly JERUSALEM" is portrayed as the model of a fortress that already protects the faithful. The kingdom of hell is portrayed antithetically with a satanic fortress that glows with the FIRES within and without. Himalayan monasteries, such as the famous Potala in Lhasa (Tibet), are true religious

fortresses, corresponding in reality to the European notion of the godly citadel. Moreover, in the time of the Turkish invasions, many churches in the southeastern part of Central Europe were enclosed by walls, further literal analogues of the Psalmist's vision. In HERALDRY the "fortress" often appears on coats of arms in highly simplified form, viewed from the front, with towers and gate, as an indication in many cases of a city's fortifications.

Fortuna The symbolic personification of fortune, luck, or chance. Originally a goddess associated with women and oracles, she

Fortuna on winged globe. Cartari, 1647

Fortress: Segeberg in Holstein (Germany). Braun-Hogenberg, 1617

later was seen as the Latin equivalent of the Greek Tyche, an embodiment of the shifting fortunes of humanity. Fortuna was often portrayed holding a rudder and a horn of plenty (CORNUCOPIA), standing on a sphere or a wheel, with a sail or wings, driven hither and thither by the changing winds. In modern times the arbitrary goddess of chance came to be understood at times as an expression of God's unfathomable providence, at times in opposition to the unerring VIRTUES (like *constantia*). In East Asia (China, Japan) "fortune" is symbolized by the "fat" BUDDHA and the "seven GODS OF HAPPINESS." (See also BLINDNESS.)

four A NUMBER of more symbolic significance than might at first be supposed, given our greater awareness of associations with the number THREE. The number four is associated with the CROSS and the SQUARE; there are four seasons, four RIVERS OF PARADISE, four humors, four points of the compass, four EVANGELISTS, four great prophets (Isaiah, Jeremiah, Ezekiel, and Daniel) and four Doctors of the Church (Augustine, Ambrose, Jerome, and Gregory). Most important, however, are the four letters in the name of God, the Hebrew Tetragrammaton transliterated as YHWH or JHVH and often pronounced "Yahweh" or "Jehovah"—although the devout Jew reveres the name too much ever to utter it.

In ancient China the imperial residence had four GATES (thought of as existing in the "middle," the "fifth" point or region of the Chinese "compass"); four legendary seas surrounded the Middle Kingdom—with its four MOUNTAINS (with names corresponding to those of the emperor's four principal nobles). The four seasons were so arranged that each began with four periods of two weeks. Four legendary kings protected the JADE emperor Yü-huang-ti, the highest divinity of the Chinese popular religion. Four amulets were used to ward off demonic influences; the four arts were symbolized by the BOOK, the painting, the guitar, and the chessboard. The four scholarly treasures were the ink-stone, the ink, the brush, and the paper. The four ethical "cords" were incorruptibility, modesty, duty, and proper observation of ceremony. "Four noble truths"

are the foundation of Buddhism, whereas Maoism decried "four outdated ways of life": the old feudal culture, habit, ancient custom, and intellectual tradition.

In the Americas, similarly, the number four provides a central cosmological principle. For the Mayans there were four colors and four "bearers" of the calendar year. In the cosmology of the Aztecs, four world-TREES (not unlike the colorful ceiba trees of the Mayans) support the HEAVENS. "The four points of the compass were said to be the origins of the winds, and the points at which the four great water-jugs were poised to pour forth RAIN" [Anders], along with the four Bacabs, the gods of the points of the compass, who had survived "the destruction of the world by water" (compare Great FLOOD).

fox In many national traditions (French "Renard," English "Reynard," German "Reineke") an animal symbolizing cunning and trickery. Its reddish coat is suggestive of FIRE, which places it (like the lynx and even the SQUIRREL) among the DEVIL's followers. In ancient Rome it was a fire demon; at the feast of the goddess Ceres, foxes were chased through the fields with burning TORCHES on their tails to ward off grain fires. A starfish painted with fox's BLOOD was nailed to the door to combat evil spells. Foxes (as in ancient China) were believed to be especially lecherous, and thus their testicles, ground up in WINE, a foolproof aphrodisiac; a foxtail, worn on the arm, was supposed to be sexually arousing. In Norse myth the fox was the symbolic animal of the trickster Loki. (The coyote plays a corresponding role in the myths of Native Americans.) Foxes were important Asian symbols of eroticism and the art of seduction: it was believed in ancient China that foxes (hu-li) first lived for a thousand years and then, endowed with NINE tails, could develop special powers of seduction. Spirits rode on foxes. Although fox-women never changed their clothing, it always remained clean; they are incredibly seductive, and their unbridled sexual demands can steal the life-force of the men who succumb to them.

Four seasons as cupids. Hohberg, 1675

Fox. Children's book illustration, Franz Pocci, 1847

In ancient Japan the vulpine spirits that can transform themselves into humans—"werefoxes," we might say—were called *koki-teno*. They possessed the ability to dazzle humans, mislead and corrupt them; they functioned like WITCHES (who can however appear in other forms) and were to be burned and their ASHES scattered over RIVERS. But the fox does not have uniformly negative associations in Japan. The rice god Inari rode a WHITE fox, and stone or wooden foxes, each with a sacred scroll or the key to paradise in its mouth, often stand beside the TORII of Inari's shrines. The tip of the fox's tail also often bears the symbol for "jewel of happiness." Shooting STARS are called "sky foxes" in Japanese.

Generally speaking, the animal's symbolic significance is predominantly negative. In Dürer's "Virgin Mary with Many Animals," we see a fox, tethered, apparently in reference to satanic associations. Foxes, however, are occasionally attributes of saints (e.g., St. Boniface, St. Genou), even though in Biblical usage they are the embodiment

Foxes stealing geese. Hohberg, 1647

of trickery and malice. Many languages contain proverbial references to a fox preaching to geese (see GOOSE)—a crafty sermon in the fox's own interest—and "the fox" is sometimes substituted for "the devil." In Grimmelshausen's *Simplicissimus*, to "foxtail" someone is to flatter him or her insincerely. Medieval bestiaries also express a negative view of Reynard as a crafty deceiver: "When he is hungry and finds nothing to eat, he burrows in reddish soil so that he looks as if he were spattered with blood, then drops to the ground and holds his breath. The birds see him lying there, (apparently) covered with blood, his tongue hanging out, and they believe he is dead. They come to rest upon him, and the fox catches and eats them. The devil acts in the same way: to the living, he pretends to be dead, until he can get them in his jaws and devour them" [Unterkircher]. "On shields or in coats of arms in general the fox represents shrewd cunning, and those who so display him usually have this quality, both in reputation and in fact" [Böckler].

Freemasonry, symbols of   Here we are in one domain of symbology where the functioning of consciously elaborated and ritualized symbols is still largely undiminished and unaltered. Since the official founding of Freemasonry in 1717, great emphasis has been placed on deliberate and consequential work with symbols as a way of making ethical goals easier to attain. "Freemasonry displays its most profound essence in symbols; the Church, in dogma," writes August Wolfstieg (1922); "in them is felt the pulse of the true inner life of the Royal Craft." He then presents quotations from the older literature on the subject: "The symbolism of work brings into focus not merely new spiritual unities but knowledge itself . . . [but] the symbols of inner experience must be discovered anew by each person . . . [in order to] familiarize those who seek understanding with the same world of attitudes, dispositions, and ideas in which those symbols originated" [Wageler]. "The symbol is the overcoming of dead matter by the human mind and the bringing of that matter

Freemasonry: Master's initiation. *Nouveau catéchisme des Francs-Maçons*, 1749

into vital life, by-passing mere scholarly conceptualization with artistic imagery, replacing [mere] knowledge with feeling for life and the possibilities of forming it, and external, utilitarian evaluation with inner evaluation, appreciation" [Gans]. "It would be amiss to see in the symbols a mere substitute for written records of transactions; otherwise, why would they have survived for so many centuries alongside written documents?" [Jacob Grimm, *Antiquities of German Law*]. In times that cherished symbols there was an indomitable urge "to make things of the intellect perceptible to the senses and to transform real life into meaningful imagery" [Freytag]. "The master builders of churches luxuriated in the profoundest symbolism. The pyramids were miracles of geometric science. Geometry was at the service of symbolism. Symbolism, we might well say, is speculative geometry" [A. Pike].

After these and other quotations indicating fundamental Masonic views, Wolfstieg (1859–1922) continues: "A symbol comes into being whenever we give a fact, a number, a word, a sign, a plant, a picture, a building—in a word, a *thing*—a deeper meaning than it possesses simply as is; when we give these things and their forms a greater value and meaning than would ordinarily be theirs; when we give the purely external thing a deeper intellectual or moral significance and thus make it an image for mental or spiritual events that could otherwise never have been expressed. The symbol is thus the exact opposite of an allegory, which is the material embodiment of a pre-existing general idea by the portrayal of a single event; . . . allegory begins with a general truth and strives to express the preconceived argument through the portrayal of a single happening; it preordains how the spectator is to think, understand, and feel. . . . The symbol, on the other hand, seeks to elevate a single concept or sensation . . . into universal relevance by repeatedly going back to a pre-existing 'thing' as the vehicle and image of the concept or sensation; seeing the image, now or in the future, will recall a specific argument, a general truth, or an exhortation to the consciousness of the spectator. Thus the symbol leaves the spectator room for all sorts of notions and interpretations." Wolfstieg adds G. F. Creuzer's formulation from *Symbolism and Mythology of Ancient Peoples* (1810–1812): "Only that which is most important should be invested with the rank of symbol. . . . It expresses everything which is proper to this domain [the religious, the artistic]—the immediacy of the moment, totality, necessity, the unfathomable—and elevates them to the highest degree. With this single word we designate the manifestation of the divine and the transfiguration of the terrestrial. . . . In the symbol, the concept itself enters the corporeal world and becomes, itself, immediately visible." Mathilde Ludendorff's low opinion of the (Masonic) symbol ("artificial stultification through symbolism")—and, apparently, of Freemasonry in general—offers a grotesque contrast to the Masonic point of view. Masonic symbols are referred to in this volume in many entries, including the following: ARK, CHAIN, DRAFTING COMPASS, DARKNESS, DRAWING BOARD, GLOVE, HAMMER, HEXAGRAM, KEYSTONE, LIGHT, PENTACLE, PILLARS, PLUMB LINE AND PLUMB BOB, PYTHAGORAS, CARPENTER'S SQUARE,

STEPS, STONE, TEMPLE, TRIANGLE, TROWEL, WORK.

frog Although a small animal, a most interesting one to the student of symbology. In ancient Egypt, because of its fertility and presumably its striking metamorphosis from EGG to tadpole to four-legged creature not entirely devoid of humanoid features, the frog was a symbol of genesis and reproductive life. The gods of the OGDOAD, born out of the primeval slime, were frequently portrayed with frogs' heads. The goddess of birth, Hekek or Hiqet, the kindly midwife of popular religion, was seen as a frog. In ancient China it was believed that frog spawn fell from the sky with the DEW, and thus the frog was often called metaphorically *t'ien-chi* ("sky-rooster") rather than the literal *wa*; a mythical association with the MOON may also explain this. An ancient text says that one of the two souls of every person is formed like a frog. Poets and emperors were believed to have the power to stop the croaking of frogs with a simple command. In European antiquity we find the myth of the Lycian farmers who muddied a thirsty goddess's drinking water by diving into it; they were turned into frogs. The frog was of great importance in magic, which led Pliny to remark that if it were up to the magicians to decide, frogs would be declared more important to the world than all laws. The frog's TONGUE, for example, laid on the

HEART of a sleeping woman, was thought to make her answer every question truthfully. In Judeo-Christian imagery the "Egyptian plague" of frogs [Exodus 8:2–14] plays an important role, and this negative association with the animal recurs in the Book of Revelation [16:13]. The early Church fathers referred to frogs' living in mud and their loud croaking, and they saw them as symbols of the DEVIL or of heretics promoting false doctrine. In Coptic Egypt, on the other hand, the earlier, positive image of the frog lingered on, and the animal appeared on oil lamps as a symbol of the Resurrection. In Europe the frog is an attribute of St. Hervé and of St. Pirmin of Reichenau, who was said to have shared the ability of Chinese rulers and poets to command croaking frogs (like those of his small island and the surrounding swampland) to silence. (Compare TOAD.)

The analytical psychologist Aeppli notes that although the amphibian frog disgusts many people it is a positive symbol in dreams. Its development to maturity "and the humanoid nature of its webbed 'hands' have made the frog an image of a lower degree of psychological transformation. Thus in the fairy tale ["The Frog Prince," Brothers Grimm] a (despised) frog can turn into a (handsome) prince. The frog is associated more with vitality, the toad with gravity. The latter, in dreams, is a distinctly feminine, maternal, animal." Freudian psycho-

Rana.

Frog. Woodcut in Pseudo-Albertus Magnus, Frankfurt, 1531

Furies. Cartari, 1647

analysis, however, sees in the slippery frog, seeking admission to the princess's little bed, a thinly veiled phallic symbol: the penis can attain "completeness" only through acceptance by the sexual partner. The frog's croaking appears to have religious import in this message from "the Lord and Savior" transmitted by the Styrian visionary Jakob Lorber (1800–1864): "The frog croaks most of the day with the sheer joy it feels to be living in its mud-hole; its croaking is a hymn of praise to Me for giving it the gift of life"; it thus might serve as a "teaching apostle" to humanity.

Furies (Greek Erinyes) Goddesses of vengeance, personifying the human need to atone for misdeeds that have gone unpunished. These three dark, powerful defenders of order (see TRIADS), whose Greek names are Alecto ("relentless"), Tisiphone ("avenger of murder"), and Megaera ("jealous"), are said to have come from the BLOOD of the god Uranus. They are portrayed with snake-like hair, holding torches and whips, as determined avengers of violence and other misdeeds committed against relatives, often parents. In some contexts they were viewed as personifications of curses, but at the same time they were defenders of moral and legal order, and were therefore also called (out of appeasement, or respect?) Eumenides ("the kindly ones") or Semnai Theai ("honorable goddesses"). In many places they were revered together with the three GRACES but as their opposites.

games Pleasurable, voluntary, non-utilitarian activities carried out in accordance with specified rules; many games conceal forgotten symbolic significance. In games, for example, we may find imitations of ancient religious rituals, translated into "child's play" and surviving as such long after adults have forgotten the original practices. Children in Central Europe play "the game of HEAVEN and HELL," in which they mark out a SPIRAL course on the ground and, hopping on one foot, move a stone through 12 fields to the center; this game is now understood to be an imitation of the sun's apparent course through the heavens. Hopscotch, derived from this game, originally simulated a

Games: Stickball player in protective clothing. Clay figurine, Jalisco, Mexico

series of ordeals to be undergone between the extremities of "heaven" and "hell." Board games, similarly, reflect cosmologies going back to the time of cave drawings (see SQUARE), which have been discovered both on horizontal surfaces (the earliest surviving game boards) and on walls (an indication that the forms were indeed also of cosmological significance and not "mere" games).

In the form of chess played in ancient India *(chaturanga)*, there were FOUR players (rather than two, as in the version that became popular in the Occident), and the moves of the figures were determined by rolling the dice. *Chaturanga* was of importance as a meditation ritual on the occasion of the Buddhist festival of the full MOON. Playing cards (with their four suits) may have been thought of as freeing players from the chess "board," a square marked out on the ground.

BALL games, which were originally imbued with ritual significance, were common not only in ancient Mexico *(tlachtli)* but also in medieval Europe, where a gilded leather ball up to a yard in diameter made its way from the east gate of a settlement to the west, in imitation of the course of the sun. These games, also played or overseen by clerics, usually took place in springtime (at Easter or on the first of May); a typical competition would pit married men against bachelors. This would suggest that soccer, like so many other games, has a symbolic tradition behind it.

Already in prehistoric times HORSE races and similar competitions accompanied funerals, as a demonstration (to the higher powers) of courage and initiative. Many games of chance, on the other hand, originated in the oracular arts; and many also represent age-old combat on the field of honor, which is why it is appropriate that gambling debts be referred to as "debts of honor."

The symbolic language of ALCHEMY refers to easy operations as "child's play" *(ludus puerorum).*

garden The path from the untamed FOREST through the sacred GROVE leads finally to the garden: an artificially established and maintained piece of nature, with a tradition of positive associations. The Garden of Eden (see PARADISE) was created by God as a safe enclosure for the first humans. In the symbology of ALCHEMY such a garden represents a domain that can be entered only with great effort and difficulty and only through the narrowest of GATES. Medieval cloisters enclosed idyllic gardens representing the paradise that had been lost. In earlier times the image of the "garden of the Hespirides" represents a distant paradise (see AFTERLIFE) where golden apples grew (see ISLANDS OF THE BLESSED). In Christian iconography the enclosed garden represents virginity in general and that of Mary in particular ("The VIRGIN Mary in the Rose Garden"). Renaissance and especially baroque landscape gardening was widely understood as the ultimate expression of the cultivation of life itself; the "French garden" is its apotheosis. The "English garden," on the contrary, suggests a return to nature as yet untamed by human hand, and is more congenial to the Romantic temperament.

The Japanese tradition of gardening strives for a harmony of all its elements (as in the tradition of flower arrangement, *ikebana*). This has its origins in traditional Chinese garden symbolism, in which natural objects like STONES, TREES, MOUNTAINS, ponds, and islands were considered manifestations of deities. The great imperial garden in Chang'an (A.D. ca. 50, Han dynasty) symbolized all of China and supposedly contained at least one of every plant and creature that was to be found there; its principal features were a central body of water ringed by ROCKS, symbolizing the SEA and the mountains around it, and FIVE hills for the five "points of the compass" of Taoist cosmology. Chinese gardeners always maintained a harmonic ratio between empty and filled space, reflecting the principles of YIN AND YANG; this was an attempt to introduce cosmic balance into the human world. From the fourth century after Christ onward, PINES, bamboo groves, and streams (see RIVERS) lent the Chinese garden a natural, idyllic air. Soon the tiered pagoda found its way

Garden in baroque style. J. Boschius, 1702

into the garden, as did a massive boulder to represent the world-mountain Meru. Flat or broad stones were "female"; conical stones, "male." The Chinese tradition of garden symbolism, which lives on to this day, encourages not only garden strolls but also reflection upon the harmony between the realms of movement and stasis. The peach-blossom festival every spring was celebrated by setting a bowl of RICE wine to float in a stream and composing a poem before the vessel ran aground. The gardens of China and Japan should always be understood as perfect reproductions of cosmic harmony, designed to have a beneficial influence on humanity.

The garden is a positive symbol in dreams as well. "It is a place of growth, a place where the inner life is cultivated," writes Aeppli. "In the garden the movement from season to season is particularly ordered and stressed, and we have the most beautiful vision of all of life's color and fullness. The surrounding wall keeps together the powers that flourish within," and the gate can often be found only by making one's way around the entire wall. "This is the symbolic expression of a long psychological development, which finally culminates with the attainment of inner riches." This set of symbols is particularly impressive when the garden of the psyche contains—like Paradise itself—a WELL, fountain, or SPRING, and the

Tree of Life: an image of our essential nucleus, the "self," the "innermost center of the psyche."

gates and portals frequently symbolize not only entrances but also the spaces hidden behind them, the secret power (as in the case of the "High Gate" standing for the power of the Turkish sultans, the "gates of hell," or the VIRGIN Mary as the gateway to heaven). The gate, portal, or gateway is associated with the entry into a space, realm, or domain of great significance, just as the BRIDGE is associated with transition. In TEMPLES, the doors to those secret chambers referred to as "the holy of holies" are usually splendid gateways through which only high priests, duly ordained, may pass. In many cultures rites of passage are symbolized by passing through a doorway or gate; times of religious solemnities are marked by the opening of these "sacred gates." The gate to the entrance hall of SOLOMON's temple in JERUSALEM was flanked by two great bronze pillars. In ancient Roman JANUS was the god of entrance and egress.

The Christian symbolic tradition of the gate goes back to Christ's words in the Gospel according to St. John: "I am the door: by me if any man enter in, he shall be saved . . ." [10:9]; the portal of a church

Gate to sanctuary of Solomon's temple in Jerusalem (see PILLARS): Masonic symbol

is often adorned with depictions of the Christian VIRTUES and VICES because of their significance along the way to salvation. The traditional guardians of the gates of heaven are the archangel Michael and the apostle Peter (the keeper of the KEYS). The story of the Biblical hero Samson, who removed the doors from the gate of the Philistine temple of Gaza [Judges 16:3], has been interpreted as a typological anticipation of Christ's liberation of the pious souls of the Old Testament after breaking the seals of limbo (*Sheol*) (the "harrowing of hell"); see AFTERLIFE.

Gate (locked) to the rose garden: alchemist's allegory. M. Maier, *Atalanta*, 1618

Gate. Etching, Ludwig Richter (1803–1884)

In many civilizations the figures of guardians keep watch at the gateways to shrines (see KARASHISHI and TORII). "A door is doubtless the most significant component of a house. It is opened and closed; it is where we knock, and it is the door that is locked. It is threshold and limit. When we pass in though or out it, we enter a space where different conditions prevail, a different state of consciousness, because it leads to different people, a different atmosphere" [Algernon Blackwood, 1869–1951].

Giant killed by the heroic knight Wolfdietrich. Book illustration, 1480

genius In the original Latin sense of ancient Rome, a specific supernatural being who accompanied each person as a tutelary spirit—corresponding to the Christian "guardian ANGEL"—from cradle to grave. Romans often consecrated altars to their genii, who may originally have represented male procreative power. The cult of household gods (*lares*) is associated with the genius and with the Greek tutelary *daimon*. In the altars of Pompeiian houses the genius of the *pater familias* was portrayed as a SNAKE. In imperial Rome the notion developed that not only an individual or a family but also a building or a city had a tutelary spirit: the *genius loci*. In the Renaissance, the genius became a symbolic figure, claimed by specific individuals but also representing specific qualities. At the time of the persecution of WITCHES, it was believed that DEVIL-worshippers had a satanic counterpart to the "good genius" in the form of a *spiritus familiaris*, a "familiar" animal; however, familiars were conjured up in magic ritual even in the absence of any pact with the devil. The Renaissance scholar Girolamo Cardano (1501–1576) claimed to have a tutelary genius who made it easy for him to learn foreign languages and lent him a supernatural radiance (see NIMBUS), which he long felt surrounded him.

The form of the genius best known to present-day readers and moviegoers is the genie of Middle Eastern tradition ("Aladdin and the Wonderful Lamp").

giants In many ancient traditions, they function not unlike (noble) SAVAGES, as symbols of nature in the wild, in its primeval state before it was annexed by civilization. The connection presumably lies in the idea that before the coming of civilization only human-like creatures with extraordinary physical powers could cope with the rigors of the environment. According to the theory of the Viennese paleontologist O. Abel (1875–1946), discoveries of the large bones of prehistoric animals (along with remains of megaliths [see MENHIR], interpreted as the handiwork of giants) may also have inspired these legends. In Greek mythology there are accounts of giants and Titans whom the gods had to defeat; similarly, Norse mythology has its Thursen and Jöten, the gigantic enemies of gods (Asen) and mortals. In ancient mythological traditions giants are seen as embodying the destructive forces of nature, causing avalanches, rockslides, and earthquakes; thus the struggle of gods and demigods against giants symbolizes that of humanity against the elements. Pre-Columbian myths of creation likewise refer to races of giants, imperfect creations of the gods

Giants: Fossilized mammoth bones, displayed in Vienna in 1443 as "giants' bones"

and necessitating natural calamities for their destruction. There are multiple accounts of ANDROGYNOUS giants (e.g., Ymir, in Norse myth) whom the gods killed, dismembered, and used as raw material with which to build the universe. The giants of legend are usually clumsy, malicious figures, ultimately overcome by the heroes' courage and cunning (e.g., the Cyclops Polyphemus, defeated by Odysseus); this cunning often takes on a humorous note in subsequent popular versions. In traditional masked processions, giants are often played off against DWARFS. Similarly, the giants of Brobdingnag appear immediately after the heroes' dwarf-like Lilliputians in Swift, *Gulliver's Travels*. The most celebrated literary giants are the heroes of the French humanist Rabelais (Gargantua and Pantagruel).

In Edgar Dacqué's (1878–1945) theory, our legends of giants and DRAGONS go back to primal memories (transmitted to *Homo sapiens* by pre-human ancestors) of huge reptilian creatures from earlier ages of the earth.

glove Frequently symbolic of the HAND itself—the part of the body that acts and executes orders—and thus a sign for power and protection, as well as the right to do business or to mint coins (powers granted by the authority of the KING). The KNIGHT's gauntlet is also famous: when it was thrown down, his challenge to do battle was certain to be accepted. In later centuries a slap in the face with a gentleman's glove was a challenge to a duel. Otherwise, gloves are frequently a symbol of high station, clean hands, and a turning away from everyday reality. They are important in the symbolism of FREEMASONRY as well. They were originally a gift from the apprentice to his lodge; later they were given to him instead. Today he receives a pair of WHITE gloves as a reminder that his hands are to remain always spotless, and a second pair as a greeting to the "sister" who is excluded from the WORK of the lodge; sometimes three pairs were given: one for the work of the lodge, one to commemorate his initiation, and a pair of women's gloves with the order: "Let these never clothe impure arms, or those of a WHORE!" (1760). Goethe sent the women's gloves that had been given to him to the chaste Charlotte von Stein. Similar customs were already in practice before the formal establishment of Freemasonry (1717) and were documented in 1686. Today the following saying commonly accompanies the conferring of the gloves: "Give these white gloves to the woman for whom you have the greatest respect, the one whom you will one day make, or have already made, your lawful partner."

goat (female) As with the BULL and the cow, the male and female of the goat have differing symbolic associations. Whereas the male goat (Greek *tragus,* Latin *caper*) is a generally negative symbol associated with lust and vitality, the contented female (Greek *chimaera,* Latin *capra*) is traditionally revered as a nurturing figure. In Greek myth, for example, the she-goat Amalthea nurses the baby Zeus; one of her horns, broken off, becomes the symbol of the bounties of nature (see CORNUCOPIA). The divine robes of Pallas Athena include the original Greek "aegis," the skin of a female goat, which according to Herodotus [IV, 189] was a garment worn by Libyan women and (along with the OLIVE tree, which was sacred to Athena and was imported from Libya) suggests the North African origin of the goddess.

Goat (female): Four goats nibbling from a tree. Fresco, Egypt, Old Empire

In Christian symbology the female goat is not of great importance. We do find her, however, in depictions of the Nativity, alongside the SHEEP as another reverent observer from the animal world. According to the medieval bestiaries, she likes to climb tall MOUNTAINS, and this is interpreted allegorically: "Like her, Christ also loves tall mountains, i.e., the prophets and the apostles. In the Song of Solomon it is written: 'The voice of my beloved! Behold, he cometh leaping upon the mountains, skipping upon the hills. My beloved is like a [wild goat] or a young hart' [2: 8–9; compare Vulgate text]. The goat's sharp vision is also a reference to the Lord, who foresees everything and distinguishes everything from afar" [Unterkircher].

Hircus.

Goat (male). Woodcut in Pseudo-Albertus Magnus, 1531

goat (male) Unlike his female counterpart, the male goat is usually interpreted negatively. Whereas pre-Christian conceptions took notice of his virility (male goats pull the chariot of the Norse THUNDER-god Thor and carry the Vedic FIRE-god Agni) or caricature it in the portrayals of composite beings (SATYRS, fauns; compare SAVAGES) noted for unbridled lust, increasing repression of sexuality brings with it a demotion of the male goat to his status as an "impure, stinking" creature "in search of gratification"; in portrayals of the Last Judgment, he is the creature condemned eternally to the fires of hell. Most of the DEVIL's physical traits, in Christian iconography, are taken over from the goat as well. In the late Middle Ages and the modern era WITCHES are often portrayed as being transported through the air on goats. In these representations the devil appears usually as a male goat whose rump the witches kiss. Books of the occult portrayed the mysterious "idol Baphomet" of the supposedly heretical Knights Templars as a goat. All of these associations may go back to Herodotus' account [*History*, Book II] of the Mendesian (Egyptian) sexual cult of the goat, and the Biblical custom of the "scapegoat" driven into the wilderness as the bearer of all the sinful impurity of the children of Israel [Leviticus 17:21–22]. Greek chroniclers associate the Mendesian goat with PAN; it may have originally been a RAM instead. Herodotus' account of the ritual coupling of the Mendesian women with the sacred goat should probably be taken as a libelous fable of Egyptian animal worship. In medieval bestiaries the male goat is a "lustful, vicious animal, always craving copulation. It is in his nature to be so hot that his BLOOD can dissolve DIAMONDS, which neither fire nor iron can break" [Unterkircher].

gods of happiness, seven (*Shichi-fukujin*; also translated "Seven Gods of Luck") A collective reference, in Japanese popular religion, to SEVEN personifications of earthly happiness; of considerable symbological interest. The first of them is Hotei (the Fat BUDDHA), the incarnation of merriment and *joie de vivre*. The others are Bishamonten, the watchman; Fukurokuju, the god of longevity; Jurojin, the god of scholarship; Daikoku, the god of nutrition; Ebisu, the god of fishing; and Benzaiten, the goddess of music. The seven appear either as individual figures or together on a treasure SHIP, often in the form of amulets, such as wooden or ivory *netsuke* figures serving primarily to fasten kimono sashes. Today the function of the seven has become primarily decorative. In ancient Chinese iconography there are FIVE gods of happiness, portrayed as old men in the red robes of civil servants. One of these *wu-fu* personifies longevity and has a CRANE and FLOWERS as his attributes; the others, wealth, virtue, well-being (attribute: a vase), and health. They are sometimes portrayed each accompanied by a BAT, and the "five bats" alone can symbolize good fortune.

Gog and Magog Symbolic designation for the powers of the ANTICHRIST and of the enemies of God in the Book of Revelation 20:8. After peace has reigned on EARTH for a thousand years, the DEVIL will be freed from his prison "and shall go out to deceive the nations which are in the four quarters of the earth, Gog and Magog, to gather them together to battle: the number of whom is as the sand of the sea." But soon the "fire came down from God out of heaven, and devoured them. And the devil that deceived them was cast into the lake of fire and brimstone" [verses 8–10]. In the Book of Ezekiel in the Old Testament, Gog is a prince of the northern land of Magog, which may simply be named for him (Gyges?); the author of the Book of Revelation turned these into the names of two peoples. In Islamic mythology an eastern nation asked ALEXANDER THE GREAT for help against the attacks of "Yajuj and Majuj," and "the Bicorn" (see HORN) put up an impenetrable wall of iron and bronze. "And this people came to believe, and praised Allah for his grace. . . ." Later legends recount that the peoples shut out by the wall tried each night to break through the wall with their razor-sharp, glowing TONGUES; but with every dawn they were compelled to flee again, for Allah had made the wall as strong again as it had been before. But Allah promised that they would ultimately "execute his wrath by breaking through the wall and destroying all the infidels and evil-doers, before Allah would cast them into Gehenna [see HELL] as a sign of his victory." Behind the names Yajuj and Majuj scholars have seen the demonic Gog and Magog of Biblical myth. "The Prophet rightly interpreted them not merely as names of individuals but as synonyms for the powers of CHAOS" [Beltz, 1980].

gold The expression "precious metal" (also for SILVER) understates the "moral" impor-

Gold as a "miniature sun" in the crucible. *Abraham Eleazar*, 1760

tance of the material to the alchemists in their pursuit of transfiguration. The rust-free, gleaming metal is associated with the SUN in almost all cultures; for the Aztecs it was divine excrement, *teocuitlatl*, "feces of the sun god." The alchemist's maxim, *Aurum nostrum non est aurum vulgi*, "Our gold is not the gold of the masses," suggests that to him "gold" meant not literally the metal, but rather esoteric knowledge, the highest state of spiritual development. Of course, even in orthodox Christianity gold symbolizes perfection and the light of heaven, as the gold backgrounds of medieval panels and Eastern icons suggest. In classical antiquity precious medicinal herbs were dug out with golden implements, so that their powers would not be diminished, and gold jewelry

Gold heated in a crucible "until it is pure." J. Boschius, 1702

was believed to ward off magic spells (especially when combined with PRECIOUS STONES). The general wearing of gold jewelry, however, was not allowed everywhere (see RINGS). Gold was widely regarded as embodying the powers of the EARTH, and, although it had virtually no practical value, it was always associated with higher powers and the gods. In many ancient civilizations gold was reserved for the production of sa-

Gold purified in a smelting furnace. Hohberg, 1675

cred articles and symbols of rulers (see CROWN). The "golden calf" of the Bible [Exodus 32:1–24], a symbol of the "idolatry" of the northern Israelites, was apparently not really the image of a calf, but of a BULL; Moses destroyed it. In ancient China gold (chin), the solar metal, symbolized the principal of yang, the dualistic complement of YIN (whose metal was silver).

golden age A symbol frequently encountered in the history of ideas, referring to a past, often prehistoric epoch of greater wisdom and greater proximity to God. The myths of the submerged island of ATLANTIS and of the loss of PARADISE have a similar basis: the conviction that in earlier times humanity had immediate access to the sources of knowledge but that they were sealed off by human wrongdoing (arrogance, reaching for the forbidden fruit). From a psychological point of view it may be decisive that childhood experience is far deeper and more intense than that in later stages of a person's development, when the multiple phenomena of one's surroundings can be confronted more rationally and more soberly. We all

believe that winters were snowier and more romantic in our childhood than today, that the wonders and mysteries of earlier times must have been more intense than those of the present. Add to this the belief in a cyclical course of human history, in which every age is succeeded by one in which mortals are farther removed from the gods or from God; a catastrophe (the FLOOD, the END OF THE WORLD) marks the end of each epoch—not only in the Old World but also, for example, in ancient Mexico. A Golden Age is described both by Hesiod (ca. 700 B.C.) and later, in poetic form, by Ovid (Publius Ovidius Naso, 43 B.C.–A.D. 17) in his *Metamorphoses*. What we see most clearly is a pessimistic view that the world is growing old: its innocent youth is over, to be replaced by an "iron age" characterized by a bitter struggle for survival. To this is added a longing for a lost primordial age of closeness to God, a return of paradise in a nobler version, a "heavenly JERUSALEM" perhaps, already announced in pre-Christian terms by Virgil (Publius Vergilius Maro, 70–19 B.C.). Many doctrines and philosophies promise groups within a society a new age in which conditions like those in paradise will be attainable.

golem A mythical symbolic figure of a robot-like being consisting of matter artificially brought to life and capable of threatening its creator. Whereas Frankenstein's monster (in Mary Shelley's novel of 1818) is supposedly put together from parts of human bodies, the golem of Jewish myth is the product of a legendary act of creation through language. "Golem" literally means something like "unformed material," like Adam before his soul was breathed into him. Tradition had it that great masters of the Cabala (Rabbi Eleazar of Worms, but especially the late Renaissance rabbi Judah Low ben Bezulel of Prague) were able to bring to (rather dull-witted) life humans formed from clay (see EARTH). A Rabbi Elijah of Chelm (Poland) was said to have created a golem who served him but grew more and more imposing and threatening, arousing fear in his creator. The word *emeth* ("truth"), pressed into the golem's forehead, brought him to life, until the rabbi erased the aleph, leaving only *meth* ("death"); the golem collapsed into a heap of clay, but the clay suffocated its creator. This can be understood as a warning against the unthinking use of magic powers, which become too much for us, making us lose control. Another persuasive interpretation is that in the course of meditating mystics can perceive themselves as foreign entities which almost crush them; this was said to have been the experience of the cabalist Hai ben Sherira (ca. A.D. 1000).

goose A bird functioning symbolically like a smaller version of the SWAN, often associated with the world of women and the household. In ancient times geese were caught with snares, and the taming of the domestic goose soon followed in Egypt. In Greece, too, the goose quickly became a sacrificial animal and a source of down and inexpensive food. In Rome the goose was fattened, its liver a delicacy. Its vigilance saved the Romans when the Gauls tried to storm the Capitol. It was believed that gooseflesh was an aphrodisiac, and that the bile of the bird augmented a man's potency. The goose was the attribute of VENUS (Aphrodite) and MARS (presumably because of the episode of the Capitoline geese), CUPID (Eros), and the phallic fertility god Priapus. The flight of wild geese fascinated the shamans of the Siberian peoples; in a trance, the priest felt that he was being carried up into the air with them and imitated their cry (which is said to have contributed to the Norse myth of Wotan's horde tearing across the sky). Since in winter the domestic goose came to

Goose. Egyptian wall painting of the Old Kingdom, 4th dynasty, Medum

adorn the holiday table of farmer and town-dweller alike, its culinary significance was also worked into legend—most notably that of St. Martin, who out of modesty refused to be made a bishop and hid in the coop with the geese; their outraged squawking, however, soon betrayed him. Eating "St. Martin's goose" is explained as "revenge" for their indiscretion. The "loquacity" of the goose in general made it a symbol for talkative old people. In medieval bestiaries geese are versions of vigilant humans; gray wild geese are like devout Christians who keep their distance from the bustle of the world and wear gray sackcloth. "Domesticated geese, however, also have white or colorful feathers and resemble town-dwellers, who dress in a similar manner. With their loud cries along the village lanes they are like people who in communal life give themselves over to chatter and malicious gossip" [Unterkircher]. The goose appears frequently in legends, fairy tales, and popular turns of phrase. A person who will "not say boo to a goose" is one too timid to say anything to anyone; if my "goose is cooked," my situation is hopeless indeed; and a particularly silly person we call a "silly goose." The shape of the goose's neck, when it reaches out to peck an unsuspecting victim, and its resemblance to a thumb upturned for a similar mission, may explain the bird's association with the indelicate practice of "goosing."

Gorgons (literally "the terrible ones") THREE terrifying figures of Greek mythology. For inhabitants of the eastern Mediterranean region they embodied the dangers of the largely unknown West. The three were named Stheno, Euryale, and Medusa; they are described as having SNAKES for HAIR (like the FURIES), WINGS, and fangs. Only Medusa was mortal. Her gaze was so horrible that anyone who looked at her was turned to STONE. The hero Perseus managed to behead her by using his shield as a MIRROR and not looking at her directly. (See also ATLAS, OCTOPUS.) The "Medusa head" later became a frightening symbol on the shield of the goddess Athena. The grotesque sisters of the

Gorgons: Etruscan Medusa. Terracotta antefix, Veji, ca. 580 B.C.

Gorgons: Medusa. Early Attic amphora drawing, Eleusis, 7th century B.C.

Gorgons form another TRIAD: the Graeae (literally "the gray ones"), old women "with beautiful cheeks," who share one EYE and one TOOTH: Enyo, Pemphredo, and Deino. When he set out to kill Medusa, Perseus was able to extort their aid by stealing their eye and tooth, returning them only after they had promised to help him.

Graces (Latin *gratiae*, Greek *charites*) Figures symbolizing the beauty and charm of young women, appearing in a TRIAD like several other groups of mythical women. They were immortal but not divine. They are usually placed among the attendants of Aphrodite (VENUS) or Apollo. They are given a variety of names, including Charis (from Greek *chairein*, "to rejoice"), Aglaia

("brightness"), Euphrosyne ("cheerfulness"), and Thalia ("the blossoming one"). Their task was to bestow charm upon young maidens and joyfulness upon people in general. They are usually said to be daughters of Zeus and Eurynome (a daughter of Poseidon). They are often portrayed in the company of the MUSES and associated with the HORAE.

Grail Also "Holy Grail," a symbolic object of great importance in medieval legend and for mystical and speculative religion; a sacred chalice associated with salvation and consecration. The apocryphal Gospel according to Nicodemus first tells of this cup used by Christ at the Last Supper and soon thereafter to collect his BLOOD. The word

Gorgons: Medusa's head painted on a round shield. Ceramic, ca. 570 B.C.

Graces. Cartari, 1647

comes from the Greek *krater* (Latin *cratale*), which later came to mean "bowl" or "dish." It is said that the Grail is preserved in a castle (see FORTRESS) on a "MOUNTAIN of salvation" (Montsalvatge) and filled by AN-GELS with the consecrated Host, a source of miraculous powers. In other legends it is a STONE that broke from Lucifer's CROWN when he fell from HEAVEN, a heavenly gem that is also the last remaining fragment of the paradise that was. The quest for the Grail is thus also a symbol of the quest for heavenly riches. The counterpart of the Grail in Eastern cosmology is the vase containing the life elixir *soma* referred to in the Vedas: a magical repository of earthly and spiritual life force. Another analogue is the goblet or (in Celtic tradition) cauldron of necromancy. The Crusaders' fanatical pursuit of relics may have played a role in developing the legend of the Holy Grail, which was then taken up and elaborated upon by a variety of authors (including Chrétien de Troyes, Robert de Boron, Wolfram von Eschenbach, Thomas Malory) in the legends of Perceval and Galahad. In Jungian psychology the Grail is a symbol of the feminine, that which receives but also gives, a sort of spiritual womb (see MOTHER) for all who give themselves over to its mystery.

grain, ears of, on Mary's robe   Frequent adornment of devotional and pilgrim's images of the Virgin in medieval and Renaissance times. This motif is reminiscent of "grain mothers" of antiquity, such as Demeter (Latin Ceres) and thus suggests the very long tradition of this expression of popular piety. Grain, which is placed in the ground ("buried"), apparently dead, but in the spring awakens to new life bearing rich fruit, was for the Ancients (in the Eleusinian mysteries, for example) a symbol of rebirth after the darkness of the grave, a source of hope and a model for the victory over death. Even independently of this tradition, the adornment of Mary's robe with ears of grain may well have expressed a prayer for bountiful harvests.

green   Like most colors, symbolically ambiguous; it can range from the positively

Ears of grain. Print, southern Germany, ca. 1450

valued "rich moss green" to "nauseous green." In many cultures it is popularly felt to symbolize hope, and dreams featuring the color are viewed positively, both in China and elsewhere. "Where green crops up, it is simply nature, and, naturally, growth . . . the experience of spring. If, say, the devil appears as 'the green one,' he has kept on the garment of an ancient god of vegetation" [Aeppli]. But there is also a negative aspect: "If in the dream there are excessive amounts of green, then negative forces of nature have taken over" [ibid.]. Christian symbolism finds green "equidistant from the blue of heaven and the red of hell . . . an intermediate and mediating color, soothing, refreshing, human, a color of contemplation, of the expectation of resurrection" [Heinz-Mohr]. Christ's CROSS, as a symbol of the hope of salvation, was often portrayed as green, the GRAIL EMERALD green, God's THRONE at the Last Judgment as made of green jasper (compare Revelation 4:3). The color was especially prized in the books of St. Hildegard of Bingen (1098–1179), who writes again and again of *viriditas* ("greenness," vitality) and, for example, esteems the emerald because of its color: the stone "originates in the early morn, with the sunrise. This is when the green of the earth and the grass is freshest, for the air is still cold, but the sun already warm, and plants suck in the green as eagerly as the baby lamb its milk. The heat of the day is barely enough to cook and feed this green. . . . The emerald is a powerful remedy against all human frailties and diseases because the sun engenders it and its substance comes from the green of the air." "The Emerald Isle" is Ireland, and green the color symbolizing the struggle for Irish independence from Great Britain. "Green" can refer to immaturity, not only of fruit but also, idiomatically, of persons (e.g., "greenhorn"); if I "give you the green light," I tell you that you are free to proceed; the Green political movement stresses ecological concerns and resists the dominance of unexamined technology. Especially in English, the color is associated with negative emotions: we become "green with envy," and jealousy is "the green-eyed monster" [*Othello*, III, iii]. In Islam, however, green is the color of the Prophet.

In traditional Chinese color symbolism, green and WHITE are paired in a DUALITY corresponding to the polar antithesis RED and white in the symbolism of occidental ALCHEMY. The green DRAGON of Chinese alchemy is associated with the *yin* principle, MERCURY, and WATER; the white TIGER, with *yang*, LEAD, and FIRE. In Occidental alchemy, the green dragon or LION symbolizes a corrosive solvent, like aqua regia, and its symbol is the inverted or "female" TRIANGLE combined with an "R." Variations in pictorial symbolism are such, however, that in some sources the green dragon is made to symbolize mercury, just as it does in China.

griffin (Also spelled "griffon" or "gryphon") A fabulous animal, symbolically significant for its domination of both the EARTH and the sky—because of its LION's body and EAGLE's head and wings. It has typological antecedents in ancient Asia, especially in the Assyrian *k'rub*, which is also the source of the Hebrew cherub (see ANGELS). The frequent representations of griffin-like creatures in Persian art made them symbolize ancient Persia for the Jews. In Greece the griffin was a symbol of vigilant strength; Apollo rode one, and griffins guarded the GOLD of the Hyperboreans of the far north. The griffin was also an embodiment of NEM-

Griffin, ancient Middle Eastern style. Relief, palace of Capara Guzana, ca. 870 B.C.

ESIS, the goddess of retribution, and turned her WHEEL of fortune. In legend the creature was a symbol of *superbia* (arrogant pride), because ALEXANDER THE GREAT was said to have tried to fly on the backs of griffins to the edge of the sky. At first also portrayed as a satanic figure entrapping human souls, the creature later became (from Dante onward) a symbol of the dual nature (divine and human) of Jesus Christ, precisely because of its mastery of earth and sky. The solar associations of both the lion and the eagle favored this positive reading. The griffin thus also became the adversary of ser-

Griffin, symbol of pugnacity. J. Boschius, 1702

pents (see SNAKES) and BASILISKS, both of which were seen as embodiments of satanic demons. Even Christ's Ascension came to be associated with the griffin. The creature appeared as frequently in the applied arts (tapestries, the work of goldsmiths) as in HERALDRY. In the latter domain, Böckler (1688) offered the following interpretation: "Griffins are portrayed with a lion's body, an eagle's head, long ears, and an eagle's claws, to indicate that one must combine intelligence and strength."

grove   Unlike the dark FOREST, a symbol of human fear of unexplored, "untamed" Nature, the spatially limited grove, consisting often of not more than a few TREES, is a place for reflection and quiet encounters with supernatural forces and beings. The grove of Dodona in Epirus was sacred to Zeus, who expressed his wishes through the oracle of its rustling OAKS. At the ancient Roman grove of Aricia on Lake Nemi, dedicated to DIANA Aricina, a sacred KING

Grove in which a hare seeks refuge. From an Etruscan vase, Caere, ca. 580 B.C.

guarded the trees. Such groves often gave asylum to fugitives. In Celtic and Germanic tradition there were similar sacred groves in which the gods manifested themselves. One more step further along the symbological continuum from the untamed forest to controlled, cultivated nature, we find the GARDEN.

hair Popularly believed to be the carrier of the life-force, continuing to grow even after a person's death; for the Biblical hero Samson, for example, the seat of his strength. The Nazarites take an oath to let "no razor come upon [their] heads" [Numbers 6:5] and to avoid all grapes and WINE, which is interpreted as a protest against the customs of settled cultures and a striving for the purity of early nomadic times. Others, living away from civilization—penitents and prophets like John the Baptist and the anchorites of Egypt—grow their hair long. Long hair enveloping the body, in the case of female penitents like the legendary Mary of Egypt, indicates a solitary life abjuring worldly concerns and the ostentation of dress but covering the body all the same. On the other hand, in the Middle Ages long hair is a symbol of vicious excess and lust (*luxuria*), associated with the Sirens (see WATER SPIRITS) and the rebellious Absalom, who is slain while suspended from a tree in whose branches his long hair has become caught [2 Samuel 18]. In Germanic cultures, since long hair was a sign of the freeborn, the hair of slaves or convicts was shorn. The monk's tonsure was understood as a sign that he renounced the liberties of ordinary citizens. In many cultures hair was sacrificed in funeral rites; the cutting off of hair also marks a woman's entry into the cloister. Specific ways of wearing the hair are frequently markers of caste or profession. Children's hair is often cut when they cease to be toddlers, or a particular lock of hair is left uncut until puberty (as in the case of the ancient Egyptian child-deity Horus Harpocrates). Supernatural creatures and demons are often portrayed with SNAKES for hair (the FURIES; the Etruscan god of the underworld, Charon; Medusa [see GORGONS]), and RED hair often was considered "diabolical." Among members of modern sub- and countercultures, long hair expresses a desire for independence from bourgeois norms or a protest against them. Legends and fairy tales often contain the motif already mentioned. Rapunzel is a good example, as are other women, usually virgins who are covered by their long hair. Old Spanish narratives or

the accounts of St. Agnes or Mary Magdalene also mention hair.

Magic rituals often involve hair, as in the tying of KNOTS out of someone's hair in order to make him or her fall in love. The custom of carrying a lock of the hair of one's beloved in a locket was wide-spread in the 19th century. Figures of speech often involve hair in a great variety of contexts (to have one's hair stand on end; not to get gray hairs over something; not to turn a hair; to let one's hair down; to escape by a hair; to get into someone's hair), thus indicating the attention accorded to this part of the body, which only the pettiest among us seek to "split." (See also HEADDRESS AND HEADGEAR.)

Hair: Necklace, gilded silver, of knights of the Order of the Pigtail. Austria, ca. 1380

hammer   Not only a tool but also an object endowed with great symbolic power, suggesting might and activity; in simple representation often indistinguishable from the double-headed AX. The hammer was first of all the tool of the blacksmith (a figure frequently surrounded with a fearful aura), who could turn iron into steel. The Etruscan death spirit Charu (see DEVIL) carried a large, long-handled hammer as a symbol of his function. Hephaestus (Latin Vulcan) also carries one, and a hammer is also the weapon of the Norse god of thunder, Thor: his trusty Mjollnir ("crusher") returns to his hand like a boomerang after it has smashed GIANTS to bits. Thor's hammer, however, can also be a positive symbol, bringing good fortune, as in the sanctioning of WEDDINGS. It also appears as an amulet, or on gravestones, to ward off evil. It is similar in form to the Egyptian tau (or T) CROSS of late antiquity. There were also club-like hammers used on the battlefield to bash in enemy skulls. The name of Charles "Martel" (the grandfather of Charlemagne) means "hammer." In the symbolism of FREEMASONRY the hammer (either a stonemason's mallet or a double-headed hammer) is the tool of the Master of the Lodge and of the two foremen. A pick symbolizes the work to be done on the "rough STONE," the apprentice. Symbols and coats of arms referring to mining contain a crossed hammer and pick; on maps, the same symbol, toppled or reversed, indicates an abandoned mine or a strip mine.

Hammer borne by Etruscan death spirit. Grave-wall painting, Tarquinia

hand   The part of the human body appearing most frequently in symbol. In paleolithic cave pictures we already find silhouettes of hands—in the caves of Gargas and Pech-Merle in France, and in the cave and rock art of other parts of the earth (South America, Australia). The Gargas cave in the Pyrenees contains depictions of many twisted finger joints and mutilated hands, perhaps commemorating acts of sacrifice. The hand can have multiple meanings: the gesture of taking hold or pushing away, for example, can express positive or negative symbolic meaning. Thus it often appears as an amulet, e.g., the "Hand of Fatima" of the Islamic world. In Semitic cultures "hand" and

Hand enlarged on male figure. Relief on a medieval Bogumile tombstone, Bosnia

"might" are one concept (*jad*) referring to a ruler's power; thus the hand is a royal symbol. Contact with the hand symbolizes "the magic touch"; the laying on of hands confers blessing and endows the person touched with one's own power or that of a higher being. A handshake is a symbol of friendly acceptance, also to show that the hand does not conceal a weapon; raised or folded hands, a symbol of prayer; specific gestures of the fingers, a solemn oath or blessing. In India the traditional system of *mudras* includes a wide array of codings for hand gestures. In Islam the FIVE fingers mean proclaiming one's faith, prayer, pilgrimage, fasting, and generosity. For the early medieval Bogumile sect of the Balkan peninsula, the hand, for example on tombstones, refers to the "five ELEMENTS" of the sect's cosmology. In Christian iconography Christ is re-

Hand of iron as a warning to grape thieves. Southern Tyrol, 19th century

ferred to as "the RIGHT hand of God," the right hand having a positive valuation in other contexts as well (as in the symbolic language of magic, where the right hand is associated with "WHITE magic" and the "path to the left hand" with BLACK). Hands covered or hidden in sleeves refer to the ancient custom of covering one's hands as a sign of respect in the presence of rulers. This is how many paintings show Moses receiving the Table of the Law on Mount Sinai. KINGS were believed to be able to cure the sick with a simple touch. The raised open hand of Byzantine rulers led to the Christian gesture for blessing. Two raised hands express a turning toward the heavens and the receptivity of the person praying (ORANT attitude, or gesture of adoration). Objects that had been blessed were not to be touched by the bare hands of unblessed persons. The right hand with three fingers extended (thumb, index, and middle finger) symbolizes an oath: "As God is my witness. . . ." The many "hand" idioms are generally self-explanatory: "to ask for a woman's hand in

Hand of the Creator. Romanesque fresco, St. Climent de Tahull, Catalonia

marriage," "to get out of hand," "to bite the hand that feeds one," "to make money hand over fist," "to lay hands on" (multiple meanings), "one hand washes the other," "to wash one's hands of the matter" (reference to Pontius Pilate, Matthew 27:24), and so forth.

In FREEMASONRY hand symbolism is of great importance; it actually dates back to the literal masons of the great cathedrals, and it includes the codes by which members of the modern fraternity recognize one another and initiate new members. Intertwined hands form the "fraternal CHAIN," and two hands extended appear frequently in seals and Masonic arms as a sign of

Hand. Islamic gate amulet at entrance to the Alhambra, Granada

brotherhood. The various Native American nations, although divided linguistically, were nevertheless able to communicate through sign language. Simple gestures of this sort are apparently part of the primordial heritage of humanity and, like facial expressions, are usually immediately comprehensible; sign languages of the hearing-impaired are derived in part from such gestures. (See also FIG, SIGN OF THE.) In Renaissance heraldry hands mean "strength, loyalty, diligence, innocence, and unity, as is widely seen in coats of arms. A hand with the fingers extended and spread apart means disunity; the closed hand or fist, strength and unity. Hands folded together mean loyalty and union. Hands feed us, dress us, comfort us; we have the hands to thank for

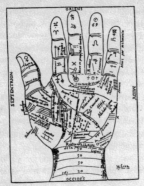

Hand: Astrology and palmistry related. Illustration, J. B. Belot's *Oeuvres*, 1640

all that humanity has wrought" [Böckler]. The lines of the palm and the varying development of its different regions are the subject of palmistry, or chiromancy, which begins with the doctrine that there are symbolic analogies linking the hand and its "hieroglyphics," planetary forces, and the talents and potential of the individual in question. "Palm reading" was especially the province of Gypsies, and it was claimed that for the sensitive palmist the sight of a person's hand simply triggered visionary experiences in which the customer's destiny was revealed.

hares Not distinguished from rabbits, either in symbolism or in popular superstition. In many ancient civilizations the hare is a "lunar animal," because the dark patches (*maria*, "seas") on the surface of the full MOON suggest leaping hares. Thus in ancient Mexico, where the hare (*tochtli*) is also the eighth of 20 day-symbols in the Aztec calendar and a sign of good luck, the animal is represented in the Codices by a U-shaped lunar hieroglyph; and in ancient China the lunar hare crushes cinnamon sticks in a mortar and is considered a symbol of longevity. In Buddhist, Celtic, Hottentot, and ancient Egyptian cultures as well, the hare was associated with the moon. Its further symbolic connotations have to do with its real or legendary characteristics, such as vigilance: the animal is said to sleep with its eyes open, and medieval physicians believed that eating its meat led to insomnia. (In classical antiquity, on the other hand, eating such a meal was believed to make a person beautiful for NINE days.) The hare is widely spoken of as easily frightened (in medieval symbology an armed man fleeing from a hare is the personification of Ignavia, or cowardice; compare the Grimms' tale of "The Seven Swabians"); its excessive fertility rate and and readiness to mate make it a symbol of lust, whereas a WHITE hare, portrayed at the feet of the VIRGIN Mary, is taken as a symbol of the triumph over "the flesh." The Easter hare, along with the EGG of fertility, plays an important role in Central European traditions for the welcoming of spring. The early Christian *Physiologus* mentions a further peculiarity of the hare: with its shorter front legs, it can run fastest uphill, eluding its pursuers. "Seek you likewise the rock, when the evil cur, the demon, pursues you. . . . If he sees you running downhill with your heart set on the earthly things of this world, he comes in ready pursuit, aided by the confusion of your thoughts. But let him see that you run along with the will of God, seeking the true ROCK of our Lord Jesus Christ, climbing to the summit of virtue, then the dog will turn back, as David writes in Psalm 34: Those who would do evil unto me must turn back and come to ruin." This

Hare undaunted by an uphill run. J. Boschius, 1702

Hare: Holy Trinity symbolized by three hares. Window, Paderborn Cathedral

sacrifice and faith in salvation. In the myths of Native Americans the hare represents a hero of the individual nation, such as GlusKabe or Manabozho, the creator of the world in its present state. A trickster figure, the hare outwits larger and stronger animals like BEARS and buffaloes. For psychologically oriented symbologists, neither the speed nor the "timidity" of the hare is critical, but rather the rate at which it multiplies: this makes the animal a symbol of fertility and passionate sexuality.

passage may explain the frequency with which the hare appears in Christian iconography. Its defenselessness makes it a natural symbol for humanity, which must put its trust in God. Hares nibbling grapes (see WINE) apparently symbolize souls in HEAVEN, who can safely enjoy the fruits of eternal life. We occasionally see depictions of three hares in a CIRCLE, their EARS forming a TRIANGLE—apparently a reminder of the Holy TRINITY, or of the fleeting (circular) course of time.

The ancients attributed predominantly positive characteristics to the hare (which was also the symbol of Iberia). Its speed and vigilance, according to Plutarch (A.D. 46–120), have a "divine" quality. According to Pliny the Elder (A.D. 23–79) this favorite animal of the goddess Aphrodite is highly beneficial to women: its meat makes sterile women fertile, and eating its testicles favors the conception of male offspring. The magician Apollonius of Tyana (first century after Christ) recommended that a hare be carried three times around the bed of a woman in labor to make her delivery easier. The hare is the fourth sign of the ancient Chinese zodiac (see STARS). A picture of SIX boys surrounding a human with the head of a hare symbolizes the wish, expressed at the time of the lunar festival, that the children in the family might rise smoothly in the civil service. Because of its lunar associations, the hare is a YIN animal. The animal plays a special role in Buddhist legend: a hare, sympathizing with the starving Buddha, sprang into the fire to provide food for him, and thus became a symbol of self-

headdress and headgear   Various sorts have greater symbolic significance than most other items of apparel. They create the visual impression that the wearer is taller, and yet they are at or near the observer's EYE-level and are thus among the first things to be noticed. Markers of rank, such as diadems, WREATHS, and CROWNS thus immediately elicit respect. Headdress is frequently symbolic of social rank or membership in specific groups and religious communities; in nonliterate societies, it may be a marker of the age group to which the individual belongs; and it also serves to adorn the wearer and (when worn by attacking warriors) to frighten the enemy.

FEATHERED headdresses frequently refer to acts of military prowess or bravery, and in some cases (as among the Papua) warriors wear entire bundles of feathers, bird-beaks, and parts of plants on their heads so as to appear more impressive. Similarly, helmets served not only to protect their wearers but were usually adorned with bull HORNS, combs made of HORSES' manes, BOAR's teeth, plumes, or spikes. The hat can stand for its wearer, like Governor Gessler's hat in the legend of William TELL. Removing one's own hat makes one appear shorter and is a sign of respect. Married women in many cultures were forbidden to show their hair in public and either wrapped it up in a sort of turban (a Germanic tradition) or covered it with a cloth (in ancient Rome); the bonnet later replaced these headcoverings, and this explains the idiomatic use of "bonnet" (*Haube*) in German in expressions referring to the fact that a woman is married. (In some parts of Swabia bridegrooms wore tall hats on the wedding day to symbolize their superiority to their newly bonneted brides.) Idioms relating to headgear abound in English as well. Since the hat can symbolize its wearer's occupation, "to wear many hats" is to perform multiple functions; a "bee in one's bonnet" is an eccentric whim; and to keep something under one's hat is to keep it secret. The present-day tendency not to wear hats or other headdress in urban environments may be the expression of a desire for social leveling.

heart "The heart is the source of all knowledge"; "What the arms do, where the legs take us, how all the parts of the body move—all of this the heart ordains." These quotations from ancient Egyptian texts show what were believed to be functions of the heart but today are for the most part associated with the brain. Because it is the central organ of the circulatory system, essential for maintaining life, and the signal of special situations in life (through the unmistakable "pounding of the heart"), in many older civilizations the heart was lent attributes that are not rationally defensible. It is admittedly unclear how much of this was meant literally and how much was rhetorical imagery. For the Egyptians of the time of the Pharaohs, the heart was the seat of the intelligence, the will, and the emotions. Ptah, the god of creation, first planned the universe in his heart, then with his spoken word called it into existence. In the judgment of the dead, the heart of the deceased person is compared in weight with

Heart: Four saints revere the arms of a Sacred Heart society. Lucas Cranach, 1505

a FEATHER (the symbol of Ma'at, the goddess of justice), to make sure that it has not been made heavy through misdeeds; "heart" is here the equivalent of "conscience." In the Bible the heart is the "inner" person: "the Lord seeth not as man seeth; for man looketh on the outward appearance, but the Lord looketh on the heart" [I Samuel 16:7]. It is said of God himself that "it grieved him at his heart" that he had created the human race [Genesis 6:6]. In the New Testament Paul prays "that Christ may dwell in [the] hearts [of the Gentiles] by faith" [Ephesians 3:3]. In Hinduism the heart is repeatedly referred to as the seat of Atman, the counterpart in mortals of the absolute (Brahman). Islam sees the heart, variously enclosed, as the corporeal seat of spirituality and contemplation. The Aztecs believed that the SUN appearing at the horizon had lost its strength in the course of its nocturnal journey through the underworld, that it was reduced to skin and bones and could gain new strength only from the BLOOD in the hearts of ritually sacrificed humans. The heart, *yollotli*, was considered to be the seat of life and the soul. Before cremation a GREEN jewel (see PRECIOUS STONES) was placed in the mouth of the dead person to represent the heart. From the late Middle Ages onward love poetry romanticizes the heart (see

Heart as a symbol of loving ardor. Wilhelm Busch

René of Anjou's "A Heart Enflamed with Love"), and in art it is soon stylized with anatomically incorrect bosom like upper edges and associated at times with earthly, at times with mystical and heavenly, love (in the latter cases, as a mystical altar, on which the impulses of the flesh are consumed by the FIRE of the Holy Ghost). The heart pierced by an ARROW symbolizes the Savior, loving and suffering for humanity; visions (like that of St. Margaret Mary Alacoque, ca. 1647) helped establish the veneration of the Sacred Heart. The heart of the VIRGIN Mary is portrayed, following the prophecy of old Simeon to her ("Yea, a SWORD shall pierce through thy own soul also"—Luke 2:35), as pierced by one or SEVEN swords. (The Mass of the Immaculate Heart of Mary is celebrated in the Roman Catholic Church 20 days after Pentecost.) "A merry heart maketh a cheerful countenance: but by sorrow of the heart the spirit is broken. The heart of him that hath understanding seeketh knowledge. . ." [Proverbs 15:13–14].

heaven, or the heavens In most languages similar or identical expressions refer to the sky above and to the abode of the gods, or of God, his "celestial armies," and (in the AFTERLIFE) the souls of the elect. Thus a single concept brings together meteorology, astronomy, astrology, theology, and notions of the origin of the cosmos. In many ancient cultures myths of creation refer to a primordial unity of heaven and EARTH, either in a jumbled CHAOS or as a sexual union of celestial woman (or man) with terrestrial man (or woman)—separated only later to make room for air and mortals. The heavens came to be invested with religious significance because LIGHT and life came from ABOVE, and these regions became metaphors for God, or the gods, themselves. The sky was often seen as a solid dome or vault (the "firmament") upon which the celestial gods lived and moved, observing mortals from above and deciding whether their behavior was to be compensated with fertilizing RAIN, CLOUDS, drought, or LIGHTNING. In the Bible God's THRONE is in heaven, and Christ ascends into heaven after the Resurrection. This heaven is composed of layered regions (in Hebrew *shamayim*, a plural) or spheres, only the first of which is visible to us; the various orders of ANGELS inhabit different spheres, as detailed in the writings of Dionysius Areopagita (ca. A.D. 500). The domes of churches, often adorned with scenes in heaven, are thus symbolic counterparts of what was believed to be God's abode; the portals (see GATES) represented the gates of heaven, and the entire structure, God's throne room or the "Heavenly JERUSALEM." An apparently innate symbology of "above and below"—with our feet planted in the dust, we raise our heads to the STARS—led to an ethical DUALITY that postulated an "evil" HELL as a polar opposite to a "good" heaven. In ancient Chinese cosmology the sky symbolizes the force of destiny that determines everything that happens on earth. The Temple of Heaven in Peking (today Beijing) is an architectural expression of the desire for harmony between these two cosmic realms, the EMPEROR representing heavenly authority on earth. In the *Book of Songs* it is written: "The sublime Emperor, our father, enters the Temple of Heaven. He bows in the motionless center of the Middle Kingdom. He speaks: The briars (see THORNS) and wild shrubs on my lands have been burned. The fields that are planted bring forth rich harvests. Our storehouses are full— I bring a sacrifice to mighty heaven. . . . The bells, the drums, the pipes will celebrate this sacrifice." Around 100 B.C. Emperor Chao said the following prayer: "Most sublime heaven, ruler from above, you who

Heaven. Hohberg, 1675

envelop the earth, bring forth life, and set the course of the waters! Most sublime heaven, O eternal one! I, the first among mortals, Emperor Chao, thank you for all of your acts of benevolence. The most fertile earth, which the heavens govern, and the sun and the rain let your gifts thrive. . . ." Clearly, in this cosmology heaven does not represent something utterly foreign to this world: it is a superior realm, but one mediated by the person of the Emperor and exercising supreme authority over events on earth.

In the Occident "heaven" is often endowed with earthly attributes—everything beautiful on earth raised to the highest power—so that it can be imagined at all, and yet it is ultimately an otherworldly goal for the earthly traveler. Only in exceptional cases do we find notions of heaven that are more spiritual in conception, without "vault," clouds, stars, and transpositions of earthly delights. Jacobus de Voragine's *Golden Legend* (ca. 1270) includes an example of an utterly naive notion of a heavenly realm: a dreamer sees "a beautiful meadow . . . on which there stood many lovely flowers; a gentle wind passed through the leaves on the trees, producing sweet sounds and fragrance. There were fruits in the trees, splendid in appearance and light to the taste; there were benches of gold and jewels, and gleaming divans adorned with costly coverlets. Clear springs flowed past. He then was led into the city proper, its walls of pure gold, gleaming wondrous bright. But in the

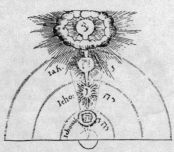

Heavenly spheres and the syllables of the name of God. Robert Fludd, 1617

air the heavenly host sang music such as no human ear had ever heard; and a voice spoke: This is the city of the blessed!" With this naive symbolic depiction we might contrast the more spiritual vision offered by St. Hildegard of Bingen (1098–1179) in her *De operatione Dei*: "Heaven is those who see God and speak of his coming; and it was heaven when the Son of God manifested himself in human form. Heaven is likewise the name of those who reflect the light of God's face like fiery SPARKS; through them, God has triumphed over all of his enemies. But when God created heaven and earth he placed man and woman in the middle of the universe. . . . The Lord prepared his throne in heaven, and 'from heaven did the Lord behold the earth' [Psalm 102:19]. This passage is to be understood as follows: The Son of God . . . prepares his throne in heaven, as human thought secures the instrument of his work in accordance with his wishes. . . . Thus does his kingdom reign over all things, in heaven and on earth." Here the concept of heaven is clearly distinguished from that of the "firmament" (the vault or dome of the heavens, which can also be a perceptible reality), which "is secured by the stars as if locked in place, as we lock our house with a key lest harm come to it. . . . The firmament is the throne of all beauty, that is, the earth that holds the throne." The concepts of heaven and PARADISE are also distinguished in many religious systems: heaven a spiritual realm, and paradise a restoration, after the Last Judgment, of the lost Eden (see GARDEN).

Outside of Europe we find a similar symbolic description of heaven in ancient Peru, whose cosmology the Inca Garcilaso de la Vega describes as follows: "They called heaven *hana pacha*, or 'upper world'; the good went to this heaven, it was believed, as a reward for their virtues. They called the world of procreation and ruin *hurin pacha*, or 'lower world.' When the evil died they went to *uru pacha*, 'world beneath the other,' the center of the earth; to make it clearer, they gave this third *pacha* another name, *zupaya huacin*, or 'DEVIL's house.' . . . They believed that peace in the upper world meant quiet life free from the care and burdens of this life. . . . They saw those who had lived good lives on earth as being rewarded with great pleasure, peace, and joy. Their afterlife pleasures, however, were not those of the flesh: they consisted rather in mental and physical peace, freedom from care and physical suffering." Now, Garcilaso de la Vega lived from 1539 to 1616, thus admittedly in the colonial era and subject to the influence of missionary teachings. But parallels to his text, promising "unearthly" pleasures in the afterlife, are found in ancient Egypt, as in this dialogue from the Book of the Dead: " 'You live with peace in your heart.' 'But there is no sexual pleasure there!' 'I gave you transfiguration in place of water, air, and sexual lust, and peace in your heart in place of bread and beer' " [Dondelinger].

Hedgehog: "It is protected by the fear it inspires." J. Boschius, 1702

hedgehog (Greek *echinos*, Latin *erinaceus*) The animal that is "armed, and yet a hero of peace," respected throughout the areas, in the Old World, where it is found. In antiquity its spines were used to roughen cloth, and its meat to make herbal medicine, e.g., against hair loss, since its spines evoked the image of resilient hair. The skin of a hedgehog hung from a grapevine was thought to ward off hail. The "shrewdness" of the hedgehog as a storer of food was extolled by Pliny the Elder (A.D. 23–79), among others. According to the early Christian text *Physiologus*, the hedgehog goes into a vineyard and climbs up "to the grapes and throws them down . . . then rolls on them, impaling them on its spines, and takes them to its young. . . . So should you, Christian, approach the true and sacred vine. . . . St. Basil says: Be thou like the hedgehog. Be it merely an unclean animal, its ways are loving and it cares for its young. . . . Revere the grapes of the true vine, namely the words of our Lord Jesus Christ, and bring them to your children, so that they, reared in his spirit, may give praise to our Father in heaven." There are also references to the enmity between the hedgehog and the SNAKE. Medieval bestiaries praise the "sagacity" of the hedgehog, who rolls up into a spiny ball in times of danger, and also uses those spines to collect berries; it is also said to have a nest with two exits, blocking the northern exit when the north wind is blowing and waiting until the south wind has dispersed the chilly FOG. On the other hand, the hedgehog was accused of being "miserly" and pugnacious (because it flares out its quills in a fight). Hohberg's baroque book of emblems (1675) contains the following rhyme: "When autumn's bounty heavy weighs the tree,/ The hedgehog's busy, fills its lair with fruit;/ When God has brought you bounties rich and free,/ See to it that they're wisely put to use." The hedgehog's "miserliness" made it a symbol of wealth in East Asia.

hell The traditional opposite of HEAVEN has its origins in the notion of a dark underworld (see CAVE) but was enriched by the theologically grounded image of a place of punishment where sinners go after death to suffer endless torment. As heaven or the heavens house God or the gods, so hell is the domain of the DEVIL or of the merciless rulers of the underworld. The joyless underworld of pre-Christian religions (in Hebrew *sheol,* in Greek *Hades*) was already portrayed as dark and unappealing—and inaccessible to the living; there were also descriptions of punishments for especially godless mortals.

(The word "hell" comes from the same Germanic root as "Hel," the name of the Norse goddess of death, and "hole," "hollow," and "conceal.") The notion of a fiery hell, reeking of sulfur, is derived partly from Ge Hinnom (in Latin Gehenna, in Arabic Jehenna), a ravine outside Jerusalem used first for sacrifices, then for the burning of refuse, and partly from observations of volcanic phenomena. The prophet Isaiah already refers to a fire in which the bodies of those who rebel against God will burn eternally [66:24]. Volcanoes are evoked by Tertullian (ca. A.D. 150–230) as proof of the real existence of a subterranean hell, which Dante Alighieri (1265–1321) later describes at length in The Divine Comedy. Symbolic images of reward and retribution in the AFTERLIFE are also derived in part from the figurative language of the Zoroastrian religion of ancient Persia, in which the dead must cross the Bridge of the Requiter (Chinvat peretu): for evildoers it becomes as narrow as the edge of a knife, and they plunge into the eternal abyss. In addition to the fires themselves, Christian symbols of hell include the "jaws of hell" (portrayed like those of a DRAGON), the death mask, and the three-headed DOG Cerberus from Greek mythology. As a warning to the living, the torments of hell were often portrayed in graphic detail: for example, the damned were eternally punished for the sin of lust by having

Remembre frendes grete and small.
Foz to be redy whan dethe dothe call:

Hell: Death rides forth from the jaws of hell. W. Paxton, London, 1507

their breasts and genitals gnawed by TOADS and bitten by SNAKES. (See also LAZARUS.)

The underworld of the Aztecs, Mictlán, was similarly conceived. Only those who drowned, or died in battle, sacrificial rites, or childbirth, could avoid it and look forward to other forms of afterlife—just as, in Norse mythology, those who died the "straw death" (i.e., in their beds) could not escape the dark realm of the goddess Hel: only those who died as heroes were borne by the VALKYRIES to Valhalla, the realm of light. Pessimistic notions of the afterlife with satanic death-gods and -demons are similarly characteristic of late Etruscan grave iconography, replacing earlier symbols of a peaceful afterlife along the lines of the ISLANDS OF THE BLESSED. Etruscan gods of the underworld, with their HORNS and pointed EARS, holding snakes, apparently had a lasting influence on the Christian notion of the devil. East Asian Buddhism also has its version of hell. In the great halls of Japanese temples the ruler of the underworld, Emma-o, is portrayed as sitting in judgment upon sinners, with his judicial staff as a symbol of his powers. Life-size wooden figures represent the condemned as demons carry them off to be punished, with sword, rack, iron bars, and pillory. In modern times these tableaux have come to be thought of primarily as intimidations for disobedient children. The Islamic tradition speaks of hellfire SEVEN times hotter than any earthly fire. Similarly, the bodies of the damned are said to be enlarged, so that they will suffer more.

Hell. "Warning against False Love of This World," woodcut (detail), Nürnberg, 1495

The cruelty of all of these notions can be understood only as a symbolic expression of the hope that those whose misdeeds escape punishment on earth will still not go eternally free. In Europe the Church condemned as heresy the idea of apocatastasis, i.e., an apocalyptic reconciliation that would include hell, a notion found, for example, in Parsiism, in which "even the land of hell will be restored to cosmic joy." In the world of Islam, Sufi mystics also reject the notion of eternal condemnation, as we see from the words of Abud Yazid al-Bistami: "What is this business of hell? On the day of judgment I shall certainly stand with the damned and say to Thee: Take me as their ransom. And if Thou wilt not, then I shall teach them that [even] Thy paradise is but a game for children. . . . If, O Allah, in Thy perfect knowledge of things to come, Thou knowest that Thou wilt torment one of Thy creatures in hell, then let my being take up so much space there that there might be none for any other" [quoted by Gardet].

hen The adult female of the chicken has different symbolic associations from the ROOSTER: she is the quintessential MOTHER. "Just as the mother hen protects her brood,/ Lets nothing near which to them harm might bring,/ So can we too, the children of the Rood,/ Be touched not by life's care, life's woe, life's sting" [Hohberg]. The hen's protective love for her defenseless offspring figures also in Christ's analogy: "O Jerusalem, Jerusalem, . . . how often would I have

Hen guarding her young. Hohberg, 1647

gathered thy children together, even as a hen gathereth her chickens under her wings . . . !" [Matthew 23:37]. The hen's patient "brooding" stood for grammar in the allegorical representation of the "SEVEN liberal arts": it, too, requires great patience. The ancients believed that hen's blood could regulate an excessive sex drive. Whereas in Africa female initiation rites implore the hen's spiritual guidance, Central Europeans think of the bird as ignorant or foolish, as Jungian theory also indicates: hens in dreams symbolize "an intellectually impoverished flock, highly susceptible to outside influence. They often go into a panic over nothing, suggesting the restless confusion in the mental processes of foolish people. . . . In this way something that the dreamer takes too seriously in waking life is appropriately seen in all its noisy triviality" [Aeppli]. In fairy tales and nursery rhymes, the bird who, in one story, can be frantic with worry that the sky is falling, can also (like the GOOSE of other traditions) lay "GOLDEN EGGS": it would be foolish to kill her. In legend, the hen sitting on her eggs symbolizes supernatural forces guarding treasures (including mineral deposits).

Hen as the embodiment of love and patience. J. Boschius, 1702

heraldry, symbols in In various historical periods the symbols in coats of arms have been taken to be more meaningful than they indeed were; more was read into them than was really there (compare COLORS, SYMBOLISM OF). Whereas some "canting" arms contain rebuses that "spell out" by means of homonyms—and thus without any necessary etymological relevance—some version of the names of the families or places in question (e.g., shells for Shelley, a spear for Shakespeare), it would be a mistake to take seriously all of the latter-day speculations on the deeper significance of heraldic symbols. This sort of heraldic exegesis was very popular in mannerist and the baroque periods, examples of which appear in this volume in the form of quotations from Georg Andreas Böckler's *Ars Heraldica* (1688): they are of interest as documents of intellectual history and have been given too little heed as such. It is clear that "royal" animals like EAGLES and LIONS often appear in rulers' coats of arms (and are also used simply to express confidence). But to say that the LYNX actually denotes "quick, rapid cunning and alert, precise intelligence," or the BOAR "the dauntless and well-armed soldier, who in battle opposes the enemy with valiant courage," is to offer manneristic interpretation rather than scholarly accuracy. In the 19th century these interpretations were widely discussed, but they are rejected by those who see heraldry as an ancillary discipline to the study of history. (See also TOTEM.)

hermit The symbolic figure of the person who, through ascetic isolation from the world and worldly affairs, can attain special visionary gifts and the ability to help those who come in search of wisdom and counsel. In the strictest sense the word refers to those who have taken up a religious life based on abstaining from communication with others and on being alone with God. The first such form of monastic life (the word "monk" comes from Latin *monacus,* Greek *monos,* "alone") was practiced in Egypt by Coptic (Christian) anchorites, who lived in CAVES in the wilderness (see St. ANTHONY), whereas the hermitages of Central Europe were built in FOREST settings. The miraculous powers attained by hermits, through their isolation and prayer, are legendary, and "hermits of the woods" are known not only in the Christian world but also among the religions of India. Gautama Buddha himself spent a considerable part of his life in isolation from

Hermit: Indian hermit of the forest. Farmer's almanac, Austria, 1911

the world before he undertook his mission of teaching.

heron (Greek *herodius,* Latin *ardea*) A large WATER BIRD with a pointed beak. In ancient legend the enemy of the EAGLE and the LARK, the ally of the CROW, and sacred to the sea god Poseidon (Neptune); its appearance was a good omen. In Aesop's fable the heron is to extract a bone from the wolf's throat but must risk its own head in the process. In the early Christian text *Physiologus* the heron is spoken of as the most contented of birds: "its bed and its food are in the same place," it need not "fly to and fro" like the other birds. It is thus a symbol for the Christian to emulate, not seeking out the many abodes of the heretic, shunning the "food of heresy." In the medieval bestiaries it was written that the heron detested the RAIN and would fly high above the CLOUDS to avoid it; this came to serve as a warning of impending bad weather. "This bird is a symbol for the souls of the elect, who, fearing the storms of this world, direct all their efforts beyond the temporal sphere toward their lofty heavenly home. Some herons are WHITE, some ash-gray; white is the color of innocence, ash-grey that of

Heron. Hohberg, 1675

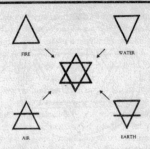

Hexagram constructed from alchemist's symbols for the elements

penitence . . ." [Unterkircher]. Hohberg, in his emblem-book of 1675, offers verses in a similar vein: "Each time a heron sees another storm approach,/ It soars above the clouds that threaten rain./ So, when on Christian hearts life's troubles do encroach,/ Their refuge is God's mercy yet again." Because of the belief that the heron could shed tears, the bird also became a symbol for Christ on the Mount of Olives; it was also thought of as the extirpator of the "satanic" serpent (see SNAKE), and the prophet Jeremiah may have intended to include it among the birds who "know their appointed times" (although it is more likely that the reference in 8:7 is to the STORK). The long beak of the heron makes it, in some contexts, a symbol for curiosity ("sticking its nose in everywhere"); but it is also occasionally portrayed with a white STONE in its beak, making it a symbol of discretion.

In Chinese art the heron (*lu*) is often portrayed alongside the LOTUS blossom (*lien*). Because of the homonymy of the respective syllables with the words for "path" and "ascent," the combination becomes a rebus to express the wish: "May your path always take you higher and higher."

hexagram SIX-pointed STAR, composed of two overlapping TRIANGLES; a symbol found in a wide array of cultures around the world. It is traditionally interpreted as the combination of a "watery" (female, pointing downward) and a "fiery" (male, pointing upward) triangle, representing together a

closed, harmonically ordered DUALITY. The Biblical king SOLOMON, son of DAVID and Bathsheba, was said to have exorcised demons and summoned ANGELS with it until his death (ca. 930 B.C.), although most traditions view his use of the Tetragrammaton (YHWH—Yahweh—the four-lettered name of God) as having been the decisive factor. Because of its association with Solomon, the six-pointed star came to be known as the *sigillum Salomonis* ("Solomon's seal") or *scutum Davidis* ("David's shield"); today, appearing in the coat of arms of the state of Israel, it is usually referred to as the Star of Zion or Star of David. When cosmological speculation went beyond the fire-water duality to posit the FOUR "ELEMENTS," the hexagram came to be seen as having four components, including a symbol for "air" (a triangle resting on one side, with a line parallel to that side intersecting the other two) and for "EARTH" (the

Hexagram constructed from interlocking triangles

Hexagram: Masonic emblem with the name of God at its center. Ca. 1800

same symbol inverted). In the symbology of ALCHEMY, the combination of the four elements usually designates primal matter, in which all components are present. Similarly, in the world of FREEMASONRY, the hexagram is often part of the SEAL of an individual lodge; it is also referred to as a symbol of totality, although the "flaming star" (the PENTACLE or pentagram) is more common in this sense. The hexagram also appears frequently in alpine ROCK drawings and in popular books of spells and exorcisms as a powerful magic symbol, without any necessary reference to Judaism. For Jungian psychology the hexagram, especially inscribed in a CIRCLE, is most prominent as a MANDALA, a simple geometrical figure to be used as an aid to meditation. The Indian *sriyantra* mandala (composed of NINE interpenetrating triangles within multiple frames; see YANTRA) can be understood as a refinement upon this basic structure. In the I CHING of ancient China the 64 possible pairings of trigrams of solid and broken lines are also called hexagrams.

hippopotamus (Greek, literally "RIVER HORSE") The massive herbivore of the marshlands is thought to be the primeval monster "behemoth" [Job 40:15–24], which is also expected to return as a hostile, satanic beast in the last days of the earth (see END OF THE WORLD). In ancient Egypt the hippopotamus was frequently hunted (with harpoons) because of its destruction of crops, and it was thought of as a follower of Seth,

the adversary and slayer of Osiris. The mass of its belly, however, is suggestive of the physical form of pregnant women, and thus the hippo also became a positive symbol and finally a divinity. Ta-uret (Greek Thoëris), "the great one," was a hippopotamus standing on its hind legs, with a woman's breasts supported by the "Sa loop" (an amulet and symbol of protection). In this form figures of the hippo-goddess were placed on the beds of women in childbirth; the goddess's influence extended especially to the birth of royal children who would one day ascend to the THRONE. In Christian art the hippopotamus appears frequently in depictions of the creation of the animal world.

Homer For the ancient world the ideal symbolic figure of the epic poet with divine insight, BLIND (like the seer Tiresias) to everyday reality, and inspired by the MUSES. There has almost always been uncertainty as to his historical identity and his birthplace (Smyrna in Asia Minor? the island of Chios?). He is now believed to have lived in the eighth century B.C., but we know nothing about his life. The two hexameter epics, *The Iliad* and *The Odyssey*, seem to be written by a single author, at least for the most part; but the attribution of *The Homeric Hymns* and *The War between the Frog and the Mice (Batrachomyomachia)* to the great poet was clearly erroneous. The division of each of the epics into 24 books might suggest some numerical symbolism relating to the NUMBER 12, but this division appears to have been introduced only after the fact, in the Hellenistic period in Alexandria; still, Achilles takes his revenge on

Hippopotamus figurine painted with water plants. Blue pottery, Egypt, ca. 1500 B.C.

Hector for 12 days; Odysseus has 12 adventures and shoots his ARROW through 12 AX holes. The two epics contain many symbolic echoes of ancient traditions, such as the double source of the RIVER Scamander ("One of these two SPRINGS is warm, and steam rises from it as smoke from a burning FIRE, but the other even in summer is as cold as hail or snow, or the ICE that forms on WATER"—*Iliad* [translated by Butler], XXII, 147–150) or Zeus' weighing of the lots ("Then . . . the FATHER of all balanced his GOLDEN SCALES and placed a doom in each of them, one for Achilles and one for Hector"—ibid., 208–210). In the Middle Ages Virgil, who sought to equal Homer with his *Aeneid*, was for a time more esteemed than his model, but since the end of the 18th century, Homer has been recognized as the unrivaled master, the quintessential epic poet.

honey Whether in association with the BEE or not, honey is a privileged symbol for "sweetness" in every sense of the word. Wild honey was gathered by both inhabitants of the Spanish Levantina (as cave paintings from before 3000 B.C. document) and the ancestors of South African Bushmen. The land of Canaan promised to Moses in the Bible is described as "a good land and large, . . . a land flowing with milk and honey" [Exodus 3:8]. The words of God are "sweeter than honey" [Psalm 119:103], and the BOOKS or scrolls literally devoured by prophets as a sign of their incorporation of God's word are said to be "as honey for sweetness" [Ezekiel 3:3] or "sweet as honey" [Revelation 10:9]. Mead and honey were frequently food for the gods, e.g., for Zeus as a toddler. In Hindu myth the Asvin TWINS, messengers of the gods in the morning sky, bring honey, and the devout refresh themselves at a legendary SPRING that flows with honey. The Scythians and Spartans used honey to embalm KINGS and, in the Mithraic cult of late antiquity, as a sacramental fluid that cleansed mortals of sin, since it was produced by a sinless creature that "did but touch blossoms and flowers." Ancient Cretan tablets in Linear B script refer to the sacrifice of honey "for the goddess." In a curious story in the

Honey gathered in ancient Egypt. Tomb relief, Thebes, ca. 600 B.C.

Old Testament, the heroic Samson tears apart a lion with his bare hands, then finds honey and a swarm of bees in its carcass, which inspires his riddle, "Out of the eater came forth meat, and out of the strong came forth sweetness" [Judges 14:14], a symbol of the emergence of new life out of death. In the time of the early patriarchs of the Church, the words of revelation flowing from God's mouth are called "the RIVER of honey that flows through the new Eden," and the body of Christ "the ROCK from which honey pours."

In many civilizations honey is a sacrifice for the dead, food for supernatural beings, protection used to ward off demons; it is likened to "the heavenly dew." One of the many gods of nature associated with protecting honey bees was Noh-yum-cab ("ruler of the bees"), revered in the Mayan civilization of Central America, where a weak alcoholic ceremonial beverage was made from water, honey of non-stinging bees, and the bark of the lonchocarpus or balché tree; it is still made by the Lacandón. In ancient China honey was associated with the "fifth point of the compass," the center, and was used to sweeten the food of the emperor. The same word, *mi*, refers to honey, sweetness, and sexual pleasure. Dreams of honey were believed to presage good fortune; similarly, in Jungian psychology, honey is believed to symbolize the goal of attaining emotional maturity (individuation). Medieval physicians, who thought that honey was congealed dew which bees merely collected, used it not only for sweetening but also as a balm for wounds. In figurative usage, "honey" is a term of endearment, and a "honey of a deal" is a particularly advantageous one. Corresponding to the English use of "honey" as a verb (meaning to cajole or flatter) is the more vivid German expression, "to spread honey around someone's mouth." It is IN Röhrich's hypothesis that this goes back to the Chinese custom of putting honey on the lips of (the image of) the god of the kitchen and the hearth (who reports annually to the god of the heavens about the inhabitants of the house); this custom, which is supposed to win the household god's sympathy, may have been reported in Europe by early travelers to Asia.

hoopoe (Greek *epops*, Latin *upapa*) A migratory BIRD of the Mediterranean regions, considered unclean because it picks larvae out of animal waste; it is also known as the enemy of the BEE. According to Ovid's *Metamorphoses*, the hoopoe was a king of Thrace (Tereus) who was transformed into a bird for his misdeeds. (His wife Philomela, whom he pursued with drawn sword, became a NIGHTINGALE.) The ancients associated the hoopoe with a magic root (identified in some Central European traditions with the MANDRAKE) capable of opening any lock, and with the growth of grape vines.

In the early Christian text *Physiologus* it is written that young hoopoes pluck the old FEATHERS from their aging parents and lick their bleak eyes until the parents are rejuvenated. The young say to their parents: "We were your little baby birds and you brought us up, exhausted yourselves caring for us, feeding us; now we do the same for you. How can humans be so unfeeling as not to love their own parents, who cared for them and taught them the ways of love?" The same story is related in the medieval bestiaries, but they also portray the hoopoe as an unclean bird, digging in feces, and thus a symbol of sinners, who stubbornly take delight in the filth of sin. The bird is also said to be fond of sorrow, which brings about "the death of the spirit."

Horae Although their name literally means "hours" in Greek, the Horae were mythical personifications of the seasons, as defined in a tripartite division of the year into Thallo (blooming), Auxo (growth), and Carpo (vegetation). (Persephone, in Latin Proserpina, had to spend one third of the year in Hades; see POMEGRANATE.) The three were the daughters of Zeus and Themis (the goddess of human order), and they came to be identified not only with divisions of time (*hora*) but also, through their shared associations with "temporal and legal order," with the abstractions Eirene (peace), Dike (right), and Eunomia (legality). The Horae were often portrayed as attendants upon Aphrodite (VENUS), like the three GRACES, or Hera (Juno). (See TRIADS.) *Die Horen* (published 1795–97), an influential literary journal of German classicism, was named for the Horae.

horns are characteristic of BULL-deities, even when their bodies are otherwise portrayed as human, or when the horns stand alone (e.g., the "cult horns" of ancient Crete, between which the double-headed AX often stood) as symbols in the strictest sense of the word. Horns are the animal's weapons, and thus stand for its strength and aggressiveness. They were frequently used as a visible representation of the powers of horned deities, especially in association with strong animals like the wild buffalo of early-Holocene North African cave paintings, between whose horns a disk appears, representing the SUN. In ancient Egypt Hathor, the goddess of the HEAVENS, who was often portrayed with the head of a cow, has a similar sun between her horns. Later the god Amon, or Amen, was portrayed at the Siwa Oasis with RAM's horns; this was the origin of the word "ammonite," originally "horn of Amon," for the fossils that were thought to resemble these horns. After a visit to the shrine ALEXANDER THE GREAT had himself portrayed as the "son of Zeus Amon" with the same headgear. The Bible mentions altars with horns at the corners, overlaid with brass; the blood of sacrificial animals was painted on the horns. Anyone accused of crimes was granted asylum upon reaching the temple and touching the horns. When Yahweh angrily breaks them off and

Horned helmet on warrior. Votive figure, Sardinia, ca. 1000 B.C.

dashes them to the ground [Amos 3:14], this is a terrible gesture of divine condemnation. There is some controversy as to the proper translation of verses in Exodus that apparently refer to MOSES as wearing "horns" (in Hebrew *karan*) when he descends from MOUNT Sinai (34:29–35). The Near East specialist A. Jirku points out that masks made from the skulls of cattle, including horns, were not unknown in ancient Palestine, and the Vulgate uses the expression *facies cornuta*, a "horned face." Following this reading, Michelangelo's statue of Moses portrays him with horns. Subsequent translations, however, interpret the word in question as meaning "beams of light"; in the King James Version, for example, it is said that "the skin of Moses' face shone." The horn is a symbol of divine strength in the New Testament as well: the Lord "hath raised up an horn of salvation for us in the house of his servant David" [Luke 1:69]. In the Book of Revelation the LAMB has "SEVEN horns and seven EYES, which are the seven Spirits of God" [5:6]; the satanic DRAGON has "seven heads and ten horns" [12:3], symbolizing his infernal powers. Horns were used in many cultures as containers for sacrificial beverages and those consumed by celebrants. Hunting horns are attributes of saints Hubert, Oswald, and Eustace, as well

as Cornelius (because of the similarity of his name with the Latin word *cornu*, "horn"). (See also CORNUCOPIA and TRUMPET)

The headdress of Native Americans of the prairie regions was often adorned with pared and polished buffalo horns, one on either side of the head, lending the headdress particular significance. "This horned headdress is worn only on special occasions . . . [and only by] a man whose bravery and status is recognized by the entire tribe, and whose voice has the same weight in the deliberations of the council as a chief of the first order. . . . This headdress has a striking similarity with Jewish costume, namely with the horns worn by Abyssinian chieftains and the Israelites as a sign of might and power in great parades and victory celebrations" (George Catlin). The famous painter of Native American subjects refers here to a verse from the Old Testament— "And Zedekiah the son of Chenaanah made him horns of IRON: and he said, Thus saith the Lord, With these shalt thou push the Syrians, until thou have consumed them" [I Kings 22:11]—which, however, is probably meant allegorically.

horse In the symbolic tradition, an embodiment of power and vitality on a higher plane than that of the BULL. Already in the cave art of the Ice Age wild horses and cattle are the most important subjects, and it has been concluded (by A. Leroi-Gourhan and others) that horses and cattle formed a fundamental duality for prehistoric painters.

Horse (outline). Cave painting, Las Monedas, Spain (Prov. Santander)

Horse (pregnant) under the net. Cave painting, La Pileta, Andalusia, Ice Age

Horses were not tamed until thousands of years later, in Eastern Europe or Central Asia, and their nomadic riders often disturbed the fixed peoples who had settled in the Mediterranean region (see CENTAURS). Because of the original strangeness of the animal it was frequently associated with the realm of the dead (e.g., Wotan's horde) and sacrificed to the dead; later, however, because of its speed and vitality, it came to symbolize the sun or pulled CHARIOTS (of Apollo, Mithras, or Elijah) through the HEAVENS. Its symbolic import often remained ambiguous, as we see from the gleaming white horse of "Christ triumphant" on the one hand and the mounts of the "Horsemen of the Apocalypse" (Book of Revelation) on the other. The early Church Fathers found the animal haughty

Horse-goddess Epona. Gallo-Roman relief, Bregenz (Vorarlberg, Austria)

and lascivious (it was said to neigh longingly when it saw a woman); yet it appeared at the same time as an image of victory (e.g., that of martyrs over the world). The positive aspect was anticipated in classical antiquity in the WINGED horse PEGASUS. (See also DOLPHIN.) In FAIRY TALES horses are often prophetic creatures with magical powers, speaking with human voices and providing advice for those who are entrusted to their care. Saintly horsemen include St. Hubert, St. Eustache, St. Martin (see COATS AND CAPES), and the DRAGON-slayer St. George. In depictions of the Crucifixion Romans are shown mounted on horses whose heads, averted from Christ, symbolize their riders' unbelief.

Horses' skulls on the gables of houses were supposed to ward off misfortune. Germanic

Horse. Stone relief, "El Cigarralejo" shrine (Murcia, Spain), ca. 380 B.C.

sacrifices of horses, followed by the eating of the meat of the animal, led after the Christianization of Europe to the taboo that is still attached to the consumption of horsemeat in many societies.

Psychological symbology sees in the horse a "noble" and intelligent creature, but one easily disturbed or frightened; the id and the ego are likened to horse and rider, respectively; dreams of horses striking out blindly are often interpreted as a longing for integration.

hourglass A symbol not primarily of death but of the transitory nature of time and human experience, which, however, implies a certain *memento mori*, a reminder of our mortality. The hourglass is one of the attributes of CHRONUS or Eon, the personifica-

Hourglass, symbol of the passing of time. Wilhelm Busch

tion of time. Since it must be continually turned over if it is to function, it has also been associated with cyclical theories and notions of the "eternal return" of the same cosmological situations. In another tradition, it urges mortals to live in moderation and virtue, lest their allotted time be arbitrarily curtailed as the result of intemperance. The ascetics St. Ambrose and St. Magdalene are each depicted with an hourglass. In the ritual of FREEMASONRY, an hourglass is placed in the *chambre des réflexions* along with other symbolic objects upon which the candidate is to meditate. (See also DARKNESS.)

house Since the end of the hunter-nomadism of the Ice Age, the symbol of the center of existence for the human race as it

House of death. Terra cotta funeral urn, Etruscan, ca. 780 B.C.

settled; usually laid out (as were cities) using cosmic principles as guidelines, also to determine its location. The oldest known houses, in our sense of fixed, lasting residences, were unearthed in Jericho (see SEVEN) and Catalhuyuk (in the highland of Asia Minor) and date from around 6500 B.C., a time long before the actual development of cities, agriculture, or cattle breeding, as we understand them. The house was the center around which the subsequent progress of civilization crystalized; it was the symbol of humanity itself, once it had found its lasting place in the cosmos. Even before the discovery of pot-making, this part of the Near East had real houses made of sun-dried bricks; in Catalhuyuk they were equipped with sanctuaries and burial chambers (under the floor). We use the word "house" to refer to a family line (the House of Hapsburg, the House of York) or a firm (a brokerage house, i.e., the House of Rothschild); a synagogue or church is "the house of God" (see TOWER), and the grave is the *domus aeterna*, the "final house" or resting place—until the Last Judgment (see END OF THE WORLD). In other cultures the house is a meeting place for communal festivities, rites, and deliberations, e.g., the "men's house," a ritual covenant house where men also gather by age group (among the Tambaran of New Guinea) or the longhouse, a symbol of the Iroquoi confederation and the center of Iroquoi life (Hodenosyauné, "people of the longhouse"). In Jungian psychology, the house is an important symbol, in dreams, for example: "There are important dreams involving the house in general. . . . What happens inside it, happens within ourselves. We often are the house. Of course, Freudian psychology associates the house with the woman, the mother, in a sexual or childbearing sense; and the nature of a house is in fact more feminine or maternal than masculine. Still, the orderly, dilapidated, old, or remodeled house in a dream can stand for the dreamer, male or female" [Aeppli]. (See also FIRE.)

hyacinth One of the flowers that, according to mythology, were originally human or that came to be through the death of a human. (See also ADONIS, NARCISSUS.) The Spartan prince Hyacinthus—in what legend calls the first homoerotic love between two men—was the beloved of the musician Thamyris, but also of the god Apollo, who accidentally killed him with a throw of the discus; the west WIND Zephyrus, who was similarly enamored of Hyacinthus, was said to have diverted the discus out of jealousy. From the blood of the dying youth sprang the hyacinth [Ovid, *Metamorphoses*, Book X], whose flowers bear the letters that spell out Apollo's cry of woe: "Ai, ai!" Hyacinthia, the greatest annual feast of the Spartans, honored the grave of Hyacinth in Amyclae (where CASSANDRA's grave was also to be found). Cultural historians believe that Hyacinth was a pre-Hellenic god of vegetation whose claim to divinity dwindled next to Apollo's as the story evolved over the centuries; Hyacinth was left with the status of a legendary hero.

hyena An animal despised on the basis of anthropomorphic prejudice, long endowed with negative symbolic associations. Its name (Greek *hyaena*, from *hys*, "swine") marks it as an unclean scavenger, often believed to be a mongrel offspring of a DOG and a WOLF [Pliny] or ready to cross-breed with the wolf [Aristotle]. In Ovid's *Metamorphoses* it is said that the hyena can change its sex; the early Christian text *Physiologus*, similarly, says that it "is now male, now female, and altogether unclean, changing its nature as it does." This is why Jeremiah also says: "The cave

Hypnos carrying a sleeping person. Detail from an Attic vase, ca. 450 B.C.

of the hyena is not of my inheritance [compare 12:9]. See to it that you likewise are not like the hyena, loving now the male, now the female nature" (a warning against homosexual tendencies). This fable was passed on from author to author, although Aristotle had already recognized it as erroneous. According to Pliny, the hyena can not only imitate the human voice and call out names but also hypnotize other animals by touching them with its paw or even with its SHADOW. It was popularly believed that the hyena had magical powers: its skin could drive away hail, its first cervical vertebra brought about reconciliations (according to ancient sources), and the PRECIOUS STONE "hyaenia" (tiger-eye?) that supposedly came from its eye brought prophetic dreams. When the hyena itself appeared in someone's dreams, this was taken as an omen of the birth of a sexually malformed child. In Christian art there are portrayals of the legend of Macarius the Egyptian, who heals a BLIND boy whom a hyena has brought to him: a symbol of "having one's eyes opened" despite negative predispositions. Otherwise, the animal's role in iconography is to symbolize avarice; in depictions of the "SEVEN-headed beast" of the Book of Revelation, which stands for the seven VICES, one of the heads is that of a hyena.

Hyena. From E. Topsell's *The History of Four-footed Beasts*, 1658

Hypnos (Latin *Somnus*) The allegorical personification of the dream, son of the Night (Greek *Nyx*) and brother of Death

(Greek THANATOS). In Homer's *Iliad* Hypnos is presented as a god and persuaded by Hera (who promises him one of the GRACES in marriage) to put Zeus into a deep sleep; Hera and Thanatos can then bring the body of Sarpedon, a hero killed before the gates of Troy in battle against the Greeks, back to his native Lydia. In pictorial art Hypnos is portrayed as a youth with a poppy in his hair, holding a small horn containing soporific drink. His precise symbolic significance varies between "sleep" and "dream," and his name is the source of our word "hypnosis."

I-Ching (in older transliteration also "I-Ging"; today, "Yijing") The "Book of Changes," not itself a symbol, it is rather a guide to oracular readings growing out of speculation on the ancient Chinese DUALITY of male and female. The system of divination to which it refers was developed in the Chou dynasty, probably as early as 1000 B.C., and is said to have been first practiced with yarrow stalks, which were subsequently replaced in graphic representation with solid and broken lines. Solid lines represent the masculine, broken the feminine element. Three lines together form a trigram, and each such combination of solid and broken lines is characterized by a prevalence of one possibility or the other. The eight possible combinations stand for HEAVEN, EARTH, WATER, FIRE, moisture, WIND, THUNDER,

and MOUNTAINS. There are 64 possible pairings of the trigrams, called HEXAGRAMS, which together provide a formula or encoding for the entire universe; this is the basis for the I-Ching, the famous guide to "reading the sticks." Six solid lines, for example, stand for "heaven, KING, FATHER, donor"; six broken lines, for "earth, MOTHER, subjects, receiver." Explanatory remarks of varying length make it possible to answer specific questions that are posed by those seeking advice or information. The striving for harmony of polar opposites (see YIN AND YANG) that is expressed by the entire system was particularly stressed in the school of Confucius (or Master Kung, 551–479 B.C.); the I-Ching was also highly respected in Taoism. Present-day students of the occult often look to its system of symbols for answers to questions about personal strengths and weaknesses, as well as possibilities for success and sources of danger.

ibis (in Egyptian *hibi*; scientific name *Threskiornis aethiopica*) For the ancient Egyptians a bird of great symbolic significance, still referred to as the "sacred ibis." Some 30 inches tall, poking about in marshy ground with its SICKLE-shaped beak, it seems to be constantly searching. The curve of its beak has lunar associations (see MOON), intensified in symbolic tradition by the fact that the bird remains near the WATER. The ibis was sacred to Thoth (Djhuty), the Egyptian god of wisdom, or was considered his earthly manifestation; for this reason ibises were embalmed and buried in clay urns, and the burial crypts of Saqqarah are said to contain several million ibis mummies. It was popularly believed in ancient times that an ibis FEATHER tossed onto a SNAKE could keep it pinned to the spot, and that an ibis EGG kept away all wild animals. For the Jews, however, the ibis was a negative symbol, presumably because in Deuteronomy all wading birds are included among the "unclean" animals. But God, in a reference to the wonders of the Creation, asks in one reading of Job 38:36: "Who hath given the ibis wisdom and the ROOSTER insight?" The early Christian text *Physiologus* and medieval

I Ching: The 64 combinations of six lines, broken or unbroken

Ibis. Egyptian bronze, ca. 500 B.C.

bestiaries refer to the ibis as unable to swim and thus eating dead FISH from the shore; it prepares food for its young from these fish and from snakes. "Those who live a life of the flesh are like the ibis: they devour their deadly deeds and even feed their children with them, to their ruin" [Unterkircher]. "And the ibis is the worst of all, for out of sinners do sins sprout forth and grow" [*Physiologus*].

Icarus The mythical figure who symbolizes the human wish to soar through the clouds like a BIRD, to float in a state of weightlessness—but his story also constitutes a warning against arrogance. Daedalus, Icarus' FATHER and the builder of the Cretan LABYRINTH to house the Minotaur (see BULL), had given the princess Ariadne the ball of thread with

Icarus's fall. G. Whitney, *A Choice of Emblems*, Leiden, 1586

which she was able to assure the hero Theseus' escape from the labyrinth after he killed the monster. Her father, KING Minos, had Daedalus and Icarus imprisoned, but Daedalus made WINGS out of wax and FEATHERS, with which they were able to escape. Icarus, despite his father's warning, flew too close to the SUN, which melted the wax, and he plunged into the SEA and drowned. For humans, although hang gliding and bungie jumping come close, the desire to fly (propelled by their own muscles) has remained unfulfilled, except occasionally in dreams. Dreams of flying are interpreted generally as the result of a physiological unbalance while sleeping or (psychologically) as an expression of the desire to be freed from the restraints of gravity, of the world in which we live.

ice Naturally associated with cold and the far north, with the homeland of the "hoary giants" of Norse mythology. In this account of the beginning of the world, the first creature is a COW, Audumla, formed from melting ice, who then licked the first man out of ice. Ice naturally has no place in the cosmologies of southern lands. In the Middle Ages it was transported from the Alps to Italy and recommended to persons with "warm constitutions" as a way of cooling their internal heat. In China ice (*ping*) is associated with childlike piety: in a moral tale, a child whose mother is ill and longs for a carp sits on the ice of a frozen river until it melts and the FISH jumps out. What is on top of the ice is considered male (yang); the water below, female (YIN). "Broken ice" is a Chinese metaphor for marital pleasure in old age. There is a wealth of similar idioms in Western languages. We look for ways to "break the ice" in conversation, and we say that something "cuts no ice" with us if we are not impressed by it. Ice, however, can be deceptive, and when we "walk on thin ice" we are asking for trouble. To "put something on ice" is to delay action on it. An "icy heart" belongs to a person who knows little of pity or mercy.

idols "Graven images" were always a source of displeasure for representatives of revealed religions: they believed that the "heathens" were worshipping not supernatural beings represented by the images but rather the images themselves. According to early Christian legend, 365 graven images were toppled as Jesus, Mary, and Joseph went by in their flight into Egypt. Idolatry was treated as spiritual BLINDNESS: "How ign'rant they who graven image make,/ Abandon Christ for heathen idols' sake;/They helpless look for help where none's to find—/ What measure foolisher, what eyes more blind?" [Hohberg]. In Islamic tradition the idols of the past were knocked off their pedestals when Amina (see MOTHER) gave birth to the Prophet or, in a different version, were shaken at the moment of his conception and subsequently collapsed. The basis for this is probably a prophecy in the Book of Isaiah: "Behold, the Lord rideth upon a swift cloud, and shall come into Egypt: and the idols of Egypt shall be moved at his presence" [19:1]. Toppled idols are attributes of St. Justa, St. Rufina, and St. Susanna, and, on the icons of the Eastern Church, St. Nicholas. According to Jewish legend, ABRAHAM, at the time of KING NIMROD, was the first "iconoclast," destroying his FATHER's wooden and STONE idols: " 'They neither smell nor hear nor speak. They have a mouth and do not speak, EYES and do not see, HANDS and do not reach out and grasp, feet and do not walk. So, too, will it come to pass with those who believe in them and worship them.' And Abraham fetched an AX and

Idol worshippers. Hohberg, 1675

smashed his father's idols" [bin Gorion, 1980].

incense (Hebrew *lebonah*, Greek *libanos*, Latin *tus*) The symbol of the otherworldly "fragrance of holiness." Incense is traditionally frankincense, the gum of the shrub *Boswellia carteri*, which in antiquity was imported from southern Arabia but is also to be found in India and East Africa. In the Middle East incense was burned in sacrifices and to ward off evil spirits; in Egypt, Babylonia, Persia, and Crete, in ancestor worship. From the seventh century B.C. onward, incense was used in Greek sacrifices, especially in mystery cults; it was also recommended by PYTHAGORAS. In Rome it was used at funerals and in the worship of the emperor, and for this reason was rejected at first by Christians before its use was finally integrated into their services. Incense was also burned in everyday life. Its smoke rising to the HEAVENS symbolized the path of the ascendant soul or the prayers rising from the assembly.

In the Jewish tradition, incense was burnt only as a sacrifice to God—a symbol of worship that also served to placate divine anger. The Wise Men brought the baby Jesus frankincense from the East; in the Book of Revelation it is written that "the four beasts and four and twenty elders fell down before the Lamb, having every one of them harps, and golden vials full of odours [i.e., incense], which are the prayers of saints" [5:8]. "The incense, which becomes a sacramental through the blessing that precedes its use, serves also to purify. The censer can be swung in the form of a cross, to refer to Christ's sacrifice; or in a circle, to set apart the blessed gifts as belonging to God" [Lurker, 1987]. Censers were often adorned with reliefs of the PHOENIX or Shadrach, Meshach, and Abednego, whose songs of praise from the midst of the fiery furnace [Daniel 3:28; see OVENS] were likened to the clouds of incense. Censers were attributes frequently shown in the hands of great priestly figures from the Old Testament (Melchizedek, Aaron, Samuel), as well as the saints Stephen, Lawrence, Vincent, and Pelagia.

Incense "drifts away as it brings pleasure." J. Boschius, 1702

The use of incense at funerals may have begun as a way of masking the odor of decomposition, and the clouds of rising smoke only later have come to represent the soul going up to heaven.

In the Mayan civilization of Central America the fragrant gum of the copal tree (*pom, Protium copal*) was burned as a sacrifice. Gum balls sent their fragrance "up into the center of the sky," and incense was also called "the brain of the heavens." The censers were named after the god Yum Kak (the Lord of FIRE).

In the Far East incense (in Chinese, *hsiang*) was originally made from fragrant sandalwood. In modern times, the same incense sticks, mostly from India, have been burned in East and West. The ASHES have been gathered on occasion and swallowed to ward off disease. The use of incense seems to have spread throughout the Far East with Buddhism itself. It is now generally found in all temples and chapels, and in the shrines in private homes.

In European magic rituals conjuring up spirits of the cosmos (e.g., those of the PLANETS), there was extensive use of incense, apparently the heritage of the mystery sects of late antiquity. In some cases narcotic materials were burned as a way of inducing visionary experiences. The alchemist Leonhard Thurneysser (1530–1596) refers to "various spices, such as ALOE, frankincense, myrrh, tomato-wood, sandalwood, mastic."

Incense was also burnt by early physicians as a way of driving off harmful "miasmas" (pernicious vapors).

iron Within the entire history of civilization, iron has been put to use only relatively recently; in myths of the ages of the EARTH, it represents the last stage in a progression that began with the GOLDEN AGE. Iron is an attribute of the god of war, MARS (Greek Aries), and the REDDISH COLOR of rust suggests that of BLOOD. In the ancient world it was believed to be a metal of which demons and evil spirits were afraid; for this reason, many people wore iron RINGS and amulets, a practice that the Church found it necessary to forbid as late as the seventh century after Christ. Superstitions about horseshoes are the joint product of the belief in the metal's own power to ward off evil, the MOON-like shape of the horseshoe, and the assocation with the HORSE itself—a symbolic animal of great importance. Since ancient times people have used iron spikes to scratch magic CIRCLES in the ground for protection against demons. Many medicinal herbs could not be dug out of the ground with the iron implements used to dig graves, lest the herbs lose their curative power. The ancients found one indication of the supernatural powers of iron in its ability to be magnetized. It was believed that a lodestone could even pull away disease, arouse "sympathy," and bind married couples together. Rust was also seen as magically "infectious," poisoning plants. In ancient China iron stood for strength and justice; it was believed that it would keep hostile WATER-DRAGONS in check, and thus iron figures were buried on RIVER-banks and in dams.

Islands of the Blessed Islands were widely thought of as ordinarily unattainable paradises, symbols of a more literal PARADISE (i.e., a second Eden), associated with the AFTERLIFE, but a paradise that some attempt to locate in a "mythic geography." One example, in the Sumerian Gilgamesh epic, is the island country of Dilmun, to which the "Noah" of the Great FLOOD, here named Ziusudra or Ut-Napishtim, is carried off. Dilmun was identified as corresponding to the Bahrain Islands of the Persian Gulf, which however do not correspond with what we think of as an "island paradise." In classical antiquity there were many references to the Islands of the Blessed (Greek *macaron nesoi*, Latin *insulae fortunatae*, from which comes the Arabic *al-djaz'ir al-chalidat*), located in the western Oceanus and equated with Elysium, where the chosen went after death. Here another attempt was made at pseudo-geographical identification, this time with the Canary Islands, as Plutarch (ca. A.D. 50–125) wrote: "It seldom rains there, and when it does, then in moderation. The winds there are mostly mild, and they then bring so much dew that the earth of its own accord brings forth the best fruit in such plenty that the inhabitants have nothing more to do than to enjoy their leisure. The air is always pleasant, so that even barbarians assume that these are the Elysian fields, the abode of the blessed, which Homer portrayed in his magical verses." The historian Flavius Josephus (A.D. 37–95) associates the Islands of the Blessed with notions of a duality opposing matter and spirit, along the lines of Gnostic polaristic belief that souls are SPARKS of light that must be freed:

Islands of the Blessed: Thomas More's *Utopia*. Woodcut, 1515–16

they come from the "finest ether" but are imprisoned in the "bondage of the flesh" until death; only then do they float, purified, over the ocean to a place of rapture in the Islands of the Blessed, whereas souls besmirched by the "material" element are punished in a "dark CAVE." Fabulous paradises in the West Sea (the Atlantic) are referred to in Celtic, especially Irish, myth, which described such islands and voyages to them even before the influence of Christian missionaries. These notions were then incorporated into Christian ideology, for example in the legend of the seafaring abbot St. Brendan, who was said to have sailed to a "promised land of the blessed" (which was later interpreted as a pre-Columbian discovery of America). Visionary or mythical cosmologies, however, resist efforts to subsume them in geography as we know it.

The same can be said of traditional Chinese cosmology and its version of the Islands of the Blessed: Fang-chang, P'eng-lai, and Ying-chou, said to lie in the Pacific off the east coast of China. The "EIGHT Immortals" lived there in bliss. In earlier times the clothing of the dead was often adorned with images of the mythical islands, in order to suggest to the souls of the dead that they had already attained the joys associated with the islands. In the traditional Chinese GARDEN there bizarrely formed rock islands symbolizing the islands of legend. Similar islands of other peoples, such as those in the traditions of Native American nations of the Southeast United States, with its "Fountain of Youth," belong more in the context of myth than of symbol. Such fabled islands often resemble the longed-for land of COCKAIGNE.

ivy *(Hedera helix)* A sometimes poisonous, sometimes medicinal plant with multiple symbolic significance. Since its leaves always remain GREEN, it suggested immortality, but in other contexts it was considered demonic. The THYRSUS-staffs of Dionysus, the god of ecstasy, were twined not only with vine-leaves but also with ivy. Ivy was spoken of

Ivy: "Climbing not by my own strength." Hohberg, 1675

as cooling, and inspiring profound thoughts, and thus compensating for the heat-inducing WINE. Thalia, the MUSE of comedy, was also portrayed with an ivy WREATH. Because of the way ivy clings it also became a symbol of true love and friendship; the vigor of the plant associated it with the clandestine enjoyment of life's pleasures, so that it adorned images of SATYRS and Sileni, and it also plays a role in the Egyptian cult of the god Osiris, who is resurrected after death. Ivy wreaths were thought to cool the brow even in the course of heavy drinking. Since ivy clings to dead trees and continues green, medieval Christian symbolists elevated ivy to a symbol of the eternal life of the soul after the death of the body. Hohberg on the allegorical significance of the plant: "As swift as ivy's tendrils climb the tree,/ They hold so fast, no storm have they to fear./ Thus we ascend if God our mainstay be,/ Nor can harm come to us whilst He is near" (1675).

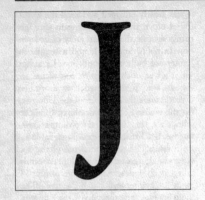

sexual metaphors that include the syllable for jade (e.g., *nung-yü*, "jade play," for intercourse). In popular Taoism the "jade emperor" (Yü Ti) is the supreme heavenly god. Jadeite (in Aztec *chalchihuitl*) was similarly prized in ancient Mexico from the time of the Olmec (ca. 800 B.C.) onward and was used in the making of religious carvings and the stones symbolizing the HEART that were placed in sarcophagi with the remains of princes. Chalchihuitlcue ("she with the jade loincloth") was the name of a WATER goddess. The hieroglyph for "PRECIOUS STONE" refers in ancient Mexico primarily to jade, less often to TURQUOISE.

jade A light-green gemstone composed of either of two minerals, jadeite (imperial jade) or nephrite (mutton-fat jade), each of which was used for making AXES in the Neolithic Age. In China jadeite was considered the most precious of all minerals, primarily because of the beauty of polished jade, finely veined with a variety of shadings, and seeming to glow from within; despite its hardness, it gives an illusion of fluidity. Translucent, emerald-green pieces were most prized and felt to symbolize purity, wisdom, and courage. As early as 3000 B.C. ritual instruments and jewelry were made from this jade; around 1500 B.C., carved FISH, BIRDS, and DRAGONS. The lasting beauty of these objects led to the belief that jade had within it the quality of immortality. Jade amulets were placed on the lips, faces, or chests of the dead, and buried with them. A famous archaeological discovery was the remains of two persons buried in "jade garments" near Manch'eng: countless thin pieces of jade had been sewn together with GOLD thread, clothing the bodies like coats of armor (around the time of the birth of Christ). In later times huge blocks of nephrite were ornately sculpted to portray entire landscapes or GARDENS. Jade carving is still actively practiced in China, with extensive use of the traditional "vocabulary" of symbols and forms. Because of the cool smoothness of its polished surface, poets often liken jade (*yü*) to the skin of a beautiful woman, and there are numerous

Janus The god with two faces, symbol of entry and exit, guardian of GATES and THRESHOLDS in ancient Rome; there is no corresponding Greek deity. All gates were sacred to him, in the belief that the beginning of any undertaking, symbolized by passing through a gate, was decisive for its completion. Janus' blessing was necessary for the first month of the year (Januarius) and for the beginning of every subsequent month and of every day. Military campaigns set out from the shrine at the archway Janus Geminus, whose gates remained open in times of war.

Their closing thus symbolized the less frequent times of peace. As the god of the doorway (*janua*), he was the guardian of the entrance to the house, with a doorkeeper's staff and a KEY as his attributes. He was

Janus as an embodiment of duality. Cartari, 1647

considered a transmitter of knowledge about agriculture and living in accord with the law; he also had his place in the state religion. As the guardian of beginnings and endings (sowing and reaping) he was portrayed with two faces, one looking forward, one back. The "head of Janus" has today in some cultures similar symbolic associations to those of the knife that "cuts both ways": the ambiguous, the combination of the positive and negative qualities of a situation or an action. Apparently independently of this Roman symbolic tradition, there are in Central Africa wooden MASKS with two faces, one with African features, one with European.

Jerusalem (Hebrew Yerushalayim, "abode of peace") The principal CITY of the Biblical world and a prime symbolic locus in Judaism, Christianity, and Islam, Jerusalem was already settled in the fourth millenium B.C. and is referred to in Egyptian documents of the 18th century B.C. as "Aushamen, Rushalimum" and ca. 1400 B.C. as "Urushalim." Ca. 1000 B.C. KING DAVID conquered the city, which was at that time controlled by the Jebusites, and made it his capital. With the help of the Phoenicians, his successor SOLOMON built the palace and the TEMPLE on Mount Zion, the sacred MOUNTAIN of Israel, considered to be the permanent abode of God. In 586 B.C. the city was destroyed by Nebuchadnezzar; from 538 B.C. on, resettled by the Jews. The construction of the "second temple" was completed in 515 B.C.;

Jerusalem, "City of the King of Kings." Crusader's coin of King Baldwin I

it was greatly enlarged by Herod the Great (37–4 B.C.), then destroyed again after uprisings against the Roman army of occupation (A.D. 70 and 135), and a temple to Jupiter was built on Mount Zion. Jerusalem was a major Christian center under the EMPEROR Constantine, but after the city came under Arab rule (A.D. 638) the Umayyad "Dome of the Rock" came to stand on the foundation of Herod's temple. (See OMPHALOS.) Countless Biblical passages document the religious importance of Jerusalem, which is far greater than its objective role as a city in Judea. At the time of Christ, Jerusalem had a population of about 25,000. "The temple is the palace of 'King Yahweh,' the place of his throne, the place of the soles of his feet [Ezekiel 43:7]. As the temple was selected and chosen to be God's property, so too the city of Jerusalem" [A. Stöger, quoted by Bauer]. Visions of the END OF THE WORLD and the Last Judgment (see also TRUMPET) make Jerusalem a mythic place in which all of humanity will be separated into the saved and the damned. The "heavenly" or "new Jerusalem" is a counterpart to the terrestrial city, elevated and transfigured (see PRECIOUS STONES and CUBE); this city, in the Book of Revelation, descends from heaven as the "city of God," in which no temple is necessary any more, "for the Lord God Almighty and the Lamb are the temple of it. And the temple had no need of the sun, neither of the moon, to shine in it: for the glory of God did lighten it" [21:22–23].

The difficult question—for people living today—of the relationship between the real (terrestrial) and the "heavenly Jerusalem" is treated by E. Aron [1973] as follows: the temple lies in a sense at the point of intersection between heaven and earth, experience and transcendence, and it "corresponds somehow, on the terrestrial level, to the inaccessible sanctuary in which the Messiah awaits, perhaps, the moment to enter the world. 'There is a Holy of Holies in heaven that corresponds to the one on earth.' According to Rabbi Simeon ben Jochai, who lived in the first century after Christ, Mount Moria is the counterpart of the sanctuary in

Jerusalem. Woodcut in Salomon Schweigger's travel memoirs, 1638

the other world. When the sanctuary below is completed, a new one of the same sort spontaneously comes into being in heaven. A structure built by human hands is reflected in the heavenly spheres." These mental structures based on correspondences between ABOVE AND BELOW are also characteristic of other cultures that perceive otherworldly primal images and terrestrial reflections as analogues. To return to Jerusalem was for many centuries the dream of the Jewish people, who in the time of the Romans had been banished and scattered in the new Diaspora (Hebrew *Galuth*; see also AHASUERUS)—driven out, often, with the catcall "hep, hep" (from the initials of *Hierosalyma est perdita*, Latin for "Jerusalem is lost"). In the symbolism of FREEMASONRY it also plays a major role as the site where the Temple of Solomon was built; the XVIth Degree of the Scottish Rite, for example, is called "Prince of Jerusalem."

Jizo (literally "bowels of the EARTH") A Japanese personification of MOTHER Earth, appearing nevertheless in masculine form. He is portrayed as a mendicant friar (see BEGGAR), simply dressed, bald, and holding a plate for alms (*Jizo bosatsu*), often wearing a RED sweater and a woolen cap. Jizo is foremost among the popular deities of Japan, and figures of him are common along the roadside. He is supposed to be a source of blessings, functioning as a "guardian ANGEL" for children. Sometimes STONES are placed atop statues of him, to serve as stepping stones when he guides the souls of children who have died young across the RIVER between this world and the next (see AFTERLIFE).

Joan of Arc (French Jeanne d'Arc; 1412–1431) The Maid (see VIRGIN) of Orléans, a national symbol in France not unlike William TELL in Switzerland. The farm girl from Domrémy on the Meuse was a visionary who claimed to have heard the voices of the archangel Michael, St. Catherine, and St. Margaret, and to have received divine inspiration to restore the greatness of France. Her charisma enabled her to bring about the coronation of Charles VII at Reims and to win several victories in the Hundred Years' War before fortune turned against her and she was captured by the Burgundians in 1430 and turned over to the English. Accused of blasphemy, sorcery, and the unnatural wearing of men's clothing, she was interrogated under torture, initially pardoned but then—in a time of ever greater fear of WITCHES—condemned to be burned at the stake. At the time of her successes it was said, among other things, that a swarm of WHITE BUTTERFLIES surrounded her FLAG. When Joan was put to death—at the age of 19—an English soldier saw a white DOVE emerge from the flames and ascend into the HEAVENS. Not long thereafter (1456) an ecclesiastical and judicial proclamation ex-

Joan of Arc. Drawing made during her lifetime, Clément des Fauquembergues

onerated her; her unsullied reputation, despite all of the accusations leveled against her, contributed to her posthumous ability to fascinate increasingly wider circles of admirers; Joan, who was canonized in 1920, is commemorated in plays by Schiller [*The Maid of Orléans*, 1801], Shaw [*Saint Joan*, 1923], and Anouilh [*The Lark*, 1953].

Job A Biblical figure symbolizing the person whose faith in God remains unshaken despite severe trials and blows of fate. The story of Job begins with his use by God and the DEVIL as an "experimental subject," to be tested to determine his true attitude toward God. Satan has God's permission to inflict any imaginable torment upon Job, and, as God predicts, Job's faith and love never waver: "For I know that my redeemer liveth" [Job 19:25]. Job sees that he cannot dispute God, must recognize his wisdom, and he is thereupon blessed by God, getting back twice what he had lost; and "after this lived Job an hundred and forty years, and saw his sons, and his sons' sons, even four generations" [42:16]. The Book of Job was especially prized in the Middle Ages, as the Prayer for the Dead shows: "Redeem, O Lord, his soul, as you freed Job from his afflictions!" Christian typological interpre-

tation, for which the contents of the Old Testament are anticipations of the New, sees the suffering Job, mocked by his former friends, as corresponding to Christ suffering and scorned on the Cross; the mocking friends, to heretics; Job vindicated and restored to happiness, to the devout Christian restored to PARADISE after the Last Judgment. Temporarily afflicted with leprosy, then healed, Job has frequently been viewed as a patron saint of hospitals, especially of those treating lepers. Compare LAZARUS.

Joseph The foster FATHER of Jesus, descended from the house of KING DAVID, popularly canonized in the Christian world, and a figure whose name boys frequently receive at baptism. In the Gospel according to St. Matthew, he is identified as "Joseph the husband of Mary, of whom was born Jesus, who is called Christ" [1:16]. An ANGEL informed him that Jesus was sired by the Holy Ghost, and from then on Joseph brought the boy up as his son, until Jesus was 19, as legendary accounts report [*The History of Joseph, the Carpenter*]. "The good foster father withdraws, effacing himself like one who knows that his task on earth is completed. . . . He had protected the child, as he had allowed the MOTHER to accept her

Job learns of his afflictions. Gustave Doré (1832–1883)

Joseph as the foster father of Jesus. W. Auer, 1890

Judas Iscariot devoured by Lucifer. From Dante's *Inferno*, Venice, 1512

supernatural calling. . . . The apocryphal text is surely not mistaken when it shows us an angel of the Lord keeping vigil at the death of this decent man" [Daniel-Rops]. Joseph the carpenter (in Aramaic *naggar*, "joiner, cabinet maker, master builder") has become a symbol of selfless renunciation: "Mary, engaged to Joseph, then the virginal mother of the holy child, chooses to remain a VIRGIN forever" [Bauer]. This doctrine explains the German word *Josefsehe* ("Joseph's marriage") to refer to a marriage that the partners refrain from consummating.

Judas He betrayed Jesus to his enemies, then so regretted his deed that he hanged himself, and came to symbolize all traitors. Thus for example the farmer Raffl, who

betrayed the Tyrolese freedom fighter Andreas Hofer to the French, leading to Hofer's execution (1810), was called "the Judas of the Tyrol." Legends, however, often reveal hints of something like pity for the traitor, whose betrayal paved the way for the redemption of humanity through the Crucifixion. In the *Navigatio Sancti Brandani*, the sea voyage that took the Irish saint Brendan (ca. 484–577) to the mythical ISLANDS OF THE BLESSED, it is also written that once a year the soul of Judas is granted one day's "vacation from HELL" on an island in the northern sea, a cooling respite from the eternal FIRE, because he once gave a poor man a sheet. At day's end, however, his soul is once again seized by demons and carried back to hell. In painting and sculpture Judas is often portrayed holding the traitor's purse containing the "thirty pieces of silver" [Matthew 26:15], or betraying Christ with the kiss that identifies him to the agents seeking him [27:49]. The traditional Passion play offered the ultimate (although naively atemporal) depiction of Judas, disdaining the logical sequence of events, as in the following words, which the actor playing Judas spoke to the Pharisees: "I will betray to you Jesus Christ, who died for us on the Cross. . . ."

Jupiter or Jove (Greek Zeus) The lord of the HEAVENS who resided on Mount Olym-

Jupiter as ruler of the calendar year. J. Hassfurt, 1491

Jupiter with his lightning bolts. Cartari, 1647

pus, an omnipotent ruler with bolts of LIGHTNING ever at hand. His astral counterpart is known today to be the largest PLANET in the solar system, circling the sun in approximately 399 days. The orbit of Jupiter, like that of Mars, is irregular when viewed from the EARTH, characterized by S-curves that may help to explain the multitude of ancient myths about the irregular love life of the father of the gods. In astrology Jupiter is considered "the great benefactor" or "bringer of good fortune"; its "diurnal house" is Sagittarius and its "nocturnal house" Pisces (see FISH). Those born under the influence of Jupiter are said to be "jovial," benevolent, friendly, kind-hearted, or, in negative manifestations, haughty and self-satisfied. Jupiter is a planet of the daytime, masculine, supportive of life, ruling religion, law, and the human ages from 57 to 68. Its color is reddish-purple or GREEN; its metal, zinc; the PRECIOUS STONES associated with it, EMERALD, AMETHYST, turquoise, and jasper, and, as a decorative STONE, also fine serpentine. In ancient China, the gleaming yellowish-white planet is the "lord of the East," its color BLUE, and its associated ELEMENT WOOD.

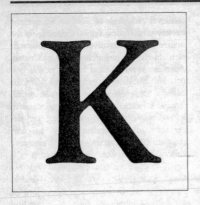

karashishi The animal figures "guarding" the gates (see TORII) of Japanese shrines; also called "dogs of Buddha" (*fo-chi*). Although they guard Buddhist temples, these "Chinese LIONS" originated in the Shinto religion. Because the Chinese had never actually seen lions, the *karashishi* resemble a Pekinese more than the predatory beast known in the Occident. The "lion" to the right side of the gate is conceived of as male and has its mouth open; the one to the left, as female, its mouth closed. Although they are more comical than frightening in appearance, the *karashishi* are symbols of vitality and endurance: it is said that when they are cubs their MOTHERS throw them off

Karashishi guarding entrance to a Japanese shrine

high precipices so that only the strongest survive. It is also popularly believed that they can take hollow balls that are rolled to them and fill them with precious MILK.

key Because it both locks and unlocks, frequently associated with its bearer's power to confine and set free. (Compare KNOTS.) In ecclesiastical tradition it is St. Peter who holds "the keys of the kingdom of heaven" [Matthew 16:19]. Because Peter is so frequently portrayed with great keys, he is also popularly referred to as the gatekeeper of heaven. Other saints also have keys as attributes: King Ferdinand of Spain, who conquered ("freed") the Moorish city of Córdoba, or Hippolytus, the dungeon guard converted by St. Lawrence; Martha and Notburga (patron saints of housekeepers and maids) are each portrayed with a bunch of keys. In depictions of the Last Judgment a giant key is used to lock the DEVIL in the "bottomless pit" for a thousand years [Revelation 20:1–3].

In many systems of FREEMASONRY the key is one of the "jewels of office," symbolizing the rank of Master or Treasurer. It also appears in a T-shape, resembling a tau CROSS or a HAMMER. The TONGUE is also spoken of as a key: of those not present, for example, it is to speak only good; otherwise, it is to remain silent, locking in evil, as it were.

Turning over the keys of a city under siege was a tangible symbol of surrender to the victor; even today the keys to the city are handed to honored guests (or to the king and queen of Mardi Gras, who rule for three days of merrymaking). Popular speech has long made reference to the keys to a beloved person's HEART: in the 12th century Wernher of Tegernsee sang, "You are locked up in my heart; the key is lost, and you must abide within forever." A "key" is also the process by which messages are decoded or symbols interpreted, as in Luke 11:52: "Woe unto you, lawyers! for ye have taken away the key of knowledge"—i.e., through false interpretation of the Scripture you have blocked access for those who seek to know God.

Key: It "opens and closes." J. Boschius, 1702

In civil law the keys that hung from the belt of a married woman took on great importance as a symbol of her status. She ordinarily received them from her new mother-in-law when she married, which gave her sole access to all the recesses of the house. Böckler writes as follows of the significance of keys in coats of arms: "Keys refer to mastery, to the power to lock and unlock—for which reason they are also the attribute of two-faced JANUS, who had the power to lock up the old year and unlock the new. It is also customary to present the keys of the city to those who have sovereignty over it, as an indication that the city is entirely theirs. Keys in a coat of arms also indicate trust and proven loyalty to one's lord and master" [1688]. Keys appear in the coats of arms of the cities of Regensburg, Bremen, Soest, and Stade, and of the Benedictine monastery in Melk (Lower Austria). The two keys in the Papal arms, in reference to the power to "bind" and "loose" [Matthew 16:19], were originally of GOLD and SILVER, the former to "bind," the latter to "loose." Avignon, temporary seat of the Papacy and under Papal rule from 1348 to 1797, included a third key in its coat of arms, as a symbol of the city's submission to Papal authority.

keystones The stones that adorn and secure the apex of an arch or dome. In the medieval cathedrals of Western Europe the keystones often bear symbols identifying the master builders involved in the construction. In the Mayan architecture of Central America, in which there are no "true" ("Vitruvian") arches but rather "false" or corbelled arches, these overlays that bind wall to wall are often adorned with paintings of gods or princes and hieroglyphic texts; the corbels thus symbolically "crown" the completion of the structure much as keystones do in the Old World.

king A symbolic figure of rule—understandable only in advanced civilizations or within their sphere of influence—extending the patriarchal principle (see FATHER) of the world of the gods to human society, or serving as the terrestrial counterpart of the masculine sovereignty associated with solar religions. (QUEENS are less frequently of symbolic significance and indicate matriarchal [see MOTHER] qualities of the civilization in question. They are usually associated with domains considered sacred.) In many ancient civilizations the king must be vigorous and at the height of his powers, showing no signs of age; otherwise he must do away with himself or be killed. It is often required that he appear to be the greatest of heroes, but he may not play an active role in battle. Through divine analogy he is supposed to have supernatural powers—such as the ability to heal the sick simply by touching them—with which he was supposedly endowed at the solemn ceremony of coronation (see

King: One of the "Three Kings." Coptic fresco, church of Faras in Nubia, ca. A.D. 1200

King: The "Three Kings," actually astrologers (magi), in Bethlehem. W. Auer, 1890

CROWN). Within his kingdom he embodies the divine order of the cosmos, parallel to the SUN in the HEAVENS. Thus the Pharaoh is the earthly counterpart of Rê; the Inca (not unlike the emperor of Japan or the baroque "sun king" Louis XIV), of the sun god Ynti. The successor in this ideological tradition is the adulation of the rulers of Rome in the period following the deification of Julius Caesar, and the ensuing creation of the title of EMPEROR—subsequently modifying by the phrase "by the grace of God"; this found ready acceptance in the Christian world through ecclesiastical sanction and participation in the ceremony of anointment and coronation. The common basis for all such belief is the desire for an embodiment of authority that will guarantee the welfare of the people.

The Wise Men at the stable in Matthew 2—Magi, Eastern astrologers—soon came to be referred to as kings (e.g., "We three kings of Orient are") and representatives of the three known continents (Asia, Africa, and Europe); the traditional names for them, such as Caspar, Melchior, and Balthazar, do not appear in the Bible. They also represent three stages in a man's life (Caspar, European, old age; Melchior, Asian, maturity; Balthasar, "Moorish," young manhood) and respect shown to the Christ child by the heathen world—which although not yet converted nevertheless has some premonition of the possibilities of salvation—for the newborn Christ. In the symbolism of AL-CHEMY the king usually appears in conjunction with the queen, representing the sun-and-MOON DUALITY (Gabricius and Beya, VENUS and MARS, and so forth), in accordance with the theory of SULFUR AND MERCURY, which together, after alchemistic purification, form the "philsopher's STONE," usually represented by a crowned ANDROGYNE. Jungian psychology has subjected the alchemistic tradition to extensive analysis and views the king less as an image of paternal authority (a "father imago") and more as an archetype, in the psyche's great store of inherited symbols, of higher insight and wisdom. In European fairy tales the figure of the king predominantly represents the end-point of all the hero's travels and adventures on his way to education and maturity. Noble birth is not involved here: the "kingship" of the protagonist, who is usually of modest social origins, consists in his identifying himself symbolically with "the finest of the land" and developing his own abilities as fully as possible. Major symbolic figures of legend include King Arthur of ancient England, and Frederick I (called "Barbarossa"), who is said to be asleep in the Kyffhäuser Mountains or on the Untersberg near Salzburg.

knight   A member of a warrior class, order, or noble rank with its own code of honor and a conventionally established mode of behavior, now elevated to the status of symbol through the concept of "chivalry." Ancient Rome distinguished between *equites equo publico*, those whose horses were provided by public funds, and *equites equo privato*, who could provide their own horse and battle gear. In the heyday of the Roman Empire, the *eques Romanus* emerged more

Knight battling dragon. *Tristan und Isolde*, 1484

Knight in armor. Wallhausen, *Art of War on Horseback*, 1616

Knighthood was at first not hereditary but had to be attained through one's own feats and honors. Hereditary knighthood began only in 1186, with certain knights responsible only to the (Holy Roman) Emperor and others in feudal relationships with princes or other sovereigns. The knight's education began at the age of seven with service as a page; at 14 he became a squire, and at 21 he was dubbed a knight, having the flat blade of the SWORD laid upon his shoulder or the back of his neck. An episode in the Hundred Years' War (see JOAN OF ARC) illustrates the importance of this ritual: a country squire was about to take the Earl of

and more clearly as a privileged class including not only officers but also landowners, orators, and grammarians. In the Imperial period the importance of the *equites Romani*, of patrician or noble birth and linked with the EMPEROR, increased; they became prefects, procurators, and holders of other important civil posts, and in the second century after Christ were the pillars of the imperial bureaucracy.

In the Middle Ages a "knight" was at first simply a member of the class of professional soldiers in the employ of individual kings; around the year 1000, what we understand today as "knighthood" came into being.

Knights as symbols of vain power. Hohberg, 1647

Suffolk prisoner when Suffolk questioned whether the man was truly a knight; he insisted on dubbing him on the spot before he would let the man arrest him—anything rather than submit to a man of low rank.

In Bavaria and Austria, "knight" *(Ritter)* designated a rank between "baron" *(Freiherr)* and the untitled nobility. In England, knighthood is a nonhereditary honor conferred by the KING or QUEEN; knights are addressed as "Sir" plus their given name. Members of certain military orders, and recipients of certain state honors, are also referred to as knights.

knots In string and ribbons, associated with the themes of tying and untying, retention and release. Their essential quality is one of uniting, binding, and thus also of confining;

Knight: St. George slaying the dragon. W. Auer, 1890

Knots: "Whoever pulls at me will only make me more solid." J. Boschius, 1702

the undoing of knots frees energies and individuals. The image of cutting through a knot originally referred to an unconventional but speedy and most direct path to one's goal, and to the setting free of previously confined power. The most famous such symbol is the Gordian knot, in the FORTRESS of the Phrygian capital Gordium: an elaborately knotted strap connected the pole of the legendary, eponymous KING Gordius' CHARIOT to the YOKE. It is possible that this knot was an object used in religious ceremonies to symbolize the link between the AXIS MUNDI and either the EARTH or the HEAVENS. Tradition had it that whoever managed to undo the knot would be master of the entire world. It is said that in the winter of 334–333 B.C. ALEXANDER THE GREAT simply cut the knot with his SWORD. "Cutting the Gordian knot" became a proverbial expression for solving a difficult

Knots: Ancient Chinese endless knot, symbol of longevity

problem by taking forceful action that others could not have conceived. It was popularly believed in antiquity that tight knots could not only restrain evil demons but also cast a spell to hold a lover; "love knots," symbolizing an engagement, are not as binding as a RING, and thus can still be untied, or used in situations where marriage is impossible. Knots can be a hindrance when the goal is deliverance—as in the case of childbirth ("delivery"): no one was allowed to enter the temple of Juno Lacinia, the Roman goddess of childbirth, with anything knotted on his or her person. Pliny the Elder (A.D. 23–79) describes the custom of the father wrapping a BELT or sash around the expectant mother and then saying to her, "I have tied you up, and now I set you free," in order to make her delivery easier. In ancient Greece, several statues of the gods were tied up so that they would not escape

Knots: Fabric pattern, shroud of the "Iron" Archduke Ernest, ca. 1420

(or rather so that the higher beings dwelling within would not leave the statues representing them; see OMPHALOS). In the Christian world Romanesque "braided" ornamentation is related to the Germanic notion of "knots of destiny" tied by divine power. In Anglo-Saxon art this power was ascribed to Christ, the only one capable of freeing humanity from terrestrial bonds and entanglements. Knots have long been tied in garments to ward off evil, and such knots carry over into carvings and metalwork. Knots in the garments of bride and groom are especially common (see WEDDING CUSTOMS). In the monastic world, the knotted cord around

the monk's waist symbolizes that he is bound
by the vows that he has taken; three knots
refer to poverty, celibacy, and obedience.
WITCHES were said to practice a misan-
thropic form of knot magic by (symbolically)
tying up the drawstrings on the trousers of
married men so tightly that they were unable
to undo them and sire offspring.

Various ancient Egyptian symbols refer to
knots, such as the "noose of Isis" (associated
with the BLOOD of Isis), the cord tied to
form a ring or CIRCLE as a symbol of eternity,
and presumably also the ANKH. Similarly,
the oval cartouche enclosing the hieroglyphs
for the name of the Pharaoh is to be understood as a cord tied in a knot. In the Alps
we occasionally find magic knots in stone
drawings, ornamental "endless" knots presumably intended to keep evil spirits away
from hikers. In Hinduism the acts of devotion of religious penitents are represented by
knots. In Buddhism the "mystic knot," one
of the "eight treasures," symbolizes the duration of spiritual life: never-ending wisdom
and vigilance. In the symbolism of FREE-
MASONRY, knots—for example, in the "cord
of union," symbolizing also the binding nature of the Mason's duties—apparently go
back to medieval artisan-builders and their
world of images. The two Romanesque PIL-
LARS in the Würzburg cathedral are named
Jachin and Boaz after the pillars in Solomon's temple [I Kings 7:21]; one ornamental
cord is wrapped eight times around Jachin
and knotted once, another four (see NUM-
BERS) times around Boaz and knotted twice—
apparently referring to symbolic traditions

Kukri emblem of the Gurkha Regiment (India)

of pillars and knots which we are unable to
explicate today. Knots and braids are of
great symbolic importance in China. The
endless knot p'an-chang is a Buddhist symbol, also called "the knot of happiness."
Following Indian tradition it is likened to a
knot formed from the intestines of slain
enemies. The knot, with its six loops over
a central square, is a frequent ornamentation
in handicrafts. In general, for ancient cultures the magical act of tying or untying
knots is of greater importance than the knot
itself as a symbol in the stricter sense.

kukri The curved dagger of the Nepalese
Gurkhas, with its cutting edge on the inside
of the curve. Two crossed kukris were the
symbol of these mercenary troops, who were
recruited by English trainers, then stationed
in various parts of Asia, where they were
the most feared combatants. This double-
kukri symbol corresponds to the European
image of two crossed SWORDS, which signifies
"battle."

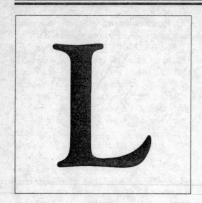

labarum The royal flag of Rome, carried before the Roman army; in a narrower sense, in the Christian symbolism, the flag of victory with the CHI-RHO (the monogram of Christ), which is said to have accompanied the emperor Constantine I at his victory over Maxentius in the Battle of Milvian Bridge (in the year 312). In the Middle Ages this labarum became the insignia of the resurrected Christ, a symbol of his victory over death. In Easter processions the "LAMB of God" is represented with this victory flag.

labyrinth A specific sort of tortuous path, originally constructed around a system of

Labyrinth: Floor mosaic, Chartres Cathedral

co-ordinate axes (see CROSS) in fretwork or SPIRAL-like curving lines. The near universality of similarly constructed labyrinths suggests that they were significant as religious symbols, indicating in a compact space a long and difficult path, often one of initiation. Subsequently designated as "Trojan fortresses," these labyrinths apparently served as a sort of notation for religious dances. It is because of this association that they appear in ancient Greek floor mosaics and, in Scandinavia (especially on the island of Gotland), in the arrangements of rows of stones. In medieval cathedrals they were understood as "roads to Jerusalem" which the faithful followed, praying and on their knees, in lieu of a pilgrimage to the Holy Land; the labyrinth on the floor of the Chartres cathedral has a diameter of almost 40 feet, and the path through it measures approximately an eighth of a mile. In many myths and legends of distant cultures there are labyrinths through which the hero must make his way in order to attain a great goal. The Greek myth of the demigod Theseus, who killed the minotaur in the labyrinth at Crete, also indicates the association of the labyrinth with rituals of initiation (see ICARUS). In later times, especially in the baroque and rococo periods, labyrinths—which originally had been clearly, if elaborately, constructed—became garden mazes of cropped hedges with blind alleys, serving merely as distractions for park visitors.

Psychologists see the labyrinth as an expression of the "search for the center," something of an incomplete MANDALA.

ladder A symbol in the Judeo-Christian world of the link between HEAVEN and EARTH, and of the possibility of ascending into heaven. In Jacob's famous dream vision, heavenly angels go up and down a ladder [Genesis 28:12], an expression of ongoing communication between God and humanity. Ladders have appeared in naive descriptions of other ascents into heaven: Christ's Ascension, that of the prophet Elijah (ordinarily shown in a CHARIOT of FIRE), or that of any unblemished soul. Ladders appear in abstract allegories like the ladder of

Labyrinths in baroque emblems. J. Boschius' *Symbolographia,* 1702

ric, logic, arithmetic, geometry, music, and astronomy (or variations thereupon).

The symbol of a ladder with seven rungs (compare PLANETS) appeared already in the cult of Mithra, and perhaps of ORPHEUS as well. In non-European cultures, shamans entering a trance have been spoken of as ascending a ladder. The ancient Egyptian expression *asken pet* (the ladder of the SUN god) refers, however, to a staircase rather than a ladder in our sense.

lamb A young SHEEP; symbol of the lambs sarificed by the Israelites to escape the tenth plague that God meted out to Egypt for refusing to let Moses and his people go [Exodus 11–12]. The image of God as a SHEPHERD caring for his flock (his people), and of God's servant who is brought to the slaughter like a sacrificial lamb [Isaiah 53:7], yielded the image in the New Testament of the "good shepherd" Christ, who seeks lambs who have gone astray. In John 1:29 John the Baptist refers to Jesus as "the Lamb of God [Latin *agnus Dei*], which taketh away the sin of the world." The Book of Revelation refers to the triumphant lamb: "Lo, a Lamb stood on the mount Sion" [14:1]. The Lamb of God (paschal lamb) as a Christ symbol appears already in the Roman cata-

VIRTUE, with its SEVEN rungs; martyrdom as a ladder to heaven; or the ladder of asceticism, whose first rung is the DRAGON of sin, which must be tread upon. In Byzantium the VIRGIN Mary is addressed as the heavenly ladder which God descended to reach sinners and through which he enables them to reach heaven. In nonecclesiastical contexts, philosophy is often personified as one of the "liberal arts" with a ladder on its breast. Like the CHAIN, the ladder also symbolizes a link to the higher spheres (see ABOVE/ BELOW). In the symbolism of Freemasonry, the "mystic ladder" with two times seven rungs is, in the Scottish Rite, the symbol of the 30th degree; the rungs are, in one grouping, justice, mercy, humility, loyalty, work, duty, and generosity (informed by shrewd insight), and, in the other, the "liberal arts" of medieval scholasticism: grammar, rheto-

Ladder to heaven, with the four impediments: Poverty, disease, lust, early death. Cicero, *Duty,* 1531

Lamb of God with nimbus and cross: Symbol of the sacrificial death of Christ

Lamb with cross banner, and rose with cross inscribed: Martin Luther's imprint

combs; the Council of Trullo at the end of the 17th century forbade the portrayal of Christ as a lamb in Byzantine iconography. In the West, however, the triumphant Easter lamb with the flag of victory over death is a favorite symbol of the Resurrection, and figures portraying this lamb, made from consecrated wax, were worn as amulets. The sacrificial lamb also symbolizes martyrdom, e.g., the lamb between the WOLVES in the Roman Praetextatus catacomb. The shepherd Abel sacrificed a lamb in the Old Testament, and the lamb later became the attribute of such saints as Susanna, Agnes (because of the homonymy Agnes/agnus), and Wendelin, the patron saint of shepherds. Baroque "pastoral dramas" were saccharine romances about the shepherd's life, with coy allusions to the innocence of "sweet little lambs" caught up in erotic imbroglios.

laurel   (Greek *daphne*, Latin *laurus*) A bush or tree of the Mediterranean region, sacred to the cult of the SUN god Apollo. The myth of the metamorphosis of DAPHNE, the nymph of whom he was enamored, into a laurel, is cited to explain his association with the tree. Through it Apollo provided

Lamb: Agnus Dei on a key from the abbey at Cluny (France), 12th century.

oracular wisdom, purging himself of guilt for killing the DRAGON or SNAKE Python, and Orestes for killing his mother Clytemnestra. Laurel leaves were prized not only for their medicinal properties but also for their ability to cleanse the soul of guilt. Laurel GROVES surrounded the shrines of Apollo, and the oracular priestess Pythia in Delphi chewed laurel leaves when she mounted the wreathed tripod on which she received Apollonian wisdom. Laurel was sacred to Dionysus (see BACCHUS), along with IVY, and, in ancient Rome, to Jupiter as well. It came to symbolize peace after the defeat of one's enemies: notices proclaiming victory, and the weapons with which it had been won, were adorned with laurel sprigs and placed in the lap of a sculpted Jupiter. In Roman ritual, as for the Greeks, the laurel had the power to purge those who had shed the BLOOD of others, and legend had it that the laurel was the one tree planted on earth that was never struck by LIGHTNING. Burnt offerings were kindled with laurel branches, whose crackling was considered a good omen. Laurel WREATHS and branches figured on coins and gemstones as attributes of Jupiter and Apollo. Laurel leaves were prized in the early Christian world as well, as a symbol of eternal life and of the renewal brought by Christ's sacrifice. The allegorical goddess Victory (Greek Nike) has been portrayed throughout the centuries as crowning victors with laurel wreaths.

Lazarus   (Hebrew Eleazar) The name of two unrelated figures referred to in the New Testament gospels. The Lazarus in Christ's parable of the rich man and the beggar [Luke 16:19–31] symbolizes the person who suffers

Laurel, whose wood is said to withstand lightning. Hohberg, 1675

poverty and disease on earth and is rewarded in heaven; his high-living opposite dies and comes to know the torments of HELL. Lazarus rests in the bosom of ABRAHAM, while the rich man's entreaty that the beggar might be sent to "dip the tip of his finger in water and cool [the rich man's] tongue" is denied: for "between us and you there is a great gulf fixed: so that they which would pass from hence to you cannot; neither can they pass to us, that would come from thence." Because the beggar in his lifetime was "full of sores," he, like JOB, came to be thought of as the patron saint of lepers' hospitals, and then later of hospitals in general; hence the English word "lazaretto" (or "lazaret") and its cognates in other European languages. It is the other Lazarus, the brother of Mary and Martha of Bethany, whom Jesus raised from the dead [John 11:1–44]. In the visual

Lazarus as a leprous beggar. Illustration in Merian Bible, Strasbourg, 1625

arts Lazarus, bound in graveclothes, frequently served as an embodiment of the belief in the resurrection of the dead. European charitable societies (e.g., the Lazarists) often derive their names from these two symbolic traditions.

lead Viewed in antiquity as a metal with magic powers; lead tablets into which had been scratched curses upon one's enemies, were thought to be particularly effective. Thin plates of lead were worn over the chest as protection against magic spells, especially demonic love-spells. In Greek mythology it was with lead that the hero Bellerophon slew the fire-breathing CHIMERA: riding the winged horse PEGASUS, whom he had tamed with the help of Athena, he shot ARROWS down upon the monster and finally hurled a lead ingot impaled on his spear into its

Lead: The sickle-like symbol of the planet Saturn (astrology, alchemy)

maw. The lead, melted by the monster's breath, flowed down its throat and destroyed its viscera. Lead was considered the terrestrial counterpart of the planet SATURN, which was represented by an old man with a wooden leg and a scythe, with the qualities "cold" and "damp." In ALCHEMY lead was believed to be closely related to GOLD, and there were tales of successful "transmutations" of molten lead into gold by sprinkling in bits of the "philosopher's STONE": an image of the ennobling of the terrestrial, material human being to a "more SUN-like" spirituality. Colloquial and poetic speech ("like a lead balloon," "a leaden heart") and Christian similes ("The burden of sin weighs upon a man like lead") frequently refer to the heaviness of the metal.

Lent-cloth (Latin *velum quadragesimale*, German *Hungertuch*) A cloth or curtain hung in the apse of a church to cover the altar during Lent, especially in alpine regions in earlier centuries. Around A.D. 1000 a white cloth was customary, but Lent-cloths were soon adorned with colors (BLACK, VIOLET, BROWN), then with scenes from the Bible as well. Famous Lent-cloths include those of the cathedrals of Gurk (1458) and Millstatt (1593), both in Carinthia, Austria. Because it symbolized Lenten fasting, the cloth became popularly associated with hunger; in German, a destitute person is said not only to be "as poor as a churchmouse" (as in English) but also to be "gnawing on the Lent-cloth"—like, indeed, the poor MOUSE, who also has few other options.

light The universal symbol of divinity and the spiritual; after the primeval CHAOS of DARKNESS, light flooded the universe and bade obscurity be gone. Light and darkness form the most important DUALITY of opposing forces, light frequently being symbolized by its most powerful source, the SUN. Sunlight is direct "illumination," whereas the light of the MOON is obtained through reflection, speculation. Darkness, it should be noted, is not always the hostile opponent of light: it can function as its complement (see YIN AND YANG). Patriarchal civilizations take light to be masculine and darkness feminine. The religion of ancient Persia focuses on the struggle between light (Ormudz) and darkness (Ahriman), the realm of light having divine—and that of darkness, demonic—qualities. The immediately "clear" idea of the ascent through darkness to the light is the subject of most theories of initiation. In the Cabala the primeval light is the essence of divinity, just as in Christianity the Savior is called "the light of the world." The association of light, sun, and God to do battle against evil is clear in a late Babylonian hymn to the sun god Shamash (ninth century B.C.): "Thou who dost

Light created by God's spirit (dove); the first word. Fludd, *History*, 1617

illumine darkness and the sky, destroyer of evil above and below, god Shamash. . . . All princes rejoice to gaze upon thee; all the gods of heaven exult in thee. In thy brilliance do they see even that which is hidden, and thus do they walk secure in thy light. . . . All the gates of heaven are open wide, and all the gods of heaven do sacrifice unto thee!" The sunlight hymn of the Egyptian "heretic king," Akhenaton ("sun"), is famous: "Beautiful art thou in the bright spot in heaven, thou living sun, first living thing! Thou art brilliant in the East, and every land hast thou filled with thy beauty. . . ." The symbolic association of light and spirit marks the Manichaean and Gnostic traditions as well. The founder of the former religious philosophy, the Persian prophet Mani or Manes (ca. A.D. 215–275), taught that there were three ages in the history of the world: that of creation, that of the intermingling of light and darkness, and the present age, in which the particles of light are believed to be returning to their heavenly home. They flow out of terrestrial nature and form the sun, the moon, and the STARS above. A PILLAR of splendor, they ascend to the moon during the first half of each month, until the lunar disk is a full circle. From there they are raised up to the sun and luminous PARADISE. The purified soul, as soon as it has left the human body, is led by three ANGELS to this realm of light, where it receives its prize from the Judge of

Truth: the CROWNS (WREATH and diadem) and vestment of light.

In the Judeo-Christian world as well, light has a quality all its own and is not thought of as simply emanating from the sun. In the Book of Genesis, God's separation of light and darkness occurs on the first day of the Creation [1:4–5]; not until the fourth day does he create the sun and the moon, "lights," simply, which he places in the firmament of heaven [1:14–19]—apparently a deliberate distinction between this conceptual world and the worship of sun gods as practiced by the "heathen" peoples of surrounding lands. In Jewish legends this peculiarity of the Genesis account of creation is explained as follows: the Creator hid the light that he created on the first day, because he foresaw that the future peoples of the earth would arouse his wrath. "He said unto himself: the doers of evil are not worthy that this light should shine upon them; they must make do with the sun and the moon—lights that will one day disappear. The first light, however, which is eternal, shall be the light of the just" [bin Gorion, 1980]. Subsequently, however, Christian iconography was to draw upon stylized sunbeams to express, through the halo or the NIMBUS, the association

Light created through the word of God. Gustave Doré (1832–1883)

between God and light—in reference to such Biblical passages as the following, from Psalm 104: "O Lord my God, thou art very great; thou art clothed with honour and majesty. Who coverest thyself with light as with a garment . . ." It is clear that Jesus' statement, "I am the light of the world" [John 8:12], has had great influence on the Christian symbology of light; in Catholic churches a lamp designated as "the Eternal Light" is implored to shine even for the dead. Light is also shed by candles, such as the Easter candle, or the household candle that is blessed in the church on February 2 at the Mass for the Light of Mary. Baptismal and communion candles offer the believer not merely abstract symbolism but profound emotional meaning. It is popularly believed that the simple act of lighting blessed candles will bring protection against storms, hail damage, flooding, and disease, provided that the faithful ask for heavenly assistance by their light. The Eternal Light shines in synagogues to symbolize God's constant care for his people.

This symbolism is of course not restricted to the Judeo-Christian world. In Buddhism, too, light symbolizes the recognition of truth and the transcendence of the material world on the way toward absolute reality: colorless, formless Nirvana. In Hinduism, light is a metaphor for wisdom, for grasping spiritually the divine part of the personality (*atman*) and manifestation of Krishna, the lord of light. In Islam, light has a sacred name (Nûr) because "Allah is the light of heaven and earth." Light plays a major role in the Cabala, for example, in the Book of Zohar (Sefer ha-zohar), the primal light Or (or Avr), "which emanates from out of the secrecy of the hidden primal ether, Avir," and is the revelation of "the abyss En-Zof." In this mystical cosmology, darkness comes into being only after light. An arch intervenes to "settle the quarrel between the forces of light and darkness," which recalls the symbolism of the "royal arch" in FREE-MASONRY—where there is an extensive tradition of light symbolism. "The Mason is a seeker of light; light is bestowed upon the candidate; in ritual work the temple is illuminated, and the lights, greater and lesser, are of great importance. . . . The symbolism of this cult of light is further expressed in the Masonic reverence for the East, and explains why the East is the most sacred point in the temple of mysteries. . . ." [Lennhoff-Posner]. The "greater lights" refer to three symbolic objects (the carpenter's SQUARE, the drafting COMPASS, and the holy BOOK); the "lesser lights" to the Master of the Lodge and the two "foremen" (or the sun and the moon). The officers of individual lodges are also referred to as "lights." (See also BLINDNESS and WINDOW.)

lightning All older civilizations saw in the impressive discharge of electricity from the HEAVENS, bringing FIRE and destruction to the EARTH, an expression and symbol of supernatural power. It is usually the sky-god or KING of the gods who destroys enemy creatures on earth, or punishes insubordinate humans, with an AX or a HAMMER. Because it comes from the skies, lightning also functions as a symbol of extraterrestrial illumination. In dry regions, which depended upon rainstorms, lightning was also associated with making fields fertile and came to symbolize masculine vitality. The Etruscans interpreted lightning as an omen: in the eastern sky, it was a good augur; in the west, unfavorable; the northeast was the best, and lightning in the northwest foretold catastrophe. Priests at Roman oracles adopted this system. Lightning was attributed to Zeus Ceraunus (JUPITER Fulgur), and to the Slavic THUNDER-god Perun (Latvian Perkons,

Lightning. J. Boschius, 1702

Lithuanian Perkunas) or in earlier times the West Semitic god Hadad. Persons killed by lightning were thought to have been marked by the god in question and had to be buried on the spot. In Judeo-Christian thought lightning is a symbol of God's immediate presence (the revelation of the Ten Commandments on Mount Sinai) or of the Last Judgment. In the Renaissance lightning came to emblematize the inscrutable ways of Providence: "What use are fortress, trench, can moat or wall prevail/ Against the lightning hurled by Heaven's Lord and Master?/ And sentry's watch, but little can avail, alas!/ 'Tis God's protection only can avert disaster" [Hohberg].

Native American tradition attributes lightning to supernatural "thunder-birds" and represents lightning with the same zigzag strokes that are familiar in Western Europe. The Aztecs of Mexico represented lightning with the god Xolotl in the guise of a DOG, that also accompanied the dead. Lightning splits open the earth and thus opens the way to the underworld for gods and humans. (See STORM.) The Incas of ancient Peru had a common word, *illapa*, for thunder and lightning, and they used the name for the blunderbusses (literally, "thunder-boxes") of the conquistadors as well. Garcilaso de la Vega (1539–1616) records that thunder and lightning were not revered as being them-

Lightning strikes a fortress. Hohberg, 1675

selves divine, but rather as servants of the sacred SUN; the servants lived not in heaven but in the air. In analytical psychology lightning is seen as a symbol of masculine vitality. But the "fiery passion and intellectual fervor" that it can ignite "are also flames that can consume us. . . . A bolt of lightning can strike from out of a sky of BLUE or gray" [Aeppli].

In many cultures lightning is portrayed as a SNAKE cast down from heaven. Thus the Aztecs had not only the canine Xolotl but also the "obsidian serpent" Itzcóatl, and the ancient Finns a "snake of many colors," which is said to have fallen to the depths of the SEA and been eaten by a salmon, from whose belly humans extracted the bright flashes of heavenly FIRE (see SPARKS). The superhuman powers of the gods of heaven is symbolized in the myth of the Greek princess Semele, where Zeus, father of the gods, appears as a procreative bolt of lightning. "When Zeus promised to grant her every wish, she asked him to come to her as a suitor exactly as he had gone to Hera. He could not take back his word, and he rode into her chamber in a chariot, with bolts of lightning and thunder, and he hurled the lightning. The horrified Semele went mad; she gave birth to a premature child, whom Zeus saved from the flames [that he had himself unleashed] and sewed up in his own thigh" [Apollodorus, Library]. The child was Dionysus (see BACCHUS), the god of ecstatic intoxication, whom Zeus turned into a young GOAT to protect him from the jealous Hera.

Lightning: Zeus (Jupiter) hurls lightning bolts at the Titans. Cartari, 1647

Lily. Fresco, Thera (Santorini), ca. 1500 B.C.

lily "The lily white in stately splendor reigns,/ Her rivals bests—but lasts brief days, then dies./ We, too, would age swift and perish with our pains,/ Did not God's grace sustain, extend, our lives" [Hohberg]. Even before the formulation of its symbolic meaning, the lily was held in great esteem, a favorite motif in the decorative arts in Egypt, Minoan Crete, and Mycenae. In poetry, the voices of the CICADAS and the MUSES are said to be "lily-like" (i.e., gentle). According to myth, lilies came from the MILK of Hera, some drops of which fell to EARTH; the Milky Way was formed at the same time. The love goddess Aphrodite (VENUS) hated the flower for its chaste appearance and added its pistil—which resembles a DONKEY'S penis (compare LINGA). Nevertheless, the lily became for the Christian world a symbol of pure, virginal love. Gabriel, the ANGEL of the Annunciation, is usually portrayed holding a lily, as are Mary's husband Joseph and her parents, Joachim and Anne. The "lilies of the field"—which "do not toil" but are praised in the Sermon on the Mount as models of those who, in their faith, ask no questions—made the flower the attribute of many saints (including Anthony of Padua, Dominic, Philip Neri, Vincent Ferrer, Catherine of Siena, and Philomena). The fleur-de-lys motif is important in HERALDRY: lilies "are royal flowers . . . , especially because the form of the flower is like that of a SCEPTER, or because SNAKES flee from lilies, which give off a fragrance that stimulates the HEART" [Böckler]. An angel was said to have presented a lily to Clovis I (481–511), king of the Franks; from 1179 onward the fleur de lys (actually it looks more like an iris) adorned the coat of arms

Lilium album.

Lily. Hohberg, 1675

of the kings of France. Through Louis XI it became part of the arms of the Medicis and thus of Florence and Tuscany. The Florentine lily, unlike the Bourbon version, includes the stamens. In popular symbolism the lily represents not only purity (as in church processions) but also "pallid death": legends (of Corvey, Hildesheim, and Wroclaw) tell of a lily appearing mysteriously to announce the death of a friar. A traditional song also refers to "three lilies" planted on a grave (see DEATH, SYMBOLS OF).

linden   A tree of the genus *Tilia,* whose Old World species are sometimes called "lime trees" (unrelated to the other "lime tree," *Citrus aurantifolia*) and New World species "basswoods." There are about 60 species found in the Northern Temperate Zone. In

Lily: The fleur-de-lis of French heraldry. 15th century

the German-speaking world the linden was a favorite source of shade at the meeting place at the center of each village, sacred (in the Dark Ages) to the goddess Freyja. It was believed to ward off lightning and was a symbol of local judicial authority. The tree, mentioned in medieval German poetry from Walther von der Vogelweide onward, came to symbolize the village community. In Slavic countries it had a similar significance, also as a source for the special honey that BEES gathered from its blossoms. "Lime-blossom tea" (used to induce perspiration) is actually made from the entire flower, including the wing-like bract. Hildegard of Bingen (1098–1179), following the theory of the four humors, called the *Tilia* a "very warm" tree: "all of its warmth resides in the roots and rises from there to the branches

Linden. Medieval seal of the city of Lindau on Lake Constance

and leaves. The linden is a symbol of fragility. A person suffering from a heart ailment should take a powder made from the inside of its roots, along with bread." It clears the EYES, she continues, if one sleeps with one's eyelids and face covered with fresh linden leaves.

In HERALDRY the linden is often portrayed with stylized HEART-shaped leaves (e.g., in the seal of the imperial city of Lindau). The heraldic figure of the linden-leaf CROSS has such leaves at the four extremities, and they also appear alone (or on bent linden branches) as an ornament on the shield or helmet (counties of Thuringia and Hesse).

linga (or lingam) In ancient Indian iconography an abstract phallic symbol epitomizing the creative principle as embodied by the god Shiva, the lord of all living things. This representation of the phallus goes back to prehistoric fertility cults, but the sculptures usually bear little resemblance to the natural penis: the lingas are short columns, rounded at the top, at times suggestive of a Mediterranean OMPHALOS. The linga may also be related to representations of the AXIS MUNDI. The Shiva cult often pairs the linga with the YONI symbol: a ring of stone encircles the base of the linga column, symbolizing the greater unity of the two sexes, which is essential for all life (see DUALITY). The Lingayat sect of southern India, founded in the 11th century after Christ, worships the creative lingam, which is also often worn in a locket as an amulet; this phallic symbol is referred to as a thing "of great moral worth." Linga pillars are often portrayed with the kundalini SNAKE, the symbol of vitality, coiled around them: this combination represents the combination of matter and idea in a higher form of knowledge, attainable through spiritual discipline. The CADUCEUS of Hermes (Latin MERCURY) and the snakes wrapped around it are similarly interpreted in speculative philosophy. The sexual organ of the god Shiva Mahalinga, who is still worshipped in India today, is visited by countless pilgrims to the CAVE of Armanath in the mountains of Kashmir. In the cave itself the pilgrims can see a stalagmite that is more or less phallic in form. According to historical documents from the medieval Khmer kingdom (Kampuchea), in the Hindu period the city of Angkor (whose structure is patterned after the SQUARE of the cosmos) had at its center the sacred linga of Shiva.

lion (Latin *leo*) Like the EAGLE, an animal symbolizing dominion, important in heraldry, and referred to in fable as the "KING of the beasts." The lion of ASTROLOGY—the sign Leo—has as its "planet" the SUN; the characteristics attributed to those born under Leo are thus solar in nature. The basis for the association between Leo and the sun is presumably the lion's strength, its golden-brown color, and the ray-like mane of the male. Like the eagle, again, the lion was believed to be able to gaze directly at the sun without blinking. The lion's "masculinity" enabled the animal to serve as a counterpart of great goddesses (Cybele, Artemis, FORTUNA), although the lioness occasionally appeared in similar contexts. In Egypt the lioness was the manifestation of the goddess of war Sekhmet; the male lion, with the solar disk on his head, was that of the god Re. It seems that in early times the HEAVENS were also represented by a lion which swallowed the sun every evening at dusk; the lion, however, was soon replaced by a COW, or by Nut, the wife of the heavens. In classical antiquity gods and demigods, e.g. Hercules, were often portrayed as defeating lions in combat—a representation of the victory of the human intellect over animalistic nature. In Judeo-Christian symbolism the figure of the lion has conflicting associations: it represents the strength of the tribe of Judah, but also the ravenous opponent against which only God can offer protection ("Daniel in the Lion's Den"). The early Christian text *Physiologus* contains allegorical fables about the lion, e.g., that the lion obliterates its tracks with its tail ("So, too, did Christ, my Savior, the victor from the tribe of Judah, obliterate his spiritual tracks, i.e., his divinity"), or that it sleeps in its CAVE with its eyes open ("So, too, did the body of my Lord sleep on the Cross; his

Lion as king of the beasts. *Book of Wisdom*, Ulm, 1483

divinity, however, watches and never sleeps, at the right hand of God the Father"). The same source, finally, relates the wondrous circumstances of the lion's birth: "When the lioness gives birth to her cub, it is born dead, and she keeps watch beside the body, until on the third day the father comes and blows into the cub's face; . . . [the lioness] sits across from it for three full days and gazes at [her offspring]. But if her gaze ever falters, it never comes to life." The male lion awakens the cub by blowing the breath of life into its nostrils. "So did the unbelieving heathens gaze upon our Lord Jesus Christ during his three days of burial and his resurrection, and they were given [spiritual] life. . . . When the male lion came, i.e., the living Word, [the Holy Ghost] breathed upon them and gave them life." The negative interpretation follows: the Christian should continue to walk in the way of God, avoiding the temptation of the lion, "that is, of the devil: for Satan, even though he is invisible, seeks with temptations whom he will devour next, like the lion. . . ."

In the symbolism of ALCHEMY the lion stands at times for the primal element SULFUR and at others, as "the RED lion," for the finished "philosopher's stone." A GREEN lion stands for a potent solvent to induce decomposition. Usually the lion is at one extreme or the other—a model for the heroic individual or a symbol for the devil's presence in the world [I Peter 5:8]. Christ is often represented as victorious over allegorical creatures like the lion, the DRAGON, or the BASILISK. His typological forerunner

Lions receive Daniel in their den. Grave decoration, Bordjel-Youni, Tunisia

in the Old Testament is Samson, who tears a lion limb from limb. In East Asia lions were known only through accounts transmitted from distant lands; the word for the lion, *shih*, comes from the Persian word *sir*. Lions in paintings and sculpture thus bear little resemblance to the animal itself. Pairs of stylized lions appear as doorkeepers guarding the entrances to sacred confines. The lion on the right is understood to be male and holds a BALL or a PEARL under one paw; the lion on the left, female, holds a cub. For the "Dance of the Lion," which is celebrated on the 15th day of the first lunar month, someone dons a lion's mask with golden eyes and SILVER teeth; this "lion" can be appeased only with (small) gifts of money. Men riding on lions symbolize divine power. In Japan the lion has given up even more of its natural appearance: it is called a KARASHISHI or "DOG of Buddha" and, as in China, guards the entrances to temples and shrines.

In European HERALDRY the lion—second in importance only to the eagle—usually appears standing erect on its hind legs ("rampant") or roaring with its front paws (and its mane) raised, exaggeratedly lean and shaggy; it is usually red or GOLD, with its TONGUE and claws in a contrasting color. Because the lion, as "king of the beasts," symbolized strength and military valor, it was already a popular heraldic animal in the Middle Ages; as time went by and it ap-

Lion. Woodcut in Pseudo-Albertus Magnus, Frankfurt, 1531

peared more and more frequently, its symbolic import became diluted and it constituted less of a distinction or obligation for the noble in whose arms it appeared. In the world of astrology, Leo (July 23–August 23), the fifth sign of the zodiac, is a "FIRE sign," associated with the sun and gold, a "royal" sign. Leos are believed to love splendor and riches, to be vain, to tend to dominate others, but to be natural leaders, intelligent, magnanimous—a set of characteristics obviously derived from those of the lion. The symbolic significance of the lion in Jungian psychology is in general accord with the animal's role in other traditions and systems. For the Jungians, the lion combines tremendous energy with serene self-control; it is effortlessly masterful, the aggressor against whom all are defenseless, the opponent who always destroys. When in a DREAM the lion "raises its powerful, manly head, the dreamer is so impressed, so transfixed by this great and dangerous force, that even a person ignorant of dream symbolism somehow knows that a great, savage energy within is demanding a breakthrough: a new personality more able to resist the onslaughts of drives and urges" [Aeppli].

lizard The early Christian text *Physiologus* reports that, when the lizard grows old and its EYES lose the power of sight, it crawls into a crack in a wall facing east. When the SUN rises, the lizard's "eyes are opened and their sight restored. Thus, likewise, when

Lizard. Maori carving, from a doorpost in the village of Ohinemutu, New Zealand

you find . . . the vision of your heart grown dim, seek out the rising sun of righteousness, our Lord Jesus Christ, and he will open the eyes of your heart." As a hibernating animal, the lizard became a symbol of death followed by resurrection, but it is also shown on coins being killed by the sun-god (Apollo Sauroctonus). On Roman coins it is associated with Salus, the goddess of safety and welfare, presumably because of its ability, if its tail is cut off, to grow a new one; in Artemidorus' dream-book it is said to indicate a "contemptuous disposition." Christian theology took over the positive valuation (rebirth, rejuvenation through shedding of its skin, longing for—spiritual—LIGHT) and represented the lizard on candle-holders, censers, and the like. Like the BEE, the lizard could embody the soul; in this form it could slip out of the mouths of sleeping persons, who after the lizard's return would be able to recall its experiences.

locust A kind of grasshopper with a peculiar set of symbolic associations; it often arrives in swarms to do severe damage to vegetation, and plagues of locusts are both feared and legendary. They figure prominently in the story of Moses in the Old Testament: "And the locusts went up over all the land of Egypt . . . ; before them there were no such locusts as they, neither after them shall there be such. For they covered the face of the whole earth, so that the land was darkened; and they did eat every herb of the land . . . : and there remained not any green thing in the trees, or in the herbs of the field, through all the land of Egypt" [Exodus 10:14–15]. For the prophet Joel as well, the plague of locusts is the embodiment of divine retribution and the occasion for Joel's call to repentance. In the Book of Revelation smoke pours out of the bottomless pit, "and there came out of the smoke locusts upon the earth: and unto them was given power, as the scorpions of the earth have power. And it was commanded them that they should not hurt the grass of the earth, neither any green thing, neither any tree; but only those men which have not the seal of God in their foreheads"

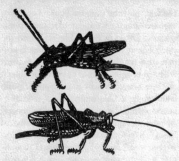

Locusts. E. Topsell, *History*, 1658

[9:2–4]. They seem not to be migrating locusts but demons: "And the shapes of the locusts were like unto horses prepared unto battle; and on their heads were as it were crowns like gold, and their faces were as the faces of men. And they had hair as the hair of women, and their teeth were as the teeth of lions. And they had breastplates, as it were breastplates of iron; and the sound of their wings was as the sound of chariots of many horses running to battle. And they had tails like unto scorpions, and there were stings in their tails; and their power was to hurt men five months. And they had a king over them, which is the angel of the bottomless pit, whose name in the Hebrew tongue is Abaddon, but in the Greek tongue hath his name Apollyon ['destroyer']" [9:7–11]. In the *Moralia in Job* (by Gregory I, 540–604), the locust is Christ's comrade in battle against the heathens; because of its shedding of its carapace, the insect is made to symbolize Christ resurrected. In medieval bestiaries the locust is included among the "worms," but as one that does not stay in one place like the caterpillar but buzzes about, eating everything. In ancient China the locust symbolized "the blessing of having many children," but swarms of them were taken as an indication that the order of the cosmos had been disturbed.

lotus A flower as meaningful in the southeast Mediterranean region and in Asia as the ROSE or the LILY in Europe. Different botanical varieties are called "lotus" in dif-ferent cultures: in Egypt the word designates the WHITE lotus (*Nymphaea lotus*) and the BLUE lotus (*Nymphaea cerulea*); in India, the white and reddish hydrophytes *Nelumbium nelumbo* and *Nelumbium nucifera*; and in many books, the white water-lily of Central America, *Nymphaea ampla* (in Maya, *naab* or *nicté há*). In ancient Egypt the lotus blossom is mentioned in the myth of the creation of the world (see OGDOAD): it originated from the primordial ooze, and the divine creator of the world ("a handsome lad") arose from its calyx. The blossoms, which open at sunrise and close at sunset, were linked with the SUN god and the mythical emergence of LIGHT from the slime in which the universe began. The graves of Thebes contain many paintings showing lotus ponds on which the dead person floats in a boat made of rushes, and pillars representing bunches of lotuses are common in the monumental architecture; lotus WREATHS were buried with the dead. The combination of papyrus and lotus symbolized the union of the two parts of the kingdom. The fragrant blue lotus blossom was prized even more than the white. The blue was the attribute of Nefertum, the young god of the ancient city of Memphis, who was known as the "lord of sweet fragrances"; the blue lotus was called "the beautiful" (*nen-nufer*; hence the French *nénuphar*, "water-lily").

In India the lotus blossom is the most important symbol for spirituality and art. Its goddess, Padma, is of pre-Aryan origin and

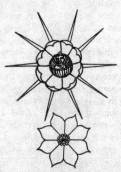

Lotus blossoms (blue and white). Tantrist meditation images, Tibet

Lotus: Resurrection from one of its blossoms. Egyptian Book of the Dead, from the Ani Papyrus

is linked with the conceptual world of WATER and fertility; in Aryan times the flower became associated with Vishnu's wife Laksmi and with Brahma: in Hindu myth, Brahma, the creator of the world, was born from a lotus blossom growing from the navel of Vishnu, who was sleeping on the water. In Buddhist tradition the lotus is of even greater significance: Gautama Buddha has "lotus eyes, lotus feet, and lotus thighs." The teacher, or guru, who brought Buddhism to Tibet (in the eighth century after Christ), was known as Padmasambhava ("born from out of the lotus"). One manifestation of the *bodhisattva* Avalokitesvara is called Padmapani, literally "holder of the lotus," the flower symbolizing compassion; another manifestation, Padmanartesvara ("lord of the dance with the lotus"), holds a RED lotus. The lotus is also the great symbol of knowledge: knowledge leads out of the cycle of reincarnation to Nirvana. The formulation "*Om mani padme hum*" of Tibetan prayer (translated "Om, jewel in the lotus, amen") is interpreted in Tantric Buddhism in terms that we might call "Freudian": the expression is taken as a metaphor for the (spiritual) sexual union of female blossom and male energy. In the various systems of yoga the highest spiritual knowledge of the currents of energy rising through the body is symbolized by the blooming of a lotus blossom on the crown of one's head; in Taoism,

similarly, by the "GOLDEN blossom" as the "highest lotus." In China, too, lotus symbolism is linked to Buddhism. The lotus—which has its roots in the mud but arises from it clean and pure, fragrant, devoid of twigs or branches, unfolding an empty blossom that gazes upward—is an image of pure aspiration; it is also one of the "jewels" of Buddhism and Taoism, and the attribute of Ho-hsien-ku, one of the EIGHT IMMORTALS. The syllable *ho* ("lotus") in masculine names formerly indicated that the bearer was a Buddhist. The blue lotus blossom (*ch'ing*) is associated with the concept of "cleanliness," which is denoted in Chinese by a homonym. Another word for "lotus," *lien*, sounds like the words for "bind" and "modesty"—the basis for many rebus-like expressions of congratulation and well-wishing. Thus a boy holding a lotus blossom signifies: "May you always enjoy times of plenty." The binding of upper-class women's feet was supposed to turn them into "bent lotuses," on which it was thought that the women would walk and dance more daintily. This cruel practice was not outlawed until the end of the 19th century. The eighth day of the fourth month of the Chinese calendar was traditionally celebrated as the birthday of Fo (Buddha), "the day that the lotus blooms." Among the Maya of the Yucatán, the lotus-like white water-lily was called "the flower of the water" and frequently depicted on clay vessels and in architectural relief-work. The flower may have been added to narcotic beverages, such as *balché* mead mixed with *loncho carpus* rind, to produce the ecstatic states of the jaguar priests. (See also HONEY.)

lynx The beast of prey known for its acuity of vision (as in the expression "lynx-eyed") is relegated in Christian iconography to the realm of the DEVIL. In HERALDRY the lynx or "tiger-wolf" symbolizes "rapid cleverness and mental alertness; in the Duchy of Brandenburg nobles with these qualities have the lynx in their coat of arms, along with their names" [Böckler].

modern era, then in literature (e.g., in Hugo von Hofmannsthal's play *Jedermann*, 1911), the personification of money, especially ill-gotten gains. In the writings of Agrippa von Nettesheim (1486–1535) Mammon appears as a demon, one of the followers of the DEVIL—a reference to Luke 16:13: "Ye cannot serve God and Mammon." Mammon is usually portrayed as a GOLDEN IDOL, often a devil strewing about gold pieces. In this way he lures men and women to a preoccupation with the pleasures of this world, then abandons them when they die. In the Renaissance, those who were obsessed with the pursuit of wealth were called "servants of Mammon."

magpie From Central Europe to the New World a creature associated with talkativeness (in reference to a person, "magpie" is synonymous with "chatterbox") and thievery ("to steal like a magpie"). In Ovid's *Metamorphoses* a woman is turned into a magpie. Whereas the black-and-white-feathered bird is viewed negatively in the Occident, in China the magpie (*hsi*) is a symbol of good luck (*hsi-ch'iao,* "magpie of happiness"); its cry is believed to announce good news or the coming of welcome visitors. A text from the fifth century after Christ relates that in ancient times husband and wife would break a MIRROR in two pieces when they were to be separated for a while; if either was unfaithful, the adulterous partner's half of the mirror was transformed into a magpie which flew to the other partner with news of the deed. For this reason, magpies are often etched into bronze mirrors. The magpie was also an embodiment of *yang* (see YIN AND YANG) and, as the bird of happiness and good fortune, was the opposite of the raven (see CROW). Images of 12 magpies thus convey the sender's best wishes, and those showing magpies, BAMBOO, and a PLUM, or a pair of magpies, symbolize marital bliss (especially with congratulations on a marriage; see WEDDING CUSTOMS).

Mammon (from the Aramaic *ma'mon,* "riches") In the magic books of the early

mandala (Sanskrit, literally "circle") An aid to concentration and meditation consisting of CIRCLES and derivations thereof, used in Buddhist India and Lamaistic Tibet. Such structures are usually drawn and painted, but can also be given architectural form, as in the designs of TEMPLE grounds. They are actually "cosmograms," imagistic represen-

Mammon's servant with death; the "money devil." Hans Holbein, 1547; France, ca. 1660

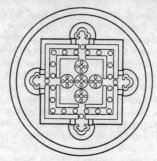

Mandala-like cosmogram. Indo-Tibetan

Mandorla: Christ's ascension. Farmer's almanac, Austria, 1913

tations of the world-order, often incorporating quadripartite (see FOUR and SQUARE) divisions and organization. A center is targeted so as to "narrow the mind's field of vision" [Jung] for the sake of contemplation and concentration: the attention is directed toward spiritual and intellectual matters and intuitive knowledge, which, it is hoped, will in this way be internalized by and become rooted in the psyche. In the center are found various symbols, in accordance with the doctrine or the degree to which the individual has progressed: in Indian Tantrism, for example, the DIAMOND "THUNDERbolt" at the center symbolizes the final union of the masculine and feminine principles, the transcendence of the Shiva-Shakti DUALITY of Kundalini yoga. The symbolic designs of ALCHEMY also often resemble mandalas, although no historical connection with Asian sources is conceivable. Indeed, Jungian psychology understands the mandala and its various symbolic forms as innate archetypes, occurring spontaneously (e.g., in DREAMS, visions, or free sketches) even in individuals with no education in the area of cultural history. Mandalas, according to Jung, symbolize submersion and internalization after periods of chaos; they express something of the spiritual essence or kernel, a deeper reconciliation and wholeness within. When used specifically as aids to meditation, mandalas are designated by the Indian word YANTRA.

mandorla (Italian for "almond") This almond-shaped variation on the halo or NIMBUS (consisting of two intersecting arcs) surrounded the entire body of (the transfigured) Christ, or of the Virgin Mary after the Assumption, in many medieval depictions. The almond (Greek *amygdale*) is an ancient symbol for the closing up of valuable contents in a hard, almost impenetrable shell. In the Book of Jeremiah, however, the "rod of an almond tree" [1:11]), because of the similarity between the Hebrew words *shaked* ("almond tree") and *shakad* ("to keep watch"), is associated with vigilance. The simultaneously luminous and embracing mandorla is a mysterious image of concentration upon the LIGHT that shines from

Mandorla: Mary as Queen of Heaven. Farmer's almanac, Austria, 1913

within: Christ's true nature lies beneath the surface of his corporeal being. In medieval times the almond was also interpreted as a symbol of the embryo enclosed in the uterus. The form of the almond, which suggests a stylized vulva (see also YONI), may have contributed to this interpretation.

mandrake (*Mandragora officinarum*) A Eurasian plant of great symbolic significance, not to be confused with the North American May apple (*Podophyllum peltatum*), which is sometimes called "mandrake." Its branching root, which (especially when properly adapted) is suggestive of the human form, was prized even in the early years of the modern era. According to the traditional doctrine of "signatures," which held that external characteristics of a plant indicated specific medicinal properties and applications (a sort of "labeling" with nature's own "directions"), the mandrake bore the divine signature of "the whole person" and was thus seen as a panacea. In fact, the plant, which is of the nightshade family, contains a number of poisonous hallucinogens (including hyoscyamine, atropine, and scopolamine). It was thus an important ingredient in WITCHES' ointments and came to symbolize every sort of necromancy. According to legend the plant grew under gallows from the sperm of hanged men and could be removed from the ground only with the strictest precautions: because the plant was said to give such a blood-curdling, indeed lethal, cry when it was uprooted, DOGS—who died in the process—were made to harvest the root. Such stories were presumably used to drive up the price of mandrake root and helped to foster belief in its magical powers. It was at once prized and feared, as numerous legends show. For Greek antiquity it was the symbol of the sorceress CIRCE; for the Jews, an aid in attaining pregnancy (compare ELEPHANT). In general, the mandrake symbolized forces humans must approach only with great caution. In poetry the mandrake is also referred to by its Latin name, "mandragora": "Not poppy, nor mandragora,/ Nor all the drowsy syrups of the world,/ Shall ever medicine thee to that sweet sleep/ Which thou owedst yesterday" [*Othello*, III, iii, 330–333].

maple   The various species of maple tree have symbolic associations in China and in Canada. In China this goes back to the homonymy of the word for the tree (*feng*) with the word meaning "to bestow honors upon." When an ape holding a package tied with string is shown in the branches of a maple tree, this is read *"feng-hou,"* freely translated: May the receiver of this picture attain the rank of count. The maple leaf has been the national symbol of Canada since the 19th century. The tree in question is the sugar maple (*Acer saccharum*), the source of maple syrup and other products. The coat of arms of Canada includes three red maple leaves in the base of the shield, and the crest is a LION holding another. The flag also shows a red maple leaf, and three are in the coats of arms of Ontario and Quebec.

marriage and weddings as symbols   (Symbolic customs observed in real-life marriage ceremonies are treated separately in the article WEDDING CUSTOMS.) The wedding itself is an almost universal symbol for the uniting of polar opposites (see DUALITIES) which from that point on function no longer antagonistically or competitively but complementarily, forming together a higher unity, a whole that is more than the sum of the parts. For the ancients, the *hieros gamos*

Mandrake root as a woman's body. P. Schöffer, *Garden of Health*, 1485

Marriage bath of alchemy's Sulfur and Mercury. *Rosarium Philosophorum*, Frankfurt, 1550

("sacred wedding") was a symbol for the creative uniting of HEAVEN and EARTH, MALE and FEMALE, god and goddess, often acted out through the copulation of the KING with a priestess representing the goddess or the female element in the universe; only in this way could fertility and cosmic order be assured for the coming year (e.g., the New Year's festival of the ancient cultures of Mesopotamia). There were many attempts to transpose the obvious sexual aspect of the tradition into an intellectual register, making it an image for the coming together of a different pair of opposites, e.g., the mystic melding of God and humans at the moment of enlightenment, or the "marital" union of God and his people (Yahweh with the Israelites, Christ with his Church), with even the wedding song of the Old Testament, the Song of Solomon, taken only figuratively: the Church is "the Bride of Christ." In the Catholic Church nuns also receive a bridal veil when they take their vows, becoming "mystic brides" of the Savior. In ALCHEMY the frequent visual depictions of the wedding, and even sexual intercourse, between KING and QUEEN symbolize the joining of the hypothetical primal elements SULFUR AND MERCURY, which then together constitute a higher, ANDROGYNOUS unity, dissolving in a "chemical wedding" the original dualities of "*sol* and *luna*" (SUN and MOON), MARS and VENUS, and so forth—not

unlike the ideas of Gnostic antiquity, which proposed a union of *sophia* (wisdom) with *dynamis* (power) and can be seen as surviving (in veiled form) in alchemy.

Mars   (Greek Ares) Roman god of war and of agriculture, for whom the month of March (Latin *Martius*) was named. With one of the vestal VIRGINS Mars sired the TWINS Romulus and Remus. His symbols were the shield and the spear; his sacred animals, the WOLF, the BULL, and the woodpecker. There are relatively few depictions of Mars in the pictorial arts. The Romans viewed him as the equivalent of the Germanic sword god Tiu (in Old Norse, Tyr), and thus Tuesday ("Tiu's day") was for them "Mars' day," *dies Martis*. The association of the god of war with the reddish glimmering PLANET that was given his name and with (rusty) IRON, requires little explanation. (His PRECIOUS STONES are the RUBY, garnet, and carnelian—all of which bear his color, BLOOD RED.) In ASTROLOGY the planet is called "the little troublemaker," ruling Aries (see RAM) by day and Scorpio by night. It is "hot, dry, keen, cruel . . . the planet of tyrants, war, unforeseen disaster" (J. W. Pfaff, 1816) and governs such qualities as activity, will, energy, and aggressive sexuality. A person under the influence of the planet is said to be bellicose, "martial." Both in astrological symbolism and in Greek myth, VENUS and Mars are seen as a pair of complementary opposites, a DUALITY not unlike YIN AND YANG. Agrippa of Nettesheim (1486–1535) described the spirits of Mars—which the sorcerer's rituals sought to conjure up—as

Mars with Aries and Cancer, signs of the zodiac that he rules. *Hausbuchmeister*, 1475

"furious and ugly in appearance, brownish red in color, with HORNS, like a DEER'S antlers, and claws like a GRIFFIN'S. They bellow like raging bulls and move like flames that consume; their sign is LIGHTNING, and THUNDER." The overall image is very much like that of the DEVIL. In the astrology of ancient China, Mars is associated with the color red, fire, and the direction south. The orbit of the planet as viewed from the earth is characterized by regressive curves, which may help to explain some of its symbolic connotations (confusion, impulsivity, sudden calamity).

Mask of satyr held by actor. From a vase decoration, Greece, 4th century B.C.

masks   In nonliterate as well as in highly civilized cultures, expressions of the presence of supernatural entities. The person wearing the mask feels internally transformed and takes on temporarily the qualities of the god or demon represented by the mask. As a result of this, masks came to be thought of not only as disguises for the face but also as independent cult and art objects, e.g., the diabase masks of the Teotihuacán civilization in ancient Mexico. In many parts of sub-Saharan Africa and Melanesia, wooden masks have great ritual importance, especially in the rites of secret alliances. For Mediterranean antiquity masks provided a means of identifying with a "supernatural" being. Theatrical masks go back to the masks worn in the cult of Dionysus (see BACCHUS). Fright-masks (see GORGONS) were used as decorations to ward off enemies and evil spirits. In Mycenaean times gold-leaf masks were placed on the faces of the dead ("Aga-

memnon's mask" is a well-known example), presumably to conceal the collapse of the features; this custom has been documented occasionally in the Central Europe of the Hallstatt period (ca. 750–450 B.C.), e.g., in the hill graves of Gross-Klein in the Austrian province of Styria. The helmet-masks of Roman times presumably not only served as protection but also lent their wearers a heroic appearance. In East Asia the wooden masks of Noh theater (representing maidens, men, old men, old women, and demons) are especially noteworthy. They are supposed to offer compact expressions of character and add emphasis to the gestures of the actors. (See also JANUS.)

medicine   In books about traditional Native American life, a collective designation for everything that is sacred, elevated above the everyday world, and involved in religious customs. Examples include contents

Mask of cedar with carved antlers, 11½ inches high. Native American, Spiro, Oklahoma

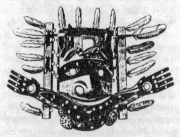

Mask. Inuit, Bering Strait

of the "medicine bundle": amulets and symbolic objects such as arrowheads (see AR-ROW), STONES, FEATHERS, BONES, pollen; "to make medicine" is to meditate, to seek visions. The "medicine man" is the shamanistic healer. Since healing and religion were inseparable in Native American cultures, shamans in full ritual dress—who in fact performed additional rituals beyond those of consecration—were generally called medicine men, even when they simply led ceremonial dances. Their special abilities, it was believed, extended to anything involving religion or magic. On occasion they wore women's clothes: in the Cheyenne culture, for example, changing gender was seen as a way for the shaman to come into contact

Medicine man wearing bear skin. Great Plains, U.S., George Catlin

with the cosmic whole (see ANDROGYNE). "Medicine wheels" are circular arrangements of stones, apparently relating to ceremonies of the Plains nations. The circumference or "rim" of the wheels measures almost 100 feet, and the inner circle or "hub" is some ten feet in diameter; the "spokes" number 28, apparently corresponding to the 28 days of the lunar month. Piles of stones on the periphery mark the points at which the STARS Aldebaran, Rigel, and Sirius rise over the horizon on summer mornings. The ethnologist K. H. Schlesier (1985) associates these "spirit wheels" with the Cheyenne ceremony of "the gift of the earth": "Since they are found on mountain tops and are not visible from below, they

are directed to heaven, to the spirits of the Higher World."

menhir The upright "long STONE" (Breton from *men*, "long," and *hir*, "stone"), resembling an OBELISK but rough-hewn or undressed. The practice, prevalent in Northwestern Europe from the Neolithic onward, of building stone structures out of roughly assembled, often monumental blocks of stone, is assuredly related to the endurance of stone in general (see ROCK). Megalithic construction, apparently religiously motivated, produced first and foremost burial structures, like the dolmens (literally "table stones") of Brittany or the *Hünengräber* ("giants' graves") of Northern Germany: they were presumably intended to assure that the nation would continue to benefit from the presence of deceased priests and heroes. In close proximity to dolmens we often find menhirs—whose purpose and symbolism are subjects of controversy. The menhirs, considered by some to be phallic monuments (compare LINGA) to bring about lasting fertility, are believed by ethnologists to be rather "seats for the soul," in or on which the souls of those buried in the nearby dolmens can watch over the land. Other possible explanations interpret the menhir as a conspicuous marker for a "sacred place" or as a more permanent representation of the AXIS MUNDI than the (usually wooden) POLES of other religious traditions. Large stone

Menhir with suggestions of head, sword, dagger. Filitosa (Corsica), Bronze Age

PILLARS, e.g., grave monuments, are sometimes called menhirs even when there is no demonstrable connection with the megalithic tradition. Near Carnac (in Morbihan, Brittany) there are whole fields containing alignments of megaliths, apparently less regular in form and positioning than proper menhirs, which are believed to be situated with respect to astronomical (seasonally) fixed points on the horizon (as in the case of Stonehenge)—although such principles have not been firmly established. It is possible that the menhirs served to commemorate processions (see PILGRIMAGE) to sacred places (the megalithic graves of important personages), or that they were part of a system of religious symbols to which we no longer have access.

Mercury (Greek Hermes) Greek god of commerce and industry, associated especially with prosperity and the merchant class. As the messenger of the gods, he carries the herald's staff or CADUCEUS; he is both associated with profit and referred to as the god of thieves. His winged shoes and helmet suggest the speed with which he travels. As Hermes Psychopompus ("escort of souls") he symbolizes the safe journey of the deceased to the other world (see AFTERLIFE); carrying a RAM, he stands for "the good SHEPHERD" (Hermes Criophorus). He is also said to be the inventor of the lyre. The Roman counterpart of Hermes is believed

Mercury (Hermes) with the caduceus. Cartari, 1647

to derive his name from the Latin *mercari*, meaning "to engage in commerce."

The PLANET Mercury is the most difficult to observe. In many parts of the world it can be seen with the naked eye for only 12 to 18 hours per year, and it remains so close to the SUN that it can be seen only at twilight or when the sky is slightly overcast, especially in autumn and spring. Its "fleetingness," the way it eludes the observer, is apparently the reason for its symbolic meaning: it is "ambiguous in nature and, because of its mobility, uncertain" (J. W. Pfaff, 1816).

In ASTROLOGY the planet is associated with such characteristics as eloquence, dexterity, agility, and inconstancy (also friendship). It is referred to as an ANDROGYNOUS planet; its metal, of course, is mercury (see SULFUR AND MERCURY). It rules the sign of Gemini (see TWINS) by day and Virgo (see VIRGIN) by night. Its color is sky BLUE, and its PRECIOUS STONES are AGATE, jasper, topaz, opal, and AMBER.

milk The first nourishment of humans and other mammals, has—because of its whiteness and its mild flavor—often symbolized the food of the gods and "pure sacrifice." It was often associated with lunar forces (see MOON), and in some contexts it was believed to have the power to extinguish the "masculine" FIRE of LIGHTNING itself. In the ancient Hindu account of the creation of the world, the cosmos was a primeval sea of milk which the gods (with the help of a SNAKE coiled around the MOUNTAIN of the world) churned to make firm butter. The sacrificial drink soma was likened to milk; the milk heated in Vedic sacrifice was understood as a symbol of the divine RIVER of life. Indeed, sacrifices of milk (libations) were customary in many pastoral cultures. In ancient Egypt there were depictions of the goddess Isis nursing the pharaoh at her BREAST, which in some cultures (the Etruscan—where Hercle [Hercules] is nursed by Uni [Juno]—and the Berber) is understood as a ritual of adoption. In the cults of Attis and Mithra, milk and HONEY were consumed in rituals. The "promised land" of Canaan

Milking technique of ancient Egypt. Tomb relief, Sakkara, ca. 2400 B.C.

was a land of plenty, "a good land and a large, . . . a land flowing with milk and honey" [Exodus 3:8]. There are abundant Biblical references to the symbolic importance to the elect of the pure, nutritious liquid, but it is also mentioned as nourishment for those undeveloped and childlike men and women to whom solid food can be given only when they have grown mature [Hebrews 5:12–14]. In ancient China milk was never drunk, but was used in the preparation of food. Mother's milk was believed to impart sexual potency and long life.

In medieval Christian art, the nursing *Maria lactans* is often shown with the baby Jesus at her breast, and this image contrasts with that of the "bad mother" who "nurses vipers at her bosom." Wet-nurses were especially drawn to this aspect of the Virgin Mary and bought cakes containing soil from Bethlehem, where drops of Mary's milk,

Milky Way and lilies originate from Hera's milk. Cartari, 1647

according to legend, fell to the ground. They also revered St. Catherine of Alexandria, who, when she was beheaded in A.D. 307, was said to have shed not BLOOD but milk. In the time of the minnesingers, drinking the pure "milk of pious thinking" (Schiller's formulation, centuries later, in *William Tell*) symbolized respect for courtly morality. In ancient cultures, sacrifices of milk were often understood as rituals of purification.

In the imagery of ALCHEMY, milk, along with blood, is a symbol for the two primal ELEMENTS, SULFUR AND MERCURY, as in Stolcius' "Chemical Garden" (1624): "Two noble streams especially fine,/ Of whitest milk and rich red blood,/ That you can tell are pure and good,/ . . . The two of which when they've been boiled/ Will give you precious heavy GOLD." Milk may well be a circumlocution for sperm here, since in the ancient theory of procreation new life came from the union of white sperm with red menses. Traditional proverbial expressions include many references to milk. What we have "always" known or believed in, we say that we drank in "with our mother's milk." "There's no use crying over spilt milk," because it cannot be gathered up again (i.e., what is done cannot be undone). "Milk" is whatever is sweet, pleasant, refreshing— e.g., "the milk of human kindness" [*Macbeth*, I, v, 18], or "adversity's sweet milk, philosophy" [*Romeo and Juliet*, III, iii, 55]. According to classical mythology, the Milky Way (Greek *galaxis*) was formed when Hera (Juno) removed the vigorously sucking young Hercules from her breast; the milk of the gods was spilled and flowed across the sky. (See also LILY.)

mill, millstone In many cosmologies of early advanced civilizations the turning of the fixed STARS around the celestial North Pole (which is linked to the center of the earth [see MUNDUS, OMPHALOS] by a crystalline AXIS MUNDI) is thought of as a "great mill." The cyclical ages of the earth are associated symbolically with the notion of the rotations of this mill. In this context the mill also represents the equalizing effect of fate, which

Mill and plow. Illustration, Elke of Repgow's *Sachsenspiegel*, ca. 1230

provides equal justice in the same way that a mill grinds every grain without prejudice. The association with BREAD, which the grain is processed to produce, is obvious. In ancient Rome the vestal VIRGINS hung garlands on mills on the feast day of Vesta, the goddess of the hearth. In medieval Christian symbolism we find the "mystic mill": the prophet Isaiah pours the grain of the Old Testament into the hopper and the apostle Paul collects the flour into which it is turned. In some pictorial representations the four EVANGELISTS pour in the grain while the apostles direct the course of the RIVERS that will drive the mill wheel. The Church fathers collect the flour, and Jesus distributes to the faithful the communion wafers baked from it; Christ is the very "bread of life." A millstone hurled down from HEAVEN to EARTH appears on several occasions in the Bible as a sign of divine punishment, especially in the Book of Revelation: "And a mighty angel took up a stone like a great millstone, and cast it into the sea, saying, Thus with violence shall that great city Babylon be thrown down . . ." [18:21].

Mill, sickle and plow. From an early Boccaccio edition, Ulm, 1473

mirrors derive their symbolic importance from the ancient belief that persons or objects were magically linked to their reflections. Thus a mirror could hold on to a person's soul or life force. This belief explains the custom in some cultures of covering all the mirrors in the room in which a person has died; otherwise, it was feared, the person's soul would be kept in the room and could never cross over into the AFTERLIFE. Demons and supernatural creatures are revealed by the fact that they have no reflection in a mirror; some incarnations of the devil (e.g., the BASILISK) cannot bear to gaze upon their own image, and die if they catch sight of their reflection in a mirror. Mirrors are thus also amulets, offering protection against satanic creatures and forces. This tradition appears to have referred originally to the reflecting surfaces of bodies of water, which also functioned as aids for augury, since they made visible a sort of "anti-world," an alternate version of our own.

In antiquity mirrors were generally made of silver or polished bronze. Etruscan disklike mirrors are famous for their engraved ornamentation and their depictions, on the reverse side of the mirror, of mythological motifs (e.g., the labors of HERCULES)—strengthening the importance of mirrors beyond mere functionality.

In ancient Mexico there were mirrors made from polished volcanic glass (obsidian). The name of the Aztec god Tezcatlipoca literally means "smoking mirror." Here, too, it seems likely that the mirror played a role in divination, perhaps in the calling up of visions.

The mirror has special significance in the Shinto tradition of Japan, where it is an attribute of the SUN goddess Amaterasu. A sacred mirror named Yatano-kagami is among the imperial treasures (along with PEARLS and a SWORD) and is kept in the shrine of Ise, beyond the reach of ordinary mortals. It is said to be made of bronze, in the form of an eight-petalled lotus blossom, ten inches in diameter. It is handed to each new EMPEROR as a symbol of office. According to one tradition, which cannot be verified, the mirror bears the Hebrew inscription of "I

Mirror "returns to each of us what we give." J. Boschius, 1702

am who am" (God's self-revelation in Exodus 3:14; King James Version: "I AM THAT I AM").

In European iconography the significance of mirrors is ambiguous. On the one hand, they appear in the hands of the deadly sirens of antiquity, or of Luxuria, the personification of lust and vanity; on the other hand, they are also attributes of the virtues of self-knowledge, Veritas and Prudentia. Moreover, the mirror is also associated with the VIRGIN Mary, because she gave us God's image and reflection, Jesus Christ, without the mirror (Mary herself) being changed or broken in the process. (The MOON is simi-

Mirror shows vain woman the devil's backside. Der Ritter vom Thurn, 1493

larly associated with Mary, because it reflects the light of the SUN.) All of creation is seen as a reflection of God's being; for Jakob Böhme (1575–1624), creation is both an EYE and the mirror in which the eye sees itself. The eyes are popularly referred to as the "mirrors of the soul." A bright mirror symbolizes marital bliss; a broken one, divorce or seven years' bad luck. Dark mirrors that send no reflection back to us (in dreams, for example) are also warnings of bad luck or even death. The Islamic mystic Jelaleddin Rumi (1207–1273) saw the mirror as a symbol of the HEART, which must be clean and pure if it is to reflect undiminished Allah's intense LIGHT. The mirror also frequently symbolizes those who, rather than acting on their own behalf, entrust themselves to divine wisdom. There have frequently been literary reworkings of the theme of an apparent anti-universe to which one gains access through a mirror (e.g., Lewis Carroll's Through the Looking-Glass, or Jean Cocteau's Orphée). (See also MAGPIE.)

The symbolic significance of mirrors for Jungian psychologists is derived from traditional lore and superstition. According to Aeppli, for example, dreams of mirrors are to be taken seriously. He explains the traditional belief that such dreams are omens of death as follows: "Some part of us is missing because in a mirror we stand outside ourselves. This brings about a primal feeling that our soul has been taken from us. Those who gaze at themselves in a mirror for a long period of time become transfixed and feel impaired. . . . Some people cannot bear to look at themselves in a mirror. Some few, like the Narcissus of myth, 'lose themselves' when they gaze at their image in the water. Others, after an exhaustive exploration of other regions, can return to themselves and their reality only when they have looked into a mirror and verified their actual existence." Thus in this context the ambivalence of mirrors as symbols varies with the personal attitudes and maturity of those who are examining themselves in them.

mistletoe (*Viscum album*) A plant favored in modern times as a Christmas symbol; in ancient times it was considered sacred in many cultures. This semiparasitic plant, which draws water and minerals from its host, was considered neither TREE nor bush; according to legend, it sprang up where LIGHTNING had struck a tree (especially an OAK). Mistletoe growing on oak trees was especially prized, e.g., by ancient Romans or the Celtic Druids. According to Pliny the Elder, the Druids cut it with GOLDEN SICKLES, gathered it in a WHITE cloth, and then offered it in sacrifice to the gods, along with a BULL. Mistletoe was considered a panacea, and, because it always remained GREEN, a symbol of immortality. Robert Graves writes that the mistletoe was thought to be the sexual organ of the oak tree, and when "the Druids cut it, using a golden sickle for reasons of ritual, they were performing a symbolic castration. The viscous juice of the berries was thought of as the sperm of the oak and a fluid (*chylus*) with great powers of rejuvenation." In modern times the medicinal effects of the plant have been studied: it yields a weak diuretic which also lowers the blood pressure somewhat; anthroposophic medicine stresses the plant's effectiveness against cancer, which is still subject to clinical verification. The English and American custom of hanging up sprigs of mistletoe at Christmas time—and of feeling free to kiss anyone standing under them—seems to go back to the Celtic enthusiasm for the plant. In Germanic myth, a plot hatched by the wicked Loki turned mistletoe in the hand of the BLIND god Höd into a lethal spear, which killed Balder, the god of light and vegetation; only after the END OF THE WORLD (Ragnarök) can Höd and Balder begin a new life in PARADISE (Gimle). Here the mistletoe symbolizes the innocent tool that becomes an instrument of doom through evil magic, as does the god who throws it, Balder's blind brother.

Moon as a vessel containing a hare. Codex Borgia, ancient Mexico

moon For symbology the most important heavenly body next to the SUN. The moon is usually thought of as "female," primarily because of its passivity (see YIN) as the receiver of the sun's light, but also because of the similarity of the lunar month and the menstrual cycle. The waxing and waning of the moon, and the inevitable return of the same lunar form, make a striking symbol for all philosophies combining death and rebirth. Infrequently the moon is considered—and personified as—masculine (as in German: *der Mond*, from the Germanic Mani, whose sister is Sól, or in a Southern variant Sunna, the sun; or, in English, the man in the moon) but for most languages and cultures it is feminine, e.g., the Latin Luna, the Greek Selene or Artemis, the East Asian Kuan-yin or Kwannon, or the Mayan Ixchel. In the imagery of ALCHEMY Luna represents SILVER, as well as the QUEEN, who, wedded with the KING, forms an ANDROGYNE. It was always believed that the phases of the moon influenced events on earth: not only the ebb and flow of the tides but also the rising and falling of sap in plants; haircuts and blood-letting were scheduled with reference to the lunar cycle. "Moon-herbs" (plants blooming at night) were prescribed for gynecological disorders. In Christian iconography the VIRGIN Mary, MOTHER of God, is often likened to the moon or portrayed standing or enthroned on a lunar crescent, which in Austria was readily seen as a symbol for the victory over the Turks (whose military emblem was the half-moon) but in fact goes back to Revelation 12:1: "a woman clothed with the sun, and the moon under her feet"—symbolizing victory over hostile forces. The double-headed AX, with its two whetted blades curving like half-moons, is often thought of as a lunar symbol and is for this reason referred to (like the crescent-shaped bow) as the weapon of the AMAZONS, the legendary women warriors of the ancient world. In the TRIADIC figure of the dark goddess Hecate Trioditis ("three-faced"), the three most striking phases of the moon (first quarter, full, and dark or new) are associated with the three phases of a woman's life (maiden, mother, old woman). (See DUALITIES, ABOVE AND BELOW, and SPINNING.)

In Jewish legend we find an impressive symbolic myth, based on the duality of sun and moon, that seeks to explain why the moon sheds a weaker light. The Creator explains to the moon that there are two realms, this world and the AFTERLIFE, and that the existence of the two lights refers to this polarity. The moon, since its realm is the greater of the two, the afterlife, feels that it would be only fitting for it to give off more light than the sun. "Then the Lord said: It is perfectly clear to me: you think that I will make you bigger and the sun smaller. But because you set out to cheat the sun, you shall be the smaller, and your brilliance only one-sixtieth of that of the sun. Then the moon said to the Lord: O, Lord of the world! I spoke but this one word, and for this I am to be punished so severely? And the Lord said: One day [i.e., presumably after the Last Judgment] you will be as big as the sun once more, 'and the shining of the moon will be as the shining of the sun' " [bin Gorion, 1980]. One harbinger of the Day of Judgment (see END OF THE WORLD), however, is an eclipse of the moon [Joel 3:15]. In the Jewish world, however, the moon is linked not only with the nocturnal or the otherworldly but also, as in other traditions, with femininity (an association suggested by the temporal similarity of the lunar and menstrual cycles) and fertility (in multiple senses). Women and domesticated animals wore moon-like necklaces. The Greek apologist Theophilus of Antioch (second century after Christ) saw the sun and the moon as dualistic symbols, "images bearing a great mystery: for the sun is the symbol of God; the moon, of humanity," whose light is a reflection of God's. Similarly, Origen (A.D. 184–254) interpreted the moon as a symbol of the Church, which receives illumination and then transmits it to all believers. Every month, moreover, the moon is "reborn"—an obvious symbol for the Resurrection.

In ancient Peru the worship of the moon was subordinated to that of the sun. The Inca Garcilaso de la Vega (1539–1616) calls the moon "the wife of the sun" and writes that the interior walls of the lunar temple were covered with SILVER, "so that their whiteness might immediately proclaim this the chamber of the moon. As in the case of the sun, this temple contained a likeness of the moon, portrayed as a woman's face formed and drawn on a great silver ingot. This was where one came to seek out the moon and to commend oneself to her protection. The moon was the sister and the wife of the sun as well as the mother of the King and the entire race, and thus was called 'Mamaquilla,' or 'Mother Moon.' There were no sacrifices to the moon like those to the sun. On either side of the figure representing the moon were the bodies of the deceased queens of the Incas, arranged in order of age and royal succession. . . ."

In astrology the moon is still considered a "planet," as in the geocentric system of the ancient world; the moon and the sun together are the "principal lights" of the astrologer's universe. The moon is the clos-

Moon: Mithras altar with lunar crescent to be lit from behind. Bonn, Roman period

est heavenly body to the earth, showing it always the same "face," a face whose lines and shadows are the stuff of legend, as we have seen. Because of its different phases, the moon is thought of in astrology, as in other traditions, as "fickle, producing transitory effects," but also as a benevolent, "feminine" "planet," influencing the emotions, the female sex, mothers, and the entire populace of the earth. It is exalted in the sign of Taurus (see BULL), whether because of the resemblance between the tips of the lunar crescent and the horns of a bull, or because of myths associating lunar goddesses with virile partners in taurine form. Modern astrologers view the moon as influencing a woman's superficial personality but a man's deeper being, his soul. In ancient Rome the moon was spoken of as a liar, *"luna mendax,"* in part because its form resembled a C when it was waning (*decrescere*) and a D when it was waxing (*crescere*). Because of their traditional symbolic associations, PEARLS, opal, selenite, and mother-of-pearl were spoken of as "moonstones." The fact that the moon is not only a "symbolic place" in the heavens but has now been visited by humans, seems to be of little importance to astrologers: their cosmology is geared to those who remain on earth, and its version of the influence and symbolism of the traditional "planets" has remained unchanged. In iconography the moon is usually portrayed as a crescent, its profile turned to the left. Lunar crescents appear in the coats of arms of many Islamic countries. Böckler, speaking of lunar images in heraldry, noted that the hundred senators of Romulus wore a C-shaped half-moon on their shoes as an indication "that they trampled under foot as vain and worldly everything under the moon, or simply to distinguish themselves as senators. Nobles whose arms include the moon, which means 'growth' or 'prosperity,' presumably took this symbol from the Turks long ago" (1688).

Moses Great prophet and lawgiver of Israel, received the Ten Commandments (or Decalogue) from God on Mount Sinai (see MOUNTAIN). The FIVE BOOKS of Moses

(Genesis, Exodus, Leviticus, Numbers, and Deuteronomy) form the Pentateuch or the sacred Torah of Jewish tradition. The authorship of these books was long ascribed to Moses, hence their title. Most scholars now say the books have not one author but four principal sources, Yahwist, Elohist, Priestly, and Deuteronomic; over the course of many years, it is believed, the strands were woven together to form these first five books of the Old Testament canon. Most scholars believe Moses was a historical figure. The name is Egyptian and means "son" or "child" (compare Ramses or Ra-Meses, "son of Re"); the Hebrew interpretation of it is "pulled from the water." Our most reliable calculations place Moses' life around 1450 B.C.: the "darkness" in Egypt (in Exodus 10:21–23, the ninth of the "plagues" of Egypt; compare FROG, LOCUST) before the Jewish exodus has been linked to the eruption of Thera (Santorini), which yielded such great quantities of volcanic ash as to eclipse the light of the sun. Moses bound the Jewish people departing from Egypt in a covenant with the monotheistic ("Thou shalt have no other gods before [or besides] me", Exodus 20:3) Yahweh, establishing an order based on law, including moral law. But he was "neither

Moses with the Tablets of the Law, crowned by sunbeams. Gustave Doré (1832–1883)

Moses. Etching, Schnorr von Carolsfeld

an officer nor a member of the caste of priests, neither a member of an ecstatic cult nor a descendent of old nobility"; he was rather a "prophet and a man of God" [O. Schilling, in Bauer] who through his angry outburst over the "water of Meribah [literally 'contention']" [Numbers 20:8–13] lost the right to enter the Promised Land and died on Mount Nebo; "but no man knoweth of his sepulchre unto this day" [Deuteronomy 34:6]. "It is characteristic of Jewish views of religion that no cult was to be attached to the person of Moses. But legend soon seized upon Moses and endowed him with those wondrous characteristics—typical of ancient Middle Eastern folklore—that abound even in the account of his life in the five books that bear his name" [Bertholet]. "Without his overwhelmingly powerful experience of the burning bush [on Mount Horeb in Exodus 3:1–6; see THORNS], his life's work—towering over that of his contemporaries, indeed hardly measurable in human terms—would have been inconceivable" [Schilling in Bauer].

mother   The great symbol of grounding and protection is associated in every context with the transmission of life to the individual personality; this association is independent of the dominant social order—as common in clearly patriarchal as in matriarchal societies. "Our experience of our own mother is immense and long-lasting, from the beginning of our life onward; it fills our child-

hood. The figure of this woman—to whom we belong more completely than to any other woman—accompanies us all the days of our lives. Although corporeally separated from her, we are nourished for years through her efforts, her devotion" [Aeppli]. When the mother, however, does not allow the "umbilical cord" to be cut, does not allow the child to develop independently of her, "the unconscious, sensing danger, withdraws much of its veneration for her and she appears as a negative figure"—what Erich Neumann calls the "terrible mother." In this situation, Aeppli recommends, one should carefully re-examine one's relationship to one's parents. Carl Gustav Jung understood the maternal archetype very broadly and found it in the person of the individual's grandmother, wet-nurse, or nanny, as well as the mother herself. She is, "in a higher or figurative sense, the goddess, especially the Mother of God, the VIRGIN, SOPHIA [. . .], and by extension the Church, the university, the CITY, the country, HEAVEN, the sea, any enclosed body of water; matter, the underworld; in a narrow sense, the locus of procreation and birth, the field, the GARDEN, the ROCK, the CAVE, the TREE, the SPRING; in the narrowest sense, the womb, and every hollow form; the oven, the pot; as an animal, the COW, the helpful animal in general." The negative quality of the maternal archetype is expressed in the WITCH, succubus, SNAKE, grave, abyss. The essential association, however, is with "wisdom beyond knowledge, benevolence, sheltering, sustaining; the giving of

Mother and son, resembling Christian-era pietàs. Votive bronze, Sardinia, ca. 1000 B.C.

Mother-goddess statuette (saurian head), holding child. El Obeid (Iraq), ca. 4000 B.C.

fertility, growth, nourishment; the locus of magical transformation and rebirth; all that is secret and hidden." Negative maternal images are found, for example, in DREAMS in which the mother appears as a "primitive, selfish force": "She does not let go, is always demanding; she contains that which threatens the son inside the man, and alienates the mother's daughter, until late in life" [Aeppli]. The task of the individual is to detach the maternal archetype—the primal, collective, communal, psychic content of all the experience of humanity—from the individual's personal image of his or her own mother. "Every dream movement with the greater archetypal mother frees us from our ties to our own mothers, ties which ultimately are not really part of her, do not belong to her. In this way, when we learn to make this distinction, the maternal complex is dissolved and we attain a natural relationship to our real mother" [Aeppli]. In symbolism the MOON or the EARTH is often associated with the image of the mother, as is Mary, the Virgin Mother of God. Mary's virginity—a paradox, if thought of in purely rational terms—is an article of faith for most Christian believers, unfathomable in terms of nature, science, or human experience. (See also BLACK, FATHER.)

mountain   A virtually universal symbol of God's proximity, the mountain rises above the ordinary level of humanity and extends close to the HEAVENS. If the peak is concealed by CLOUDS, this stimulates our imaginations; volcanos especially are felt to be eerie, awe-inspiring points of contact with a superhuman realm. Sacred mountains or those that are sites of divine revelations (Fuji, Elbrus, Sinai, Horeb, Tabor, Carmel, Gerizim, Kailas, Olympus . . .) frequently became symbols of divine power and were so portrayed in the fine arts. The cosmos, too, is often represented as a terraced mountain, such as the world-mountain Meru in Indian art, or as a terraced pyramid (e.g., Burubudur, Java). The ziggurat structures of ancient Mesopotamia were also architectural translations of divine mountains. PILGRIMAGES to holy mountains symbolized spiritual elevation, step by step, above the level of everyday life. Thus the Spanish mystic St. John of the Cross (1542–1591) called his path to God "the ascension to Mount Carmel." Mountain pilgrimages are common today; many make the "Four Mountain" pilgrimage in Carinthia (Austria); about 200,000 pilgrims per year climb to the top of Mount Fuji (Japan) or sacrifice at one of the countless Shinto shrines at its foot. In ancient Mexico Mount Tlaloc (in the Iztaccíhuatl massif) bore an idol of the RAIN god of the same name; on its head were placed seeds of all cultivated fruits, in hopes of rich harvests. The mountain, closer to the heavens than the surrounding land, is thus already an easily imaginable abode for the gods; moreover, clouds frequently gather around mountains and pour forth rain. Mountain peaks are obvious symbols of "el-

Mountain: Deity atop mountains. Akkadian seal, ca. 2500 B.C.

Mountain: Moses receives the Ten Commandments.
Bible illustration, Hans Holbein, 1530

evation" above the level of everyday life,
and the AXIS MUNDI is frequently imagined
as a mountain in the far north under the
polar star, around which the other STARS
revolve. For the ancient Chinese there were
five holy mountains, corresponding to the
four points of the compass and one central
point. Of particular importance were the
Kunlun Mountains "with NINE levels." In
representations of the world, mountains with
clouds symbolized the mainland, where YIN
AND YANG alternately predominated. In pre-
Columbian Mexico cloud-like crenelations
and representations of the firmament often
crowned the temple pyramids, which were
thought of as artificial mountains upon which
the gods lived.

In Christian iconography the Christ of
the Last Judgment is often portrayed seated
on a mountain, far up in the clouds. All
other mountains were to be symbolically
leveled, however, which we may take as a
conscious turning away from heathen mountain worship. It is not surprising that after
the spread of Christianity to Central Europe
old mountain shrines came to be seen as
gathering places for evil spirits; WITCHES,
led by the DEVIL, were believed to celebrate
blasphemous rites there (e.g., on the Brocken
in the Harz Mountains in Germany). But
frequently churches or chapels were built on
mountaintops as a way of taking them over
from pre-Christian cults. Crosses placed on
mountaintops in the modern era are further
expressions of the belief in God's proximity
to these sites. Compare CAVES, OMPHALOS,
ROCKS, STONE. The archetypical sacred
mountain of the Bible is Mount Sinai, where
God appeared to MOSES. He commanded
Moses as follows: "Thou shalt set bounds

unto the people round about, saying, Take
heed to yourselves, that ye go not up into
the mount, or touch the border of it: who-
soever toucheth the mount shall be surely
put to death: There shall not an hand touch
it, but he shall surely be stoned, or shot
through; whether it be beast or man, it shall
not live: when the trumpet [shofar] soundeth
long, they shall come up to the mount"
[Exodus 19:12–13]. In the Bible Mount Zion
in the former Jebusite city of Jerusalem,
which the Israelites conquered, is another
abode for the glory of God: "Thus saith the
Lord of hosts; I was jealous for Zion [. . .].
I am returned unto Zion, and will dwell in
the midst of Jerusalem: and Jerusalem shall
be called a city of truth; and the mountain
of the Lord of hosts the holy mountain"
[Zechariah 8:2–3]. For the SAMARITAN religious community, however, Mount Gerizim,
a wooded knoll with many SPRINGS, had this
status and was spoken of as a sort of Eden
(see PARADISE). Each of these groups has,
within its symbolic view of the world, its
own "mountain of the Lord's house [. . .]
established in the top of the mountains, and
[. . .] exalted above the hills" [Isaiah 2:2].
In the Middle Ages Mont Sauvage (Montsalvatge, Munsalvaesche), site of the Castle
of the GRAIL, became the quintessential sacred mountain of legend.

mouse (Latin *mus*, Greek *sminthus*) Despite (or precisely because of) its smallness,
the mouse is of considerable importance in
popular tradition and belief, and thus in the
history of symbols as well. It has often been
thought of as analogous to the soul: the
mouse scurries off in haste, hardly visible,
just as the spirit leaves the body at the
moment of death. According to ancient
zoologists a mouse had the ability to terrify
an ELEPHANT; two mice could reproduce by
licking one another; mice originated in Egypt,
from the mud of the Nile; the livers of mice
wax and wane with the phases of the MOON.
Timid animals preferring dark spaces, they
were said to have demonic and prophetic
powers. Their squeaking and footsteps were
taken as portents of STORMS; their gnawing
at religious artifacts, of cruel blows of fate.
The supposed lasciviousness of mice led to

Mouse. Miniature bronze, late Egyptian

their representation on coins together with Aphrodite (VENUS), the goddess of love. The anonymous satire *The War between the Frog and the Mice (Batrachomyomachia)*, which was at first attributed to HOMER, is an early parody of the heroic epic. In DREAMS (as in death) a mouse could embody the soul of the dreamer and as such leave the body and then return to it. The mice who ate Bishop Hatto in his "mouse tower" in Bingen (Germany) are said to be the souls of those whom he allowed to starve in order to satisfy his own miserly greed. The most negative aspect of the popular image of the rodent goes back to the observation that mice not only destroy stores of grain (Apollo Smintheus, in the ancient world, and St. Gertrude, in the Christian, were believed to protect against such damage) but also—along with RATS— spread pestilence. Thus they came to be associated symbolically with satanic demons and with all powers hostile to humanity. In medieval times "to mouse" could mean "to pillage"; in German, alcoholic deliriums feature visions of "white mice" (corresponding

Mouse. Wilhelm Busch

to the English "pink elephants" or the Aztec "400 rabbits"). In the Greek world, Apollo Smintheus was also said to shoot ARROWS bearing the plague. "This is why the sight of these ravenous creatures fills us with nausea and revulsion," writes Aeppli on the role of the mouse as a dream symbol. "Now and then a single mouse appears in a dream signifying something splendid, if not totally devoid of danger, just as the word 'mouse' can be a term of affection in the unconscious language of love. . . . On the level of analogy with organs of the body, the mouse appears occasionally in the dreams of young men to represent the female sex organ. The other aspect of the stealthily gnawing rodent is far more common. . . ." The frequent appearance of whole armies of mice clearly

Mouse: Mice in the pantry. Aesop's *Fables*, Ulm, 1475

suggests, Aeppli continues, "that bits of our psyches or souls are scurrying around inside us, scattered, dissociated, voracious, in the dark pantries of our lives." (See also RAT.) In modern comics and cartoons, the mouse plays a different role: it is the weaker but smarter combatant who triumphs over its physically superior adversary, the CAT, just as the young DAVID defeated the GIANT Goliath. Papyri of ancient Egypt already offer their version of this war between cats and mice.

mouth In symbolic tradition not only the orifice through which food is taken in and speech is articulated but also the primary locus associated with the breath of life. The ceremony in which the ancient Egyptians "opened the mouth" of the mummy being buried (touching the face with a flint prong and a curved AX blade) was thought to restore the life force of the person who had died. In the mythology of Heliopolis, or On, the divine couple Shu ("breath") and Tefnut ("saliva" or "moisture") came from the mouth of the god Atum (see NINE); in the ancient Hindu myth of creation the other gods came from the mouth of the first god, Prajapati, whereas humans came from his penis (LINGA) and demons from his anus. There are many symbolic associations between the mouth and the womb (as in the expression os uteri, "the mouth of the uterus"); as a sexual symbol, the mouth often stands for the vulva. The mouths of Parsi fire-priests were covered with cloth so that their breath would not desecrate the FIRE; in Jainism the mouth was bound to prevent the swallowing of insects. For St. Hildegard of Bingen (1098–1179) the human mouth is subject to the most austere moral obligation, because it is through the mouth that "the entire person is kept alive. As the world is illuminated by the brilliance of the sun, so does the breath [that passes through the mouth] temper and inspire every higher breath [i.e., of the Spirit]." The mouth appears in figures of speech referring to facial expressions ("down in the mouth") or speech ("word of mouth," "a foul mouth"), including references that distinguish mere words from sincere intention ("to mouth pieties"; compare "lip service"); by extension, the word can refer to any opening, including the point at which a RIVER flows into the sea. In the account of the Last Judgment (see END OF THE WORLD) in the Book of Revelation, Christ appears as the great judge, "and out of his mouth goeth a sharp sword, that with it he should smite the nations" [19:15]. In medieval depictions of exorcism, BLACK DEVILS (the demons who had taken possession) come out of the mouths of those who have been healed; GOLDEN threads from the mouths of persons in prayer link them with HEAVEN. On baroque tombstones we sometimes see a kneeling woman whose mouth is covered by a cloth: the wife or widow of the deceased is so represented if she died before the stone was carved.

Münchhausen   The symbolic figure of the merry boaster with his tall tales of adventure was actually a historical person. Carl Friedrich Hieronymus Baron von Münchhausen (1720–1797), of a line of Lower Saxon nobility dating from 1183, did lead an adventurous life, fought in two wars against the Turks, and was a passionate hunter. On his estate Bodenwerder (in the Weser region of Germany) he regaled his guests with accounts of his astonishing adventures, earning him the sobriquet "baron of lies"—and a place in popular tradition. Several of these stories were published (1781–83), and the librarian R. E. Raspe, who lived in England, published more in English (Oxford, 1785). G. A. Bürger translated these into German (1786, 1788), adding tales drawn from Lucian, Rabelais, Swift, and others; his extraordinarily popular book provided material for the further adaptations, dramatizations, and even films, of subsequent centuries. In psychiatry, patients displaying the "Münchhausen syndrome" (technical name: *Pseudologia phantastica*) adorn their life stories with incredibly exaggerated details.

Münchhausen carried through the air by wild ducks that he has shot. Gustave Doré (1832–1883)

mundus The Latin word for "world" designates a sacrificial pit which in ancient Rome symbolized the center of the ordered world. Romulus, the founder of the city, was said to have excavated it at the intersection (on what later became the Palatine) of the streets that divided Rome into quadrants. In a sacrificial rite, the Romans placed into the pit lumps of earth from their legendary original homeland, along with the year's first fruits of every variety. The mundus is the symbolic navel (see OMPHALOS) both of the city of Rome and of the (human) cosmos, as well as an altar for sacrifices to the divinities of the underworld, or *inferi*. Any city with a central mundus could view itself as the center of the universe. The Roman custom was actually derived from an earlier, quite similar Etruscan one [Pfiffig].

muses The symbolic figures that have become proverbial for symbolic inspiration: "Happy the one whom the muses love, the one from whose lips language flows sweet" [Hesiod]. In Greek myth they were sired by Zeus with the nymph Mnemosyne ("memory") to inspire verses commemorating the heroic victories of the gods over the pre-Olympian Titans. Apparently thought of at first as MOUNTAIN and water nymphs (see WATER SPIRITS), they came to be defined with individual "specialties" and associated specifically with Mount Parnassus, Mount Helicon, the spring Castalia (near Delphi; "One drink from her waters, and the poet sings"), and the Hippocrene (the "horse spring" created by the winged horse PEGASUS with a stamp of his hooves). European schoolchildren used to memorize the names of the muses using the rhyme "Clio-Me-Ter-Thal/ Eu-Er-Ur-Po-Call," which is made up of the first syllables of the names Clio (the muse of history), Melpomene (tragedy), Terpsichore (dance, choral songs), Thalia (comedy), Euterpe (flute), Erato (hymns), Urania (didactic poetry, astronomy), Polyhymnia (dance), and Calliope (heroic epic); there are great variations in the assignment of these "specialties." Originally, it is said, there were only three muses (see TRIADS); the subsequent number, NINE, is understood to have originated through the squaring of the three. In art they are portrayed as young women accompanied by the SUN god Apollo ("For it is thanks to the Muses, and to Apollo, whose beams strike true from afar, that there are poets on earth, and that the harp resounds"—Hesiod): Apollo Musagetes, carrying the lyre and wearing a WREATH of LAURELS, leads the chorus of muses.

mushrooms Often symbols of good fortune; surprisingly, it is especially the poisonous toadstool that is given this symbolic import. The fact that the peoples of Siberia once used the toadstool as a hallucinogen would hardly explain this Central European tradition, which presumably comes from the unusual—and supposedly "happy" —appearance of the toadstool with the white spots on its red top. Some mushrooms (morels) may have been associated with potency and fertility becasue of their phallic shape. Mushrooms growing in CIRCLES were sometimes called "WITCH's rings," apparently because they were interpreted as the botanical spoor of witches' or elves' nocturnal round dances. In ancient China the mushroom (*ku*

Mushrooms: Sprang up "in a single night." J. Boschius, 1702

or *chih*), which symbolized longevity, was thought of as miraculous ambrosia and associated with immortality. On the Chinese counterpart of the mythical ISLANDS OF THE BLESSED there stood a "mushroom palace" made of SILVER and GOLD.

Modern Western usage focuses most often on the rapid growth of the mushroom (buildings spring up on the urban landscape "like mushrooms") or on its physical form (the "mushroom cloud" that follows an atomic explosion).

nail Associated in many archaic cosmologies of Northern European peoples with the North Star, and imagined as an AXIS MUNDI around which the heavenly firmament rotated (see HEAVEN). In Central Africa many human figures carved from wood have been found with nails pounded into them ("nail fetishes"). The nails, which are usually hammered in by sorcerers as part of a ritual, serve to remind a spirit (thought of as inhabiting the figure) of a tutelary obligation; the nail is to assure that the spirit inside the IDOL does in fact heed those who implore it to lend its assistance (for good or ill). In Central Europe, the pounding of nails into particular significant trees or wooden figures is often a traditional sign of someone's presence or the visit of an outsider. In Christian symbolism the nail is a reminder of the crucifixion of Christ (see CROSS). In the High Middle Ages FOUR nails appeared in depictions of Christ crucified; later his feet came to be portrayed as pierced by a single nail, making a total of only three. Three nails are also part of the "ARMA CHRISTI." Clove (from the Latin *clavus*, "nail") flowers were widely viewed as botanical symbols of the nails of the Crucifixion, owing to the nail-like form of their dried buds. "As pungent whiff of clove revives, restores,/ So that refreshed we can resume our course,/ When God's own will the faithful always do,/ Their way can be but happy, bless'd and true" [Hohberg]. Nails are among the attributes of saints who were so martyred:

Cyrus or Quirinus, Pantaleon, Severus, Ingratia. Cold or rugged individuals are frequently said to be "as hard as nails," and "to hit the nail on the head" is to come up with a precise analysis or expression.

nakedness symbolizes the primal state of humanity, the individual portrayed without the social or hierarchical markers that clothing constitutes. This we see especially in rites of initiation, e.g., into the Mithras cult of late antiquity, in which the initiate's nakedness was supposed to suggest that of a newborn. The cult also required that each adherent give himself over completely to the higher powers or forces, that he make no effort to preserve any sort of invulnerability; the initiate was thus required to undo all the constraints and KNOTS that had previously served to protect him, exposing even his genitals (ordinarily covered as protection against any sort of aggression, including that of the "evil EYE"). It was to return to the legendary state of primeval innocence in the Garden of Eden (see PARADISE) before the Fall that worshippers in various "Adamite" sects, both ancient and modern, disrobed; this is still the practice in the Canadian Dukhobor sect (British Columbia, Saskatchewan), which originated in Russia. Asceticism (i.e., renouncing clothing) is the prime consideration behind the nakedness of the Digambara ("clothed in air") cult of Indian Jainism. Eroticism plays no role in the nakedness of simple, nonliterate peoples in tropical regions: the genitalia are "ignored," and there is a great sense of modesty about sexual behavior. This attitude is suspended only in the context of special rituals. In the art of Christian Europe ADAM AND EVE are shown naked (although usually with leaves or long hair covering the genital areas), as are WITCHES (e.g., in the engravings of Hans Baldung-Grien)—with the implication, in this case, of licentiousness. Renaissance art brought the return of the "nude"—for the first time since antiquity, and justified within the context of the classicist return to that tradition. Thus symbolic and mythological figures could be portrayed undraped, despite the prudery that attached to other subjects and is seen, for example, in the painting-over of Michelangelo's "Last Judgment."

Narcissus In Greek mythology as recounted by Ovid [*Metamorphoses* III, 339–512], a beautiful youth, the son of a river god (Cephisus) and a nymph; the seer Tiresias prophesied long life for the infant Narcissus provided that he "never know himself." The nymph Echo, whom the goddess Hera had deprived of original speech and thought (as a punishment for talkativeness), loved Narcissus beyond all reason but was unable to manifest herself to him: she was but a disembodied voice, capable only of repeating the words of others. Because of Narcissus' heartless rejection of all prospective lovers, the goddess of revenge, Nemesis, led him to drink from a spring on Mount Helicon (see MUSES) and fall madly in love with his own reflection (see MIRROR) in the water. Unable to tear himself away, he could only watch himself languish and die, the slave and victim of his own seductive beauty. He was transformed into the flower that bears his name. That flower has come to be widely viewed as a symbol of spring, but also of sleep, death, and resurrection, because it seems to withdraw in the summer but is highly conspicuous in the spring. Because its form resembles that of the LILY, it often appears in paintings of the VIRGIN Mary. Still, the association that has most marked our linguistic usage is with the youth Narcissus as a symbol of "narcissistic" self-love (and pathological vanity) at the expense of any real awareness of the rest of the world. In China the narcissus (*shui-hsien*, literally "water immortal") is a New Year's symbol of happiness and good fortune. It was not originally native to China but was introduced by Arab traders and has appeared in Chinese FAIRY TALES since the Middle Ages. In conventional Chinese rebus-like punning, images containing the combination narcissus-STONE-BAMBOO mean "The EIGHT IMMORTALS wish you a long life."

Nemesis (Greek, literally "distribution of that which is due; retribution; righteous anger") The personification of opposition to injustice, both the avenger of misdeeds and the impartial referee at tournaments; her attributes are SCALES, a SWORD, and a measuring stick. (In addition, she was originally portrayed as winged.) Her divine powers include that of bringing back to reality those mortals whose good fortune is undeserved. In Greek myth she is referred to as the daughter of the NIGHT (Nyx). It is further recounted that Zeus became enamored of her and she took on different forms to escape his advances; while she was in the form of a GOOSE, however, he assumed that of a SWAN and impregnated her. In another version, Zeus, again as a swan, pretended to be fleeing from an EAGLE and sought refuge in Nemesis' lap; Nemesis, as a result, soon produced an egg, which Leda, the queen of Sparta, hatched and from which emerged Helen, whose abduction led to the Trojan War. The swan and the eagle were made into constellations as memorials to Zeus. Gladiators sacrificed to Nemesis at small altars placed at the entrances to the arenas of Roman amphitheaters. (See also APPLE.)

net A sculptural representation of a net (Greek *agrenon*) covered many OMPHALOS STONES; its function is not clear. (Was it supposed to confine supernatural creatures who had chosen the omphalos as a possible abode?) In Greek myth the fire god and metal-smith Hephaestus (Latin Vulcan) catches his unfaithful wife Aphrodite (VENUS) and her lover Ares (MARS) *in flagrante delicto* and casts over them a net made of sturdy bronze wire, so that he can expose them to the scorn of the gods. This net for Aphrodite (as Robert Graves suggests) can be understood as a reappearance of an implement important in her initial role as goddess of the sea and fishing. Indeed, nets are generally symbols of catching or capture, in accordance with their normal use. The Norse sea goddess Ran, the daughter of Aegir, uses a net to gather up those who have died by drowning and then carries them off to her personal realm of shades. The trickster hero Maui of Polynesian myth caught the SUN in a net and stole its FIRE,

Net. Hohberg, 1675

in order to give it to humanity. In ancient Persia the net is the symbol of the mystic, who seeks to "capture" enlightenment with it. St. Luke's gospel recounts the miraculous "draught of the FISHES" (using nets) on the lake of Gennesaret [5:1–11], an anticipation of Peter's subsequent success as an apostle: "from henceforth thou shalt catch men" [verse 11]. In India, the net-like web of the SPIDER is a symbol for cosmic order, and, because of its radial structure, for the radiance of the divine spirit. The "demon nets" of the Himalayas are similarly constructed from sticks and thread; these traps are supposed to destroy evil spirits. In India the spider's web also symbolizes the illusory world of the senses (maya): it captures the weak, but the wise can tear it apart. In Hugo von Trimberg's (1230–1310) "The Devil's Net" (1290) a pious hermit persuades the DEVIL to betray his strategy: his servants (Pride, Envy, Hatred, Avarice, Gluttony, Lust, and Anger) are going about with a gigantic net in which to catch persons of all social classes and occupations—a satanic counterpart to the image in Luke.

night (Greek *nyx*, Latin *nox*) Not always thought of simply as the absence of sunlight (see SUN), but rather associated symbolically with mysterious DARKNESS and the protection of the womb (see MOTHER). Greek mythology had an ambivalent view of night. In one of its manifestations it was the great goddess Nyx in a BLACK, STAR-studded robe; during the day she lives in a CAVE far off in the west, until the time comes for her to emerge from it and cross the sky in her CHARIOT pulled by black HORSES. She is also portrayed with black WINGS. In Aeschylus' poetic image, the MOON is the EYE of the black night. As the bringer of sleep and of respite from care she bore the name Euphrosyne or Euphrone. Her son is HYPNOS ("dream"). Nyx is thus the mother of sleep, dreams, and sexual pleasure—but also of death. Her uncanny appearance also makes her the mother of such pernicious offspring as Moros ("doom"), the revenge goddess NEMESIS, and the FATES (Greek Moirae, Latin Parcae). The goddess (whom the Romans called Nox) appeared in mythology as a creature of CHAOS, born with Erebos ("darkness"), Gaea ("earth"), Eros, and Tartarus. With her brother Erebos she conceived Ether and Hemera ("day"). When Hemera withdraws into her nocturnal abode, Nyx begins her voyage across the face of the earth. There was no cult of Nyx, and yet Zeus (JUPITER) himself was said to fear her greatly. In many cultures, rituals honoring the dead or the earth itself were celebrated at night— in early Christianity, primarily because of the necessity of keeping the gatherings secret. It was later said that WITCHES celebrated nocturnal orgies (Walpurgis Night). For Roman Catholics the Easter vigil service is the pivotal moment in the liturgical year, with the blessing of the FIRE, the lighting of the Easter candle, and the blessing of the

Night (Nyx) with the brothers Sleep (Hypnos) and Death (Thanatos). Cartari, 1647

baptismal water—frequently used immediately for the sacrament of baptism. Most important, however, is the joy of anticipation as the dawn of the day of Christ's resurrection approaches. In the Alps there are legends of a ghostly race of spirits that haunt the night, frightening those who venture out of their homes after dark.

nightingale (in poetic language: "philomel" or "philomela") Thought of in antiquity as a plaintive mother, weeping for her child and crying "Itys!" [Ovid, Metamorphoses] (compare HOOPOE). It also symbolized the human goal of producing truly melodious language; poets referred to themselves as disciples of the nightingale. The name of the bird often stands for "song" or "poetry." Because the parent birds taught their young to sing, the nightingale became an allegorical reference to pedagogical ability. In folk medicine the flesh of the bird was prescribed for those who seemed to require excessive sleep, and the HEART of the bird in particular was to be eaten to beautify one's voice or sharpen one's rhetorical skills. But already in antiquity the rich came under attack for eating nightingale (especially the TONGUE) simply as a curiosity. In Europe as in Asia, the bird was prized for the sweetness of its song, which was also generally considered to be a good omen. In certain areas, however, it was interpreted as a cry for help

Nightingale: "My song is of my love." J. Boschius, 1702

from some "poor soul in PURGATORY" or as a plaintive warning of an impending death; whereas Christians often heard in it a longing for PARADISE or HEAVEN. In Arnim and Brentano's collection Des Knaben Wunderhorn (1805ff.) it is written: "O Nightingale, I hear thy song,/ And in my breast my HEART would burst," and the first of these lines has been transformed into a Berlin idiom meaning, "I get the point." (See also OWL.) Jacobus de Voragine's Legenda aurea (ca. 1270) contains a parable about the nightingale in the section entitled "Of Saint Barlaam and Josaphat." A hunter, it seems, freed a nightingale that he had captured. The bird called down to him: "A great TREASURE has slipped through your fingers: in my entrails is a PEARL larger than an OSTRICH EGG." The hunter tried to lure the bird back, but it only mocked his gullibility: "You actually believed that I had a pearl inside me bigger than an ostrich egg—why, I myself am not that big! You're like the fools who put their faith in graven idols. They worship what they have made and call 'tutelary' or 'guardian' things that they themselves must guard." In the medieval collection Gesta Romanorum (ca. 1300) the nightingale is similarly associated with a jewel. A knight, imprisoned for a misdeed, is consoled by the beautiful song of a nightingale that visits him in prison; he feeds the bird BREAD crumbs. It flies off, then returns with a small jewel in its beak. "When the knight saw the stone, he was filled with wonder. He swiftly took it from the bird, applied it to his iron chains, and they fell away from him." The PRECIOUS STONE similarly enables him to open the prison doors and escape. The spiritual or symbolic moral of the story is not spelled out, but it seems to involve the bird's gratitude: acts of charity will be rewarded.

nimbus (Latin, "rain cloud") or halo The symbol for the aura that radiates from superhuman beings, especially surrounding their heads. (Compare the MANDORLA, which surrounds the entire body.) The luminous disk was not an innovation of Christian iconography: it is used earlier in Eastern art and

Nimbus: Christ with cross nimbus. Byzantine church at Daphni, ca. A.D. 1100

in Hellenistic art of late antiquity as an expression of the divinity of those who are so portrayed. The nimbus was accorded to Zeus (JUPITER), Apollo as god of the SUN, and Dionysus (BACCHUS), as well as great KINGS and the images on coins of deified Roman EMPERORS.

As early as the second century there were depictions of Christ with the nimbus (as found in the Calixtus catacomb in Rome); the VIRGIN Mary and the ANGELS were later similarly depicted. Christ is often portrayed with a CROSS nimbus: the CIRCLE is divided into quadrants by the beams of the cross, and the lower portion of the vertical beam is not visible. Symbols of the four EVANGELISTS have the nimbus from the fourth century onward. It later serves to single out saints in group portrayals and is usually executed in GOLD paint.

Nimrod A symbolic, at times humorous, designation for a hunter, going back to the "table of the nations" in Genesis 10, in which cities and countries, like people, are named for their mythic ancestral fathers: in this account, Nimrod "began to be a mighty one in the earth. He was a mighty hunter before the Lord: wherefore it is said, Even as Nimrod the mighty hunter before the Lord. And the beginning of his kingdom

was Babel, and Erech, and Accad, and CALNEH, in the land of Shinar. Out of that land went forth Asshur, and builded Nineveh, and the city Rehoboth, and Calah" [verses 8–11]. Nimrod is the personification of the Assyrian empire, and the name "Nimrud" seems to have originally designated an Assyrian god of war and the hunt. The city of Calah, founded around 1270 B.C. south of the present location of Mosul on the Tigris, was also called Nimrud; according to the Biblical view, Nimrud or Nimrod was thought to be the ancestral father of its inhabitants. In the Islamic tradition KING Nimrod plays a role corresponding to that of Herod in the New Testament. Nimrod learned through a prophecy that a child named ABRAHAM, greater than gods and kings, was to be born; Nimrod, a mighty king afraid lest he lose his power, had all the male children killed. Allah, however, arranged for Abraham to escape. The legend of Abraham's birth, his concealment in a cave until he came to know God, is recounted in Jewish popular tradition in exactly the same terms [bin Gorion, 1980]. (See also STARS.)

nine In the symbolism of NUMBERS, nine is initially significant as the square of the number three (see TRIANGLE, TRINITY, TRIADS). This "higher power" of three was of greatest importance in the religion and cosmology of ancient Egypt, where any of several groupings of nine gods was called a *pesedjet*, or ennead. In the priestly mythology of the city of On (Greek Heliopolis) the creator and supreme god was Atum; his children were Shu (air) and Tefnut (moisture); then came Geb (EARTH) and Nut (HEAVEN) and their children Eset (Isis) and Usire (Osiris), Setekh (Seth) and Nebhat (Nephthys). Other gods were also grouped in enneads, although some of them actually consisted of seven (the "great ennead of Abydos") or 15 (Thebes) gods. In ancient China the number nine was important in the I CHING and in the *Book of Rituals (Li Chi)*, which speaks of nine ceremonies (puberty rite for men, WEDDING, audience, ambassadorship, burial, sacrifice, hospitality, drinking, and military rituals). In the Han dynasty (see SIX) a nine-based cosmology was for a time especially favored (the realm of the dead—"nine SPRINGS"; the ninth day of the ninth month was a men's festival of "yang raised to a higher power" [see YIN AND YANG]; there were nine earthly provinces, nine great MOUNTAINS, nine fields of heaven, and so on). The center of Peking (today Beijing) had eight roads leading into it, and these, added to the one central point, made for a similar nonary structure. In the Occident there were nine orders of ANGELS, nine cosmic spheres in medieval cosmology, nine MUSES. We say that a CAT has nine lives, and a person who is "dressed to the nines" is wearing his or her most elaborate finery.

Noah In the Biblical account of the Great FLOOD, the second great progenitor of the human race (after ADAM), corresponding to Ziusudra or Utnapishtim, whom King Gilgamesh (in Babylonian myth) met on the island Dilmun (see ISLANDS OF THE BLESSED). Like St. JOSEPH, Noah, the builder of the ARK, is considered a patron saint of carpenters; because of his discovery of the intoxicating power of WINE, he is also called the first vintner. Common attributes of Noah include the DOVE with OLIVE branch, and the RAINBOW, divine symbols of reconciliation after the destruction of the world by WATER. Typolgical Christian interpreters understood the mockery of Noah, who in his drunkenness had fallen asleep with his private parts exposed, as an anticipation of the moment in which Christ is stripped of his garments before the Crucifixion.

In early writings of Freemasonry (1738), Masons were called "sons of Noah," meaning that they adhered to an ancient order older than the Ten Commandments. Their precepts involved worshipping God and not IDOLS; rejecting murder, infidelity, and theft; leading upright lives; and never eating the flesh of an animal "suffocated in its own blood." These ethical and religious principles correspond to the moral laws enumerated in Genesis 9:1–7.

Norns In Germanic myth the personifications of fate, corresponding to the Parcae (see FATES) of the Romans or the Moirae of the Greeks. Represented as three SPINNING women, Urd ("fate"), Verdandi ("becoming"), and Skuld ("guilt"), they determine the birth, life, and death of every newborn mortal, just like the fairies in the Grimms' version of "Cinderella." As they sit near Urd's well and the world TREE Yggdrasill, Urd spins the thread, Verdandi winds it into a skein, and Skuld cuts it off. The myth promotes a fatalistic approach to life, or, viewed somewhat differently, encourages us to accept our lot; compare VALKYRIES. It is possible that the TRIAD and their symbolic associations are not unrelated historically to their Mediterranean counterparts.

nose "The human nose is the air that moves the waters," writes Hildegard of Bingen (1098–1179), alluding to the spirit-like breath (Hebrew *ruah*) of God that moves "upon the face of the waters" in Genesis 1:2. That same nose is arguably the most characteristic feature of a person's physiognomy. DEVILS are usually portrayed with misshapen noses, and thus children used to mock those who had a "Longish nose and pointed chin—Satan surely dwells within." In another tradition, it was popularly believed that there was a relationship between a man's nose and his penis; Melanesian

Nose accentuated on devil's mask (with genuine goat's horns). Salzburg, ca. 1820

Nose: "Tweaking one's own nose." Bookplate, A. Kubin

ancestor figures often have a beak-like nose that extends down to meet the genitals. The nose appears frequently in colloquial idioms: "to have a good nose for" (the sense of smell as a metaphor for discernment), "to lead a person by the nose," "to look down one's nose at," "to pay through the nose." From the 17th century onward we find drawings of a bird pinching in its beak a human nose protruding from its breast. This motif refers to the old legal custom according to which a person admitting to having slandered another was forced to pinch his or her own nose and repeat the slander. In Mayan iconography (e.g., the mask friezes of temple grounds) the RAIN god Chac is portrayed with a proboscis-like nose (see also SCEPTER).

numbers In the view of the Pythagoreans (sixth century B.C.), the key to the harmonic laws of the cosmos, and thus symbols of divine order. The discovery that vibrating strings whose lengths can be expressed in simple numerical ratios yield pleasing chords led to the concept of "harmony" as we know it and was also the first step toward a mathematical analysis of our experience of the world. Every form can be expressed in numbers, which are concealed in our universe like "divine archetypes" waiting to be discovered. An example of this is in the theorem of PYTHAGORAS, which reveals the (at first apparently miraculous) relationship of squares constructed on the three sides of a right TRIANGLE. "Numbers were not cast blindly into the world. They came together in orderly balanced systems, like the formation of crystals or musical chords, in accordance with all-embracing laws of harmony" [Koestler]. Numbers were not viewed as units of measure but rather as the beginning (*arche*), "the ruling, uncreated, steadfast bond internally linking all things" — Philolaus, fifth century B.C. Similarly, the periodicity of cosmic cycles, which seems to follow numerical patterns, must have suggested to the ancients that numbers were not simply organizing tools introduced by humans but primal realities of the universe, "absolute" (literally, "detached") traces of superhuman forces and thus sacred symbols of the gods. For Novalis (1772–1801) numerology was mystic: "It is very likely that there is in nature a miraculous mysticism of numbers, and in history as well. Is not everything significant, strangely interconnected? Cannot God manifest himself in mathematics, just as in any other branch of learning?" Novalis, like the ancients, understood numbers not as the practical invention of humanity but as symbols of the absolute, with their special appeal to the aesthetic sensibilities of those who were able to appreciate them and the special harmonies of the "music of the spheres." In this tradition certain numbers are truly "sacred," especially the primal One as the Creator, which through a process of revelation and renunciation yields a DUALITY (see, e.g., YIN AND YANG). In Hegelian dialectic, thesis and antithesis are joined by synthesis, and three is a number rich in association with perfection (*"omne trium perfectum"*) and mystery (see TRINITY, TRIANGLE, TRIADS): it is often said that "the third time's the charm," and heroes in FAIRY tales must prove themselves by accomplishing three feats. The masculine-feminine duality is integrated in the triad of mother, father, and child.

The number FOUR owes its archetypal power to more than a simple doubling of duality. Jung saw in the Catholic doctrine of the bodily Assumption of the Blessed Virgin Mary, which presents difficulties for many present-day Christians, an attempt to bring the feminine element into the "masculine" Trinity of Father, Son, and Holy Spirit, producing a new structure with the regularity and plenitude of the SQUARE. The grids on which we plot our world are inevitably based on the number four, starting (perhaps) with the four ELEMENTS or the four points of the compass. But there is a fifth critical point, the "origin" of the graph, the center—for the ancient Chinese, the fifth "point of the compass," and to the five points in the Chinese system there correspond FIVE, rather than four, elements. (See also PENTACLE.) The number SIX is expressed symbolically in the HEXAGRAM, "SOLOMON'S SEAL," the STAR of DAVID. NINE—three squared—is the number of orders of ANGELS and of cosmic spheres in medieval cosmology.

Ten is associated with completion and perfection (the Ten Commandments; 1 + 2 + 3 + 4 = 10; the sum of its own digits, 1 + 0, is one, unity); this symbolism is well established in virtually all cultures, since counting began on the ten fingers. The ten *sephirot* (divine manifestations) of the Cabala are also thought of as a TREE whose roots are in HEAVEN and whose branches extend all the way to the earth, corresponding to the ten secret names for God: Eheie, Yah, El, Elohim, Eloi Gibor, Eloah, Jehova Sabaoth, Elohim Sabaoth, Shadai, and Adonai.

The number 11 ("the devil's dozen" of Central Europe) usually has negative asso-

Numbers: Triskelion "trumpet" design, early medieval Ireland

ciations. Twelve is a number of great importance (12 signs of the zodiac, tribes of Israel, Apostles; the duodecimal system; see also HOMER). From the fifth century B.C. onward, there were 12 gods in the Greek pantheon: Zeus, Hera, Poseidon, Demeter, Apollo, Artemis, Ares, Aphrodite, Hermes, Athena, Hephaestus, and Hestia (often supplanted by Dionysus [BACCHUS]). In Athens, an altar was sacred to "the Twelve."

Thirteen is almost always an unlucky number. Hesiod cautioned farmers against beginning the sowing on the 13th of the month. In the Babylonian leap year there was a 13th month under the sign of the "unlucky RAVEN." The DEVIL was believed to accompany a coven of 12 WITCHES as the 13th member.

Twenty-four is the number of hours in the day and of elders in the Book of Revelation (4:4). In the Cabala, 26 is the sum of the digits associated with the four letters of the Tetragrammaton (YHWH: 10 + 5 + 6 + 5 = 26). Thirty-three is the age at which Christ died, the number of cantos in each book of the *Divine Comedy* (except for the "Inferno," which has 34, so that the three books total 100) and the number of rungs in the Byzantine "mystic LADDER."

Forty is the number of fasting, trial, and seclusion: the Old Testament prescribed that a woman who gave birth to a son required 40 days of isolation and purification afterwards (and for a daughter the time was doubled; see Leviticus 12:1–5); the ancient Greeks held a funeral banquet 40 days after a person's death; the Great FLOOD continued for 40 days and 40 nights; and Moses waited

Numbers: Gothic tracery filling of round windows, based on the numbers 3 and 6

for 40 days on Mount Sinai for the Ten Commandments. The Israelites spent 40 years in the desert; Christ fasted for 40 days after his baptism, and there are 40 weekdays in Lent. St. Augustine associated the number 40 with our journey through this world and our expectation of the world to come.

In the Old Testament the number 50 is associated with the "jubile" or jubilee year (one year beyond seven sabbath years, and thus occurring every $7 \times 7 + 1$, or 50 years) in which debts are forgiven, slaves freed, and land returned to its original owners [Leviticus 25:8–28]. In the Church calendar, Pentecost (from the Greek word for 50th) was fixed on the 50th day counting from Easter.

The number 70—the sacred seven multiplied by ten—lies behind such concepts as the Septuagint (from the Greek word for 70 because of the ancient tradition that this Greek translation of the Old Testament was completed by 70 or 72 scholars in 70 or 72 days), Septuagesima Sunday (the third Sunday before Lent; a reference to the 70 days following), and in the number of additional followers of Jesus beyond the Twelve (Luke 10:1,17; in some manuscripts, 72).

Other symbolic numbers can be derived from astronomical data and calendar cycles. The religious year of the Aztecs (tonalpohualli) and the Mayas (tzolkin) was 260 days long; its dates coincided with those of the 365-day solar calendar every 52 years, an interval called xuihmolpilli (73×260 days = 52×365 days).

Other cultures also viewed numbers as symbolic principles. For the ancient Chinese "10,000" meant "countless," and the EMPEROR was called "10,000 years" as a way of wishing him long life. From ca. A.D. 700 onward the SWASTIKA was used as a numerical symbol for this "infinity"—like the sideways-eight of the Occident, which presumably goes back to a KNOT symbol. (See also I CHING.)

E. Staufer has persuasively linked the number 666 in the Book of Revelation (13:18) to Greek numerical values inscribed on a coin of the emperor Domitian.

Numerology was of great interest to the Neo-Platonic philosophers of late antiquity and to Cabalistic scholars of the Middle Ages, because both Hebrew and Greek letters had numerical values. The principle of "isosephia" (numerical equivalence) suggested associations between names with equal numerical values; for example, "Abraxas" and "Meithras" each yield 365, the number of days in the solar year. Or the Hebrew words "Vehenna shalisha" ("and, lo, three men") in Genesis 18:2 have the same numerical value, 701, as "Elo Mikael Gabriel ve-Raphael" ("these are Michael, Gabriel, and Raphael"). This Cabalistic art of numerical speculation is called "gematry." Similar equivalencies were sought in the monastic schools of the Middle Ages. Hrabanus Maurus (A.D. 776–869) wrote: "Thus Holy Scripture contains many secrets suggested only numerically; thus only those who understand numerology can gain access to them. Thus everyone who seeks a higher understanding of the Holy Scriptures must first make an assiduous study of arithmetic." "Sacred numbers," according to this way of thinking, reveal the structure of all creation; from the earliest times onward they have belonged to the esoteric traditions of the seminary.

oak A TREE of great symbolic importance; because of its hard wood a frequent symbol of immortality or endurance. Because oaks were thought to be struck by lightning particularly often, they were associated in antiquity with the god of LIGHTNING and the HEAVENS, Zeus or JUPITER, who made his will known through the rustling of the oak leaves in the GROVE at Dodona. In ancient Rome an oak-grove on Lake Nemi ruled by a FOREST-KING was consecrated to Jupiter, and wreaths of oak leaves symbolized the rank of rulers. Celtic Druids revered oaks, upon which MISTLETOE grew, as did the Germanic peoples, who often planted them around their assembly squares and viewed them as sacred to Thor (Thunor), the god of THUNDER (as the Lithuanians associated them with Perkunas). Ancient Japan also had an oak-god (Kashima-no kami). For the ancient Greeks, oaks were inhabited by nymphs known as dryads (from the Greek *drys*, "oak"). Oak leaves were believed to have the power to transfix LIONS; the ashes of burnt oak-wood, to protect crops against disease; an ARROW made from the wood, to keep SNAKES away from dunghills. For the German Romantic poets the oak symbolized unshakeable power ("loyal, unshakeable, like German oaks"), and for this reason oak leaves appeared as a military insignia of Nazi Germany. In the U.S. Army a gold oak leaf insignia denotes the rank of major; a silver, lieutenant colonel. Druids ate acorns before

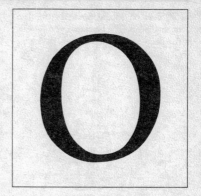

Oak being felled by a monk. French book illustration, ca. 1120

making prophecies, but otherwise they became a male sexual symbol. The word "glans" (as in "glans penis") is the Latin for "acorn"; in 1629 Oswald Crollius wrote: "The acorn shows and represents the head of the male organ." For this reason acorns are also worn as amulets. ("Acorns" are also one of the suits in the traditional German deck of playing cards.)

obelisk (from a Greek word meaning "rod for broiling, spit") A sculpted STONE PILLAR, of great symbolic importance in ancient Egypt. The first of these holy obelisks is said to have stood in the city of On (Greek Heliopolis) and to have been the first object to be struck by the rays of the SUN when the world was created. The four-sided tapering monoliths were topped by a pyramid, which was often covered with GOLD so that it would gleam in the sunlight. They often stood in pairs as entry pylons of temples, or individually in the middle of the space in front of the temple. In present-day Egypt few obelisks are still in their original places: most of them were taken off to other countries as curiosities, and some 15 of them are to be found in the squares of European or American capitals (notably in Paris on the place de la Concorde). The largest, weighing over 1000 tons, was never completed and still lies in a quarry in Aswan. It is impossible to decide today whether the first obelisk was

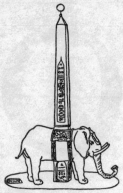

Obelisk on elephant, symbol of early civilization. *Poliphili Hypnerotomachia*, 1499

a phallic fertility symbol or a stone AXIS MUNDI.

octopus The eight-armed sea mollusk often found on GOLD medallions of the late Minoan or Mycenaean period, apparently with a mythical or symbolic meaning lost to us today. Its arms, depicted as rolled up in SPIRALS, form an impressive symmetry around the body with its two EYES, the whole suggesting a head surrounded by snake-like HAIR. Later misinterpretations of these depictions may have been the source of the mythic tradition of the head of Medusa (the most famous of the three GORGONS, beheaded by Perseus). The octopus, with its highly developed eyes and flexible prehensile arms, appears bizarre to residents of landlocked regions and may have been the model for the mythical sea-monster Scylla, who men-

Octopus on small gold disk. Mycenae, ca. 1300 B.C.

aced Odysseus and his crew. Otherwise, inhabitants of coastal regions already prized cephalopods as food in ancient times, especially the squid. The dark liquid secreted by the cuttlefish (Latin *sepia*) was used as writing ink, and its bite was considered poisonous. The dark, inky cloud surrounding the animal was thought of as a symbol of its ties to mysterious, otherworldly forces. Along with the CRAB, the cuttlefish was occasionally associated with the astrological sign Cancer.

Oedipus (Greek, literally "swollen foot") The central character in a group of legends that originated in the Greek city of Thebes and have become an important source for ancient and modern literary adaptations. Oedipus defeated the SPHINX by solving her riddle; never having known his parents, he killed his FATHER Laius and married his MOTHER Jocasta. As punishment for these

Octopus. C. Gesner, *Nomenclator*, Zürich, 1650

offenses (of which Oedipus himself suspects nothing) the gods sent a plague that would not be lifted until the guilty were punished. Jocasta hanged herself, and Oedipus blinded himself. Later the gods exonerated Oedipus, making a hero of the man whose offenses had been committed in perfect innocence. Details of the myth have their parallels in numerous tales in which the birth of a child is predicted who will bring great misfortune; the child is exposed to the elements but does not die; it goes on to solve a riddle and eventually fulfills the oracle. Robert Graves sees in Oedipus the figure of a "new KING" who kills the "old king" (seen as his symbolic father) and assumes the THRONE, since every ruler was to reign only for a specified period of time—"a custom, that the patriarchal victors [over this older social order] misunderstood as patricide and incest. Freud's theory that the 'Oedipus complex' is universal to all humans, is based on this misunderstanding." In fact, the Oedipus of Greek myth never desired a woman known to him as his mother, but simply "married into" a ruling position in a matrilineal political order; similar marriages are found in fairy tales in which a traveling artisan wins the HAND of a princess and thus comes to rule the entire kingdom. It was not until the myth was given poetic form that the story of Oedipus took on the depth and complexity that we associate with it: especially in the dramas of Sophocles (496–406 B.C.; *Oedipus Rex, Oedipus at Colonus*) and Euripides (480–406 B.C.; *The Phoenician Women*) it becomes an exploration of ethical questions of guilt and responsibility.

Ogdoad, or the eight A symbolic-cosmological concept from the priest-schools of the ancient Egyptian city of Khmunu (literally "City of the Eight"; in modern Arabic Al-Ashmunayn; Hellenistic name Hermopolis). Whereas other religious centers emphasized the concept of the ennead, or the NINE, in Khmunu creation out of primordial chaos was personified speculatively in male-female DUALITIES: Nun and Naunet were primordial WATER in male and female form; Huh and Hauhet, infinite space; Kuk and Kauket, darkness; Amûn and Amaunet the hidden, or the void. This ogdoad brought forth life in the form of FROGS and SNAKES, living in the primordial slime, from which then the first hills arose, on which the SUN-god created the first LOTUS-blossom. This "Hermopolitan cosmology" is noteworthy because one of its figures, Amûn, became for the Egyptians the imperial god of Thebes.

olive tree Associated in antiquity with the goddess Athena, who was said to have created it on the Acropolis as part of her competition with the sea god Poseidon for the mastery of Attica; of great practical

Olive tree symbolizing peace. Hohberg, 1675

importance in the Mediterranean region. Images of the gods were carved from its wood; the sacred GROVE in Olympia consisted of olive TREES, and at tournaments olive branches were presented to the winners. The olive branch had a dual association with both war and peace. It was primarily a Roman symbol of the goddess of peace (Pax), and messengers asking for peace or asylum often carried olive branches wrapped in wool. However, Athena (Latin Minerva) was the goddess not only of wisdom but also of war, and thus olive, as well as LAUREL, WREATHS adorned the brows of military victors.

In the Bible the DOVE that Noah sends out from the ARK after the FLOOD returns with an olive branch in its beak as a sign of the restoration of peace with God; "pouring oil on troubled waters" is not merely a figure of speech, and (olive) oil also softens, cleanses, serves as fuel and food. Jacob poured oil on the stone of Bethel after his dream vision of a LADDER extending to HEAVEN [Genesis 28:10–22, especially 18]. The etymological meaning of "Messiah" in Hebrew is "the anointed one." Oil is also used in treating wounds, as we see in the parable of the Good Samaritan [Luke 10:30–37]. In the Christian tradition pure olive oil is mixed with balsam and aromatic spices to make the "chrism" used in baptism, confirmation, holy orders, and the anointing of the sick. Since the seventh century coronation ceremonies have included anointing with oil.

"Although on barren mountains th'olive tree does stand,/ It still gives us its oil, so precious, valued, grand;/ So, too, may God's own word come slowly to our ears/ Yet no wise lacking pow'r, or strength to soothe our fears"; and "Tend well the olive tree and keep it in your sight,/ And peace's emblem will reward your yeoman toil./ So too is peace the prize for rich and poor alike/ When rulers tend their land and till its waiting soil" [Hohberg].

In Islamic legend the two forbidden trees in the earthly PARADISE were the olive and the FIG.

omphalos (Greek, literally "navel") In many parts of the ancient world, a familiar symbol for the birthplace of the cosmos or the site of the Creation. The most famous omphalos was in the temple of Apollo in Delphi and is now displayed in the museum of that city: a ROCK carved in the form of a beehive with the suggestion of a NET covering it, it symbolized the ideal midpoint of the cosmos, the point at which the subterranean, terrestrial, and celestial worlds all met. For this reason, it was also believed to inspire oracles. A similar omphalos STONE (*umbilicus urbis Romae*) stood in the Forum. Similar shrines were to be found in Gordium (the Phrygian capital) and in Baghdad. A rock in the Holy of Holies of the JERUSALEM temple (located in the space underneath the altar for burnt offerings) was likewise thought of as the site of the Creation and the ideal midpoint of the world—and also as sealing in the subterranean waters of the "Tehom," which, according to Talmudic tradition, came

gushing forth whenever the omphalos was removed. It was supposedly through the hole that it now seals that the waters of the first great FLOOD were drained off to the lower depths. The name of the rock, Shetiya, is derived from the Hebrew word *shata* ("to found, establish, posit") [Müller]. Today the Dome of the Rock—viewed by Muslims as housing the sacrificial altar of their ancestor ABRAHAM—stands on the same site, next to the al-Aqsa mosque.

Polaris, the pole STAR, around which the other fixed stars appear to rotate, was frequently referred to as the "navel of the HEAVENS." Its terrestrial counterpart was often a sacred MOUNTAIN (e.g., Mount Meru in India).

In general, the omphalos, as a stone sealing off a conduit between different realms, combines elements of stone worship, shamanism, and the worship of "mother EARTH." The Delphi omphalos is said to have been sacred first to the earth goddess Gaea and only later to Apollo. A similar stone is said to have been in the Hall of the Mysteries at Eleusis. (See also AXIS MUNDI, MUNDUS.)

onion (*Allium cepa*) A vegetable already popular in the time of the ancient Egyptians, frequently mentioned in ancient Greek writings (Homer, Aristophanes) as well. In time the onion and its cousins (leek, garlic, chive, shallot), because of their powerful odors, came to be thought of as food for the masses and rejected by the gentry—although in more recent centuries precisely these odors

Omphalos of Delphi. Stone sculpture, covered with net weave

Onion. J. Meydenbach, *Hortus Sanitatis*, 1491

Orant prayer in pre-Christian era. Terra cotta idol, Crete, ca. 1150 B.C.

(and especially that of garlic) were believed to ward off vampires. In folk medicine the onion was recommended against congestion, impotence, dropsy, digestive disorders, colds, scurvy, and hair loss.

The most immediate association with onions is their capacity to produce tears. According to one saying, for example, "marriage is like an onion: you weep and swallow it anyway." Its general symbolic significance is that of something that is very useful, however unpleasant its surface (suggestive of life's woes).

orant A posture for prayer in which the HANDS are not folded but raised to the level of the shoulders or the head, the palms turned upward, as if to receive the bounties of HEAVEN. This is said to be the oldest and most natural posture for prayer; it is still

Orant prayer. Sarcophagus relief, Tarragona, 5th century after Christ

assumed by priests in the celebration of Mass. Orant prayer, common in Mediterranean regions, was taken over by the early Christian Church, where it was seen as appropriate for imploring divine blessing and assistance. Figures on tombstones often portray the deceased in this posture. In the Eastern Church the VIRGIN Mary has often been portrayed orant, but in the West the posture has lost currency and significance.

Orpheus A mysterious figure in Greek myth and a symbol of the musician who was able with the overwhelming power of his art to move animals and plants, even STONES, and to inspire the divinities of the underworld (see AFTERLIFE) to acts of mercy. The son of a MUSE and a RIVER god in Thrace, he became a master of song and the lyre. When his wife Eurydice died from the bite of a snake, he went down into the underworld and charmed its KING and QUEEN (Dis, or Pluto, and Persephone), along with the shades of the dead. He was allowed to convey Eurydice back to the world of the living, but only under the condition that he not turn to look at her until journey's end. His longing was so great that he forgot this stipulation—and Eurydice was forever lost to him. Later the wine god Dionysus set his maenads (women mad with ecstasy) upon Orpheus because the musician revered Apollo more than him, and Orpheus (like Dionysus Zagreus himself before his rebirth, in Orphic myth) was torn limb from limb. The muses gathered up his scattered body parts for burial, but his head floated off toward Lesbos, the island of women poets.

Only portions of the doctrines associated with the Orphic mysteries have been reconstructed. In their precepts of purity, and in their rituals for purification, they are reminiscent of the doctrines of the Pythagoreans (see PYTHAGORAS). In the Orphic myth of the beginning of the world, CHRONUS created an EGG from which the ANDROGYNOUS ancestral god Phanes broke forth. Phanes gave birth to Nyx (the NIGHT); Uranus (HEAVEN), Gaea (EARTH), and Cronus were the children of Phanes and Nyx. Zeus, the son of Cronus (Latin SATURN), came to be

Orpheus. Detail from floor mosaic. Palestine, 5th century after Christ

the foremost of the gods and had a son by his daughter Demeter. This son, Zagreus, however, was torn apart and devoured by the Titans; this is why Zeus destroyed them with bolts of his LIGHTNING. Mortals were formed from their ASHES, and this is why mortals carry about in their bodies "titanic" (evil) as well as good (coming from the body of Zagreus, who was later restored to life as Dionysus) elements. Orphic rituals of purification sought to liberate these divine SPARKS from their material prison—an anticipation of Gnostic and, later, alchemistic doctrine.

There are many depictions of the myth of Orpheus and Eurydice in opera (Gluck, Monteverdi, Haydn) and painting (Tintoretto, Breughel, Rubens, Tiepolo).

A floor mosaic in the old synagogue of Gaza shows Orpheus playing a harp, surrounded by wild animals listening to his music. The Hebrew inscription of this typical scene indicates that the Greek bard was seen as an equivalent of DAVID, the harp-playing king of the Old Testament.

ostrich (*Struthio camelus*) In Greek the word for "ostrich" was originally the same as for "sparrow" (*struthus*); the confusion was avoided by adding the qualifier *megas* ("large") or using instead the form *struthocamelus* (literally "camel ostrich"), a reference to the bird's size and the form of its legs and feet. The ostrich was already known in Mediterranean regions in the fifth century

B.C., when it was still found in northern Africa; its African habitat is confirmed in pre- and early-historic cave drawings. Aristotle believed that the ostrich was part bird, part land mammal. The FEATHER symbolizing the Egyptian goddess Maat was apparently an ostrich plume. The early Christian text *Physiologus* (second century) praises the "beautiful, iridescent" feathers of the ostrich and offers the following account: the bird "flies low over the face of the earth. . . . It eats whatever it finds. It even visits the blacksmith, devouring red-hot iron, passing it immediately through its intestine, from which it emerges still glowing. This iron, however, is lightened and purified through the process of digestion, as I saw with my own eyes in Chios. The bird lays EGGS but does not brood them in the usual way: it sits facing them and stares at them intensely; they grow warm in the heat of its gaze, and its young are hatched. . . . This is why in church its eggs are proposed as a model for us: when we stand together and pray, our eyes should be watching God, because he took away our sins."

The other notion, according to which the heat of the SUN hatched the eggs of the ostrich, served as an analogy for Christ's awakening from the tomb; the emergence of its young without parental involvement (which, of course, has no zoological validity) came to symbolize the virginity of Mary (see VIRGIN).

Ostrich as eater of horse shoes. J. Boschius, 1702

Ostrich portrayed like eagle. Bestiary, Bibliothèque de l'Arsenal, Paris, 12th century

In medieval bestiaries, the inability of the ostrich to fly makes it, like the SWAN, a symbol of religious hypocrisy. It often spreads its wings as if to fly, but it cannot leave the earth, "just like hypocrites, who give the appearance of holiness but in their actions are never holy. . . . Thus are hypocrites weighed down by their worldly goods and will never rise to attain the bounties of heaven" [Unterkircher]—unlike FALCONS and HERONS, whose bodies are lighter, enabling them to take flight easily.

The ostrich appears also as a HERALDIC symbol, as in the arms of the poet J. A. Eisenbart (1666–1727), whose name literally means "iron beard", and (along with horseshoes) of the Austrian city of Leoben, long associated with the iron industry; both commemorate the bird's legendary ability to digest iron.

ovens, stoves, and furnaces are rich in symbolic associations. In the Old Testament the smelting furnace so hot that not even IRON retains its form, is an image for trials and tribulations [Deuteronomy 4:20; I Kings 8:51; Jeremiah 11:4]. In colder latitudes such devices have different associations, especially in the case of the stove that heats the living space; in the cold months domestic life is centered upon this both real and symbolic "hearth" at which meals were also formerly prepared. It is the location of the FIRE (vital energy), here domesticated, that serves human needs, and, when the fire is not lit, a hollow form, and thus a maternal

symbol in the Jungian sense (see MOTHER). In FAIRY TALES like the Grimms' "Goose Maid," things can be confessed to the stove that no human ear would be allowed to hear. The oven in which Hansel and Gretel burn up the WITCH can be understood as standing primarily for the stake at which witches (and JOAN OF ARC) were burned so that no physical traces of them remained. (Their ASHES were usually strewn into RIVERS.) Only those who are pleasing in God's sight—like Shadrach, Meshach, and Abednego in the Book of Daniel—can withstand the flames: King Nebuchadnezzar had the three youths cast into the "fiery furnace" when they refused to worship the "golden statue . . . sixty cubits high" (see IDOL), but an ANGEL "drove the fiery flames out of the furnace, and made the inside of the furnace as though a dew-laden breeze were blowing through it. The fire in no way touched them or caused them pain or harm" [Daniel 3:1, 49–50 (deuterocanonical), New American Bible].

owl Familiar in the European world in association with the goddess Pallas Athena; the German equivalent of "coals to Newcastle" is "owls to Athens." The symbolic import of the bird is ambivalent. Owls, in their different varieties, appear to humans to be wise, patient, introspective, brooding, and able to see in the dark. After noting that "the owl by nature has special signifi-

Ovens: Alchemist's purifying furnace. Geber, "De Alchimia," Strasbourg, 1531

Owl representing the soul, used in masked drama. Tsimshian nation, Pacific Northwest

cance, primarily because it stays awake at night, and is thus the special bird of soldiers on watch and those who study far into the night," Böckler [1688] mentions a non-European example of the bird's symbolic importance: "The arms of the Tatar rulers contain a black night-owl in a golden shield, because the first of them, Genghis Khan, saved his life with the help of such a bird." As a symbol of knowledge and of erudition that can see through obscurity (and as the bird of Athena/Minerva, the goddess of wisdom), the owl appears frequently in the emblems of scholarly publishing houses and book stores. But owls have negative associations in popular thinking: with their nocturnal ("furtive") habits, solitude, silent flight, and plaintive cry ("eerie," "harbingers of death"), they came to symbolize a turning away from spiritual light—or, conversely, Jesus Christ in the "night of suffering and death." The baroque poet Hohberg speaks of the screech owl under attack from diurnal birds: "As daytime birds attack the bird of shade/ And fall upon with beaks as

if to kill,/ Thus read'ly world would Church's realm invade,/ And sanctum swift with monstrous murder fill" [1675]. In Judaism the female night-demon Lilith is described in the company of the owl; the dark and terrible Hindu goddess Durga, in her manifestation as "Camunda," rides an owl; the Mayan death-god Hunhau is often depicted with a head like an owl's. In China the owl is the negative counterpart of the PHOENIX, a harbinger of misfortune, apparently because of its "demonic" gaze and a fable according to which owls learn to fly only when they have irreverently pecked out the eyes of their parents. And yet the bird seems to have been a positive symbol in the Shang dynasty, since many bronze containers bear its image. In the pre-Aztec civilization of ancient Mexico (Teotihuacán) the owl was

Owl: Screech owl attacked by birds. Hohberg, 1675

the sacred animal of the rain-god, whereas for the Aztecs it symbolized a demonic night-creature and was considered an evil omen.

ox   For the symbologist and the cultural historian, the domesticated (castrated) counterpart of the wild BULL; an image of patient servitude and peaceful strength, and for this reason both respected and used as a sacrificial animal. In ancient China it was considered immoral to eat the meat of the animal who pulled the plow. In Christian iconography the ox appears with the DONKEY in the stable at Bethlehem, on the basis of a passage in an extracanonical gospel purporting to be written by St. Matthew. The

Owl. Attic cup, ca. 470 B.C.

ox is also an attribute of St. Cornély (who, it is said, came to Brittany in a wagon pulled by oxen and transformed his persecutors into rows of megaliths; see MENHIR); Leonard, the patron saint of cattle; and Sts. Sylvester and Wendelin. Many legends feature oxen that pull a wagon containing a relic or the body of a saint only to a certain point (which later becomes a shrine for pilgrims), thus carrying out God's intentions. For reasons that are no longer clear, images of oxen on Romanesque PILLARS are supposed to symbolize the NIGHT. "Where there are no oxen, the crib remains empty" [Proverbs 14:4, New American Bible]. Böckler [1688] similarly focuses on practical (not to say prosaic) considerations and praises the strength and servility of the ox, "a benevolent animal, and well suited not only for working the fields and such but also for eating; in sum, there is nothing there that cannot be used."

palm trees (Usually date palms are described and depicted.) The Judeo-Christian symbolism of the palm TREE generally goes back to Psalm 92:12: "The righteous shall flourish like the palm tree." In 1675 Hohberg wrote as follows: "All that the palm produces has its vital use:/ Fruit, milk, oil, wood, bark, leaves, and fiber, even juice./ The faithful, too, all serve the ends of God above,/ As long as they do strive to live in Christian love."

In the arid regions south of the Mediterranean the date palm was prized for obvious reasons. It was considered holy, and the SUN god Assur was often portrayed above it. The Egyptians laid palm fronds on coffins and mummies, and the people of Jerusalem placed them in Christ's path as he entered the city. (In some Christian observances of Palm Sunday, the palm fronds are replaced by willow catkins.) From early Christian times onward, there are frequent depictions of the martyr's "palm of victory" and the flourishing palm tree of the PARADISE to come after the Last Judgment, often in combination with LILIES and GRAPES. The Greek word, *phoenix*, indicates an association with the SUN and Helios Apollo; see PHOENIX. Nike, the goddess of victory (Latin Victoria), was often portrayed with the palm branch; in Egypt, the goddess of HEAVEN, Hathor, was the "lady of the date palm." In general, the tree (because of its straight, slender trunk and abundant foliage) symbolized ascent,

victory, and rebirth. It also served as the emblem of the 17th-century literary group "the Fertile Society," of which Baron von Hohberg (quoted above) was a member, and whose motto was "Nothing wasted, a use for everything." From the legend that the palm tree will grow tall even if a heavy weight is suspended from it, comes the motto of the principality of Waldeck-Pyrmont, "*Palma sub pondere crescit,*" which is understood to mean that difficulties only make us stronger. "The palm tree bends not, staunchly bears the weight,/ Victorious, dauntless, yielding sweetest dates./ When God's our trust and we pray unafraid,/ Come angel legions ever to our aid" [Hohberg].

Pan (Latin Faunus; compare FLORA, SATYRS) A Greek shepherd-god from the MOUNTAINS of Arcadia; the word "panic" is derived from his name. He was portrayed with a hairy body and the legs and horns of a goat: an embodiment of the life of mountain CAVES and meadows. SHEPHERDS believed that he so loved his regular nap in the heat of the day that no one would dare to interrupt it; if anyone did, the raging Pan would suddenly appear, and this apparition filled the offender with a paralyzing horror. This fate is said to have befallen the Persians at the battle of Marathon, and the Greeks erected a temple to Pan on the Acropolis as an expression of their gratitude. The "pipes of Pan" which he played are also called a

Palm. Hohberg, 1675

Pan with syrinx and shepherd's staff. Cartari, 1647

syrinx—so named for the nymph Syrinx, who eluded his amorous advances by transforming herself into a bed of reeds. In order to retain her precious voice, Pan fashioned his simple pipes from those very reeds. Since Pan's name also means "all" in Greek, the shepherd-god evolved into a figure of all-encompassing nature. Plutarch (A.D. 46-120) relates that during the reign of the emperor Tiberius sailors on a ship passing the island of Paxos heard a voice saying, "When you reach Epirus, make it known that the great Pan is dead." When they did so, a mournful cry arose from all the animals, ROCKS, and TREES. This was interpreted as the death of an older, simpler order in which the gods of nature were worshipped, and the coming of a new age—that of Christianity, in which the oracles fall silent and the IDOLS are toppled. Many legends repeat (with different names) a similar story: a voice from out of the FOREST brings a message of death to the friendly creatures who inhabit the wild (see SAVAGES). This story may have originated in a seasonally determined cult festival for one of the "gods dying and rising from the dead" (see ADONIS).

Pandora The principal figure in a myth contained in Hesiod's *Theogony* and *Works and Days*, symbolically attributing all the ills of the world to the female sex. After PRO-METHEUS had eased the lot of early man with the gift of FIRE, the gods decided that human existence was not to become utterly idyllic. The metalsmith and god of FIRE Hephaestus (Latin Vulcan) crafted a female figure, into which the four WINDS blew the breath of life. Gods and goddesses lent her beauty. Then the seductive figure was sent among mortals. Although Zeus had made her lazy, ill-natured, and stupid, the naive Epimetheus, the brother of Prometheus, readily married her. She brought with her a box (see BOX-TREE), or in some versions a jug, out of which emerged all the torments of humanity: age, pain, disease, madness. Only hope, which the box also contained, could keep mortals from immediately ending their lives. "Thus did the pernicious female sex come to be, a great misfortune for the male. . . . She is the mother of the hordes of women who have become the ruin of mortal man" [Hesiod]. "Pandora" ("all-giving") may have been an early epithet of the EARTH-MOTHER Gaea, but this image was subsequently transformed into a profoundly misogynist myth.

According to Hyginus, Pyrrha, Pandora's daughter, was the first mortal woman to be born (i.e., not molded by Hephaestus). In the Greek legend of the Great FLOOD, she and her husband Deucalion are the two who survive.

panther A predatory animal (*pardalis, pantera, leopardalis*) once found throughout the Near East and in parts of North Africa; the big cat's savagery and cunning, as well as the superior fighting courage of the female, are frequently mentioned in ancient texts. Among the fabulous details of these documents are reports that the panther longs to drink WINE and needs human feces to protect itself from aconite, or monkshood, poisoning. Many mythological heroes wore panther skins (ORPHEUS, Jason, Antenor), and the cat was counted among the followers of Dionysus (see BACCHUS), Aphrodite (see VENUS), the enchantress CIRCE, and Cybele. Beginning in 186 B.C., panthers were brought to Rome from Africa to fight. In the early Christian text *Physiologus*, strangely enough,

Panther as exotic mount for Dionysus (Bacchus). Mosaic, Pella (Macedonia), ca. 300 B.C.

the panther is described as "the friendliest of animals, an enemy only of the SNAKE. . . . A powerful but sweet fragrance emanates from its voice, and other animals follow the fragrance and come quite close to the cat." So, too, the text goes on, did Jesus Christ proclaim the salvation of the world upon his resurrection, "and he became an utterly sweet fragrance for us, to all near and far." His garment is "colorful like that of the panther," adorned with virginity, purity, mercy, faith, VIRTUE, harmony, peace, and generosity, and he is an enemy of the fallen serpent. The belief that the panther always slept three days after feeding and returning to its cave, and only upon waking sent forth its "fragrant" voice, also contributed to associating it symbolically with Christ. In the various medieval bestiaries we also find the following: the DRAGON alone is filled with dread when it hears the voice of the panther; it hides then in underground caves where it "is paralyzed with fear, for it cannot bear the smell of the panther. So, too, did Christ, the true panther, descend from heaven, to save us from the power of the diabolical dragon. . . . After death he descended into the underworld, where he tied up the great dragon. . ." [Unterkircher]. In other details the bestiaries generally repeat the details of the older *Physiologus*.

In ancient China the panther was seen ambivalently. It was seen primarily as a highly dangerous, cruel, savage animal, and its tail was attached to chariots of war as a military insignia. A beautiful young woman is called a "brightly colored panther" if she is found to be aggressive. Through Chinese homonymy, panthers (*pao*, also "announce") and MAGPIES (*hsi*, also "joy") together in a picture connote a joyous announcement. The BLACK panther is considered especially dangerous.

In European HERALDRY the panther (not occurring in nature in this part of the world) came to be portrayed as a curious combination of lion, dragon, and bull (the source of its horns), whose breath, described in the *Physiologus* as sweet, is represented by flames shooting from its mouth. From the 14th century onward it has EAGLE's claws on its front feet, and in the 16th century it has flames emerging from all of the orifices of its body. In this form, it is the heraldic emblem of the Austrian province of Styria. In the region around Lake Constance, it has cloven hooves on its hind feet; in Italy, it has a head like that of a HARE, and is called *la dolce* ("the sweet one") in a reference to the *Physiologus*.

In the New World the corresponding animal is the jaguar, which for example in ancient Mexico was the symbol of the Aztec warrior order (Ocelotl) and also of the 14th

Panther in stylized form. From the coat of arms of Styria, Austria

Panther, "adorned by its spots." J. Boschius, 1702

of the 20 day-signs of the Aztec calendar. The Maya called the jaguar *balam*, which was also the epithet of a divinatory priest; on earthenware vessels the jaguar often appears with water-LILY tendrils or pierced by a javelin thrown by the god of the PLANET VENUS. In the myths of the native peoples of Latin America, the jaguar is often the tutelary spirit of shamans; tales of TWIN jaguars also abound.

paradise The image of a GARDEN of delights, free of all danger, the domain of the sinless men and women of earliest times. The etymological (ancient Persian) meaning of the word is "walled-in park," suggesting the enclosed preserves of KINGS. In the Biblical paradise, "the TREE of the knowledge of good and evil" [Genesis 2:17] was declared off limits by God—a taboo not respected by the first humans. In the primordial time of myth, paradise was the primordial midpoint of the universe, marked by the FOUR RIVERS flowing out of it and, above all, by the presence of the Creator himself. This "paradise lost" became the goal of the righteous believer, who hoped to find it again in HEAVEN. Islamic descriptions of paradise are different from those of other religions only in their inclusion of sexual pleasures for the man who is admitted into it: "large-eyed beauties, untouched by any person or demon" [Beltz, 1980]. Among

PALM and POMEGRANATE trees, fragrant shrubs, and shady GROVES, the righteous delight in the primordial garden restored after the Last Judgment. In one of its four rivers flows the clear water of life; in the second, WINE that does not intoxicate those who drink of it; in the third, MILK that never spoils; and in the fourth, HONEY— unclouded, fragrant, and nourishing. This is "no mere dream world but a highly realistic world of pleasures . . . an image of life lived in peace and leisure, as was typical in the resort oases of the Eastern, male-dominated world. Notions of paradise were already anticipated in the gardens of Arab caliphs" [Beltz, 1980]. Four different gardens were imagined, corresponding to the four rivers of paradise.

In classical antiquity the notion of the Elysian ISLANDS OF THE BLESSED in the region of the setting SUN was largely displaced by that of a dark underworld (Hades, Orcus). The Celtic conception of the AFTERLIFE frequently combines the idea of "happy islands" in the western sea with that of an underwater paradise, inaccessible to the living, with sensual pleasures comparable to those of the Islamic paradise. Sailors' tales from this part of the world mention for example "three times fifty" islands on which thousands of beautiful women wait, sweet music is heard, and deceit, care, disease, and death are unknown. Among these mythical islands are Mag Mell, the richly flowered plain of pleasures; Mag Mon, the plain of games; Ciuín, the gentle land; and Imchiuín, the very gentle land. The island

Paradise of the animals. M. Merian, 1633

Paradise: Adam, Eve, Tree of Knowledge. Schedel, *Weltchronik*, Nürnberg, 1493

Emain is also called Tir na'm Bán, the land of women, where countless women and maidens wait, all aglow. Such myths apparently sought (by promising an exaggerated paradise suggestive of the land of COCK-AIGNE) to reduce people's fears of dying and to prepare them for the miracles of the hoped-for afterlife, where the just will live on after death without torment or care, like in the Jaru Fields of ancient Egyptian myth. A similar version of paradise is that of the RAIN god Tlaloc (reserved primarily for victims of drowning) in the ancient Mexican tradition.

We repeatedly encounter the notion of a prelapsarian GOLDEN AGE, generally symbolized by a splendid garden, and restored for the elect after the END OF THE WORLD and the Last Judgment. The historian of civilization will be quick to point out that the symbolic landscape hardly corresponds to the reality of prehistoric hunters and gatherers; it owes much more to the later epoch in which humanity cultivated the plant world to grow fruit orchards. The image of the Garden of Eden, familiar in the Occidental world, is associated with an indeterminate location in the Middle East or beyond; in the Middle Ages, however, it was believed that the earthly paradise must be situated not far from JERUSALEM. (See MOUNTAIN, OMPHALOS, ROCK.) ANGELS with fiery swords were thought to guard it, or, in another version, it existed in a different realm to which human understanding had no access: a domain of happiness only roughly analogous to any terrestrial site, not unlike the island of Dilmun in Sumerian myth, which is superficially associated with the Bahrain Islands in the Persian Gulf but understood to exist on a different plane. In the same way the "heavenly Jerusalem" of the Book of Revelation corresponds to the terrestrial city of the same name only as an ideal to a tangible archetype.

The great Gothic cathedrals were understood as providing an image of paradise; this is why the main portal was often adorned with a relief of the Last Judgment.

Eastern images of paradise are far removed from terrestrial notions: the ideal state is one of spiritual nearness to God. In the Buddhist concept of Nirvana (which Westerners often falsely equate with "nothingness"), the individual personality is absorbed into the all-embracing totality of absolute being.

The desire not to view any form of paradise for the just and holy as the one ultimate goal of absolute existence is expressed in a legend attributed to the Sufi master Rabi'a, who died A.D. 810. When asked why she

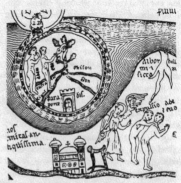

Paradise: Eden. World map, Richard of Haldingham, 13th century

carried in one hand a bowl of WATER and in the other one of FIRE, she replied: "I rush to set fire to paradise and to flood hell with water, so that these veils might be lifted from the eyes of pilgrims on their way to God, and that they might recognize their true goal; so that the servants of God might see him, him alone, hoping for no reward, fearing no reprisal. . . ." A somewhat later Sufi, Abud Yazid Bistami, provided the following commentary: "Paradise is the last of all the veils, for those who are chosen for paradise remain there; and those who remain there do not dwell with God. God is He-who-is-veiled."

parrot (Greek *psittacus*) Imported from India to ancient Greece, and prized for its ability to imitate human speech. Callimachus (300–240 B.C.) saw the BIRD as a symbol of babbling humans; in one of Aesop's fables, the parrot is the rival of the weasel. In the early Christian text *Physiologus*, the bird's imitation of human speech is related to the teaching of St. Basil: "In the same way must you imitate the voice of the Apostles praising God, and praise him yourself. Imitate the conduct of the just, so as to be worthy of attaining their luminous throne." The parrot's beak was thought of as an amulet against fever and demons.

In medieval bestiaries the parrot is spoken of as recalcitrant: its head is so hard that the bird must be beaten with an IRON rod if one wants to teach it anything. According to Conrad of Würzburg, the bird's feathers do not become wet in the RAIN, and it is thus a symbol for the VIRGIN Mary, who was not stained by original sin. The bird appears in German depictions of PARADISE under the assumption that it has learned to pronounce the name of Eve—in German, "Eva," and thus the reverse image of the (Latin) "ave" with which the angel Gabriel greets Mary (the sinless reverse image of the sinful Eve) at the time of the Annunciation [Luke 1:28].

In China the parrot of southern regions (*ying-wu*) was a symbol for the engagingly prattling prostitute, but also, with a PEARL in its beak, an attribute of the kind goddess Kuan-yin (in Japan, Kwannon).

peacock (Greek *taós*, Latin *pavus*) This splendid bird comes from India, where its lavish spread of tail FEATHERS (in the male, that is; the peahen is so lacking in ostentation as to be virtually ignored by symbologists) made the bird a symbol for the SUN. The peacock journeyed by way of Babylonia, Persia, and Asia Minor to Samos, where he became the sacred bird at the shrine to Hera. In the fifth century B.C. Athenians paid to see peacocks displayed as sideshow curiosities; in the second century B.C. the Romans considered them sacred to the goddess Juno. In India many gods were portrayed riding on peacocks; in the Western world the peacock was referred to as a slayer of serpents, and the shimmering colors of his tail feathers were explained by his supposed ability to transform SNAKE venom into solar iridescence. In the Middle East, the Kurdish Jezidi ("devil worshippers") sect viewed the bird (referred to as Melek Taus, "KING Peacock") as a messenger of God; for Muslims the peacock symbolized the cosmos or the sun and MOON. In early Christianity, as well, the peacock had generally positive associations: it was believed that the bird's flesh was immune to spoilage (a symbol of the buried Christ), and his moulting and new growth of feathers in the spring similarly made him a symbol for renewal and resurrection. The Christian era also preserved an ancient superstition according to which peacock BLOOD dispelled evil spirits. Thus the peacock often appeared among the animals in the stable in depictions of Christ's Nativity; two peacocks drinking from a chalice symbolize spiritual rebirth, and cherubim

Peacock (stylized). Pillar relief, Rusucurru (Mauritania, North Africa), early Christian

Peacock, symbol of vanity. J. Boschius, 1702

(see ANGELS) often have four WINGS consisting of peacock feathers. Their "EYES" were symbols of divine omniscience, and the flesh of the bird was long thought of as an ideal restorative meal for the sick.

Negative traits crop up in the early Christian text *Physiologus:* the peacock, it is written, "struts about, prides himself on his appearance, displays his feathers, and gazes haughtily about. But when he catches sight of his feet, he lets out an angry shriek: they ill befit his otherwise splendid appearance." The symbolic interpretation follows: Christians may rejoice over their good qualities, but "when you see your feet, i.e., your shortcomings, then cry out to God in your lamentation, and hate that in you which is unjust, as the peacock hates his feet, so that you can appear before your [heavenly] bridegroom free of sin." This introduces the symbolic association that continues from the medieval bestiaries into our own time: the peacock as a symbol of vanity, luxury, and arrogance. Even the clergy are warned not to fall into these attitudes. "When the peacock is praised, he raises his tail, just as a priest, praised by flatterers, lifts up his spirit in vainglory. When he raises his tail, his hindquarters are bared, and he cuts a ridiculous figure, vainly pluming himself. The peacock should walk with his tail lowered, just as all that a teacher does should be executed in humility" [Unterkircher]. In ba-

roque depictions of the Stations of the Cross, Jesus stripped of his garments expiates for humanity the sin of vanity, symbolized by a peacock portrayed nearby. For minnesingers the bird represented arrogant pride (*superbia*).

Under the influence of the Indian tradition (the goddess Sarasvati rides a peacock, and Indra sits on the peacock THRONE), the bird was viewed favorably in China. The peacock (*k'ung-ch'iao*) was the embodiment of beauty and dignity, able to dispel evil spirits, and dancing when its gaze fell upon a beautiful woman. Peacock feathers were symbols of rank for the Manchu emperors and were displayed in vases. Peacocks were also kept in the traditional Chinese GARDEN.

In the symbolism of ALCHEMY the iridescent fan of the peacock (*cauda pavonis*) refers in certain texts and images to steps in the transformation of base metals into GOLD; in others, to a process gone awry, yielding only dross (*caput mortuum*, the death's head).

In HERALDRY the peacock (or its fan, or a single feather) appears only infrequently, referring naturally not to *superbia* but to the positive tradition of resurrection and glory.

pear A fruit cultivated in the Neolithic Age out of varieties growing in the wild. Homer mentions the pear, which was the sacred fruit of great goddesses (Hera, Aphrodite/VENUS, Pomona). The statues of Hera in Tiryns and Mycenae were carved from the wood of the pear-tree, as Pausanias tells us. In ancient China the pear (*li*) was a symbol of longevity, because pear-trees can live to be very old. Since the word for separation is also *li*, lovers and friends were not supposed to slice pears and divide them between themselves. The WHITE blossoms of the pear-tree are a symbol of mourning and the transitory nature of life, but of beauty as well. The shape of the pear suggests that of a woman with a wide pelvis, and this may be why in analytic psychology the pear is seen as a sexual symbol. Around 1290 Hugo of Trimberg associated an elaborately developed allegory with a pear-tree some of whose fruit fell among THORNS, some into the water or into green grass. The

Pear. Detail from a figure in *Das contrafeyte Kreuter-buch* ("The Illustrated Herbal"), Brunfels, 1536

pear-tree is the ancestral mother Eve, and the pears are her descendents; whoever does not fall into the green grass of repentance, dies in mortal sin.

pearl Grouped in symbological tradition with PRECIOUS STONES, the pearl with its delicate shimmer is thought of as lunar (see MOON) and feminine; its spherical form is associated with perfection (see CIRCLE). Because of the rarity of perfectly formed pearls, and the pearl's enclosure in oysters or other BIVALVES, it symbolized for the Gnostics of late antiquity hidden knowledge and esoteric wisdom, and for Christians the teachings of Jesus, which were inaccessible to nonbelievers. The early Christian text *Physiologus* tells of a curious bivalve, the "purple oyster," which "comes up from the bottom of the sea, . . . opens its mouth and drinks in the dew of heaven and the rays of the sun, moon, and stars; it thus produces the pearl from the lights above. . . . The two halves of the shell are like the Old and New Testaments, and the pearl is like our Saviour, Jesus Christ." Other bivalves in the Red Sea "stand near the shore, all of them with their mouths open, so that something edible will find its way in. . . . When a storm comes, as is often the case in this region, the power of the lightning penetrates inside the shellfish, which takes fright and

closes up its shell. . . . It has the lightning inside it. That lightning wraps around the eyeballs of the shellfish, and thus makes pearls out of its eyes. The shellfish dies a wretched death, but the pearls shine in the Red Sea. . . . The divine lightning from heaven entered the utterly pure oyster, Mary, the Mother of God, and a pearl of great price came forth from her, as it is written: she gave birth to Christ, the pearl begotten by divine lightning" [John Damascenus, born A.D. 675]. The shimmering white pearl is also, as in ancient Persia, a symbol of the VIRGIN. According to the Book of Revelation, the gates of the "heavenly JERUSALEM" are made of pearl (hence the expression "pearly gates" for the gates of heaven); a string of pearls is a frequent analogy for the multitude of God's powers.

A Gnostic "Hymn of the Soul," attributed to Bardesanes and dating from the early Christian era, is impressive in its sym-

Pearl oysters. Hohberg (1647) and J. Boschius (1702)

Pearl: One of the "eight jewels" of ancient China

bolic richness: a child (representing humanity) is sent out into distant EGYPT on the long pilgrimage of life, to fetch a pearl out of a deep WELL guarded by a dragon. But he eats the customary food of the country and forgets his mission, until a letter (saving doctrine) brought by an EAGLE reminds him of it. Now the task of recovering the pearl (enlightenment, gnosis) from the well can be undertaken. "Coiled 'round the well, the dragon guardian hissed. I began its lullaby, singing songs, and pronouncing names rich in magic power—names of my beloved father, mother, brother—until at last the dragon slept. I snatched up the pearl and fled the foreign land, leaving my unclean garment [i.e., the body] behind me." The pilgrim is then taken up to his heavenly home and clothed in a royal mantle [Schultz]. The medieval collection *Gesta Romanorum* (ca. 1300) contains the story of a maiden who possesses a precious pearl (free will). FIVE brothers (the senses) attempt to persuade her to give it up, but she refuses to give up her treasure in exchange for sensual pleasures. Only when "the KING" comes does she give him the pearl, and he in turn makes her his bride.

In ancient Greece the pearl was a symbol of Aphrodite (VENUS), who was born of the sea-foam. In the ancient Chinese language of symbols it was one of the "eight jewels," standing for the precious and the pure; tears were referred to as "little pearls" (a metaphor echoed in some European sayings). In wealthy families it was customary before burial to place a pearl in the MOUTH of the deceased (which similarly has its parallel in Greek antiquity: the "obol" for the ferryman Charon; see AFTERLIFE). The legendary pearls of eternal youth or seduction of Asian fairy tales—supposedly offering access to extraordinary sexual pleasure—are not actually pearls

in our sense but WHITE "love pills" produced by a form of "alchemy." Real pearls, by contrast, retain their association with chastity. In China, as in the West, we find the belief that oysters are "impregnated" by storms (THUNDER, in this version) and that pearls then grow inside them in the moonlight. This poetic fable notwithstanding, it is reported that pearls were cultured in China long before the practice developed in Japan.

In the Japanese tradition, too, "pearls" play an important role. They constitute one of the three imperial insignias (*shinki sanshu*), along with the SWORD and the MIRROR; pearls are said to have been the creation of the god Tama No-oya, and to have the form of EYES.

In general, despite their association with tears, pearls serve as symbols of virtue which (according to the medieval scholar Lonicerus) "fortify the living spirits that come from the heart." S. Golowin (1986) quotes a saying of Eastern European jewelers: "The pearls we believe in bring us moon-silver tears—but tears of joy."

Pegasus The familiar animal symbol for poetic inspiration acquired this association only in the modern era, although it is clearly grounded in ancient myth, where the wondrous HORSE was said to have opened up the Hippocrene spring on Mount Helicon (the MOUNTAIN of the MUSES) by stamping his

Pegasus opening up the Hippocrene spring with his hooves. J. Boschius, 1702

Pegasus: "From Parnassus to the stars." J. Boschius, 1702

hooves. WINGED horses appear in many Old World FAIRY TALES. Pegasus was said to have sprung from the torso of the beheaded GORGON Medusa. The hero Bellerophon tamed the wild creature with the help of a bridle provided by the goddess Athena; riding on Pegasus, Bellerophon was able to defeat the fearsome CHIMERA. Mythologists associate Pegasus with the sea (originally following Poseidon) or with the LIGHTNING that bolts across the sky. Symbologically speaking, he combines the vitality and strength of a horse with the weightlessness (and freedom from terrestrial concerns) of a BIRD; thus it was only natural that Pegasus should later come to symbolize the indomitable poetic spirit overcoming the impediments of this world. The figure of Pegasus illustrates the favorable aspect of the horse in the mythic tradition; the animal's darker side is frequently visible in myths of the CENTAURS.

pelican An important bird in symbolic tradition. The fact that adult pelicans dipped their beaks into their pouches to extract fish with which to feed their young led to the misperception that the parents were ripping open their breasts to offer their BLOOD to their young. In this way the pelican came to symbolize the sacrificial death of Christ, as well as parental self-denial. In the *Physiologus* text of late antiquity, the bird kills

its disobedient young (or they are killed by SNAKES) but can restore them to life three days later with its heart's blood, whereby it gives up its own life.

This symbol also appears in the imagery of ALCHEMY, not only as a specific sort of laboratory retort, whose "beak" bends down towards its "pot belly" but also as an image for the philosopher's STONE pulverized and scattered in molten LEAD: when the magic "stone" itself melts and dissolves, it brings about the transformation of the lead into GOLD. Thus the pelican functions as a symbol of selfless striving for purification. In this sense it is also associated with the "Rosicrucian" degree of the Scottish system of FREEMASONRY. In earlier times a "Knight of the Rosae Crucis" was also called a "Knight of the Pelican."

In medieval bestiaries we find references to a forgotten hymn containing the words "*Pie pelicane, Jesu domine*" ("O merciful pelican, Lord Jesus") and to the bird's consuming no more food than is actually necessary to keep it alive. "So, too, does the hermit live, who consumes only bread, not living to eat, but only eating to live" [Unterkircher].

pentacle A FIVE-pointed STAR drawn with five strokes without lifting one's pencil; it is also referred to as a "pentagram," or by its Latin names, *pentangulum*, *pentaculum* (a designation also for other magic signs used in rituals), *signum Pythagoricum* ("sign for

Pelican. Eysenhut, *Defensorium inviolatae virginitatis b. Mariae*, Regensburg, 1471

Pentacle on baptismal font of Sibenik Cathedral (Dalmatia). Marble relief, medieval

Pythagoreans"; see PYTHAGORAS), *signum Hygeae* ("sign of Hygieia", goddess of health), and *signum salutatis* ("sign of health"), according to the symbolic significance attached to it. Pythagoras and his disciples considered the pentacle a sacred symbol of mind-body harmony; it thus became a symbol for health. In Gnostic and Manichaean groups, for whom five was a sacred number (a reference to the five ELEMENTS which they recognized: LIGHT, air, WIND, FIRE, WATER), the pentacle was a fundamental symbol; later sects (e.g., the Bogumiles of the Balkan Peninsula) then took it over, frequently placing it on their tombstones, or only suggesting it with a five-fingered HAND. The five-pointed star was as frequent on the "Abraxas" amulets of antiquity as in the later magical literature of the Occident. It is possible that in the Christian era the pentacle was a manifestation of a secret "undercurrent" of Gnosticism which sought to conceal itself from the ecclesiastical authorities, as was presumably the ideology of ALCHEMY. In magic ritual the pentacle is frequently used in administering ritual oaths (as in Goethe's *Faust I*). The figure must be completely closed, its lines unbroken. Traditionally the pentacle pointing upward is associated with "white," and downward, with

"black" magic. The pentacle of white magic was drawn beginning with a horizontal stroke from left to right, then with a diagonal stroke to the lower left, and so forth. The pentacle of black magic often had a GOAT's head inscribed in it; the upright or white pentacle, an outline of the human form.

The pentacle also appears in Christian iconography, where it is associated with the five stigmata of Christ, or, because of its closed form, with the coming together of beginning and end, ALPHA AND OMEGA, in Christ (compare CIRCLE). Its use in the Occident goes back long before Christ, however: to Etruscan ceramics, or to Egyptian grave drawings (where five-pointed stars, with no internal drawings, stand for all the stars in the HEAVENS). We might seek models in nature for the pentacle, e.g., the starfish or other echinodermata, but the drawing of pentacles can also be understood simply as a playful striving for graphic dexterity. In rock drawings found in alpine regions, mostly dating from the late Middle Ages and the early modern era, the pentacle clearly appears to have apotropaic (i.e., seeking to ward off evil) significance, to judge from its use alongside Christian and genital symbols, which were employed similarly.

The pentacle is of particular significance as the "blazing star" in the symbology of FREEMASONRY, with beams or flaming clusters in each point of the star and a G in the center. The symbol "reminds us of the sun, which illuminates the earth with its rays and

Pentacle: Esthetically appealing construction of concentric pentacles within a circle

Pentacle: Amulet ring, letters in "hygieia" "salus" (health, well-being). Cartari, 1647

makes us mindful of our blessings, as it gives light and life to all who are on earth" [Lennhoff-Posner]. In Freemasonry the blazing star has been documented as early as 1735; the G has been variously interpreted as standing for "gnosis," "geometry," "God," "glory," and a variety of other concepts. The alchemists, like the Gnostics, had associated the number five with the elements, but specifically with the spiritual QUINTESSENCE (*quinta essentia*) of the usual four. As a sign to ward off demons, the pentacle often is found carved in the wood of old door frames, thresholds, and gates.

Stars with more points are found less frequently; the most significant include the HEXAGRAM and the eight-pointed star (see EIGHT IMMORTALS), a symbolic doubling of the FOUR (of the CROSS, for example) and standing for the law.

peony The flower often identified in Europe with "the ROSE without thorns" of choral tradition (the Virgin Mary). In ancient folk medicine the garden peony (*Paeonia officinalis*) was thought to have a great variety of beneficial effects. A necklace made from its seeds was placed around the neck of an infant as an amulet against teething pains. Its petals and roots were believed to be effective against asthma, gout, and epilepsy; bunches of peonies were tied to the necks of epileptics. The flower was recommended to seafarers as protection against storms.

In East Asia the *Paeonia suffructicosa* and *Paeonia lactiflora* (white-blossomed and smelling like roses) were held in particular esteem; their petals are also represented in designs on costly fabrics. These peonies are considered to be symbols of dignity and honor.

pheasant In the symbolism of the Occident, the bird appears only when it provides the real-life basis for the invented PHOENIX, and this involves primarily the GOLDEN pheasant (whose excrement was a source of strength, according to ancient superstition). The pheasant is important in China, however, where the bird with the loudly flapping wings came to be associated with THUNDER and the principle of *yang* (see YIN AND YANG); it is said, however, to be able to turn into an oyster or a SNAKE and thus embody *yin*. Although the pheasant was one of the 12 insignias of the Hapsburg emperors, and the symbol of the empress herself, it has generally negative associations. Its cry can stand for flooding or for immorality and seduction, and in fables the bird is often a figure of supernatural calamity. In China the golden pheasant was the insignia of a high-ranking civil servant; in Nazi Germany, a nickname for anyone who wore the golden badge of Party membership. Hohberg's emblem-book

Peony. B. Besler, *Hortus Eystettensis*, 1613

Pheasant hiding its head. Hohberg, 1647

of the baroque period (1675) attributes behavior to the pheasant that has since become associated with the OSTRICH: "As foolish pheasant, when he hides his head,/ Thinks all of him is hidden, so he's caught,/ The world believes concealed its every vice,/ Yet One's not fooled: all-wise, all-seeing God."

phoenix A legendary HERON-like BIRD of considerable symbolic importance, widely associated with notions of immortality and resurrection. Its name goes back to the Greek word for red—the color of FIRE—because the bird was said to arise again perpetually from its ashes after a purifying fire had consumed it. Its origin is the sacred Egyptian bird Benu, or Bynw, a heron said to have been the first creature to alight on the hill that came into being out of the primordial ooze. Benu was revered in Heliopolis as a manifestation of the SUN god; it was said that it appeared only once every 500 years. The mythologists of classical antiquity came up with additional details: the phoenix ate only DEW (compare BIRD OF PARADISE); it

Phoenix. Bas-relief, Chinese, ca. A.D. 100

flew to other lands, gathered fragrant herbs, brought them back to Heliopolis, heaped them on the altar, set fire to them, and burned itself to ashes, only to arise out of them in three days' time. In later versions the bird was said to have GOLDEN or multicolored plumage. In ancient Rome the phoenix came to symbolize the ever-renascent vitality of the Empire, and for this reason it is found on coins and in mosaics of the imperial period. The fathers of the Church logically viewed the bird as a typological symbol of the immortal soul and the resurrection of Christ "on the third day." In the text *Physiologus* (second century after Christ) it is written: "If it is granted even to this unreasoning creature, who does not know the Creator of all things, to be raised from the dead, will we not be raised, who praise God and keep His commandments?"

Phoenix. Hohberg, 1675

In Christian iconography the phoenix often appears as a pendant to the PELICAN; for ALCHEMISTS it symbolizes the destruction and new formation of *materia prima* on its way to becoming the philosopher's STONE.

In ancient Chinese imagery the counterpart of the phoenix is the fabulous *feng-huang,* the bird in which (as in the UNICORN *ky-lin*) YIN AND YANG are united in a totality that transcends their DUALITY; the *feng-huang* is thus a powerful symbol of conjugal union. The analogy between the phoenix and the quetzal of ancient Mexico, however, is problematic.

In Jewish legend the phoenix is called "Milcham," and its immortality is explained

Phoenix: Benu of ancient Egypt, with the crown of Osiris. Tomb fresco, Thebes, ca. 1150 B.C.

Eleusinian mysteries of Greece the pig was the sacred animal sacrificed to the goddess Demeter. On Hierro (Canary Islands) the pre-Spanish inhabitants prayed to a pig that was supposed to intercede for them with the deity capable of granting them rain. In ancient China the pig was the 12th and last sign of the zodiac, symbolizing "manly strength." In ancient Egypt a sow eating her piglets was the symbol of Nut, goddess of the heavens, whose children (the STARS) disappear every morning and are reborn every evening. This is why the Egyptians wore amulets depicting pigs, although the animal is most frequently thought of as one of the followers of Seth (Sutech), the slayer of Osiris. Although they kept pigs and ate pork, the Egyptians considered pigs unclean, if not as rigorously as did the Jews and the Muslims. Trichinosis is often used to explain the Jewish and Muslim aversion to the pig, but it is also a deliberate rejection of the practices of "heathens," for whom the pig stood for fertility and wealth and who thus chose it as a sacrificial animal and pork as a special food.

In Christian iconography we find many depictions of Christ's casting demons out of the possessed and sending them into a herd of 2,000 swine, which then plunged into the sea [Matthew 8:28–34; Mark 5:1–20]. The pig is a symbol of ignorance and voracious appetite, as well as an emblem used in mockery of Judaism, whose personification, "Synagogue," is sometimes portrayed riding a pig. In a favorable context, the sow was an attribute of St. Anthony, because bacon was considered a remedy for measles (which were also called "St. Anthony's fire").

as follows: When Eve had sinned by eating the fruit of the tree of knowledge, she became jealous of the sinless state of the other creatures of the earth; one by one, she enticed them to eat of the forbidden fruit. Only the bird Milcham refused, and as its reward God instructed the ANGEL of death that this one obedient creature was forever to be spared. Milcham was given a walled city, in which he could live undisturbed for a thousand years. "One thousand are the years of his life, and, when the thousand years are past, a fire goes forth from his nest and consumes the birds. Only an egg remains, but this egg becomes a baby bird, and Milcham lives on. Others, however, say that when Milcham is a thousand years old his body shrivels and his wings lose their feathers, so that he looks like a baby bird again. Then his plumage grows back, and he soars like an eagle, and death never overcomes him" [bin Gorion, 1980].

pig (German *Schwein*) For modern Westerners primarily a symbol of uncleanliness, the pig often represented fertility and prosperity in the cultures of antiquity. From Neolithic Malta we retain a depiction of a sow nursing 13 piglets. The Norse goddess Freya had the cognomen Syr ("sow"). Ceridwen, the "old wise woman" of the Celts, was a swine goddess; the hero Manannan had a pig as one of his attributes. In the

Pig as a symbol of luck. Woodcut from the wrapper of a deck of cards, 1660

The modern-day association of the pig with good fortune in some cultures (e.g., in German celebrations of New Year's) seems to have its origin in the old custom of giving a pig as a booby (or consolation) prize to the person who came in last in a competition. (The BOAR has a distinct symbolic tradition of its own.)

The Jungian psychologist Aeppli points out that pigs resemble humans anatomically more than do other mammals, and that "the human unconscious clearly affirms the pig" and that dreaming of a pig is readily taken as a promise of good things to come. ("Schwein haben" is a German idiom meaning "to be fortunate.") "One look at a pigpen makes it clear: the sow is an eager, happy universal mother of the muddy realm, many-teated, heavy set, surrounded by her brood. . . . Today as always she appears in our dreams bathed in the shimmery light of her motherhood." The great esteem in which the pig was held in pre-Christian times (so different from its place in much of Christian iconography) is readily understandable in the face of all the evidence of modern psychotherapy.

pilgrimage The meditative journey, often a procession, to a sacred place or shrine. The pilgrimage culminates not only at a point in space but also in a heightened spiritual state. These journeys presuppose the existence of consecrated end-points (memorials, saints' graves, mystic shrines, churches). In Greek antiquity Athenians journeyed in a solemn procession to the shrine of Demeter at Eleusis. In the Judeo-Christian world pilgrimages to Santiago de Compostela, Lourdes, Rome, or JERUSALEM have taken on almost the same importance as Muslim pilgrimages to Mecca. It is possible that the the Breton alignments of megaliths near Carnac (see MENHIR) were to commemorate similar processions by Stone Age pilgrims. Among Roman Catholics there is a strong tradition of pilgrimages to MOUNTAIN shrines (e.g., Montserrat, Monte Gargano, Odilienberg in Alsace, Maria Plain near Salzburg).

The pilgrimage can also involve the movement of sacred objects and symbols themselves, for the purpose of bringing a special blessing (e.g., fertility) to the surrounding countryside. The physical proximity of the sacred object (a divine image or representation, a sacrament) is believed to heighten its positive effects, as in the case of the processions of the goddess Nerthus in a CHARIOT pulled by cows [Tacitus, *Germania*]. Ecclesiastical pilgrimages serve a further purpose: they constitute a public declaration of faith, in a space extending far beyond the physical confines of the church

St. Gerold, Pilger und Martyrer.

Pilgrimage: St. Gerald, "pilgrim and martyr." W. Auer, 1890

itself. In the Roman Catholic tradition, the most significant are on Easter (celebrating the Resurrection) and for the solemnity of the Body and Blood of Christ (Corpus Christi), established in 1264 by Pope Urban IV to celebrate Christ's presence in the Holy of Holies, the consecrated Host in the monstrance.

pillars Not merely functional components holding up massive structures: they are of great symbolic significance. They often flank the entrance to a shrine or temple (or to an inner sanctuary, the holy of holies) and are

Caroli V. Imperium fuum in novum orbem proferentis. Aquila fupra Columnas Herculis evolans. L. PLUS OUTRE : PLUS ULTRA.

Pillars of Hercules (Gibraltar), Emperor Charles V's motto ("Beyond"). Boschius, 1702

Pillars of the temple brought down by Samson. Gustave Doré (1832–1883)

associated symbolically with the "pillars of the earth" (see AXIS MUNDI). Greek mythology preserves the notion of the "pillars of Hercules" standing at the edge of the *oecumene*, or inhabited world. In the Bible God alone has the power to shake the pillars of the earth (see Job 9:6) on Judgment Day, like the hero Samson at the entrance to the temple of the Philistines [Judges 16:25–30]. Paired pillars are reminiscent of the Egyptian use of paired OBELISKS as gateways to temples. Among the most famous pillars, especially because of their importance in the traditions of FREEMASONRY, are the bronze pillars "Jachin" ("God is our foundation") and "Boaz" ("Strength is in Him") of SOLOMON'S TEMPLE, which are believed to have been almost 30 feet in height. (The sectioned DJED-POLES of ancient Egypt similarly symbolized endurance and stability.) In Masonic symbolism these two bronze pillars stood for "justice and benevolence, the two pillars of humanity." There may be an association with an esoteric system of DUALI-

TIES, e.g., the alchemist's primal elements SULFUR AND MERCURY. In time the image of two pillars was expanded to include a third, and together they were known as *Sagesse, Force,* and *Beauté* ("wisdom, strength, beauty"), corresponding also to the three leading officers of the Lodge. (See also KNOTS.)

According to Coptic legend, at King Solomon's command a "winged spirit" provided him with a pillar on which all the wisdom

Pillars, Jachin and Boaz, at the entrance to Solomon's temple. Masonic symbols

Pillars: "Ever changeless," even in fire. J. Boschius, 1702

of the world was engraved. The Bible mentions a pillar of FIRE and CLOUDS that accompanies the Israelites on their way through the Sinai Desert; it may well be related figurally to the pillars of Solomon's temple. Christian tradition associates the "SEVEN pillars of wisdom" in the Old Testament (see Proverbs 9:1) with the "seven gifts of the Holy Spirit"; in the Book of Revelation Christ's apostles are the pillars of the "Heavenly JERUSALEM."

Pillars do not always have religious associations: they can also commemorate military victories (e.g., the Trajan colum in Rome), and they sometimes have the same symbolic associations as TREES; for the psychoanalyst, the pillar is primarily a phallic symbol.

pine, Scots (*Pinus silvestris*) Despite its widespread occurrence, a TREE of little importance in European popular symbology. In East Asia, however, the Scots pine is actually the "tree of life," appearing GREEN and vital even in advanced age; it is prized as a symbol of long life and undiminished married bliss. In Chinese art in particular the Scots pine (*sung*) symbolizes permanence, because even in the coldest winter it retains its needles, whose appearance in pairs is associated with marital companion-

ship. "Through its repose it prolongs its life" [Confucius]. Scots pines were also planted on graves, and especially old trees of this species were revered.

planets (from the Greek; literally "wandering" heavenly bodies) Initially distinguished from the fixed STARS, which appear to move in regular patterns around the polestar, the planets seemed to follow paths of their own, and it was subsequently discovered that they received their LIGHT from the SUN. All of the cultures that concerned themselves with the symbolism of heavenly bodies accorded great significance to the planets, and in most cases associated them with divinities. Their orbits, when viewed from the earth, often appear arbitrary and strange; a person's horoscope is greatly influenced by the position of the planets at the moment of his or her birth. The observed color and trajectory of the planets were decisive for their symbolic associations with divinities. Including the sun and the MOON, traditional astrology counted SEVEN planets circling the earth, a sacred number corresponding to the number of days in the week; the other five were MARS, MERCURY, JUPITER, VENUS, and SATURN. The planets discovered later (Uranus, Neptune, and Pluto, with their longer "years") are of less importance in astrology, and the planetoids with orbits between Mars and Jupiter are omitted entirely.

Scots Pine: Characteristic of East Asian landscapes. Woodcut, China, ca. 1600

Ancient China recognized FIVE planets, corresponding to the five points of the (Chinese) compass: Saturn was associated with the center, the ELEMENT EARTH, and the color YELLOW; Mercury with north, WATER, and BLACK; Jupiter with east, WOOD, and BLUE; Mars with south, FIRE, and RED; Venus with west, metal, and WHITE. The symbolic analogies between planets and divinities, colors, elements, personality traits, and the like, were worked out in detail in all speculative systems. The Greek Pausanias (second century after Christ), for example, mentions the following guardians for the planets in his cosmology: the sun was governed by Theia and Hyperion; the moon by Atlas and Phoebe; Mars by Dione and Crius; Mercury by Metis and Coeus; Jupiter by Themis and Eurymedon; Saturn by Rhea and Cronus. In later centuries the Cabala and traditions of ritual magic used other names for the polar forces (the *intelligentia* and *daemonium*) governing the individual planets, as well as specific squares of numbers, symbols, perfumes, and colors associated with each one.

Astrologers spoke of "children of the planets," individuals in whose horoscopes and personalities one of the seven traditional planets played a dominant role and who therefore displayed traits corresponding to one or another of the gods of ancient myth. Thus for example persons whose horoscopes were ruled by Mars were referred to as being "martial"; by Jupiter, as being "jovial." In a famous series of "children of the planets" produced by the artist Hans Sebaldus Beham between 1530 and 1540, each of the planets symbolized a characteristic trait that it passed on to its "children" and that was thought to determine their personality. The sun was associated with LIGHT; the moon with magic and mysticism; Mars with vitality and aggression; Mercury with illumination and mobility; Venus with love; Jupiter with law; Saturn with self-possession and peace. The sequence of the seven planets and their gods is, of course, preserved in the Roman names of the seven days of the week, and in their Romance language names today, as well as, through Germanic equiva-

lents, in many of the corresponding German and English names. Mars, for example, lends his (or its) name to the third day of the week, *dies martis*, and his Germanic counterpart, the god of war Tyr or Ziu, to the German *Dienstag* and the English "Tuesday."

plow This peaceful (see Isaiah 2:4: "They shall beat their SWORDS into plowshares") symbol for the agricultural life replaced the older dibble. (See ANTS.) In ancient agricultural societies the plowing of "MOTHER EARTH" was likened to a phallic sexual act. The hook-plow, which tears up the surface of the earth without turning the clumps over, was actually established in typology long before the asymmetrical plowshare of today. The pre-Columbian civilizations of the Americas had no plows or animals to pull them; they relied on the dibble. In HERALDRY the plow appears only occasionally (in the arms of the city of Straubing in Bavaria, in certain punning contexts, and in the new arms of Ethiopia.)

Legend has it that ANGELS drove the plow of the rustic St. Isidor, who was unwilling to labor for his masters during Mass; other saints symbolized their mastery over nature by hitching unusual animals to their plows (St. Gentius: an OX and a WOLF; St. Kontigern: a WOLF and a DEER; St. James of Tarentaise: BEARS).

Empress Kunigunde was cleared of suspicion of infidelity to her husband, Emperor Heinrich II, by surviving an ordeal in which, it was believed, the innocent could tread on

Plow. Hohberg, 1675

Plow: Dance of death scene. Hans Holbein, 1547

red-hot plowshares without being injured; this scene is depicted in a relief by Tilman Riemenschneider in the Bamberg Cathedral.

plum In East Asia a favorite symbol for a maiden's early youth, because the plum blossom (Chinese *mei-hua*) appears even before the tree is covered with leaves. The erotic association is seen also in the expression "plum blossom blanket" for the coverlet on the bridal bed. The FIVE-leafed plum blossom symbolized the five GODS OF HAPPINESS

Plum tree in bloom. China, 19th century

of ancient China, as well as a specific oracle; together, the plum, Scots PINE, and BAMBOO trees were called the "three friends of the cold season."

For the Jungian psychologist, the plum is a promise "in a man's dream of very realistic sexual pleasure. The name for the fruit [the German *Pflaume*] is also a term of disfavor applied by women to certain others of their sex" [Aeppli]. In northern Germany, "when plums are ripe for Pentecost" is comparable to the English "cold day in August."

The ancient Greek word for the plum (*coccymelon*) literally meant "CUCKOO apple."

plumb line and plumb bob Apparatus from the world of medieval architecture, of enduring importance in the symbolic language of FREEMASONRY. The bob, or plummet, makes for "straightness and veracity" and belongs to the "movable jewels," along with the SCALES and the carpenter's SQUARE. The plumb bob is "dropped into the conscience and verifies the straight line of the spiritual structure"; it is associated with the rank of Second Foreman. Symbols referring to the vertical axis were originally references to the making of the cosmos, with the AXIS MUNDI, linking HEAVEN and EARTH, at its center.

pole Traditionally the trunk of a TREE, driven into the ground; in many ancient cultures, one symbol of the AXIS MUNDI, which is otherwise portrayed as a MOUNTAIN or tree at the center of the (flat) world. From a superficial point of view, sacred poles have often been understood as phallic symbols, an interpretation that seldom lends itself to verification. First and foremost these wooden pillars signify the connection between HEAVEN and EARTH, like the Irminsul, the tribal shrine of the Saxons, destroyed by Charlemagne in 772. The maypole, an emblem of the forces of awakening nature as they become visible in the spring, also resists simple classification as a phallic symbol: it must be understood in the tradition of the axis mundi, and the Central European competition to climb the pole symbolizes all

Pole with Moses's "serpent of brass" (cf. ASCLEPIUS). Bible, Reims, 11th century

striving to "make it to the top" (see ABOVE/ BELOW).

Stone versions of the cult pole include the megalithic MENHIRS and the OBELISKS of ancient Egypt.

Pole-like PILLARS became the abode of saintly, if somewhat theatrical, men who vowed to honor God by standing indefinitely atop the pillars. St. Simeon Stylites (approximately A.D. 396–459) was said to have remained steadfast on a 50–foot-high pillar for 40 years, although the DEVIL, in the form of a massive SNAKE entwined around the pillar, sought to disrupt his composure. We find here the same symbolic association of a snake with a staff or pillar as in the CADUCEUS or the staff of ASCLEPIUS.

political symbols In modern times, simply formed graphic images with immediately recognizable significance have often served as symbols for political movements; their undeniable subconscious impact has yet to be systematically analyzed. Symbols organized around horizontal and vertical axes have conservative, defensive, or static associations; those in which diagonals are emphasized suggest dynamic or aggressive political movements. Those who conceive of or embrace individual symbols have doubtless been unaware of these principles of design; political symbols correspond "auto-

matically" to the nature of individual movements. The Nazi SWASTIKA provides an example of these principles: traditionally displayed horizontally, it suggests mobility, torsion, rotation, a spirit of aggression. With its severe vertical-horizontal design, the *Krückenkreuz* (see CROSS), which the Austrian Fatherland Front sought to oppose to the swastika, seemed immobile and stodgy by contrast. Symbols with zigzags and arrows are typical of radical political movements, whether of the right (the double LIGHTNING bolts of the SS, the arrows of the Phalange) or, traditionally, of the left (the three arrows of the Social Democrats, the SICKLE in the hammer-and-sickle, the points of the Soviet STAR). In recent times, however, there has been a perceptible move away from the banality of such symbols.

The figures of animals appear only occasionally as political symbols, and then usually with some humorous intent, as in the case of the DONKEY and ELEPHANT that symbolize the Democratic and Republican Parties of the United States. Flowers generally symbolize *joie de vivre.* (See CARNATION.)

pomegranate (Old French *pome grenate,* "apple with many seeds") Long cultivated in the eastern Mediterranean region and Near East, the pomegranate TREE is believed to have been propagated by the Phoenicians and became a popular source of both fruit and herbal medicine throughout warmer regions. The many seeds embedded in the pulp of the fruit came to symbolize fertility; the entire fruit, goddesses like the Phoenician Astarte (or Ashtoreth), Demeter and Persephone (Latin Ceres and Proserpina), Aphrodite (VENUS), and Athena. Pomegranate trees were planted on the graves of heroes, perhaps to ensure that they would have many successors. In the mythology of the cult of Eleusis, Persephone would not have had to stay on in Hades after her abduction had she not eaten a pomegranate there; because she had, she could not dwell perpetually with the other gods but had to spend one third of each year in Hades. The MOTHER of Attys, the lover of the "great mother" Cybele, was said to have become

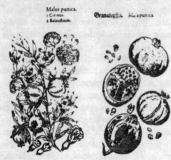

Malus punica.
1 Cierous.
2 Balaustium.

Granatopffici. Malapunica.

Pomegranate. Joachim Camerarius the Younger, *Hortus Medicus*, 1588

pregnant by touching a pomegranate tree. Specific nymphs, the Rhoeae, were believed to inhabit the trees. In Rome Juno was represented holding a pomegranate as a symbol of marriage. The tree, with its fragrant, fiery red blossoms, was also seen as a symbol of love and marriage, followed by childbirth. Brides wore WREATHS made from its twigs. In the Judeo-Christian era the symbolism was made more spiritual, and the fruit came to refer to God's bountiful love. The red juice of the pomegranate became a symbol of the BLOOD of martyrs; the seeds enclosed in a single fruit, the individual Christians united in the Church community. Since the rind of the fruit is tough but its juice sweet, the pomegranate came to symbolize the priest: severe on the outside, indulgent on the inside. In baroque symbolism the image of a pomegranate, split open to reveal its wealth of seeds, stood for generosity (CHARITY, Hospitaler orders). In heraldry the pomegranate adorns the arms of Granada and Colombia (formerly "New Granada").

precious and semiprecious stones By virtue of their beauty, these stones have more than ornamental function: with their COLORS and other characteristics they also influence the imagination. We are concerned here with relatively hard minerals that can be cut, and also (in accordance with common usage) organic materials like CORAL and AMBER, which are of importance primarily as talismans and amulets but can also function symbolically. Polished and shiny, gems can also serve as MIRRORS. JADE, which occurs in countless varieties, is for the Chinese a symbol of multiplicity and the infinite; its durability was believed to conserve bodies after burial. Throughout the world these STONES in general, since they reveal their beauty only when they are cut and polished, came to symbolize humanity itself, in its need for refinement. On the other hand, CRYSTALS occurring gem-like in nature, symbolized perfect virtue; in Christian iconography, for example, ROCK-crystal was a symbol of the Virgin Mary, because it is not a source of light itself but sparkles when a beam of God's light strikes it. In Asiatic religions, jewels symbolize the treasures of the right religious teachings. The philosopher's stone in ALCHEMY is either a mythical precious stone or a carved building stone (in association with medieval construction guilds and their beliefs). Reflecting gems, especially crystals, were often used as aids to meditation and were also believed to have healing properties. Ancient books of stonelore, called "lithica," treat the magic correspondences between planets, personality types, and "power-stones," which are supposed to have a great variety of effects. In symbology, along with rock-crystal, DIAMONDS, AMETHYSTS, RUBIES, jade, TURQUOISES, SAPPHIRES, and EMERALDS are especially important. In the Book of Revelation (see CAVE) the "HEAVENLY JÉRUSALEM" of the promised future is constructed out of precious stones of different colors, which in a sense constitute a return in permanent form of the pure, sparkling water of the

Precious stones in J. Sporer's *On the Powers of Precious Stones*, ca. 1495

Precious stones: Opal. From *Hortus Sanitatis*, 1499

springs (see WELLS) of Eden (see PARADISE). Twelve precious stones adorned the breastplate of the Jewish high-priest: ruby, peridot, beryl, turquoise, lapis lazuli, jasper, jacinth, AGATE, amethyst, tarsis, carnelian, and nephrite. The name of one of the 12 tribes of Israel was to be engraved in each of the stones.

In ASTROLOGY, similarly, the 12 signs of the zodiac (see STARS) have gems associated with them and as "birthstones" symbolize the powers of the individual signs. The lithica of antiquity, especially those of Theophrastus, Orpheus, Damigeron Latinus, Aetius, and Psellus, were the primary sources for these correspondences. The association of stones with individual signs of the zodiac varies somewhat from lithicum to lithicum, but the following is the most frequent: Aries—hematite; Taurus—emerald; Gemini—multicolored stones; Cancer—adularia; Leo—ruby or diamond; Virgo—beryl; Libra—agate; Scorpio—amethyst; Sagittarius—turquoise; Capricorn—onyx; Aquarius—amber; Pisces—coral. The individual PLANETS with their special powers are also symbolized by gems, from which pieces of jewelry were made to be worn by persons feeling themselves particularly linked to the heavenly body in question. The most common pairings are as follows: thus SUN—diamond, rock-crystal, bright-colored varieties of zircon, tourmaline, and cairngorm; the MOON—pearls, adularia, agate; Mars—ruby, garnet, coral, carnelian; Mercury—beryl, tiger-eye, topaz, agate, amber, zircon; Jupiter—emerald, GREEN turquoise, jade, serpentine, malachite; Venus—lapis lazuli, sapphire, aquamarine; Saturn—amethyst, dark varieties of onyx and sapphire.

The fact that there were 12 tribes of Israel, 12 Apostles, and 12 signs of the zodiac often led to symbolical speculations and analogies; the crosses of the Eastern Orthodox Church were often adorned with 12 small jewels (for the Apostles) and one large one in the middle (for Christ), which was likened to the sun. In the early Christian Gnostic "Hymn of the Soul" (see PEARL), the royal robes, which are given to the enlightened soul who has returned home to the kingdom of heaven, are described as follows: "They glimmered with agates, rubies, diamonds, beryls, onyxes, pearls, gleaming pure. And from out of a blue sapphire there shone the iridescent image of the King of Kings. . . ." St. Hildegard of Bingen (1098–1179) has the Son speaking to God the Father at the Last Judgment as follows: the world shall not pass away "until you see my body and all its members . . . filled with precious gems, perfected in all those who . . . worship you, just as the gems glitter with the power of virtue." In her book of natural history, *Liber Subtilitatum*, she ascribes supernatural powers to gems, as well as a symbologically interesting history of their origin: "The devil draws back in fear before precious stones; he hates them and despises them, because they remind him that their brilliance was already manifest before he plunged from glory [see GRAIL] . . . and because some gems came to be, in that very fire in which he is punished. . . . Gems have their origin in the East and in especially torrid zones. There the sun heats the mountains like fire, and the rivers are always boiling hot. . . . Where the water touches the burning-hot mountains, they foam [and that foam solidifies and is left behind]. The temperature as [the gems] dry determines their color and their powers. . . . The mountains upon which many large precious stones come into being in this way, are as bright as the light of day. Thus gems originate from fire and water, and for this reason they also contain heat, moisture, and many powers and serve many good, decent, and useful ends. . . . There are [however] other stones; they do do not originate on these mountains and not in the way described, but rather from whatever other, worthless things. With them, according to their nature, and with God's consent, good and evil can be brought about." The initiate is to see to it that they are all used to honor God, to good ends, and for the purpose of healing.

Prometheus   A Titan in Greek mythology whose name means "the one who thinks in advance"; he symbolizes belief in humanity even against divine decree. According to tradition, Prometheus created man out of clay; in the course of a ritual sacrifice, he outwitted Zeus for the benefit of mortals, leading Zeus to withhold from them the gift of FIRE. Prometheus stole it from the HEAVENS and brought it to man, thus making the birth of civilization possible; Zeus sent PANDORA as a punishment for mortals. Prometheus was bound to a ROCK in the Caucasus, where his liver was torn from his body by an EAGLE—only to grow back every day, until Hercules killed the bird with an ARROW. For many writers (Voltaire, Schlegel, Herder, Byron), artists (Titian, Rubens, Böcklin), and composers (Beethoven, Liszt, Orff), Prometheus symbolizes the creative thinker's stubborn refusal to yield to fate.

Prometheus and the eagle. Detail from a drinking cup, Hellas, ca. 540 B.C.

Purgatory: Illustration for All Soul's Day (Nov. 2). W. Auer, 1890

Purgatory   In Roman Catholic teaching, a state of purification in the AFTERLIFE, in which the souls of those who have died in a state of grace are prepared for HEAVEN. The idea of purification or refinement is expressed already in Plato's (427–347 B.C.) dialogue *Gorgias;* the Church fathers Tertullian, Ambrose, and Augustine derived it from canonical writings. Around the middle of the second century after Christ it had become so established that inscriptions on tombstones commonly sought intercession for the souls of deceased Christians. The symbol of this process of refinement (a metallurgical concept!) is FIRE, which is seen as being like HELL but of limited duration. In iconography we often find the souls of the dead, portrayed with human forms, standing in the flames, making beseeching gestures; when they have atoned for their venial sins they are received by ANGELS and carried up to heaven. The Catholic Church feels profound, mystic sympathy for the fate of these "poor souls." (See also LIGHT and WATER.) There are numerous accounts of the "poor souls" in purgatory in Jacobus de Voragine's *Golden Legend* (ca. 1270), in the section on the Feast of All Souls' Day ("In Memory of the Souls of All Believers"), which, with its information about the many notions of the afterlife prevailing in the Middle Ages, is often of great symbological interest.

Pygmalion KING of Cyprus and a symbol both of the artist in love with his own creation and of the man who grooms a woman to his liking. According to legend, Pygmalion was a gifted sculptor who created the ivory statue of a maiden so perfect in its beauty that he could not bring himself to wed any mortal woman; he implored Aphrodite (VENUS) to bring the statue to life. His wish was granted, and the artist was able to wed his own creation. This myth was the source for numerous adaptations, including a Bach cantata, operas by Cherubini and Rameau, an operetta by Suppé (*The Beautiful Galatea*), dramas by Rousseau and Shaw (the latter the source of the musical *My Fair Lady*), a painting by Burne-Jones.

Pythagoras of Samos (ca. 540–500 B.C.) Greek philosopher, a symbolic figure representing great wisdom and learning. He is said to have traveled through EGYPT and BABYLON and finally established a school of religion and ethics in southern Italy that promulgated a variety of mystic doctrines (reincarnation, purification, striving for harmony) and developed into something of a general "school of mysteries." Its NUMBER symbolism influenced various subsequent schools of mystic thought. The "Pythagorean theorem" became part of the symbolic tradition of FREEMASONRY (see TRIANGLE); in a similar formulation, it was known in Egypt and Babylon before the time of Prometheus. The symbolic "sacred mathesis" of the Pythagoreans viewed numbers not merely as values for counting or measuring but as

Pythagoras researching principles of harmony. Woodcut, Italy, 1492

the essence of the real world; *geometria* has been associated with the G in the "blazing star" of Masonic symbolism (see PENTACLE). In Rosicrucian and alchemistic works of the Renaissance (e.g., Michael Maier's *Atlanta Fugiens*, 1618) we find the following advice to seekers of wisdom: "Pursue eagerly the science of geometry." Interpreted as a figure of transcendent harmony, the "Pythagorean triangle" with sides measuring 3, 4, and 5 units respectively, is a Masonic symbol of the Master of the Lodge and serves as a symbol of the past master who has striven for moderation and balance. From it the cube (the cubic STONE), the carpenter's SQUARE (with sides measuring 3 and 4 units), and a CROSS (from the lattice of the cube) can all be constructed. In this way the "mystical mathematics" of Pythagoras provided symbols for the Mason's approach to the secrets of creation and the Creator, "the almighty master builder of all worlds."

queen In the history of symbols the importance of the queen is not necessarily comparable to that of the KING: she appears rather as a complementary term in dualities, rarely standing alone, at least in secular contexts. Her importance apparently stems from social conditions of the Occident, where women had only secondary status in the everyday world. In FAIRY TALES and legends, on the other hand, we often find female royalty from the supernatural realm, for example the queen of the fairies, or, negatively valued, the queen of the WITCHES (called "*la dama*" and "*la señora*" in the Basque country). These figures suggest that in older times, at least in nonsecular contexts, women were allowed more influence than in the Judeo-Christian era, although this fact does not constitute a historical justification for speaking of a "gynocratic" or "matriarchal" period in human history. In the context of psychology, great queens, when they appear in dreams for example, appear to symbolize "the great feminine principle," or simply "the MOTHER."

quintessence A concept imported into everyday usage from the world of ALCHEMY, where it was believed that the FOUR elements of ancient cosmology (EARTH, air, FIRE, and WATER) were complemented by a "fifth essence": the pure, ethereal world-spirit. The alchemist's spiritual focus on essence, rather than matter, was supposed to increase the proportion of the fifth essence in the make-up of the entire world. The quintessence was thought to be present within each of the other four elements as its sublime creature: in water as the DOLPHIN, in fire as the PHOENIX, in the air as the EAGLE, and on earth as the human race. At the same time, the quintessence was believed to envelop and extend beyond each of the others. The graphic symbol corresponding to the quintessence is the PENTACLE.

rain The saintly abbess Hildegard of Bingen (1098–1179) likened rain to the vital energy of the soul, which makes the body flourish and "keeps it from drying out, as the rain moistens the earth. For when the rainfall is moderate and not excessive, the earth brings forth new life. But if it is inordinately heavy, it destroys the earth and drowns its new shoots. From the soul there emanate certain forces to vitalize the body, just as rainwater with its moisture vitalizes the earth. . . ." Hildegard also compared tears and rainfall. "The spiritual person is so shaken with fear of the Lord as to break out in tears, just as CLOUDS draw their water from the upper reaches and pour it forth as rain"; thus the gift of repentance irrigates, fertilizes the soul, "washing sin away."

In ancient agricultural societies the fertilizing rain was symbolized universally by a comb-like figure, with the horizontal stroke standing for the cloud and the vertical lines coming down from it standing for the rain itself. The ancient Mexican rain god Tlaloc was portrayed with teeth like those of a comb growing out of his upper jaw. The moisture from the sky that made the earth bring forth fruit was frequently represented as a flow of semen from the god of the heavens to "MOTHER Earth."

In Psalm 72 ("of" or "for" Solomon) it is written that the just and peaceful king "shall come down like rain upon the mown grass: as showers that water the earth" [verse 6].

In ancient China the not infrequent droughts were seen as divine retribution, and bone oracles from the beginning of the historical era seek to respond to the question of when rain would come. It was believed that only the proper union of the feminine principle YIN with the masculine yang would yield rain. (See YIN AND YANG; RAINBOW.)

Ancient cave paintings reveal that in the civilizations of southeast Africa rain was symbolized by a SNAKE coming down from heaven—a creature perhaps associated with LIGHTNING as well. In other contexts a gigantic horned snake appears to have stood for rainwater. And in many ancient cosmologies clouds were thought of as reservoirs of rainwater, waiting to be split open by thunderbolts.

rainbow (Greek *iris*) In many cultures this impressive phenomenon is understood symbolically as a manifestation of divine benevolence, e.g. God's covenant with Noah in Genesis 9:11–13 that never again from that time onward would a great FLOOD cover the face of the earth. We also find many depictions of the Last Judgment in which a rainbow serves as the divine throne.

In ancient Greece Iris was the virginal rainbow goddess, rushing down from Mount Olympus to communicate to mortals the commands of Zeus and Hera; Iris is portrayed with WINGS and the CADUCEUS, clothed in the "iridescent" dew. (The similarly irides-

Rain god Tlaloc. Sculpted jade vessel, Zapotec, ancient Mexico

Rainbow: The heavenly messenger Iris. Cartari, 1647

cent pigmented membrane of the eye is thus called the "iris.")

It is not clear whether Bifrost, the BRIDGE of old Germanic cosmology, is to be understood as the MILKY WAY or as a rainbow. In medieval Christian symbology the three principal COLORS of the rainbow, BLUE, RED, and GREEN, were viewed as symbols, respectively, of flood, fire, and the earth restored after destruction (Gottfried of Viterbo, ca. 1125–1192), or the seven colors of the rainbow as symbols of the seven sacraments and seven gifts of the Holy Spirit; the entire rainbow was also thought of symbolizing the Virgin Mary, bringing heaven and earth together in restored harmony.

In ancient China the rainbow was seen as a symbol of the union of YIN AND YANG, but also in some contexts as standing for fornication and represented as a seven-headed SNAKE. (Similarly, the rainbow was portrayed in the myths of ancient Java as a snake with a head at each end of its body: one head drinks in water from the northern sea and the other spews it out into the sea of the south.) It was considered irreverent to point at a rainbow. The Incas of ancient Peru associated the rainbow with the (divine) sun, and Garcilaso de la Vega (1539–1616) reports that their kings included a rainbow in their coats of arms.

In the European popular tradition a rainbow has often been taken as an omen of future wealth or the finding of a treasure (the proverbial "pot of GOLD" at its end). Ancient Celtic gold coins were called "rainbow saucers."

ram (Latin *aries*) The male SHEEP is the first of the 12 signs of the zodiac (see STARS). (In the Mesopotamian ordering of the signs this region of the heavens was called "the Laborer.") In Greek myth a ram with fleece of gold carried Phrixus and Helle (children of King Athamas) across the sea toward Colchis. As a reward it was transported into the heavens, where it became the constellation Aries. But the Golden Fleece was left behind in Colchis, which, it is said, is why the light of the constellation appears to be so feeble.

Aries is one of the FIRE signs, along with Sagittarius and Leo (see CENTAURS, LION). It is ruled by MARS by day, and thus its color is RED; its metal is steel and its birthstone AMETHYST. Those born under Aries (March 21 – April 20) are believed by astrologers to be aggressive, to be strongly oriented toward progress, but to squander love and energy.

For the Yorubas of Western Africa, the ram is the symbol and attribute of the thunder god Shango, the AX-bearer; THUNDER is thought of as the deafening bleating of the ram. The Germanic storm god Thor (or Donar), the hammer wielder, was associated with the ram, as were the Egyptian god Khnum and later "JUPITER Amun" with ram's HORNS. In the Greek tradition Hermes was occasionally referred to as the "carrier of rams" (*criophorus*) and shepherd god.

Ram "of the sun," praying man. Rock drawing, Fezzan, North Africa

Ram. Mosaic, Rusguniae, North Africa, early Christian

Rat catchers. Woodcut, England, ca. 1650

According to the Jungian psychologist Ernst Aeppli, the ram, in comparison with the BULL, is also "a wild symbol of the creative forces of nature, but more linked with problems of the intellect"; thus the ram is less clearly associated with the destructive forces of elemental nature.

In the Bible the ram is also the replacement for the human sacrifice that ABRAHAM was ready to perform upon his son Isaac [Genesis 22:1–14]. "Rabbi Hanina ben Dosa tells us that no part of the animal died in vain. The ashes [or embers] were an essential part of the fire that blazed on the altar of the temple. The ram had ten tendons, and this is why DAVID's harp had ten strings. Its skin was used to make Elijah's belt. Then we come to the two horns of the ram. The Lord blew the left one on Mount Sinai, as it is written: 'the voice of the trumpet [i.e., shofar, ram's horn] exceeding loud' [Exodus 19:16]. The right one, however, grew larger than the left, and it is the right one that the Lord will blow when he gathers the scattered out of exile, about which it is written: 'And it shall come to pass in that day, that the great trumpet shall be blown' [Isaiah 27: 13]."

rat Like the MOUSE, a creature with predominantly negative symbolic associations, nevertheless representing in certain contexts the human soul. (The Pied Piper of Hamelin, for example, frequently stands for Satan, the tempter and captor of souls.) As a destroyer of stored food and a transmitter of disease, the rat acquired the reputation of being in league with the DEVIL, demons, and witches in their efforts to bring the unsuspecting to ruin. Rats were often not distinguished from mice, primarily because sewer rats were so common.

The rat plays a very different role in the cultures of South and East Asia. In some places in India, temples were erected to them—perhaps, admittedly, to appease demons associated with disease. The rat is also the mount of Ganesha, the ELEPHANT-headed god of learning; in Japan, the rat is the companion of the god of good fortune. In both Japan and China, the absence of rats from a household was cause for concern (analogously, perhaps, to the Western image of "rats leaving a sinking ship"). When the rat nibbled, it is said to be "counting money"; in China, a miser is called a "money rat." In South China the rat is celebrated as the mythical bringer of RICE to humanity. On the other hand, the Chinese also often viewed rats (ta shu or lao shu) as demonic figures, the male counterparts, more or less, to the

Rats' tails as a symbol of confusion. Children's book illustration, F. Pocci, 1846

female FOX demons. In the Chinese zodiac the rat appears as the first sign, like the RAM (Aries) in the West; the "years of the rat" are 1972, 1984, 1996, and so forth.

In some Western contexts rats are associated idiomatically with tangles or concatenations of misfortune or rumor (from the observation that baby rats in the nest, when sick, appear to get their tails entangled) or with deep sleep (from the confusion of rats, which do not hibernate, with hamsters and dormice, which do).

raven (Latin *corvus*, Greek *corax*) A BLACK BIRD whose symbolic tradition largely overlaps with that of the CROW, from which it is not clearly distinguished from culture to culture. We generally find negative associations with these birds, although the raven is occasionally valued for its wisdom. In the Bible NOAH sends a raven from the ARK to search for land [Genesis 8:7], and ravens bring the prophet Elijah (and, later, the anchorites ANTHONY and Paul) BREAD and meat in the desert [I Kings 17:4, 6]. The raven has negative associations in the Babylonian calendar, where it governs the (variable) 13th month. In Greek mythology, it is portrayed as indiscreetly revealing secrets (the reason for which it was replaced by the OWL as the companion of the goddess Athena). It is said that the raven's feathers were originally WHITE but were then blackened by Apollo to punish it for divulging secrets. In another myth, when Apollo had sent the raven for water, the bird saw a tree with green figs, waited underneath it until the

Raven as constellation. Map of heavens, Abderahmanas Sufi, 15th century copy (Gotha)

fruit ripened, and only afterward fetched the water; as punishment, Apollo placed the bird (as the constellation Corvus) where the monstrous (constellation) Hydra would forever keep it away from the "bowl" (the constellation Crater). On the positive side of the ledger, however, the bird was the SUN god's companion (as in ancient China, where it was believed that a three-legged raven lived in the sun). Curiously, the ancients believed that ravens laid eggs through their beaks, and for this reason they were kept away from childbearing women, for fear that contact might lead to a difficult labor. Pliny the Elder speaks of the bird's cry as sounding "choked"; the raven, he suggests, is the only bird that seems to understand what it augurs. It appears in a positive light when Apollo, in the guise of a raven, guides the inhabitants of Thera (Santorini) to Cyrene; when a white raven guides the Boeotian emigrants; and when two ravens guide ALEXANDER THE GREAT to the shrine of Amon (see HORNS). Sculpture of the Mithraic cult also often portrays ravens.

In early Christianity the raven was berated for not reporting to Noah that the floodwaters had receded. It became a symbol of those who are so caught up in worldly pleasures that they keep putting off their conversion—like the bird who cries "*cras, cras*" (Latin "tomorrow, tomorrow"). The fact that the bird lives from carrion (with a special predilection, in popular belief, for the corpses of hanged men) and was thought to neglect its young, led to its being viewed

Raven (Yehl, Yelch) as hero in Native American iconography (Pacific Northwest)

Raven's young. Wilhelm Busch

as a harbinger of misfortune, disease, war, and death; Poe's choice of the bird for the celebrated poem to which it lends its name (1845) follows this tradition. In Norse myth, however, two ravens, Hugin and Munin ("thought" and "remembrance"), accompany the god Odin, whom they inform about everything that happens on earth. In many fairy tales ravens are humans upon whom a curse has been placed; in Native American myths of various nations of the Northwest, the raven is a supernatural creator. Many Christian saints have ravens as their attributes: Benedict, Boniface, Oswald, and especially Meinrad (whose pet ravens helped find his body) and Vincent (whose body ravens defended against beasts of prey).

In the symbolism of ALCHEMY, the raven represents the blackened *materia prima* on its way to becoming the philosopher's STONE; in this context, the bird was often portrayed with a white head, an indication of the enlightenment to be expected in the course of transformation.

We have noted that in ancient China the three-legged raven was associated with the sun; according to legend, ten such ravens once gave off unbearable heat until an archer

Coruus.

Raven. Woodcut in Pseudo-Albertus Magnus, Frankfurt, 1531

killed NINE of them. A RED raven was the symbol of the rulers of the Chou dynasty (ended 256 B.C.), who identified with the sun. Ravens serve as messengers of the fairy goddess Hsi-wang-mu and bring her food; in heavenly tournaments they fear only the UNICORNS.

In HERALDRY the raven appears from the Middle Ages onward, in the arms of the Corbet and Biron families, the Ravenstein estate, the Saxon city of Rabenau, and the Einsiedeln monastery in the Swiss city of Schwyz (because of the association with St. Meinrad).

Ravens, like MAGPIES, are popularly referred to as "thieving" birds; in Iceland it is said that children must not use raven quills as drinking straws, or else they will grow up to be thieves.

A Ukrainian legend reported by S. Golowin is rich in poetic and symbolic resonances. In Eden (see PARADISE) the ravens had feathers of many colors, but after the Fall (see ADAM AND EVE) they began to eat carrion and turned black. Only in the new paradise at the end of time will their former beauty be restored, and their croaking will become a melodic song of praise to the Creator.

It is only natural, given these traditions, that the raven should be a significant symbol for the Jungian psychologist. The bird is associated with the dark side of the psyche but can function positively if the individual in question is able to come to terms with the issues involved there.

red A frequent choice of persons asked to name their favorite COLOR. In the form of iron oxide (red ochre) it accompanied humanity from prehistoric times onward, and it was used again and again in the CAVE art of the Ice Age. Even earlier, Neanderthals had sprinkled the bodies of the dead with red pigment as a way of restoring to them the "warm" color of BLOOD and life. In general, red is thought of as the color of aggression, vitality, and strength, associated with FIRE and symbolizing both love and mortal combat. Introverts and melancholics find it intrusive or repulsive.

Its symbological significance, properly speaking, is similarly diverse. In ancient Egypt it had positive associations only in the "red CROWN" of the Lower Egyptian delta; otherwise it was the color of the hostile god Sutech or Seth and of the evil serpent Apep or Apophis. These names were written in papyri in red ink; reddish animals (dogs, for example) were shunned, since the color was associated with acts of violence.

In ancient Mexican art red was used only sparingly, when needed for the depiction of blood, fire, the SUN, or (blended with other colors) leather. In the Mayan culture it is the color of the east; for the highland nations of ancient Mexico, the south—as is also the case in ancient China, where red (hung) was also the sacred, vitalizing color of the Chou dynasty (1050–256 B.C.). The red flags of communist China seem almost to be linked with this ancient tradition. Red was the color of the god who brought riches and good fortune. The combination of red and GREEN was a Chinese symbol of vitality, as in the "green socks and red skirt" worn by young girls or the red lamps and green WINE of taverns. On the other hand, men who found marital love-making strenuous were called "red-faced," and this was thought to presage an early death.

In the Christian artistic tradition, red was the color of the sacrificial blood of Christ and the martyrs, of fervent love (e.g., in the garment of John, the disciple whom Jesus loved) and of the "tongues like as of fire" [Acts 2:3] of the Holy Spirit at Pentecost. The red worn by cardinals suggests their readiness to die for the Church. But women of easy virtue wore red, and the IDOLS of heathen peoples were often painted red. In the Book of Revelation "Mystery, Babylon the Great, the Mother of Harlots and Abominations of the Earth" is "arrayed in purple and scarlet colour"; she rides "upon a scarlet coloured beast, full of names of blasphemy, having seven heads and ten horns" [17:5, 4, 3]. Thus red also became known as the color of HELL and the DEVIL, as well as of the "suspicious" animals associated with this domain: the FOX and the SQUIRREL.

The color has positive associations—as the color of victorious love—in depictions of the Creator and of the risen Christ. In the Catholic Church, red appears as the color of vestments on feast and memorial days of martyrs (and the Holy Spirit: Pentecost), and, because of its association with Christ's Passion, on Passion Sunday and Good Friday.

In popular tradition red is the color of love (in association with flowers, for example, and especially ROSES), but also of life (e.g., rosy or ruddy cheeks) or of anger ("to see red"). Houses of prostitution are found in "red-light districts"; in traffic, a red light orders automobiles (and pedestrians) not to enter an intersection, warning that it may be fatal to do so. In the world of bullfighting the red of the cape is supposed to enrage the BULL and move him to attack, although in fact the animal may not distinguish colors in the same way that humans do: it is probably the movement of the muleta and not its color that provokes the bull.

In ALCHEMY red, standing for SULFUR, forms a DUALITY with white. This polarity may be related to ancient theories of procreation, in which new life comes out of the union of (menstrual) blood with (white) sperm. In this way the two colors came to be associated symbolically with creation in general.

In FREEMASONRY red is the color of the elevated ranks of the "Scottish Rite," as contrasted with the "BLUE" degrees (Apprentice, Journeyman, Master).

As a dream symbol, the color red reveals something of the dreamer's emotional functioning: "Where red appears, the psyche is ready for action; conquest and suffering set in; there is surrender, but also affliction, and, most of all, emotional connectedness" [Aeppli].

rice The East Asian analogue, materially and symbolically, of such Western staples as grain or BREAD. In ancient China it was said to have been introduced by the mythical primeval emperor Shen-Nung, along with the annual ritual of rice planting. In some provinces the DOG or the RAT was credited with having brought rice to humanity. Rice was placed in the MOUTHS of the dead, and rice was piled high in bowls (a practice otherwise avoided) to be sacrificed to ancestors. There was also a taboo prohibiting the discarding of leftover rice, supposedly enforced by the god of THUNDER, who would strike down anyone who violated it.

In Japan the SUN goddess Amaterasu was credited with the introduction of rice farming. When the STORM god Susano-o savaged her fields, she became enraged and hid in a CAVE; only later could she be persuaded to end her exile and illuminate the world again. (Compare BAUBO.) In another Japanese tradition, the god Inari is the "rice bearer." He is said to have appeared around 800 B.C. as an old man with two bundles of rice, revealing himself as the protector of the rice fields. There are many shrines to Inari, reportedly some 40,000 across Japan. Each is marked by a line of gates (see TORII) constructed one behind the next. Ceremonial meals were eaten in the presence of Buddhist priests to insure wealth and happiness in private and public life.

right and left The two sides form a DUALITY in which usually (but not always) the right is viewed more favorably. Tracings of the HAND in Ice Age cave temples (along with other evidence) suggest that humans have always been predominantly right-handed. It is probably for this reason that the right side has been treated predominantly as better and luckier than the left. It may be of some significance that the left arm traditionally remained passive, holding the warrior's shield, while the right carried and thrust the weapon. The place of honor at an Occidental table is at the right hand of the host. At the Last Judgment the just take their place on the right side and the damned on the left, and the risen Christ "sits at the right hand of God the Father Almighty." In depictions of the Crucifixion, the repentant thief is on Christ's right, the unrepentant on his left.

In the Cabala, the duality of God's hands—which in this tradition can have no negative aspect—is expressed as follows: the right

(the "hand of blessing") symbolizes mercy, and the left (the "hand of the king"), justice. In many cultures the right side is thought of as masculine and the left as feminine; this division implies a negative view of women, but it may also be related to an association of the right hand with everyday activities and the left with magic. African magicians, however, carry out sacred actions with the right hand and prepare poisons with the left.

Ancient China, with its understanding of YIN AND YANG as perfect complements, did not have a clear preference for one side or the other. The male head of the household traditionally sat on the left and his wife on the right, but they slept in the reverse of this position. When groups of deities of both sexes are portrayed together, the Chinese custom places gods to the right and goddesses to the left, whereas in Tibetan iconography this arrangement is reversed.

In the tradition of European magic, the "path to the right hand" is referred to as "white," and the one "to the left" as "black" magic.

The origin of the use of "right" and "left," respectively, to designate conservative and liberal parties or political leanings, is unclear. It seems likely that in the British Parliament the more influential Tories first claimed the "better" (right) side of the chamber for themselves, leaving the less favored side for their opponents.

ring A traditional symbol of infinity or eternity, the transposition of the CIRCLE into the real world of tangible, functional objects. In Greek and especially Roman antiquity, the privilege of wearing iron rings was reserved for prominent citizens. Priests of Jupiter were allowed to wear GOLD rings (the origin of the bishop's ring), and this privilege was subsequently extended to senators and KNIGHTS. There were also magical associations with rings, e.g., Solomon's signet ring (see HEXAGRAM). In an oracle mentioned by Aristotle (384–322 B.C.), the sound made when two rings suspended by threads came together announced that it was time for action. Rings suspended over a Ouija

Rings: With Udjat eye (ancient Egypt), seven-spotted snake (Bavaria, ca. 1800)

board were said to have spelled out the names of the conspirators plotting against the emperor Flavius Valens (A.D. 328–378). In early Christian times Macrobius (ca. A.D. 400) wrote of rings adorned by such symbols as the FISH, the DOVE, and the ANCHOR (see also CROSS). The Pope's ring, called the "fisherman's ring" or *annulus piscatoris*, portrays the apostle Peter casting his NET [Luke 5:1–11]; the ring is broken at the death of each of Peter's successors. In the Middle Ages rings came to symbolize betrothal (compare KNOTS) and MARRIAGE. Jeweled rings were also worn as amulets to ward off specific diseases (e.g., carnelian against hemorrhaging, or "spasm rings" against palsy). Since the time of Agrippa of Nettesheim (1486–1535) books of magic have contained instructions for making rings with every sort of secret power. Broken rings symbolize broken vows; the loss of a ring was popularly thought to bring misfortune. The signet ring (see SEAL) with its HERALDIC symbols (usually passed down from generation to generation) was used to certify deeds and other documents. The rings of the dying were removed so that it would be possible for them to depart this world; by classical times, the wearing of rings was forbidden in the observance of many cults, since they were thought to impede contact with the world of the gods. In the Germanic tradition, the early Middle Ages attached great significance to rings (e.g., *Der Ring des Nibelungen*): they were associated with great blessings or curses. Fairy tales and popular legends

contain many accounts of magical rings with the power to make wishes come true.

G. A. Böckler writes as follows of the occurrence of rings in heraldry: "Coats of arms often contain rings symbolizing honor, fidelity, and perseverance. When a vassal receives a ring from a prince, it is a sign of extraordinary high favor. Aristotle recounts that the citizens of Carthage gave their military commanders a ring for every victory over the foe; thus rings were even then symbols of nobility—as they remain to this day" (1688). Modern heraldry see rings in coats of arms as references to the rank of bishop; nevertheless, gold and silver rings with PRECIOUS STONES also appear in the arms of cities and families.

An anticipation of Lessing's ring parable in *Nathan the Wise* (but without the Enlightenment notion of humanity as transcending all limits) is contained in the medieval *Gesta Romanorum* (ca. 1300): a king has three sons, one of whom he especially loves. To this favorite son he wishes to leave a ring with a valuable jewel, and to each of the others a copy of it, identical in appearance. "After the father's death, each son believed that his ring was the valuable one with the real jewel. Hearing of this, a man proposed to settle the dispute as follows: 'We shall see which ring has the power to drive off disease; this, then, must be the most valuable.' " Two of the rings have no effect, but the favorite son's has the power to heal. The collection offers the following interpretation of the story: "The three brothers are the three races of the earth. The first [corresponding to the favorite son] are God's children through Christ, the spirit made flesh; the others are the Jews and the Saracens [Muslims]. Now, it is clear that God loves the Christian people best, and for this reason He left them the ring that makes the blind see and heals disease, drives out demons and works every other miracle. This ring is the true faith. . . ."

E. bin Gorion's collection of Jewish legends, *The Judas Spring*, on the other hand, contains the parable of two precious stones (religions), identical in appearance; only the "Father in Heaven," it is written, can tell which is better. Bin Gorion presents this legend as Lessing's prototype.

rivers The "cradles of civilization" of the ancient world were river basins, around 3000 B.C. The comparative and collective importance of the Yellow River (Hwang Ho), the Ganges, the Indus, the Tigris and Euphrates, and the Nile as base lines for the history of civilization has never been explored; no parallel phenomenon has been found in the New World. It is important for its symbolism that the river is not a "body" of water but a stream: with its flow and its floodings, it functions not statically but dynamically, and it becomes the basis for the historical reckoning of time itself. Ancient Jewish tradition divides the land surrounding Paradise into FOUR quadrants, which serve as points of the compass: Pison (Indus?), Gihon (Ganges?), Hiddekel (Tigris), and Euphrates. The dividing line between this world and the next (see AFTERLIFE) was also commonly thought of as a river; similarly, in Greek mythology, a river (Oceanus) surrounds the entire inhabited world (*oecumene*). Within a given civilization, its focal river was often believed to have an extraterrestrial source: the Nile (in Egyptian, Yotru) in a cave; the major rivers of Asia (Brahmaputra, Ganges, Indus, and Oxus) on the world-MOUNTAIN Meru. In ancient China the taming of the river gods by the primeval emperor Yü is a mythical event of great importance, and human sacrifices were once offered to appease these divinities. DRAGON-kings (symbols and personifications

River landscape (Tigris and Euphrates?). Engraving, Maikop (Caucasus), ca. 1800 B.C.

of the dangers of rapid currents and flooding) were said to live in rivers and await these sacrifices; similarly, the drowned, wishing to return to life, lay in wait for swimmers to replace them in the realm of the dead. The ancient Greeks sacrificed BULLS, HORSES, SHEEP, and locks of HAIR to river gods (including Achelous, Scamandrus, Cephissus), who are usually portrayed as part human, part animal, such as humans with bull's heads, or CENTAURS (Nessus). In ancient Rome the Tiber was revered as "Tibertinus pater," the father of all other rivers. In Christian times baptismal fonts often bore representations of the rivers of Eden, and the baptismal water was likened to that of the Jordan, in which John baptised Christ. To the four rivers of paradise were opposed four rivers of HELL (a borrowing from Greek mythology): Acheron, Cocytus, Styx, and Phlegeton or Pyriphlegeton ("river of fire").

In India, and especially in Varanasi, the veneration of the Ganges continues to this day; its waters are said to be capable of washing away all human shortcomings ("As fire consumes wood, so does Ganga consume sins"). The Ganges is seen as coming down from HEAVEN, sent by Brahma to wash away every trace of sin, from both the ASHES of the dead and the bodies of the living, once the god Shiva takes hold of it and places it in the riverbed. Pilgrimages to SPRINGS along the holy river serve to expunge misdeeds that mar the pilgrim's karma (the sum-total of a person's deeds, decisive for future reincarnations). According to Böckler (1688),

River god Tiber. Cartari, 1647

River: Pharaoh's daughter rescues Moses from the Nile. Gustave Doré (1832–1883)

in heraldry rivers and waves mean "either that the noble's father made great voyages overseas in the service of his lord, or was the first to cross a river to attack or pursue the enemy, or performed a praiseworthy act at sea. Just as the sea, constantly in motion, will suffer no stagnation, no dead body, but will cast up the same with the agitation of its waves, so too must the high-minded not fritter their time away with those who would burden them with idle chitchat. Clear water cleanses away all that besmirches, like a loyal friend, who not only points out short-comings but also teaches us how to rid ourselves of them."

robbers As noble champions of social equality, stealing the ill-gotten gains of the rich and distributing them among the poor, robbers are romantic symbols of protest against unequal distribution of property; for the psy-chologist, they may symbolize the rebellion of the young against authority and parental (especially paternal) power (Robin Hood). In popular literature, but also in Schiller's play *Die Räuber*, this subject matter is richly treated. (See also FOREST.)

rocks Because of their durability, rocks and boulders usually symbolize that which

is stable, unchanging, eternal, and by ex-tension that which is divine, as well—es-pecially in the case of rocks distinguished by the unusualness of their form, which tend to be understood as the abodes of specific supernatural beings or as persons who have been turned to stone (as punishment for misdeeds). On ancient Chinese scrolls, rocks symbolize longevity and the principle of *yang* (as opposed to YIN, whose symbol is the waterfall). In many regions of the country rocks and STONES were prayed to, and struck, for RAIN; gravel was used in magic rituals to enhance fertility. For the Jews, the boulder beneath the Holy of Holies in the Jerusalem temple was the point at which the world was created and the center of the earth (see OMPHALOS). The gods and heroes of many civilizations (e.g., Mithra) were born as rocks. In Christianity, the WATER obtained by Moses from the rock (during the exodus of the Jews from Egypt) symbolizes baptismal water and the life-giving water of faith. The apostle Simon Peter (in Greek, Petros, "rock") symbolizes the unshifting ground upon which the Church is built (see Matthew 16:18). Boulders are fundamental for building: in northwestern Europe megaliths (literally "great stones") were combined as early as 4800 B.C. in monumental structures. Here, too, their durability may have been a symbol for the eternal. Stone pillars (MENHIRS), which have often been interpreted as phallic symbols, were more probably elevated seats for the souls of departed ancestors, located near stone graves.

Rock of "steadfast faith" on which the City of God is built. Hohberg, 1675

Rock: Mithras, god of light, born from rock. Relief, Rome

In the symbology of FREEMASONRY, "rough" (unfinished) stone is the apprentice, who still needs education; the "finished" stone, the end-stage of that process. The rough stone represents a person's still latent abilities, and a variety of "refining" rituals, their realization (see PRECIOUS STONES). Rocky MOUNTAIN-tops were of particular importance in the rituals of many civilizations, as were pinnacles (e.g., the rock Idafe, for the original inhabitants of La Palma in the Canary Islands). Specific stones were also considered to be invested with powers ("hot stones," in Brittany) and capable of bestowing life-force, e.g., when infertile women sat on them (and in ancient China, similarly). (See also HELL.) Rock symbolism is found frequently in the Old Testament, for example in Psalm 31:2–3—"Be thou my strong rock, for an house of defense to save me. For thou art my rock and my fortress . . ."—or in David's prayer of thanksgiving: "The Lord is my rock, and my fortress, and my deliverer; The God of my rock; in him will I trust . . ." [II Samuel 22:2–3]. The rock as a divine image was of great importance to the Hurrians and the Hittites, who believed that Kumarbi, the ancient father of the gods, drew Ullikummi, his "diorite son," from a rock. Ullikummi threatened the supremacy of the new god of the heavens, Teshub, until the former was cut down with a COPPER SICKLE from his position on the shoulder of the ATLAS-like Upelluri and thus defeated. The Incas of Peru referred to

those "very high mountains which tower above the others, . . . shooting up almost as steeply as a wall" as being *huaca,* i.e., holy and mysterious [Garcilaso de la Vega]. On these rocky towers they placed their sacrifices to the gods; when the Spanish missionaries converted the former kingdom to Christianity, they placed CROSSES on such sites.

Roland Behind the hero of folklore there actually is a historical figure, the military commander of the Frankish border province Hruolandus, roughly corresponding to modern-day Brittany. In 778, in the course of an unsuccessful campaign waged against the caliph Abd er-Rahman by Charlemagne in the Roncevaux valley in the Pyrenees, Roland died in a Basque attack as he attempted to pull back the rear guard. In popular accounts derived from Turpin's *Historia Karoli Magni et Rotholandi,* this defeat is blamed on a plot by the traitor Ganelon: thus Roland, like SIEGFRIED, was a victim of betrayal. Fatally wounded, Roland attempted to destroy his SWORD by thrice striking a block of marble with it, lest it fall into enemy hands; but the STONE itself was cleft and the sword remained whole. Roland blew his horn, breaking it in the process (see TRUMPET), and died in the arms of a faithful servant. In many German cities we find a statue of Roland in front of the town hall: the gigan-

Roland Column. Wedel (Holstein), Germany, 1558, 1651

tic hero, outfitted with sword and shield, is a symbol of judicial authority.

rooster or cock (Latin *gallus*) Known to European antiquity variously as an animal of the SUN, crowing to announce daybreak and to drive off nocturnal demons, or (especially the black rooster) as a magical and sacrificial animal for subterranean powers. The positive symbolism triumphed, however, and the image of the rooster—whose crowing was believed to ward off even LIONS and BASILISKS—appeared on amulet stones, shields, and grave markers. It was said that a rooster's comb gave protection from nightmares; his testes were considered an aphrodisiac and capable of causing a woman to give birth to male children; similarly, the bird that delivers us from the confines of the night was believed to facilitate the delivery of babies from the womb. For many cultures his bright RED comb and his dazzling feathers make him a symbol of FIRE and the sun; to put the "red rooster" on someone's roof was to set it on fire. By the early 19th century roosters were appearing on church towers as harbingers of dawn and to summon parishioners to morning prayer. The bird's territoriality and unflagging readiness to mate make him an obvious symbol of masculinity, but Christians also see him as a symbol of Christ, the bringer of a new dawn of faith.

Rooster crowing. Hohberg, 1675

St. Gregory proposed the rooster as a model for the clergy: he smites his midsection (does penance) before he opens his mouth to speak. The "triple" crowing of the cock, portrayed on early Christian sarcophagi (a reference to Peter's three denials of Christ before the cock crowed, Matthew 26:33–35, 69–75), was a warning against arrogance. The image of the bird as a watchful guardian made him an early attribute of divinities (Athena, Demeter), as did his readiness to do battle (MARS), his abilities as a "healer" (ASCLEPIUS), and his heralding of the sun (Apollo). In late antiquity Abraxis, a deity thought to master all the days of the year, was portrayed with a rooster's head and SNAKES for feet. In Norse mythology the cock "Goldcomb" guards the RAINBOW bridge leading to the abode of the gods. In East Asia the bird has a similar symbolic tradition. The tenth sign of the Chinese zodiac, he is not eaten. The reddish rooster protects against fire; the white drives off demons. The rooster is considered not only brave but also kind-hearted (calling the hens to share the feed) and reliable (with his wake-up summons, which in Japan is also addressed to the sun goddess). In Hindu legend the "rooster king" sits in the branches of a TREE in the land of Jambudvipa; his daily crowing is a signal to all the roosters in the world to join in. In Chinese homonymic symbolism, the rooster (*kung-chi*) with his crowing (*ming*) stands for *kung-ming*, merit and fame. Civil servants (*kuan*) were given a rooster with a large comb, or *kuan*. A rooster with chicks symbolized a

Rooster as attribute of Mercury (Hermes). Cartari, 1647

father's providing for his children, or, more narrowly, his sons. Cockfighting, although outlawed, is still a popular (and brutal) attraction in parts of Latin America and in South China; the bird's aggression is reduced to a betting matter, despite the bird's mythical significance: in many traditions, the sun is occupied by a fiery rooster. In medieval Europe the rooster took on a negative association (like the male GOAT) as an embodiment of lechery (as when young men were said to be driven by "rooster demons") and pugnacity. At the same time he was given a place in the arms of Gaul (France) and St. Gall; St. Vitus was also portrayed with a rooster (perched on a BOOK). Because of his morning "alarm," the bird also adorned splendid clocks. St. Peter, portrayed together with the crowing rooster, became the

Roosters preparing to fight. Wilhelm Busch

patron saint of watchmakers. Hohberg (1675) penned the following edifying verses: "When watchful cock first cries them all awake,/ His fellows add their voices one by one./ So, let your voice not falter, never quake,/ But join in strong each time God's praise is sung." (See also IBIS.) There are wide-ranging associations with the English word "cock": it can refer by extension to any male bird, occasionally to other male animals (e.g., "cock lobster"), and, of course, to the penis, a usage labeled vulgar but one so widespread that it has led to the general replacement of "cock" (in the sense of *gallus*) by "rooster."

rose For the ancients, roses were associated with the myth of ADONIS, the lover of Aphrodite (Latin VENUS), from whose BLOOD the first RED roses (or pheasant's eye, a variety of Ranunculus) were said to have grown. They thus became symbolic of love that transcended even death, and of resurrection itself.

The ancient Roman festival "Rosalia" was part of the cult of the dead from the first century after Christ onward; it was celebrated on different dates in different regions, but always between May 11 and July 15. The tradition of Rosalia is preserved in present-day Italy in the celebration of Pentecost Sunday (*domenica rosata*).

Participants in Dionysian festivals (see BACCHUS) were adorned with rose garlands because it was believed that roses had the ability to counteract the intoxicating power of WINE, thus keeping revelers from revealing secrets in their drunkenness. Thus the rose came to symbolize discretion, and FIVE-leafed roses were often part of the carved adornments of confessionals. "Sub rosa," under the seal of secrecy, literally means "under the rose."

In Christian symbolism the red rose stood for the blood shed by Jesus on the Cross, and thus for God's love (compare "*rosa candida*" in Dante's *Divine Comedy*). The troubadours, however, saw the rose as a tangible symbol of earthly love, and this tradition continues into our own time (see FLOWERS, LANGUAGE OF). The WHITE rose, however, is a legendary symbol of death.

Rose on cruciform stem, bees. Rosicrutian symbol, Fludd, *Summum Bonum*, 1629

Rose. Pseudo-Albertus Magnus, Frankfurt, 1531

Christian iconography made the rose (the "queen of flowers") a symbol for Mary, the Queen of Heaven, and for virginity: in the Middle Ages only VIRGINS were permitted to wear rose garlands, and the Madonna was frequently portrayed as surrounded by roses.

In ALCHEMY red and white roses enter into the general red/white DUALITY, symbolizing the primal elements SULFUR AND MERCURY, and a rose with seven concentric rings of petals stands for the seven metals and the corresponding planets. The association of the rose with the Cross led to the symbol of the Rosicrucians, a mystical Christian fraternity (or *collegium philosophicum*) dating back to the Renaissance. Their symbol, a five-leafed rose in a cross, resembles Martin Luther's personal seal, in which a cross grows out of a heart at the center of a five-leafed rose. The coat of arms of Johann Valentin Andreae (1586–1654), through whose writings the Rosicrucians became known throughout the world, was a St. Andrew's cross (in the form of an X) with a rose at each of its four corners.

The rose is of great importance in the symbolism of FREEMASONRY. Three roses are placed in the grave of a Mason when he is buried. The three "St. John's roses" stand for "LIGHT, love, and life": on the Masonic "St. John's day," June 24, the lodge is decorated with roses in three different colors, and some lodge names refer to this custom (e.g., the Hamburg Lodge of the Three Roses, into which the 18th-century dramatist Lessing was inducted).

Rosicrucian and Masonic symbolism appear in Goethe's poem "The Secrets," which describes a cross entwined with roses: "Who added roses to the cross?/ The garland swells, surrounds the rood on every side,/ Brings softness to its rugged edge;/ And lightest silver clouds do float suspended,/ Just to lift up cross and roses all;/ And from the midst flows holy life,/ In triple stream from single source . . . ." The baroque poet W. H. von Hohberg remarked in 1675 that there is "no rose without a thorn" (or, more precisely, without a prickle): "As rose was never seen, that thorns did not afford,/ So are people, too, a motley mix, wheree'er you turn,/ With some, the godly ones, the people of the Lord;/ And others, wicked, fully certain yet to burn."

In traditional Chinese symbolism the rose is considerably less important than in the West: it signifies "youth" but has no specific association with love.

Böckler writes about the rose in HERALDRY as follows: "Flowers generally signify a state of flourishing, full of joyful hope, which will be propagated, it is hoped, in the descendents of the noble line and in their glorious deeds. One such flower is the rose, . . . whose royal status among flowers is explained by its special association with comfort, generosity, and discretion. Red roses

Roses adorn death. Poetry illustration. E. Fitzgerald, 1859

have an inevitable association with the redness of the blood that all must shed for freedom, for the Fatherland, for the Church: just as a red rose by the grace of God steadily grows and grows, so must an officer be prepared at any moment to shed blood. The rose came to have special significance as a military insignia because of the Roman belief that Mars was born from a rose" (1688).

In general the heraldic rose appears (like the LILY) in highly stylized form, as a blossom viewed from above with leaves bent inward: not only the five-leaved but also six- or eight-leaved roses, and occasionally silver or gold in color rather than the more common red. Roses are best known in English heraldry, and specifically as symbols of the houses of York (a white rose) and Lancaster (a red rose); this is why the conflict between the two houses is referred to as the War of the Roses. The "Tudor rose" is a combination of the roses of York and Lancaster. The arms of the city of Southampton contain one red rose and two white. In Germany the arms of the princes of Lippe and those of the barons of Altenburg contained roses, as did subsequently those of the cities of Lemgo and Lippstadt.

rubies and garnets The ruby is one of the most valued of PRECIOUS STONES; because of its RED color, associated symbolically with the planet MARS. In legends and FAIRY TALES the tradition of the ruby overlaps with that of the garnet or "carbuncle" (from the Latin diminutive of *carbo*, "coal": these gems were popularly believed to glow in the dark like smoldering lumps of coal). Albertus Magnus (1193–1280) ascribed to the carbuncle "the power of all the other stones" and believed that it drove off poison in the form of gas or steam. Hildegard of Bingen (1098–1179) had already written as follows: "Wherever there is a carbuncle, the demons of the air cannot carry out their diabolical mission; . . . so, too, this stone suppresses all human disease." Because of their intense coloration, these stones were often referred to as antidotes to depression, melancholia, and bad dreams. Ancient books of "stone" lore refer to their power to protect against

shipwreck. The ruby came to symbolize vitality, royalty, and passionate love. In the Book of Revelation God's glory is likened to DIAMONDS and rubies. The alchemist Leonhard Thurneysser wrote: "The ruby brings joy, and strengthens the heart" (1583).

runes Symbolic markings resembling (in function) the letters of our alphabet. They developed (presumably through loose imitation of Mediterranean models) mostly among the various Germanic peoples. The traditional sequence of runes does not correspond to our ABC's, which suggests that they developed independently and were not simply an encoding of the Roman or Greek alphabet. The individual runes were thought to be linked symbolically with the magical powers of specific Germanic deities. Although it was not until the early Middle Ages that runes became widely used in ordinary writing in Scandinavia and Jutland, their use at oracles apparently dates back to the first century. With the spread of Christianity, however, such writing (because of its association with older, polytheistic religions) became less common, until it was finally prohibited. In the fervor of modern-day fascistic movements, runes have been lent an almost religious significance for which there is scant historical justification. The *Sigrune*, a LIGHTNING-bolt version of the letter S used in the Third Reich, comes from a rune associated with the SUN, fertility, and the warding off of demons; the *Lebensrune*, used at the end of a word in

Runes. Woodcut from Olaus Worm's book on runes, Copenhagen, 1636

place of an R, originally had ambivalent symbolic associations, with both good and bad fortune, and was traditionally coupled with an inverted triple antler to form a symbol for a pair of twin gods. The "thorn," corresponding to the English sound -th-, was associated with curses. Another rune, symbolizing cattle, property, and wealth, was associated with Freyr, the god of fertility.

Since 1945 neo-Nazi groups in Germany (in their graffiti, for example) have tried to turn individual runes into POLITICAL symbols (compare SWASTIKA)—a complete distortion of their original significance.

salamander In symbolic and folk tradition, not the amphibian known to modern zoologists but rather a creature believed to inhabit the element FIRE as its (divinely appointed, and thus not demonic) guardian and vital source. Paracelsus (1493–1541) believed that the fiery salamander was constitutionally incompatible with humanity, unlike such WATER SPIRITS as undines and melusines, which were known for their great affinities with humans. In speculative writing of the Renaissance salamanders are also referred to as "*vulcanales*"; when they mate with other creatures, the offspring are called "tinder." In the early Christian text *Physiologus*, the salamander is referred to as a reptile, not inhabiting fire but capable of putting it out: "When the salamander enters the boiler of the bath, even those flames are extinguished." The Christian moral drawn from this particular mythic tradition is as follows: the story of Shadrach, Meshach, and Abednego in the fiery furnace [Daniel 3:8–30] must be factual, since God's protection (similarly evoked in Isaiah 43:2: "When thou walkest through the fire, thou shalt not be burned; neither shall the flame kindle upon thee") can be no less powerful than the natural ability of an animal. The *Physiologus* mentions a further attribute of the salamander, but without drawing a moral

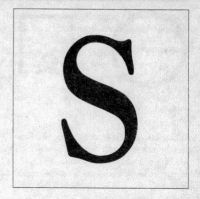

De Salam. A. Lib. II.

Salamander. C. Gressner, *Historia Animalium*, 1585

conclusion from it: the salamander is also referred to as a "bird colder than any other," dwelling in the volcano of Mount Etna but never consumed by its fires. (This may be simply a distortion of the myth of the PHOENIX.)

salt (Greek *hals*, Latin *sal*) A mineral traditionally viewed as indispensable (in the form of sodium chloride for cooking), mentioned in Plato's *Symposium* and also used for the preservation of food. The Latin word *sal* also means "wit," and *salsus* (literally "salty") means "ironical." Homer calls salt "divine"; it was also used for symbolic purification in expiatory offerings and the celebration of ancient mysteries. In ancient Rome salt was rubbed on the lips of infants as protection against danger. There are Syrian myths recounting how the gods taught humans to use salt. Gabiya, the ancient

Salamander "lives from fire and extinguishes it." J. Boschius, 1702

Salt as the "third principle," and salt in the chemical sense. Alchemist's symbols

Lithuanian goddess of sacred FIRE, was honored by throwing salt into the flames. Salt was believed to drive off demons, and, even in the modern era, legends of "WITCHES' sabbaths" refer to the absence of salt from all foods served at the feast.

In the Bible, "salt" symbolizes God's covenant with his people (e.g., "And every oblation of thy meat offering shalt thou season with salt; neither shalt thou suffer the salt of the covenant of thy God to be lacking from thy meat offering: with all thine offerings thou shalt offer salt," Leviticus 2:13); Elisha purified a SPRING by casting salt into it [II Kings 2:19–22]. In the Sermon on the Mount, Jesus referred to his disciples as "the salt of the earth" [Matthew 5:13], and St. Jerome calls Christ himself the redeeming salt that penetrates HEAVEN and EARTH.

There are also references to the destructive effects of salt. After the destruction of Carthage the Romans scattered salt over the surrounding countryside to make it forever barren, as did Abimelech with the conquered city of Shechem [Judges 9:45].

Lot's wife is turned into a "pillar of salt" when she looks back upon the destruction of SODOM AND GOMORRAH [Genesis 19:26].

In India salt was believed to be a powerful stimulant, and ascetics, Brahmans offering certain sacrifices, and newlyweds were all forbidden to consume it.

In the language of ALCHEMY, "salt" refers not to sodium chloride but to the third "principle," alongside SULFUR AND MERCURY, representing the "tangible" (an interpretation that seems to originate with Paracelsus). *Sal*, however, is also mentioned in other symbolic contexts, e.g., *sal sapientiae*, the "salt of wisdom."

The idiom "with a grain of salt" (going back to the Latin *cum grano salis*) is associated with caution, but it has not always implied skepticism as it does today. It originated in a warning from Pliny the Elder (A.D. 23–79) that certain antidotes for poison were to be taken only in combination with a grain of salt.

Samaritan, The Good A symbolic figure originating in the Gospel according to Luke [10:29–37] and standing for all who selflessly come to the aid of the wounded. "A certain man went down from Jerusalem to Jericho, and fell among thieves, which stripped him of his raiment, and wounded him, and departed, leaving him half dead. And by chance there came down a certain priest that way; and when he saw him, he passed by on the other side. And likewise a Levite . . . . But a certain Samaritan, as he journeyed, came where he was: and when he saw him, he had compassion on him, and went to him, and bound up his wounds, pouring in oil and wine, and set him on his own beast, and brought him to an inn, and took care of him. . . ." The city of Samaria (Hebrew Shomron) was the seat of a religious community (on Mount Garizim, and still existing today in Nablus) viewed as heretical by the orthodox Jewish priests of Jerusalem. In the Samaritan tradition Mount Garizim replaced Mount Zion as the "hill of eternity," the "blessed mountain" with PARADISE at its summit. "The water of the Samaritans, according to the rabbis, was more impure even than the blood of swine. . . . Halfway be-

The Good Samaritan. Farmer's almanac, Austria, 1911

tween Jericho and Jerusalem, at a bend in the gorge, an old 'khan,' now utterly dilapidated, is still called 'the Inn of the Good Samaritan,' and in Syria oil and wine are still sometimes poured into wounds when they are bound up" [Daniel-Rops]. Christ's parable teaches that even members of despised groups can act compassionately. In subsequent tradition, the Good Samaritan has come to stand for all of those who selflessly care for the sick and wounded.

sapphire A PRECIOUS STONE symbolically associated, because of its BLUE color, with the HEAVENS and the "ELEMENT" air. In ancient books of stone-lore, it is often confused with lapis lazuli and associated with the planet VENUS, whereas it is otherwise associated with SATURN: in Hindi it is called *saniprijam* ("beloved of Saturn") or *saurinata* ("sacred to Saturn"). The medieval scientist Lonicerus wrote that sapphires make people "joyful, fresh, and devout" and more inclined to peaceful dealings. Traditional symbology associates the stone with heavenly virtues, chastity, and veracity. Albertus Magnus (1193–1280) also believed that sapphires brought "peace and harmony" and made those who came in contact with them "devout and pure in their relationship with God." An Indian sapphire is prominently placed on the crown of the German kaiser. According to the alchemist Leonhard Thurneysser, "The sapphire heals the bite of spider and snake, and when it is rubbed over the bite it improves the victim's eyesight" (1583).

Sappho (in antiquity also "Psappho") Celebrated Greek poet (ca. 612 – ca. 540 B.C.), now symbolically associated with lesbianism (from "Lesbos," the island on which she lived and wrote). In modern terms, Sappho might be considered "bisexual, since, although her erotic poems were not addressed to men, she was married and had a daughter" [Pomeroy, 1985]. Because of the immediacy of her poetic expression and the beauty of her language, Plato referred to her as the "tenth MUSE." Not only Sappho's lyric poetry but also her expressions of po-

litical views and social criticism survive: she criticized her brother, for example, for purchasing a concubine (see COURTESANS) and then setting her free. Sappho's lifestyle should be understood in the context of the cultural influence of nearby Lydia: both there and on Lesbos adolescent girls were entrusted to prominent women for guidance and protection. It is easily conceivable that this also included an erotic component, an arrangement as readily tolerated as male homosexuality. On Lesbos as in Sparta, women were far more highly esteemed than in Athens, and their education was in no way inferior to that of their male counterparts.

In ancient times Sappho had become a legendary figure, her love for girls viewed as a perversion by those who knew nothing of the mores of her culture. It was also said that she had loved a mythical boatman named Phaon (whom a magic ointment from Aphrodite had turned into the most handsome man in the world) and threw herself from a cliff (island of Leucas) to a watery death when he rejected her.

Saturn (Greek Cronus) In Greek myth the father of JUPITER, who deposed him. His reign, in the early days of the universe, was the "GOLDEN AGE." Nevertheless, the PLANET Saturn, in the symbolism of ASTROLOGY, is the great bringer of misfortune, represented as an old man with a peg-leg and a scythe, and having its home in the houses of Aquar-

Saturn and Venus: Astrological personifications. *Practica Teütsch,* 1521

Saturn watering silver and gold trees. Alchemist's symbol, M. Maier, 1617

ius and CAPRICORN. The planet rules the period of a person's life from the age of 69 onward; referred to as "melancholy," Saturn is considered cold, dry, and unfriendly (the opposite of the planet Jupiter). It is associated symbolically with old men, fathers, ancestors, orphans, inheritance, diligent research, great powers of recollection, patience, and meticulous attention to detail, but also with prisons, long solitude, weights and measures. The theme of patience may derive from the long (and, when viewed from the earth, often back-looping) orbit of the planet as it moves across the heavens. Saturn's astrological metal is LEAD, its colors the darker shades of brown and blue, its PRECIOUS STONES onyx, violet SAPPHIRE, dark CORAL, and dark AMETHYST.

In ancient Chinese astrology, Saturn is associated with the center (the fifth point of the traditional Chinese "compass") and with the (yellow) element earth.

Depictions of Saturn as an old man with a scythe play an important role in the symbolism of ALCHEMY, because of the man's supposed proximity to GOLD; there are many legendary Renaissance accounts of the transformation of the gray, terrestrial Saturn metal lead into solar gold after a tiny bit of the philosopher's STONE was dropped into the cauldron.

In Indian astrology the planet Saturn was represented by an ugly, elderly, crippled (probably because of the slow progress of the planet across the sky) ruler, Shani or Manda, riding through the heavens on a black VULTURE or RAVEN.

satyrs Half men, half beasts—with the horns and feet of a GOAT, snub-nosed, and with tails—satyrs seem to have been made in the image of the god PAN, and at the same time to represent an ancient version of the SAVAGE celebrated in modern times. Like Yeti in central Asian legends, they are generally hostile to humans but lusty in their pursuit of sexual gratification. They pursued nymphs and naiads (TREE spirits), who in late antiquity were often portrayed as teasing the satyrs and only pretending to flee their advances. Satyrs were portrayed among the followers of Dionysus (BACCHUS), the god of WINE; the Dionysian drama festivals included bawdy farces known as "satyr plays" (the origin of our word "satire"). "Satyriasis" is a term used in modern medicine to designate an uncontrollable male sex drive.

In Greek mythology we also find the Sileni, similar creatures to satyrs, with hooves, tails, and ears like those of HORSES. Silenus was Dionysus' (usually drunken) tutor, often shown as a fat, old man riding on a DONKEY.

Satyr: Companion of Orpheus. Floor mosaic, Palestine, 5th century

savages and spirits of wild nature Inhabitants of the wild play a significant role in symbology and heraldry. They traditionally personify nature in its untamed state, before the coming of civilization, and thus are in many ways comparable to GIANTS. Savages are also frequently described as being larger than ordinary human size. The SATYRS, Sileni, and fauns of ancient legend, along with the nature god Pan, are classical versions of the inhabitants of the wild whose traces a great variety of cultures have followed. Similar humanoid, half-animal creatures also appear in Native American legends and the folklore of Central Asian peoples. In recent years it has often been debated whether these creatures are mere projections of the unconscious (embodiments of unrestrained drives, a yearning for total realization of desires) or whether there is also a primordial memory of earlier life forms at work here. It has even been hypothesized that in remote regions there could be extant "survivors" of the earliest forms of human life (e.g., *Homo erectus* or the Neanderthal) and that they explain ever recurring rumors of Yeti, Dremo, Mihgö, Almas, and Almasti (Asia) and Sasquatch and Bigfoot (North America). In Central America, too, there are tales of a savage forest-dweller, Yum K'ax of Lacandón myth. In many of these cases, the oc-

Savages: Father and child. Woodcut, H. Schäuffelen, ca. 1520

casional findings of footprints lend some element of credibility to the otherwise apparently incomprehensible traditions. Some have hypothesized that these creatures inhabit a middle realm between worlds of occult imagery and "hard facts." There are historians of religion, on the other hand, who believe that the collective memory of the human race retains old beliefs in guardian spirits of the forests and nature in general, and that at times of stress, excitation, or loneliness (especially in forest surroundings) these spirits can produce visions or hallucinations of hairy, APE-like forest dwellers. (See also HORSE, GOAT.)

In HERALDRY we find these "wild men" most often appearing to hold the coat of arms (e.g., the arms of Prussia).

In the medieval collection *Gesta Romanorum* (ca. 1300), the spirits of the wild are monstrous beings (called *"monstra et portenta"*) symbolically reflecting the shortcomings of (civilized) humans, who are all too prone to complacency. The man with the head of a DOG, the Cynocephalic, for example, "speaks with a bark and wears animal pelts," and symbolizes penitents, who "should wear animal skins, i.e., do penance openly, so that others might profit from their example." Other models for emulation are the

Savages: Civilized satyr. Aubrey Beardsley (1872–1898)

Savages: Horse-Silenus in dancer's pose. Vase painting, Greece, ca. 450 B.C.

"Complaint of the Wild People of the Woods, about the Faithless World," which includes the following indictment: "How ill-bred is our youth, how devoid of virtue our elders, how shameless the image of woman, how savage that of man," so that by contrast even the "real" savages seem civilized, living far from supposed civilization and the corruption that it brings.

According to analytic psychologists, such creatures come from the darkest "FOREST," the "uncleared" part of the psyche. Aeppli notes that this realm is traditionally perceived as dangerous, "because we are not supposed to be creatures of the forest, nor

Savages: Silenus. Wilhelm Busch

women in distant India "who have BEARDS that reach to their breasts but whose heads are totally bald. These are the just, who follow the correct path of Church teachings and cannot be diverted from it by love or hatred" (presumably because their unusual appearance assures that they will not be tempted to yield to the desires of the flesh; for a similar legend about St. Cummernus, also known as Wilgefortis or Liborada, see BEARD.) Negative examples, on the other hand, are "people with HORNS, pug noses, and goat's legs. They are the proud, who display the horns of their arrogance for all to see, and have for their own salvation only the tiniest nose for introspection and when they run after pomp and splendor have the legs of a goat. For the goat runs fast and climbs with ease. This applies to the haughty of this world."

As a result of the ambiguity of these creatures of the wild as models for human behavior, they evolved away from the lusty prototypes from the ancient world (satyr, faun, Pan, Silenus) or Scandinavian legend (trolls) and often became on the contrary symbols of unspoiled life, far from the intemperance that ruined SODOM. A woodcut by Hans Schäuffelein (Nuremberg, late 16th century), inspired a text by Hans Sachs, a

are we supposed to return to that state, or to that of goblins or dwarfs. Even the gentlest hermit, if he never leaves his grassy ravine and humble cottage, if no one seeks him out in his solitude, ceases to be truly human: he himself becomes a tree, an old animal, the forest itself, and thus totally nature."

In the Chinese tradition, the yeh ("forest," "savage state") has similar associations: uncultivated terrain surrounds the "savage" (yeh-jen), the barbarian thought of as inhabiting the forests that once covered most of the land. ROBBERS were called the "people of the green forests."

Scales and fasces, attributes of Justice. Cartari, 1647

scales Symbolically important not only as the sign of the zodiac Libra but as a general symbol for justice and the just proportion; in many cultures, associated with the judicial system, earthly justice, and Justice with her blindfold (as an indication that when meting out justice she must not be subject to influence). According to the ethical doctrines of retribution held by many religions, there is a court of justice in the AFTERLIFE as well, to consider our good and bad deeds from this life—e.g., the ancient Egyptian court of the dead in which the god Osiris, in the presence of Maat, the goddess of justice, weighs the HEART of each person

who has died and thus decides that person's fate in the afterlife. The Tibetans and ancient Persians likewise believed in otherworldly courts of justice to examine lives led on earth. In ancient Greece, Zeus was said to use scales to measure out the fates of mortals. In the Christian tradition, the scales symbolize most importantly Christ as the great judge who will hold them on the Last Day and determine whether each of us, as we stand before the Seat of Judgment, is to be remanded to the PARADISE of HEAVEN or the eternal torments of HELL.

The witch's scales of the Dutch city of Oudewater were of more than symbolic importance: they were used to determine whether an accused person had been levitated by the DEVIL or had the normal weight of an ordinary mortal.

In the astrological interpretation of the STARS and their apparent movements, Libra is the seventh sign of the zodiac; those born under this sign are said to be characterized by moderation, "deliberation," justice, harmony, peaceful temperament, and hesitancy—a choice of qualities influenced by a belief that names predict reality (*"nomina sunt omina"*). "A false balance is abomination to the Lord: but a just weight is his delight" [Proverbs 11:1].

In the symbology of FREEMASONRY, a set of WATER scales is the insignia of the second

Scales: "Here pushed down, there uplifted." J. Boschius, 1702

Scales: Level helps to satisfy upward longings. J. Boschius, 1702

foreman of the Lodge, so that he can "maintain equality in each Lodge, without regard to the social rank" [Baurnjöpel].

scarab The dung beetle; of great symbolic importance, first in ancient Egypt, then throughout the Eastern Mediterranean. This originated in the phonetic resemblance of the words meaning "scarab" (*chepre*) and "to come into being (in a specific form)" (*cheper*), and in the theory formulated by Plutarch as follows: "It is assumed that this species of beetle consists exclusively of males, and that they place their semen in the material that they roll into balls. They then roll these balls onward with their hind feet. They imitate the movement of the sun, except that it moves from east to west, and the scarabs move their dung-balls in the opposite direction." This theory led to a symbolic association of BALL, SUN, autogenesis, and renewal; the god Chepri was the symbolic figure of the rising sun, "generated from the earth." Mummies wear a "heart scarab" as an amulet on their breasts, and scarabs lent their form to both SEALS and jeweled charms that protected their wearers against evil. The Phoenicians and Carthaginians imitated the Egyptian scarabs and

Scarab from necklace of King Tutankhamen. 14th century B.C.

executed them in hard semiprecious stones like jasper and carnelian; by the fifth century B.C. they were popular among the Greeks and Etruscans as well. Etruscan scarabs were found in all Mediterranean markets and were traded as far off as the Crimean Peninsula.

The scarab was also an early Christian symbol for the Resurrection.

scepter (Latin *sceptrum*) A sign of the power and majesty of a KING or EMPEROR, ceremonially held by him like the "imperial APPLE" in some traditions. Typological forerunners of the scepter may include branches, clubs, and SHEPHERD's staffs. The European scepter has a knob at the top called a *sphaera* (compare "sphere"), representing the all-embracing nature of royal or imperial power. The "THUNDER-bolt" (Sanskrit *vayra*, Tibetan *dorye*) of Lamaism is also called "the

Scepter with goat heads. Bronze, Nahal Mishmar, Dead Sea, ca. 3200 B.C.

DIAMOND scepter" and "the symbol of indestructible wisdom."

An unusual version was the "little man scepter" used ceremonially in the southern Mayan region of Central America, which had a grotesque deity with a long, snout-like nose (presumably a representation of the RAIN god Chac) in the place of the *sphaera*. At the lower end was frequently the head and body of a SNAKE.

In Christian iconography canonized rulers (e.g., Sigismond of Burgundy, Charlemagne, Stephen of Hungary, St. Louis) often have the scepter as an attribute. In depictions of the Passion, Christ is often shown with a reed scepter corresponding to the CROWN of THORNS (see Matthew 27:29).

The scepter (*ju-i*) of ancient China was a symbol associated not with the emperor but with reverence for elders. The *ju-i* (homonymous with the words "as it is desired")

Scepter with ring, wreath, and diamond, together symbolizing the necessary ingredients for marital bliss. Hohberg, 1675

was made of JADE and presented to revered old men, or to the family of the bride at traditional weddings. In Chinese rebuses it expresses a wish that the recipient might be successful.

scorpion This arachnid, with its dangerous venomous sting, has for obvious reasons long been associated symbolically with deadly menace, but also with veracity. A king of ancient Egypt, ruling before Menes united the country and formed the first dynasty, was named Scorpion (Selek), and the feminine form of the word (Selket) named the patroness of magical healers. Ancient incantations to ward off "stinging reptiles" express the hope that divine magic will be stronger than any poison. The goddess Isis (Eset), fleeing from Seth (Sutech), the slayer of Osiris (Usire), took SEVEN scorpions with her.

According to the astral mythology of ancient Greece, Artemis, the goddess of the hunt, sent Scorpius to kill the mighty hunter Orion, and they were both translated to the sky. This is why, whenever (the constella-

Scorpion to ward off Gyalpo demons. Tibet

tion) Scorpius appears in the eastern sky, the otherwise undaunted Orion flees below the horizon.

In the Bible the scorpion, like the serpent (see SNAKE), symbolizes demonic powers and is mentioned in the Book of Revelation in this function among the creatures of HELL. Dangerous sects are also likened to scorpions, but they also appear as symbols of logic and dialectic in depictions of the "seven liberal arts" (see LADDER). In medieval art the scorpion also symbolized the continent of Africa.

In the religion of the Mayas the black god of war Ek-Chuah was portrayed with the tail of a scorpion.

In ASTROLOGY Scorpio is the eighth sign of the zodiac, through which the sun moves from October 23 until November 21. Its

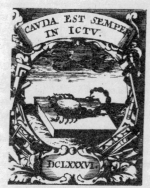

Scorpion, "always prepared to sting." J. Boschius, 1702

principal star is the reddish Antares (the "anti-MARS"); the sign is governed by the planet Mars (color: RED; metal: IRON). Traditionally Scorpio has been associated with male sexuality, destruction, the occult, the mystical, illumination—and, to offset the arachnid's venom (as in ancient Egypt), healing and resurrection. In this way even a potentially dangerous sign is understood as ambivalent: a source of change, a symbol of the triumph of life over death. (See also LOCUST.)

Seal of city of Meersburg on Lake Constance. Middle Ages

Seal. Stone, Larissa (Greece), ca. 4500 B.C.

seal (Greek *sphragis* [origin of the word "sphragistics," the study of seals and signets], Latin *signum* [origin of the word "sign"]) In Greece and Rome signet RINGS (later superseded by the first stamps and stamppads) were used to attest to the authenticity of a document. (Seals were first commonly used in Mesopotamia, in the form of a rolling apparatus adorned with drawings and cuneiform characters.) The seal came to symbolize legitimacy and the personality of the individual. Thus in the Bible it is written: "Bind up the testimony, seal the law among my disciples" [Isaiah 8:16]. The Book of Revelation is famous as the "book of the seven seals," which the LAMB opens one by one. Numerous idioms refer symbolically to the use of seals: "under the seal of silence," "under hand and seal," "signed, sealed, and delivered," "to put one's stamp on something."

seven After THREE, the most significant of sacred NUMBERS of the ancient civilizations

Seal of knight (Henry de Percy), 1301

of the Middle East. In Sumerian and Akkadian texts there are said to be seven demons, represented by seven points and figuring in the constellation Pleiades (see STARS). In Judaism the traditional number is echoed in the seven branches of the Menorah (see CANDELABRA AND CANDLESTICKS). The number may originate in the division of the 28-day lunar month into four weeks, or in the seven "planets" (SUN, MOON, MARS, MERCURY, JUPITER, VENUS, and SATURN). In the Book of Revelation the number seven plays a major role: seven churches, the seven horns and eyes of the LAMB [5:6], seven heads of the dragon [12:3], the seven vials of the wrath of God [15:7] in the book "sealed with seven seals" [5:1]. A famous "seven scene" in the Old Testament is also associated with divine wrath: seven priests with seven rams' horns (i.e., shofars; see TRUMPET) circled the walls of Jericho for seven days. On the seventh day they "compassed the city seven times," the Israelites gave a battle cry, and the walls of Jericho fell [Joshua 6:6–20].

In the Parsi religion of ancient Persia seven "immortal saints" were revered as the supreme spirits (Amesha Spentas): good intentions, utmost fairness, the longed-for kingdom of God, pious modesty, perfect health, rejuvenated immortality, and watchful obedience.

In medieval Europe there was a predilection for series of seven: the seven gifts of the Holy Spirit (represented in the Gothic era by DOVES), seven VIRTUES, seven arts and sciences, seven sacraments, seven "ages

Seven "planets" associated with days of the week; seven-pointed star

of man," seven deadly sins, seven petitions in the Lord's Prayer.

Although in ancient China the number seven, being uneven, must have been associated with the masculine principle *yang* (see YIN AND YANG), it was used in determining the ages of a woman's life: when she is 2 x 7 years old, the "way of yin" (i.e., menstruation) begins; at the age of 7 x 7 it ends (menopause). Seven times seven days were involved in the cult of the dead: on every seventh day after the person's death (until the 49th day) there were sacrifices on his or her behalf. On the seventh day of the seventh month there was a major festival for

women and girls. In China the enumeration of seven planets was of less traditional importance than the earlier system (presumably imported from India) including only FIVE (Mars, Mercury, Jupiter, Venus, and Saturn). (See also GODS OF HAPPINESS.)

In German, a nagging, disagreeable (married) woman (see also XANTHIPPE) is called a *böse Sieben* (literally an "evil seven"). This usage may go back to the "seventh house" of a person's horoscope, associated with marriage; an unfavorable aspect in the seventh house was believed to bring marital strife. According to another explanation, the *böse Sieben* comes from the seven in one older version of the deck of cards: on this seven there appeared the devil's likeness, and the card could beat any other. A third

Seven stars around eye of God. Emblem of German mystic Jakob Böhme (1575–1624)

theory mentions Mary Magdalene, "out of whom went seven devils" [Luke 8:2].

shadows In symbolic tradition, shadows are not merely the result of obstructions to the passage of light, but rather dark entities with a nature all their own. They are mysterious doubles of the persons who cast them, and are often understood as images of those persons' souls. (Thus some languages have a common word for "image," "soul," and "shadow.") H. Kolmer has suggested that the often severely elongated, silhouette-like representations of men and women in the rock drawings of the early Holocene epoch, may have been taken from shadows cast by the SUN when it was close to the horizon— presumably because the direct representation of the human figure was taboo. In many cosmologies the souls of the dead in the

Seven Liberal Arts, Philosophy. Reisch, *Margarita Philosophica*, Strasbourg, 1508

AFTERLIFE are thought of as shadows—hence the word "shades" in this sense—so as to represent their lack of corporeality. The absence of a shadow (e.g., if it has been sold to the DEVIL) implies the loss of one's soul. In legend, being unable to see one's own shadow (or stepping on one's own shadow) is taken as a sign that one is marked for death. We find repeated references to avoiding contact with the shadows of dreaded persons (e.g., WITCHES), lest one come under their power. Philosophers often speak of the material world of appearances as a mere shadow of the true ideal world (see, for example, the metaphor of Plato's CAVE).

For the Jungian psychologist, the shadow symbolizes the unconscious layers of the personality that are integrated into the complex structure of the experienced world—and susceptible of transformation—only through the process of individuation.

Idiomatic references to shadows require little explanation: "to stand in someone's shadow," "to be afraid of one's own shadow," "to confuse shadow and substance," "foreshadowing," "a shadowy existence." (Note, also: "to put someone in the shade.")

The angel's annunciation of Christ's birth includes the statement: "The power of the Highest shall overshadow thee" [Luke 1:35]. "In the shadow of God's wings" [from Psalm 17:8] was a frequent motto of the devout, e.g., J. V. Andreae (1586–1654), the spiritual father of the Rosicrucians ("*Sub umbra alarum tuarum Jehova*").

Of considerable symbological significance is the view presented in the Letter to the Hebrews that the rituals and offices of the levitical priesthood of Christ's day amount to merely "the example and shadow of heavenly things" [8:5; compare 10:1]. The early Christians saw the events of the Old Testament as symbolic anticipations and prophecies of the story of Christ and the institutions and rites of the Church—a more advanced stage of the story of salvation, duly "foreshadowed" by what had gone before. The "typology" of the illuminated manuscripts of the Middle Ages, such as the *Bible Moralisée*, offers an allegorical exegesis of the Old Testament, finding for almost every passage a corresponding text in the New Testament and thus a Christian interpretation.

sheep The ewe and the RAM are opposed symbolically much like the cow and the BULL, or the male and female of the GOAT. Our associations with the undifferentiated "sheep" go back to the "ewe" tradition of a harmless, or even stupid, creature, the most likely to fall prey to the WOLF. The ram, on the other hand, is a symbol of strength, vitality, and unwavering determination.

The sheep, one of the first domesticated animals, had to be watched over by SHEPHERDS; it came to symbolize helplessness in the face of any and all predators. Its ingenuousness made it easy to lead astray, and W. H. von Hohberg presents it as a pious parishioner listening to the wolf's sermon: "Simplicity doth fall a victim swift to guile/ Like sheep that harken to a wolf's shrewd homily./ The devil, when he speaks, assumes an angel's style,/ Yet every word is nought but Godless travesty" (1675).

In the symbolism of the LAMB, the innocence of the sheep is further intensified; there are many depictions of the lamb's ultimate triumph over the DEVIL.

Sheep: St. Saturnalia, who hid from a wooer among a herd of sheep. W. Auer, 1890

The proverbial bellwether (the sheep that leads the flock) is a castrated ram ("wether") wearing a "bell."

shepherd (Latin *pastor*) The symbolic image of the herder of sheep and lambs, caring for his flock and protecting it against enemies; the flock represents the submissive followers of a spiritual leader. The image was an obvious one to nomadic peoples, like the Jews of ancient times, in whose lives animal husbandry played a major role. The young DAVID defended his flock against the LION and the BEAR; the God of Israel was

Shepherd. Etching, Ludwig Richter (1883–1884)

Shepherd as worshipper, with baby lamb. Mari, Mesopotamia, ca. 1750 B.C.

referred to as the shepherd of his people [Psalm 23:1], and kings were his representatives on EARTH. Later Christ referred to himself as "the good shepherd" [John 10:11, and elsewhere], a familiar motif in Christian art, but one that also appears in non-Christian contexts (e.g., Hermes Criophorus: see RAM): the shepherd, carrying on his shoulders a lamb that has been placed in his care, symbolizes caring for the helpless. MOSES, leading his people through the wilderness to the Promised Land, and later the Pope, have been likened to shepherds. According to the Gospels, Christ's birth in Bethlehem was announced to shepherds. Common attributes of the shepherd are most often the crooked staff, after which the bishop's crosier (often a richly adorned object with ivory carvings) is modeled, and in many cases, a

straight staff with a spade-like end, with which the shepherd can pick up STONES and cast them away. The insignias of the KINGS of EGYPT, the lash and the crooked SCEPTER, are modifications of the fly-flap and shepherd's staff, respectively. Communications from bishops to the members of their dioceses are called "pastoral letters," and Christian clergy are routinely called the "pastors" of their "flocks." The young JOAN OF ARC is frequently shown tending her sheep before she is summoned by the voices of ANGELS. The "pastoral romances" of the baroque period and thereafter sentimentalized the supposedly idyllic life of shepherds, written by city dwellers with no notion of its rigors.

Shepherd: Christ as the Good Shepherd. Austrian farmer's almanac, 1911

Shepherd: The Good Shepherd. Early Christian cata-comb relief, Sousse, Tunisia

ship In symbolic tradition, the vessel that transports heavenly bodies, especially the SUN, through the HEAVENS (the ship replacing the CHARIOT), or the dead to the other world (see AFTERLIFE). Neolithic drawings of ships—clearly symbolizing the voyage to the ISLANDS OF THE BLESSED—frequently adorn the walls of megalithic graves. Similarly, Bronze Age Swedish drawings of ships (each with a double stem suggestive of the front of a toboggan) are presumably symbolic representations of cosmic events rather than depictions of real ships. The sun boats placed in the water near the Gizah pyramid stand for the ships that were believed to transport the sun across the sky every day; when this world was in darkness, the sun was understood to be illuminating the realm of the dead, making its way back to the point on the eastern horizon where it would appear on the morrow. In Christian iconography and elsewhere, ships and boats frequently symbolize voyages, including our voyage through life. "The life of this world is a raging sea which we must navigate on our journey homeward. If we are able to withstand the sirens' song (*Odyssey*), we will reach the harbor of eternal life" [St. Augustine]. The Church is often referred to as a ship, especially as a sort of Noah's ARK, carrying the faithful to salvation: the church tower is likened to a mast and its buttresses to oars. The CROSS is spoken of at times as a mast, at times as the ANCHOR of our hope. Scenes in the New Testament by the Lake of Gennesaret (Sea of Galilee) and along the routes of the Apostle Paul's voyages provide further connections.

In many cultures real-life ships have been thought of as having a magical life of their own, as the frequent carving of animals'

Ship: Nicholas, patron saint of seafarers. W. Auer, 1890

heads on the stems (and, later, the figureheads) of ships suggests. For reasons of technical necessity, the ancient Egyptians built boats for Nile voyages with severely upturned bows, but depictions of such crescent-shaped vessels may also be references to the MOON: near the equator the lunar crescent appears less severely bowed than in higher latitudes.

Many Christian saints have ships as attributes—Brendan the Seafarer, Athanasius, Nicholas (patron saint of seamen), Peter,

Ship of the sun, with falcon-headed Horus holding ankh. Egypt

Ship: Voyage to the afterlife. Coptic grave marker, Terenuthis, Egypt, ca. 450 B.C.

Vincent, and Ursula—as does the goddess Isis, who was revered in late antiquity in many Roman provinces.

Ships are endowed with symbolic significance in ancient China as well. Hsün-tsu, for example, in the third century B.C., offered the following comparison: "The ruler is the boat, the people the water. The water carries the boat forward, but can also capsize it."

sibyls In modern languages the word "sibylline" is applied to darkly oracular hints or pronouncements. This is a reference to the inspired women prophets of ancient Greek tradition, whose number and origin are given differently by different authors. Most often we read that there were ten sibyls. They are referred to as Chaldean or Hebrew, Persian, Delphic (a daughter of Apollo), Italic, Cimmerian, Erythrean (the sibyl who took up residence in Cumae); Cymerian (named Amaltheia or Herophile), Hellespontian (from Marpessos), Phrygian, and Tiburtian (named Albunea or Aniena) in origin.

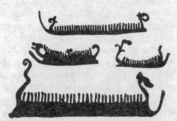

Ships with embellished stems. Cave drawings, southern Sweden, Nordic Bronze Age

The sibyl of Cumae is referred to most frequently. She is said to have traveled from her native Asia Minor to Italy, then led Aeneas to the underworld and lived on for a thousand years. Like Pythia of Delphi, she is an oracle of Apollo. The last three of her "books" (said to treat omens, catastrophes, monsters, processions, and sacrifices) were preserved in Rome in the Capitoline temple but burned in 83 B.C. The sibyls live on in the frescoes of the Sistine Chapel.

The *Sibylline Oracles*, on the other hand, are hexameter verses composed much later (in the fifth century), Christian warnings of disasters to come.

Sickle aloft: attribute of St. Notburga. W. Auer, 1890

sickle This ancient harvest tool of prehistoric farming societies (dating from the Neolithic) was first made from flint; it later became a cult symbol, associated with the lunar crescent (see MOON). Curved SWORDS were often called sickles (e.g., the weapon of the god Marduk, the tutelary deity of the city of BABYLON). The god Cronus used a sickle to castrate the primeval god Uranus, before he himself was struck down by his son Zeus' (JUPITER) lightning, deposed, and banished. The sickle remained the attribute of Cronus (Latin SATURN), who must be viewed as a pre-Hellenic god of fertility. His name later became confused with that of

Sickle held by Priapus, god of fertility. Cartari, 1647

the personification of time (CHRONUS), who came to be portrayed with the sickle (or, later, the scythe) as a reminder of the unrelenting flow of time. In this sense the sickle and the scythe became established as symbols of DEATH.

Siegfried A legendary figure from the world of the *Song of the Nibelungs (Nibelungenlied)*, who came to be stylized as the heroic ideal of the blond Germanic youth, especially through German romanticism (early 19th century) and Wagner's *Ring*. References to Siegfried are found outside German-speaking countries as well: the bunker system along the Western boundary of Hitler's Germany (called the "West Wall" in German) was referred to in England and the United States as the "Siegfried Line."

The hero of the Old Norse *Prose Edda* is the DRAGON-slayer Sigurd, the son of Sigmund and Hjördis. When he has killed the

Sickle-sword, insignia of the Mangbettu king Munsa. Africa, 19th century

dragon, Sigurd eats its HEART and is able to understand the language of BIRDS. He later meets the VALKYRIE Brynhild, seeks her HAND in marriage for King Gunnar, and himself marries her sister Gudrun. Still young, Sigurd is murdered in his sleep by Gunnar's half-brother Gutthorm.

In the Danish version the hero, named Sivard, rescues the proud Bryniel from the glass mountain on which she is imprisoned (the counterpart of the "flickering flame" that surrounds Brünhilde's mountain in Wagner's version, for example).

In the earliest versions widely circulated in written German, the hero is the "horned Siegfried," who bathes in a dragon's BLOOD to make his skin impervious to his attackers. There are old ballads in which he is said to have slain both GIANTS and dragons.

The fascination of the Siegfried motif seems to have been extraordinary: a young hero with features "like those of the sun itself" is treacherously betrayed and loses his life, then is avenged through the intrigues of his widow (Kriemhild, in the modern version), but at the cost of countless other lives. "Sigurd was struck down, south of the Rhine,/ And from his branch the RAVEN cried out:/ Atli's blade ere long will taste your blood, /And treachery seal the murderer's fate!" [*The Old Song of Sigurd*, 5]. (For Atli, see ATTILA).

silver One of the "noble" metals, like GOLD; generally associated with the MOON itself or lunar deities, and valued somewhat less than gold ("Words are silver; silence is golden"). In ancient Mexico silver was called "the white excrement of the gods" and was also thought of as the terrestrial counterpart (or feces) of the moon god. In the writings of European alchemists the name of the moon goddess Luna is usually used for silver. Because it was somewhat cheaper than gold, silver jewelry came to be associated with middle-class prosperity; it was frequently used to make devotional objects. Silver was popularly believed to ward off demons. Priests were said to have buried silver statues along the borders of the Roman Empire to ward off barbarian invaders, whom they believed to be demonic; when the statues were re-moved, Goths, Huns, and Thracians swept over the empire. Silver bullets were believed to wound or kill storm WITCHES when they were fired into dark CLOUDS.

six A NUMBER of interesting symbolic sig-nificance. The creation of the world is the "hexaemeron" (six days' labor) after which God "rested on the seventh day" [Genesis 2:2]. St. Augustine considered the number six significant because it is the sum of the first three (1 + 2 + 3). The six acts of corporeal mercy described in the Gospel according to Matthew [25:35–36] form one of the few symbolic series in the Christian tradition that are based on the number six. One important visual symbol incorporating the number is the HEXAGRAM, the STAR of DAVID formed from two TRIANGLES.

In ancient China the celebrated first EM-PEROR, Shi Huang-ti (ruled 221–210 B.C.), founder of the Middle Kingdom, preferred a six-based system and divided his empire into 36 military provinces, each administered by one civil and one military governor; the subsequent Han dynasty introduced a NINE-based system. The predominant conceptual system of ancient China was based on the number FIVE, but there were traditionally six parts of the body (head, torso, two arms, two legs), six emotions (anger, pain, hatred, joy, desire, love), six RIVERS, and six great kings. To the traditional five points of the Chinese "compass" (the Occidental four, plus the center) was occasionally added a sixth: the vertical axis (see ABOVE/BELOW).

skeleton In shamanistic cultures human skeletons, or scrawny human figures with highly visible bone structures, symbolize the emotional experience of disintegration undergone by initiates to the world of the trance. Similar depictions can also symbolize ascetic renunciation. Most often, however, skeletons are viewed as symbols of DEATH, since bones last beyond the decay of the flesh and under favorable conditions can be conserved for thousands of years. Depictions of the Last Judgment (see END OF THE WORLD) often show skeletons arising from their

Skeleton: "Burial" of *"materia prima."* Alchemist's al-legory, *Musaeum Hermeticum,* 1678

graves—which, in the symbolism of AL-CHEMY, promise resurrection and rebirth of "primal" or "first" matter (*materia prima*) after "blackening" (*nigredo*) and "putrefac-tion." Usually, however, a skeleton is a visual metaphor personifying death—hold-ing an HOURGLASS and a scythe (or SIC-KLE)—serving in depictions of the DANCE OF DEATH as a reminder that "in the midst of life, we are surrounded by death" (*"Media in vita in morte sumus"*), an especially pop-ular motif in periods in which epidemics (like the "black death") ravaged Western Europe.

slipper In Central Europe this traditional footwear of women is (perhaps through im-

Skeleton, representing death, comes for a fool. Sebas-tian Brant, *Ship of Fools,* 1494

plicit genital symbolism) frequently their "heraldic emblem" in male jokes and cautionary tales about the "henpecked" husband (in German, *Pantoffelheld,* "slipper hero," who is also said to "stand under the slipper"). The sandal is said to have been the signature of the Lydian QUEEN Omphale, whom Hercules was forced to serve as a slave in woman's clothes. There is a Hellenistic sculpture that shows Aphrodite brandishing a sandal, threatening a lecherous faun. Various explanations have been offered for the modern association of the slipper with female domination. For example, in certain regions of Austria it was customary that during the wedding ceremony each partner tried to step on the other's foot; the loser was destined to spend the rest of his or her life under the slipper. The gesture of kissing a person's feet as a sign of submission, e.g., the Pope's slipper with its embroidered CROSS, is also mentioned in this context. In Lower Austria a *Pantoffelheld* is also called a "*Simandl,*" perhaps meaning "she-man"; in Krems he is immortalized by the "Simandl Well." Mythic accounts of the AMAZONS and of ancient matriarchies appear to have arisen as comparable male-to-male warnings against female domination.

snail   This mollusk, best known in popular speech for its slow rate of movement (a "snail's pace"), is of symbolic importance for its harmonically formed spiral shell. Because the escargot seals itself inside its shell with a "lid" that it subsequently knocks off to re-emerge after winter or drought are past, snails came to symbolize the resurrection of Christ. The fact that they carry about their own "houses," moreover, made them allegorical figures of self-sufficiency: the snail is the creature that has all its "belongings" with it at every moment. Hildegard of Bingen explored the medicinal properties of substances extracted from snails (their shells, powdered, were effective against worms; extracts from slugs soothed boils like similar preparations from earthworms). She used the word for TURTLES (*testudines*) to refer to snails.

Snail: "I take all my property with me." J. Boschius, 1702

snake   A symbolic animal with highly ambiguous associations. For many ancient civilizations, the snake symbolized the underworld and the realm of the dead, apparently because it spends much of its life in hiding and in pits below the surface of the earth, but also because of its apparent ability to be rejuvenated through the shedding of its skin. The snake moves effortlessly without the aid of feet, emerges from an EGG like a BIRD, and can often kill with its venomous bite.

The snake has such remarkable natural associations with life and death that it plays a significant role in most cultural traditions.

The Biblical serpent, the embodiment of Satan in the Garden of Eden, later becomes the "serpent of brass" "put upon a pole" by Moses [Numbers 21:8–9], interpreted as an archetype of Christ crucified [John 3:14–15]. Aaron's rod was transformed into a serpent capable of devouring those of Pharaoh's sorcerers [Exodus 7:9–12].

In Norse mythology a huge snake (Jörmungandr) is wrapped around the earth, a symbol of the sea, not unlike its ancient Egyptian counterpart, the gigantic Apophis, which threatens to capsize the boat of the SUN god.

The early Christian text *Physiologus* offers curious versions of the snake's symbolic significance: because it sheds its skin, the snake is associated with rejuvenation (the Christian, too, should slough off the "old age of this world" and strive for the rejuvenation of eternal life); when the snake drinks from the SPRING it leaves its venom behind in its CAVE so as to keep the water pure (thus the Christian in pursuit of the water of eternal life must leave behind the poison of sin); snakes bite only those who are clothed, shying away from the NAKED (thus we should cast off the "fig leaf of lust" and be "naked of sin," so that evil cannot have its way with us); finally, a snake in danger protects only its head, leaving the rest of its body open to attack (thus we are to protect only our head, i.e., Christ, never denying him, but sacrificing our bodies like the martyrs).

Of particular symbolic significance is the snake biting its own tail (Greek UROBORUS), which stands for the cycle of eternal return, or for eternity in general. In the alchemistic tradition it is associated with cyclical processes (evaporation and condensation, alternating successively), the state of "sublimation" often being represented by WINGS.

Symbolic traditions tend to stress the negative role of the snake (e.g., the danger of its venomous bite); thus the creatures thought of as killing snakes (EAGLE, STORK, FALCON) have come to have positive associations. Older systems of myth, however, include mysterious positive aspects of the snake, often because of its associations with the

Snake rejuvenated by shedding its skin. Hohberg, 1647

Snake: Giant stone head of plumed serpent. Main temple of Tenochtitlán (Mexico City)

earth and the underworld. A house snake, for example, can represent the blessings of departed ancestors. (Crowned, milk-fed snakes appear in many popular legends.) The snake is also associated with healing and reincarnation (e.g., the sacred snakes of ASCLEPIUS; see also CADUCEUS). For the ancient Egyptians, the snake Uraeus (the bellicose cobra) stood for the CROWN, spitting venom at the Pharaoh's enemies; it was also represented as coiled around the solar disk associated with various sun gods.

In the pre-Columbian civilizations of Central America, the snake (Aztec *coátl*) appeared as the fifth day-sign of the calendar. The snake being thought of as poor and homeless, it mostly portended ill for those born under this sign, who were expected to become peddlers and warriors, forever wandering with no fixed abode. The plumed serpent Quetzalcóatl (adorned with the green feathers of the quetzal bird), however, was a divinity of great religious significance, apparently representing a harmonization of the duality bird/snake (and thus heaven/earth). (The Mayan name of the plumed serpent was Kukulcan.) The bird/snake polarity is represented, for example, in the arms of Mexico City (in Aztec, Tenochtitlán), which show an eagle perched on a cactus with a snake in its claws. Throughout the world such pairings are of great significance as symbols of the union of polar opposites. [See M. Lurker, *Adler und Schlange*, 1983.]

In Goethe's prose work entitled "Fairy Tale," the snake symbolizes the spread of pure humanity. Traditionally, however, snakes are thought of as fear-inducing. Such mythic creatures as BASILISKS and DRAGONS

Snake: Naga, guardian of temple gates in Hindu iconography

are exaggerated versions of the snake and its menace. In psychoanalysis snake phobia is interpreted as fear of a "phallic symbol."

In philosophic systems of Asiatic origin the kundalini snake, coiled at the base of the spinal column, symbolizes vital energy to be awakened and elevated through meditation. (See also CROCODILE.)

Snake-like creatures play an important role as "guardians of the TREASURES of the earth" in ancient Indian symbolic tradition. These benevolent demigods, called "Nagas," are often portrayed by sculptors as humans with snakes' bodies, standing guard at temples. Poisonous snakes, however, were seized by the GRIFFIN-like "golden-plumed sun bird Garuda" and destroyed, according to myth. Still, the snake was the most revered of animals after the COW and the APE, primarily because of its shedding of its skin (associated once more with renewed life) and because of its proximity to WATER, the element of life (associated with fertility). The god Vishnu rests on a world-snake; the gods and Titans rolled the body of the snake Vasuki around the world-mountain Meru when they churned the primeval "sea of MILK" into butter. The cobra goddess Ma-

nasa ruled the earth whenever Vishnu slept. Snake-like creatures came to embody the powers and aspects of various divinities.

The snake (she), the fifth symbol in the Chinese zodiac, is thought of as dangerously sly. A person whom we might call "two-faced" was described by the Chinese as having "the heart of a snake." On the other hand, meandering RIVERS were spoken of as snakes, and legends and fairy tales relate how grateful snakes reward their benefactors with PEARLS. Owning a snake skin was thought to assure that one would attain wealth. As in Western psychoanalysis, dreams of snakes were interpreted sexually: the snake's body represented the penis, and the triangular head the female pubic triangle. In Chinese astrology, the snake governs 1989, 2001, and every 12th succeeding year.

Rock paintings reveal that in the cultures of southeast Africa giant snakes stood for RAIN and for water in general; in addition, they are depicted as horned fantasy creatures, as in the myths of this region. In eastern Africa we also find paintings in which a great snake seems to represent the surface of the earth, its undulations suggesting peaks and valleys [H. Kolmer].

In the Shinto tradition of Japan we find a myth not unlike those of Hercules (struggle with the three-headed hydra), Perseus (see GORGONS), and St. George: the storm god Susano-o finally defeated the giant eight-headed snake Yamata-no-orochi, discovering in its tail a sacred SWORD and freeing the snake's prisoner, the princess Inadahime, whom he married. Storm winds are generally portrayed as destructive in Japanese myth (they destroyed the sacred RICE fields planted by the sun goddess Amaterasu), but they also purify, which made it possible for Susano-o to assume the role of the slayer of the great snake.

The serpent in the Garden of Eden, which led Eve to disobey God's commandment not to eat of the fruit of the Tree of Knowledge, is called Samael in medieval Jewish legend, a name also associated with Lucifer, the Prince of Darkness. The serpent, it is written, thinks as follows: "If I speak with the man, he will not listen, for a man is inflexible. Thus I shall address the woman first, who is more susceptible. I know that she will listen to me, because a woman will listen to anyone!"

Jungian psychology views the snake (like all other reptiles) as a symbolic creature going back to the earliest ages of the earth and the human race. In Ernst Aeppli's words, the snake "inhabits an incomprehensible natural region"; it is "an image of exceptional, primordial forces. All of our experience indicates that it is a major symbol of psychic energy. When a snake appears in a dream it represents powers from the depths of the psyches of others, powers as old, we might say, as this primordial reptile itself."

In figures of speech it is usually the negative aspect of the snake that is stressed: a "snake in the grass," a "cold-hearted snake," and a "viper" are all treacherous persons. Indeed, the expression to "nurse a viper to one's bosom" (to give protection to a person of whose treachery we suspect nothing) goes back to ancient times. (Compare medieval sculptures portraying a naked woman with two snakes at her breast, representing the VICES Lust and Sexual Pleasure.)

Sodom and Gomorrah   In the Old Testament, the names of two Canaanite cities in the plain of the RIVER Jordan, which are said to have been destroyed as the result of divine judgment; they are also mentioned by Strabo (63 B.C.–A.D. 19) and Tacitus

Sodom and Gomorrah. Copy of a drawing in the Merian Bible, Strasbourg, 1625

(55 B.C.–A.D. 16). So far no archaeological evidence has been found to support the tradition of the two godless cities beside the Dead Sea (referred to in rabbinical literature as "the Sea of Sodom"). The Book of Genesis speaks of the moral turpitude of the citizens of Sodom, whose men wanted to rape two male visitors to the city (actually ANGELS sent by God). "Then the Lord rained upon Sodom and upon Gomorrah brimstone and fire from the Lord out of heaven; and he overthrew those cities, and all the plain, and all the inhabitants of the cities, and that which grew upon the ground. But [Lot's] wife looked back from behind him, and she became a pillar of salt. . . . The smoke of the country went up as the smoke of a furnace" [19:24–28]. Sodom thus came to symbolize an immoral city like BABYLON. (The use of the word "sodomy" in the sense of "bestiality" seems to have no grounding in the Biblical passage.) In the Book of Deuteronomy it is written: "For [the] rock [of our enemies] is not our Rock, even our enemies themselves being judges. For their vine is of the vine of Sodom, and of the fields of Gomorrah" [32:31–32].

The medieval collection *Gesta Romanorum* (ca. 1300) offers a strange explanation for the moral decay of the city of Sodom: it was gluttony that "lured the people of Sodom to sin. . . . Their godlessness came from having eaten too much bread and sated themselves with it. . . . Thus let us ask the Lord that we might remain temperate on earth, so as to be invited to his table in heaven."

When Adit, Lot's wife, looked back, she was turned into a pillar of salt, which, according to Jewish legend, is still to be found at the same place: "The OXEN in this region lick at it every day, until only the toes of her FEET remain, but by the next day the part they had licked away has grown back" [bin Gorion, 1980].

Solomon   (in Hebrew Shelomo or Shlomo) The wise KING of Israel (961–931 B.C.), is best known today for his famous judgment determining the true mother of a disputed child ("Divide the living child in two") [I

Solomon: "Divide the living child in two" (I Kings 3). Gustave Doré (1832–1883)

Kings 3:16–28]. He was the son of King DAVID and Bathsheba; he established peaceful relations between EGYPT and Phoenicia, undertook merchant voyages, reorganized the army, simplified the administration, and brought prosperity to his people. In intellectual history his construction of the temple in Jerusalem is of great importance; this temple is of particular importance in the legend of FREEMASONRY, in which the master builder Hiram Abif, who was murdered by three journeymen laborers, is the great martyr for his rank and for the conservation of its secret watchword. "Through Solomon's construction of the temple, God came to choose in Jerusalem his fixed abode. The holy site, previously transient with or within Jerusalem, came to rest; similarly, the Chosen People will come to rest in the Promised Land. The glory of God inhabits the temple, and it is filled with his presence. Yahweh chooses the temple as the abode of his holy name" [A. Stöger, quoted in Bauer]. In Biblical tradition Solomon is known as an author of Proverbs, part of the deuterocanonical Book of Wisdom, and, most prominently, the Song of Solomon, a collection of wedding songs full of erotic ardor, often understood as the text of a cult celebration of the *hieros gamos* (see MARRIAGE AND WED-

DINGS AS SYMBOLS) of heaven and earth, or as a celebration of conjugal love; in Church tradition, however, the text is understood as an allegory, the love of husband and wife standing for God's love for his people, Christ's love for his Church, and the mystical union of the soul with the divine prime mover.

The HEXAGRAM, or six-pointed star, came to be known as the *sigillum Salomonis* ("Solomon's seal") or *scutum Davidis* ("David's shield"), then as the Star of David.

Somnus (Latin for "sleep, dream"; Greek *Morpheus* [hence, "morphine"]) The god of DREAMS. There is no consensus on the equating of the Latin and Greek names, since this figure is more a literary than a mythological one. In Ovid's *Metamorphoses* the god of dreams has a thousand sons, corresponding to the multiplicity of dream visions. In poetry the name Morpheus can refer to dream visions in human form; Icelus or Phobetor, those in animal form; and Phantasus, to any inanimate object in a dream. To be "in the arms of Morpheus" is to sleep or dream. (See also HYPNOS.)

Sophia (Greek "wisdom") A philosophical concept, associated with scholarship, mastery, skill, and devices. Complete *sophia*

Sophia as mother of Faith, Hope, and Charity. W. Auer, 1890

was attainable only by the gods; a human could only strive for it, aspiring to be a *philosophos* ("lover of wisdom")—a view that seems to originate with PYTHAGORAS. In the later doctrines of the Gnostics, the *Pistis Sophia* was revered as a person and a divinity of symbolic origin; in Christianity, as divine wisdom (*Hagia Sophia*), human wisdom being a mere symbolic reflection of the divine. Among Christian saintly legends we find that of St. Sophia (Latin *Sapientia*), the mother of (the three theological VIRTUES) Faith (Fides), Hope (Spes), and Charity (Caritas), who are said to have been martyred under the Emperor Hadrian (A.D. 117–138).

Sphinx of Greek mythology. Cartari, 1647

soul-hole   (German *Seelenloch*) A term for the round opening in stones used to seal prehistoric megalithic graves; presumably symbolic in significance. It has been suggested that these holes were to enable the souls of the dead (thought of as fog-like shapes) to leave their graves, watch over the living, then return; or that they served as actual entrances for practitioners of ancestor worship, who brought sacrifices to the interior of the tomb (although the openings are mostly too small for this purpose). According to a theory proposed by D. Evers of Wiesbaden, the first hypothesis is correct, and the openings were supposed to correspond to the heavenly North Pole, the point through which the AXIS MUNDI passed. Thus the grave openings also offered access to the heavens, linking the underworld, the world of the living, and the world above for those who had moved on to the AFTERLIFE. Evers

Soul-hole: Soul-hole in the entry stone of a megalithic grave. Paris basin, Neolithic

sees the stone graves themselves as representing the underworld.

sparks   Symbolically speaking, tiny bits of actual LIGHT, floating upward from the domain of base matter into the higher realms—across the DUALITY ABOVE/BELOW. The duality spirit/matter, as it appears in Orphism, Pythagoreanism, Essenianism, and other philosophies and religions with Gnostic leanings, begins with the belief that minute bits of the divine spirit or of the ether are buried in us and that they attain the realm of light, as souls without bodies, when they have freed themselves from the "bondage of the flesh." The Chassidic mystic Rabbi Samuel Rav Shmelke of Mikulov (died 1778), formulated the duality as follows: "All souls are divine sparks. When any spark is sunk in the swamp and mire, will we not feel sorrow for it? Will we not help it to free itself, so that it can once more light up with its full brilliance? It is, after all, a part of God himself . . ." [Langer].

sphinx   The Greek designation for a mythical creature with the body of a LION and a human head, known especially through the monumental sculpture at Giza (187 feet tall). Whatever fantastic hypotheses have circulated, the sphinx at Giza does not date back to the earliest ages of the earth: it is a depiction of the pharaoh Chephren (ca.

Sphinx with head of Queen Hatchepsut. Ca. 1490 B.C.

2600 B.C.), with a lion's body to symbolize his invincibility. (The "king of the beasts" was supposed to indicate the ruler's superiority to the rest of the human race.) Other KINGS of ancient Egypt (e.g., Sesostris III, Amenemhet III) were also portrayed in this form; queens were so portrayed only in rare cases.

The female sphinx of Greek tradition has its origins in a fairy tale motif. This sphinx was often winged, always female, a demon lurking at the side of the road, challenging travelers to solve her riddle and devouring all those who could not—until Oedipus succeeded in matching wits with her. She thus came to symbolize the riddle of human existence, the existential question that hu-

Sphinx, winged. Ivory, 2 inches high, Asia Minor, ca. 500 B.C.

manity is challenged to answer. It is this sphinx with her "mysterious" smile that was a favorite subject of mannerist and baroque painters and sculptors.

spider (Greek *arachne*) In the myths of many peoples, a symbolic creature with negative associations; occasionally, a cunning "trickster," as in the often comic Ananzi tales of West Africa. Most of these traditions begin with a feeling of distance from a creature capable of spinning a web and lying in wait to paralyze FLIES and gnats and suck them dry. In Christian symbolic tradition the spider is the "evil" counterpart of the good BEE; the spider generally stands for the sinful urges that suck the BLOOD from hu-

Spider of Native American myth. Shell engraving, Mississippi Mound civilization

manity. In popular tradition, however, it can also stand for the soul: it was believed that the souls of sleeping persons could leave their bodies in the form of spiders (or, in another version, LIZARDS) and subsequently return.

" 'Come into my parlor,' said the spider to the fly": most cultural traditions conserve the image of the spider as a treacherous creature never to be trusted. (See, for example, Jeremias Gotthelf's 19th-century novella "The Black Spider.") Nevertheless, in some alpine regions of Central Europe the garden spider, because of the CROSS on its back, is considered a good-luck symbol and a sacred creature that must not be killed. In ancient China as well, a spider is an omen of impending good fortune, e.g., the return of a "prodigal son." The spider, lowering itself on its thread, was associated with the expectation of joys descending from HEAVEN.

In Ovid's *Metamorphoses* the goddess Athena (in other contexts a paragon of fairness) is described as furiously jealous of the Lydian princess Arachne's skill as a weaver. When Athena saw that Arachne had produced a flawless tapestry depicting the amorous adventures of the gods, one finer even than any the goddess herself could weave, she destroyed the tapestry and transformed the proud princess into the creature she most hated, a spider; filled with trepidation, the transformed Arachne crawled off into the recesses of her web. (See also SPINNING.)

Spinning: The Three Fates with the thread of life. Cartari, 1647

spinning Frequently associated with supernatural female triads (FATES, Moirae, NORNS) who spin, gather up, and cut the threads of fate. Women's spinning in general has often been associated with the MOON, whose three major phases (full moon, first or third quarter, and new moon) suggest the three figures of Hecate (*Hecate Triformis*) [Graves]. (The *weaving* of the threads of fate is similarly considered to be the task of supernatural females.) Spinning and distaffs play an important role in the symbolism of FAIRY TALES, where they are likewise associated with fate and death ("Sleeping Beauty") and often

Spinning. Fairy tale illustration, Ludwig Richter (1803–1884)

with triads (Brothers Grimm, "Of Wicked Flax Spinning"). Through the moon's apparent death and resurrection, the spinning goddesses of fate are associated with the themes of the underworld and rebirth. In Christian iconography the Virgin Mary is often portrayed holding a distaff (e.g., with the archangel Gabriel in depictions of the Annunciation); this is also a reference back to Eve, who was also frequently portrayed spinning. The association of Mary and the lunar crescent is frequent throughout the centuries.

Spinning was thought of as the domain of the goddesses and priestesses in a great variety of contexts. For example, in the ancient Mayan culture of the Yucatan, Ixchel (under the aspect of the goddess Chac-chel) is a moon goddess portrayed with a weaving stool; as Ixcanleom, she is also associated with the SPIDER.

In medieval Europe the spindle, a symbol of the contemplative life, is also an attribute of certain female saints (JOAN OF ARC, portrayed as a shepherdess; St. Margaret; St. Genevieve).

We speak idiomatically of spinning "yarns" and every other product of the imagination; here our association is not only with the spinning of thread but also with the spider's construction of its web. Even in present-day usage, the word "distaff" is used to replace "female": e.g., the "distaff side" of a family.

spiral An ancient graphic symbol, found throughout the world, and related to the CIRCLE, especially to systems of concentric circles, which are not always distinguishable from spirals at first glance. Although there have been very different interpretations of the two symbolic forms, it is possible for hastily drawn concentric circles to become a spiral, and thus overlapping readings of the two cannot be ruled out. The spiral is fundamentally a dynamic system incorporating a movement of either rolling up ("involution") or unwinding ("evolution"), according to whether the movement is considered to proceed from the center outward or from the outside inward. The spiral, whose macrocosmic manifestation (in the winding fog of the cosmos) is invisible to the naked eye, may have first been observed in the movement of flowing water, or of any liquid descending through an opening. In any case, the spiral may have become associated with a sinking into the "waters of death" (see AFTERLIFE), as did the pattern of concentric waves generated when something breaks through the surface of a lake; this would explain the frequent occurrence of spirals on megalithic graves of prehistoric times. It is also possible, however, that these designs referred to the movement of the STARS through the night sky. It has frequently been seen that these petroglyphs are struck by rays of the SUN coming through cracks in the structure, on solstices in par-

Spiral: Coiled snake as playing board. Limestone, predynastic Egypt, ca. 3500 B.C.

ticular. Since the sun also "sinks into the western sea" every evening, only to reappear the next morning in the east, the presence of these spiral drawings may also relate to notions of death and resurrection.

In cultures familiar with the potter's wheel, spirals may be grounded in the simple observation that these forms are produced by moving an object (or finger) through the damp, spinning clay. Mere "doodling" can also produce figures of this sort; there need not be any deep symbolic significance.

The double spiral is of particular interest, since it combines evolution and involution in a single unity. It is thus possible to read in the double spiral both waxing and waning, growing up and falling off, and in whichever order one chooses. It is in this double sense, perhaps, that we should interpret the double spiral in the pubic TRIANGLE of a Neolithic "mother goddess" statuette from Trace. In Romanesque sculpture double spirals are sometimes placed in the folds of Christ's garments.

In prehistoric burial structures we also find triple spirals, whose significance (beyond mere decoration) is lost to us. Similarly, the association that symbologists have proposed between spirals and LABYRINTHS remains only a hypothesis, although the notion of "a difficult path in and out again" is consonant with the symbolic tradition of death and rebirth.

Spiral (triple) adorning the megalithic grave "New Grange." Ireland, Bronze Age

springs Considered sacred places in many ancient cultures, often because of the notion that the WATER that fertilizes the earth comes to its surface not only as RAIN from the HEAVENS but also as a gift from the subterranean divinities below. This is especially prevalent in the case of hot or warm springs, whose water has medicinal properties because of its mineral content. Naiads and other supernatural beings were revered at these sites, often within the cults of gods and goddesses of healing and purification. In the Greek, Roman (the Fontinalia festival), Celtic, and Germanic traditions it was usually female figures, often in TRIADS, who were associated with springs, and simultaneously with fertility, childbearing, and marriage. In China and Japan small shrines were often placed alongside springs. The Chinese character for "spring," *ch'üan,* can be constructed from elements meaning "pure" and "water"; it is also a cognate of the word for "origin."

The Bible refers to the FOUR RIVERS of PARADISE as flowing from a single source [Genesis 2:10–14], which becomes a symbol of rebirth and eternal life. In the Book of Revelation it has its counterpart in the "heavenly JERUSALEM" [see esp. 22:1–2], the wellspring of life in the new-found paradise of the Last Day. In the typological tradition of scriptural exegesis, which interprets events in the Old Testament as prefiguring moments in the life of Christ, MOSES' striking of the ROCK to produce the water of Meribah [Numbers 20:7–13] is related to the stigmata of Christ, whose blood brings salvation, and similarly to the water of baptism. Van Eyck's Ghent altar shows the heavenly spring dividing into SEVEN rivers, corresponding to

Spring symbolizing God's inexhaustible benevolence. Hohberg, 1675

the seven gifts of the Holy Spirit. (See also WELLS.)

The medieval collection *Gesta Romanorum* (ca. 1300) contains several novellas in which springs are important symbols; in one, a spring in Sicily that makes sterile women fertile and another makes fertile women sterile. "Interpretation: In the case of the former, we are to think of Christ, who makes a sterile person—a sinner—fertile and able to carry out works of mercy. The other spring is the devil, who opposes such transformations and often brings a good person to a bad end. . . . In Epirus there is a spring that extinguishes blazing TORCHES and ignites torches that have gone out. Interpretation: In the same way Christ puts out the bright torches—the 'wise'—of this world, and lights up the poor, whose flame this world has extinguished." In dream symbolism a spring, often near a TREE, is interpreted as a distinctly positive symbol of the "water of life." "When the dreamer hears the rustle of the tree and the rush of the spring, security is not far away: the fountain of youth is at hand" [Aeppli].

Springs. From J. Boschius's *Symbolographia,* 1702

square In symbological tradition often designated by the successively more comprehensive terms "rectangle" and "tetragon"; a geometrical symbol associated with quadripartite spatial orientation, the organization of our domain according to the points of the compass and their supernatural guardians. As with the CROSS, the square is an indication of our wish to find our way in an apparently chaotic world by introducing di-

Square: Gothic window pattern, adapted to the square

rections and coordinates. Inherent in the square is an ordering principle that seems innately present in all humans; the figure forms a DUALITY with the CIRCLE, a form associated rather with the heavenly powers. The legendary "squaring of the circle" (i.e., constructing a square equal in area to a given circle, using only geometrical means) symbolizes the wish to bring the heavenly and terrestrial elements into an ideal harmony (Latin *coincidentia oppositorum*).

The design of many TEMPLES is based on the square, their gradations suggesting the cosmic MOUNTAIN of the universe (e.g., Angkor Wat in Cambodia). In the Temple of the Heavens in Peking (Beijing), as in the Borobudur (Java) the square is joined with the circle. Not only the city planning of the ancient Romans (cities made up of equal quadrants) but also such imaginary cities as the "heavenly JERUSALEM" of the Book of Revelation or J. V. Andreae's "Christianopolis" (17th century) further illustrate this model for the ideal city—a version of the cosmos, built to human scale, with its own AXIS MUNDI erected at the center. In ancient China, Persia, and Mesopotamia, the earth is represented as a square; in ancient India, it is referred to as *chaturanta* ("having four sides"). According to Chinese tradition, the *ho-t'u* ("river map"), a cosmological "magic square" divided into nine fields, came from the Hoangho. In the Old World, similar squares were constructed, in various contexts, from letters

and numbers; the interchangeability of the letters to form intelligible words, or the uniformity of the sums of rows or columns, was intended to symbolize harmony with the laws of the cosmos.

In GAMES, too, we find expressions of a tetradic cosmology, as in *patolli* (ancient Mexico) or the chessboard of the Old World, or the board on which the German game of *Mühle* is played, with its three concentric squares and the "ladders" that connect them. The design of the *Mühle* board is anticipated in cave drawings found in Austria, Italy, France, on the Isle of Man, the Balkan peninsula, and in Afghanistan (the Pamir region), as well as in prehistoric ceramics of the Villanova and Este civilizations (Italy). The cave drawings are found not only on horizontal but also on vertical surfaces, indicating that the designs were not used solely for "board" games but had symbolic significance as well, as representations of the cosmos.

In the MANDALAS used for meditation in Indian Buddhism we find a combination of the circle (a symbol of enlightenment, *bodhi*, directed toward the community, *sangha*) and the square to form a figure of harmonious union (see YANTRA).

See also EARTH and CUBE.

square, carpenter's Like the drafting COMPASS, an architect's instrument of considerable symbolic importance, appearing both

Carpenter's square and drafting compass held by master builder. Woodcut, 1536

Carpenter's Square: The right angle. J. Boschius, 1702

in Dürer's etching "Melancholia" and as an attribute of the apostle Thomas (the patron saint of builders). It continues to be significant in the symbology of FREEMASONRY, in the context of "right": the right angle stands for that which is right, for justice, the true law. The Master of the Lodge wears a miniature carpenter's square on his chest as a symbol of the powers and duties of his office. Otherwise, the right angle is often combined with the PLUMB LINE and the scales (the "three movable jewels" symbolizing the Master and his two lieutenants; the "immovable jewels" are raw stone, hewn stone, and the DRAWING BOARD, representing apprentice, lodge brother, and Master, respectively). A carpenter's square with unequal arms in the ratio 3:4 refers to the Pythagorean theorem, since it makes it possible to draw a TRIANGLE whose sides are in the ratio 3:4:5. According to J. Baurnjöpel (1793), the carpenter's square represents "the love of God and neighbor, with which [the Master] must be richly adorned; this jewel—which embraces all laws—also urges every brother, from his first entry into the temple onward, to practice every virtue of which a person is capable."

The carpenter's square was an important symbol in ancient China also. It appears in the hand of the mythical scholar Fu-hsi (or Fuxi), who is said to have invented the I CHING and is depicted with the underbelly of a SNAKE. The square symbolizes both edification and the sanctifying power of magic.

squirrels Once viewed with distrust. The squirrel Ratatöskr ("rat-tooth") of Norse mythology constantly ran up and down the world-tree Yggdrasill and sowed strife between the EAGLE atop it and the DRAGON Nidhogg, by repeating to each one what the other had just said about it. The squirrel was also associated with the fiery Loki and consequently then in the Christian era with the DEVIL, who seemed to be embodied in the reddish, scurrying, elusive rodent.

stars "Fixed stars" light the HEAVENS at night and are considered symbols of cosmic order because of the regularity of their movement around the pole star (see AXIS MUNDI); they also stand for the "light from above," which is not always discernible. In many mythic traditions the stars are understood as resulting from metamorphoses of those who have died. Jewish speculative cosmology believed that every star had a guardian ANGEL and that constellations were harmonious groups of heavenly spirits. In Christian iconography the presence of stars indicated heavenly occurrences. The ceilings of ancient Egyptian burial chambers were adorned with depictions of a starry firmament. The VIRGIN Mary was often depicted not only standing on the lunar crescent but also surrounded by a halo (see NIMBUS) in the form of a star-studded CROWN. The great number of stars in the sky was used to symbolize the countless descendants

Sciurus.

Squirrel. Woodcut in Pseudo-Albertus Magnus, 1531

Stars: "Blazing Star," with G. Masonic symbol

of ABRAHAM. Christ proclaims himself "the bright and morning star" [Revelation 22:16]. The Star of Bethlehem, usually surrounded by eight beams, is of particular importance: it guided the Wise Men from the East to the manger where the Christ child lay. The six-pointed star (today called the Star of Zion or Star of David), made up of two triangles, was known as the *sigillum Salomonis* ("Solomon's seal") or *scutum Davidis* ("David's shield"). (See HEXAGRAM.) The five-pointed star, or PENTACLE, played a major role in the tradition of magic; it is considered a favorable symbol when one of its points is at the apex, and in the inverted position a sign of BLACK magic.

In ancient China the stars were closely observed (11,520 had been counted by the second century after Christ), and they play a major role in Chinese legends and customs. On New Year's Day, for example, everyone offered a sacrifice to "his" or "her" star.

In the symbolism of FREEMASONRY the "blazing star" (usually five-pointed, surrounded by beams, and with a G in the middle, for "geometry," "God," or "Gnosis") is of particular significance: it symbolizes the LIGHT of the spirit.

The PLANETS (literally "wanderers") are distinguished from the "fixed" stars throughout the tradition of symbology. (See PLANETS, CIRCLE.)

The Incas of Peru believed that the stars were "the handmaidens of the moon, and therefore gave them the chamber next to their mistress (in the temple of Cuzco), so that they might be at her beck and call. They believed that the stars moved through the heavens with the moon, as her servants, and not those of the sun: after all, they were visible at night, not during the day" [Gar-

Stars: Correspondences of zodiac, body parts. Ratdolt, *Flores Albumasaris*, 1488

cilaso de la Vega]. The Aztecs of Mexico viewed the stars as heavenly manifestations of the first fallen or sacrificed warriors; this is why they are sometimes represented in Aztec art by empty skulls.

Ancient cultures had differing interpretations for shooting stars—they marked the death of important men (ancient China) or the birth of a child, whose soul was descending from heaven to earth, where it would come to life.

Colloquial references to a person's "lucky star," or to something as "not being in the stars" (i.e., not meant to be), indicate the widespread acceptance of certain astrologi-

Stars: "Count them if you can." J. Boschius, 1702

Stars: Jupiter as ruler of the zodiac. Cartari, 1647

cal themes. "To reach for the stars" is to attempt to bring about the apparently impossible. If we "see stars" we are perceiving flashes of light after sustaining a blow to the head or some comparable experience. "Stars" (or "luminaries") are also illustrious celebrities, especially from the world of show business.

The symbolism of constellations is not always easily explained. Only a few of them clearly form connect-the-dot images of the figures for which they are named. Without a considerable leap of the imagination it is difficult to recognize a SWAN, lyre, maiden, and LION in the constellations Cygnus, Lyra, Virgo, and Leo, respectively; indeed, it is only the rare constellation (e.g., Orion, Cassiopeia) whose stars can be readily seen as forming a separate entity. This is why old maps of the heavens superimpose drawings of figures over the stars themselves; the

drawings often seem to have little connection to the actual constellations. In fact, other cultures refer to the constellations by different names from those used in the Western European tradition, or even group the stars differently. The earliest use of constellations was as a navigational guide for the first seafarers; it was at this time that they were linked to legends and myths. The most important constellations were those that seemed to disappear, in turn and according to the time of year, at dusk and reappear with the sun at dawn. These were organized into a system based on the number 12 and referred to as a "circle of animals," the zodiac (from Greek *zoidion*, diminutive of *zoion*, "animal"), which divides the ap-

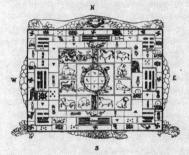

Stars: Tibetan cosmogram with zodiac figures bordering the central field

parent path of the sun into 12 "houses": Aries, Taurus, Gemini, Cancer, Leo, Virgo, Libra, Scorpio, Sagittarius, Capricorn, Aquarius, and Pisces (see RAM, BULL, TWINS, CRAB, LION, VIRGIN, SCALES, SCORPION, CENTAUR, CAPRICORN, WATER SPIRITS, and FISH). Some of these names were already in use in the ancient civilizations of Mesopotamia and were taken over or altered by the Egyptians and the Greeks. The sun is associated with each constellation for the approximate duration of one lunar cycle (one month). Popular astrology attributes to each sign characteristics generally derived from the symbolic tradition of the constellation; the "sun sign"

Stars: Paths of fixed stars around the celestial North Pole. Time exposure, 1898

is thought to determine, or at least influence, the character of those who are born "under" it.

(The ancient Chinese zodiac is made up of entirely different signs: RAT, OX, TIGER, HARE, DRAGON, SNAKE, HORSE, SHEEP, MONKEY, ROOSTER, DOG, and PIG. Each year is associated with one of these animals, and the year of a person's birth determines which animal's characteristics he or she shares.)

Incidentally, the region of the heavens associated with a "sign" of the Western zodiac is no longer the same as the region in which the corresponding constellation is actually to be found; the zodiac is in this sense regularly "displaced" as a function of time. The signs and the constellations were perfectly aligned some 2500 years ago, which suggests that the signs of the zodiac were first defined around that time. A Babylonian text from the year 420 B.C. referred to them as Laborer (for Aries), Pleiades (for Taurus), Twins (Gemini), Crab (Cancer), Lion (Leo), EAR OF GRAIN (held by a maiden, or Virgo), Scales (Libra), Scorpion (Scorpio), Centaur (as an archer, hence Sagittarius), "Goat-Fish" (for Capricorn), Gula (for Aquarius), and "Two Tails" (for Pisces).

The 12 signs of the zodiac have been grouped in a variety of ways, e.g., in three "crosses," to each of which four signs belong: the "cardinal cross" (Aries, Cancer, Libra, and Capricorn, associated with the four archangels Gabriel, Raphael, Michael, and Uriel); the "fixed cross" (Taurus, Leo, Scorpio, and Aquarius, associated with the ancient "guardians of the four corners of the earth" and thus with the four EVANGELISTS: Luke/bull, Mark/lion, John/EAGLE, Matthew/ANGEL [or -/man]); and the "movable cross" (Gemini, Virgo, Sagittarius, and Pisces). They were also grouped in threes, with one of the "four ELEMENTS" associated with each group (fire: Aries, Leo, Sagittarius; earth: Taurus, Virgo, Capricorn; air: Gemini, Libra, Aquarius; water: Cancer, Scorpio, Pisces). In classical antiquity the individual signs had already been associated symbolically with the same characteristics as today, as the text "Trimalchio's Banquet" by Petronius (d. A.D. 66) indicates. (It was also said that "nomina sunt omina" ["names are portents"]; parents took great care in selecting names for their children, as is still the case today.) The basis of the entire doctrine of correspondences between signs of the zodiac and personality traits seems to have been formulated and promulgated most significantly in Hellenistic Alexandria in the second century after Christ.

The rejection of traditional star worship, as it was still practiced in historical times by the Sabeans in Harran, is grounded in Islamic tradition in the legend of the patriarch ABRAHAM, who, it is said, spent the first 15 years of his life hidden in a CAVE and eating from Allah's hand. (Abraham was evading the pursuit of King NIMROD, who feared the loss of his kingdom.) Then his mother led him out into the open, under the protection of the ANGEL Gibreel (Gabriel). "When Abraham glimpsed the evening star, the sole light in the night sky, he thought that it was the supreme being and wanted to worship it; but the star grew dim, and Abraham swore never to worship anything that dropped from sight. He had the same experience with the rising moon and with the early-morning sun. Each time he was tempted to view them as supreme and worship them. But when they had dropped below the horizon he was saddened and thus came to see that he must worship only the one who had created these lights and put

Stars: Ursa Major never sets. J. Boschius, 1702

Stars: Zodiac. Engraved brass plate, Middle Ages

them in orbit" [Beltz]. In strict monotheistic doctrine the lights in the heavens are only symbols of the Creator. The search for the ultimate master has a different manifestation in the Christian legend of St. CHRISTOPHER.

In Christian systems, the signs of the zodiac, being 12 in number, were readily associated with the 12 Apostles: Aries with Peter, Taurus with Andrew, Gemini with James the Greater, Cancer with John, Leo with Thomas, Virgo with James the Less, Libra with Philip, Scorpio with Bartholomew, Sagittarius with Matthew, Capricorn with Simon, Aquarius with Jude, and Pisces with Matthias. (See also PRECIOUS STONES.) The traditional number of the planets, SEVEN, takes on special symbolic associations through the reference in the Book of Revelation to "seven stars" which are "the angels of the seven churches" in Asia to which John's message is specifically addressed [1:16, 20]. The number of signs of the zodiac, 12, appears in the form of 12 stars, which crown the heavenly woman in Revelation 12:1. Stars falling from the heavens are harbingers of the END OF THE WORLD. The Christmas star, which the three Magi (astrologers) followed to Bethlehem, is often portrayed in art as a comet.

Stars appear frequently in coats of arms: in German HERALDRY often in the form of six-pointed stars, in English five- (or, less frequently, eight-) pointed. Goethe chose as his coat of arms a six-pointed star on a BLUE field, in memory of the appearance of the morning star (VENUS) in a clear sky (1775; recognized 1782). A constellation (the Southern Cross) has adorned the arms of Brazil since 1889. White stars on the flag of the United States, symbolize the individual fifty states. In the arms of Singapore there are five stars, standing for democracy, peace, progress, law, and equality.

stepmother (German *Stiefmutter*) Unlike the mother-in-law, who plays a negative maternal role only in modern-day humor, the stepmother as the wicked anti-mother—the selfish enemy of her stepchildren—is found in fairy tale and idiom; she is ready even to kill her wards, and is thus not far removed from the most negative of female figures, the WITCH. The cause for this devaluation of a female figure who in real life is rarely characterized by her proverbial "wickedness," may lie in a relationship to the birth mother which has not been properly processed but whose direct negative expression convention has rendered taboo. The prefix "step-" comes from a root that means "bereft" and is related to the words "stub," "stoop," "stint."

The stepmother is of particular importance in the German-speaking world, where the idiom that is translated literally as "to complain to one's stepmother" means "to waste one's breath"; similarly, "to weep at one's stepmother's grave" is to feign sorrow. In the Brothers Grimm the figure of the stepmother is often literally a witch (as in "Snow White"). "Since Mother died, we haven't a moment of happiness. Our stepmother beats us every day, and when we go to her, she kicks us away" ("Little Brother and Little Sister"). (The one German exception to this general trend is the use of the diminutive *Stiefmütterchen* as the word for "pansy," the flower *Viola tricolor* prized in folk medicine. This usage, which dates back to the 16th century, has not been satisfactorily explained; the highly sentimental 19th-century language of FLOWERS offers an interpretation particularly surprising in the German context: the pansy "looks so sweet, so loving, so good, like the gentle mother's heart that gives faith, hope, and love to the child of another.") In German or in English, the lot of a "stepchild" is to be neglected: "Public assistance programs became the stepchild of the new administration."

steps and stairways Symbolize the ascent to a higher plane, closer to HEAVEN. In ancient cultures TEMPLES are often terraced (the ziggurat of Mesopotamia, stupa of South Asian Buddhism [e.g., the Borubudur of Java], teocalli of ancient Mexico, or similar structures on the Peruvian coastline). The temples of ancient Greece were built on terraced foundations. Climbing steps clearly corresponds to an "archetypal" longing of the psyche to approach the heavenly spheres of the cosmos; this same longing underlies the notion of sacred MOUNTAINS. To rise above the everyday sphere and attain a higher one is to approach God. Terraced temples were constructed not only as surrogate mountains for flat regions like Mesopotamia but also in mountainous areas, e.g. the Mexican highland (Teotihuacan). This structure suggests that the actual construction of steps enabling a sort of ascent into heaven was itself important, and not merely the ascent *per se*.

Steps to philosopher's stone. Alchemist's allegory, St. Michelspacher, 1616

In the symbolism of FREEMASONRY the steps depicted in allegorical tapestries represent degrees of initiation. Three steps correspond to moderation, justice, and benevolence. SEVEN steps (also depicted as rungs of a ladder) represent the seven liberal arts of the medieval world, the seven ages of man, and the seven "cardinal virtues," believed to lead to self-knowledge, -mastery, and -improvement. The point seems to be that this material cannot be communicated all at once but must come gradually: the candidate must not be taxed, but rather shown the way step by step.

stone With its characteristic durability and permanence, stone is for many cultures a symbol of divine power. Other important features are that SPARKS can be made by striking some stones, and that others (meteorites) have fallen from the sky or have unusual forms. In the early stages in the progress of humanity, stones were used to make tools and weapons; this procedure presumably required that our remote ancestors distinguish between stones of varying qualities. The practice of building sacred structures from massive stones (megalithic dolmens, stone circles, alignments) is widespread and goes back to around 6000 B.C. (see MENHIR). In several myths supernatural beings and even humans are made from stones (see FLOOD). In the ancient Middle East a stone was a sign of God's presence and was covered with libations or anointed with oil and BLOOD. It thus became an altar (Beth-El, "the house of God"). Even simple heaps of stones (Kerkur in Northern Africa, Obo in Central Asia) have symbolic religious significance. The prestige of stone blocks formed by nature, not fashioned by human hands, is expressed in Exodus 20:25: "And if thou wilt make me an altar of stone, thou shalt not build it of hewn stone: for if thou lift up thy tool upon it, thou hast polluted it." For this reason strictly observant Jews disapproved of the splendor of the JERUSALEM TEMPLE [Aron].

In ancient Greek myth a stone replaces the supreme god in the pantheon. The primeval god Cronus (SATURN) feared that a son of his would supplant him as he himself had castrated and driven out his father Uranus; Cronus therefore devoured his children. His wife Rhea, however, wrapped a stone in a diaper; Cronus (see also CHRONUS) swallowed it, and the boy Zeus was able to grow up in hiding and later defeat his father. Later in Delphi Zeus erected the stone, that Cronus had spat out; it was anointed with oil, covered with a woolen NET, and revered as the OMPHALOS (literally "navel").

Stone: Neolithic dolmen structure. Keryval, near Carnac, Brittany

In the Greek legend of the great FLOOD, the surviving human couple, Deucalion and Pyrrha, create a new human race out of stones (the "bones of Mother Earth") thrown over their shoulders—to replace the old human race drowned in the flood.

PRECIOUS STONES, distinguished by their COLOR, brilliance, and durability, are of particular symbolic interest, but the block of stone used in construction ("The stone which the builders refused is become the head stone of the corner," Psalm 118:22; compare Matthew 21:42) is also significant.

In the symbolic tradition of FREEMASONRY, the as yet unformed "rough stone" stands for the rank of apprentice; he aspires to become a "hewn stone," ready for incorporation in the great structure ("temple") of humanity. This notion goes back to the world of the builders of the great medieval cathedrals, for whom stone carving was of central importance. The KEYSTONE of an arch was often engraved with the master's personal, RUNE-like insignia.

In Christian symbolism stones are often associated with the ancient Jewish practice of stoning those who had been condemned to death (especially as blasphemers), as in depictions of St. Stephen, the first martyr, and, less frequently, of the penitent St. Jerome, who is occasionally shown beating his breast with a stone as a sign of contrition. Liborius of Paderborn was believed to come to the aid of those who suffered from kidney, gall, and bladder "stones," and is thus portrayed with three stones placed on a BOOK.

In the imagery of ALCHEMY the philosopher's stone (lapis philosophorum) is the sought-after substance with which "base" metals could be transformed into GOLD.

Stones (and THRONES made of stone) are often mentioned in accounts of coronation ceremonies from the distant past. In ancient Ireland, for example, there was said to be a stone that would cry out when it was touched by the rightful KING. This "stone of knowledge" is on a hill in the city of Tara; it was called Fal, and said to be the penis of the hero Fergus (see also LINGA). Two other stones in Tara were so close together that ordinarily no one's HAND could pass between them (Blocc and Bluigne). But when they accepted a man as the future king, they parted before him and let his carriage (see CHARIOT) pass between them. When he drove on to Fal, it rubbed against the axle of his carriage so that everyone could hear its piercing cry [A. and B. Rees]. The Stone of Scone, originally associated with the crowning of Scottish kings, was moved to England in 1296. Its place under the Coronation Chair at Westminster Abbey symbolizes the rule of English monarchs over Scotland.

Rocks placed in crevices and other gaps could be removed, enabling a person to squeeze through, magically "scraping off" diseases and other disorders. Another superstition related to stones over which childless women would slide, bare-bottomed, in the hope of acquiring fertility from contact with these "bones of Mother Earth." Similarly, many prehistoric dolmens in Brittany were known as "hot stones" and believed to transmit their powers to infertile women who sat on them. Their "heat" symbolized life force and the ability to bring children into the world. The stones were believed to store up energy from the earth and pass it along to those who came into contact with them. (See also VULTURE.)

The archaeologist K. J. Narr sees in the construction of tombs out of stone "certainly a taste for the monumental, and also a desire for a lasting burial place; it would not be surprising, at the same time, if a desire for continuity with past and future generations were decisive here. Megalithic monuments from prehistoric times offer some concrete indications that they represented a vital link to the deceased, that they were part of an elaborate tradition of ancestor worship, often associated with the establishment of sacred preserves, meeting places, even megalithic places of worship." Even today Jewish visitors to cemeteries place small stones on the grave marker to symbolize their respect for the dead.

stones, pitted Carved blocks of STONE, or rocks occurring in nature, that are covered with indentations, are important in many ancient cults. The indentations may symbolize the womb; in ancient China, for example, those who wished to have children tossed pebbles at the surface of such stones. If they remained in the indentations, the pebble-thrower understood that the wish would be fulfilled. In other cultures the indentations, often erroneously referred to as "holes," symbolized WELLS or SPRINGS from which fertilizing water was thought to flow, or mouths from which the WIND emanated. (A Breton custom required that women pound with HAMMERS in the indentations of prehistoric stones whenever the waters were becalmed and fishing boats were unable to sail.) The pitted stones could also serve as receptacles for liquid sacrifices (libations), or be scraped to yield a fine powder that was ingested as a folk medicine (in part because the stone symbolized endurance). It is thus impossible to come up with a single, universally valid interpretation of this symbol.

Since these stones also occur naturally, not all of the so-called "sacrificial stones" that survive today are actually relics of pre-Christian cults. Nevertheless, popular legend generally associates them with "heathen ritual," "blood sacrifice," and the like. The persistence of this interpretation simply documents how deeply rooted our beliefs are in the magic powers of BLOOD—and our associations with stones as focal points for "primitive" rituals. In fact, when pitted stones were used as sacrificial receptacles, the liquids in question were more often MILK or water than blood.

It has been suggested that the pitted stones were deliberately hammered as representations of heavenly constellations; little proof has been offered, however, in support of this hypothesis. It should also be noted that the stones may have come into being in different ways in different locations, independent of all historical connections and influences.

stork Although the Old Testament includes all wading birds among the "unclean" creatures of the earth (see IBIS), the stork is otherwise considered a favorable symbol, primarily because it is the scourge of SNAKES. It thus came to be associated with Christ and his disciples, who destroyed satanic creatures; in northern latitudes, moreover, its regular return every spring was linked to Easter and the Resurrection. This pattern seems to explain the notion that the stork brings babies, although other factors also

Stork eating snake. C. Gesner, *Icones Avium*, 1560

contributed: it is a bird associated with the soul, and, as a WATER bird, it was believed to have access to the "waters of creation," the source of all fertility. In one ancient legend the stork feeds its elderly father, and this made the bird a symbol of filial love and devotion. The stork was also believed to have a long life, which made it a symbol (especially in China) of human longevity. In the Netherlands, storks nesting on rooftops are traditionally believed to be harbingers of good fortune. Standing calmly on one leg, the bird seems dignified, contemplative, and alert, which makes it a symbol of meditation and contemplation. In the psychoanalytic interpretation of the stork as a symbol, its beak represents the phallus, and the waters from which it fetches babies represent the womb.

Storms as bad omens. "Practica Teütsch," 1521

storm In mythic and symbolic tradition, usually clearly distinguished from the blowing of the WINDS, the storm represents a powerful manifestation of the gods and their will. The destructive power of the storm wind (e.g., that of the Japanese god Susano-o, or of the Mayan Huracan [source of our word "hurricane"]) led to special rituals to appease the gods; but storms often bring needed RAIN, which makes their personifications ambivalent figures (e.g., the Babylonian storm god Adad [Syrian Hadad], who was also called the "Lord of Abundance," since he also was responsible for making the land fertile). Storm gods are often identical with those associated with THUNDER and LIGHTNING. The *maruts* of ancient India, storm spirits and companions of the god Indra,

Storm caused by witch's spell. Olaus Magnus, *Historia*, 1555

struck the CLOUD "fortresses" with their battle-axes so that rain could pour forth. In Germanic tradition the storm wind was often said to be Wotan's horde, the rush of a ghostly army, then later the passing of an impious spirit breaking the sabbath rest. In the Alps flour and bread crumbs were often scattered into the storm wind to appease it (a practice condemned as devil worship by the Inquisition). In the baroque period storms were likened to the blows of fate, the sorrows of life on earth: "When storm wind blows and thunder crashes down,/ The dove hides in the hollows of the cliff./ So Christians, from the ragings of this world,/ In His own wounds do find their shelter sure" [Hohberg].

sulfur and mercury Designated in the symbolic language of ALCHEMY as the two primal essences, or "elements," one "burning," the other "volatile." All matter was believed to be composed from the two terms of this DUALITY (combined in varying proportions and in different degrees of purity). When the alchemist's task was understood literally as the transformation of base metals into GOLD, this transformation was to be achieved by greater purification of sulfur and mercury and increasing the proportion of (the "spiritual") mercury in their union.

Sulfur and Mercury: Alchemist's symbols for the "burning" and "volatile" elements

Paracelsus (1493–1541), or a historically undocumented alchemist named Basilius Valentinus, added *sal* ("salt") as the third of the "philosophical" elements, the one associated with the "tangibility" of matter: when wood burns, the flame comes from the sulfur, the mercury goes off in the form of smoke, and the "salt" is left behind in the form of ASHES. This version of how matter is constituted is not totally dissimilar to the modern account, proposed by atomic physicists, in which the "elemental" components are protons, electrons, and neutrons. The alchemistic version was abandoned only in the modern era, when it was discovered that the real element sulfur does not occur in metals that have been fully purified. (See also CADUCEUS.)

sun The "daytime star" is naturally the most prominent of all heavenly phenomena. Countless religions associate a sky god with the sun, and there are countless names that designate this sun god as the destroyer of DARKNESS. (In one Babylonian formulation, the sun god is addressed as "you who illuminate darkness, light up the heavens, and annihilate evil above and below. . . . All princes are gladdened when they behold you; all the gods rejoice in you.") The solar cult of the Egyptian god Amon-Re was transformed by the pharaoh Amenhotep IV (Ekhnaton, 1365–1348 B.C.) to a monotheistic system. ("So beautiful do you appear at the heavenly locus of light, O living sun,

who first began to live. . . .") Only in the Old Testament is the sun considered to be merely one of two "great lights" [Genesis 1:16] placed by God in the firmament—a dramatic contrast to the solar cult of the "pagans." In Christian iconography the sun, rising over and over again in the East, symbolizes immortality and resurrection. There are fourth-century mosaics showing Christ as a Helios-like figure in a solar CHARIOT surrounded by sunbeams, or surrounded by a solar NIMBUS. Since Christ is also triumphant over time (*chronocrator*), he is frequently associated with the sun (which measures out the length of each day) in Romanesque art.

Graphic symbols for the sun include both the still-current CIRCLE surrounded by beams and the earlier basic form, the "solar wheel": a circle with a point at its center and perpendicular lines dividing into quadrants. In ALCHEMY the sun is associated with glittering GOLD ("the earth's sun, the KING of metals"); in ASTROLOGY, with the LION. In patriarchal societies the sun is usually thought of as masculine (although the German language, with its feminine *die Sonne*, is an exception), as is the sun deity (with the exception of the Japanese sun goddess Amaterasu Omikami—who, nevertheless, was created by the sky god Isanagi).

In regions subject to the threat of drought, the sun, with its heat, can take on ambivalent or negative aspects, or it must be

Sun design on buffalo-skin coat. Blackfeet civilization, U.S. Plains

fortified for its course across the sky with the BLOOD of human sacrifices, as in ancient Mexico. See also CHARIOT, BALL, and KING.

The most striking example of sun worship in an ancient culture was in Peru, where the sun was believed to be the divine ancestor of the Inca nation. The Inca Garcilaso de la Vega (1539–1616) describes the sun temple of the capital Cuzco as follows: "All four walls were covered from top to bottom with gold sheets and bars. Toward the front was what we would call the principal altar; this is where the figure of the sun stood, consisting of a sheet of gold twice as thick as the sheets that covered the walls. This figure, with its round face surrounded by darting flames, was made from a single sheet of gold, and looked just the same as in paintings. It was so big that it took up the entire forward part of the temple, extending all the way across from side to side. . . . On each side of the figure of the sun were its 'children': the bodies of the dead kings, embalmed (however this was accomplished) so that they looked as if they were still alive. They sat on their accustomed golden thrones, which were positioned on golden girders. . . . The temple gates were gilded like portals. On the exterior of the temple was a golden cornice, made of planks more than a yard in width, which surrounded the entire temple like a crown." The association of sun and gold was apparently nowhere so persistently realized as in the Andes, and

Sun: Apollo as sun god and archer. Cartari, 1647

the symbolic linking of the immutable "noble" elements with mummification is equally striking: in the ancient Peruvian Temple of the MOON, the female ancestors of the ruling family were "preserved" and revered in surroundings made of SILVER.

Japan is actually named for the sun. The Japanese word for Japan, Nihon, is made up of elements meaning "sun" (ni) and "source" (hon); thus the country is often called "the Land of the Rising Sun."

In astrology, as in classical antiquity, the sun is spoken of as one of the "PLANETS," because of its apparent revolutions around the earth (which determine the length of our years). The sun is one of the "principal lights" (like the moon), and it is frequently referred to as "masculine, dominant, hot." The sign of the zodiac in which the sun is located at the time of a person's birth determines the "birth sign." The sun is said to rule the sign Leo (see LION); in Aries it is "exalted," and Aquarius is the sign of its "detriment." Its color is reddish orange; the PRECIOUS stones associated with it are DIAMOND, RUBY, topaz, chrysolite, and hyacinth. Traditionally, the sun is associated symbolically with KINGS, paternal authority, worldly status, fame, victory, life force, and force of will. The sun and the moon are referred to in the symbolism of FREEMASONRY as "the two great lights of the physical world, the images of the first and second supervisors or foremen; they signify the obligation of

Sun god (?) on bull. Siberian cave drawing, Alma Ata, late Bronze Age

Sun: Creation of sun as center of universe. Fludd, *Utriusque Cosmi Historia*, 1617

every good Freemason to seek the true light, day and night, and never linger in the darkness of vice" [Baurnjöpel].

In iconography the sun is usually portrayed either as the sun god crowned with sunbeams, or as the solar disk, with a human face, surrounded by beams. Prehistoric Asian cave drawings often show human figures with a "solar wheel" surrounded by spikes in place of the head; the wheel is divided into quadrants, each containing points (possibly indicating a division of the year into quarters and months or weeks). Prehistoric northern African art includes images of "sun BULLS" and "sun RAMS" (not unlike later religious images found in Egypt), each with a disk on its head.

In coats of arms the sun (with or without a face) is usually drawn surrounded by alternating tickmarks and flaming darts.

swallow The symbologists of antiquity did not distinguish between swallow, martin, and swift: they were each simply called *chelidon* (Greek) or *hirundo* (Latin). According to legend they are always punctual in their southward migrations; they were believed to spend their winters devoid of plumage (Aristotle, Pliny the Elder). There are songs in ancient Greek celebrating the swallow as a harbinger of spring and likening its cry to the speech of "barbarians." The reddish stone chelidonius, found in the stomachs of young

swallows, was supposed to have magical powers. Swallows nesting on rooftops have not always been thought of as promising good fortune, as they are today. Plutarch (A.D. 46–120) mentions the Egyptian myth of the metamorphosis of the goddess Isis into a swallow. The proverb "One swallow doesn't make a summer" appears already in texts of Aristotle and Aristophanes. The swallow (like the DOVE) was a frequent attribute of the love goddess Aphrodite. Consuming the ASHES of a swallow that had been sitting on its eggs was believed to make a man irresistible to women, and the blood (and even the excrement) of the bird promoted HAIR growth. In the Middle Ages the swallow (like the CRANE) and its annual return symbolized spring and the Resurrection. Swallows in fables give their young the ability to see by feeding them juice squeezed from the swallowwort or celandine plant (*Chelidonium majus*), all of whose names refer to its association with the bird; this legendary practice came to symbolize the opening of the eyes of the dead at the Last Judgment.

In China as in Europe the swallow (*yen*) was a symbol of springtime, and it was believed that the bird spent winters inside a BIVALVE at sea. Its nesting at someone's house promised childbirth, happiness, success, and marital joy. The swallow was also associated symbolically with the relationship between an elder and a younger brother. The nests of the Indian water martin, which are made from algae, are still prized today for strengthening sexual potency.

Medieval bestiaries contain an abundance of positive interpretations of the swallow.

Swallow. Fresco, Thera (Santorini), Greece, ca. 1600 B.C.

Its cry is likened to that of the repentant sinner. "The swallow does not sit down to eat, but eats on the wing; so, too, should we seek out the heavenly realm, far from the terrestrial. . . . The swallow traverses the seas when winter and cold weather are impending; so, too, should we flee the bitterness and cold of the world and wait in the warmth of love for the frost of temptation to depart from our spirits" [Unterkircher].

swan (Latin *cygnus* or *olor*) A BIRD of great symbolic significance for the ancient world (despite its rarity in Mediterranean regions); its limber neck and WHITE plumage made it a symbol of noble purity. This is why Zeus chose to approach the unsuspecting Leda in this guise. It is interesting that Homer (in Hymn 21) praises the singing swan, which (unlike the mute swan) lives only in more northern latitudes. This swan is associated with Apollo, who also was said to be revered especially by the northern mythic race of Hyperboreans. The swan was present at the god's birth, carried him across the sky, and derived from him its gift of prophecy. At times the swan is referred to as the enemy or opponent of the EAGLE or (like the eagle) of the SNAKE, each of which the swan frequently defeats. The proverbial "swan song" (the significant final words or performance of a great person) goes back to the prophetic talent of the swan, already mentioned by Aeschylus (525–456 B.C.): it supposedly foresees its impending death and emits extraordinary cries bemoaning its own passing. In fact, the singing swan of Northern Europe (*cygnus musicus*) can produce a powerful

Swan song. J. Boschius, 1702

Swan: "Unblemished radiance." J. Boschius, 1702

trumpet-like note in the upper register and a weaker one in the lower, even shortly before it is paralyzed by severe cold. If several of these swans cry at once, they do give the impression of song. According to Germanic superstition, VIRGINS could be transformed into prophetic swan maidens (as in the *Nibelungenlied*); similar myths (in which the maidens can doff their plumage) are found in a variety of cultural contexts. In Christian thought the *cygnus musicus* came to symbolize the Savior crying out from the Cross *in extremis*. The association of the bird with song (and hence lyrical beauty) led Ben Jonson to call Shakespeare "the sweet swan of Avon."

The swan often symbolizes feminine grace; Aphrodite and Artemis (Latin DIANA) are often portrayed as accompanied by swans. It is in part because of the association of swans with physical grace that Tchaikovsky's *Swan Lake* is for many the quintessential classical ballet.

In the imagery of ALCHEMY the swan symbolizes the element mercury (see SULFUR AND MERCURY) in its volatility.

The swan is important in HERALDRY as well, frequently appearing in coats of arms (e.g., those of Boulogne-sur-Mer and the Saxon city of Zwickau, whose Latin name was Cygnea). A chivalric Order of the Swan was founded in 1440, then renewed in 1843 by the German king Friedrich Wilhelm II as a charitable secular order, but never came into operation.

A strange, negative symbolic interpretation of the swan surfaces in medieval bestiaries. In contrast to its snow-white plumage, it is written, the bird has "utterly BLACK flesh": "Thus it is a symbol of the hypocrite, whose black sinful flesh is clothed by white garments. When the bird's white plumage is stripped away, its black flesh is roasted in the fire. So, too, will the hypocrite, once dead, be stripped of worldly splendor and descend into the fires of hell" [Unterkircher]. Böckler, on the other hand, writes that swans do battle even with eagles if attacked. They "are the royalty among water fowl; the meaning that they carry is of the whiteness of peace" (1688). This poetic formulation is reminiscent of the swan knight, Lohengrin.

swastika A particular form of CROSS, most familiar as a POLITICAL SYMBOL associated by Adolf Hitler's followers with that which is "Aryan," Germanic, or Teutonic. From 1935 until 1945, the swastika (BLACK against a WHITE background) with an EAGLE atop it symbolized Nazi Germany. The swastika is found in many different cultures of both the Old and the New World; it is actually a variation on the cross formed by two axes of a WHEEL. The bending of the ends of the four arms in a single direction suggests a circular or dynamic movement. (The arms can be bent either clockwise or counter-

clockwise.) The swastika thus suggests, for example, the recurrence of the seasons of the year. It has been documented in the pre-Aryan civilization of Mohenjo-Daro on the Indus River (ca. 2000 B.C.); in ancient China the swastika (*wan tsu*) is a symbol of the four points of the compass. Since ca. A.D. 700 the Chinese have also associated it with the NUMBER 10,000, or infinity. In the Buddhist tradition of India it is referred to as the "SEAL on Buddha's HEART"; in Tibet, too, it is associated with good fortune and serves as a talisman. In Indian Jainism the four arms represent the four levels of existence: the world of the gods, of humans, of animals, and the underworld, respectively. In Mediterranean cultures the perpendicular tips of the four ends were sometimes curled, or further bent to form mazes. Thought of as a quadruplication of the Greek letter gamma, it was also called the *crux gammata*. The Old Norse amulet referred to as "Thor's HAMMER" was also formed like a swastika. The symbol appears less frequently in pre-Columbian cultures of the Western hemisphere.

Gnostic sects of late antiquity used a sort of swastika, formed by four legs bent at the knee, as a secret symbol, not unlike the (three-legged) TRISKELION.

sword Neither the weapon itself nor the sword as symbol goes back to "the earliest times," since swords could obviously not have been produced before the Bronze Age. (The "wooden swords" of the first inhabitants of South America are closer to clubs than to what we think of as swords.) When cherubim (see ANGEL) are placed at the east of the Garden of Eden with "a flaming sword which turned every way" [Genesis 3:24] after ADAM AND EVE are driven out of their earthly PARADISE, this is an indication that the Biblical account itself does not date from the era that it describes. The swords of the Bronze Age were often richly decorated, which indicates that their function was not merely utilitarian. In the Germanic tradition we find accounts of "sword dances," and the names given to the swords of legendary heroes (names like Balmung,

Swastika: Labyrinthine floor mosaic, Roman villa in Sparta

Sword as a guarantee of chastity. *Tristan and Isolde*, 1484

"anointing," or Nagelring, "ring of nails") suggest that swords were endowed with magic or symbolic values. Medieval KNIGHTS were dubbed using the tip of a sword. A sword placed between a man and a woman in bed symbolized chastity (*signum castitatis*).

There are Egyptian pylon reliefs of the Rameses period (14th-11th century B.C.) showing the pharaoh in a ritual pose, raising a hand to seize a sword that a god is holding out to him: the SICKLE-like sword called a *chopesh*, which suggests some Asian influence. The foreign *shirdana* mercenaries from the North, however, carry long swords.

In ancient Chinese depictions we find magicians with swords to drive off demons. There was also a tradition of distinct "male" and "female" swords, forged from the liver and kidneys of a mythic HARE that ate metal

Sword held by archangel Michael. From a woodcut by Lucas Cranach, 1506

and lived in the Kuenlun Mountains. When a woman dreamt of drawing a sword, it was believed, she would give birth to a boy (as in the Freudian psychology of the 20th century, the sword was a phallic, or masculine, symbol); the possession of a sword, in a woman's dream, promised good fortune, whereas, in a man's dream, a sword falling into WATER foretold the death of a woman.

In Japan the proper use of the sword was the art of the samurai, who had two different weapons: the *katana*, a long sword used in battle, and the *wakizashi*, a short sword for hand-to-hand combat and for ritual suicide (*seppuku*, referred to in the West as "hara-kiri"). The makers of swords had to obey certain commandments of abstinence because of the sacred nature of their craft. The hilt (*tsuba*) separating the blade from the

Sword hilt (*tsuba*). Japan, ca. 1750

handle was richly adorned. Today a sword fight (*iai-do*) with a training partner is carried out only as an exercise with narrowly-defined safety precautions; fencing with BAMBOO swords (*kendo*) is derived from the old samurai tradition. In Shinto myth the STORM god Susano-o (see CAVE, RICE) kills an eight-headed SNAKE and draws from its tail the sword "*Ame no murakomo no tsuguri*," which today, accompanied by PEARLS and a MIRROR, is among the imperial treasures of Japan.

In the Occident the sword is the weapon of the archangel Michael, King David, and Judith, who used one to behead Holofernes. In the Book of Revelation a sword comes out of Christ's mouth [1:16], a symbol of indomitable power and divine truth, coming down from heaven like a bolt of LIGHTNING.

The sword is a symbol of sovereignty in the hand of St. Stephen of Hungary or Charlemagne; of a martyr's death when it is an attribute of the saints Paul, James the Greater, Thomas Beckett, Catherine, or Lucia. In the Gospel according to Luke, Simeon tells the Virgin Mary that her soul will be pierced by a sword, a prediction of the extraordinary suffering that she will undergo. In baroque iconography we occasionally find depictions of SEVEN swords, a reference to the seven sorrows of Mary.

In general, the sword is a symbol of vitality and strength, most frequently an attribute of gods of war (see MARS) or (as a symbol for lightning) THUNDER. In Catholic doctrine the "two swords" symbolized spiritual and temporal dominion; Pope Innocent III, among others, spoke of EMPERORS or KINGS as his vassals to whom he turned over the temporal sword as a fief.

The most familiar sword in English tradition is King Arthur's Excalibur, which only the young Arthur was able to draw out of the stone in which it was lodged. In Thomas Malory's *Morte d'Arthur*, however, it is the Lady of the Lake who hands Excalibur to Arthur.

Only in exceptional cases do we find the decidedly masculine symbol of the sword in a woman's hand. JOAN OF ARC (burned at the stake in 1431) claimed that St. Catherine (see above) had told her of a sword buried underneath a village church: "The sword was underground, totally rusted, with FIVE CROSSES on it. I had learned from my voices that it was there. . . . I had a letter written to the local Church authorities, asking for the sword. They sent it to me" [from the trial records, as quoted by A. Holl]. After great military victories, however, the inspired soldier (who was canonized in 1920) was to perish by the sword (compare Matthew 26:52).

We speak of a threat of impending disaster as a "sword of Damocles," referring to the sword that Dionysius of Syracuse suspended over the head of his courtier Damocles at a banquet to teach him how precarious a king's lot was.

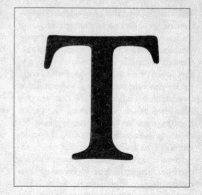

tarot Usually refers to a symbolic tradition making use of certain cards from the tarok deck for the purpose of fortunetelling and philosophical speculation. Although some theories would place its origins in the mysteries of ancient Egypt, historians generally believe that the deck was invented in 14th-century Italy when images from a pictorial encyclopedia (used for teaching children) were combined in Venice with the Spanish set of numbered playing cards. The names given to the 22 trump cards (the Major Arcana) seem closely related to medieval imagery and readily capture the symbolic imagination; this explains the appeal of tarot for those embracing mystical doctrines and practices. "The close association between mysticism and tarot has become so well established that it often seems that tarot exists only to serve as a symbolic vehicle for occult theories and speculation" [Tegtmeier]. The names of the Major Arcana are as follows: 0—The Fool (French *Le Mat*, associated with the ELEMENT air); I—The Magician (*Le Bateleur*, MERCURY); II—The High Priestess (*La Papesse*, the MOON); III—The Empress (*L'Impératrice*, VENUS); IV—The EMPEROR (*L'Empereur*, Aquarius); V—The Pope or Hierophant (*Le Pape*, Taurus); VI—The Lovers (*L'Amoureux*, Gemini); VII—The CHARIOT (*Le Chariot*, Cancer); VIII—Justice (*La Justice*, LIBRA); IX—The HERMIT (*L'Ermite*, Virgo); X—The WHEEL

Tarot: Two cards from the Major Arcana (Judgment, Devil). France, ca. 1840

of Fortune (*La Roue de Fortune*, JUPITER); XI—Strength (*La Force*, Leo); XII—The Hanged Man (*Le Pendu*, WATER); XIII—Death (*La Mort*, Scorpio); XIV—Temperance (*La Tempérance*, Sagittarius); XV—The DEVIL (*Le Diable*, CAPRICORN); XVI—The LIGHTNING-Struck TOWER (*La Maison-Dieu*, MARS); XVII—The STAR (*L'Étoile*, Aries); XVIII—The Moon (*La Lune*, Pisces); XIX—The SUN (*Le Soleil*, the sun); XX—Judgment (*La Trompête*, or *Le Jugement*, FIRE); XXI—The World, or The Universe (*Le Monde*, SATURN).

In esoteric speculation these cards are associated with the "channels" that combine the ten *sephirot* or forces of the Cabala and correspond to the letters of the Hebrew alphabet. For example, in the "sephirotic TREE" the channel of the letter *beth* with its associated trump I (The Magician) links the sephirot Kether (the CROWN) and Binah (understanding), and the channel of *aleph* with the trump 0 (The Fool) links Kether and Chochmah (wisdom). [See in particular Golowin, Nichols, and Tegtmeier.]

The four suits of the Minor Arcana are SWORDS, Wands, Cups, and PENTACLES, associated with the elements air, fire, water, and earth, respectively.

tea In the Far East, tea is not merely a beverage but also a symbol of cultivation and meditation. *Sado*, the "way of tea-drinking," is part of the life-discipline of the

Japanese Zen tradition. In Buddhist legend, the first tea leaves came from the eyelids of the meditating Bodhidharma (Japanese "Daruma"). The Holy One, it is said, cut them off himself so as not to fall asleep, and this is why the leaves that grew from them function as stimulants. In Chinese tradition it is written (ca. A.D. 800) that tea was discovered by a Lu-Yü, who supposedly was hatched from an EGG. The Japanese tea ceremony goes back to the year 1286 and is attributed to the monk Shomei, who imported the beverage and all associated utensils from China. Tea is to be taken in a GARDEN (*roji*) containing a tea house (*chah-itsu*); it is not to be swallowed hastily, but rather enjoyed in a state of inner composure in which one concentrates on inner and outer harmonies; each step in the process is meticulously prescribed. According to Zen philosophers, the feeling of peace and fulfillment that comes with the tea ceremony then carries over into the rest of one's daily life. For this reason the teacups (*chawan*) used should be beautiful but simple (*wabi*), both in form and in color. Collectors are especially fond of teacups from Kyoto, which are traditionally BLACK and RED in color.

Tea has a special place in the British Isles as well: its popularity there still surpasses that of coffee, and for many the beverage and accompanying snacks have almost ritual status.

Tell, William (German Wilhelm Tell, Tall, or Thäll) A legendary figure symbolizing the Swiss longing for independence and liberty. According to tradition, Tell was a hunter from the village of Bürglen (Uri), forced by the tyrannical Hapsburg governor Gessler to shoot an APPLE on his son's head with an ARROW from his crossbow. He is successful but soon thereafter kills Gessler himself, thus giving the signal for the Swiss uprising against Hapsburg rule and the establishment of the new Confederation.

Modern interpreters, while understanding the legend as symbolizing the Swiss people's aspirations for political control of their own destinies and their own land, note that the theme of the hunter forced to shoot at his

William Tell shoots the apple from his son's head. Woodcut, Meister D. S., 1707

own son is far older than the period in which the incident is supposed to have taken place in Switzerland. In Saxo Grammaticus' account (ca. 1200) the hunter is named Toko (in the Palnatoki legend); in the Old Norse saga of Thidrek, Egill; in Scottish legend, William Cloudesly. The first treatment of the material in the context with which we are now familiar, is a "Song of Tell" (14th century), subsequently extended in popular ballads and linked around 1470 with the conspiracy to overthrow Hapsburg rule. The Tell legend became famous beyond the borders of Switzerland through Schiller's play *William Tell* (1804) and Rossini's opera (1829), the latter written in the spirit of the Italian *Risorgimento*. Tell came to symbolize the staunchly fearless hero, rebelling against oppression in the name of liberty.

One element in the Tell legend, the placing of the governor's hat on a pole, should be understood as an ancient symbol of judicial or military authority and not of tyrannical rule.

temple Not only a structure erected for sacred purposes but also a symbol for any sort of sanctuary or holy place, or for any higher striving to establish a place for things of the spirit in the midst of the secular world. In Christian symbology the individual is spoken of as a "temple of God" (compare I Corinthians 6:19), or it is said that "Christ is the true temple to which we must go. . . . The temple of God is His word given form; in the temple of the Holy Spirit God's word is taught. . . . We must make our way past all of Satan's armies into the temple of Jesus Christ" [Jakob Böhme, 1575–1624].

The word "temple" goes back to the same root as the Greek *temenos*, "secluded realm," referring to the space for worship, sealed off by walls from the secular world. Symbolically, however, these walls, although they are to protect the shrine against desecration and outsiders against the extraordinary powers contained within, are also to be movable, so that the holy realm within can be extended as far as possible.

Temples are often constructed along the lines of the prevalent cosmological model of the universe; they thus stand for the ordered world as a whole. (See also AXIS MUNDI, OMPHALOS, CROSS, SQUARE.) The ziggurats of ancient Mesopotamia (see BABEL, TOWER) often have names that when translated reveal their status as divine mountains, centers of the universe, or points of contact between the divine and human realms: "House of the Foundations of Heaven and Earth" (Babylon); "Temple of the Seven Guardians of Heaven and Earth" (Birs Nimrud); "House of the Mountain of the Uni-

Temple of Augustus (Rome). Coin, Ephesus, 19th century B.C.

verse." The name of the great altar of SOLOMON's temple, 'Ar'el, comes from the Akkadian *arallu*, which can mean either "underworld" or "mountain of the gods." Thus both the altar and the STONE Shetiya beneath it were presumably thought of both as a symbolic mountain and as an umbilical center of the universe. Greek and Roman temples, for many Westerners, are the most significant suriving examples of classical architecture.

This temple symbolism, along with the notion of an ideal central point, is of great importance in the philosophic tradition of FREEMASONRY. King Solomon's temple, work on which began in 966 B.C., was considered in Jewish cosmology to constitute an idealized image of the world. The outer vestibule (*ulam*) corresponded to the sea; the shrine itself (*hekal*), to the land; and the dark holy

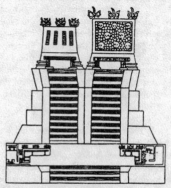

Temple: Double shrine on pyramid. Colonial period, Mexico, Codex Ixtlilxóchitl

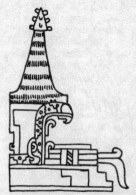

Temple: Shrine of cave god, portal in form of dragon's mouth. Mexico, Codex Borgia

of holies (*debir*), to HEAVEN. In the world of the builders of the great medieval cathedrals, this temple in JERUSALEM became an ideal prototype for the construction of a spiritual "temple of humanity" (or "all-encompassing brotherly love") that was to admit a peaceful brotherhood consisting of those "who were to build it and who were identical with it. For the idea of the construction of the temple can be understood only when the act of building and the human race are seen as equivalent" [Lennhoff and Posner]. The Freemason's tools (carpenter's SQUARE, drafting COMPASS, TRIANGLE, HAMMER, etc.) are symbolically linked to the construction of an ideal temple in honor of "the almighty master builder of the universe"; each individual enters the fraternity as a "cubic STONE." Meeting-places of individual lodges are also called "temples." (See also MOUNTAIN.)

Thanatos   Ancient Greek personification of death; described as the twin brother of HYPNOS (Latin SOMNUS), the DREAM, and the son of Nyx, the NIGHT. In European art and literature Thanatos is portrayed as a serious, winged youth with an extinguished (or flickering) TORCH in his hand. In the ancient world he was a negative figure, and even the gods hated him. He was said to accompany the souls of the dead to the underworld (see AFTERLIFE), except in those myths in which this was the duty of the FURIES. In one of the plays of Euripides (ca. 480–406 B.C.), Thanatos attempts to take the soul of Alcestis (who gave up her life to save her husband Admetus) from her grave and transport it to Hades, but Heracles (HERCULES) overpowers Thanatos and restores Alcestis to the world of the living (operas by Lully and Gluck; oratorio by Handel).

thistle   A plant associated today with "prickliness," is the national emblem of Scotland. In earlier times a number of varieties of thistle were more esteemed, both for their medicinal applications and for a different set of symbolic associations. It was believed in classical antiquity that thistles could reverse evil omens and dispell demonic powers. Although they are generally eaten only by DONKEYS, humans can eat them as well; if a pregnant woman ate them, it was believed, she would give birth to a son. The variety *Centum capita* arouses irresistible feelings of love in the opposite sex (a statement attributed to Pythagoras). Since cut thistles do not lose their form, they are a Chinese image for loyalty and longevity. In the Christian Occident the sufferings of Christ and the martyrs were symbolized by the prickly plant, and especially the teasel ("the more suffering is inflicted upon them, the higher they grow"). The MILK-thistle (*Silybum marianum*) with its white markings is associated with the mother's milk of the

Thanatos burying the dead. Detail from an Attic vase, ca. 450 B.C.

Carduus Benedictus.

Thistle. Hohberg, 1675

Virgin Mary and was used as a medicinal herb. Portraits of martyrs are often framed by thistle-shoots. The "Benedictine thistle" (*Cnicus benedictus*) is an old medicinal herb that was used under the name "cardobenedictine" or "cnicin" in treating internal disorders. In 1675 W. H. von Hohberg treated its symbolism in the following edifying verses: "Though cardobenedictine's bitter/ And to the palate most unkind/ Yet still it doth the stomach good./ Thus though the word of God to ear severely rings/ 'Tis soul's well-being, sooth, eternal life it brings." (See also FLOWERS, LANGUAGE OF.)

thorns and briars The symbolism and typology of the thorn-bush is determined by the following Bible verses: "And the angel of the Lord appeared unto [Moses] in a flame of fire out of the midst of a bush: and he looked, and, behold, the bush burned with fire, and the bush was not consumed. . . . God called to him out of the midst of the bush . . ." [Exodus 3:2, 4] and summoned him to lead God's people. Holy fire does not consume what it inflames, and Mary could become a MOTHER and yet have her VIRGINITY remain intact. Thus some altar paintings of the 15th and 16th centuries show Mary and the Christ-child in the Burning Bush. Thorny tendrils are also primarily associated

Thorns and briars: The bush burns but is not consumed. J. Boschius, 1702

with Christ's suffering under the CROWN of Thorns. Thorns play a role in the brutal self-mutilations of ancient Mexico: e.g., agave thorns were strung together and pulled through a hole in the tongue. Long-standing idioms illustrate vividly the immediate associations: "to fall among thorns" (i.e., into a life of sin), "a thorny question," "to be a thorn in someone's flesh," "to sit on thorns."

threshold Like the entire GATE or portal, the threshold, as a symbol of transition between inside and out, requires special rites and attention. In many cultures a tutelary spirit—who was under no circumstances to be trifled with—was believed to guard the threshold. The custom of carrying the bride over the threshold may have originated as an attempt to deceive this spirit, to make it believe that she had always lived there. The spirit had the power to keep out intruders, demons, and WITCHES. It is for him that the Japanese sprinkle SALT on the threshold (so that he will keep ghosts away); in Europe a PENTACLE was often carved in the threshold (or, in the Balkan regions, over the doorway). Jews affix a mezzuzah to the doorframe of their homes. A Jewish priest was to wear golden bells on the hem of his robe, "and his sound shall be heard when he goeth in unto the holy place before the Lord, and when he cometh out, that he die not" [Exodus 28:34–35]. Thus entrance and exit were to be clearly announced, lest supernatural powers be surprised. Dagon, the Philistine god of agriculture, had a TEMPLE in Ashdod whose threshold was not to be tread upon but stepped over [I Samuel 5:5; compare Zephaniah 1:9, with its warning against the pagan practice of leaping over thresholds].

The word "threshold" is frequently used figuratively to mark a moment of transition; the importance attached to such thresholds recalls both the tutelary spirits of which we have spoken and the "rites of passage" of ancient tradition, marking the attainment of adulthood.

In many traditions the entrances to shrines are flanked by statues of tutelary divinities or of supernatural animals (see KARASHISHI, JANUS).

throne (from Greek *thronos.*) Every hierarchical society has used elevated, consecrated seats for its chieftain, KING, or EMPEROR, so that on official occasions the ruler could take a superior position (even when seated) to that of "mere mortals." The throne subsequently took on a symbolic value of its own; in many expressions it stands for the power of the ruler or realm. The so-called "throne of Minos" in Knossos (Crete) is especially famous. HOMER portrays gods, kings, and nobles on thrones. Empty thrones were sometimes maintained as seats for the gods, who were thought of as present but invisible. From the seventh century B.C. onward, Greek thrones were richly adorned, showing the influence of Middle Eastern cultures. Among the most famous thrones for the gods were those reserved for Zeus in Olympia (statue by Phidias) and Apollo in Amyclae. In Rome there were thrones for the emperor and for the goddess Roma; adorned with a crown and scepter, these thrones were themselves worshipped, as in the Hittite civilization of Asia Minor.

There are many passages in the Bible referring to God's throne. King SOLOMON, as God's deputy, "made a great throne of ivory, and overlaid it with the best GOLD" [I Kings 10:18]. Jesus promises his apostles that they will sit on 12 thrones and judge

Throne: King Ahiran of Byblos on sphinx throne. Stone relief, Phoenician, ca. 1100 B.C.

the 12 tribes of Israel, "when the Son of man shall sit in the throne of his glory" [Matthew 19:28]. In the Book of Revelation it is written: "And I saw a great white throne, and him that sat on it, from whose face the earth and the heaven fled away" [20:11].

Peter's throne (*cathedra Sancti Petri*) is the symbol of the Papacy; bishops and abbots also had their thrones. In the symbolic art of the Eastern Church the motif of Christ riding a throne (*etimasia*) was a frequent emblem for Christ's return at the time of the Last Judgment.

In civilizations outside Europe, the "PEACOCK throne" of the Persian Shah, and, in Western Africa, the "golden throne" of the Ashanti, were especially famous.

thunder Understood in many ancient cultures as the powerful expression of creatures—usually gods—who dwelt in the HEAVENS; LIGHTNING was also attributed to them. The rumbling of the heavens was understood as a manifestation of power from above, in the Bible as the voice of God: "Hear attentively the noise of his voice, and the sound that goeth out of his mouth. He directeth it under the whole heaven, and his lightning unto the ends of the earth. After it a voice roareth: he thundereth with the voice of his excellency; and he will not

Throne: Isis wearing a symbolic throne. 15th century B.C.

Thunder: Thunder-bird, stylized like the double eagle. Painting, Haida, Northwest U.S.

stay them when his voice is heard" [Job 37:2–4]. Thunder was often understood as an expression of divine wrath at a disturbance of cosmic order: among Native Americans as the beating of the wings of the thunder-bird; in Norse myth as the sound of Thor's HAMMER Mjollnir (literally, "the pulverizer"), which the thunder-god hurled at the GIANTS. In ancient China thunder was perceived in a variety of ways: as "heaven's laughter," as supernatural drum-rolls, as the expression of a RED-haired sky-demon, or as the rumbling of a WAGON carrying the souls of the dead across the sky. Heavenly thunder gods were sometimes thought of as being one-legged: the Aztecs' Tezcatlipoca, or the Quiché Mayas' Huracán (from whose name our word "hurricane" is derived). In Central Europe belemnites, which are fossil remains of mollusks, are popularly known as "thunderbolts" or "thunderstones," as were

Thunder: Vajra, thunderbolt. Lamaist ritual object, Tibet

also, in some areas, the Neolithic pickaxes placed by the *pater familias* under the ridge of the roof to ward off storm damage. Frequently the god of thunder, lightning, and the weather in general is also the supreme god of the heavens, like Zeus Ceraunus in ancient Greece, or, in Slavic traditions, Perun, whose symbol is a club. "Thunderbolt" (*vajra* or *rdo-rje*) is the name of a symbolic object used in Indian and Tibetan ritual, known also as the "DIAMOND-SCEPTER"; it is used in Tantric Buddhism to "split open ignorance and liberate knowledge." It was originally the weapon of the Vedic sky-god Indra, with which he chopped up the clouds, freeing the RAIN. In Japanese iconography the thunder-god is the divinity Raijin, painted red and surrounded by eight tambourine-like drums. In general thunder is perceived as an impressive and concretely perceptible expression of heavenly powers, at times threatening us, at times protecting us from hostile entities. See also STORM.

thyrsus A characteristic staff associated with Dionysus (Latin BACCHUS), the god of intoxication and ecstasy who spread the cultivation of grapes for WINE from land to land. As their SCEPTER, Dionysus and his followers carried the thyrsus, a staff wrapped in grape and ivy vines and crowned with a large pine-cone. Our other associations with Dionysus lend credence to the hypothesis that the thyrsus is to be understood as a phallic symbol. It was originally the stalk of the giant fennel (Greek *narthex*, Latin *ferula*), whose natural height can extend to several yards. PROMETHEUS was said to have used this giant stalk to carry the SPARK from Mount Olympus that would bring FIRE to the human race. In schools it came to be used as a "rod" with which to discipline pupils.

tiara The Papal CROWN. In ancient Greek literature the term originally referred to the traditional felt HEADDRESS (shaped like a truncated cone) of the Persians, then especially to the crown of the Persian king, crenelated and adorned with STARS. Another form of the tiara is the miter, with mouth covering, worn by Darius III in the Pompeian mosaic depicting his battle with ALEXANDER THE GREAT. The Phrygian cap—symbol, at the time of the French Revolution, of rule by the people—has been referred to as a sort of tiara. In the Middle Ages it came to designate the three-tiered crown of the Pope, a symbol of his "triregnum": ruling over HEAVEN, EARTH, and the underworld, or the three classical continents Asia, Europe, and Africa (settled by the descendents of NOAH's sons, Shem, Japheth, and Ham). Another explanation of the three rings of the Papal tiara is that they symbolize the Church suffering, doing battle, and triumphant. The form of this tiara was established in the time of Pope Urban V (d. 1370) but also used in depictions of earlier saints (e.g., Peter, Gregory I, SOPHIA). Popes who abdicated or saints who refused canonization are portrayed with the tiara beside them on the ground. The FIVE-tiered tiara is worn exclusively by God the Father in depictions of the Holy TRINITY.

tiger A predatory animal first known to the ancients of the Occident through ALEXANDER THE GREAT's campaign to India. Its Greek name, *tigris*, goes back to the Iranian word *thigra* ("sharp, pointed"). Along with the PANTHER and the LYNX it appears as an attribute of the WINE god Dionysus (Latin BACCHUS); it also seems to have symbolic associations with the wind god Zephyr and with Cybele, the mother goddess of Phrygian myth (Asia Minor). The first tiger appeared in Rome in A.D. 19 as a gift to Augustus from an Indian delegation.

In ancient symbolism, the tiger appears naturally only in Asian traditions, where its

Tiger. From a drawing in E. Topsell's *The History of Four-footed Beasts,* 1638

power inspired fear and wonder. Gods and heroes wear tiger skins, especially the fierce tutelary divinities of popular religions. In ancient China the third sign of the zodiac (corresponding roughly to Gemini) was named for the tiger. The animal was so revered that the Chinese avoided speaking its name, *hu;* they substituted for it such formulas as "the king of the MOUNTAINS" or "the giant reptile." The tiger was esteemed because it drove off (or devoured) the wild boar that threatened the farmer's crops. The tiger's vitality and energy explain its association with yang; the white, or albino, tiger, however, is associated with YIN (as well as autumn and the west). ("White tiger," in Chinese, is also a term of opprobrium for a quarrelsome woman.) Even demons were said to fear tigers; this is why stone figures of tigers were often placed on grave markers. The image of a tiger on a door post was also believed to keep demons away from a dwelling. Tutelary gods were depicted riding on the backs of tigers. In South China there was a "were-tiger" tradition, according to which humans could be turned into tigers.

Medieval bestiaries praised the "motherly love" of the female tiger and noted that hunters routinely exploited her maternal instincts, placing a round MIRROR on the ground where she would look into it and mistake it for a tiger cub—which she would then attempt to nurse. (A similar ruse is proposed to save humans who are being pursued by a tigress.)

It is not clear whether the "manticore," described by Pausanias and others as a fabulous monster, was in fact a tiger. The most

Tiger woman as siren in wait for male swimmers. Moghul painting. Bombay, ca. 1750

familiar literary tiger for Western readers is the one addressed in William Blake's *Song of Experience* (1794): "Tyger! Tyger! burning bright/ In the forests of the night. . . ."

Titanic The 45,000-ton SHIP, 270 meters (over 885 feet) in length, with 2201 persons on board—a "floating palace"—sank on April 14, 1912 after colliding with an iceberg in the North Atlantic, causing 1502 casualties. The most famous catastrophe at sea of the modern period, the sinking of the *Titanic* was interpreted as a "punishment" for the attempt to set records at whatever cost and for the presumption of those who worshipped "progress" and "technology" above all else. The sinking of the *Titanic* thus became a modern symbolic counterpart of the dramas of classical antiquity in which human hubris leads to divine retribution. The very name of the ship—which declares a total disregard for any "limits of growth"—helped to make the *Titanic* legendary. Decades later, the catastrophe continued to be the dramatized in books and films; it appears to have lost none of its macabre fascination.

toads Having predominantly negative symbolic associations because of their unattractive appearance and their corrosive secretions, toads have been viewed most often as demonic creatures: members of witches' households, say, or part of the bill

Toad nursed and weaned (alchemist's emblem). M. Maier, *Atalanta,* 1618

of fare at a witches' feast, or tormenting the damned in the regions of HELL. In ancient China, the (three-legged) toad was a symbol of the MOON; it was believed that lunar eclipses were caused by a toad swallowing the moon. In other contexts as well the toad, because of its seclusion and fondness for dampness, is associated with the lunar realm, and in China with the principle of YIN. In Europe, from antiquity onward, the toad was on the one hand a despised creature, "full of evil magic," but on the other hand a symbol of the womb (see MOTHER), and women seeking relief from gynecological disorders often made votive offerings of statuettes of toads at places of PILGRIMAGE. In popular legend a toad is often the embodiment of a "poor soul" that has not yet attained salvation; thus, after the death of a person who has failed to carry out a vow, the person's soul must do so in the form of the despised animal, and can enter HEAVEN only when it has, say, crawled all the way to the altar at a shrine. In other legends the toad occasionally appears as the embodiment of maternally protective household spirits who must be catered to so that they will bless the house in return. There are also many legends in which toads guard TREASURES.

In the imagery of ALCHEMY, the toad symbolizes the watery, earthy part of the primal matter to be purified; it is to be united with the volatile (symbolized by the EAGLE), and this union is at times depicted with a winged toad. There is curious symbolism in the alchemistic allegory of a toad placed at a woman's BOSOM: as the text of an engraving in the book of emblems *Atalanta Fugiens* (1618) explains, "If you set a toad at the woman's breast, and let it be suckled and the woman die, then the toad will grow large from the milk." This strange depiction is related to the description of a (pseudo-) chemical process in which primal matter (on its way to becoming the philosopher's STONE) must be drenched (or "nursed") with "maiden's milk" (philosophical milk, the fluid of the moon). The growing "child" is indeed nursed by its mother, who dies in the process: this is called *ablactatio* ("weaning").

Toad-like mythic creature. Native American ceramic, Mogollon, ca. A.D. 800

Alchemistic symbolism, as this case suggests, is rarely to be fully explained by rational means.

In ancient Mexico the earth was often represented by the toad, who lived on and dug beneath its surface. Poisonous secretions of toads may well have been used as consciousness-altering drugs. Frequently the toad (like the FROG), because of the conspicuous transformations in its life cycle, came to be associated with resurrection and rebirth, as prehistoric rock drawings of tadpole-like figures suggest.

tomahawk Many languages have expressions corresponding to the English "to dig up the tomahawk" (or "hatchet"), understood as the opposite of "to smoke the peacepipe" (see CALUMET) or, of course, "to bury the tomahawk" (or "hatchet"). The tomahawk was a weapon (and tool) of the Native American peoples of Eastern and Central North America; this AX, which also had ritual and symbolic significance, was often painted and adorned with FEATHERS. Through the Leatherstocking novels of James Fenimore Cooper readers throughout the world became familiar with the custom of "burying the hatchet" upon the conclusion of peace.

Tomahawk of the Missouris. 19th century

In the 19th century white traders sold Native Americans a version of the tomahawk that had been combined with a tobacco pipe and had an iron blade. This tomahawk, like the calumet, often appears in 19th-century portraits of chiefs.

tongue (Greek *glossa,* Latin *lingua*) An organ of the body frequently symbolizing "language," since it is critical for the articulation of most consonants. "To speak in foreign tongues" can refer to a mastery of foreign languages, or to xenoglossia, the paranormal ability to speak languages that one has not studied. In the mythology of ancient Egypt, "HEART and tongue" are the tools with which the god Ptah created the world: reason and language (i.e., the Creator's "word"). There are maxims warning people against being led by the tongue alone.

In the Bible, the word "tongue" frequently refers to speech or language. "The tongue of the just is as choice SILVER" [Proverbs 10:20], or "Many have fallen by the sword, but not as many as by the tongue" [Sirach 28:18]. At Pentecost the Holy Spirit descended upon the Apostles in "cloven tongues like as of fire" and they "began to speak with other tongues, as the Spirit gave them utterances" [Acts 2:3–4], the miracle of xenoglossia and the first Christian instance of this particular charism. "Speaking in tongues" is the ecstatic stammering of incomprehensible sounds (Greek *glossolalia,* a frequent practice in many charismatic churches. Similar speech was already attributed to the prophet Isaiah (the stammering Hebrew "*sau lasau, sau lasau, cau lacau, cau lacau, ze'er sham, ze'er sham*" of Isaiah 28:10; translated in the King James Version as "For precept must be upon precept, precept upon precept; line upon line, line upon line; here a little, and there a little"). Members of Pentecostal religions believe that these ecstatic utterances are divinely inspired, that they "speak with tongues of ANGELS." (See also Acts 10:46, I Corinthians 12:10, 14:5, etc.)

In Christian iconography the tongue is an attribute of martyred saints whose tongues were cut out, e.g. John of Nepomuk (the

Tongue: St. John of Nepomuk with his tongue in his hand. W. Auer, 1890

patron saint of the seal of confession) and Emmeram of Regensburg, who was said to have preached even without a tongue. St. Hildegard of Bingen associated the tongue with the ELEMENT WATER: "The tongue as it forms words is like waters surging to the point of overflowing their banks. This shows that the soul, in its longing for heaven, strains against its physical confines to sing the praises of its creator."

"To speak with a forked tongue" is to use one's speech as treacherously as a SNAKE (which, it was once popularly believed, transmitted venom with its tongue)—perhaps the serpent of the Garden of Eden (see ADAM AND EVE, PARADISE).

A particularly gruesome form of self-torture practiced in ancient Mexico called for penitents to pull strings of THORNS through their tongues.

tooth Teeth often symbolize vitality, procreation, sexual potency, and sperm. In ancient legends, armed men grew out of soil sown with DRAGON's teeth. Teeth also had "occult significance" [Stemplinger]: when teeth were bared in a MIRROR, it was believed, the mirror darkened. North African Christians mocked or combatted IDOLS by baring their teeth at them, and "the first

baby tooth, if it does not touch the ground when it falls out, prevents genital pain. The tooth of a seven-year-old boy, set in gold or silver, prevents conception."

In Christian iconography St. Apollonia is usually portrayed with teeth and a pair of tongs, since her teeth were extracted as a part of her martyrdom. Through this association she became the patron saint of dentists.

In the symbology of dreams teeth are thought to have sexual associations: strong teeth, biting and chewing food, symbolize vitality, and "the urge to bite when making love is significant. The love for one's partner is so intense that one could 'just gobble him or her up.' Dreams of losing teeth . . . , like dental pain itself, have to do with sexual potency and impotence. Masturbation, above all, brings on dreams of losing teeth, as an expression of the sapping of energy" [Aeppli].

The Chinese believed that a person who dreamt of losing a front tooth would soon lose a parent. The gnashing of teeth was thought to keep ghosts away.

"Toothsome" means delicious, and, by extension, sexually attractive. A person "dressed to the teeth" (or "to the nines") is in his or her best attire.

torch Symbolically and in ceremonies more than merely a source of LIGHT. The torch has a characteristic flame, flickering in a way that seems to bring its surroundings to life, and thus often carried in processions, demonstrations, and political rallies. Torches play a role in many mystic cults and were used, for example, in Mithraic ritual to symbolize life and death: next to the bull-slaying sun-god Mithra stand the spirits Cautes (Life, Light) with a raised torch and Cautopates (Death, DARKNESS) with a lowered torch. The extinguished torch symbolizing death, often in the hands of allegorical CUPIDS, appears frequently on old tombstones. In the Book of Revelation, seven torches are interpreted as symbols of the seven powers or spirits of God [4:5]. A torch is the attribute of martyrs who were tormented with one (e.g., Theodotus, Eutro-

Torch. Hohberg, 1675

pia), and a DOG with a torch in its mouth
often appears with St. Dominic, the founder
of the Dominican order (punningly interpreted as *domini canes*, "dogs of the Lord").
In Hohberg's emblem-book (1675) the torch
of divine wisdom sheds its light: "A traveler,
forced the darkest night to brave,/ Sights
torch's shine and puts his cares to rest;/ So
does God's light his fold both guide and
save,/ When darkness comes to put them to
the test." The fact that the torch's flame
appears to be alive made it a symbol of
awakening, also in relays, where the torch's
FIRE has often been understood as almost
sacred ("the torch is passed")—although
the athlete's torch has generally been transformed into a sort of portable lantern. The
most familiar torch today is the the symbol
of the Olympic Games.

torii The GATE to a Japanese shrine, constructed with a characteristic form and designating that one is entering holy ground.
The torii is usually made of reddened wood
or, less often, of STONE, although in recent

Torii: Yoke-shaped gate at entrance to many Japanese
shrines

times concrete has also been used. The gate
is often hung with intertwined rice straw,
which is thought to have a purifying effect,
keeping anything unclean from entering the
temple grounds (*shimenawa*), and with strips
of WHITE paper, which also symbolize purity.
KARASHISHI usually stand at either side of
the gate.

torque A necklace or collar customarily
worn in Celtic cultures to designate that the
wearer had attained manhood or was a warrior. Roman sculptures showing Celtic (Gal-
lic) warriors in a variety of roles almost
always include the torque, leaving little doubt
as to its symbolic importance. It was not a
closed RING but rather had an opening worn
toward the front; the two ends were often
adorned with heads of animals or stylized
human faces. Archaeological excavations
have revealed that, contrary to the impression given by ancient documents and works
of art, warriors were not always buried with
the torque. Gods and demigods—not only
mortal members of the warrior caste—were
portrayed with the torque.

totem In ethnology, a supernatural tutelary spirit or clan ancestor, usually represented in animal form. The term became
more generally familiar through the totem
POLES carved in TREE trunks by Native
Americans of the Pacific Northwest (Tlin-
git, Haida, Tsimshian, Kwakiutl). Most of
them have an oval opening near the base,
originally the entry to a ceremonial house
(which, however, is rarely preserved). The
carvings are depictions of the animals associated symbolically with the group in question and their myths—BEAR, RAVEN, EAGLE,
killer WHALE, beaver—the creatures with
which the group feels the deepest inner
bonds. The carving and painting of totem
poles often is of great artistic value. For
many decades the poles were museum pieces,
but with the recent revitalization of Native
American culture they have been reinte-
grated into the spiritual life of members of
the various nations.

Individual ethnic groups of ancient Egypt,
later grouped in administrative districts, car-

Totem pole topped by raven. Haida nation, Pacific Northwest, 46 feet tall

ried sculptures of supernatural totemic animals (e.g., BULLS, COWS, oryxes) on bannerlike structures (poles with cross-beams); however, ethnologists have been unable to reconstruct the myths that led to the choice of individual animals.

In classical antiquity there were similar totemic animals for individual ethnic groups, "a vestige of the original animal fetishes" [Stemplinger]. Legends frequently recount how sacred animals showed the way to what were to become dwelling places or shrines. Apollo, for example, is said to have taken on the form of the RAVEN (one of his sacred creatures) and guided the inhabitants of the island of Thera (Santorini) to Cyrene around 630 B.C. Two ravens showed ALEXANDER THE GREAT the way to the shrine of Zeus Amun. When the inhabitants of Picenum went in search of a new homeland in the fourth century B.C., a woodpecker rode on their leader's FLAG. Aeneas and those colonizing Cyme were led by DOVES. The founders of Epidaurus followed a SNAKE; the Samnites a bull, the Hirpines a WOLF; a HARE pointed out the spot where the city of Boiai was to be established; a swarm of BEES

led the way to the CAVE where the oracle of the Boeotian demigod Trophonius was found. With totems, however, as with the occurrence in family names of words for animals, it is not always clear whether there is actually a powerful sense of attachment to the animal in question—and this same uncertainty extends to representations of real animals or mythical creatures in coats of arms (see HERALDRY, SYMBOLS IN). The creatures may simply be an encoding for positive characteristics (e.g., courage, strength, military preparedness) with which the bearers (of the arms in question) wished to associate themselves; hence the preference for such "royal" figures as the eagle or the LION.

tower A predominantly vertical structure, associated by the symbologist with the idea of an AXIS MUNDI linking HEAVEN and EARTH. The Biblical Tower of BABEL (BABYLON) is a mythical symbol of the hubris of our early ancestors, who believed that they could master even the heavens themselves. There are positive associations, however, with certain towers frequently depicted in the Christian tradition: the lighthouse, whose LIGHT guides the SHIP of life, or the citadel tower that protects the faithful against the forces of Satan. The VIRGIN Mary is referred to in litanies as the "Tower of David" or "a tower

Tower: "Eternally immovable." J. Boschius, 1702

Tower: Lighthouse. J. Boschius, 1702

of ivory," showing the way to heaven, as does the entire Church. In the early Christian text *Pastor Hermae* ("The Shepherd of Herma," ca. A.D. 140), the Church is likened to "a great tower over the water, made of splendid ashlars." Literal towers for churches were not built until the Middle Ages, when they served to make the sound of the BELLS resonate at a great distance. The earliest such structures were bell towers isolated from the sanctuaries.

The TAROT card "The LIGHTNING-Struck Tower" (French "La Maison-Dieu") in the Major Arcana—as lightning strikes, people plunge from the tower to the earth below—is interpreted as a reference to human presumptuousness, as in the story of Babel.

In HERALDRY enclosed towers with pinnacles and gates appear frequently in the arms of cities, especially when the name of the city ends in "-burg" or "-bourg" (literally, "fortress"). According to the speculative interpretation of Böckler (1688), towers in the arms of families refer to strongholds that the founder of the line successfully either stormed or defended. "It is thus clear that the tower must designate persons of great merit."

As an attribute of saints, the tower is associated with Bernard of Aosta, Leocadia of Toledo, and Barbara (who was imprisoned

in a tower by her father). Towers as prisons appear frequently in fairy tales (e.g., "Rapunzel"), legend, and history (e.g., the Tower of London).

treasures The ones that play a major role in old tales of magic, spells, and adventure can be understood as "hoards" or "troves" from earlier eras, buried or hidden at a time of danger but then never retrieved by those who had left them behind. It was believed that they offered a relatively easy way to get rich—if one knew a few magic words and were willing to brave the curses attached to the treasures. There are many legends in which such treasures are almost recovered, only to sink back into the EARTH once more.

Viewed rationally, the search for buried GOLD had little prospect of success; the basis for such legendary quests may lie in symbolic traditions of late antiquity, like Gnostic doctrine, in which "treasures" stood for specific attainments sought on the path to wisdom and knowledge. Guardians block access to these inner treasures and can be commanded only by those who possess secret passwords and geometrical symbols—comparable, perhaps, to the mantras and MANDALAS of other cultures. Later traditions may be seen as literalizations of Gnostic doctrine by those with no understanding of its symbolic significance: the treasures become "real" hoards, but access to them continues to depend upon knowing the proper magic words and geometric forms.

tree Rooted in the EARTH but with their branches pointing to the HEAVENS, trees are, like humans themselves, creatures of two worlds, intermediaries between ABOVE AND BELOW. Not only were specific trees or an entire GROVE revered in many ancient civilizations as the abodes of supernatural beings (divinities, elemental spirits), but also the tree was widely seen as the AXIS MUNDI around which the cosmos is organized—for example, the world-tree Yggdrasill in Norse mythology, or the sacred ceiba or yaxché tree of the Yucatan Mayas, which grows in the center of the world and supports the layers of the sky: in each of the four regions

Tree of Knowledge (Eden) as death symbol. Colophon, Frankfurt, 1531

Germanic god of THUNDER and the (Greek) king of the gods, Zeus. Sacred trees of this sort are found among virtually all ancient peoples, to some extent real trees occurring in nature, to some extent trees idealized into cosmic symbols.

In Christian iconography the tree symbolizes life lived in accordance with God's plan: its annual cycle refers to life, death, and resurrection: a barren or dead tree, to the sinner. The Tree of Knowledge is believed to have provided the wood for Christ's CROSS, thus making it from then on, for the believer, the Tree of Life. It was frequently depicted with branches and leaves or likened to the family tree of the "root of Jesse." Tree symbolism and reverence for trees carry some trace, finally, of the natural religion of old, in which trees were not merely a source of wood but the abode of nymphs, and entities to which humans related emotionally. Trees with saints' images on their trunks (called "forest devotions" in Austria) go back to this, as does the Christmas tree, today an almost universal symbol, consoling us in mid-winter with the prospect of greening and rebirth.

Above all, the Virgin Mary was seen as the "tree of life," blessed by the Holy Ghost, and giving the world its fruit, the Savior. Through this association, old village shrines, places of pilgrimage, seem to carry into the present the tradition of "sacred trees": Triple-Oaks of Our Lady, Mary's Green, the Mary Linden, and so forth; Bishop Ezzo of

of the world one colored tree of this species serves as a corner-pillar for the heavens. The importance of forbidden trees in Eden is well known; for Buddhists the peepul or bo tree (*Ficus religiosa*) under which Gautama Buddha attained enlightenment, is the symbol of the "great awakening." Ancient Egypt venerated the sycamore, from out of which the goddess Hathor extended fortifying drink and nourishment to the souls (the mobile, winged *ba*) of the dead. The Sumerian god of vegetation, Dumuzi (Tammuz) was revered as the tree of life. For the ancient Chinese the PEAR and mulberry trees were sacred; for the Druids it was the OAK, which was also the sacred attribute of the

Tree of the planets with two alchemists. Basilius Valentinus, *Azoth*, 1659

Tree-like drawings and ships. Rock drawings, Sweden, Bronze Age

Bamberg celebrated the Cross as a tree of blessings: "Your bough did heaven's burden bear. Your fruit is sweet and good, sublime the blood upon you there." Throughout the Christian Occident we find legends of dead trees, branches, or sticks that turned green again as a sign of God's grace. Medieval sculptures of the Cross as a tree, with the beginnings of branches, are related to this symbolism of resurrection, an association suggested by the way the new growth of spring follows defoliation and winter's repose.

A Jewish legend recounts that the progenitor ABRAHAM planted trees everywhere he went, but that they did not thrive; only one, in the land of Canaan, shot up tall. Through it Abraham could tell whether someone believed in the true God or was an idolator. Over the believer the tree would spread its branches and offer its SHADE for protection, but not over the idolator, from whom the tree would turn aside, refusing shade, stretching its branches upward. Abraham, however, did not forsake the idolators but rather sought to convert them. "By eating from the Tree of Knowledge Adam brought death into the world. But when Abraham came, he healed the world by means of another tree." The legend of the tree that brings redemption may be a transposition, into the world of the Old Testament, of the Christian symbolic tradition of the tree of the Cross. The early Christian text *Physiologus* tells of the Indian tree Peridexion, on whose fruit DOVES feed eagerly but which the SNAKE cannot come near, fleeing even the shadow that the tree casts. The tree is a reference to the Savior, the "true tree of life," whose fruit sustains believers but which the DEVIL cannot approach. In medieval bestiaries this tree is called Perindens; it protects the doves that live in its shade from the DRAGON. "The heavenly fruit of the tree is the wisdom of the Holy Ghost, wisdom that we are given in the sacraments" [Unterkircher].

An antitype of the trees of paradise restored appears in Islamic mythology as the zaqqum-tree, whose foliage and fruit feed the condemned sinners and blasphemers after the final judgment. "Its thorny branches and bitter fruit will swell up in their bodies like molten ore" [Beltz, 1980]. The garden of the new paradise is filled with shade-trees with delicious fruit, of which the just and faithful may eat. Another tree in the Islamic religious tradition is the world-tree, on whose leaves the name of every person is written; Israfil, the ANGEL of death, gathers the leaves that fall by Allah's will and fetches from the earth those who are destined to die. See also DEATH, SYMBOLS OF, and FIG, SIGN OF THE.

triads   Along with triadic structures of female mythical figures, characteristic of classical antiquity and its conceptual world. There seems to have been a more pronounced desire to see powerful female divinities in threes than was the case for their male counterparts: consider the GRACES, the HORAE, the FATES, the GORGONS, the Graeae, the FURIES. Even the number of the NINE MUSES suggests a structure of three-times-three. Later mythologists attempted to interpret the goddess of the night and magic, Hecate, as a triadic figure (girl, woman, crone), which is not unequivocally supported by classical sources. (See SPINNING.) In south-central Europe at the time of the Romans three MOTHERS (*matres, matronae, matrae*) were revered; cults of similar female

Triad in Hindu iconography: Brahma, Vishnu, Shiva with linga. Ca. A.D. 500

Triad: A god with three faces. Gallo-Roman, Reims

triads carried over into alpine regions in the form of the worship of legendary female saints, the three "Beths," with names like "Ainbeth, Wilbeth, and Warbeth" (or Catherine, Barbara, and Lucia; there were many variants). The symbolism of the female triad may also have influenced the Norse myth of the three Norns, spinning human destiny like the Fates of the Greeks. The Hindu Trimurti shows a triadic organization, portraying jointly Brahma, Shiva, and Vishnu, in a way that has often been likened to the Christian Trinity. Its roots in intellectual history, however, involve the efforts of Indian theologians to bridge the widening gap between followers of Shiva and of Vishnu. The Buddhist notion of knowledge (*bodhi*) as the *tri-kaya* ("three bodies") is composed of *dharma-kaya* (true being), *nirmana-kaya* (the earthly mode, Gautama Buddha), and *sambogha-kaya*, the blessed functioning of the community of believers. From this is derived the symbolic

Triad: Sirens. Cartari, 1647

image of the "three jewels" (*tri-ratna*): law, Buddha, and community, which are interpreted in Jainism as "right conduct," "right faith," and "right knowledge." In the imagery of ALCHEMY, the division of the world into *corpus, anima,* and *spiritus* (body, soul, spirit; also, salt, SULFUR, AND MERCURY) is often portrayed with three figures (often disguised by symbols of the TRINITY). (See also BLACK.)

triangle One of the simplest of geometrical symbols; at its origin it represented the first possibility of enclosing an area, and creating a figure, with straight lines. For this reason, not every triangle has symbolic significance. Archaeologists found Stone Age masonry made of triangularly applied flagstones at the Lepenski Vir site on the Danube (seventh millennium B.C.); triangular bone-carvings are even older. There is a wide variety of interpretations for this symbol. The female pubic triangle is most frequently mentioned, with its apex pointing downward and, in some cases, a vertical line beginning at that apex. In later civilizations triangles appear frequently in designs on ceramics, those pointing downward traditionally interpreted as WATER-symbols (suggesting the direction of falling rain) and those pointing upward, as FIRE-symbols (the direction of the flame). The two triangles superimposed form a complete DUALITY, the SIX-pointed star (HEXAGRAM, Star of David). A triangle is also inscribed at times in the conjurer's magic CIRCLE. The triangle can also be used in place of the trefoil (three-leaf CLOVER), as a sort of euphemism for this masculine symbol. In the system of the Pythagoreans, the Greek letter delta, with its triangular form, was the symbol for cosmic birth, and similarly in Hinduism for the female, life-giving deity Durga. In the early Christian period the Manicheans used the triangle as a symbol of the TRINITY, which led St. Augustine (A.D. 354–430) to reject its use for this purpose. It did subsequently prevail as a symbol for the Trinity (the hand, head, and name of God, complemented by an EYE), signifying the Father, the Son, and the Holy Ghost; this "God's-

Triangle: The sign Hrungnir's Heart. Gotland (Sweden), Viking era

eye" in the triangle was particularly frequent in the baroque period, and in the symbology of FREEMASONRY this "all-seeing eye," with nine beams emanating from it, is also a symbol of the Godhead. In the Cabala the Book of Zohar ("splendor") contains the sentence: "In heaven God's two eyes and his forehead form a triangle, and their reflection forms a triangle in the waters." In pre-Christian times the philosopher Xenocrates (339–314 B.C.) had viewed the equilateral triangle as "divine," the isosceles as "demonic," and the scalene as "human" (imperfect).

Arthur Koestler portrays the fascination of number harmony in the context of the proportions of the right triangle, as elucidated by PYTHAGORAS (sixth century. B.C.): "There is no apparent relationship between the lengths of the sides of a right triangle; but if we construct a square on each side, the combined area of the smaller squares is exactly equal to the area of the largest. If such wonderfully ordered laws, previously invisible to the human eye, could be discovered by plunging into numerical formations, were there not grounds to hope that under mathematical examination the universe would soon reveal all of its secrets?" (1959). In the light of the symbolic associations already mentioned, FREEMASONRY also found significance in the Pythagorean right triangle with its sides of three, four, and five units, respectively; it appears, with squares contructed on the three sides, on Masonic instructional tapestries, and is referred to simply as the "Pythagoras." As "Euclid's 47th problem" it is the symbol of the "Master of the Lodge" and the insignia of the past-master.

In ancient China the triangle is a "female symbol" but is not the subject of great speculation. In Tibetan Tantrism the hexagram, as the combination of two equilateral triangles, symbolizes the "penetration of femininity by male fire." In the illuminated manuscripts of ancient Mexico a triangle resembling a capital A is the symbol for "year." In Occidental art triangular composition was frequent in both architecture and painting, especially where subjects relating to the Trinity were being addressed.

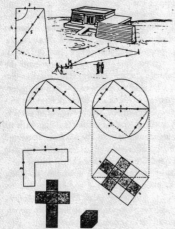

Triangle: Egyptian sailmakers construct a Pythagorean triangle; a geometry lesson

trident   A fishing spear with three barbed prongs, is the symbol and attribute of the sea-god Poseidon (Latin Neptune). As a piece of fishing apparatus it occasionally appears in coats of arms, e.g. on the flag of Barbados. In Hindu symbolism the trident refers to the god Shiva, i.e., to his three aspects (creation, being, destruction) or to his past, present, and future. Worshippers of Shiva paint the sign of the trident on their foreheads as a visible symbol. The ancient Indian FIRE-god Agni (cognate of Latin *ignis*, "fire"), who rides a RAM, also holds a trident in his hand.

Trident and fish. Floor mosaic, House of Fish, Ostia, 4th century A.D.

Trinity (from the Latin *trinitas*; also Holy Trinity) A theological concept of great symbological import, and not to be confused with TRIADS or triadic structures in general. The Trinity is the doctrine of unity of God in three persons—God the Father, Christ the Son, and the Holy Spirit (or Holy Ghost)—formulated at the time of the confrontation with Arianism (Council of Nicaea, A.D. 325). In the Occident it led to the doctrine of "tritheism," espoused by Roscelin of Compiègne and declared heretical in 1092. In the fine arts the Trinity was first portrayed by three persons sitting side by side. but after the tenth century it was forbidden to represent the Holy Spirit in human form. He was replaced by the figure of the DOVE, or the Trinity, following classical prototypes, was portrayed as a body whose head had three faces, or by a head whose three faces blended in with one another. A TRIANGLE with its apex pointing upward and "God's eye" inside it, is another symbol of the Trinity. For the Jungian school of analytic psychology the trinity is a masculine symbol that the doctrine of the (physical) Assumption of the Blessed Virgin (officially proclaimed on November 1, 1950) augmented to form a quaternity (see FOUR), the archetype of totality and perfection (see SQUARE). Other traditional symbols of the Trinity include three overlapping CIRCLES, three arcs enclosed by a circle, the three-leaf clover, the tau CROSS with three arms

of equal length, the Y-shaped "fork"-cross, three tendrils on a grapevine (see WINE), a pair of SCALES with three weights, three HARES whose ears form a triangle, or three FISH, LIONS, or EAGLES with a common head. In portrayals of the "Seat of Grace," God the Father appears as a BEARDED man, holding in his arms the Cross with Christ upon it, as the Holy Spirit hovers overhead in the form of a dove. The Quaternity (including Mary), often understood as the coronation of the Mother of God, was a frequent subject of sacred art from the mid-15th century onward. The old portrayal of God with three faces was forbidden and declared heretical by Pope Urban VIII in 1628, but

Trinity as three suns, equilateral triangle, rainbow. J. Boschius, 1702

Trinity of body, soul, and spirit in alchemy. *Rosarium Philosophorum*, 1550

many such portrayals survive from the Middle Ages. The reason for this prohibition was Protestant ridiculing of such images as "Catholic Cerberuses" (see DOG).

triskelion   A design dividing a CIRCLE into three parts, not unlike its division into four by the bent arms of a SWASTIKA. Triskelions appear, for example, on prehistoric earthenware vessels of the late Bronze Age, and triadic structures of SPIRALS adorn the walls

Trinity. Rustic altar panel, Tyrol, ca. 1600

of Irish megaliths—surely with symbolic intent and not as mere decoration. There are also triskelions formed from three human legs bent at the knee, e.g. on Pamphylian coins or in the arms of the city of Agrigento (Sicily). Armored legs in this configuration appear in the arms of the Isle of Man, with the motto *"Stabia quocunque ieceris"* ("It will stand erect, wherever it is thrown"). The arms of the city of Füssen (Bavaria) also contain three legs. As in the case of the swastika, the triskelion is associated with rotation. The form of three overlapping circles, frequently found in the WINDOWS of Gothic churches, is associated with the Holy TRINITY. Medieval stained-glass windows often portray three rabbits or HARES chasing one another, with their ears meeting at the center to form a TRIANGLE.

Triskelion in Celtic art; triadic structure.

trowel   A mason's tool significant in the symbology of FREEMASONRY, especially in references to those who have already completed their "apprenticeship" and are "brothers" (the "journeymen") of the order (but not yet "masters"): the "STONE" has already been "hewn," and the trowel serves to apply the "mortar" (binding WORK that secures the brother within the fraternity). While the other symbolic tools of this system are more those of the stonecutter than of the "mason" in the present-day sense, the trowel is actually used to bind "building blocks" together: this is also its symbolic role in the building of the symbolic "TEMPLE" of Freemasonry. In some versions of Masonic doctrine, the trowel—which can be used to "wall up" or seal off an area—

Trowel and level, Masonic symbols of the work of the Lodge

signifies the injunction of secrecy to be maintained with respect to outsiders (the "profane") in order to guarantee the "arcanum," i.e., the secret (enclosed, as it were, in a "chest" [in Latin, *arca*]) of the validity and significance of Masonic symbols and rituals as personally experienced by the "brothers" of the fraternity.

Miniature GOLD and SILVER trowels serve to commemorate gatherings of Masonic brothers. Baurnjöpel mentions that officers of the lodge wear a trowel and a KEY "over their hearts . . . the former of the purest, brightest gold, and the latter made of ivory." (1793).

trumpet A horn capable of producing a single pitch, derived from the ancient Jewish shofar (a RAM'S HORN), which was sounded during marches through the desert, when enemies were approaching, when God ap-

Trumpet: Fall of Jericho. Detail, Luther Bible, Wittenberg, 1682

peared to Moses on Mount Sinai, or to announce the freeing of slaves in the year of "jubile" [Leviticus 25:8–17]. Tradition also has it that the shofar was a reminder of the ram that God commanded Abraham, the ancestral father of the Jewish people, to sacrifice in place of his son Isaac [Genesis 22:1–14]. It was said that only those of the Jewish faith could produce sounds from the horn. The shofar brings forth "lasting, calling, broken, resounding, pealing, or mournful sounds, in a specific order" [de Vries, 1986] and is still blown on the Jewish New Year as ordained in Numbers 29:1.

Trumpet: Horn players with helmets. Cave drawings, Scandinavia, Bronze Age

A great trumpet, it is said, will announce the reuniting of the lost and the exiled. Christian depictions of the Last Judgment follow the Book of Revelation, and ANGELS blow trumpets to announce the END OF THE WORLD; this tradition, and the use of bugles in the military, are behind the use of "trumpet" as a verb meaning to spread news.

In the Bronze Age large curved horns apparently played a role in the religious practice of Northern Europe; they are also depicted in the prehistoric cave drawings of the period.

turquoise A BLUE-GREEN gemstone that symbolizes in Western tradition, according to its coloration, either the planet JUPITER (green) or VENUS (blue); the turquoise is the birthstone of those born under the sign of Sagittarius. The name of the STONE refers to the notion that it is of Turkish or Middle Eastern origin. It was thought to protect rulers from evil influences.

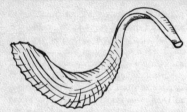

Trumpet: Shofar, made from twisted ram's horn, blown on Rosh Hashanah

In ancient Mexico, also, the turquoise (in Aztec, *xihuitl*) was one of the most admired gemstones; only JADE was more valued. Turquoise mosaics adorned the DIADEM of the KINGS and their ornamental shields. The FIRE god was called "Lord of the Turquoise" (Xiuhtecutli)—the sky-blue turquoise symbolizing the unity of heavenly (i.e., solar) and earthly FIRE. He was adorned with the "turquoise serpent" (Xiuhcoatl), which also constituted his "alter ego"; the Aztec king was considered to be his earthly counterpart.

turtle For the psychologist, a symbol of quiet strength and the possibility of taking refuge from any external attack. "It retains about it something of the age-old hush of life constantly able to withdraw into itself at the approach of danger" [Aeppli]. The turtle plays such a role, for example, in the highly symbolic novel *Momo* by Michael Ende. In ancient Chinese cosmology we find mention of the primordial Ao, a sea-turtle of cosmic dimensions: it carries the world on its back. Stone sculptures of turtles, with armored backs, were believed to preserve the stability of the cosmos. There was said to be an Ao-shan (Ao mountain) on the ISLANDS OF THE BLESSED. Ao itself was said to be a fire-eater, and an Ao figure on the roof was thought to protect a house against FIRE. In the Chinese system of symbolic analogies, Ao was one of the five sacred animals, specifically associated with the north, WATER, and winter. In the earliest periods of Chinese civilization, bits of turtle shell were used in augury, apparently because the

number of peripheral sections (24) corresponded to the number of divisions in the agrarian calendar. Because of the great age it attained, the turtle served as a symbol for longevity; because of its imperviousness to attack, as a symbol for universal order which nothing could dislodge. At the same time the turtle also had negative associations: it was believed that all turtles (*kui*) were female, that they could reproduce only by mating with SNAKES, and that they had no sense of shame (*kui* also being the word for "penis"). The positive associations, however, were predominant.

In European antiquity the turtle, because it produced so many EGGS, was a symbol of fertility; because of its "quiet reserve," chaste love; because of its long life, unwavering vitality. In patristic writings, the turtle, living in mud, came to symbolize all that is earth-bound; St. Ambrose (ca. 340–397), however, pointed out that the shell of the turtle could be used to make a seven-stringed instrument whose music gladdened the hearts of all who heard it. Even in ancient times the protective function of the shell was exploited symbolically in magic rituals (to ward off hail and black magic); turtle EYES set in GOLD served as an amulet against the "evil eye." In Aesop's fable, the patience of the tortoise enables it to "outrun" the HARE.

In the art and mythology of ancient Mexico, as well, turtles are of considerable importance. (Sea-turtles, for example, are the mounts of mythical ancestors.)

In India the turtle was the second embodiment (*avatara*) of the god Vishnu.

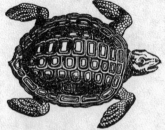

Turtle: Sea turtle. C. Gesner, *Nomenclator*, Zürich, 1650

Twins: Arabian portrayal of the constellation Gemini. El Sufi, A.D. 1009

twins In some cultures, considered regrettable accidents of nature; often one of them is killed at birth, in some cases because it is supposed (in parts of West Africa, for example) that the two have committed a sort of incest in the mother's womb. In Native American myths they represent a DUALITY of good and evil. In other traditions twins are greatly esteemed, as in the case of the Greek and Roman myths of Castor and Pollux (Greek Polydeuces). The rulers of the island kingdom of Atlantis, according to Plato's account, are also twins: ATLAS and Gadirus (the demigod for whom the city of Gades [Cádiz] was named), Ampheres and Eudemon, Mneseus and Autochthon, Elasippus and Mestor, Azaes and Diaprepes. These may refer not to "real" sets of twins

out to the ancient custom (also observed by the first inhabitants of the Canary Islands [see ISLANDS OF THE BLESSED]) of two KINGS sharing a single throne. According to Robert Graves, this arrangement was also known in Mycenaean Greece. In addition to Castor and Pollux (Sparta), Idas and Lynceus ruled in Messina, Proetus and Acrisius in Argos, Heracles (Hercules) and Iphicles in Tiryns, and Eteocles and Polynices in Thebes.

Twins are often so portrayed as to symbolize dually opposed temperaments. One is soft, passive, and introverted; the other, dynamic, bellicose, extroverted. Or one is mortal, the other immortal. In other cases, they complement each other perfectly, forming an invincible duo so dangerous to the cosmic order that they must be eliminated from the world of the living.

The third sign of the zodiac (see STARS) is Gemini ("the twins," May 22–June 21), an "air sign" associated with duality, separation, contradiction, similarity, duplication, repeated actions, and the like. The constellation is named for the stars Castor and Pollux, which are of almost equal brightness.

In ancient China twins of different sexes were an unlucky omen. They were said to constitute a "ghostly couple" and were generally not allowed to live. A pair of male twins, on the other hand, was sometimes viewed as a divine recognition of great piety.

UFO, or **unidentified flying object** In the view of many authors, especially those writing in the 1960s, spaceships bringing intelligent visitors from other planets or solar systems—superior beings who contemplate life on earth with grave concern and contemplate constructive intervention. Some psychologists, on the other hand, believe that the supposed sightings and ensuing interpretations are mere visions—an updating (for the technical age) of the traditional notion of guardian ANGELS: symbols of a yearning for help from "heaven" to eliminate (or at least reduce) the existential distress of humanity. The angel of yore has now become a UFO. It should be noted that in recent times, since space flights and the various possibilities for investigating outer space have virtually eliminated the possibility of extraterrestrial life, the number of UFO sightings has been reduced almost to zero, just as the general interest in cosmic phenomena on the part of the general population has greatly diminished. In earlier times people looking at comets saw heavenly SWORDS and rings of fire, "signs from heaven"; similarly, UFO's, in the years following the middle of the 20th century, symbolized the hope for an intervention from on high (see ABOVE/BELOW)—a hope manifested also in books and motion pictures, and an extraordinary symptom of the times.

unicorn A fabled creature important in ancient and medieval symbology, usually portrayed as a WHITE DEER with a HORSE'S mane, cloven hoofs, and a SPIRAL HORN growing out of its forehead. It seems to have its origin in the writings of the Greek historian Ctesias (ca. 400 B.C.), who refers to a wild animal whose single horn has healing powers—presumably a misunderstanding of descriptions of the Indian rhinoceros. Cattle breeders can also produce one-horned BULLS by surgical means: the calf's dermal bumps (papillae), from which two horns would normally grow, are made to overlap, then heal, and grow together. Rhinoceros horn was valued for enhancing potency, and the horn apparently is of phallic significance. In Occidental iconography, however, the horn is still shown as growing out of the unicorn's forehead; thus what was originally a symbol of sexuality is associated with the intellect. The unicorn indeed became a symbol of purity and strength, and medieval miniatures and tapestries show that it could be caught only with the aid of a VIRGIN, in whose lap the trusting animal seeks refuge, whereupon it is caught by hunters and killed. This is seen as a symbol of the Virgin Mary's conception of Christ, and of the subsequent crucifixion of the Savior. Gabriel, the ANGEL of the Annunciation, is sometimes portrayed as a hunter, driving the "precious unicorn" to the Virgin, with the help of his DOGS, who are named either "Faith, Hope, and Charity," or "Truth, Righteousness, Peace, and Mercy," for the cardinal virtues. Mary, meanwhile, sits in an enclosed garden (*hortus conclusus*) or in a rose-arbor (as in tapestries at the Musée Cluny in Paris). The Christian interpretation of the unicorn goes back to ancient myths and early Christian instructional texts, which were subsequently adapted and illustrated in medieval bestiaries. There are frequent references to the efficacy of the horn as an antidote to poison; ground up, it was said to heal wounds quickly. Such horns (in truth tusks of the narwhal, a North Atlantic sea mammal, *Monodon monoceros*, imported from the waters off Iceland and Greenland) were displayed not

Unicorn of ancient Chinese tradition. Stone relief, ca. 100 B.C.

sing lullabies; the elephant fell asleep in the lap of one of them, the other killed it with a SWORD, and the king dyed a cape in its BLOOD. It is not clear what animal is meant in the Bible by the Hebrew word *re'em*. Although it is probably a wild buffalo, the word is translated "unicorn" (Greek *monoceros*), as in Psalm 22:21: "Save me from the lion's mouth: for thou hast heard me from the horns of the unicorns." The Chinese unicorn (*ky-lin, ch'i-lin*) bears little resem-

only in Renaissance collections of curios but also in pharmacies. The early Christian *Physiologus* describes as follows the power of the horn to counter the effects of poison: before the other animals come to drink, "the snake comes forward and spits its venom into the water. The animals, however, knowing that the water is poisoned, do not dare to drink. They await the unicorn. The unicorn comes, goes right into the lake and makes a cross with its horn. This removes the effect of the poison. Only after the unicorn has drunk do the other animals approach and do likewise." This is clearly a mythical transformation of the belief in the wondrous power of the rhinoceros' horn. In the medieval collection *Gesta Romanorum*, incidentally, the ELEPHANT takes what is otherwise the role of the unicorn: a king, wishing to hunt one down, is said to have ordered two beautiful virgins to go into the forest naked and

Unicorn ridden by a savage. Antique playing card ("Vogel-Unter") by Meister E. S.

blance to its European counterpart: it can best be described as a deer-like animal with scales, an oxtail, and a furry horn on its forehead. It stands for happiness and blessedness, especially being blessed with male offspring. Portrayals of the gentle goddess Kuan-yin towering over a reclining unicorn are reminiscent of the Occidental pairing of virgin and unicorn. In the imagery of ALCHEMY the unicorn is a symbol for the primal essence mercury, which is to be joined with the LION, SULFUR, in a higher unity. In HERALDRY the unicorn, as a bearded horse with cloven hoofs and a spiral horn, appears only rarely within the shield itself (e.g., of the Austrian city of Bludenz), but often as a supporter, along with the lion, as in the arms of Great Britain.

Unicornis ein Einhorn.

Unicorn. From C. Gesner's *Historia Animalium*, Zürich, 1551

Uroborus around Demogorgon, god of time. Cartari, 1647

Uroborus. Etching on bronze vessel, China, Chou dynasty, ca. 1200 B.C.

Uroborus around young sun god: Symbol of (circular) course of time. Ancient Egypt

uroborus A SNAKE biting (or "swallowing") its own tail. This symbolic image (found in a great variety of cultures) presents in animal form the circle as an embodiment of "eternal return" and suggests that for—indeed, *in*—every end there is a new beginning, in a cycle of endless repetitions. Along with the symbolic associations already present in the "constantly rejuvenated" snake, the "closing of the circle" through its body offers an expressive metaphor for cyclical repetition, for the sequence of "ENDS" OF THE WORLD and restorations of it, for death

Uroborus, Greek text: "The One is everything." Codex Marcianus, Venice, 11th century

Uroborus as two-headed, winged dragon. Illustration, 12th century codex, British Museum

and rebirth—and, by extension, for eternity (like the simple circle). In the symbolism of ALCHEMY, the uroborus symbolizes a closed, cyclical process in which the heating, evaporation, cooling, and condensation of a liq- uid helps to refine or purify substances. In this uroborus the single snake is often replaced by two creatures, each biting the tail of the other, the upper one a winged DRAGON (a symbol of volatility).

Valkyries (Old Norse *valkyrjar*, "choosers of the slain") Figures in Old Norse mythology associated with the honorable death of warriors. They are handmaidens of the god Odin, who is seeking brave soldiers from earthly battles—those, precisely, who have no fear of death—to become his comrades in the great battle Ragnarök at the end of time (see END OF THE WORLD). The Valkyries ride through the clouds on swift HORSES, snatching up the elect and carrying them off to Valhalla, Odin's AFTERLIFE home for the valiant. In the *Edda*, the names of the Valkyries include Skuld (the last of the NORNS, who brings death), Brünnhilde, Göll ("she who calls out"), Gondul ("she-wolf"), Hrist ("storm"), Mist, and Thrud ("force"). Those who have fallen in battle and been borne off to Valhalla are called *einherjar* ("individual combatants"); they face one another daily in training matches, then every evening carouse together unwounded. The entire myth of the Valkyries expresses on one hand the great prestige attached to death in combat (not unlike the Aztec celebration of death on the field of battle or the sacrificial altar) and on the other hand a fearless anticipation of the great battle at the end of time—in which all the gods and their adjutants must fall, and after which a new era can begin, a version of PARADISE lived out in "Gimle" in the southern sky.

The Valkyrie Brünnhilde has become most familiar, playing a tragic role in the *Song of the Nibelungs* and bringing about the ruin of the hero SIEGFRIED, who has won her hand for King Gunther. Brünnhilde is always thought of as "robust," and it is this quality which has become proverbial.

Vandals The name of a Germanic people from the period of the great migrations; in modern usage, it ascribes senseless destruction by the Vandals of old and their present-day imitators. The historical Vandals first settled by the rivers Oder and Vistula, divided into two groups, the Asdings and the Silings (for which "Silesia" is named). When the time of the great migrations came, the Silings wandered long and far, then settled in 411 in the south of Spain. (The name "Andalusia" may be a corruption of "Vandalusia.") There they learned seafaring and were soon led by their king Geiserich to North Africa (429); in 439 they conquered Carthage and founded an empire there. From Carthage they undertook "Viking raids" in the Mediterranean area, and in 455, they unexpectedly defeated the utterly unprepared city of Rome. "The plundering went on for a fortnight. But there was no wanton destruction, and the lives of the populace were spared. . . . In comparison with the horrible defeat of Carthage in 146 B.C., the sacking of Rome was relatively mild, and involved no real violations of accepted military procedures of the time. The word 'vandalism' was first used by the French bishop Grégoire of Blois in 1794 to describe the

Vandal coin portraying King Gunthamund (d. A.D. 496). North Africa

Veiled bride. Turkish miniature, 17th century

savage destruction that characterized the French Revolution, which he likened to the sacking of Rome in 455. But he gave the Vandals a notoriety that they hardly deserved. The carrying off of the spoils of war, mostly from public property, was accepted practice, observed especially by the Romans themselves when they were the victors" [Nack]. Under Geiserich's great-grandson Gelimer the North African empire of the Vandals collapsed, and the territory was restored to Roman rule. The Vandal captives were not executed but integrated into the Roman army and thus scattered over the provinces of the dissolving empire.

veil A partly transparent covering for the face, generally a symbol of modesty, virtue, and withdrawal from the outside world. In earlier times women and girls wore veils to church to indicate their removal from the vanities of this world. Nuns were veiled in public (hence the expression "to take the veil" for entry into cloister life). The veil was commonly worn at court in the Middle Ages and survives in the veils of bride and widow. In Muslim countries women are required to be veiled in public so as not to arouse the desires of male strangers. On the other hand, it is customary among the Tuaregs of the Central Sahara that men veil their faces, a practice presumably originating as protection against sand storms.

Fog and cloud cover are often referred to as veils. Both the noun and the verb are used in extended senses to refer to intentional (if at times partial) concealment (e.g., "thinly veiled references"). The veil is the attribute both of St. Ludmilla, who was strangled with one, and of Margravine Agnes of Austria: in fulfillment of a sacred vow, St. Leopold founded the cloister Klosterneuburg on the spot where Agnes' veil was found after it had been carried off by the wind.

Venus (Greek Aphrodite) The PLANET, originally referred to as a STAR—"the" morning, or evening, star, and yet one that is never above the horizon at midnight; this "star" was also known as Phosphorus or Lucifer ("the bearer of LIGHT") in the Western tradition. In ancient Rome Venus was associated with romantic attraction and sexual desire; the goddess "ruled" in springtime, and her festival, Veneralia, was celebrated on the first day of April. In Greek mythology the goddess was said to have been born off the coast of Cyprus from out of the sea foam (as Botticclli painted her). (Her Greek name, Aphrodite, comes from *aphrus*, "foam.") Her metal was COPPER (from the Greek *cyprius*, literally "Cypriot"). Her cognomen Anadyomene means "climbing from the sea." The erotic cult of the goddess goes back to even earlier times; Plato, however, introduced

Venus as morning star precedes the sun; as evening star, follows it. J. Boschius, 1702

Venus with Taurus and Libra. Astrological guide, 1499

the distinction between a popular and a heavenly symbol of love (Aphrodite Pandemos and Aphrodite Urania, respectively). She was also the goddess of fertility (in Rome, Venus Genetrix).

In ASTROLOGY Venus is thought of as a clearly feminine planet, ruling Libra by day and Taurus by night. Venus is thought of as "gentle, sensual, motherly, a planet of music and joy, loving harmony and sympathy," a "benefactor" of the imagination and of love matches. The COLORS associated with it are pink and light BLUE; its stones the aquamarine, the light SAPPHIRE, bright red CORAL, lapis lazuli, and sky-blue TURQUOISE.

In ancient China the planet was associated with WHITE (the color of death), autumn (the time of year when it is particularly visible as the evening star), the male sex, and the "ELEMENT" metal. It thus had completely different astrological associations in the Eastern and Western traditions.

In the Maya civilization of the Yucatan, Venus was observed very closely, and its orbit as morning and evening star calculated at length in the manuscript known today as the "Codex Dresdensis." Five Venus years, numbering 2920 days, correspond to eight solar years, as the Mayas noted, and in this time the planet appeared five times each as the morning star; five gods were associated with these appearances. The first of these appearances in each cycle was considered a sign of bad luck, because the star "fired its spears at various creatures." There were sim-

ilar beliefs in the Mexican highland, where the planet was associated with the divine Quetzalcoatl, or plumed serpent (see SNAKE). In ancient Peru Venus was known as "Chasca," which the Inca Garcilaso de la Vega explains as meaning "long- or curly-haired." It was revered as a page in the court of the divine SUN, at times preceding it and at times scurrying along behind it.

In early scholarship about prehistoric art, certain statuettes and reliefs were referred to as depictions of "Venus," apparently as a way of mocking Paleolithic ideals of beauty. These sculptures, however, clearly are not expressive of erotic desires or aesthetic notions: they depict distant female ancestors, and their corpulence is to be understood as a symbolic accentuation of plenitude and the ability to bear and nurse children. (Compare CORNUCOPIA.)

vices Cardinal sins or deadly sins are usually personified in the visual arts by ugly persons, often doing battle with the VIRTUES; the number, assortment, and attributes of the figures vary. The most important are the following: Pride—a crowned woman with bat's wings, riding a LION and holding a SCEPTER; Envy—a woman riding a DOG with a BONE in its MOUTH; Gluttony—a woman riding a FOX with a GOOSE in its mouth; Covetousness (or Avarice or Greed)—a man sitting on a money-chest, often with

Vices: Invidia (Envy) strangling herself. Cartari, 1647

Vices: Seven Deadly Sins as demons. Baldung Grien's *Pomegranate Book,* 1511

a BADGER; Sloth—a man sleeping on a DON-KEY; Anger—a man tearing his garments, or two men dueling with SWORDS; Lust—a woman riding a PIG or goat, or a Siren (see WATER SPIRITS) holding both of her fish-tails in her hands (an image also appearing, however, on amulets to ward off evil); Unbelief—a person before an IDOL; Despair—a man hanging himself (JUDAS); Folly—a man biting STONES; Cowardice—a man fleeing a HARE. In the baroque period, Envy (*Invidia*) was also portrayed as a bare-bosomed woman strangling herself; Blame or Slander, as the Greek god Momus with a club; Deceit (*Fraus*), as a SNAKE with a human head and SCORPION tails. Late baroque sculptural groupings often portray the Stations of the Cross as individual scenes in which Christ atones for specific vices of humanity.

villagers, foolish In different cultures the inhabitants of specific villages or towns (usually not far from that of the storyteller in question) have become symbols of collective stupidity in the solution of problems. In ancient times the inhabitants of the Thracian city of Abdera were the butts of jokes. The inhabitants of the village of Gotham in Nottinghamshire (England) were said to have feigned stupidity in the early 13th century to dissuade King John from establishing a residence there. In the Renaissance the in-habitants of the Saxon city of Schilda or Schildau (hence the present-day generic *Schildbürger*) became famous for their antics (*Schildbürgerstreiche*) as recounted in the *Lalenbuch* of 1598, a reworking of material from the EULENSPIEGEL tradition and the writings of Hans Sachs. (In earlier collections similar stories had been told about the "Lalebürger," residents of a fictitious town.) In Jewish folklore of Eastern Europe the inhabitants of the shtetl Chelm played a similar role. In modern times the populations of entire countries have come to function in this way. In France, the Belgians, and in the United States, Polish people sometimes are the butt of such humor.

violet (color) A mixture of BLUE and RED, named for the FLOWER of the same name; the color traditionally stands for spirituality, linked with the blood of sacrifice. In liturgical usage it is associated with repentance, penance, expiation, and contemplation. Violet is made from equal parts of the primary colors blue and red, and thus symbolically combines wisdom and love. In old representations of Christ's Passion, he wears a violet mantle. Also, violet is the color used in the Church during the Advent season, the period of contemplation that precedes Christmas.

A similar, more reddish color is the purple of the ancient imperial capes or the fine clothing of the rich. Purple dye came from the secretions of two species of sea snail and thus was very costly; this made purple cloth a prized status symbol. In antiquity and the Middle Ages the lichen orchil (Latin *Roccella tinctoria,* Spanish *orchilla*) was used to make an "imitation" purple dye. Orchil was harvested primarily on the coast of the Canary Islands (ISLANDS OF THE BLESSED). (See also AMETHYST.)

violet (flower) (Latin *Viola odorata,* Greek *ionia*) A small, highly fragrant FLOWER, said in Central Europe to "teach the virtue of modesty" because, tiny though it is, it is a favorite symbol of springtime. According to Greek mythology, the meadow from which Hades, the god of the underworld, abducted

Violet (flower). Hohberg, 1675

Persephone was covered with crocuses, ROSES, HYACINTHS, and violets. On the Roman *dies violaris*, or violet day, the dead were commemorated and their graves decorated with violets. Garlands of violets were worn at banquets because the flower was believed to have a "cooling" effect. It was also believed to reduce the intensity of a reveler's hangover the morning after.

An old German superstition recommended that the first three violets found at the edge of the forest be swallowed as a medicine to ward off all maladies. Hohberg (1675) offered the following allegorical verses: "Sweet violet tall grass doth oft conceal,/ And yet its lovely fragrance makes it known./ So, too, the Christian leads a quiet life,/ Yet one for which great honors are in store." The bluish color of the blossom, associated with loyalty and constancy, made it a favorite gift for lovers to exchange. In the Middle Ages the finding of the first violet of the year was an occasion for great festivities and outdoor dancing. (See also VIOLET [COLOR].)

virgin, maiden, maid (Latin *virgo*, Greek *parthenos*) A young woman, unmarried and chaste, symbolizes in many cultures an ascetic turning toward the otherworldly; in some cases this abstinence is associated with a magical cult of abstinence rather than strictly moral considerations. A period of virginity was required of the women seers (see SIBYLS) and vestals of ancient Rome so that they would be constantly available to receive communications from their divinity.

Many gods, heroes, and rulers were said to have been conceived nonsexually by virgins, e.g., Hebe (the Greek goddess of youth), Perseus, ALEXANDER THE GREAT, Genghis Khan, Lao-tzu, and, in ancient Mexico, the god Quetzalcóatl (see SNAKE). The emperor Augustus was said to have been miraculously sired by a snake, the sacred creature of Apollo, in one of the temples of the god. The vestal virgin Rhea Silvia was made pregnant with Romulus and Remus by MARS, the god of war. Christian theologians interpret these myths as anticipations of the conception of Christ; in medieval paintings of the Annunciation, God's procreative power is depicted as a DOVE within a beam of LIGHT striking Mary's head or EAR. WINDOWS and CRYSTALS (see also PRECIOUS STONES) that transmit light intact are symbols for the Virgin Mary.

Ancient Peru also had its sacral virgins, as the Inca Garcilaso de la Vega (1539–1616) and others report: "They lived until the end of their lives in constant seclusion, preserving their virginity to the last . . . for they said that the wives of the SUN must not be of the ordinary sort, that anyone could see. And this seclusion was so extreme that not even the KING himself would make use of his privilege . . . , i.e., would see or speak with them. . . . The principal activity of the solar virgins was SPINNING and weaving. . . . The nuns produced all of these [fabrics] by hand and in great quantity—for the sun, their husband. And, since the sun could neither wear nor set aside the finery, they sent it to the King as the sun's natural and legal successor . . . and since

Virgin with eagle's wings. Medieval heraldic insignia

Virgin: St. Juliana keeps the devil in chains. W. Auer, 1890

they had been made for the sun, and by the hands of the Coyas, his wives, who because of their station were of the very blood of the sun, these fabrics were venerated above all others." If a solar virgin was found in an unchaste relationship with a mortal man, her punishment was to be buried alive; her lover, however, was hanged, and his birthplace destroyed. Among nonliterate peoples we also encounter the notion that virgins have superior powers to those of married women. The mythologist F. Karlinger comments as follows upon an Australian aborigine myth about the constellation Pleiades: "The two [STARS of] Pleiades who married Wurunnah do not shine as brightly as those who remained virgins. The belief in the greater power [here, brightness] of virgins as compared with married women, prevails among the majority of exotic peoples." See also MOTHER.

The sun is in the house of Virgo, the sixth sign of the zodiac, from August 23 until September 22. BEES, the FOX, and barnyard fowl have a magical association with this sign, which is one of the "EARTH signs," along with Taurus (see BULL) and CAPRICORN. Traditional astrological symbology associates with Virgo such qualities as self-denial, intellectual clarity and cool-headedness, untapped possibilities, the transmutability of primal matter (the alchemist's *materia prima*: the sign is ruled by the

planet MERCURY; see SULFUR AND MERCURY). According to the astral legend communicated by Aratus in his didactic poem *Phaenomena* (third century B.C.), Virgo is the personification of justice (Greek Dike), who in a distant GOLDEN AGE lived among mortals but then became disenchanted with them as their mores became cruder; she spread her WINGS and flew up into the HEAVENS, where she is visible only as a distant constellation. It is no accident that the sign of the zodiac next to her is Libra (see SCALES).

virtues   (from Latin *virtus*, "manliness") In Christian art, personifications of the "three theological virtues," faith, hope, and love (or charity), and the "four cardinal virtues," courage, justice, prudence, and temperance—SEVEN in all. The "theological virtues" Fides, Spes, and Caritas are said to be the daughters of St. SOPHIA (Wisdom), and their most important attributes are as follows: Faith—a burning HEART, CROSS, candle, and BOOK (the Bible); Hope—an ANCHOR, DOVE, SHIP, LABARUM, CORNUCOPIA; Love—CHI-RHO, LAMB, children, PELICAN, BREAD. The attributes of the four cardinal virtues include the following: Courage (Fortitudo)—a KNIGHT's armor, LION's skin, SWORD and buckler, Samson's PILLAR, FLAG; Justice (Justitia)—SCALES, carpenter's SQUARE, globe, law book; Prudence (Prudentia)—a SNAKE ("Be ye therefore wise as serpents"—Matthew 10:16), MIRROR, TORCH, coffin (memento mori); Temperance (Temperantia)—two containers for mixing WATER and WINE, a CAMEL and an ELEPHANT for riding, HOURGLASS, windmill.

Other virtues are also personified: Patience (Patientia) with the OX; Gentleness (Mansuetudo) with the LAMB; Humility (Humilitas) with the DOVE; Obedience (Oboedientia) with the camel; Perseverance (Perseverantia) with the brooding HEN; Chastity (Castitas) with the LILY or the UNICORN; Peace (Pax) or Harmony (Concordia) with the olive branch or a pair of doves. All these figures are generally portrayed as young women in long dresses; at times they are shown struggling against the VICES (psychomachia). Symbolic plants associated with the individual Virtues include the cedar (Humility), the PALM (Sophia, Wisdom), the CYPRESS (Pietas, Piety), the grapevine (Temperance), the ROSE bush with THORNS (Courage).

The assortment of virtues and the choice of attributes vary, within both the Gothic architectural tradition and the world of painting.

vitriol In modern times, a general term for water-soluble sulfates of heavy metals (e.g., copper, iron, zinc); in the symbology of ALCHEMY, however, a symbolic name for the combination of ABOVE AND BELOW, an acronym formed from the Latin sentence *"Visita inferiora terrae, rectificando invenies occultum lapidem"* ("Seek out the lower reaches of the earth, and when you have completed this task, you will discover the hidden stone," i.e., the philosopher's stone). Some variations in the sentence are found in the writings of alchemists, e.g., ". . . invenietis occultum lapidem, veram medicinam" (". . . you will discover the hidden stone, the true medicine"), which yields "vitriolum" in the place of "vitriol." Although these sentences seem to suggest a normal technical process for refining ore, they are meant allegorically, referring to a process through which people are purified, and that which is "down below" is led to ascend into the spiritual realm.

Because sulfuric acid, also called "oil of vitriol," is so corrosive, the words "vitriol" and "vitriolic" have come to be used figuratively to refer to vituperative feelings and utterances.

vulture The individual species (e.g., great bearded vulture, Egyptian vulture) are not symbologically distinct. Vultures are considered less "regal" than eagles, since they are known only as eaters of carrion; the Iberians and the Persians left bodies (especially of those killed in combat) for them to eat, and this is still the custom in Tibet, and in Parsiism, in which bodies are laid out in the *dakhmas* ("towers of silence") for this purpose. Only in ancient Egypt was the vulture highly revered, primarily in the form of Nekhbet, the vulture goddess of Elkab in

Vulture: Aztec calendar symbol Cozcaucuauhtli. Codex Borgia

Upper Egypt. The vulture is frequently portrayed hovering protectively over the pharaoh, and the queen wore the "vulture headdress." Nekhbet was the patron goddess of childbirth and of motherhood (see MOTHER) in general. Vultures also appear in the form of the goddess Mut, and together with the SNAKE they adorn the pharaoh's crown. It was noticed in classical antiquity that vultures frequently followed behind campaigning armies, and this apparently led to the legend of their gift of prophecy: they were said to gather, three days before the fact, at sites where battles were to occur. Zeus can also transform himself into a vulture, and in Homer's *Iliad* (VII, 59) Apollo and Athena are said to be sitting in a tree, in this form. The underworld demon Eurynomus was portrayed sitting on a vulture's remains; a vulture or eagle ate PROMETHEUS' liver. For the Romans, the vulture was sacred to the god of war, and it was a sacrilege to kill the bird. Its use in augury as an oracular animal (e.g., at the founding of Rome) apparently goes back to Etruscan tradition.

It was widely believed that vultures were hatched without fertilization by the male, whose role was assumed by the east WIND. Thus the bird came to symbolize the VIRGIN Mary. The early Christian text *Physiologus* reports that when it is "pregnant" the bird flies to India to get the "birthing STONE," which is hollow and contains a rattling pit (like the "eagle stone," or *aëtites*). "When the female feels the beginnings of labor, she takes the stone, sits upon it, and gives birth [!] painlessly." The symbolic meaning is as follows: "You who are pregnant with the Holy Ghost, take the spiritual birthing stone—which the builders have cast aside and which has become the cornerstone—

and, seated upon it, you will give birth to the spirit of salvation. . . . For in fact this birthing stone of the Holy Spirit is Jesus Christ our Lord, hewn without human labor, that is, come to be, out of a virgin, without human seed. And, just as the birthing stone has within it a second, rattling stone, so does the body of the Lord have godliness resonating within it." In India Shani or Manda, the old, feeble, ugly personification of the PLANET SATURN, rides a vulture. In ancient Mexico the vulture is the 16th of the 20 day-signs (*Cozcacuauhtli*), and it was believed that the bird could live to a very old age because the king vulture (*Sarcoramphus papa*) is bald.

walnut   According to the *Historia naturalis* of Pliny the Elder (A.D. 23–79), the shade of the walnut TREE is particularly dark, and harmful for plants and persons. The nut itself, which in many fairy tales and legends contains secret riches, is of considerable symbolic importance in general: a hard shell surrounds valuable contents. In the Jewish tradition of Biblical exegesis (*Midrash ha-ne'elam*), Holy Scriptures are likened to a walnut: the shell corresponds to the historical facts they recount, which contain symbols and mysteries. St. Augustine (A.D. 354–430) writes of the nut as involving three substances: the leathery fruit or "flesh" that surrounds the nut, the "bones" of the shell, and the kernel or "soul" inside. The fruit is also the flesh of Christ with the bitterness of suffering; the shell is the wood of the CROSS; and the kernel is the sweet interior of divine revelation, which nourishes us and, through the oil that it yields, also provides LIGHT. We refer to a difficult problem as "a hard nut to crack," and eccentric or mentally unstable persons are said to be "nuts" (noun and adjective). The slang use of "nuts" to mean "testicles," although peculiar to English, is not totally dissociable from a European symbolic tradition linking the walnut to fertility (and that which is hidden): walnuts are a common wedding present, and Sextus Pompeius (second century after Christ) mentions the custom of pelting newlyweds with walnuts (as we might

with RICE). It is said in France that a rich harvest of walnuts means that many children will be born as well. Psychologists in the Jungian tradition seem to view the nut similarly: "Dreams of walnuts may refer to attempts to solve a difficult problem in which something valuable is at stake. But far more often walnuts, like so much graffiti, simply represent female genitalia" [Aeppli].

wampum   A symbolic object associated with Native Americans of the Eastern regions of what are now the United States and Canada; less familiar internationally than the peace pipe (CALUMET) or the TOMAHAWK. The Iroquois nations wore wampum BELTS constructed as mosaics from porcupine quills and sometimes adorned with white shell beads; the word "wampum" (or "wampumpeag") originally referred to these beads themselves. Emissaries wore wampum belts for purposes of identification, much as the CADUCEUS was carried in European antiquity. "Belts or strips in varying length and a great variety of designs served as simple documents; chains of varying length and varying arrangement of light and dark beads served as devices for remembering legends, historical events, and covenants. Specialists were trained in the significance of specific numbers of chains and belts so as to be able to interpret any 'document' that they were handed. These men were living libraries who could narrate a long story as their fingers moved over the beads" [La Farge]. In colonial times settlers used wampum belts made of porcelain beads from Europe as currency for transactions with Native Americans; thus the word "wampum" came in time to be slang for "money."

water   In many myths of the creation of the world, water is the primordial fluid from which all life comes, but it is also the ELE-

Wampum belt with symbol of treaty between William Penn and the Delaware

Water or rain god. Iran, ca. 2500 B.C.

MENT in which creatures drown and matter dissolves. There are many myths in which great FLOODS close cycles of creation and destroy forms of life that were displeasing to the gods. For the psychologist, water can symbolize the deeper layers of the psyche, inhabited by mysterious life forms (compare FISH). This elemental symbol is highly ambivalent, since it is associated both with life and fertility and with submersion and destruction. The SUN descends every evening into the water of the Western Sea, to warm the realm of the dead; thus water is also associated with the AFTERLIFE. The "waters under the EARTH" have frequently been associated with primordial CHAOS; the rainwater that falls from the HEAVENS, however, with life-giving blessings from on high. Whirlpools (see SPIRAL) offer a graphic symbol for life's difficulties and upheavals; quietly flowing RIVERS, for life continuing smoothly as planned. In many cultures ponds, pools, and especially SPRINGS were believed to be dwelling places for nymphs, water sprites, or prophetic (and often dangerous) demons of various sorts. Here, too, is an indication of the ambivalent symbolic character of water.

WINE mixed with water in the Eucharist constitutes a special DUALITY—the "FIRE" of the wine mingled with the passive element, water—a reference to the dual nature (divine and human) of the person of Jesus. (The personification of temperance, Temperantia, e.g., in the TAROT cards, includes a depiction of mixing wine and water.) In other Christian contexts, water is generally the cleansing element that washes away sin in the sacrament of baptism.

Water was used in witches' ordeals because it was believed that this "pure" element would reject those who were in league with the DEVIL. Those suspected of witchcraft were bound hand and foot, then thrown into the water; those who sank were deemed innocent (and pulled out with a rope), because it was assumed that the guilty would float like a cork.

Holy water is of great importance in Roman Catholic practice, both the holy water which has not yet been mixed with oil (chrism) and the *aqua benedicta* from specific holy days which the faithful take with them and place in receptacles at the THRESHOLDS of their homes—where it is used for moistening one's fingers before making the sign of the CROSS, and formerly for sprinkling in the interior of the house. Drops of holy water sprinkled on the ground are also popularly believed to help the "poor souls in PURGATORY" and reduce the intensity of the fires in which they are being cleansed.

The New World conception of the AFTERLIFE as a watery realm is a foreign one to most Europeans. It is clearly documented, however, on earthenware vessels (presumably Mayan) of the Yucatán. The Aztecs called the paradise of the rain god Tlaloc "Tlalocan"; it was a far more pleasant region than the underworld, Mictlan, the abode to which ordinary mortals were consigned after death. (Compare HELL.) In the 20-day calendar of Central America, however, the ninth day sign, water (Aztec *Atl*, Maya *Muluc*), was associated with excessive rain-

Water springs from the rock by the power of God. Hohberg, 1675

Water: Baptism by immersion. *Legenda Aurea,* Esslingen, Germany, 1481

fall; it was considered a sign of bad luck and predicted disease and fever. It was depicted as a bluish, forked stream, capped by waves. It was part of the Mexican hieroglyph for "war," *atl-tlachinolli,* literally translated "water/fire," the conflict between the two elements being the essence of this duality.

In many cultures special reverence is given to water that flows directly from the depths of the earth, like a gift from the subterranean gods—especially when it is hot (thermal) or has special curative properties because of its mineral content. Several Ice Age CAVE TEMPLES have been found in the Pyrenees near such springs, and they continued to be revered in classical antiquity, as remains of special offerings indicate. Hot springs were of particular importance in Celtic regions, where the water was considered to be part of the bounties of Mother Earth

Water: Divinity, overflowing vessel. Seal of King Gudea, Sumeria, 3rd millennium B.C.

(e.g., the goddess Sulis, worshipped at the thermal spring in Bath, England). The custom of throwing coins into fountains seems to be a vestige of symbolic sacrifices to water deities believed capable of fulfilling wishes (because of a linking of the notions of earth, fertility, and fortune). Nymphs, incidentally, were revered in these contexts as personifications of the effects that the faithful hoped to obtain from the waters. (See WATER SPIRITS.)

The belief that ritually consecrated water can bring divine blessings—a belief that unites the cleansing and fertilizing properties of water in religious ritual—is not limited to Catholicism; it is also found in non-European religions, such as Parseeism. In Indonesia trance-dancers are sprinkled with consecrated water to bring them back to reality. Water is thought of as having a purifying effect in the Isis cult of late antiquity. In the Christian world, the water of baptism is believed to wash away all of the faults inherited from a person's ancestors; the person is, as it were, reborn. In ancient Mexico, too, a similar ritual was connected with the washing of newborns: the midwife prayed that the water might remove any evil clinging to the baby from its parents. There were ritual BATHS, such as the Jewish mikvah, in many older civilizations, fulfilling not only hygienic but also symbolic functions. The most noteworthy include the artificial bathing ponds in the pre-Aryan ruins of Mohenjo-Daro, the Hindu bath in the Ganges, the "lustration pool" in Knossos (Crete), purification baths before the Eleusinian mysteries, and similar symbolic practices in Greek cults of late antiquity. ("For pious folk a single drop's enough; whole oceans leave the wicked still uncleansed.") There were symbolic purification baths in ancient Mexico as well: the priest-king of the holy city of Tollan performed midnight ablutions, and the city of Tenochtitlan had three sacred baths. At the festival of Xochiquetzal the entire populace was supposed to bathe in the early morning; anyone who failed to would be visited with venereal and skin infections. Ritual washings are part of the rules of Islam; only where water is not

Water: Sea god Neptune with wife Amphitrite and trident. Cartari, 1647

available (i.e., in the desert) can pure sand be substituted for this purpose.

An exhaustive discussion of the relevant rituals would lead us too far from symbology into the realm of religion proper; however, a few additional beliefs from European antiquity and thereafter should be mentioned. It was believed that moving water, especially seawater, could wash away all evil spells. Those who called upon subterranean gods used water from springs; for celestial gods, rain water. The morning DEW, according to Pliny the Elder (A.D. 23–79), is "a true medicine, a gift from heaven, for eyes, ulcers, and intestines"; the ancients believed that it came from moonbeams or the tears of the dawn-goddess EOS. In the Judeo-Christian tradition the dew symbolizes God's bounties raining down from heaven.

In ALCHEMY, too, this ros coelestis was gathered up in cloths, according to the Mutus Liber (1677). This may, however, be a veiled reference, meaning not literally dew but the volatile element mercury (see SULFUR AND MERCURY). There are frequent references to the use of "May dew" as a solvent "impregnated with Nature's SALTS"—although it is difficult here to separate allegory and popular belief.

In the symbolic theories of analytic psychology as well, water—an element that is essential for life but has no nutritional value— is considered to be of great importance, standing for the source of human life (children come from ponds or wells into the world of the living) or that which keeps us alive. It is the fundamental symbol of all the energy of the unconscious—an energy that can be dangerous when it overflows its proper limits (a frequent dream sequence). Still, water is a favorable, salubrious image when it stays within its normal confines (pond, river—or even the sea itself, remaining beyond the shore) and thus, as in many FAIRY TALES, can truly be called "the water of life."

water spirits Even more so than FISH (which are themselves often depicted with supernatural features), water spirits symbolize the vitality of water and especially its status as a source of life—an association that explains its traditional place in the YIN, or "feminine," half of the cosmos. For the analytical psychologist, water spirits—occasionally masculine but usually feminine—personify specific material from the unconscious. In ancient Hindu myth the apsaras were originally heavenly dancers following the god Indra, but who live in bodies of water (usually LOTUS ponds) when they come down to the earth and use their wiles to keep ascetics from pursuing their strict practices. The love between the water nymph Urvashi and King Puruavas is the subject of a compelling narrative by Kalidasa (ca. 500 B.C.). There are similar legends in the European tradition, although the marriages between humans and water creatures (often named Undine or Melusine) rarely prove to be lasting or fulfilling. These creatures often have the form of mermaids and are thus "women" only in part. Their seductive appeal comes from their beautiful song and their long, golden

Water Spirits: Fabulous creatures from the Chinese text Shan-hai-jing

Water Spirits: Melusine bathing in her chamber. Illustration, Antwerp, 1491

Water Spirits: The nymph Galatea. Cartari, 1647

HAIR, through which they pass GOLDEN combs (e.g., the Rhine Lorelei)—usually to destroy the men whom they captivate. There are many legends in which mermaids long to wed humans as a way of getting a soul (which they, like all spirits of the elements, lack). The classical forerunners of medieval European mermaids were the naiads, Nereids, and sirens of Greek mythology—portrayed, on the one hand, as shy nymphs

Water Spirits: Sea monster Scylla, the bane of seafarers. Cartari, 1647

inhabiting SPRINGS, but, on the other, as treacherously seductive figures.

In the imagery of ALCHEMY a mermaid with two fish-tails represents the DUALITY of SULFUR AND MERCURY in the state of separation.

In HERALDRY a mermaid in a coat of arms refers to the legendary marriage of the earliest male ancestor of the line with such a creature—although such unions, as we have noted, were generally not believed to be lasting.

Aquarius is the 11th of the 12 signs of the zodiac (see STARS), especially familiar from references to an "Age of Aquarius"—already begun or about to begin—believed to succeed that of Pisces. Those born under Aquarius (January 21–February 19) are said to have mystical tendencies and a longing for freedom of movement; they seek to bridge the gap between the conscious and unconscious realms, the everyday world and the supernatural.

wedding customs MARRIAGE ceremonies throughout the world are accompanied by symbolic actions; a wedding frequently offers an image of the ideal fusion of two cosmic elements. A wedding is usually a public,

Wedding of symbolic complements Gabricius and Beia. Alchemist's emblem, M. Maier, *Symbola,* 1618

officially recognized event that makes known to the entire community the fact that the bride and groom are exchanging their previous status as "youth" and "maiden" (see VIRGIN) for new rights and responsibilities. Especially in monogamous societies, the marriage is celebrated as a permanent, legal bond; the bride is often thought of as the principal figure (we often use the word "bridal" to mean "nuptial"), and most of the symbolic customs are centered upon her. She has the splendid clothing, jewelry, VEILS, WREATHS, and CROWNS; the bridegroom, by comparison, is quite modestly adorned. The exchange of RINGS goes back to the symbolism of the CIRCLE: with no end and no beginning, the circular ring seems to refer to the romantic ideal of "marriages made in HEAVEN" (i.e., predestined from birth). This is no purely Occidental notion, for marriage was spoken of in similar terms in ancient China, where the "Old Man in the MOON" paired up newborn boys and girls, linking their legs with an invisible RED thread; as the boy and girl grew to adulthood, they felt a powerful attraction to each other and finally married.

Certain modern wedding customs, such as the throwing of RICE (a symbol of fertility), are of Asian origin (like the rice itself) and do not derive from any Occidental tradition.

In polygamous societies, weddings are usually celebrated more quietly. If the bride was expected to be a virgin, her purity often had to be demonstrated by the exhibiting of blood-stained bed sheets upon the consummation of the marriage. (See also SLIPPER, HEADDRESS, COPPER.)

wells Often at SPRINGS, wells are traditionally shafts leading down to the world below (in the tale of "Mother Holle" [Brothers Grimm]) or to the "waters of the deep," which hold secret powers. The city-dweller of the present day can hardly imagine the importance of a well, as a source of potable water, for village communities. In Islam a SQUARE brick-lined well is an image of PARADISE. There are early Christian representations of the fountain in the Garden of Eden, from which the FOUR RIVERS originate. Here the life-giving ELEMENT WATER comes to light, and it is associated symbolically with baptism and with the BLOODY water flowing from the wound in the side of the crucified Christ. There were many portrayals of the scene from the New Testament, "Jesus and the Samaritan Woman at the Well." The belief in the curative powers of water from the earth goes back to ancient, indeed prehistoric cults. Christianity readily took up such traditions, and pilgrimages were encouraged to rivers and sources about

Wells: Christ and the Samaritan woman at the well. Detail, Psalter, 1493

which miraculous legends had spread. They were associated with the Virgin Mary and often especially with the curing of eye ailments (through an association between the eye as the MIRROR of the soul and the water-surface as mirror). In the secular domain there are legends of a "fountain of eternal youth." Among the Mayas of the Yucatán well-shafts running through limestone (Tzenotes) were holy sites where sacrifices were made. As analytic psychology has recognized, wells often appear in fairy tales and dreams as places of penetration into the unknown worlds of the unconscious, of what is hidden and, in everyday life, inaccessible; wells are associated with the symbolic notions of the cleansing BATH, drinking from the sources of life, and quenching our thirst for higher knowledge. An opposing image is the "bottomless pit" of Revelation 9, out of which fire and brimstone issue and in which the devil, defeated, is imprisoned for a thousand years. In ancient Chinese literature the well is associated with eroticism and "The Feast of Pleasure of the Heavenly Lovers" on the seventh day of the seventh lunar month.

whale Traditionally, the sea monster Cetus that Perseus slew to free the princess Andromeda has been thought of as a whale, as has the "great fish" that swallowed Jonah: "And Jonah was in the belly of the fish three days and three nights. Then Jonah prayed unto the Lord his God out of the fish's belly. . . . And the Lord spake unto the fish, and it vomited out Jonah upon the dry land" [Jonah 1:17–2:1, 10]. Christian thought frequently finds anticipations of scenes in the Gospels in the Old Testament; thus Christ in Matthew 12:40 offers the

Whale: The prophet Jonah, swallowed and vomited. Ravello Cathedral, 12th century

following prediction of his own resurrection: "For as Jonah was three days and three nights in the whale's belly; so shall the Son of man be three days and three nights in the heart of the earth." This passage has repeatedly been understood as a general symbol of the resurrection of the dead and has provided a favorite motif for Christian art.

The legend of St. Brendan (*Navigatio Sancti Brandani*) includes the Sinbad-like scene in which the sea-faring monks end up on the back of a sleeping whale. The medieval bestiaries offer the following remarks: there are bushes growing on the back of the sea monster, and thus "sailors mistake it for an island, land their ships there, and build fires. But as soon as the creature feels the heat, it plunges suddenly under water and pulls the ship down into the depths of the sea"— a fate which Brandan and his brothers are spared. "The same thing happens to those who know nothing of the devil and his wiles. . . . He pulls them down into the fiery depths of hell." It is also written that a fragrance emanates from the mouth of the whale and attracts FISH for the whale to devour. (Compare PANTHER.) "This is also the fate of those whose faith is not steadfast, who give themselves over to every passing desire, following every temptation, until the devil suddenly swallows them up" [Unterkircher].

wheel An important element in the history of civilization, but one not in use in the pre-Columbian New World even in the most highly developed civilizations. The *principle* of the wheel, however, was not unknown in the Western Hemisphere, as we see from toy figures made of clay, found in the region of the Gulf of Mexico, that

Whale. Rock engraving, near Drammen, Norway, Stone Age

moved on disk-like wheels. In the Old World, the wheel made possible the constructions of carts (see CHARIOTS), which had not only practical but also religious applications. In prehistoric representations their wheels often have spokes in the form of a CROSS (the "wheel-cross"), and such wheels also appear by themselves in similar drawings. Symbologists associate the wheel both with the CIRCLE and with quadripartite organization (see FOUR), as in the cycle of the four seasons. Whereas the circle seems to remain stationary, the addition of spokes gives it a symbolic association with rotation, the dynamic, the cyclical, becoming and passing away, and freedom from any spatial confinement. Wheels and wheel-crosses frequently symbolize the SUN, which "rolls around HEAVEN": we find this association in the custom of rolling burning wheels over cliffs in solstice rituals. In a broader sense the wheel stands for the entire cosmos in its cyclical development, and at times even the divinity who created it and who is perceived as being in perpetual movement. In Asian cultures the wheel is associated with the cycle of rebirth, and in Buddhism in particular with the "wheel of apprenticeship," whose movement through successive reincarnations frees humanity from suffering. In addition, the wheel is a symbol of cosmic order, represented in miniature in the architecture of cities. W. Müller describes the "circle cities" of ancient Iran as follows: "Iran is the classic land of cities formed like wheels, each with its precise circumference mathematically determined . . . in conformity with the Iranian cosmology of the extended, round, strictly bounded earth, divided into six *karshvars* (sectors) placed around a central seventh karshvar to form a 'gleaming, resounding wheel.' The Iranian metropolis likewise has its hub, spokes, and rim" (1961). From ancient Ceylon (Sri Lanka) we find traces of an "empire of the wheel," and similarly in Brahman, Jainist, and Buddhist writings. "The only ruler who can become emperor of the wheel is one who goes through heavenly transformation and one to whom the jeweled wheel of the heavens shows itself. This charkravartin in-

habits (and this is a first indication of the cosmological structures beneath the surface here) a fortress fortified seven times, its walls studded with seven sorts of PRECIOUS STONES, its four gates gleaming with gold, silver, beryl, and crystal. . . . As the new king went through his heavenly transformation and followed the moral commandments, the wheel arose with its thousand spokes, with hub and rim—rose again after disappearing upon the death of his predecessor—and rolled eastward." The king followed its course, subjugating the regions lying at every point of the compass. "Thus the jeweled wheel was triumphant over the entire earth and the waters that surround it, and could roll homeward to the fortress of the king" [Müller, ibid.]. Müller likens this wheel to the "wheel brooch of the kings of Ireland, a similar jewel, similarly bequeathed from one ruler to the next."

In the Old Testament flaming wheels appear around God's head in the Book of Daniel, and in Ezekiel's vision he saw wheels whose "rings were full of eyes" and which "turned not when they went" [Ezekiel 1:15–20]—symbolizing omniscience and dynamic power. Medieval art frequently portrays the "wheel of life," which raises mortals up and then brings them down, or the "wheel of fortune," which never stands still, being constantly subject to the turns of fate. (In modern usage, frequent references to the "wheel of history" or "of time" and their inexorable course, suggest something of the appeal of this fatalistic image.) The goddess FORTUNA is usually portrayed standing on a

Wheel of apprenticeship: the dharma chakra symbol

sphere, but occasionally on a wheel. (Similarly, the tenth card of the Major Arcana, the trumps of the tarot deck, is the Wheel of Fortune, symbolizing life's ups and downs, fate, the inevitable.) Depictions of the zodiac or the cycle of the seasons are usually arranged in the form of a wheel. Already in ancient times Anacreon (580–495 B.C.) said of the inconstancy of fate: "Human life rolls along, shifting like the spoke of a wagon wheel"—with the movement of the wheel soon compensating, it is true, for moments of excessive hardship.

Since the cherubim (or, in some early texts, a different order of ANGELS, the "thrones") are represented in the form of fiery winged wheels, often depictions of PARADISE contain a wheel in the place of the angel at the gate.

In a Christian context, the "wheel-cross" represents Christ's lordship over the earth. Such symbols (as rock drawings, for example) are thus not necessarily prehistoric: they can be understood within the context of Christian symbology. Medieval cathedrals often contain a form of rose-window called *rota* (Latin for "wheel"), with the image of Christ at the center, symbolizing the Savior's central importance in the plan of God the Father. Such rose-windows recall the structure of the Indian MANDALA, used in meditation to help center the personality upon the unconscious divine nucleus of the soul.

Crosses on old Irish graves combine the form of the cross with that of the wheel or circle: they resemble the traditional wheelcross, except that the extremities of the cross extend beyond the circumference of the circle, suggesting that the Cross of Christ transcends the terrestrial.

The symbolic wheel on flags of rebels in the Peasants' Wars (16th century, Central Europe) refers not to the inexorable course of history but to the phonetic resemblance between the German words for "wheel" and "file" (as in "rank and file") and to the idea of forming a strong, unified RING.

The wheel appears occasionally as an attribute of saints, especially St. Catherine, and also St. Willegis of Mainz, who used the wheel to recall his humble origins in a family of artisans.

white   Since white can be defined either as the absence of all pigmentary COLOR or as the presence of all the colors of the spectrum of light, it thus can symbolize either the undisturbed innocence of prelapsarian Eden or the ultimate goal toward which all imperfect mortals strive—purification and a heavenly restoration of that "lost" innocence. In many cultures, white or simply uncolored garments are priestly vestments, associated symbolically with purity and truth. Newly baptized Christians wore white robes, and the souls of the just are similarly depicted in paintings of the Last Judgment. The Pope's white garments symbolize transfiguration, glory, and the road to heaven. PYTHAGORAS recommended that singers of sacred hymns should wear white. White animals were sacrificed to heavenly deities; BLACK, to those of the underworld. The Holy Spirit is portrayed as a white DOVE.

White, however, also has negative symbolic meanings, primarily because of its association with "the pallor of death." In dreams a "white HORSE is often linked to the notion or experience of death. The 'rider on a pale horse' appears in regions where death can intervene" [Aeppli]. In many cultures ghosts are thought of as wearing, or being, white—reverse images, as it were, of "shades" (see SHADOWS).

In the Chinese symbolic tradition, white is the color of age, autumn, the West, and misfortune, but also of virginity and purity. ("White Lotus" was the name of a secret society that sought to improve the mores of the populace.) White is generally considered the Chinese color of mourning, but this is in fact the "uncolor" of undyed mourning garments.

In ALCHEMY brightening or whitening (*albedo*) is a sign that the *materia prima*, after the stage of *nigredo* (see BLACK), is being transformed into the philosopher's STONE. (Compare LILY.)

whore Term of opprobrium for a prostitute, derived from the Indo-European root *karo-s* ("beloved, desirable"), as is the Latin *carus* ("beloved, dear, expensive"). Prostitution for religious reasons, e.g., to honor a goddess of fertility and life, was widespread in the Middle East and was understood as an expression of a woman's sacrifice of herself to the deity in question (or to the stranger or priest representing that deity). This practice explains the Hebrew word *kedeshen* ("sanctified") and the Greek word *hierodule* ("sacred maiden"). The law of Moses forbade this custom: "There shall be no whore of the daughters of Israel. . . . Thou shalt not bring the hire of a whore, or the price of a dog, into the house of the Lord thy God . . . for even both these are abomination unto the Lord thy God" [Deuteronomy 23:17–18]. But, asks the Epistle of James, "was not Rahab the harlot justified by works, when she had received the messengers?" [2:25]. This quote refers to the prostitute Rahab, who had hidden Joshua's messengers in Jericho and prepared the conquest of the city [Joshua 2:1–24]. The aversion to extramarital sexuality prevailed, however (BABEL, SODOM AND GOMORRHA), as is seen most clearly in references in the Book of Revelation to the "great whore" of Babylon (see RED). The COURTESANS of

Whore. Woodcut, Luther's New Testament, Wittenberg, 1522

Greece *(hetaerae)* had a higher social rank and are not to be confused with "common" prostitutes.

willow Some symbols have similar meanings in Europe and Asia; the willow, however, has very different associations in the two traditions. In the ancient Mediterranean world it was generally believed that the seeds of this TREE were dispersed before they matured, and that the willow therefore did not reproduce "sexually." This belief made it an image of chastity and an ideal first ingredient for preparations to promote sexual continence. In another sense, because green branches can be cut from each willow seemingly endlessly, the tree was likened to the Bible, the (inexhaustible) source of wisdom. Origen (A.D. 185–254) promised "the harvest festival of eternity" to all those who preserved the "willow branches of their chastity." In the Middle Ages and thereafter, the willow was considered to be one of the trees in which the saliva of the sick could be placed in order to heal them. Willow catkins are blessed on Palm Sunday and placed in the household to ward off all evil (especially LIGHTNING). The weeping willow, because its branches droop so "sorrowfully," was a symbol of DEATH frequently planted in cemeteries.

There are contradictory reports about the role of the willow in the cult of ASCLEPIUS, the ancient Greek god of healing. It was the custom in Athens, during the fertility festival of the Thesmophoriae to place willow branches in women's beds, supposedly to ward off SNAKES (but perhaps in truth to attract serpentine fertility demons). The priests of Asclepius are said to have sought often to cure sterility. In any case, an extract of willow bark was thought to cure rheumatism.

In ancient China, however, the willow was clearly an erotic symbol associated with springtime. COURTESANS were referred to as "flowers and willows." A woman's waist was called a "willow tree"; a beautiful woman's eyebrows were likened to the movement of willow leaves; her pubic hair was called "deep willow shadows." A young maiden was "gentle willow, fresh flower." The tree had other associations, however. Willow branches were thought to ward off evil spirits; they were also a common gift to civil servants who had been transferred to the provinces.

windows In symbology, openings that admit supernatural LIGHT. Thus magnificent stained-glass windows adorn sacred structures such as the great cathedrals of the Middle Ages (e.g., Reims, Chartres, Sainte-Chapelle de Paris), to suggest the coming glory of the "heavenly JERUSALEM." Light from outside or from ABOVE corresponds to God's spirit, and the window itself to the VIRGIN Mary (since the window is not itself a source of light but transmits the light that comes from God). The framework holding the stained glass in an individual window was often designed in accordance with the principles of NUMBER symbolism, in threes (for the TRINITY) or FOURS (for the EVANGELISTS), or in rosettes (see ROSE), which often meant a division into SEVEN sections. As to COLOR symbolism, luminous BLUE was particularly important, but out of doors this color is particularly susceptible to environmental damage. In the symbolism of FREEMASONRY, allegorical tapestries show three windows, each facing a different point of the compass (SOLOMON's temple in Jerusalem had no window facing north, because none of the SUN's rays come from that direction); S. Prichard (1730) divulged that these windows were called "fixed lights," as

Windows of the Temple, in Masonic tradition, face east, south and west.

opposed to the "moveable" lights of the HEAVENS.

winds For the symbologist, winds are not merely currents of air but also supernatural manifestations of divine intentions. Two characteristics are of primary importance: the unpredictability of the wind, and its ability to produce dramatic effects despite its own invisibility. Where winds come from a characteristic direction (like the sirocco or the bora), they are easily personified, as in Greek antiquity. The bitter north wind Boreas abducts the Athenian princess Oreithyia and carries her off to his home in Thrace; Zephyrus, the mild west wind, brings the young Psyche to Eros, the god of love; the south and east winds (Notos and Euros) were depicted less often. The four were usually shown winged; Boreas had SNAKES' bodies for feet.

In ancient China the wind (*feng*) was originally revered as a BIRD god, perhaps a primordial form of the PHOENIX. Here, too, the winds were distinguished and named according to the four points of the compass. *Feng-shui* is the science of "wind and water," the geomantic choice of locations for buildings on the basis of natural features of the landscape. *Feng* also has extended meanings: "caressing" and "odor." A fortune-teller is called a "MIRROR of the winds."

In ancient Iran, as in Islam, the wind was thought of as a great organizing principle for the cosmos. In ancient Egypt the cooling north wind came from the throat of the god Amon, and the name of the Sumerian god Enlil literally means "puff of wind." In the texts of Philo of Byblus (ca. A.D. 60–140), which are founded upon ancient Syrian beliefs, the "dark wind that mates with itself" hovers over the primordial chaos. In ancient Mexico the wind (*ehecatl*) was associated with the god Quetzalcóatl, who in this context wears a beak-like mask over his face.

The most impressive wind symbolism is found in the Bible. The Hebrew word *ruah* (feminine in gender) means "wind," "spirit," and "breath." At the beginning of the world, God's *ruah* "moved upon the face of the waters" [Genesis 1:2]. The divine revelation

Winds blowing from four corners of the earth. Ptolemy's *Geography*, Basel, 1545

to the prophet Elijah on Mount Horeb is evoked with great poetic majesty: "And, behold, the Lord passed by, and a great and strong wind rent the mountains, and brake in pieces the rocks before the Lord; but the Lord was not in the wind: and after the wind an earthquake; but the Lord was not in the earthquake: And after the earthquake a fire; but the Lord was not in the fire: and after the fire a still small voice. And it was so, when Elijah heard it, that he wrapped his face in his mantle, and went out, and stood in the entrance of the cave. And, behold, there came a voice unto him, and said, What doest thou here, Elijah?" [I Kings 19:11–13]. The frighteningly powerful manifestations of the force of the elements are merely God's harbingers; his own nature is expressed in the "still small voice." The Bible contains numerous passages of this sort; there is usually a clear distinction between God's breath and the stormy winds of destruction. Thus in the New Testament we find: "The wind bloweth where it listeth, and thou hearest the sound thereof, but canst not tell whence it cometh, and whither it goeth: so is every one that is born of the Spirit" [John 3:8]. God's *ruah* is similarly portrayed in Jewish legendary tradition: "There are two things which were not created: wind and water. They were there from the very beginning, when 'the Spirit of God moved upon the face of the waters.' God is one, and there is no other alongside him; so, too, is the wind. . . . You cannot grasp it, cannot strike it, burn it, cast it from you.

. . . The whole world is full of wind, the wind alone carries the world; it is the highest; it was at the beginning of everything" [bin Gorion, 1980]. The Greek word *pneuma*, similarly, can refer to the wind or to the Holy Spirit; when a baby is blown upon in the sacrament of baptism, this symbolizes the gift to ADAM of the breath of life. The "four winds" of the ancients, named for the four points of the compass, are held by four ANGELS in the Book of Revelation [7:1–3]. In Dürer's woodcut of the Apocalypse, the winds are symbolized by winged heads of angels, blowing.

Figures of speech involving the wind draw less upon the analogy with God's spirit than upon nautical associations, e.g., "to take the wind out of someone's sails."

wine As a traditional symbol, wine has rarely been associated with intoxication: usually diluted with water, it was a "spiritual drink," in the fullest sense of the word. The custom of intemperate drinking, in various cultures that revered Dionysus/BACCHUS, was part of a religious tradition and was believed to join mortals with the god of ecstasy. Wine supposedly could break any magic spell, unmask liars (*"in vino veritas"*), and slake the thirst even of the dead when it was poured out as a libation and allowed to seep into the ground. Called "the BLOOD of the grape," wine was often closely linked symbolically with blood, and not only in the Christian Eucharist. Poured out as a libation, it could replace blood sacrifices for the dead.

Wine: Grapes as a symbol of patient expectation. Hohberg, 1647

Grapes were first cultivated for wine long ago in the Middle East and Egypt (where the practice has been documented ca. 3000 B.C., when it was called *erpi*; dark grapes were called "EYES of Horus"). At festivals in this part of the world, wine was absolutely essential: note that Christ's first miracle, in John's gospel, was to turn water into wine at the marriage feast in Cana [2:1–11]. Christ's statement to his disciples—"I am the vine, ye are the branches" [John 15:5]— was influential in medieval art. The CROSS and the tree of life were frequently represented as grapevines, and the Last Judgment as the harvesting of grapes for wine. The only negative portrayals of excessive drinking focus on Noah's drunkenness, with his son Ham's lack of respect interpreted by Christian thought as a typological anticipation of the arresting soldiers' attitude toward Christ in the Garden of Gethsemane. In the medieval collection *Gesta Romanorum* (ca. 1300) it is written that "Noah found the wild grape vine called *labrusca*—from *labra*, the borders of fields or paths. Finding the wine sour, he took the blood of four animals (a LION, a LAMB, a PIG, and an APE), mixed it with dirt and made a fertilizer from it which he spread around the roots of the *labrusca*. Thus the blood sweetened the wine. . . . The wine turned many who drank it into lions, they grew so angry; others lambs, they grew so modest; others apes, so curious and so raucous in their laughter." The text makes no references to imbibers being turned into swine, but this presumably went without saying.

Wine: The drunken Silenus on a donkey. Cartari, 1675

For Hildegard of Bingen (1098–1179) wine is of both medicinal and symbolic importance. She, too, begins with Noah: "Now the earth, which had been damaged by the blood of Abel [see CAIN], brought forth the new wine, and wisdom began anew." Wine can have positive or negative effects, but its inner powers remain essentially mysterious. "We cannot see that secret vital force [*viriditas*, literally 'greenness'] which gives life to the grape and the grain." The same force is at work when the bread and wine of the Eucharist are transformed into the flesh and blood of Christ.

The Islamic attitude toward wine is ambiguous. According to legend, the archangel Gibreel (Gabriel), who led ADAM and his unnamed wife out of the GARDEN, took pity on them and gave them a grape tendril from the PARADISE from which they had been expelled. In another version, his staff, moistened by his tears of sympathy, bore fruit: grapes as round and soft as an angel's tears. But Iblis, the DEVIL, put a curse on the plant; thus, even though wine was originally an angelic gift, it is no longer a blessing. All of the faithful are still forbidden to drink alcohol in this life; in heaven, however, the elect will drink "the wine that is sealed with musk and that so awakens the appetite that all will call out for it. And the wine will be mixed with water from the spring of Tasmin, from which all those close to Allah, all his friends, will drink." A brook also flows through paradise with a "wine that delights the palate but does not intoxicate."

A dream of wine, according to the analytic psychologist Aeppli, refers not to alcohol itself but to aspects of the individual spirit, the psyche. "The religious experience has elevated wine to represent the blood of the Lord. Wine is that which stimulates us, the power of the spirit to overcome the force of gravity and give wings to the imagination. . . . When golden or dark red wine glows in the dreamer's goblet, life is positive and meaningful. The miracle of wine, from the point of view of the soul, is a divine, life-giving one in which terrestrial, vegetative existence becomes spirit and takes wing."

Winged demon Pazuzu. Miniature Assyrian bronze, ca. 800 B.C.

The Japanese counterpart of wine is *sake*, referred to as "rice wine" but in fact more closely resembling beer, with a higher alcohol content (12–16 percent). It is consumed ritually at weddings and New Year's; drunk from small red cups, it is also associated with the sealing of contracts.

wings Associated not only with Christian ANGELS but also with the fairies, spirits, and demons of ancient cultures. This partial assumption of BIRD-like form is an expression of their association with the HEAVENS, their FEATHERS lifting them above the human realm. What wings suggest symbolically is thus not the physical ability to fly but an "elevation" of, or improvement upon, the merely corporeal, subject as it is to the earth's gravity. Thus the cherubim, the highest order of angels, are represented as most richly endowed with wings. In Ezekiel

Winged Egyptian sun symbol as adapted to represent the god Ahura Mazda

1:4–25 they are described as having FOUR faces and four wings *(tetrapteryx)*, standing on wheels covered with STARS like EYES: they form a living CHARIOT bearing God himself. In the Book of Revelation they are described as having SIX wings; in the illustrations of medieval books, the number varies. Classical personifications are also portrayed with wings, e.g., CHRONUS, the victory goddess Nike (Latin Victoria), and (fleeting) FORTUNA. In medieval art of the Eastern Church John the Baptist, Christ's harbinger, is portrayed with wings; in Western Europe, the *doctor angelicus* Thomas Aquinas, and less often St. Vincent Ferrer, because of his angelic love for the rest of humanity. DEVILS are given not the light wings of a bird but the leathery ones of a BAT. In Romantic art fairies are often drawn with the wings of

Winged sun surrounding the god Assur as an archer. Assyrian, ca. 890 B.C.

dragonflies and BUTTERFLIES. (See also ICARUS and CUPID.) In Plato's dialogue *Phaedrus,* the wing is said to have the power "to soar aloft and carry that which gravitates downward into the upper region, which is the habitation of the gods"; it is also "the corporeal element which is most akin to the divine" [246d, translated by Jowett]. Mythical and symbolic animals are also endowed with wings as an expression of lightness or closeness to heavenly realms (PEGASUS). See also FEATHER. In heraldry wings designate the wish or accomplishment of "lifting oneself up through commendable deeds" [Böckler].

Wings: "One is not enough." J. Boschius, 1702

witches Their portrayal in myth, legend, fairy tale, and as symbolic figures, has little to do with the horrifying reality of the persecution of "witches" in Central Europe or Salem. Countless non-Western peoples have believed in witches and in the demonic powers of certain women whom they have characterized as cannibals, sorceresses, murderesses, and destroyers of male potency (e.g., by means of the *vagina dentata*). Such witches and related figures are symbols of a negative aspect of woman, her dark side, as feared by the—neurotic—male. In his rage he attacks them, combats them, determined to destroy them by fire if they have not been consumed in the ordeal by water (in the case of medieval Europe). Jungian psychology sees the figure of the witch as an imaginary embodiment of "the dark side of the

anima, the female aspect of man," represented for example by the BLACK goddess Kali in Hindu myth or the witch Rangda in the Indonesian theater. Such malformations are believed to result from a disturbed relationship to the MOTHER when the boy is growing up. Among the characteristic symbols of the fearful world of witches are nocturnal (see NIGHT) birds (e.g., OWLS), into which witches can transform themselves; TOADS, SNAKES, black CATS; then, alternatively, the witch's seductive beauty, or her repulsive ugliness; her NAKEDNESS, in rituals celebrated on solitary MOUNTAINS (e.g., the Brocken) with the DEVIL presiding, often in the form of a male GOAT. This image of the

Witches in Satan's embrace and flying on the back of a goat. Schaeufelein, ca. 1480

Witches as demons with animal heads. Molitoris, 1489

witch, familiar from European popular tradition, is only a particular instance of almost universal misogyny, however the manifestations of that fear may vary in detail. (In ancient Japan, for example, female demons transform themselves into FOXES; in the native culture of Siberia, into WOLVES.) The European persecution of "witches" bolstered this set of notions with pseudoscientific theory and translated it into murderous deeds. In recent years the figure of the witch has become a symbol of certain groups in the women's movement, a sign of protest against the social dominance of the patriarchy.

wolf (Latin *lupus*) A predatory animal considered dangerous to people and animals, in Central European tradition and well into the modern era. It is hardly surprising that the wolf is prominent in FAIRY TALES as a menace to humans—an image of "the enemy" in animal form—or that there are legends of bloodthirsty humans turned into wolves ("werewolves," literally "man-wolves"). In Old Norse mythology the mighty wolf Fenris must be tied up but then in the final battle (see END OF THE WORLD) breaks its bonds, swallows the SUN, then is killed in combat by Odin, the father of all the gods, who himself dies in the process.

In classical antiquity the wolf was thought of as a "ghost animal" whose very gaze could strike people speechless. Herodotus and Pliny the Elder report that the members of the Scythian nation of the Neuroi were transformed into wolves once a year, then back into humans. Behind the story could lie a memory of a wolf totem for the entire nation; Genghis Khan also claimed to be descended from a blue-gray "chosen wolf" which itself was sired by the sky (Tenggri).

For the Romans, the appearance of a wolf before a battle could be an omen of victory, since the animal was associated with MARS, the god of war. The Spartans, on the other hand, feared defeat when wolves attacked

Wolf preaching to the sheep. Hohberg, 1647

their flocks before the battle of Leuctra (371 B.C.). Although the wolf (because it sees in the dark) can symbolize the morning SUN (Apollo Lycius), its associations are predominantly negative ones: it stands for nature in the wild or for the forces of Satan. In ancient China, too, it stood for greed and cruelty; a "wolf gaze" is one of distrust and fear, such as a person might feel toward a predatory animal traveling in packs. Only on the Turkish steppe did the wolf function as a national totem, appearing on banners and flags.

There are, nevertheless, legends (in the Ordos region of northern China, for example) in which wolves nurse and raise children. The frightening predator can under some circumstances become the powerful guardian of helpless creatures, although the fear of "the big bad wolf" ultimately seems to prevail in most traditions. In Christian iconography the wolf is primarily the diabolical enemy that threatens the flock of the faithful (see LAMB). Only saints—e.g., Francis of Assisi, William of Vercelli (who saddled a wolf), Hervé, and Philibert of Jumièges—have the power to transform the wolf's savagery into "piety." St. Simpert of Augsburg is said to have rescued a child from the jaws of a wolf and forced the animal to return it to its mother. (The depiction of Sts. Wolfgang and Lupus in the company of wolves is simply a play on their names.) The "jaws of hell" themselves are sometimes depicted as those of a DRAGON, sometimes those of a powerful wolf.

In the early Christian text *Physiologus*, the wolf is described as a "crafty, wicked

Wolf (werewolf) attacking. Woodcut, H. Weiditz, 1517

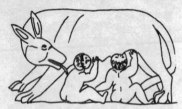

Wolf, Romulus, Remus. Relief, Avenches, Switzerland, 2nd century after Christ

Lupus.

Wolf. Pseudo-Albertus Magnus, Frankfurt, 1531

animal," pretending to be lame when it encounters a human, so as to be able to attack. "St. Basil said: This is what crafty, treacherous people are like. When they encounter good people, they pretend to be utterly innocent and harmless, but their hearts are full of bitterness and deceit." The "wolf in SHEEP's clothing" serves as a symbol of the seductive false prophet, whose goal is to "corrupt the innocent."

English idioms preserve the image of the wolf as ravenous, a menace, a predator. "To keep the wolf from the door" is to earn sufficient money to avert starvation; "to cry wolf" is to raise a false alarm; and a human "wolf" (distinguished not by his howl but by his "whistle") is a man who relentlessly pursues large numbers of women for sexual gratification.

In the imagery of ALCHEMY the *lupus metallorum* (the "wolf of metals") is said to devour the "LION" (i.e., GOLD), in order to "redeem" it. This appears to be a purification process for contaminated gold, using antimony, the "gray wolf" of the alchemist's laboratory.

Wolf emblematic of human tendency to emulate one's elders. Hohberg, 1675

The frequent portrayal of WITCHES riding on or being transformed into wolves, goes back to an association of wolves with the DEVIL.

The wolf symbolizes cunning and treachery in the fables of the wolf preaching to the sheep and "The Wolf and the CRANE." (The crane extracts a bone that has been caught in the wolf's throat, but the bird's only reward is that the wolf does not bite its head off: "such are the ungrateful rich, who live from the toil of the poor.")

Although many years of Freudian psychoanalysis were unable to free the "Wolf Man" entirely from his obsessions, Jungians hold out hope for those so afflicted. They understand the wolf (as a dream symbol) as prowling the landscape of the psyche, representing untamed external energies, "intelligent" and uncompromising. The dreamer is called upon to channel this onslaught, which entails the resolution of great conflicts. Jungians are quick to point out, however, that in fairy tales this "rapacious" predator is outsmarted by the wise child and the young goat and can certainly be no match for the mature hunter.

Incidentally, modern animal behaviorists have established that the wolf does not altogether deserve its bad reputation. With behavior modification through positive reinforcement it can be trained to co-exist with a human who adopts the manner of the "alpha wolf" (the leader of the pack).

As early as 1688 Böckler offered the following positive view of the animal: "The wolf represents alert caution, which explains the frequent appearance of its name and image in coats of arms. The wolf pursues his spoils so shrewdly that the hunter can rarely catch him on the prowl."

In the medieval bestiaries, on the other hand, the wolf is an utterly diabolical creature. The EYES of the female are said to shine at night like lanterns to bedazzle the senses of humans, just as the DEVIL takes away our ability to cry out (i.e., to pray) and his gaze is bright. His works bedazzle the fool, who is blind to their ugliness and the damnation that they bring [Unterkircher].

Presumably legendary accounts of "wolf children" (i.e., abandoned children raised by wolves) are found not only in India (see Kipling's *Jungle Book*) but also in European folklore, perhaps inspired by the Roman legend of the Capitoline wolf that was said to have nursed Romulus and Remus.

Wreath rewards "victory with peace." J. Boschius, 1702

work An everyday concept that has particular symbolic significance in the intellectual world and linguistic usage of FREEMASONRY. It refers to the work of the Lodge on the great project of building the "TEMPLE of all-embracing human love" or "of humanity," after the Master has lit the candle on the "PILLAR of Wisdom" and spoken the words "May wisdom guide the construction"; the first and second attendant light additional candles and say: "May strength carry it out," and "May beauty complete it." This lodge- or temple-work on an ideal structure brings spiritual blessings: "It is a religious mystery leading to spiritual fraternity. Its observance frees and elevates the participant as art does the artist: serving the God within us and thus, indirectly, the deification of the world" [Horneffer].

wreath or garland (Greek *stephanus*, Latin *corona*) A ring of flowers and leaves, related to the CROWN, but less permanent and usually indicating not monarchy but rather temporary honors. Wreaths, of course, need not be worn on the head: they are presented as tributes—in the form of a CIRCLE symbolizing permanence—at funerals and on other solemn occasions. For the ancient world they combined the image of the RING with that of vitality of living plants. Wreaths

and garlands crowned victorious generals, winners of athletic contests, but also, for example, sacrificial animals. In Christian symbology the wreath often symbolizes the defeat of darkness and sin, for example the bridal wreath (see VIRGIN), often in the form of a small crown, or the garlands worn by girls receiving their First Communion in the Catholic Church. In the Bible it is written that "the Lord of hosts (shall) be for a crown of glory, and for a diadem of beauty, unto the residue of his people" [Isaiah 28:5]. Garlands are often associated with the pleasures of this world and riotous living: for example, it was believed in ancient times that a garland of IVY could protect its wearer from becoming intoxicated. In modern times sanctuaries are often decorated for church holidays with wreaths of twigs and flowers, symbolizing joy, eternal life, and the Resurrection. Christ's crown of THORNS is to be understood as a parody of the ROSE garlands of Roman emperors; crowns similar to Christ's became the attributes of such saints as Mary Magdalene, Veronica, and Catherine of Siena, and crowns of roses adorn St. Cecilia and St. Flavia. Literal crowns are often representations in metal of wreaths, and there are cases where the symbolic traditions of the wreath and the crown overlap. In Latin, French, and English there is one word that, depending on context, can refer to either (*corona, couronne,* and "crown" itself). LAUREL wreaths were associated with Apollo; olive wreaths (or, at the Nemean Games, parsley wreaths), with Zeus; wreaths containing ears of grain, with Demeter (Latin Ceres); wreaths of pine-needles and -cones, with Poseidon; fennel wreaths, with Sabazius, the Phrygian god of agriculture. Wreaths of OAK leaves adorned those who had saved the lives of others.

Xanthippe (literally, "yellow horse") The wife of the philosopher Socrates (470–399 B.C.), who must have already been advanced in age when they married: when he drank hemlock and died at the age of 70, the three children that he left behind were not yet of age. The Cynics, e.g., Xenophon in his *Symposium*, portrayed Xanthippe as particularly quarrelsome. Modern commentators, however, have pointed out that the philosopher's own way of life may have given her just cause for complaint. The same perspective is offered by the Central European saying: "Xanthippes are made, not born." Still, however just her claims for our compassion may have been, her name has become a proverbial epithet (as in "a real Xanthippe") for any nagging, shrewish wife.

yantra A graphic aid to meditation, going back to ancient India and still esteemed in the modern era, consisting of geometrically balanced signs, organized symmetrically around a single center (see MANDALA). A yantra is usually constructed from successively inscribed TRIANGLES, SQUARES, and CIRCLES, which are significant to those who are aware of certain conventions but can also communicate directly with the unconscious through archetypal structures of the psyche. The best known is the "Shri" yantra, consisting primarily of artfully arranged triangles, some pointing up and some down in reference to a philosophical DUALITY; they are encircled by rings of LOTUS leaves within an extended quadratic structure. This yantra is believed to facilitate meditation upon the unity that transcends the polarity of opposites and thus to lead to a feeling of personal empowerment in the face of temporary conflicts.

yellow In ancient Chinese symbology, yellow was the COLOR of loess and thus symbolized the center and the earth. The color, of GOLD is often said to be "yellow," and gods are often portrayed with golden yellow skin. In Goethe's theory of colors, yellow is said to be "a soft and merry color, but one that is not far from being displeasing; the slightest intermingling of another color degrades it, makes it unpleasant, dirty." Only the addition of a small quantity of RED does he tolerate, judging the effect to be "warming." In Central Europe bright yellow was popularly thought to symbolize envy and jealousy (the English "green with envy" being replaced by "yellow with envy"), probably through association with "yellow bile" (Greek *chole*), which in the ancient theory of the four humors (see ELEMENTS) was believed to produce the "choleric" disposition. But yellow is referred to more frequently as the color of the SUN, and as such, according to Aeppli, its nature is ambiguous: it is "the color of easily triggered intuition and suspicion, in which there is a peculiar solar power, penetrating and illuminating." Golden yellow, with a touch of red, usually symbolizes the glow of wisdom; pale yellow, treacherous aggression (as in portrayals of the clothing of JUDAS). This is why in the Middle Ages Jews were forced to wear yellow and, in Nazi Germany, the yellow STAR of David. In the cosmology of the Maya yellow was associated with the direction south; in the color symbolism of ALCHEMY, a yellow coloration (*citrinitas*) indicates a transitional step (between "blackening" and "reddening") in the progress of matter toward becoming the philosopher's STONE.

yew (*Taxus*) An evergreen tree that can live for centuries and was thus a classical symbol of immortality. From time immemorial it has been planted at cemeteries, along with other evergreens and long-lived trees and shrubs, presumably to express the hope for a life that extends beyond the death of the body. By ancient times it was known

Yantra: Shri yantra, made up of triangles, circles and border

that the seeds of the yew are poisonous (they contain an alkaloid that can paralyze the heart), and the feared Celtic warriors dipped the tips of their spears in yew poison. The pulpy exterior of the seed, however, is not poisonous; birds eat yew berries and thereby help to propagate the tree. The wood of the tree is resin-free and utterly impervious; it was thus used for making statues and bows. Even in modern times children in southeastern Europe have been given yew crosses as amulets against evil forces.

Yin and yang, surrounded by eight trigrams (see I CHING): symbol of cosmic unity

yin and yang (Japanese *in* and *yo*) The ancient Chinese representation of cosmic DUALITY. Yin symbolizes femininity, the north, cold, SHADOW, EARTH, the passive, and dampness; yang, masculinity, the south, warmth, LIGHT, the HEAVENS, the active, dryness—and the EMPEROR. Although in the everyday life of ancient China the male was clearly dominant, the language did not reflect this by placing "yang" before "yin," as one might expect. Masculine dominance is, however, reflected in the predominantly negative associations of yin. In theory, the two principles are thought to be of equal rank. Their visual representation is based on a CIRCLE, the symbol of the primal unity (*tai-chi*) that preceded the polarity of yin and yang; this unity is a philosophical concept going back to Chu-Hsi (A.D. 1130–1200). The division into two poles is represented by the bisecting of the circle with an S-curve; the yin half is dark, the yang half light. From this polarity comes the creation of the five ELEMENTS, and from their interaction the multifaceted richness of the world (the "ten thousand things").

The mutual dependence of yin and yang is expressed by a dark (circular) center in the yang sector and a light one in the yin. This is to make it clear that light and shadow are not in conflict for domination of the whole; they strive rather for completion in one another. In the diagrams of the I CHING yin is expressed by a broken, yang by a continuous, line. Odd numbers are associated with yang; even, with yin.

In ancient CAVE temples there were yin and yang STONES. The former needed to be kept moist, the latter dry. When rainfall was excessive, the yang stone (or in times of drought or heat the yin stone) was whipped to awaken its powers, to restore the proper harmonic balance between the two principles.

yoke A word derived from the Indo-European root *yug*, "joining, arranging"; it is thus a cognate of the word "yoga." When used in a positive sense, "yoke" refers to a selfless willingness to give up autonomy, to devote oneself to a goal that demands great self-abnegation. In a negative sense, the word connotes the burden of forced labor which reduces humans to the level of OXEN. Bending one's head under the yoke is also used as a symbol of humiliation, for example by the Samnites when they had defeated the Romans in 321 B.C. and forced the Roman army to march past under the "Caudine yoke" (near the city of Caudium on the Appian Way). In the Bible it is said that God will "put a yoke of iron" on the neck of the disobedient [Deuteronomy 28:48];

Yin and yang suggested by Gothic window design

the prophet Jeremiah puts "bonds and yokes" on his neck as a sign of his submission to the rule of King Nebuchadnezzar of BABYLON, until the time has come for the oppressor's downfall. We often speak figuratively of "the yoke of slavery," "the yoke of marriage," of husband and wife being "yoked together," of "throwing off the yoke of oppression." References to "the yoke of marriage" are not necessarily meant pejoratively: they may go back to a Latin word for marriage, *conjugium*, literally "being yoked together, union," from which our word "conjugal" is derived.

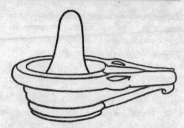

Yoni and linga combined in stylized form. Indian ritual object

yoni Sanskrit term for the womb, associated with the vulva in Indian symbology. Portrayals of the yoni in isolation (a TRIANGLE pointing downward, representing the pubic triangle) are relatively rare. In the cult of Shiva it usually appears in STONE sculptures as a ring or series of rings at the base of the LINGA (the traditional phallic symbol, usually in the form of a truncated PILLAR). The yoni and the linga constitute a fundamental DUALITY, the feminine and masculine principles without whose combination the creation of the world would have been unthinkable.

The combination of the kundalini SNAKE (the symbol of vital energy) with a representation of the yoni stands for the awareness of greater interconnectedness that arises out of matter.

Zacharius See EVANGELISTS, SYMBOLS OF
THE.

Zagreus See ORPHEUS.

Zephyrus In Greek mythology, the west
wind. See FLORA, HYACINTH, TIGER, WINDS.

Zeus In Greek mythology, son of Cronus
and father of the gods. See ANDROGYNE,
APPLE, BEAR, EGG, LIGHTNING, NEMESIS, OR-
PHEUS, PROMETHEUS, STONE, SWAN, TREE.

zinc See VITRIOL.

Zion, Mount See JERUSALEM, MOUNTAIN.

Zion, Star of See HEXAGRAM, STAR, TRI-
ANGLE.

Ziusudra In the epic *Gilgamesh*, the name
of the survivor of the GREAT FLOOD. See
also ISLANDS OF THE BLESSED.

zodiac An imaginary belt that divides the
heavens into twelve constellations, each
constellation represented by a symbol. See
ASTROLOGICAL SYMBOLS, NUMBERS, PRECIOUS
AND SEMIPRECIOUS STONES, STARS.

Zohar, Book of See LIGHT.

Bibliography

Abel, O. *Vorzeitliche Tierreste im deutschen Mythus, Brauchtum und Volksglauben.* Jena: Gustav Fischer, 1939.

Aeppli, E. *Der Traum und seine Deutung.* Zurich: E. Rentsch, 1960; Munich, 1980.

Albertus Magnus, Pseudo-. *Heimlichkeiten des weiblichen Geschlechts.* 1631. Reprint. Frankfurt, 1977.

Altus. *Mutus liber.* Introduction and commentary by Jean Laplace. Milan: Arche, 1979.

Alvarez, O. *The Celestial Brides: A Study in Mythology and Archaeology.* Stockbridge: H. Reichner, 1978.

Anders, F. *Das Pantheon der Maya.* Graz: Akademische Druck- und Verlagsanstalt, 1963.

Apollodorus, of Athens. *The Library.* Translated by Sir James George Frazer. Cambridge: Harvard University Press, 1939–46.

Aron, R. *Die verborgenen Jahre Jesu.* Munich, 1973.

Bailey, H. *The Lost Language of Symbolism.* London: E. Benn, 1968.

Bauer, J. B., ed. *Bibeltheologisches Wörterbuch.* Graz: Verlag Styria, 1967.

Baurnjöpel, Joseph. *Eine Wiener Freimaurerhandschrift aus dem 18. Jahrhundert von Bruder Baurnjöpel.* Edited and revised by Friedrich Gottschalk. Graz: Akademische Druck- und Verlagsanstalt, 1986.

Beltz, W. *Gott und die Götter.* Düsseldorf: Claassen, 1977.

———. *Die Mythen der Ägypter.* Düsseldorf: Claassen, 1982.

———. *Die Mythen des Koran.* Düsseldorf: Claassen, 1980.

———. *Die Schiffe der Götter: Ägyptische Mythologie.* Berlin: Der Morgen, 1987.

Bertholet, Alfred. *Wörterbuch der Religionen.* Revised, updated and edited by Kurt Goldammer in collaboration with Johannes Laube and Udo Tworuschka. Stuttgart: A. Kröner, 1985.

Biedermann, Hans. *Das verlorene Meisterwort: Bausteine zu einer Kultur- und Geistesgeschichte des Freimaurertums.* Vienna: H. Böhlau, 1986.

Bin Gorion, J. *Born Judas.* Frankfurt: Insel Verlag, 1981.

———. *Sagen der Juden zur Bibel.* Frankfurt: Insel Verlag, 1980.

Bloomfeld, M. W. *The Seven Deadly Sins.* East Lansing: Michigan State College Press, 1952.

Böckler, G. A. *Ars Heraldica.* Nürnberg, 1688. Reprint. Graz: Verlag für Sammler, 1971.

Boschius, J. *Symbolographia, sive de arte symbolica sermones septem.* 1701. Reprint. Graz: Akademische Druck- und Verlagsanstalt, 1972.

Burckhardt, T. *Art of Islam.* London: World of Islam Festival Pub. Co., 1976.

Burland, C. A. *The Magical Arts: A Short History.* London: Barker, 1966.

Carroll, K. *Yoruba Religious Carving.* London: G. Chapman, 1967.

Cartari, V. *Imagini delli Dei degl'Antichi.* 1647. Reprint. Graz: Akademische Druck- und Verlagsanstalt, 1963.

Casson, L. *The Pharaohs.* Chicago, 1982.

Cavendish, R. *The Black Arts.* London: Routledge & Kegan Paul, 1967.

Cavendish, R., ed. *Man, Myth and Magic: An Illustrated Encyclopaedia of the Supernatural.* London: Purnell for BPC Pub., 1970–71.

Cirlot, J. E. *A Dictionary of Symbols.* New York: Philosophical Library, 1962.

Cockren, A. *Alchemy Rediscovered and Restored.* London: Rider, 1956.

Cooper, J. C. *An Illustrated Encyclopaedia of Traditional Symbols.* London: Thames and Hudson, 1978.

Creuzer, Georg Friedrich. *Symbolik und Mythologie der alten Völker, besonders der Griechen.* Leipzig and Darmstadt: C. W. Leske, 1836–43.

Daniel-Rops, H. *Jesus: Der Heiland in seiner Zeit.* Freiburg, 1951.

Dondelinger, E. *Das Totenbuch des Schreibers Ani.* Graz: Akademische Druck- und Verlagsanstalt, 1987.

Dundes, A. *The Evil Eye: A Folklore Casebook.* New York: Garland, 1981.

Eliade, M. *Myth and Reality.* New York: Harper & Row, 1963.

Ferguson, G. *Signs and Symbols in Christian Art.* London: Oxford University Press, 1955.

Filmer, W. E. *God Counts: A Study in Bible Numbers.* Croydon, 1947.

Garcilaso de la Vega. *Wahrhaftige Kommentare zum Reich der Inka.* Berlin: Rütten & Loening, 1983.

Gardet, L. *Mystische Erfahrungen in nicht-christlichen Ländern.* Colmar, 1957.

Gesner, K., and E. Topsell. *Curious Woodcuts of Fanciful and Real Beasts.* New York: Dover, 1971.

Gimbutas, M. *The Gods and Goddesses of Old Europe.* London: Thames & Hudson, 1974.

Golowin, S. *Edelsteine, Kristallpforten der Seele.* Freiburg im Breisgau: Bauer, 1986.

Golowin, S. *Die Welt des Tarot.* Basel: Sphinx-Verlag, 1975.

Graves, R. *The Greek Myths.* London: Cassell, 1955.

Heinz-Mohr, G. *Lexikon der Symbole; Bilder und Zeichen der christlichen Kunst.* Düsseldorf and Cologne: E. Diederichs, 1981.

Hildegard of Bingen. *Heilkunde (Causae et Curae).* Salzburg: O. Müller, 1957.

———. *Naturkunde (Physica).* Salzburg: O. Müller, 1959.

———. *Welt und Mensch (De operatione Dei).* Salzburg: O. Müller, 1965.

Hohberg, W. H. Baron von. *Lust- und Arzneigarten des königlichen Propheten Davids.* 1675. Reprint. Graz: Akademische Druck- und Verlagsanstalt, 1969.

Holl, A. *Religionen.* Stuttgart: Deutsche Verlags-Anstalt, 1982.

Holm, B. *Northwest Coast Indian Art: An Analysis of Form.* Seattle: University of Washington Press, 1965.

Homer. *The Odyssey of Homer.* Translated with an introduction by Richmond Lattimore. New York: Harper & Row, 1967.

Horneffer, A. *Symbolik der Mysterienbünde.* Schwarzenburg, 1979.

Jung, C. G. *Alchemical Studies.* Princeton: Princeton University Press, 1967.

———. *Man and His Symbols.* New York: Dell Publishing Co., 1968.

———. *Mysterium Coniunctionis.* Princeton: Princeton University Press, 1970.

———. *Psychology and Alchemy.* Princeton: Princeton University Press, 1968.

———. *The Structure and Dynamics of the Psyche.* Princeton: Princeton University Press, 1969.

Karlinger, F. *Der abenteuerliche Glückstopf: Märchen des Barock.* Munich: Deutscher Taschenbuch-Verlag, 1978.

Karlinger, F., ed. *Märchen der Welt,* vol. 5: *Afrika und Ozeanien.* Munich, 1980.

Kasper, E. A. *Afrobrasilianische Religion.* Frankfurt: P. Lang, 1988.

Koestler, A. *The Sleepwalkers.* London: Hutchinson, 1959.

La Farge, O. *Die Welt der Indianer: Kultur, Geschichte und Kampf eines grossen Volkes.* Ravensburg, 1961.

Langer, G. *Neun Tore: Das Geheimnis der Chassidim.* Munich: O. W. Barth, 1959. Rev. ed. Bern, 1983.

Lehner, E. *Symbols, Signs, and Signets.* New York: Dover, 1950.

Leland, C. G. *Arcadia: Die Lehre der Hexen.* Edited by R. Tegtmeier. Munich, 1988.

Lennhoff, E., and O. Posner. *Internationales Freimaurer-Lexikon.* Vienna: Amalthea-Verlag, 1932.

Lewis, B. *The World of Islam.* London: Thames and Hudson, 1976.

Lewis, J. *Symbols and Sentiments.* New York: Academic Press, 1977.

Lurker, M. *Adler und Schlange: Tiersymbolik im Glauben und Weltbild der Völker.* Tübingen: R. Wunderlich, 1983.

———. *Götter und Symbole der alten Ägypter.* Bern, 1987.

Lurker, M., ed. *Wörterbuch der Symbolik.* Stuttgart: Kröner, 1979.

Maier, Michael. *Atalanta fugiens; hoc est, Emblemata nova de secretis naturae chymica.* Faksimile-Druck der Oppenheimer Originalausg. von 1618. Edited by Lucas Heinrich Wüthrich. Kassel: Bärenreiter-Verlag, 1964.

McIntosh, C. *The Rosy Cross Unveiled: The History and Rituals of an Occult Order.* Wellingborough: Aquarian Press, 1980.

Müller, W. *Die heilige Stadt: Roma quadrata, himmlisches Jerusalem und die Mythe vom Weltnabel.* Stuttgart: W. Kohlhammer, 1961.

Nack, E. *Die Germanien.* Vienna, 1977. Munich: Kindler, 1979.

Narr, K. J. *Handbuch der Urgeschichte.* Vol. I. Bern and Munich: Francke, 1966.

———. *Urgeschichte der Kultur.* Stuttgart: A. Kröner, 1961.

———. "Zum Sinngehalt eiszeitlicher Höhlenbilder." In *Symbolon.* New series, vol. II, 1974.

Nebesky-Wojkowitz, R. *Oracles and Demons of Tibet.* Graz: Akademische Druck- und Verlagsanstalt, 1975.

Nichols, S. *Die Psychologie des Tarot.* Interlaken: Anzata-Verlag, P. A. Zemp, 1984.

O'Kelly, M. *Newgrange: Archaeology, Art and Legend.* London: Thames and Hudson, 1982.

Ovid. *Metamorphoses.* Cambridge: Harvard University Press; London: William Heinemann, 1916.

Pager, H. *Stone Age Myth and Magic as Documented in the Rock Paintings of South Africa.* Graz: Akademische Druck- und Verlagsanstalt, 1975.

Parrinder, G. *African Traditional Religion.* London, 1962.

Pfiffig, A. J. *Religio Etrusca.* Graz: Akademische Druck- und Verlagsanstalt, 1975.

Physiologus. Translated by Michael J. Curley. Austin: University of Texas Press, 1979.

Plato. *Timaeus.* Translated by Benjamin Jowett with an introduction by Glenn R. Morrow. New York: Macmillan, 1985; London: Collier Macmillan, 1985.

Pomeroy, S. B. *Frauenleben im klassischen Altertum.* Stuttgart, 1985.

Portal, P. P. F. *Des couleurs symboliques.* Paris: Treuttel et Würtz, 1837.

Powell, T. G. E. *The Celts.* London: Thames and Hudson, 1958.

Praz, M. *Studies in Seventeenth-Century Imagery.* Rome: Edizioni di Storiae Letteratura, 1964.

Rattray, R. S. *Religion and Art in Ashanti.* London, Oxford: Clarendon Press, 1927.

Rees, A., and B. Rees. *Celtic Heritage: Ancient Tradition in Ireland and Wales*. London: Thames and Hudson, 1975.

Röhrich, Lutz. *Folktales and Reality*. Translated by Peter Tokofsky. Bloomington: Indiana University Press, 1991.

———. *Wage es, den Frosch zu küssen: Das Grimmsche Märchen Nummer eins in seinen Wandlungen*. Cologne: E. Diederichs, 1987.

Samson, J. *Amarna, City of Akhenaten and Nefertiti*. London: Aris and Phillips, 1972.

Schlesier, Karl H. *The Wolves of Heaven: Cheyenne Shamanism, Ceremonies, and Prehistoric Origins*. Norman: University of Oklahoma Press, 1987.

Scholem, G. *Major Trends in Jewish Mysticism*. New York: Schocken Books, 1946.

Schultz, W. *Dokumente der Gnosis*. Jena: E. Diederichs, 1910.

Shu ching. *Ancient China . . . The Shoo-king, or the Historical Classic*. Translated by W. H. Medhurst. Shanghai: Mission Press, 1846.

Sieverking, A. *The Cave Artists*. London: Thames and Hudson, 1979.

Spiesberger, Karl. *Hermetisches ABC*. 2 vols. Freiburg im Breisgau: Bauer, 1965.

Stemplinger, E. *Antiker Volksglaube*. Stuttgart: Spemann, 1948.

Stoltzius von Stoltzenberg, Daniel. *Chymisches Lustgärtlein*. Frankfurt, 1624; Darmstadt: Wissenschaftliche Buchgesellschaft, 1975.

Stuart, G. S. *The Mighty Aztecs*. Washington, D.C.: National Geographic Society, 1981.

Tegtmeier, R. *Der heilende Regenbogen: Sinnvolle Spiele, Experimente und Meditationen . . .* Haldenwang, 1985.

Twohig, F. S. *The Megalithic Art of Western Europe*. Oxford: Clarendon Press, 1981.

Unterkircher, F. *Tiere, Glaube, Aberglaube: Die schöensten Miniaturen aus dem Bestiarium*. Graz: Akademische Druck- und Verlagsanstalt, 1986.

Vries, S. P. de. *Jüdische Riten und Symbole*. Weisbaden: Fourier Verlag, 1986.

Wehr, G. C. G. *Jung und Rudolf Steiner*. Stuttgart: Klett, 1972.

White, T. H. *The Book of Beasts: A Translation from a Latin Bestiary of the Twelfth Century*. New York: Putnam, 1954.

Wolfstieg, A. *Freimaurerische Arbeit und Symbolik*. Berlin, 1922.

Woolley, L. *Excavations at Ur*. London: E. Benn, 1954.

Abraham, p. 1	Abraham, p. 2	Actaeon, p. 3	Adam and Eve, p. 3
Adonis, p. 4	afterlife, p. 5	Ahasuerus, p. 6	alchemy, p. 6
alchemy, p. 6	alchemy, p. 7	alchemy, p. 7	Alexander the Great, p. 7
aloe, p. 8	Alpha and Omega, p. 8	Alpha and Omega, p. 9	Amazons, p. 9
anchor, p. 10	anchor, p. 10	anchor, p. 11	androgyne, p. 11

angel, p. 12	angel, p. 12	angel, p. 12	ankh, p. 13
Anthony of Egypt, Saint, p. 13	Antichrist, p. 14	ape, p. 15	ape, p. 15
apple, p. 16	Ark, p. 17	Arma Christi, p. 18	arrow, p. 18
arrow, p. 19	Asclepius, staff of, p. 19	Asclepius, staff of, p. 20	astrological symbols, p. 21
Atlantis, p. 22	Atlantis, p. 22	Atlas, p. 22	ax, p. 23

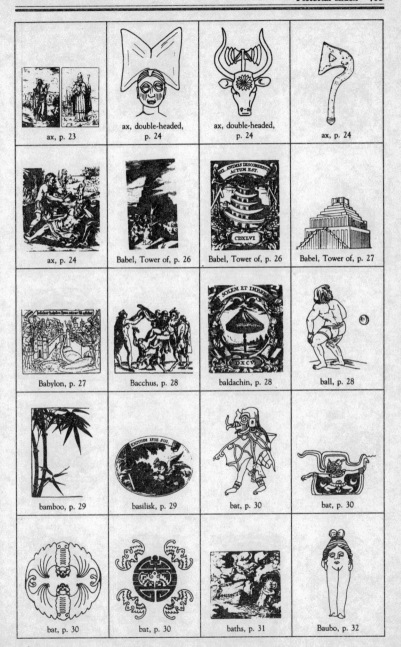

ax, p. 23	ax, double-headed, p. 24	ax, double-headed, p. 24	ax, p. 24
ax, p. 24	Babel, Tower of, p. 26	Babel, Tower of, p. 26	Babel, Tower of, p. 27
Babylon, p. 27	Bacchus, p. 28	baldachin, p. 28	ball, p. 28
bamboo, p. 29	basilisk, p. 29	bat, p. 30	bat, p. 30
bat, p. 30	bat, p. 30	baths, p. 31	Baubo, p. 32

bear, p. 33

bear, p. 33

beards and mustaches, p. 34

bee, p. 35

bee, p. 35

beggar, p. 36

beggar, p. 36

beggar, p. 36

bell, p. 37

bell, p. 37

bell, p. 37

belt, p. 38

Bes, p. 38

bird, p. 39

bird, p. 39

bird, p. 40

bird, p. 40

bird of paradise, p. 40

bivalves, p. 41

black, p. 41

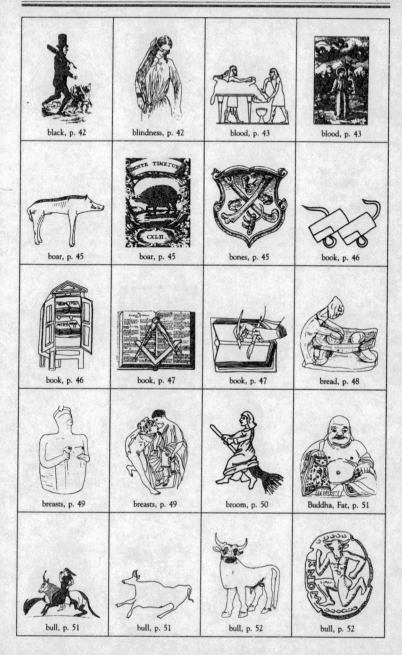

black, p. 42	blindness, p. 42	blood, p. 43	blood, p. 43
boar, p. 45	boar, p. 45	bones, p. 45	book, p. 46
book, p. 46	book, p. 47	book, p. 47	bread, p. 48
breasts, p. 49	breasts, p. 49	broom, p. 50	Buddha, Fat, p. 51
bull, p. 51	bull, p. 51	bull, p. 52	bull, p. 52

butterfly, p. 52	butterfly, p. 53	butterfly, p. 53	butterfly, p. 53
caduceus, p. 54	Cain, p. 55	Cain, p. 55	calumet, p. 56
calumet, p. 56	camel, p. 56	candelabra, p. 57	candelabra, p. 57
capricorn, p. 58	capricorn, p. 58	carnation, p. 59	cat, p. 59
cat, p. 60	caves, p. 61	cedar, p. 62	centaurs, p. 63

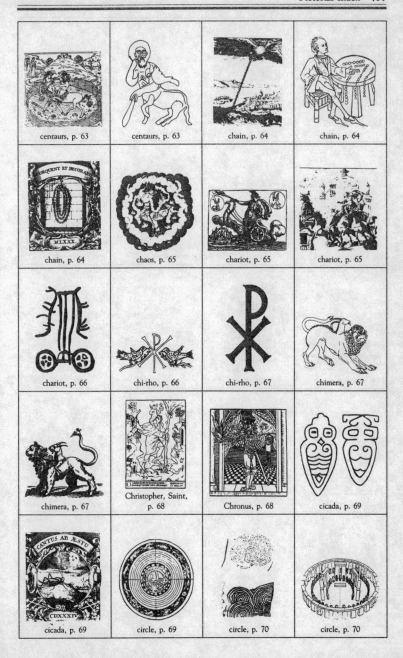

centaurs, p. 63

centaurs, p. 63

chain, p. 64

chain, p. 64

chain, p. 64

chaos, p. 65

chariot, p. 65

chariot, p. 65

chariot, p. 66

chi-rho, p. 66

chi-rho, p. 67

chimera, p. 67

chimera, p. 67

Christopher, Saint, p. 68

Chronus, p. 68

cicada, p. 69

cicada, p. 69

circle, p. 69

circle, p. 70

circle, p. 70

circle, p. 70

city, p. 71

clouds, p. 72

coats, p. 73

coats, p. 73

coats, p. 73

columbine, p. 75

compass, drafting, p. 75

coral, p. 76

coral, p. 76

courtesans p. 77

cow, p. 77

cow, p. 78

cow, p. 78

cow, p. 78

crab, p. 79

crab, p. 79

crane, p. 79

crane, p. 80

crane, p. 80

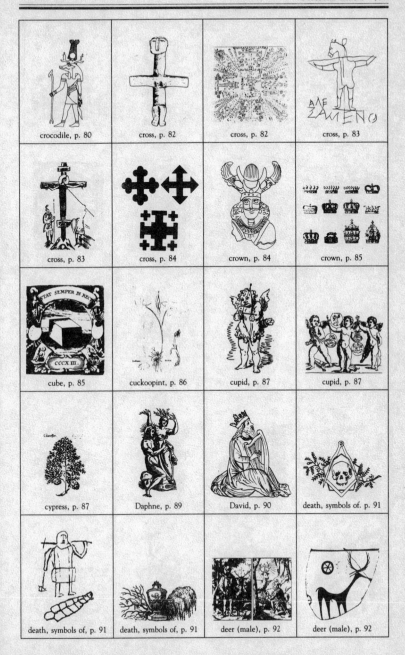

crocodile, p. 80	cross, p. 82	cross, p. 82	cross, p. 83
cross, p. 83	cross, p. 84	crown, p. 84	crown, p. 85
cube, p. 85	cuckoopint, p. 86	cupid, p. 87	cupid, p. 87
cypress, p. 87	Daphne, p. 89	David, p. 90	death, symbols of, p. 91
death, symbols of, p. 91	death, symbols of, p. 91	deer (male), p. 92	deer (male), p. 92

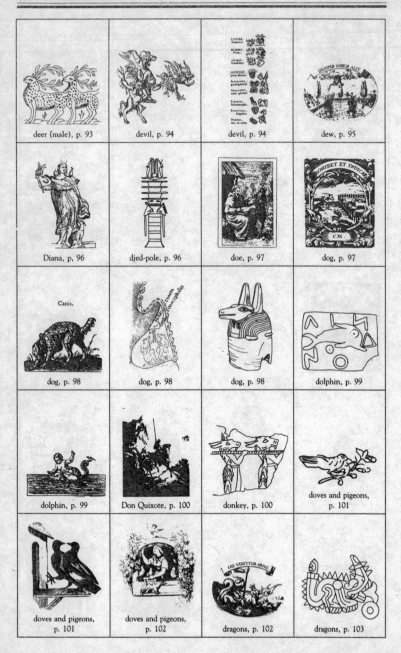

deer (male), p. 93

devil, p. 94

devil, p. 94

dew, p. 95

Diana, p, 96

djed-pole, p. 96

doe, p. 97

dog, p. 97

dog, p. 98

dog, p. 98

dog, p. 98

dolphin, p. 99

dolphin, p. 99

Don Quixote, p. 100

donkey, p. 100

doves and pigeons,
p. 101

doves and pigeons,
p. 101

doves and pigeons,
p. 102

dragons, p. 102

dragons, p. 103

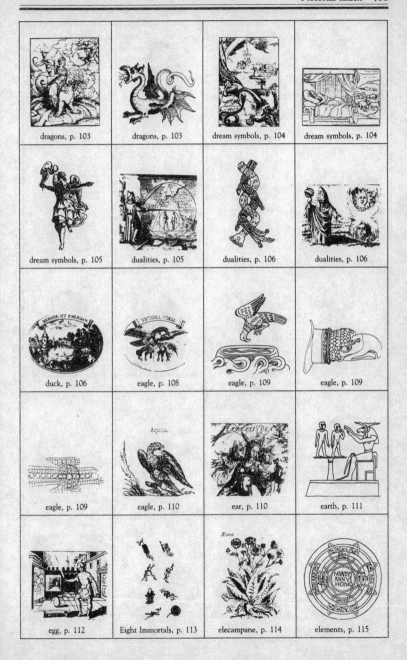

dragons, p. 103	dragons, p. 103	dream symbols, p. 104	dream symbols, p. 104
dream symbols, p. 105	dualities, p. 105	dualities, p. 106	dualities, p. 106
duck, p. 106	eagle, p. 108	eagle, p. 109	eagle, p. 109
eagle, p. 109	eagle, p. 110	ear, p. 110	earth, p. 111
egg, p. 112	Eight Immortals, p. 113	elecampane, p. 114	elements, p. 115

elements, p. 115	elephant, p. 116	elephant, p. 116	elephant, p. 116
elephant, p. 117	emperor, p. 117	emperor, p. 118	emperor, p. 118
emperor, p. 118	Eulenspiegel, Till, p. 120	Evangelists, symbols of the, p. 121	Evangelists, symbols of the, p. 121
Evangelists, symbols of the, p. 121	eye, p. 122	eye, p. 122	eye, p. 122
eye, p. 123	fairy tales, p. 124	falcon and hawk, p. 125	fasces, p. 126

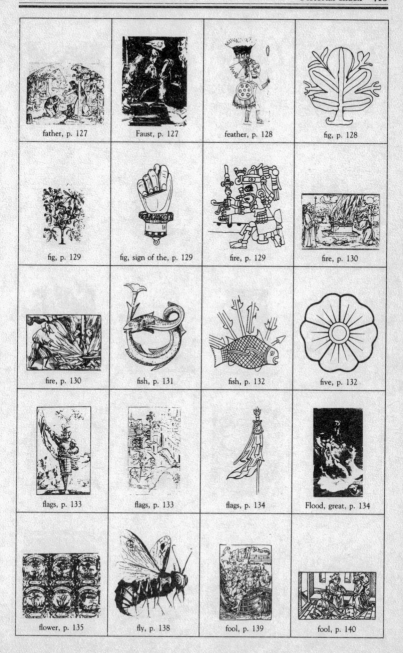

father, p. 127	Faust, p. 127	feather, p. 128	fig, p. 128
fig, p. 129	fig, sign of the, p. 129	fire, p. 129	fire, p. 130
fire, p. 130	fish, p. 131	fish, p. 132	five, p. 132
flags, p. 133	flags, p. 133	flags, p. 134	Flood, great, p. 134
flower, p. 135	fly, p. 138	fool, p. 139	fool, p. 140

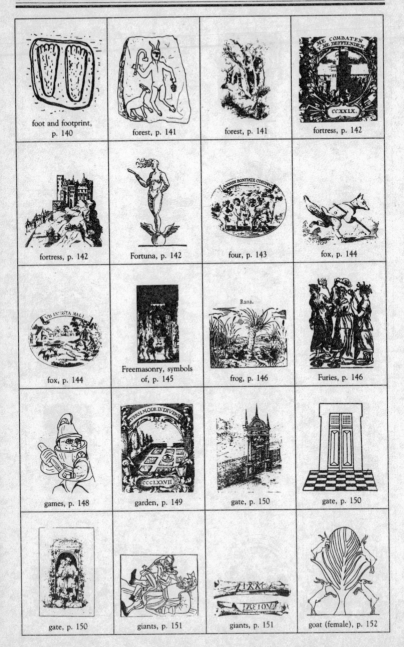

foot and footprint, p. 140	forest, p. 141	forest, p. 141	fortress, p. 142
fortress, p. 142	Fortuna, p. 142	four, p. 143	fox, p. 144
fox, p. 144	Freemasonry, symbols of, p. 145	frog, p. 146	Furies, p. 146
games, p. 148	garden, p. 149	gate, p. 150	gate, p. 150
gate, p. 150	giants, p. 151	giants, p. 151	goat (female), p. 152

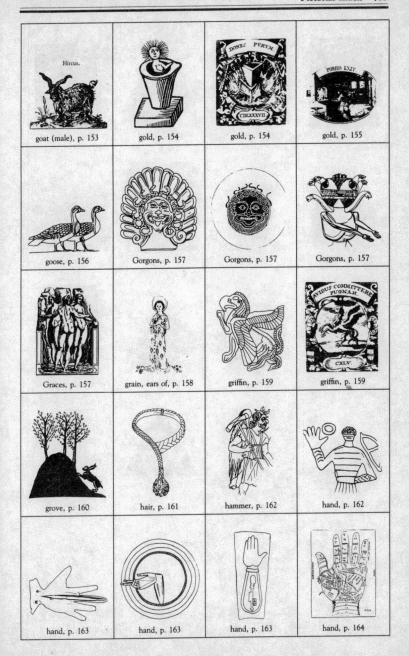

goat (male), p. 153	gold, p. 154	gold, p. 154	gold, p. 155
goose, p. 156	Gorgons, p. 157	Gorgons, p. 157	Gorgons, p. 157
Graces, p. 157	grain, ears of, p. 158	griffin, p. 159	griffin, p. 159
grove, p. 160	hair, p. 161	hammer, p. 162	hand, p. 162
hand, p. 163	hand, p. 163	hand, p. 163	hand, p. 164

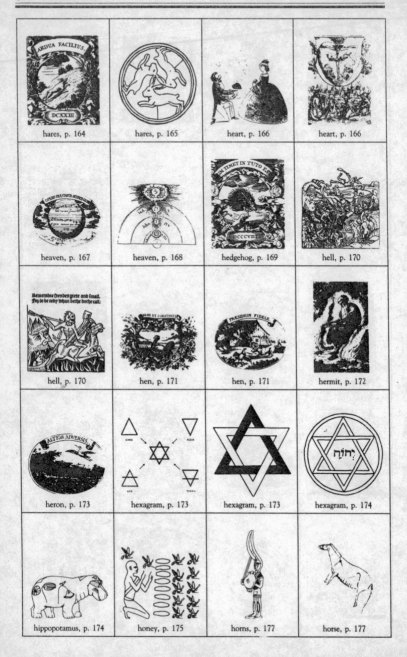

hares, p. 164

hares, p. 165

heart, p. 166

heart, p. 166

heaven, p. 167

heaven, p. 168

hedgehog, p. 169

hell, p. 170

hell, p. 170

hen, p. 171

hen, p. 171

hermit, p. 172

heron, p. 173

hexagram, p. 173

hexagram, p. 173

hexagram, p. 174

hippopotamus, p. 174

honey, p. 175

horns, p. 177

horse, p. 177

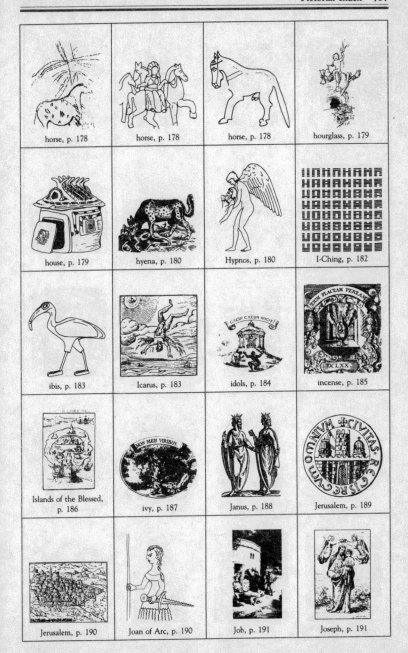

horse, p. 178

horse, p. 178

horse, p. 178

hourglass, p. 179

house, p. 179

hyena, p. 180

Hypnos, p. 180

I-Ching, p. 182

ibis, p. 183

Icarus, p. 183

idols, p. 184

incense, p. 185

Islands of the Blessed, p. 186

ivy, p. 187

Janus, p. 188

Jerusalem, p. 189

Jerusalem, p. 190

Joan of Arc, p. 190

Job, p. 191

Joseph, p. 191

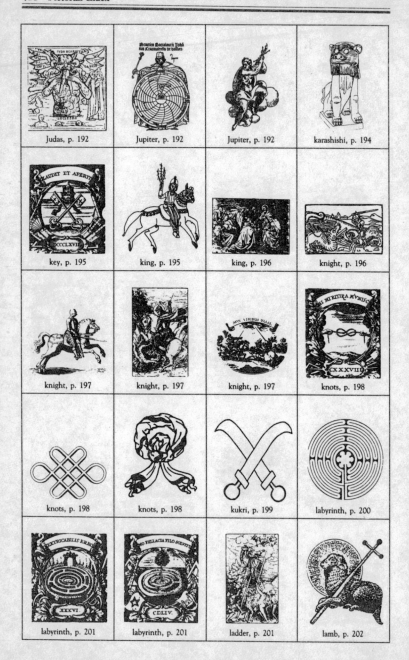

Judas, p. 192	Jupiter, p. 192	Jupiter, p. 192	karashishi, p. 194
key, p. 195	king, p. 195	king, p. 196	knight, p. 196
knight, p. 197	knight, p. 197	knight, p. 197	knots, p. 198
knots, p. 198	knots, p. 198	kukri, p. 199	labyrinth, p. 200
labyrinth, p. 201	labyrinth, p. 201	ladder, p. 201	lamb, p. 202

lamb, p. 202	lamb, p. 202	laurel, p. 203	Lazarus, p. 203
lead, p. 203	light, p. 204	light, p. 205	lightning, p. 206
lightning, p. 206	lightning, p. 207	lily, p. 207	lily, p. 208
lily, p. 208	linden, p. 208	lion, p. 209	lion, p. 210
lion, p. 210	lizard, p. 211	locust, p. 212	lotus, p. 212

lotus, p. 213

Mammon, p. 214 ·

mandala, p. 215

mandorla, p. 215

mandorla, p. 215

mandrake, p. 216

marriage, p. 217

Mars, p. 217

masks, p. 218

masks, p. 218

masks, p. 218

medicine, p. 219

menhir, p. 219

Mercury, p. 220

milk, p. 221

milk, p. 221

mill, p. 222

mill, p. 222

mirror, p. 223

mirror, p. 223

moon, p. 224

moon, p. 225

Moses, p. 226

Moses, p. 227

mother, p. 227

mother, p. 228

mountain, p. 228

mountain, p. 229

mouse, p. 230

mouse, p. 230

mouse, p. 230

Münchhausen, p. 231

mushrooms, p. 232

net, p. 236

night, p. 236

nightingale, p. 237

nimbus, p. 238

nose, p. 239

nose, p. 240

numbers, p. 241

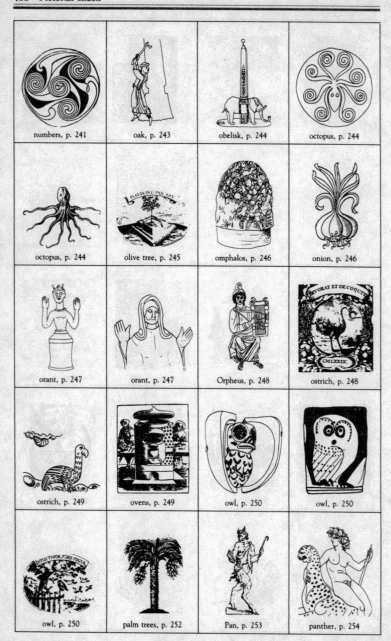

numbers, p. 241	oak, p. 243	obelisk, p. 244	octopus, p. 244
octopus, p. 244	olive tree, p. 245	omphalos, p. 246	onion, p. 246
orant, p. 247	orant, p. 247	Orpheus, p. 248	ostrich, p. 248
ostrich, p. 249	ovens, p. 249	owl, p. 250	owl, p. 250
owl, p. 250	palm trees, p. 252	Pan, p. 253	panther, p. 254

panther, p. 254	panther, p. 255	paradise, p. 255	paradise, p. 256
paradise, p. 256	peacock, p. 257	peacock, p. 258	pear, p. 259
pearl, p. 259	pearl, p. 260	Pegasus, p. 260	Pegasus, p. 261
pelican, p. 261	pentacle, p. 262	pentacle, p. 262	pentacle, p. 263
peony, p. 263	pheasant, p. 264	phoenix, p. 264	phoenix, p. 264

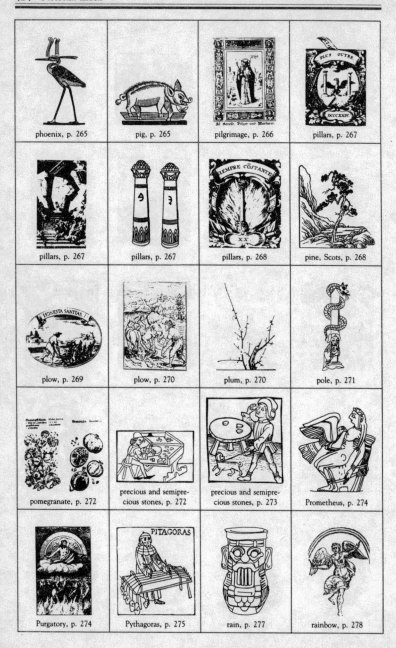

phoenix, p. 265

pig, p. 265

pilgrimage, p. 266

pillars, p. 267

pillars, p. 267

pillars, p. 267

pillars, p. 268

pine, Scots, p. 268

plow, p. 269

plow, p. 270

plum, p. 270

pole, p. 271

pomegranate, p. 272

precious and semiprecious stones, p. 272

precious and semiprecious stones, p. 273

Prometheus, p. 274

Purgatory, p. 274

Pythagoras, p. 275

rain, p. 277

rainbow, p. 278

ram, p. 278

ram, p. 279

rat, p. 279

rat, p. 279

raven, p. 280

raven, p. 280

raven, p. 281

raven, p. 281

ring, p. 284

rivers, p. 285

rivers, p. 285

rivers, p. 286

rocks, p. 286

rocks, p. 287

Roland, p. 287

rooster, p. 288

rooster, p. 288

rooster, p. 289

rose, p. 289

rose, p. 290

rose, p. 290

runes, p. 291

salamander, p. 293

salamander, p. 293

salt, p. 294

Samaritan, Good, p. 294

Saturn, p. 295

Saturn, p. 296

satyrs, p. 296

savages, p. 297

savages, p. 297

savages, p. 298

savages, p. 298

scales, p. 299

scales, p. 299

scales, p. 299

scarab, p. 300

scepter, p. 300

scepter, p. 301

scorpion, p. 301

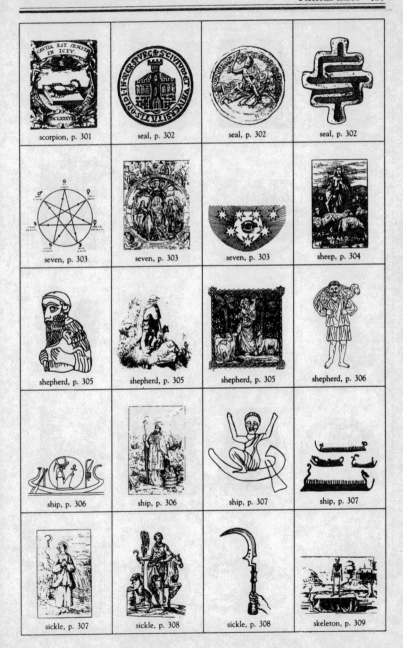

scorpion, p. 301	seal, p. 302	seal, p. 302	seal, p. 302
seven, p. 303	seven, p. 303	seven, p. 303	sheep, p. 304
shepherd, p. 305	shepherd, p. 305	shepherd, p. 305	shepherd, p. 306
ship, p. 306	ship, p. 306	ship, p. 307	ship, p. 307
sickle, p. 307	sickle, p. 308	sickle, p. 308	skeleton, p. 309

skeleton, p. 309	snail, p. 310	snake, p. 311	snake, p. 311
snake, p. 312	Sodom, p. 313	Solomon, p. 314	Sophia, p. 314
soul-hole, p. 315	sphinx, p. 315	sphinx, p. 316	sphinx, p. 316
spider, p. 316	spinning, p. 317	spinning, p. 317	spiral, p. 318
spiral, p. 318	springs, p. 319	springs, p. 319	square, p. 320

square, carpenter's,
p. 320

square, carpenter's,
p. 321

squirrel, p. 321

stars, p. 322

stars, p. 322

stars, p. 322

stars, p. 323

stars, p. 323

stars, p. 323

stars, p. 324

stars, p. 325

steps and stairways,
p. 326

stone, p. 327

stork, p. 328

storm, p. 329

storm, p. 329

sulfur and mercury,
p. 330

sun, p. 330

sun, p. 331

sun, p. 331

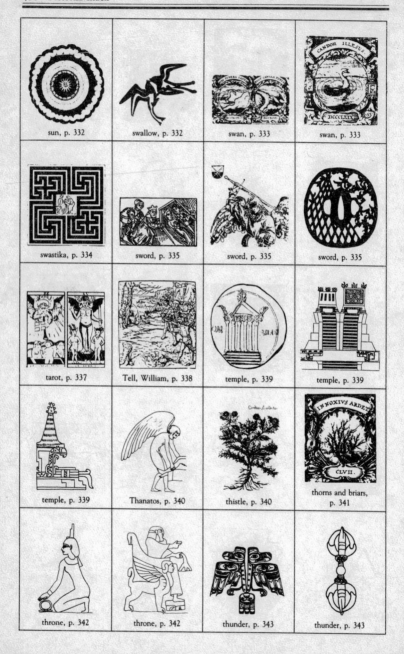

sun, p. 332

swallow, p. 332

swan, p. 333

swan, p. 333

swastika, p. 334

sword, p. 335

sword, p. 335

sword, p. 335

tarot, p. 337

Tell, William, p. 338

temple, p. 339

temple, p. 339

temple, p. 339

Thanatos, p. 340

thistle, p. 340

thorns and briars, p. 341

throne, p. 342

throne, p. 342

thunder, p. 343

thunder, p. 343

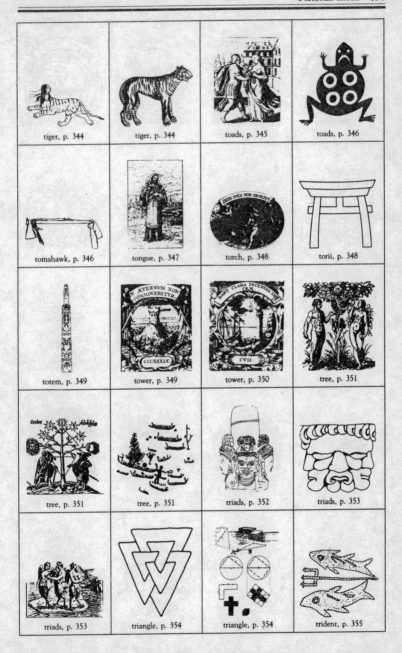

tiger, p. 344

tiger, p. 344

toads, p. 345

toads, p. 346

tomahawk, p. 346

tongue, p. 347

torch, p. 348

torii, p. 348

totem, p. 349

tower, p. 349

tower, p. 350

tree, p. 351

tree, p. 351

tree, p. 351

triads, p. 352

triads, p. 353

triads, p. 353

triangle, p. 354

triangle, p. 354

trident, p. 355

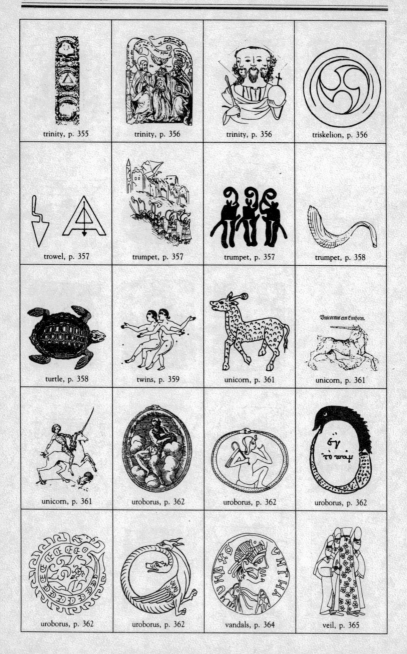

trinity, p. 355	trinity, p. 356	trinity, p. 356	triskelion, p. 356
trowel, p. 357	trumpet, p. 357	trumpet, p. 357	trumpet, p. 358
turtle, p. 358	twins, p. 359	unicorn, p. 361	unicorn, p. 361
unicorn, p. 361	uroborus, p. 362	uroborus, p. 362	uroborus, p. 362
uroborus, p. 362	uroborus, p. 362	vandals, p. 364	veil, p. 365

Venus, p. 365	Venus, p. 366	vices, p. 366	vices, p. 367
violet, p. 368	virgin, p. 368	virgin, p. 369	vulture, p. 370
wampum, p. 372	water, p. 373	water, p. 373	water, p. 374
water, p. 374	water, p. 375	water spirits, p. 375	water spirits, p. 376
water spirits, p. 376	water spirits, p. 376	wedding, p. 377	wells, p. 377

whale, p. 378	whale, p. 378	wheel, p. 379	whore, p. 381
windows, p. 382	winds, p. 383	wine, p. 383	wine, p. 384
wings, p. 385	wings, p. 385	wings, p. 385	wings, p. 386
witches, p. 386	witches, p. 386	wolf, p. 387	wolf, p. 387
wolf, p. 388	wolf, p. 388	wolf, p. 388	wreath, p. 389

yantra, p. 392

yin and yang, p. 393

yin and yang, p. 393

yoni, p. 394

Index

Entries are filed letter-by-letter. **Boldface** locators indicate extensive treatment of a topic.